A Mighty Empire

A Mighty Empire

The Origins of the
American Revolution

MARC EGNAL

Cornell University Press

ITHACA AND LONDON

Copyright © 1988 by Cornell University

All rights reserved. Except for brief quotations in a review, this
book, or parts thereof, must not be reproduced in any form
without permission in writing from the publisher.
For information, address Cornell University Press,
124 Roberts Place, Ithaca, New York 14850.

First published 1988 by Cornell University Press.

International Standard Book Number 0-8014-1932-8
Library of Congress Catalog Card Number 87-19059
Printed in the United States of America
*Librarians: Library of Congress cataloging information
appears on the last page of the book.*

*The paper in this book is acid-free and meets the guidelines for
permanence and durability of the Committee on Production Guidelines
for Book Longevity of the Council on Library Resources.*

For Judith and Barton

Contents

Maps

[ix]

Preface

This book presents a new interpretation of the origins of the American Revolution. It argues that in every colony the revolutionary movement was led by an upper-class faction whose passionate commitment to the rise of the New World was evident well before 1763. Although the membership of this group reflected the influence of self-interest, religion, and national origin, what truly gave the faction its unity was its dedication to the rapid development of America. This hypothesis, its relationship to other historical writing, and some key terms are discussed more fully in the Introduction.

Several decisions helped shape the text. While setting forth a thesis couched in the broadest terms, the book examines only five colonies: Massachusetts, New York, Pennsylvania, Virginia, and South Carolina. These particular provinces were selected because of their size (in 1770 they had 58 percent of the population), the diverse geographical areas they represent, and their prominence in the clash with Britain. The demonstration of a hypothesis for these five important and varied colonies makes likely but, of course, does not prove that the same paradigm holds for the remaining eight. As for the names of the partisans, early in the writing of this work I decided to unburden the text of the long lists that could easily accompany any description of colonial factions. The appendix identifies the prominent party adherents in each province and also presents in tabular form some of the data used in grouping these individuals. Finally, in most instances I have modernized the spelling, punctuation, and capitalization in quoted material.

» «

Like the account book of a heavily indebted colonial merchant, my scholarly ledger is brimming with obligations to those individuals and institutions who helped with this project. Several historians read portions of the manuscript, offered encouragement, and provided incisive commentaries. Setting forth valuable and, at times, far-reaching critiques were Patricia Bonomi, David Chesnutt, Emory Evans, Eric Foner, Joseph Illick, Drew McCoy, Roy Merrens, Stephen Patterson, John Selby, and Allan Tully. Thad Tate read the entire text, as did my colleague Joseph Ernst. These scholars invariably were generous with their time and thoughtful in their analyses. Nor would any set of acknowledgments be complete without recognition of two professors with whom I had the privilege of working: Frederick Tolles and Merrill Jensen.

Institutions and agencies, those lengthened shadows of dedicated employees, also must be thanked. The staffs of the archives and libraries cited in the notes to this work have been most helpful, and special appreciation must be extended to the York University interlibrary loan department for tracking down various publications. The typists in York Secretarial Services bore with me through various revisions and have my gratitude for their labors. Carolyn Gondor and Carol Randall of the Cartographic Drafting Office drew the graphs and maps. A Fulbright fellowship made possible research in English archives. Two fellowships from the Canada Council helped broaden this work beyond its initial focus, and research grants from York University allowed additional trips to East Coast repositories.

Finally, my wife, Judith Humphrey, and son, Barton, deservedly have a page for themselves. Barton may not feel that tales of the Revolution rival those of A. A. Milne and Roald Dahl, but at least George and Martha, as well as Abigail and John, are in the running. Judith has provided assistance and much needed support that go beyond any mere words of thanks. To her and Barton this book is affectionately dedicated.

MARC EGNAL

Toronto, Ontario

Note on Definitions

Any reader who jumps to the middle of this book to examine a particular colony or individual should be aware that two crucial sets of terms are used throughout this work in an unusual way. *Party* and *faction* always appear in these pages in eighteenth-century dress; that is, they refer to those loose congeries of individuals who came together because of similar views on one or more issues. Only occasionally were these groups reinforced by the formal organizational structures that the twentieth century associates with "party."

Still more important for an understanding of this book are the words *expansionism, expansionist*, and *nonexpansionist. Expansionism*, as used in this work, is the heartfelt conviction that America could and should aspire to greatness. Thomas Jefferson discoursed on this world view in the first drafts of the Declaration of Independence. Referring to the ties between Britain and the United States, he observed: "We might have been a free and a great people together; but a communication of grandeur and of freedom it seems is below their dignity. Be it so, since they will have it; the road to glory and happiness is open to us too; we will climb it in a separate state, and acquiesce in the necessity which pronounces our everlasting Adieu."[1] *Expansionists* were those upper-class individuals who held such an outlook and who were actively committed to promoting the rise of the New World. *Nonexpansionists*, by contrast, were the well-to-do

1. Thomas Jefferson, "Original Rough Draught" of the Declaration of Independence, June 11–July 4, 1776, *The Papers of Thomas Jefferson*, ed. Julian P. Boyd et al. (Princeton, 1950–), I, 423–28, quotation on 427.

citizens with little faith in America's ability to assert itself in a world of hostile nations, and hence they were unwilling to support the bold steps needed to strengthen the sovereignty of the colonies. Both sets of terms are discussed at much greater length in the Introduction.

Abbreviations Used in Notes

AAS	American Antiquarian Society
AHR	*American Historical Review*
BM	British Museum
CSM	Colonial Society of Massachusetts
CWF	Colonial Williamsburg Foundation
DAB	*Dictionary of American Biography*
FDRL	Franklin Delano Roosevelt Library
HSP	Historical Society of Pennsylvania
JAH	*Journal of American History*
JEH	*Journal of Economic History*
JSH	*Journal of Southern History*
MeHS	Maine Historical Society
MHS	Massachusetts Historical Society
MVHR	*Mississippi Valley Historical Review*
NEHGR	*New England Historical and Genealogical Register*
NYHS	New-York Historical Society
NYPL	New York Public Library
PMHB	*Pennsylvania Magazine of History and Biography*
PRO	Public Record Office, London
SCA	South Carolina Archives
SCHM	*South Carolina Historical Magazine*
SCHS	South Carolina Historical Society
SCPR	South Carolina Public Records
VMHB	*Virginia Magazine of History and Biography*
WMQ	*The William and Mary Quarterly*

A Mighty Empire

Introduction

Even before they declared independence, Americans began examining the causes of their dispute with Great Britain, and the debate over the origins of the Revolution has not slackened to this day. Modern scholars reject—and justly so—the simplest of interpretations: that the British enactments between 1763 and 1776 serve as necessary and sufficient conditions for a revolt. Of the measures adopted before 1774 only the Stamp Act, which was soon repealed, immediately disrupted the lives of the colonists. The Proclamation of 1763, restricting settlement in the West, and the Declaratory Act of 1766, affirming the power of Parliament, were not implemented; the Townshend duties taxed a few items lightly; and the Tea Act would have made that drink cheaper. The Sugar Act of 1764, as amended in 1766, raised most of the revenue Britain got from the colonies during these years but rarely was an object of complaint. Twentieth-century researchers generally accept that these measures were no more than triggering conditions, and that the fuller explanation lies in some larger development. At this point agreement among historians ends.

This book argues that in each colony the revolutionary movement was led by an upper-class faction whose fervent commitment to fostering America's rise to greatness was evident well before 1763. Although self-interest, religious convictions, and national origins helped shape the membership of this patriotic group, what truly brought these individuals together was their dedication to the rapid development of the New World. Because this interpretation both builds upon and differs from other explanations of the Revolution, a survey of modern scholarship forms a necessary introduction.

Since 1890 three schools of thought—the Imperial, Progressive, and neo-Whig—have dominated writing on the Revolution. These approaches set forth, respectively, three central themes: the rise of the colonial assemblies, the discontent of the lower classes, and the impact of political ideas.

Most historians today consider that the emphasis of the Imperial school on the maturation of the provinces and their legislatures highlights a precondition to rather than an all-important cause of the Revolution. It is hard to imagine a successful uprising of the American colonies in the seventeenth century, when most of the assemblies were little more than fractious local conclaves. The advances recorded by these bodies during the next seventy-five years provided stiffening, both psychological and substantive, for the resistance to Parliament, while, more generally, the economic and social growth of the colonies bolstered their ability to oppose the mother country. This paradigm tells us little, however, about the specific groups, events, or rhetoric of the Revolution. Indeed, an examination of collective biographies undercuts any direct link between the legislative struggles and the Revolutionary movement. Those individuals, such as the DeLanceys in New York or the Quaker party leaders in Pennsylvania, who were in the forefront of the battle for assembly rights in the 1740s and 1750s most often became tories; members of the opposing faction usually became patriots.[1]

Present-day scholars also raise serious questions about the Progressive interpretation. The Progressive historians, for example, Carl Becker, asserted that the struggle against Britain was led by a discontented lower class, which used the conflict to enhance its role in colonial society. These writers added a subordinate theme: economic self-interest initially led the elite to support the Revolution, even though fear of the populace eventually made the merchants and planters turn from the protest movement.[2] Both assertions now seem doubtful. The valuable work of the "New Left" historians during the past two decades has cast much light on the activities and mindset of the less affluent colonists. But these researchers have also made it clear that in no colony did the common folk gain control of the revolutionary movement or wrest power from the upper classes. As Gary Nash bluntly states, "no social revolution occurred in America in the

1. Charles M. Andrews, "The American Revolution: An Interpretation," *AHR*, xxxi (1926), 219–32; George L. Beer, *British Colonial Policy, 1754–1765* (New York, 1907); Herbert L. Osgood, *The American Colonies in the Eighteenth Century*, 4 vols. (New York, 1924).

2. Carl Becker, *The History of Political Parties in the Province of New York, 1760–1776* (Madison, Wis., 1909); Charles A. Beard and Mary Beard, *The Rise of American Civilization* (New York, 1927); Arthur M. Schlesinger, *The Colonial Merchants and the American Revolution, 1763–1776* (New York, 1919).

1770s."[3] The Progressives' minor thesis also appears to be wide of the mark. This approach, which devalues the role of ideas and takes a narrow, deterministic view of human behavior, seems unable to explain an event as far-ranging as the American Revolution.[4]

Since 1950 a third interpretation of the Revolution, the neo-Whig paradigm, has emerged and gradually become the accepted explanation. This school harkens back to the views of the nineteenth-century "Whig" historians, such as George Bancroft, who contended that Americans rebelled to defend their liberty. Following a similar line of reasoning, if with a far more sophisticated analysis of the revolutionaries' ideas and rhetoric, the neo-Whigs emphasize the libertarian beliefs of the colonists as the mainspring of revolt. The leading neo-Whig historians, Edmund Morgan and Bernard Bailyn, underscore this dedication to whiggish principles, although with variant readings. For Morgan, the development of the patriots' beliefs was a rational, clearly defined process. In *The Stamp Act Crisis* Edmund Morgan and coauthor Helen M. Morgan state:

> Yet in the last analysis the significance of the Stamp Act crisis lies in the emergence, not of leaders and methods and organizations, but of well-defined constitutional principles. The resolutions of the colonial and intercolonial assemblies in 1765 laid down the line on which Americans stood until they cut their connections with England. Consistently from 1765 to 1776 they denied the authority of Parliament to tax them externally or internally; consistently they affirmed their willingness to submit to whatever legislation Parliament should enact for the supervision of the empire as a whole.[5]

For Bailyn, the colonists' concern for their rights as Englishmen is characterized less by a consistent, carefully enunciated dialectic than by ill-defined but nonetheless potent fears centering on the dangers of British tyranny. In a 1973 essay Bailyn argues: "American resistance in the 1760s and 1770s was a response to acts of power deemed arbitrary, degrading, and uncontrollable—a response, in itself objectively reasonable, that was inflamed to the point of explosion by

3. Gary B. Nash, *The Urban Crucible: Social Change, Political Consciousness, and the Origins of the American Revolution* (Cambridge, Mass., 1979), 383; Jesse Lemisch, "The American Revolution Seen from the Bottom Up," in Barton J. Bernstein, ed., *Towards a New Past: Dissenting Essays in American History* (New York, 1968), 3–45; Edward Countryman, *A People in Revolution: The American Revolution and Political Society in New York, 1760–1790* (Baltimore, 1981), 36–71; Countryman, *The American Revolution* (New York, 1985).

4. On the Progressives' use of ideas, see Gordon S. Wood, "Rhetoric and Reality in the American Revolution," *WMQ*, 3d ser., xxiii (1981), 7–10.

5. Edmund S. Morgan and Helen M. Morgan, *The Stamp Act Crisis: Prologue to Revolution* (Chapel Hill, N.C., 1953; rev. ed., New York, 1962), 369–70.

ideological currents generating fears everywhere in America that irresponsible and self-seeking adventurers . . . had gained the power of the English government and were turning first, for reasons that were variously explained, to that Rhineland of their aggressions, the colonies."[6]

The neo-Whig contribution is important. Members of this school have reinvigorated the study of the revolutionaries' ideas. "We shall not understand why there was a revolution," Bailyn observed in 1967, "until we suspend disbelief and listen with care to what the Revolutionaries themselves said was the reason there was a revolution."[7] These historians have mapped out in impressive detail the complex strands of thought and rhetoric that lead from the English publicists of the seventeenth century or, in some instances, from the civic humanists of the Italian Renaissance to the political writings of the Founding Fathers.[8]

Three serious shortcomings, however, weaken the neo-Whig approach. First, this interpretation, in which motivating ideas are linked to no specific groups in colonial society, cannot explain the deep, sustained divisions within the ruling class of each colony. The universality of libertarian beliefs undercuts their explanatory force. When future loyalist Joseph Galloway announced to the First Continental Congress, "I am as much a friend of liberty [as] exists, and no man shall go farther in point of fortune, or in point of blood than the man who now addresses you," his rhetoric was little removed from that of the ardent patriots in the room.[9] The Morgans' and Bailyn's

6. Bernard Bailyn, "The Central Themes of the American Revolution: An Interpretation," in Stephen G. Kurtz and James H. Hutson, eds., *Essays on the American Revolution* (Chapel Hill, N.C., 1973), 13.

7. Bernard Bailyn, *The Origins of American Politics* (New York, 1968), 11 (orig. pub. in *Perspectives in American History*, I [1967]).

8. Caroline Robbins, *The Eighteenth-Century Commonwealthman: Studies in the Transmission, Development and Circumstance of English Liberal Thought from the Restoration of Charles II until the War with the Thirteen Colonies* (Cambridge, Mass., 1959); H. Trevor Colbourn, *The Lamp of Experience: Whig History and the Intellectual Origins of the American Revolution* (Cambridge, Mass., 1967); J. G. A. Pocock, *The Machiavellian Moment: Florentine Political Thought and the Atlantic Republican Tradition* (Princeton, N.J., 1975).

9. Joseph Galloway, Sept. 28, 1774, report of debates in Congress, *Diary and Autobiography of John Adams*, ed. L. H. Butterfield et al., 4 vols. (Cambridge, Mass., 1961), II, 141–42. Mary Beth Norton, "The Loyalist Critique of the Revolution," in *The Development of a Revolutionary Mentality*, Library of Congress Symposia on the American Revolution, I (Washington, D.C., 1972), 127–48, argues that the loyalists were "in the mainstream of 18th-century English whiggery" and adds, "Like the good Whigs they were, the loyalists had examined the proper whiggish conditions for revolution and pronounced them wanting in America" (pp. 130, 139–40). See also Robert M. Calhoon, *The Loyalists in Revolutionary America, 1760–1781* (New York, 1973), 116–18. Janice Potter, *The Liberty We Seek: Loyalist Ideology in Colonial New York and Massachusetts* (Cambridge, Mass., 1983), 85, states that "like the Patriots, Loyalists were Whigs, or Lockeans."

analyses suggest that most politically aware Americans should have been patriots. In fact, the upper classes in every province were seriously divided on the virtues of rebellion; perhaps half the wealthier citizens in Massachusetts, New York, and Pennsylvania, and a significant portion of the merchants and planters in South Carolina sided with the Crown. Even in Virginia, where few openly supported the royal cause, there were sharp splits within the elite over the wisdom of vigorous protests. Moreover, such antagonistic groups were not the creation of the revolutionary era; these factions, as this book will argue, can in every colony be traced back before 1763, and, in some instances, as far back as 1700.

Second, the neo-Whig interpretation fails to account for the specifics of colonial resistance between 1763 and 1776. If Americans objected to British enactments because they felt their liberties violated, then the protests should bear the stamp of such principles. But the resolute stand against British taxation, which the Morgans consider the hallmark of American opposition, was not evident in the colonists' deeds. Although the Sugar Act was unmistakably designed to raise a revenue, the colonists accepted it with little protest, contributing over twenty thousand pounds sterling to the royal coffers every year between 1766 and 1774.[10] Similarly, Americans paid the Townshend Act duties for a full year after the measure went into force, and the protests that emerged at the end of 1768 and continued into 1769 and 1770 were directed more toward aiding the distressed colonial economy than toward the defense of Whig rights. More generally, these historians ignore the gravity and impact of the depression of the 1760s and so leave unexplained the many actions taken in response to this slump.

Third, Bailyn, the Morgans, and other recent historians focus on but one body of thought—constitutional and political—and in the end portray the revolutionaries in terms as narrowly reductive as those of the Progressives. The neo-Whigs train a spotlight on a comparatively small group of writings, particularly the work of such English publicists as John Trenchard and Thomas Gordon and a set of American pamphleteers, but leave in a penumbra a much more extensive commentary touching such topics as trade, defense, mercantile regulation, and, more broadly, the political economy of the New World. In their efforts to avoid the economic determinism that often underlay the work of an earlier generation of writers, the neo-Whigs have moved to the other end of the spectrum and have fash-

10. For the revenue from various parliamentary exactions, see U.S. Bureau of the Census, *Historical Statistics of the United States, Colonial Times to 1970*, 2 vols., consec. pagin. (Washington, D.C., 1975), 1200.

ioned a model in which motivating ideas are divorced from day-to-day concerns.

While accepting as important the material set forth by earlier historians, this book presents a new interpretation: that in each colony an upper-class faction whose dedication to the rapid development of America was apparent well before 1763 led the revolutionary movement. Before any analysis of the history of the era can be undertaken, however, two sets of terms must be defined. These words are crucial to an understanding of this work, and are used with meanings that are not their usual ones.

Faction and *party*, as used in the pages that follow, carry the eighteenth-century sense of a group of individuals working together for one or more issues, rather than the twentieth-century denotation of a formal political structure. In certain instances, notably in New York and Pennsylvania during the last decades of the colonial period, loose factional groupings were buttressed by the rudiments of organization, including party labels, "tickets," and formal campaigns. Although such practices were more the exception than the rule, the factions detailed here are not simply artifacts of historical reconstruction; politically active colonists were usually aware that their peers could be grouped into separate, coherent camps. This book focuses on the parties formed over the issue of "expansionism," but on other questions mooted during these years, such as the incidence of local taxes or the location of a provincial capital, the same individuals could and often did form other, temporary alignments.[11]

Expansionism, as used throughout this work, is a fervent belief in America's potential for greatness. Put in other words, expansionism is a conviction that the colonies had the spiritual and physical resources to become a self-reliant, mighty New World "empire."[12] *This*

11. For a discussion of colonial factions, see Stephen E. Patterson, *Political Parties in Revolutionary Massachusetts* (Madison, Wis., 1973), 3–32; Patricia U. Bonomi, *A Factious People: Politics and Society in Colonial New York* (New York, 1971), 10–16; Bonomi, ed., *Party and Political Opposition in Revolutionary America* (Tarrytown, N.Y., 1980), v–xi.

12. I am indebted to a valuable body of scholarship that has explored, using other terms, the expansionist mindset of early Americans. Pioneering works include William A. Williams, "The Age of Mercantilism: An Interpretation of American Political Economy, 1763–1728," *WMQ*, 3d ser., xv (1958), 419–37; and Richard Warner Van Alstyne, *The Rising American Empire* (New York, 1960), 1–27. Among the more thoughtful recent studies are Walter LaFeber, "Foreign Policies of a New Nation: Franklin, Madison, and the 'Dream of a New Land to Fulfill with People in Self-Control,' 1750–1804," in William A. Williams, ed., *From Colony to Empire: Essays in the History of American Foreign Relations* (New York, 1972), 10–37; Joseph A. Ernst, "Political Economy and Reality: Problems in the Interpretation of the American Revolution," *Canadian Review of American Studies*, vii (1976), 109–18; Eric Foner, *Tom Paine and Revolutionary America* (New York, 1976), 76–106; Drew R. McCoy, *The Elusive Republic: Political Economy in Jeffersonian America* (Chapel Hill, N.C., 1980).

broad, ramifying world view must not be equated with a much narrower concept—a desire for territorial growth. The *expansionists* were those upper-class individuals who held this grand view and who were actively committed to promoting the ascendancy of America. During the colonial period these well-to-do men and, in rare instances, wealthy women generally agreed on a variety of issues, including the need for strengthened local sovereignty, a healthy domestic economy, thriving maritime commerce, and new land. Following the logic of their beliefs, most of these individuals not only supported the struggle against Britain but would later plump for the Constitution as an important step in the rise of the United States. The *nonexpansionists*, who formed the competing parties in each colony, were the affluent citizens with little faith in America's ability to assert itself in a world of antagonistic nations. While not opposed to growth, the nonexpansionists' lack of confidence in the present strength and future prospects of the New World made them unwilling to take the daring steps the patriots advocated.[13]

Where did the expansionist and nonexpansionist parties gain their adherents and commitment? In most provinces self-interest played a role in party formation. The imperial wars were the progenitors of this schism within the elite, and typically, the wealthy individuals most immediately threatened by the French, the Spanish, and their Indian allies coalesced as a party to push for defense measures. The upper-class citizens who lived farther from the frontier or, in some instances, who held investments less endangered by external enemies opposed lavish wartime expenditures and came together as nonexpansionists. Religion and national origin also helped determine the composition of the parties. In Pennsylvania, for example, Quakers, whose testimony called for a peaceful earthly kingdom, stood squarely in the nonexpansionist camp. Scotch-Irish Presbyterians, whose militant faith and dislike of the conditions they had left readily translated into a dedication to their new land, supported the expansionists. Members of the two groups soon enunciated their respective

13. Although the explanatory model presented in this book differs from the one set forth by the neo-Whigs, expansionist ideology *could* comport with libertarian beliefs. Such harmony was not invariable (some nonexpansionists—for example, Thomas Hutchinson and Joseph Galloway—accepted liberty but not a campaign to strengthen American sovereignty); however, in the eighteenth century, individuals with a boundless vision of an American "empire" often argued that an uncorrupted republic was the best government for the promotion of economic growth and that, by the same measure, abundant land, a healthy, agrarian-based economy, and strong local sovereignty were necessary for any New World regime that hoped to be free and long-lived. For one effort to demonstrate the range of ideas that complemented commonwealth thought, see Robert E. Shallope, "Republicanism and Early American Ideology," *WMQ*, 3d ser., xxxix (1982), 334–57.

views, and it was these "persuasions" that steered the activities of the parties.

Rooted in a fertile soil of self-interest, religion, and national origin and guided by deeply held convictions, the two factions were long-lived and displayed remarkable continuity in their personnel and behavior. In each colony the same individuals who vigorously opposed the encroachments of the French, Spanish, and Indians before 1763 led the struggle against Britain after 1763. Following a parallel but opposing path, the other party manifested a deep reluctance to aid British military efforts before 1763 and, during the last dozen years of the colonial period, was similarly hesitant to join the protests against the mother country. While the revolutionary crisis of 1774–1776 effectively ended the political careers of most nonexpansionists, the expansionists became ever more prominent as leaders of the new nation.

Although the focus of this work is on the initiative and leadership of the elite parties, no account of the Revolution can or should be kept within such narrow class boundaries. With an intensity that varied from colony to colony, the common people played a noteworthy part in local politics. Moreover, as the conflict with Britain intensified after 1763, the role of the artisans and small farmers became increasingly important. The expansionists realized that they required the support of the men and women who worked with their hands, and encouraged their involvement in the protest movement. But the relationship between the revolutionary planters and merchants, on the one hand, and the populace, on the other, was never an easy one. The need of the patriot elite for allies was tempered by fears that the "lower orders" might raise demands of their own. In fact, the common people grew increasingly articulate and self-conscious, and much of the story told in Parts Two, Three, and Four turns on the efforts of the wealthy factions to achieve their goals with the least possible disruption of the hierarchical social order.[14]

The chapters that follow put the flesh of names, dates, and places on this bare-bones description of the groups that shaped revolutionary America. This introduction would, however, be incomplete with-

14. Jackson Turner Main, *The Social Structure of Revolutionary America* (Princeton, N.J., 1965), 230–35, makes clear that when colonial Americans discussed social class they used both a three-fold division ("upper," "middling," and "lower") and a two-part classification ("upper" and "lower"). Usually this book relies on a dichotomy, with the most affluent individuals—typically merchants, planters, lawyers, and their families—as the upper class and the balance of society as the "common people." As the text makes clear, the more politically active members of the populace were the artisans, shopkeepers, and small farmers, rather than the poorest urbanites and rural laborers.

out, first, a discussion of the relationship between these visions of the future and the colonists' actions and, second, a brief survey of the evolving views that guided the two elite parties, particularly the expansionists, who were more dynamic, articulate, and outspoken than their provincial opponents.

The nature of expansionist and nonexpansionist ideas and their impact on the behavior of the provincial upper class must be made clear. To begin with, how coherent and carefully articulated were these bodies of thought? Within each faction a few individuals discoursed at length on their conception of the strengths and weaknesses of America, and on its proper course of development. But these men, for example, expansionists Benjamin Franklin, Thomas Jefferson, and John Dickinson and nonexpansionist Thomas Hutchinson, paid obeisance to no single text or texts. Even those in the same camp never wholly agreed with one another. Their pronouncements did not form an *ideology* if one takes that term in its narrowest sense 'as a "systematic body of concepts" or a set of "integrated assertions, theories, and aims that constitute a sociopolitical program." It would be more appropriate to describe these writings as a "persuasion" or an "outlook." Only if we accept a much broader definition of ideology, like the one Nicos Poulantzas gives ("a *relatively coherent* ensemble of representations, values and beliefs"), can these bodies of thought be called ideologies.[15]

Even granting the discursive, loosely structured nature of expansionist and nonexpansionist thought, we may ask to what degree the members of the colonial elites shared the viewpoints set forth by the most outspoken partisans. After all, the argument of this book focuses on the activity of factions, not just on the few persons who had the education and leisure to write at length.

For the majority of the provincial upper class the commitment to an expansionist or nonexpansionist world view was strong but was rarely expressed in writing as fully or as systematically as a Franklin,

15. The "narrow" definition of ideology is taken from *Webster's Ninth New Collegiate Dictionary* (Springfield, Mass., 1984), which also sets forth a "broader" alternative. Particularly valuable discussions of this concept are found in George Lichtheim, "The Concept of Ideology," *History and Theory,* IV (1965), 164–95; Peter L. Berger and Thomas Luckmann, *The Social Construction of Reality: A Treatise in the Sociology of Knowledge* (Garden City, N.Y., 1966), 5–13, 87–114; and Clifford Geertz, *The Interpretation of Cultures: Selected Essays* (New York, 1973), 191–233. Joyce Appleby, "Value and Society," Jack P. Greene and J. R. Pole, eds., *Colonial British America: Essays in the New History of the Early Modern Era* (Baltimore, 1984), 290–316, is most pertinent for colonial historians. Nicos Poulantzas, *Political Power and Social Classes* (orig. pub. in French, 1968; London, 1978), is useful not only for its definitions but also for its theoretical discussions of subgroups within social classes. See esp. 84–85, 195–208, quotation on 206.

Jefferson, or Hutchinson might have done. Instead, these merchants, planters, and lawyers underscored their beliefs with actions and brief statements, maintaining a consistency that often stretched over several decades. Typically, an expansionist trader in the 1750s avidly supported the war against the French and Indians, perhaps joined the local militia, and testified in his letters to the need for preparedness. The same individual in the 1760s and early 1770s backed strong, if peaceful, protests against the British and campaigned for such measures as nonimportation to reinflate the economy. His writings reflected concern for these immediate issues more often than speculation about a New World empire. In the 1780s this trader might well be the founder of a bank and a forceful advocate of a national government. Such individuals shared the same mental landscape as the better-known writers and at times profited from the views elaborated in a public tract or reasoned treatise. Remarked one Philadelphia merchant in 1770: "Doctor Franklin's letter [on nonimportation] . . . has had wonderful effects and plainly shows the great respect and regard a large part of the people here pay to the advice and opinion of that truly great man."[16] But while the busy traders and landowners may seldom have articulated their outlook with great sophistication or breadth, their adherence to these larger world views was as firm as that of their more eloquent peers.

What then is the relationship between these ideologies (using that term now with Poulantzas's "loose" definition) and the actions taken by members of the colonial upper class? Anyone who looks for the simplicity that comes from a deterministic approach to history will not find it in this work. All else being equal, expansionists were guided by their desire to strengthen America, while their opposite numbers responded to fears of what lay ahead. But such principles were never the only ones shaping behavior, and the text chronicles not only the broader patterns but also the aberrations. For example, in most instances the expansionists led the Revolutionary movement, but in New York between 1766 and 1768 these partisans, unnerved by the shock of an agrarian revolt, grew extraordinarily cautious. Again, although most expansionists ended up supporting independence, a few, because of their worries about the activities of the increasingly outspoken common folk, threw in their lot with the British. On the individual level, ambition and quirks of personality led to unexpected turns in the careers of such men as Benjamin Franklin, Henry Laurens, and John Adams. These exceptions do not "disprove" the contentions set forth in this book, for the argument rests with the far

16. Henry Drinker to Abel James, May 26, 1770, *PMHB*, xiv (1890), 44–45.

more extensive material that defines the norm. Rather, they convey the human dimension of the process and a sense of how individual actors wrestled with immediate problems. A shorter book could have presented the same thesis about the Revolution, but it would have sketched in only the forests and never the leaves and trees.

The broad outlines of these conflicting persuasions, which evolved over time, can be briefly reviewed. Before 1763 the tenets of expansionist thought were spelled out most fully and broadcast widely by a small but influential coterie of colonial leaders, none more significant than Benjamin Franklin of Pennsylvania and Jonathan Mayhew of Massachusetts. For the myriads who received Franklin's letters, read his tracts, or simply leafed through *Poor Richard's Almanack*, the printer expounded several of the leading themes that together helped form the expansionist outlook. One argument often underscored was the unprecedented growth of population in the New World. Poor Richard displayed lavish tables detailing the skyrocketing number of settlers, and noted the contrast between Europe and America: "I believe people increase faster by generation in these colonies, where all can have full employ and there is room and business for millions yet unborn. For in old settled countries, as England, for instance, . . . the overplus must quit the country or they will perish by poverty, diseases, and want of necessaries."[17] Furthermore, Franklin was every inch the booster in discussing the wealth of America's western reaches. In 1754 Franklin, emphasizing "the extreme richness and fertility of the land," proposed the establishment of two transmontane colonies. Because of its "natural advantages," the printer wrote, the West "must undoubtedly (perhaps in less than another century) become a populous and powerful dominion."[18]

But hailing Columbia's treasures was only one facet of Franklin's expansionist outlook in the 1740s and 1750s; equally important was his determination to oppose any foreign power that dared to hamper the rise of America. Franklin's efforts in organizing Pennsylvania resistance to the French and Indians were truly the measure of this energetic man. But as significantly, his backing for Great Britain before 1763 reflected only the coincidence of interests, never blind devotion. "O let not Britain seek to oppress us," he told a London correspondent in 1753, "but like an affectionate parent endeavor to secure freedom to her children."[19] He wrote the royal governor of

17. Benjamin Franklin, *Poor Richard's Almanack* (1750), *The Papers of Benjamin Franklin*, ed. Leonard W. Labaree et al. (New Haven, 1959–), III, 441.
18. Franklin, "A Plan for Settling Two Western Colonies" (1754), ibid., v, 456–63, quotations on 457.
19. Franklin to Peter Collinson, May 9, 1753, ibid., IV, 486.

Massachusetts, William Shirley, to suggest that a new Parliament be struck with colonial delegates. Such a body, Franklin averred, would "overcome the private interest of a petty corporation, or of any particular set of artificers or traders in England, who heretofore seem in some instances to have been more regarded than all the colonies, or than was consistent with the general interest or best national good."[20]

Paralleling Franklin's writings in the 1750s were the preachings of the Reverend Jonathan Mayhew. In sermons at the West Church in Boston and in printed "discourses," Mayhew set forth his belief in the glorious future of America. Commenting on the capture of Quebec in 1759, Mayhew declared that the colonies would become "*a mighty empire* (I do not mean an independent one), in numbers little inferior perhaps to the greatest in Europe, and in felicity to none." Mayhew continued with high eloquence: "Methinks I see mighty cities rising on every hill, and by the side of every commodious port, mighty fleets alternately sailing out and returning, laden with the produce of this, and every other country under heaven; happy fields and villages wherever I turn my eyes, through a vastly extended territory." (Mayhew, like many other colonists, used the word *empire* in the sense of a country embracing an extended area rather than with today's denotation of a metropolitan power governing scattered dominions.)[21] And like Franklin, Mayhew made clear that Americans had to be as careful to protect themselves against the wiles of the mother country as against the designs of any other power.[22]

Immediately after the Seven Years' War, with the French driven from North America, expansionist thought began a luxuriant exfoliation. Thomas Hutchinson, historian and loyalist governor of Massachusetts, closely analyzed the intellectual developments he deplored. Before 1763 "speculative men had figured in their minds an American empire . . . but in such distant ages that nobody then living could expect to see it. . . . But as soon as [the French] were removed, a new scene opened," observed Hutchinson. "The prospect was greatly enlarged. There was nothing to obstruct a gradual progress of settlements, through a vast continent, from the Atlantic to the Pacific Ocean. . . . Men whose minds were turned to calculations found that the colonies increased so rapidly, as to double the number

20. Franklin to Gov. William Shirley, Dec. 4, 22, 1754, ibid., v, 446, 449.
21. Jonathan Mayhew, *Two Discourses, October 25th, 1759*, quoted in Charles W. Akers, *Called unto Liberty: A Life of Jonathan Mayhew, 1720–1766* (Cambridge, Mass., 1964), 135–36; Jonathan Mayhew to Thomas Hollis, May 21, 1760, MHS *Proceedings*, 3d ser., LXIX (1947–50), 112, my italics.
22. Jonathan Mayhew, *Two Discourses, November 23rd, 1758*, quoted in Akers, *Called unto Liberty*, 137.

of inhabitants in a much shorter space of time than had been imagined." "These considerations," lamented Hutchinson, "produced a higher sense of the grandeur and importance of the colonies. Advantages in any respect, enjoyed by the subjects in England, which were not enjoyed by the subjects in the colonies, began to be considered in an invidious light, and men were led to inquire with greater attention than formerly, into the relation in which the colonies stood to the state from which they sprang."[23]

Between 1763 and 1770 leading expansionists in each colony detailed the world view Hutchinson had described and castigated. Among these outward-looking citizens were Thomas Cushing and James Otis, Jr., of Massachusetts, Robert R. and William Livingston of New York, Charles Thomson and John Dickinson of Pennsylvania, George Mason and Richard Henry Lee of Virginia, and Christopher Gadsden and Henry Laurens of South Carolina. In each individual's writings affirmations of the New World's potential were intertwined with demands for greater American sovereignty. George Mason's public letter to the London merchants, penned in 1766, was typical of these utterances. "Do you, does any sensible man," Mason asked, "think that three or four millions of people, not naturally defective in genius, or in courage, who have tasted the sweets of liberty in a country that doubles its inhabitants every twenty years, in a country abounding in such variety of soil and climate, capable of producing not only the necessaries, but the conveniencies and delicacies of life will long submit to oppression?"[24]

During the 1760s, however, only a few expansionists speculated that American links with London might have outlived their usefulness. "I have often viewed with infinite satisfaction," Charles Thomson remarked in 1769, "the prodigious growth and power of the British empire, and have pleased myself with the hopes that in a century or two the British colonies would overspread this immense territory. . . . But alas! the folly of a weak administration has darkened the prospect and what the issue will be, must be left to Providence."[25] Most expansionists presented solutions predicated on membership in the British empire and typically demanded that the prerogative of Parliament be narrowly circumscribed, its power limited to such areas as the regulation of trade.

23. Thomas Hutchinson, *The History of the Colony and Province of Massachusetts-Bay*, ed. Lawrence S. Mayo, 3 vols. (Cambridge, Mass., 1936), III, 61–62.

24. "A Virginia Planter" [George Mason] to the Committee of Merchants in London, June 6, 1766, *The Papers of George Mason, 1725–1792*, ed. Robert A. Rutland, 2 vols. (Chapel Hill, N.C., 1970), I, 70.

25. Charles Thomson to Franklin, Nov. 26, 1769, *Papers of Franklin*, XVI, 239–40.

The "quiet years," 1771–1773, marked a curious but important interlude in expansionist thought. The concerns for colonial sovereignty and growth were no less intense than they had been in the tumultuous 1760s, but now—with Britain conciliatory—the expansionists resolved to mute their protests and rely instead on the ineluctable growth of America as a means of achieving their goals. Thomas Cushing confided to a Virginia correspondent in 1773: "You justly observe that the government at home are daily growing weaker, while we in America are continually growing stronger. Our natural increase in wealth and population will in a course of years effectually settle this dispute in our favor, whereas if we persist in openly and strenuously denying the right of Parliament to legislate for us in any case whatever . . . there will be great danger of bringing on a rupture fatal to both countries."[26]

During the final crisis of 1774–1776, talk of accommodation gradually disappeared, and expansionists openly wondered whether their goal of a strong, ascendant America could be realized under the heavy hand of the British government. Even Henry Laurens, often a moderate voice in expansionist councils, looked to the west and opined in 1775 that "a mighty empire . . . will arise on this continent where she [Britain] cannot hinder its progress."[27]

What of independence? For the expansionists this step was never more than a means to the end of a puissant, growing America, and the majority added this blazon to their banner only during the first half of 1776. Moreover, many of them supported the call for separation most reluctantly. As a patriot upper class, they had alternately encouraged and checked the mobilization of the common people during the preceding dozen years; now many in the elite feared that any rush to independence might irreparably rend the social fabric. But the need to strengthen the American nation was, for most expansionists, a stronger imperative than their dread of militant artisans and farmers, and so these wealthy revolutionaries embraced the twin goals of a stately march to independence and limited social change. And in fact, the expansionists were generally successful in achieving their desires: no class upheaval accompanied the break from Britain. Although the working people had become more vocal and more influential (and had pushed for independence for their own reasons, most notably, to achieve social and political reform), the expansionists remained the most powerful group in the new states.

26. Thomas Cushing to Arthur Lee, Sept. 1773, MHS *Collections*, 4th ser., IV (1858), 360.
27. Henry Laurens to Thomas Denham, Feb. 7, 1775, Laurens to William Manning, Sept. 23, 1775, Laurens Papers, roll 5, SCHS.

In each colony the most articulate members of the opposing faction, the nonexpansionists, also enunciated their world view, if rarely with the fervor and energy of the expansionists. Typically, outspoken nonexpansionists did not deny the rapid growth of the New World but emphasized the dangers that lay in the future. The unavoidable corollary was the need for close ties with the mother country. "We are not ripe for a disunion," the Reverend Andrew Eliot of Boston observed in 1767, "but our growth is so great that in a few years Great Britain will not be able to compel our submission." He continued: "The colonies, if disunited from Great Britain, must undergo great convulsions before they would be settled on a firm basis. Colony would be against colony, and there would be in every one furious internal contests for power."[28] Thomas Hutchinson echoed these sentiments: "If we are under no other obligations, we certainly enjoy and cannot subsist without the protection of our mother country over our trade at sea, our personal estates ashore, the territory itself, our liberties and lives."[29] Joseph Galloway, too, writing early in 1775, limned a gloomy picture of the problems that would accompany independence: "Disputes will ever arise among the colonies. The seeds of controversy respecting their several interests and boundaries are already sown and in full vegetation." Only subordination to Britain would allow Americans to enjoy "true liberty."[30]

With independence the nonexpansionists were forced to the periphery of American political culture, and the expansionists and their views became ever more important in shaping the destiny of the new nation. New circumstances would elicit further elaborations of the expansionist outlook, but the determination to foster the rapid development of America remained a constant.

28. Andrew Eliot to Thomas Hollis, Dec. 10, 1767, MHS *Cols.*, 4th ser., IV (1858), 420.
29. Hutchinson, *History of Massachusetts*, II, 342.
30. Joseph Galloway, *A Candid Examination of the Mutual Claims of Great Britain and the Colonies* . . . (1775), is reprinted in Merrill Jensen, ed., *Tracts of the American Revolution, 1763–1776* (Indianapolis, Ind., 1967), 350–99, quotations on 386, 388.

PART ONE

The Factions Emerge,
1690–1762

The period stretching from the 1690s to 1762 has special importance for an understanding of the Revolution. During this era two upper-class groups, distinguished by their vision of American development, emerged in each colony. Moreover, during this epoch these factions clashed with one another, particularly over policies toward the French, Spanish, and Indians, and first enunciated their world views. These two elite parties, with no fundamental changes in personnel or outlook, would remain at the center of post-1762 provincial politics, with the expansionists leading the struggle against Great Britain while their circumspect opponents, the nonexpansionists, proved reluctant to support or were openly hostile to such protests.

The widely spaced dates at which these factions first appeared reflected, above all else, the impact of imperial wars. The fighting that raged from 1690 to 1713 helped divide the elite of Massachusetts into two opposing camps before the turn of the century and fostered a split in the New York upper class by the 1710s. More sheltered, Pennsylvania and Virginia largely escaped the clashes of this era, but the warfare of the 1740s shook both colonies to their cores, precipitating divisions. Expansionist and nonexpansionist parties appeared in Pennsylvania in 1740 and in Virginia about 1747. South Carolina was a special case. Conflict with the Spanish produced a first set of imperial factions at the turn of the seventeenth century; this schism endured only a little more than two decades, however, and then a lengthy period of peace coupled with social change effaced party lines. A second set of factions emerged in South Carolina in the mid-1750s.

Several considerations helped determine the makeup of the two parties, but in many colonies no factor was more important than the proximity of an individual's estate to the dangers of the frontier. Thus in New York the manor lords of the upper Hudson, such as the Livingstons, argued the need for an aggressive approach to colonial growth, as did those Virginia planters, such as the Washingtons and Lees, who lived along the Potomac. In South Carolina the wealthy Charleston merchants—for example, Henry Laurens—who owned plantations exposed to hostile incursions had bellicose views, an outlook shared by the rice and indigo planters in the parishes bordering the up-country. In Massachusetts the magnates of the Connecticut River Valley, the "river gods," were expansionists, although a well-justified fear of popular dissension complicated the behavior of this group after 1762. Similarly, the members of the elite whose lands were more protected from overland attack usually became nonexpansionists. The DeLanceys and Philipses of New York, with estates just north of New York City; the Robinsons and Randolphs of Virginia, whose holdings lay near the James River; and William Wragg of South Carolina, who spoke for the planters on the coastal lands south of Charleston, were all nonexpansionists.

Religion and national origin were also important determinants of factional makeup, at times reinforcing and at times conflicting with the geography of party formation. Expansionists could usually rely on the Scotch-Irish Presbyterians, while the nonexpansionist camp firmly embraced the Quakers, such pietistic German sects as the Mennonites and Dunkers, and many of the immigrants who had come directly from Scotland. Moreover, the divisions within New England Congregationalism had a noteworthy impact on party formation: those wealthy Puritans who were somewhat more liberal in religious matters drifted toward the expansionist camp, and those who tended toward an old-line orthodoxy favored the nonexpansionists. Other groups were less clearly divided or less constant in their loyalties. Anglicans in New York and New England often had a cautious view of colonial growth, but in Pennsylvania and the South they were split in their partisan allegiances. Germans adhering to the Lutheran and Reformed churches at first shared the pacifistic outlook of the Quakers and pietists but after 1762 increasingly favored the expansionists.

Both factions made an effort to strengthen their ranks by wooing the common people. Before 1763 the loyalties of farmers and artisans in most colonies were split between the two groups, often reflecting nothing more than the popularity of particular leaders. Class politics in Massachusetts, however, differed from the pattern prevailing in other provinces. The Boston town meeting and an unusually broad system of rural representation provided the basis for a "popular party" strong enough to compete with the two upper-class factions.

Finally, in each colony individuals articulated the "persuasions" that explained and helped guide the behavior of the upper-class factions. Many partisans, busy in the countinghouse or preoccupied with the press of plantation work, spoke with their deeds and kept affirmations of their outlook to the issues at hand. Before 1763 expansionist views were most often embodied in a vigorous concern for the defense of the colonies. "Pray God, give us success," the Charleston firm of Austin & Laurens declared in 1755, "that we may reduce the pride of that haughty, tyrannical people, the French."[1] But others who shared the same assumptions and had more opportunity for reflection explored the broader questions involved. These individuals disseminated world views that illustrated and enlarged the outlooks of their wealthy compatriots.

1. Austin & Laurens to John Knight, July 24, 1755, *The Papers of Henry Laurens*, ed. Philip M. Hamer et al. (Columbia, S.C., 1968–   ), I, 300.

CHAPTER 1

Massachusetts to 1741:
Three Parties Were Formed

"Three parties were formed," observed historian and statesman Thomas Hutchinson in his review of the debate in 1714 over issuing currency.[1] Unlike the other colonies discussed here, Massachusetts possessed, along with the affluent expansionist and nonexpansionist factions, a "popular party," the product of broad rural representation and the open town meeting in Boston. Each of these groups could trace its origins back to the beginning of the century, and each would endure with a remarkable continuity of personnel and outlook until the mid-1770s. The expansionists, who numbered in their ranks the Otises and Hancocks, took as their cynosure the image of a rising, bountiful America, while the nonexpansionists, who counted on the Hutchinsons, Sewalls, and Olivers, among other families, held a more circumspect vision of the future. Finally, the popular party, boasting such leaders as the Elisha Cookes and Samuel Adamses, advocated a set of policies—most notably inflation and democratic government—that reflected the interests of the group's lower-class following.

» «

Self-interest and religious beliefs together shaped the three factions. The popular party brought together two like-minded constitu-

1. Thomas Hutchinson, *The History of the Colony and Province of Massachusetts-Bay*, ed. Lawrence S. Mayo, 3 vols. (Cambridge, Mass., 1936), II, 155–56. Two recent overviews of colonial Massachusetts politics present a neo-Whig interpretation of the Revolution. William Pencak, *War, Politics & Revolution in Provincial Massachusetts* (Boston, 1981), emphasizes libertarian ideology and the division between a court and a country party. Richard L. Bushman, *King and People in Provincial Massachusetts* (Chapel Hill, N.C., 1985), argues that the Bay Colonists feared monarchial designs and so developed a republican outlook.

encies: the poorer farmers and the common people of Boston. The less wealthy rural communities had a potent voice in Bay Colony politics because representation in the assembly was by township and not by the much larger unit of county or parish used outside New England. Before the patriots swept all before them in the mid-1760s, roughly two-fifths of the delegates from the countryside adhered to this faction, and the villages electing popular party men described a broad arc that stretched from Essex County in the north to Plymouth and Bristol counties in the south. Several communities in southern Maine also voted with this faction (map 1). Popular party settlements tended to be poorer and less involved in commercial activities than towns adhering to the two elite groups—nonexpansionist and Connecticut Valley towns—which were their foremost opponents on social and monetary questions.[2]

Boston's common people—"the meanest inhabitants," as Governor William Shirley called them—vivified and emboldened by the town meeting, formed another mainstay of the lower-class faction. "By their constant attendance" at the town meeting, Shirley noted, these "generally are the majority and outvote the gentlemen, merchants, substantial traders, and all the better part of the inhabitants."[3] Despite Shirley's snipe at the "meanest inhabitants," it was the artisans, shopkeepers, and small traders, rather than the laborers or the indigent, who dominated the gatherings and were the most vocal adherents of the popular party in the capital. Moreover, the party leaders—such individuals as Elisha Cooke, Sr. and Jr., Oliver Noyes, and Samuel Adams, Sr. and Jr.—usually lived comfortably and occasionally were well-to-do.[4]

2. One useful measure of a town's wealth is per capita tax assessment. If the average (median) levy on the nonexpansionist settlements noted in map 1 was 100, then this index places the Connecticut Valley towns at 107, and popular party communities at 93. (In these calculations the popular party communities exclude Boston but include the four towns that overlap with the eastern expansionists; see notes to map 1.) The seven "eastern expansionist" communities (again not counting Boston) embraced four popular party towns and had an anomalously low wealth index of 88. Tax lists are presented in *Journals of the House of Representatives of Massachusetts Bay*, ed. Worthington C. Ford et al. (Boston, 1919–), xxxviii, pt. 1, pp. 103–5 (July 9, 1761). For population figures, see Evarts B. Greene and Virginia Harrington, *American Population before the Federal Census of 1790* (New York, 1932), 21–30. Van Beck Hall, *Politics without Parties: Massachusetts, 1780–1791* (Pittsburgh, 1972), 3–22, assesses the commercial development of individual towns. See also Stephen E. Patterson, *Political Parties in Revolutionary Massachusetts* (Madison, Wis., 1973), 33–62, 258–65.

3. Shirley to Board of Trade, Dec. 1, 1747, *Correspondence of William Shirley, Governor of Massachusetts and Military Commander in America, 1731–1760*, ed. Charles Henry Lincoln, 2 vols. (New York, 1912), i, 418.

4. G. B. Warden, *Boston, 1689–1776* (Boston, 1970), 68–69, 118–20; Hutchinson, *History of Massachusetts*, ii, 101, 300; Robert F. Seybolt, *The Town Officials of Colonial Boston, 1634–1775* (Cambridge, Mass., 1939); "Elisha Cooke, Jr.," *DAB*; *Selected Letters of Cotton Mather*, ed. Kenneth Silverman (Baton Rouge, La., 1971), 197, 284.

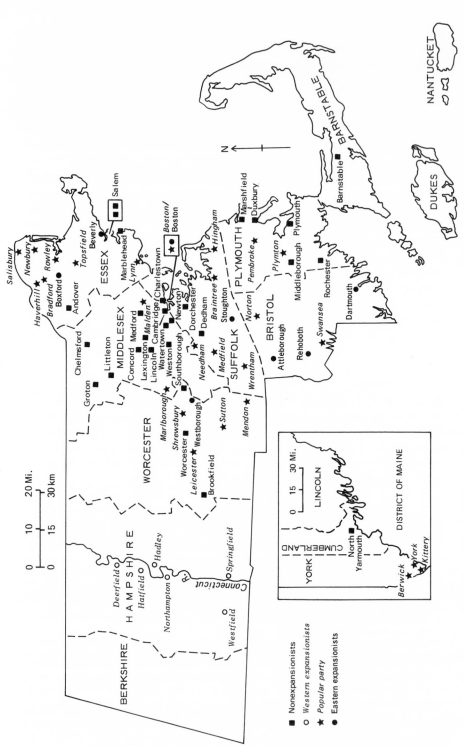

Map 1. Massachusetts: Factional continuities based on fourteen assembly votes.

Nonexpansionists
Western expansionists
Popular party
Eastern expansionists

BERKSHIRE

HAMPSHIRE
Deerfield
Hatfield
Northampton
Westfield
Springfield
Connecticut R.

WORCESTER
Groton
Littleton
Chelmsford
Marlborough
Shrewsbury
Worcester
Leicester Westborough
Brookfield
Sutton
Mendon

MIDDLESEX
Concord Medford
Lexington Malden
Lincoln Cambridge/Charlestown
Weston
Southborough
Watertown Newton
Needham
Medfield
Wrentham

ESSEX
Salisbury
Newbury
Haverhill Rowley
Bradford
Boxford
Andover Topsfield
Beverly
Marblehead
Lynn
Salem

SUFFOLK
Boston/ Boston
Dorchester
Dedham
Stoughton
Norton
Braintree
Hingham

PLYMOUTH
Marshfield
Duxbury
Plymouth
Plymton
Pembroke
Middleborough
Rochester

BRISTOL
Attleborough
Rehoboth
Swansea
Dartmouth

BARNSTABLE
Barnstable

DUKES

NANTUCKET

N

0   10   20 Mi.
0   15   30 km

YORK
CUMBERLAND
North
Yarmouth
Berwick
York
Kittery
LINCOLN
DISTRICT OF MAINE

0   15   30 Mi.

Although religious preferences were not at the root of popular party composition, supporters gravitated to those churches whose doctrines spoke most directly to those on the bottom rungs of the social ladder. In rural Massachusetts, the evangelical strain of Puritanism that blossomed in the Great Awakening of the 1740s attracted the poorer farmers in disproportionate numbers, reflecting their long-standing dissatisfaction with the clerical establishment. The revivalist's direct appeal to men, women, and children, rich and poor, and the frequent gibes at settled ministers constituted a democratizing impulse. Hence communities supporting the popular party were more likely to establish and sustain a Baptist or "New Light" Congregational church than were the towns sending expansionists or nonexpansionists to the General Court.[5] In Boston some members of the lower-class faction joined one of the separatist meetings founded in the 1740s. But in addition, many of the group's leaders, and some of their followers, sought out the settled Congregational pastors most favorably disposed to the intellectual ferment of the revival. Party

5. The link between the popular party and separate churches is based on the correlation between the political loyalties of the sixty-six towns presented in map 1 and information on the fifty-nine communities forming (if briefly in some cases) separate New Light or Baptist churches before 1776. For a list of these new meetings, see C. C. Goen, *Revivalism and Separatism in New England, 1740–1800* (New Haven, 1962), 310–18. On the democratizing nature of the Awakening, see Perry Miller, *Errand into the Wilderness* (Cambridge, Mass., 1956), 154–66; John C. Miller, "Religion, Finance, and Democracy in Massachusetts," *New England Quarterly*, VI (1933), 29–58.

SOURCES: Map 1. Partisan loyalties are based on an examination of fourteen selected votes, printed in *Mass. House Journals*. These polls are: (1) Jan. 15, 1726 (explanatory charter); (2) Mar. 25, 1740 (treasury notes); (3) Jan. 2, 1741 (land bank); (4) Apr. 5, 1751 (provincial bills); (5) Apr. 20, 1751 (provincial bills); (6) Dec. 14, 1754 (plan of union); (7) June 11, 1755 (imprison Daniel Fowle); (8) June 24, 1755 (Crown Point); (9) Oct. 12, 1758 (grant to Agent Bollan); (10) Oct. 9, 1759 (Bollan vs. Pownall); (11) Apr. 20, 1762 (superior court); (12) Feb. 1, 1764 (raising men); (13) Feb. 1, 1764 (Hutchinson as agent); (14) Feb. 1, 1765 (award for Hutchinson). Only towns voting on five or more of these issues were considered for classification. The *western expansionist* position is defined by location in Hampshire County and by agreement at least two-thirds of the time with the following pattern: affirmative votes on 1, 2, 4–10, 12, 14 and negative votes on 3, 11, 13. The *nonexpansionist* position is defined by location outside Hampshire, and by two-thirds agreement or better with the same pattern of votes. *Popular party* towns disagreed with this set of responses two-thirds or more of the time. *Expansionist* communities included towns that fell in any (or none) of the foregoing categories, and had affirmative votes on 1, 13, and two of 6, 7, and 8 and negative votes on 9, 10, 12, and 14. Thus expansionist towns opposed Hutchinson and Bollan, but favored the plan of union and the Crown Point expedition. Four of the seven expansionist towns (Beverly, Boxford, Rehoboth, and Dartmouth) could also be classified as popular party communities. If the western expansionist–nonexpansionist alliance and eastern expansionist–popular party union are considered as the two opposing groups, then similar divisions are presented in Patterson, *Political Parties*, 258–65; and Pencak, *War, Politics & Revolution*, 243–49.

adherents helped fill the pews of the Brattle Street Church, for example, whose minister, Benjamin Colman, was judged a friend of the New Lights.[6]

The lower-class group was committed above all else to two goals—popular government and inflation—and the strongest continuity in the faction's history was its concern for the rights of the common people. These partisans defended, at times fruitlessly, the open system of government in Massachusetts, against a series of onslaughts: the royal charter of 1692, the "explanatory charter" of 1726, the attempts to remodel Boston government, and the efforts of Britain after 1763 to limit representative institutions. Furthermore, this group, which Hutchinson derided as "the needy part of the province," embraced a class of debtors for whom a depreciating currency was a blessing. Popular party strength in the assembly meant that the money question was in the forefront of local politics from 1700 to 1751, when Parliament firmly banned New England's paper bills.[7]

Before 1763 the popular party was of two minds about the issue that most stirred the expansionists: the defense of the colonies against the incursions of the French and Indians. On the one hand, the common people knew that in any prolonged conflict they bore the brunt of food shortages, taxes, and military service but rarely received their share of the rewards flowing from wartime enterprises. On the other hand, these mechanics and farmers recognized that campaigns against the French often meant a surge of government spending and at least the possibility of a flood of inflationary currency. After 1762, ties with the expansionists strengthened as popular party supporters translated their defense of representative colonial institutions into an irrefragable hostility to ministerial schemes.[8]

The Bay Colony expansionists comprised a set of affluent easterners and the magnates of the Connecticut Valley. While these two groups were in many ways odd bedfellows, they shared during the wars against New France a determination to defeat the Bourbons and their native allies. In eastern Massachusetts the most influential cluster of expansionists hailed from Boston and included the Bowdoins,

6. Christopher M. Jedrey, *The World of John Cleaveland: Family and Community in Eighteenth-Century New England* (New York, 1979), 42–46, describes the members of Cleaveland's separatist church in Boston as a "ragged and despised little congregation." See also Anthony Gregg Roeber, "'Her Merchandize . . . Shall Be Holiness to the Lord': The Progress and Decline of Puritan Gentility at the Brattle Street Church, Boston, 1715–1745," *NEHGR*, cxxxi (1977), 180–89.

7. Hutchinson, *History of Massachusetts*, ii, 300.

8. Fred Anderson, *A People's Army: Massachusetts Soldiers and Society in the Seven Years' War* (Chapel Hill, N.C., 1984), esp. chap. 2.

Winthrops, and Thomas Hancock. Farther down the coast, the rocky soils of Barnstable nurtured a talented family, the Otises; several generations of this mercantile and political clan played a prominent role in party affairs even though their own town often sent nonexpansionists to the General Court. Within the legislature a set of communities as dispersed as Beverly and Stoughton usually voted with this faction (map 1), but the group's longevity and strength stemmed from its preeminence within the Boston merchant community and the ability of its leaders to work closely with many of the governors and with the other parties.

Although self-interest—including investments in the Maine land companies and contracts for provisioning the troops—brought some of the wealthy easterners into the party, social and religious leanings were more important in determining allegiances.[9] Eastern expansionists, while largely Congregationalists, gravitated to pastors who carved out a middle position within the Massachusetts religious establishment; these divines distanced themselves not only from the excesses of the revival but also from the hierarchical doctrines espoused both by the Church of England and by some of the more conservative Puritan meetings. The Brattle Street Church, for example, was established in 1699 by a merchant who disliked the Mathers' harsh counsel during the Salem witch trials. The Reverend John Colman and his successor, Samuel Cooper, kept this congregation receptive to dissenting views, attracting farsighted traders like the Hancocks and Bowdoins as well as some popular party adherents. Expansionists also frequented Jonathan Mayhew's West Church and Charles Chauncy's First Church. These ministers emphasized the worth of an individual's rational faculties and the possibility of cooperating with God in working toward salvation. Such religious teachings helped justify and encourage the worldly projects of Massachusetts expansionists, whose outlook embraced both a concern for

9. John W. Tyler, "The First Revolution: Boston Merchants and the Acts of Trade, 1760–1774" (Ph.D. diss., Princeton Univ., 1980), explores whether patriot and loyalist traders can be distinguished by their business activities and finds on both sides a preponderance of "general merchants" and dry goods wholesalers. Tyler does show, however, that a few small subgroups—such as government contractors or smugglers in the Holland trade—joined one faction or the other. Virginia D. Harrington, *The New York Merchant on the Eve of the Revolution* (New York, 1935), 349–51, presents similar conclusions for that colony. Cf. John Murrin, "The Great Inversion; or, Court versus Country: A Comparison of the Revolution Settlements in England (1688–1721) and America (1776–1816)," in J. G. A. Pocock, ed., *Three British Revolutions, 1641, 1688, 1776* (Princeton, N.J., 1980), 394–97; *Mass. House Journals*, I, 140, X, 398; MeHS *Collections*, 1st ser., V (1857), 301–302, 2d ser., IX (1907), 361–62; "Sir William Pepperell," *DAB;* Joseph Heath and John Minot to Gov. Samuel Shute, May 1, 1719, William Pepperell, Jr., to Josiah Willard, Oct. 10, 1721, MeHS *Cols.*, 2d ser., IX, 446, 447.

the social fabric and a readiness to support changes that fostered growth.[10]

Church records for these congregations indicate a preponderance of affluent patriots, if never a rigid exclusion of worshipers with other views. But Bostonians repeatedly testified to their awareness of the role played by such liberal-minded divines as Mayhew and Cooper. When Mayhew was ordained in 1747, of eleven Congregational meetings in Boston, only the Brattle Street and First Churches were invited to send their ministers to the ceremony. And in 1762 when a coalition of expansionists and popular party supporters installed Jasper Maudit as the colony's new London agent, James Otis, Jr., counseled Maudit that controversial religious matters should be "entrusted only with such gentlemen as Dr. Chauncy, Dr. Mayhew, and the Rev'd and very worthy Mr. Cooper."[11]

The expansionists of eastern Massachusetts and the clergymen they patronized readily moved from their broad philosophical and religious tenets to a range of corollaries that bore directly on political questions. Cooper, Chauncy, Mayhew, and other ministers celebrated the campaigns against the French, castigated the harsh new British policies, and rhapsodized about their dream of a mighty empire in the New World. At times they questioned anointed authorities within the empire and the colony. Thus Mayhew's sermon, "Discourse concerning Unlimited Submission," which suggested that unjust rulers need not be obeyed, was declaimed in 1750 at a time when many expansionists were angry with the contractionist program pushed through by Thomas Hutchinson and Governor Shirley. In keeping with their philosophical stance, the eastern expansionists enunciated a carefully balanced position on the money question, placing themselves between the inflationists of the popular party and the Hutchinsonian contractionists. Many of them felt that a regulated but expanding currency would be a boon to development.[12]

10. Roeber, "Brattle Street Church," 175–94; Charles W. Akers, *Called unto Liberty: A Life of Jonathan Mayhew, 1720–1766* (Cambridge, Mass., 1964), 31; Warden, *Boston*, 15, 68, 144; Edwin S. Gaustad, "Society and the Great Awakening in New England," *WMQ*, 3d ser., xi (1954), 574, 576; Robert Middlekauff, *The Mathers: Three Generations of Puritan Intellectuals, 1596–1728* (New York, 1971), 219–20.

11. James Otis, Jr., to Jasper Maudit, Oct. 28, 1762, Feb. 14, 1763, MHS *Collections*, lxxiv (1918), 77–80, 95; Charles W. Akers, "Religion and the American Revolution: Samuel Cooper and the Brattle Street Church," *WMQ*, 3d ser., xxxv (1978), 477–98; *Records of the Church in Brattle Square* (Boston, 1902); Akers, *Called unto Liberty*, 49.

12. Warden, *Boston*, 86, 134, 140, 152; Bernard Bailyn, "Religion and Revolution: Three Biographical Studies," *Perspectives in American History*, iv (1970), 111–21; Hutchinson, *History of Massachusetts*, iii, 209, 237; John Adams to Cotton Tufts, Apr. 9, 1764, *Adams Family Correspondence*, ed. L. H. Butterfield et al., 2 vols. (Cambridge, Mass., 1963), i, 20; Gaustad, "Society and the Great Awakening," 573, 576; Akers,

The wealthy families of the Connecticut Valley—including the Stoddards, Williamses, and Hawleys—led the western wing of the expansionist faction in Massachusetts. These men, often called the river gods, held estates close to the exposed western frontier and before 1760 wholeheartedly concurred with the eastern expansionists on the need for vigorous defense measures (map 1). However, the river gods and the eastern expansionists did not see eye-to-eye on other issues. The dependence of the westerners on gubernatorial patronage and their awareness that their perch at the apex of the Hampshire County social pyramid was far from secure helped frame a conservative mindset. These partisans condemned not only the Great Awakening but also the liberal Puritanism of the Brattle Street, West, and First Church parishioners, feeling that any creed that questioned constituted authority was dangerous. Moreover, the river gods viewed all currency schemes as a threat to the social order and demanded a return to a specie-based money supply. Unsurprisingly, these westerners frequently voted with the nonexpansionists in the General Court. Rightly fearing that the clash with Britain would lead to social upheaval in their section of the colony, the western expansionists would later oppose the resistance movement and would eventually become loyalists. Only a few river gods, Joseph Hawley among them, adhered to the expansionist continuities that prevailed elsewhere and opposed the British in the 1760s and 1770s.[13]

The nonexpansionists in Massachusetts were headed by a coterie of ministers and merchants who resided in Boston and its environs. At the core of the group were such prominent families as the Hutchinsons, Mathers, Olivers, Faneuils, and Sewalls. Although the nonexpansionists were often the weakest of the three parties at the Boston town meeting, their strength was never negligible, and the meeting occasionally sent nonexpansionist representatives to the General Court. Furthermore, the nonexpansionists (at least before the upheavals of the mid-1760s) enjoyed the support of many of the more affluent and commercialized farming towns, commanding a bloc of votes comparable in strength to the popular party's. Backing for the nonexpansionists came from the wealthier settlements such as

---

Called unto Liberty, 32–35, 61–75, 81–94, 134–37; T. H. Breen, *The Character of the Good Ruler: Puritan Political Ideas in New England, 1630–1730* (New Haven, Conn., 1970), 274–75.

13. Lee N. Newcomer, "Yankee Rebels of Inland Massachusetts," *WMQ*, 3d ser., ix (1952), 156–65; Stephen Innes, "Land Tenancy and Social Order in Springfield, Massachusetts, 1652–1702," *WMQ*, 3d ser., xxxv (1978), 33–56; William H. Whitmore, *The Massachusetts Civil List for the Colonial and Provincial Periods, 1630–1774* (Albany, 1870), 91–94, 139; Robert J. Taylor, *Western Massachusetts in the Revolution* (Providence, 1954), 14–15, 23–25, 52–75; Miller, *Errand into the Wilderness*, 163–66.

Charlestown and Cambridge, that ringed Boston and from several of the larger coastal towns, including Salem, Marblehead, and Plymouth (map 1).

Religious attitudes help explain why particular members of the eastern elite, engaged in economic activities similar to those of the expansionists, became nonexpansionists instead. These partisans inclined toward Anglicanism or the strain of Congregationalism emphasizing authority and tradition. Boston's Anglican churches (there were three by the 1730s) included among their parishioners such prominent nonexpansionists as the Faneuils and Apthorps. Moreover, some who preserved their ties with Puritanism found the Church of England attractive. "Had I been born and bred there," confessed Thomas Hutchinson, "I would never have left it for any other communion."[14] Most of these partisans remained within the Congregational fold and during the early decades of the century found their sentiments best voiced by such ministers as Increase and Cotton Mather, who led the Second Church. Later, the nonexpansionists praised the sermons of the pastor of New North Church, Andrew Eliot, whom John Adams acerbically labeled "Hutchinson's parish priest and his devoted idolator." These divines gave less credence to the efficacy of human reason than did ministers like Chauncy and Mayhew, and they extolled a stable hierarchical social order.[15]

While religious leanings helped define this faction, the Hutchinsonians quickly translated such beliefs into practical politics. These men were reluctant to support the campaigns against the French and Indians and urged a reversion to gold and silver coin as the answer to the colony's currency problems. In provincial affairs they favored measures—for example, the "explanatory charter" of 1726—restricting the role of the less affluent, and in Boston they labored to remodel city government and to regulate the public markets. Finally, the nonexpansionists would oppose the protests against the mother country and eventually become loyalists.[16]

Between 1690 and 1776 the three parties alternately feuded and

14. Thomas Hutchinson to Francis Bernard, Dec. 24, 1771, quoted in Bernard Bailyn, *The Ordeal of Thomas Hutchinson* (Cambridge, Mass., 1974), 23; Seybolt, *Boston Town Officials*, passim; Henry W. Foote, *Annals of King's Chapel: From the Puritan Age to the Present Day*, 3 vols. (Boston, 1882–1940), passim; [The Wardens and Vestry of Trinity Church], *Trinity Church in the City of Boston, Massachusetts, 1733–1933* (Boston, 1933), passim; Warden, *Boston*, 36, 88.

15. John Adams to William Tudor, Feb. 4, 1817, *The Works of John Adams*, ed. Charles Francis Adams, 10 vols. (Boston, 1850–56), x, 243; Bailyn, "Religion and Revolution," 88–110; Warden, *Boston*, 36–37, 86–88; *Selected Letters of Mather*, passim; Middlekauf, *The Mathers*, 231–61. Hutchinson also attended the Reverend William Welsteed's New Brick Church (Pencak, *War, Politics & Revolution*, 121).

16. Warden, *Boston*, 115–23.

allied with one another, depending on where they judged their interests to lie. But though one group or another might temporarily disappear in a coalition, each invariably emerged again to work for its distinct vision of society.

» «

During the first era of factional development, 1690 to 1725, the pressures of war divided the upper classes into two parties and provided a difficult challenge for the common people of Massachusetts. Expansionists cheered the bellicose governors and denounced the less aggressive ones. They grumbled at Governor William Stoughton's reluctance to engage the enemy during the closing years of King William's War. "We are under ill circumstances here," complained Wait Still Winthrop, "and poor management with respect to the Indian war."[17] Expansionists lauded Joseph Dudley, however, who took up the seals of office in 1702 and made the Bay Colony an active participant in Queen Anne's War, a conflict that dragged on until 1713. Dudley directed patronage to this faction and relied on Wait Winthrop, John Otis, John Higginson, and other expansionists for advice. Their counsel well pleased him. Higginson, for example, praised Dudley's grand strategy and argued in a memorial penned in 1705 that "it will be highly necessary that Canada be reduced to the crown of England."[18]

Predictably, expansionists scorned Governor Samuel Shute, who entered office in 1716 and soon demonstrated his reluctance to defend the outlying settlements in Maine against Indian attacks. When sporadic clashes with the Indians and their French advisers burst into an Indian war in 1721, John Otis, Joseph Minot, and other expansionists criticized the vacillating executive and acted on their own to bolster the colonial military effort. These politicians were happier with the administration of William Dummer, who brought the war in Maine to a successful conclusion.[19]

17. Wait Winthrop to Fitz Winthrop, [c. 1695], quoted in Richard S. Dunn, *Puritans and Yankees: The Winthrop Dynasty of New England, 1630–1717* (Princeton, 1962), 270; Philip S. Haffenden, *New England in the English Nation, 1689–1713* (Oxford, 1974); A. B. Hart, ed., *Commonwealth History of Massachusetts*, 5 vols. (New York, 1928), ii, 68–78; Everett Kimball, *The Public Life of Joseph Dudley: A Study of the Colonial Policy of the Stuarts in New England, 1660–1715* (London, 1911), chaps. 5, 6; Lt. Gov. William Stoughton to secretary of state, Apr. 28, 1701, MeHS *Cols.*, 2d ser., ix (1907), 111; Hutchinson, *History of Massachusetts*, ii, 60–61.

18. Memorial of John Higginson, [c. 1705], MeHS *Cols.*, 2d ser., ix (1907), 211; Whitmore, *Massachusetts Civil List*; Dunn, *Puritans and Yankees*, 282.

19. John Otis to William Dummer, Aug. 25, 1725, Joseph Heath and John Minot to Gov. Shute, May 1, 1719, MeHS *Cols.*, 2d ser., x (1908), 276, ix (1907), 446; Cotton Mather to Robert Wodrow, Jan. 1, 1723, *Selected Letters of Mather*, 356–57; Hutchinson, *History of Massachusetts*, ii, 216–41; Pencak, *War, Politics & Revolution*, 71–77.

Nonexpansionists saw this succession of governors through very different eyes. Joseph Dudley's bellicose ways were a particular cause for apprehension. Many lawmakers "when the war broke out . . . earnestly moved me to . . . draw in that frontier [in Maine]," Dudley observed, but those borders "being the utmost frontier eastwards, I have always positively refused to draw them in."[20] During the war years, Cotton Mather and Samuel Sewall were Dudley's most outspoken critics. Ostensibly, both men wished the colony's expeditions well, but Mather seemed only too eager to suggest how the colonists might profit from defeat, for "who can tell how far calamity may prepare them to receive a glorious gospel," and Sewall took the unusual position that New France could be conquered "with little or no bloodshed."[21] Both reprobated Dudley's conduct of the war: Mather lambasted the governor in sermons and private letters, and Sewall was the one councillor who refused to support Dudley against charges that the governor had encouraged a treasonable trade with the French and Indians. Finally, Mather and Sewell led the coterie seeking to oust the executive from his office.[22]

Nonexpansionists were more pleased by Governor Shute's pacific leanings. Cotton Mather pronounced Shute "a person of an excellent spirit" and widely broadcast his merits.[23] Similarly, Sewall applauded Shute's reluctance to prosecute the Indian war and in 1721 submitted a memorial asking whether "sufficient enquiry has not been yet made, whether the government has done all that is necessary on their part to prevent a rupture [with the Indians]." A grateful Shute repaid this support by praising Cotton Mather and appointing Sewall chief justice.[24]

For members of the popular party, the question of war or peace played only a subordinate role in shaping their response to Bay Colony governors. Between 1690 and 1715 the group typically feuded with

20. Gov. Dudley to Board of Trade, Mar. 1, 1709, MeHS *Cols.*, 2d ser., ix (1907), 252.

21. Cotton Mather to John Maxwell of Pollock, Aug. 12, 1712, *Selected Letters of Mather*, 104; Samuel Sewall to Nathaniel Higginson, Oct. 21, 1706, MHS *Cols.*, 6th ser., i (1886), 340.

22. Mather to Joseph Dudley, Jan. 20, 1708, Mather to Lord Nottingham, Nov. 26, 1703, *Selected Letters of Mather*, 77–82, 67–78, and see 56–61; Samuel Sewall to Nathaniel Higginson, Oct. 16, 1706, Mar. 10, 1708, Samuel Sewall to Sir Henry Ashurst, Feb. 25, 1708, MHS *Cols.*, 6th ser., i (1886), 334, 362, 359; Hutchinson, *History of Massachusetts*, ii, 117–21. Pencak, *War, Politics & Revolution*, 45–53, suggests the charges against Dudley were unfounded.

23. Mather to Thomas Hollis, Jr., Nov. 5, 1723, *Selected Letters of Mather*, 375.

24. Samuel Sewall, A Memorial Relating to the Kennebeck Indians, 1721, MeHS *Cols.*, 1st ser., iii (1853), 351–53; Samuel Sewall to Jeremiah Dummer, Feb. 23, 1720, MHS *Cols.*, 6th ser., ii (1888), 110; Hutchinson, *History of Massachusetts*, ii, 202–4; Mather to Thomas Hollis, Jr., Nov. 5, 1723, *Selected Letters of Mather*, 375, and see 370; Whitmore, *Mass. Civil List*.

the bellicose executives, possibly because many artisans and poorer farmers resented the burdens of the lengthy wars. In the 1690s they crossed swords with Sir William Phips, who called for a vigorous campaign against the outposts of New France in Maine. Angered by this nettlesome faction, Phips excluded them from the spoils of office. The pacific Stoughton was more to the popular party's liking, and the executive soon made himself the group's benefactor, even elevating Elisha Cooke, Sr., to the superior court. The lower-class faction clashed, however, with the imperialistic Dudley, who needed little encouragement to attack these partisans. Apart from several appointments made during his first weeks in office, Dudley rarely awarded any post to this group, and regularly vetoed popular party adherents chosen to the council; Dudley vetoed Cooke no fewer than thirteen times. The costs of Queen Anne's War, a contest Dudley so avidly joined, lay heavily upon the poorer citizens. A grain shortage, in part the product of military requisitions, produced angry riots in the capital in 1711. On another occasion, enraged housewives greeted the soldiers returning from an unsuccessful expedition by pouring their chamber pots upon them. The women shouted to one another: "Is your piss-pot charged, neighbor? So-ho, souse the cowards."[25]

After 1715, however, the lower-class faction charted a new course, endorsing military initiatives and denouncing Governor Shute for his reluctance to attack the Maine Indians. This reversal in part mirrored the mounting importance of the currency question; the party chieftains now viewed war as an excellent excuse for inflationary issues of paper money. In addition, the involvement of several of the faction's leaders in Maine land companies made them more receptive to expansionist arguments about military preparedness. Shute and his circle fully reciprocated popular party hostility. "The common people . . . are so perverse," Shute fumed after Bostonians elected to the legislature a man he had excluded from the council.[26] Remarked Cotton Mather, "There is a very wicked party in this country who fill the land with strife and sin, and who are drawing the people into continual snares." The governor's advisers particularly reviled Oliver Noyes, who, in one chronicler's words, "was strongly attached to the popular party ard highly esteemed by them." According to Mather,

25. Wait Still Winthrop's statement, 1707, recounting the welcome given the soldiers, quoted in *Selected Letters of Mather*, 60; Whitmore, *Mass. Civil List;* Hutchinson, *History of Massachusetts.* II, 60–61, 81, 96–97, 101, 111; Warden, *Boston*, 66.

26. Gov. Shute to Board of Trade, June 1, 1720, quoted in William D. Metz, "Politics and Finance in Massachusetts, 1713–1741" (Ph.D. diss., Univ. of Wisconsin, 1945), 196; Roeber, "Brattle Street Church," 180–85; Hutchinson, *History of Massachusetts*, II, 174–85; *Mass. House Journals*, I, 140, X, 398; MeHS *Cols.*, 1st ser., V (1857), 301–2, 2d ser., IX (1907), 361–62.

Noyes was little more than a "misleader and enchanter of the people."[27]

Along with military questions, the three groups also divided over monetary policy. A particularly acerbic debate surfaced soon after Queen Anne's War. Thomas Hutchinson, Jr., whose father was a leading contractionist, described the differing views.

> One [party was] very small, which were for drawing in the paper bills and depending upon silver and gold currency. Mr. [Thomas] Hutchinson, [Sr.], one of the members for Boston, was among the most active of this party. . . . Another party was very numerous. These had projected a private bank. . . . There was nothing more in it, than issuing bills of credit. . . . This party generally consisted of persons in difficult or involved circumstances in trade, or such as was possessed of real estates, but had little or no ready money at command, or men of no substance at all. . . . Three of the representatives of Boston, Mr. [Elisha] Cooke, [Jr.], . . . Mr. [Oliver] Noyes . . . and Mr. [William] Payne, were the supporters of the party. . . . A third party, though very opposite to the private bank, yet were no enemies to bills of credit.[28]

Hutchinson's analysis offers a convenient overview of the three factions. The nonexpansionists were the hard-money party; the popular party urged the creation of a "land bank," which would issue large sums of currency backed by the subscribers' real estate; and the third group, the expansionists, stood midway between the inflationists and the hard-money adherents. It was the expansionists who engineered the compromise finally accepted, a closely regulated government bank. But this contentious question did not subside. Governor Shute's adamant support for "a return to silver and gold," which he called "the only true species of money," kept currency in the foreground as an object of public debate throughout his administration.[29]

» «

There were no military ventures during the next period of factional conflict, 1725 to 1741, an era that subdivides into two periods. Between 1725 and 1733 questions of class predominated, and the two elite groups, melding into a single "prerogative" faction, united against the popular party. But after 1733 this upper-class alliance

27. Mather diary, Mar. 16, 1721, quoted in Metz, "Politics and Finance," 219. Hutchinson, *History of Massachusetts*, II, 188, was the chronicler.
28. Hutchinson, *History of Massachusetts*, II, 155–56.
29. Metz, "Politics and Finance," 75–91; Hutchinson, *History of Massachusetts*, II, 179–85; *Mass. House Journals*, I, 169–70.

dissolved as the currency question grew increasingly important. Only the popular party remained a distinct entity throughout these years.

The first battle of the period 1725 to 1733 was over the explanatory charter, a document that pitted the popular party against the united upper classes. This controversy had its origins in Governor Shute's disputes with the legislature and his appeal to the Board of Trade for assistance. The board reviewed the Massachusetts frame of government and offered a set of amendments reaffirming the governor's right to reject the assembly's choice of speaker and restricting the power of the house to adjourn itself. Only the popular party, the self-appointed Argus standing guard over the colony's representative institutions, roundly condemned this extension of the prerogative. In 1726 the two houses voted to accept the document, with the division in each chamber falling broadly along class lines. In the council such expansionists as John Cushing and Adam Winthrop voted with non-expansionists like Thomas Hutchinson, Sr., and Daniel Oliver (father of future loyalists Andrew and Peter) in favor of the charter. The few councillors, such as Elisha Cooke, Jr., and Nathaniel Byfield, who spoke against the restrictive amendments, were linked to the popular party. The lower chamber approved the document by a vote of forty-eight to thirty-two, with the two upper-class parties favoring the new charter and a familiar arc of poorer farming communities stretching from Essex to Plymouth counties forming the principal opposition.[30]

During the balance of Lieutenant Governor Dummer's term and during William Burnet's brief administration, wealthy and less affluent citizens quarreled over gubernatorial demands for a secure salary and strengthened prerogatives. Two of Governor Joseph Dudley's sons—William, who was speaker of the house, and Paul, a councillor and justice of the superior court—led the elite coalition, which was sympathetic to Dummer's and Burnet's requests. Opposing the Dudleys were Elisha Cooke, Jr., and his lower-class followers; Cooke adhered to a course set by his father, who had long battled the elder Dudley. "We have at present two parties," a Bostonian observed in 1727, "Dudley and Cooke, who from private family resentments have drawn the country blindly into differences in public management for several years."[31] Cooke, with support from the prerogative faction on crucial votes, held the line against executive demands. Governor Burnet, a refugee from the factional wars in New York, was caught up

30. Albert Matthews, "Acceptance of the Explanatory Charter, 1725–1726," CSM *Publications*, xiv (1913), 389–400; *Mass. House Journals*, vi, 458–459.

31. William Douglass to Cadwallader Colden, Nov. 20, 1727, NYHS *Cols.*, l (1917), 238.

in this second conflict. Broken by the bitter struggles, he died in 1729.[32]

During his first years in office Governor Jonathan Belcher, like his predecessor Burnet, functioned in a bipartisan world, with a prerogative and a popular faction. Belcher tried to strike a deal with the leaders of the lower-class group: his patronage in return for a multi-year salary. The resulting alliance between Belcher and Cooke was short-lived, as many well-to-do colonists surmised it would be. "The prerogative men," Thomas Hutchinson explained, "were Mr. Belcher's old friends, who were pretty well satisfied that his going over to the other side was not from any real affection to the cause, and that he must sooner or later differ with those who adhered to it, and for this event they waited patiently."[33] Belcher awarded offices to Cooke and a few other prominent individuals in the popular faction. Cooke, however, failed to persuade other members of his circle to back the governor's demands. Instead, Cooke's own popularity suffered, and in 1732 he narrowly escaped defeat when the Boston town meeting voted for representatives. With such pressure on both Belcher and Cooke, the misalliance soon dissolved, and the governor renewed his ties with the upper classes.[34]

The popular party continued to be a coherent, outspoken group, but the currency question gradually split the prerogative faction into its expansionist and nonexpansionist components. This schism, which gravely weakened Belcher's base of support and would lead to his downfall, began with the controversy over the bank scheme of 1733. Hard times in the Bay Colony revived interest in paper money, and in 1733 a set of Boston merchants associated with the expansionist party, observing that "the province is found to labor under great inconveniences through the want of a stable and sufficient medium of exchange," established a private bank.[35] The plan, which had all the earmarks of that party's balanced approach to the currency question, moderately increased the supply of treasury bills while carefully regulating and securing these new notes. Although the bank

32. William Douglass to C. Colden, Apr. 22, Sept. 9, 1728, ibid., L, 257–58, 270; Hutchinson, *History of Massachusetts*, II, 252–77.

33. Hutchinson, *History of Massachusetts*, II, 284.

34. Ibid., 284–87; Whitmore, *Mass. Civil List;* Gov. Jonathan Belcher to Thomas Palmer and others, Nov. 9, 1731, Gov. Belcher to Francis Wilks, Nov. 1, 1731, Dec. 25, 1732, Gov. Belcher to bishop of London, Apr. 29, 1732, Gov. Belcher to Richard Waldron, June 11, Nov. 16, 1733, Gov. Belcher to Jonathan Belcher, Jr., Dec. 25, 1733, MHS *Cols.*, 6th ser., VI (1893), 48, 43, 229, 131, 301, 415, 443; Warden, *Boston*, 107–8; Metz, "Politics and Finance," 433–56.

35. Quotation from "The Scheme," orig. pub. *New England Weekly Journal*, Jan. 21, 1734, reprinted in A. M. Davis, "The Merchants' Notes of 1733," MHS *Procs.*, 2d ser., XVII (1903), 204.

attracted a few popular party men, including Samuel Adams, Sr., and several nonexpansionists, such as Samuel Sewall (a cousin of the more famous Samuel who died in 1730), overwhelmingly the individuals who planned, directed, and subscribed to the institution were expansionists. Members of this faction involved in the scheme included James Bowdoin, Sr., Thomas Cushing II, and Thomas Hancock. Belcher now felt forced to choose between the elite parties, and he lashed out at the expansionists and their plans, exclaiming, "The merchants' private bank here . . . bids fair to ruin the country."[36]

The mid-1730s were quiet years politically, but after 1738 worsening economic conditions once again brought the currency question to the fore, and factional conflict resumed. In 1739 popular party supporters set up a land bank, implementing the program they had discussed for many years. The institution was to strike large amounts of money for which the subscribers' real estate was to provide security. Some twelve hundred people, drawn largely from the lower classes of Boston and from the rural areas of eastern Massachusetts, enrolled. With few exceptions, members of the elite vituperated the bank and voted against it in the legislature. A recorded ballot of June 1740 shows a familiar split between the broad swath of poorer farming communities adhering to the popular party and the wealthier towns aligned with the two elite factions.[37]

Expansionists and nonexpansionists, however, offered different alternatives to the land bank. Members of both elite factions initially backed a counterinstitution, a "silver bank," which was to issue a currency linked closely to the value of specie. For many subscribers the stratagem was intended less to expand the money supply than, as Hutchinson observed, "to lessen the temptation to receive the [land bank] bills."[38] But some expansionists, such as Jacob Wendell and Adam Winthrop, softened their opposition to the land bank by announcing that they would accept its notes as well as the currency of the silver bank. In contrast, such nonexpansionists as the Hutchinsons, Olivers, and Faneuils remained implacable opponents of the

36. Davis, "Merchants' Notes," 184–208; Gov. Belcher to Richard Waldron, Apr. 29, 1734, MHS *Cols.*, 6th ser., vii (1894), 43.

37. Andrew McFarland Davis, "List of Partners in the Land Bank of 1740," CSM *Pubs.*, iv (1910), 168–94; Hutchinson, *History of Massachusetts*, ii, 298–300. On a per capita basis subscriptions in towns linked with the popular party were higher than in communities linked to the other factions. If the (median) average for per capita participation in nonexpansionist towns was 100, then this index was 0 for Connecticut Valley settlements, 120 for eastern expansionists, and 132 for popular party towns. See map 1 and data in Patterson, *Political Parties*, 258–65.

38. Hutchinson, *History of Massachusetts*, ii, 300; *Mass. House Journals*, xviii, 47–48, 185–86; Gov. Belcher to Board of Trade, Nov. 17, 1740, MHS *Cols.*, 6th ser., vii (1894), 348–49.

land bank and gradually took over direction of the silver bank, making its bills more closely approximate specie. Thomas Hutchinson would have gone farther still; he called for the abolition of all paper money and a reversion to gold and silver currency.[39]

Meanwhile, Governor Jonathan Belcher increasingly identified himself with the nonexpansionists. During the late 1730s he awarded offices to that faction's adherents, including Samuel Sewall and Andrew Oliver, and he drew close to Thomas Hutchinson, who, Belcher remarked, "well understands the public affairs of his country, and very particularly the nature of the wicked paper currency." Belcher also praised the nonexpansionists' silver bank once he received assurances that its bills could be exchanged freely for specie.[40]

Belcher's willingness to cross the expansionists, as well as the popular party, led to his fall from power. The executive, who had long since abandoned his flirtation with the lower-class group, railed against the land bank and lobbied successfully for an act of Parliament to dissolve it. What proved his undoing, however, was his feud with the expansionists, many of whom were wealthy men with important London connections. The governor's hard-money policies irritated these partisans, as did his indifference toward defense. "I am not much displeased," Belcher stated testily during one dispute with the assembly, "that the frontier towns are like to be deserted, and that there's no powder to be had for love nor money."[41] Gradually these individuals—including the Otises, Thomas Hancock, and Paul Dudley—grouped themselves around William Shirley, an imperial-minded lawyer and politician, who they hoped would succeed Belcher. In the spring of 1741 the efforts of the expansionists were crowned with success: the ministry removed Belcher and made over the seals of office to Shirley.[42]

39. Andrew McFarland Davis, "List of Subscribers to the Silver Bank," CSM *Pubs.*, IV (1910), 199–200; Hutchinson, *History of Massachusetts*, II, 298–299; Roeber, "Brattle Street Church," 189.

40. Gov. Belcher to Richard Partridge, Oct. 30, 1740, Gov. Belcher to Board of Trade, Nov. 17, 1740, MHS *Cols.*, 6th ser., VII (1894), 342, 348–49; Whitmore, *Mass. Civil List*, 128.

41. Gov. Belcher to Richard Waldron, Mar. 21, 1734, Gov. Belcher to Board of Trade, Oct. 24, 1739, Jan. 14, 1740, Gov. Belcher to duke of Newcastle, Oct. 30, 1740, MHS *Cols.*, 6th ser., VII (1894), 29, 227, 256, 340; David Dunbar to Sec. Alured Popple, Oct. 6, 1730, Order in Council, Nov. 12, 1730, Gov. Belcher to duke of Newcastle, Jan. 1, 1731, MeHS *Cols.*, 2d ser., XI (1908), 60, 66–67, 87.

42. Gov. Belcher to Richard Partridge, Nov. 26, 1739, July 15, 1740, Gov. Belcher to Horace Walpole, Jan. 21, 1740, Gov. Belcher to Jonathan Belcher, Jr., May 19, 1740, MHS *Cols.*, 6th ser., VII (1894), 248, 313–14, 265–67, 301; John A. Schutz, *William Shirley: King's Governor of Massachusetts* (Chapel Hill, N.C., 1961), 30–44; John J. Waters, Jr., *The Otis Family in Provincial and Revolutionary Massachusetts* (Chapel Hill, N.C., 1968), 58; "Samuel Waldo," *DAB*; Whitmore, *Mass. Civil List*.

The three parties that had formed by 1700 would continue after 1741 and, indeed, until the eve of independence. A new period of warfare with the French and Indians would precipitate changed alliances and spur some individuals in each faction to elaborate their views. But the constituencies ruled by the three groups, the composition of their inner circles, and their world views—all would evolve within the lines deeply etched before 1741.

CHAPTER 2

Massachusetts, 1741–1762:
Coalition Politics

The Bay Colonists had known few executives as able as William Shirley. From his accession to the governor's chair in 1741 to his departure in 1756 Shirley worked deliberately and effectively to create a series of proadministration coalitions from the three factions. Typical of his dealings was his early success in winning over the popular party. "I have had the satisfaction to find," he announced in 1742, "that those members of the house of representatives whose relation to the land bank scheme made it expected that they would have been in opposition to the measures of the government, have been brought to concur in and promote his Majesty's service in several considerable points, which had never been before gained from former assemblies."[1] On other occasions, Shirley wooed, with favorable results, the expansionists and the Hutchinsonians.

Massachusetts politics during Shirley's lengthy administration and the years that followed turned on the workings of the three parties that had coalesced at the beginning of the century. During the midcentury era as earlier, the Otises and Hancocks led the expansionists, and the Hutchinsons and Olivers, the nonexpansionists; however, a set of new men, James Allen, John Tyng, and Samuel Adams, Sr., stood at the popular party's helm.

» «

In the 1740s, war was the overriding issue shaping the behavior of Bay Colony politicians. Expansionists flocked to Governor Shirley's

1. Gov. Shirley to duke of Newcastle, Sept. 15, 1742, *Correspondence of William Shirley, Governor of Massachusetts and Military Commander in America, 1731–1760*, ed. Charles Henry Lincoln, 2 vols. (New York, 1912), I, 91.

standard and backed his efforts to fortify the Maine frontier, to supply Britain's Caribbean campaigns, and to capture Louisbourg. Heading up the governor's forces in the council were Jacob Wendell and Samuel Waldo, while James Otis, Sr., often served as Shirley's spokesman in the house. Thomas Hancock helped provision the provincial and British troops, roundly declaring that the contract for the soldiers at Louisbourg is "what I am fonder of than anything in the world."[2] In the Connecticut Valley, another expansionist, Solomon Stoddard, organized the western defenses. In turn, Shirley bestowed a variety of offices upon these individuals and, despite the protests of the Hutchinsonians, secured the appointment of Thomas Hancock's friend Christopher Kilby as the London agent for Massachusetts.[3]

Unsurprisingly, the nonexpansionists set themselves against the governor and the bellicose measures he advocated. Many of these individuals had been close to Shirley's predecessor, Governor Belcher, and had resented the new executive from the first. They disliked Shirley's willingness to accept large wartime issues of currency, and they scored his military plans, particularly the proposed expedition against the French stronghold at Louisbourg. Hutchinson called the campaign "rash" and complained that talking about the value of the fortress was "like selling the skin of a bear before catching him."[4] Dr. William Douglass, who, like Hutchinson, was an ardent hard-money man, condemned Shirley's imperial designs and "governors in general, who may by romantic (but in perquisites profitable) expeditions depopulate the country."[5] These nonexpansionists, in league with a portion of the popular party, made a formidable opposition, and in January 1745 the house approved the attack on Louisbourg by a majority of only one. After 1745 most of Hutchinson's circle was less vehement in its criticism of the war effort, for the capture of the

2. Gov. Shirley to duke of Newcastle, May 12, 1740, Gov. Shirley to lord president of council, Nov. 1, 1742, Aug. 10, 1744, ibid., 20–21, 94, 138–39; John A. Schutz, *William Shirley: King's Governor of Massachusetts* (Chapel Hill, N.C., 1961), 82–85, 92, 107, 115; John J. Waters, Jr., *The Otis Family in Provincial and Revolutionary Massachusetts* (Chapel Hill, N.C., 1968), 88–91; Thomas Hancock, 1746, quoted in W. T. Baxter, *The House of Hancock: Business in Boston, 1724–1775* (Cambridge, Mass., 1945), 102, and see 79–112.

3. John Stoddard to Gov. Shirley, Apr. 24, 1745, Gov. Shirley to Stoddard, Apr. 10, 1747, *Correspondence of Shirley*, I, 209–10, 383; Thomas Hutchinson, *The History of the Colony and Province of Massachusetts-Bay*, ed. Lawrence S. Mayo, 3 vols. (Cambridge, Mass., 1936), II, 329n; Schutz, *William Shirley*, 70–72; William H. Whitmore, *The Massachusetts Civil List for the Colonial and Provincial Periods, 1630–1774* (Albany, 1870).

4. Hutchinson, *History of Massachusetts*, III, 255; Schutz, *William Shirley*, 90.

5. Dr. William Douglass, *Summary, Historical and Political . . . of North America*, 2 vols. (London, 1755), quoted in William Pencak, *War, Politics & Revolution in Provincial Massachusetts* (Boston, 1981), 127.

French bastion seemed to confirm the wisdom of daring tactics. But even during the last years of the conflict, several members of this faction hounded Shirley in the *Independent Advertiser,* blaming him for the colony's wildly inflated currency and once again questioning the worth of Louisbourg.[6]

Many popular party supporters rallied to Shirley's side during King George's War. Ever the consummate politician, Governor Shirley labored to win over this faction, well aware that it made up "a very considerable part of the house of representatives."[7] Shirley enforced the act of Parliament dissolving the land bank, thereby extinguishing an institution the popular party dearly loved, but he allowed patience and magnanimity to temper his actions against the participants. Moreover, he pleased this inflation-minded faction by approving sizable issues of paper money during the war years and by distributing offices to several of the party's sachems, including Samuel Adams, Sr. Such steps enticed into the executive's camp at least a portion of this group, and individuals such as Robert Hale of Beverly and John Choate of Ipswich, both of whom had been directors of the land bank, became important pro-Shirley leaders in the General Court. Nevertheless, members of the popular faction could never wholeheartedly endorse war, and some prominent partisans, including James Allen of Boston, remained critical of the governor and his policies. Moreover, many artisans, shopkeepers, and farmers grumbled at the burdens of a protracted war, and in 1741, 1745, and 1747 the Boston populace vented its anger by rioting against British navy press gangs.[8]

» «

Between 1748 and 1753, the money question replaced war as the source of contention, and new factional alliances emerged. As soon as hostilities ended, Thomas Hutchinson and his friends joined Governor Shirley in currency reform. Shirley, like many upper-class cit-

6. Hutchinson, *History of Massachusetts,* II, 309–15; Schutz, *William Shirley,* 124, 132–33, 142–43; "Samuel Adams," *DAB.* Popular party members also used the columns of the *Independent Advertiser* to harass the governor.

7. Gov. Shirley to duke of Newcastle, Jan. 23, 1742, *Correspondence of Shirley,* I, 80–81.

8. Gov. Shirley to duke of Newcastle, Oct. 17, 1741, Sept. 15, Oct. 17, 1742, Gov. Shirley to Board of Trade, Jan. 24, 30, 1743, Gov. Shirley to Josiah Willard, Nov. 19, 1747, ibid., 76–77, 91, 79, 96–97, 99, 407; Hutchinson, *History of Massachusetts,* II, 306–32; Whitmore, *Mass. Civil List;* Robert Zemsky, *Merchants, Farmers, and River Gods: An Essay on Eighteenth-Century American Politics* (Boston, 1971), 209; Schutz, *William Shirley,* 48–83, 115–25; Gary B. Nash, *The Urban Crucible: Social Change, Political Consciousness, and the Origins of the American Revolution* (Cambridge, Mass., 1979), 221–23; Pencak, *War, Politics & Revolution,* 124–26.

izens, was staggered by the amount of money in circulation in the colony—over two million pounds—and in 1749 urged the legislature to call in all treasury notes and to establish specie as the sole medium of exchange. Shirley was unstinting in his praise for Hutchinson, "in concert with whom alone this act was originally planned . . . [and who] by his extraordinary abilities and uncommon influence with the members, managed and conducted it through the opposition."[9] The governor's patronage policies shifted, and he now smiled upon the applications of Hutchinson and his associates, including Andrew and Peter Oliver. Shirley also successfully lobbied for the ouster of Hancock's friend Christopher Kilby from the agency and for the installation of Hutchinson's favorite, William Bollan. Moreover, on a visit to England, Shirley assisted the members of Parliament who pushed for and obtained an act restricting the emission of bills of credit in any of the New England colonies.[10]

The expansionists in eastern Massachusetts were divided in their views of Shirley's contractionist program, reflecting the middle-of-the-road course they had long followed on money questions. Consequently, although the expansionists had backed the governor during the war, only some of them—James Otis, Sr., and Jacob Wendell, for example—continued to support him after 1748. Others, including Thomas Hancock and Samuel Waldo, decried the Hutchinsonians' obsession with specie and feuded with the executive. "This d——d act," Hancock fumed in 1750, "has turned all trade out of doors and it's impossible to get debts in, either in dollars or province bills." In contrast to the period of King George's War, between 1748 and 1753 Shirley appointed few expansionists to any office.[11]

Predictably, the popular party anathematized the deflationary program, for as Hutchinson observed, "what was called the country party [was] . . . in favor of paper [money]."[12] This faction, now led by James Allen and John Tyng, vigorously criticized both the governor and Thomas Hutchinson. Allen and Tyng time and again tried to

9. Gov. Shirley to duke of Bedford, Jan. 31, 1749, *Correspondence of Shirley*, I, 467; Thomas Hutchinson to [Israel Williams], Feb. 1, 1749, Israel Williams Papers, MHS; U.S. Bureau of the Census, *Historical Statistics of the United States, Colonial Times to 1970*, 2 vols., consec. pagin. (Washington, D.C., 1975), 1200; Merchants' Petition to Lord of Treasury, [c. 1748], Connecticut Historical Society *Cols.*, xv (1914), 183–86; Hutchinson, *History of Massachusetts*, II, 333–37.

10. Gov. Shirley to duke of Newcastle, Jan. 23, 1750, *Correspondence of Shirley*, I, 495–96; Zemsky, *Merchants, Farmers, and River Gods*, 149–50; Schutz, *William Shirley*, 143; Waters, *Otis Family*, 96; Whitmore, *Mass. Civil List*.

11. Thomas Hancock to Christopher Kilby, May 6, 1750, quoted in Baxter, *House of Hancock*, 112; Zemsky, *Merchants, Farmers, and River Gods*, 206–7; Schutz, *William Shirley*, 135–69; Warden, *Boston*, 140; Waters, *Otis Family*, 96; Hutchinson, *History of Massachusetts*, II, 329n; Whitmore, *Mass. Civil List*.

12. Hutchinson, *History of Massachusetts*, II, 336; Warden, *Boston*, 138–40.

reduce Shirley's salary, and in Boston popular indignation against
Hutchinson reached new heights. After his defeat in the 1749 election,
the politician lamented to a friend: "I could make but 200 votes in
near 700. They were the principal inhabitants but you know we are
governed not by weight but by numbers."[13] When Hutchinson's
house caught fire, Boston firemen stood by chanting, "Let it burn. Let
it burn."[14]

» «

Between 1754 and 1760 war once again became the focus of the
struggles among the three factions. The expansionists strengthened
their ties with the bellicose Shirley while the nonexpansionists increasingly questioned his policies, and the popular party continued
to oppose him. The new allegiances of the upper-class parties, however, did not solidify during Shirley's administration, which ended in
October 1756. Shirley, who inherited General Braddock's mantle as
commander in the northern colonies, spent much of his time out of
Massachusetts and was disinclined to sever his links with the nonexpansionists. The realignment of relations between the parties and the
governor was consummated only with Thomas Pownall's assumption
of office in the summer of 1757.

With the onset of hostilities in 1754, the expansionists edged closer
to Shirley. Partisans in the Connecticut Valley, including the Williams
family and Joseph Hawley, worked with the governor to fortify the
western frontier and prepare for the attack on New France. "I have a
great desire Canada should be demolished," Ephraim Williams informed James Otis, Sr., in 1755.[15] Other members of this party joined
Shirley in supporting the Albany Plan of Union. Jacob Wendell and
James Otis, Sr., steered the governor's military program through the
legislature in the fall of 1754, and more generally the Wendell and Otis
families were active in provisioning the colony's forces. Thomas Hancock advanced twenty thousand pounds in specie and war material to
aid the Nova Scotia expedition of 1755.[16]

But relations between the expansionists and Shirley never regained the warmth evident in the mid-1740s. Shirley continued after

13. Thomas Hutchinson to Israel Williams, May 19, 1749, Israel Williams Papers;
Hutchinson, *History of Massachusetts*, III, 12–13; Schutz, *William Shirley*, 137–70.
14. G. B. Warden, *Boston, 1689–1776* (Boston, 1970), 140.
15. Ephraim Williams to Col. James Otis, Mar. 28, 1755, Israel Williams Papers;
Israel Williams to Gov. Shirley, Sept. 12, 1754, Gov. Shirley to Israel Williams, Sept.
26, 1754, *Correspondence of Shirley*, II, 86–89, 90–91.
16. Gov. Shirley to Robert Hunter Morris, Oct. 21, 1754, *Correspondence of Shirley*, II,
96; Schutz, *William Shirley*, 179, 198; Baxter, *House of Hancock*, 129–31; Waters, *Otis
Family*, 101–2.

1754 to draw his closest advisers from nonexpansionist ranks, and his dealings with the expansionists were at times marked by outright bitterness. In 1755 Shirley imposed limits on Thomas Hancock's contracting and forced him to take one of the governor's relatives, John Erving, Jr., as a partner. Erving, Hancock complained, was "pushed upon us by the governor in a way shocking and ungenerous."[17] Moreover, Shirley dismissed Hancock's plea that Kilby be reinstated as agent and excluded the Boston trader from his inner circle. Hancock lamented to Kilby that he knew nothing of Shirley's plans for the 1756 campaign, the governor "having not been in my house these sixteen months nor I scarcely in his."[18]

The nonexpansionists remained close to the governor despite their distaste for Shirley's military plans. Thomas Hutchinson served as Shirley's personal emissary to the 1754 Albany conference, where he argued, if to no avail, that the northern colonies should unite under the leadership of the Massachusetts governor. More generally, Shirley relied on Hutchinson's wisdom. For example, at Hutchinson's insistence Shirley chose Colonel William Johnson, that consistent advocate of British policies, to head the 1755 expedition against Crown Point. Shirley also continued to direct patronage toward the nonexpansionists, granting Thomas Hutchinson and Andrew Oliver additional posts and elevating Peter Oliver to the superior court.[19]

During 1754, 1755, and 1756 the popular party opposed Shirley and the war. This party had little enthusiasm for military ventures, particularly since currency reform had all but ended the possibility of wartime inflation. Led by James Allen, party members denounced the Albany Plan as "a scheme for the destroying the liberties and privileges of every British subject upon the continent" and helped transform the issue of colonial union into one that divided Bay Colony politicians along class lines.[20] Two recorded votes on the Albany Plan in December 1754 reveal the familiar split between popular party towns and the communities adhering to the elite factions. The

17. Thomas Hancock, 1755, quoted in Baxter, *House of Hancock*, 131; Sir Thomas Robinson to govs. in North America, Aug. 28, 1755, Henry Fox to Gov. Shirley, Mar. 31, 1756, *Correspondence of Shirley*, II, 243, 425; Hutchinson, *History of Massachusetts*, III, 28, 34–35; Schutz, *William Shirley*, 204–25.

18. Thomas Hancock to Christopher Kilby, [c. 1756], quoted in Zemsky, *Merchants, Farmers, and River Gods*, 188–89.

19. Gov. Shirley to General Court, Apr. 2, 1754, *Correspondence of Shirley*, II, 45; Hutchinson, *History of Massachusetts*, II, 14–20; Schutz, *William Shirley*, 181–84; Lawrence H. Gipson, "Thomas Hutchinson and the Framing of the Albany Plan of Union, 1754," *PMHB*, LXXIV (1950), 5–35. *The Papers of Benjamin Franklin*, ed. Labaree et al. (New Haven, 1959–), V, 374–87, discusses Hutchinson's role at the Albany conference.

20. Dr. William Clarke to Benjamin Franklin, Feb. 3, 1755, MHS *Cols.*, 1st ser., IV (1795), 85; Schutz, *William Shirley*, 183.

popular party also condemned other facets of Shirley's imperial program. In 1755 John Tyng led the fight against raising troops for the Crown Point expedition, even though in this squabble, which followed hot upon Braddock's defeat, many of the less affluent settlements for once showed themselves willing to support defense measures. Tyng continued his onslaught against Shirley, and in 1756 so vitriolic were his comments that he was forced to apologize to the chair.[21]

During Thomas Pownall's term the shift in relations between the upper-class parties and the governor, a change underway during the last years of Shirley's administration, was completed. Observers underscored the changes occurring after Pownall's accession to the governorship in 1757. In a wonderfully partisan essay of 1775, John Adams recounted: "Shirley was a crafty, busy, ambitious, intriguing, enterprising man. . . . Mr. Hutchinson and Mr. Oliver . . . were his principle ministers of state. . . . Mr. Pownall seems to have been a friend to liberty and to our constitution, and to have had an aversion to all plots against either, and consequently to have given his confidence to other persons than Hutchinson and Oliver."[22] Describing the same changes, Hutchinson remarked, "In a short time most of the chief friends of Mr. Shirley became opposers of Mr. Pownall, and most of Mr. Shirley's enemies became Mr. Pownall's friends."[23]

Although the nonexpansionists cooperated with the new executive during his first months in office (and a grateful Pownall secured the post of lieutenant governor for Hutchinson), they could not stomach Pownall's military policies, and a rift soon developed. "I am really of less consequence than I have been these twenty years," Hutchinson confessed in the summer of 1758.[24] In 1757 he, along with Chief Justice Stephen Sewall, vigorously opposed General Loudoun's demand that Boston quarter British troops, and the following year he clashed with Pownall over the prosecution of the war and sighed for "a peace if but tolerable."[25] In 1759 Hutchinson opposed suggestions

---

21. *Mass. House Journals*, xxxi, 152–53, 182, xxxii, 116; Schutz, *William Shirley*, 242n.

22. John Adams and [Daniel Leonard], *Novanglus and Massachusettensis: Political Essays Published in the Years 1774 and 1775.* . . . (Boston, 1819), 15–17; John Adams to William Tudor, Feb. 4, 1817, *The Works of John Adams*, ed. Charles Francis Adams, 10 vols. (Boston, 1850–56), x, 241–44.

23. Hutchinson, *History of Massachusetts*, iii, 42.

24. Thomas Hutchinson to Israel Williams, July 17, 1758, Aug. 25, 1757, Israel Williams Papers; Bernard Bailyn, *The Ordeal of Thomas Hutchinson* (Cambridge, Mass., 1974), 41–43; Malcolm Freiburg, "How to Become a Colonial Governor: Thomas Hutchinson of Massachusetts," *Review of Politics*, xxi (1959), 650.

25. Thomas Hutchinson to Israel Williams, July 17, 30, 1758, Israel Williams to Thomas Hutchinson, Aug. 7, 1758, Israel Williams Papers; Hutchinson, *History of Massachusetts*, iii, 37–38, 43–48; Zemsky, *Merchants, Farmers, and River Gods*, 44–45.

that the Bay Colony supplement its voluntary recruitment efforts with a draft—a step that New York, Connecticut, and New Hampshire had taken. And he scored the expansionists' insistence on additional defense spending, grumbling to a friend: "The bounty is extravagant and more than I would vote for on the [joint] committee [of house and council], and will be a bad precedent. . . . I assure you, [I] often think of the deplorable state we must be in if we have no [Parliamentary] reimbursement."[26]

The eastern expansionists, however, developed warm ties with the imperial-minded Pownall. Thomas Hancock, now Boston's largest military contractor, helped Pownall mobilize the colony's resources for the campaigns against New France. In the council Jacob Wendell and James Bowdoin supported the governor's cause against the onslaughts of Hutchinson and Oliver, while in the house James Otis, Sr., marshaled the expansionist forces, much as he had done during King George's War. Pownall, in turn, lavished offices upon his expansionist friends, providing the younger James Otis with a lucrative place in the vice-admiralty court and promising the elder Otis the next available seat on the superior court. In 1760 the governor happily approved the senior James Otis's elevation to the speaker's chair. Pownall also cooperated with the expansionists (at least those in the eastern part of the colony) in their unsuccessful attempt to remove Hutchinson's friend William Bollan from his post as colonial agent.[27]

Although the popular party was hesitant to back the campaigns against the French, it supported Pownall on other issues. Representatives from the popular party towns joined the executive in seeking to oust Bollan. These communities bore their own grudge against the agent, who in 1749 had been a key advocate of Hutchinson's contractionist program. Pownall, for his part, did his best to cultivate popular party adherents, consulting with the bumptious John Tyng and appointing several partisans to the local courts.[28]

For a somewhat different view of the quarrel between Hutchinson and Pownall, see Pencak, *War, Politics & Revolution*, 151–54.

26. Thomas Hutchinson to Israel Williams, Apr. 24, 1759, Israel Williams Papers. As lieutenant governor, however, Hutchinson did assist the war effort by bringing Massachusetts military accounts into order for General Jeffrey Amherst. See Lawrence H. Gipson, *The Great War for Empire: The Victorious Years, 1758–1760*, vol. VII of *The British Empire before the American Revolution* (New York, 1949), 316, 321.

27. Thomas Hutchinson to Israel Williams, June 5, 1758, Feb. 10, Apr. 5, 1759, Israel Williams Papers; Stephen E. Patterson, *Political Parties in Revolutionary Massachusetts* (Madison, Wis., 1973), 50–52; Waters, *Otis Family*, 116–17; Baxter, *House of Hancock*, 136–40.

28. Thomas Hutchinson to Israel Williams, Feb. 10, 1759, Israel Williams Papers; Patterson, *Political Parties*, 51–52, 266–68; Whitmore, *Mass. Civil List;* John Adams to William Tudor, Feb. 4, 1817, *Works of John Adams*, x, 241–43; *Mass. House Journals*, xxxv, 96–97, xxxvi, 69.

The end of Pownall's administration coincided with the defeat of the French in North America and signaled the onset of a new era of factional politics in Massachusetts. In a province where the popular party heightened political sensitivities and trumpeted the dangers of Whitehall's oppressive new policies, Britain soon replaced France as the colony's foremost imperial opponent.

» «

Two patterns of factional alliance were evident during the first years of Francis Bernard's administration, which began in August 1760. When conflict with Britain was in the foreground, the nonexpansionists stood with the executive and confronted the united forces of the eastern expansionists and the popular party. But when imperial questions receded, the royal governor had the opportunity to stitch together an upper-class union that isolated the popular party in opposition. The partisan battles of 1760, 1761, and 1762 are important because they suggest in microcosm the bivalent nature of Massachusetts coalition politics in the years after 1762. Moreover, beginning in 1760 the Connecticut River towns unmistakably became part of the nonexpansionist faction. These western communities had long voted with the Hutchinsonians on questions of prerogative and currency reform but shared common ground with the eastern expansionists on defense.

Although Bernard often professed a desire to rise above faction ("I hope I shall not want to be directed by a junto or supported by a party," he pronounced in April 1760, contemplating his new assignment), he was forced to choose between the two upper-class groups shortly after taking office.[29] Chief Justice Stephen Sewall died in September, and the two competitors for his post were James Otis, Sr., and Thomas Hutchinson, the leaders respectively of the expansionists and nonexpansionists. For a governor concerned that the prerogative be upheld there was, as Bernard confessed, no "balancing between the two candidates."[30] Despite Hutchinson's reluctance and Otis's eagerness for the post, Bernard chose Hutchinson, for he was well aware that the bench would have to determine the legality of writs of assistance, the general search warrants used by customs officials. Otis appeared undecided on the issue, but Hutchinson, a nonexpansionist to his marrow, affirmed their validity.[31]

29. Gov. Bernard to Lord Barrington, Apr. 19, 1760, *The Barrington-Bernard Correspondence and Illustrative Matter, 1760–1770,* ed. Edward Channing and Archibald Cary Coolidge (Cambridge, Mass., 1912), 12.

30. Gov. Bernard to Earl of Shelburne, Dec. 22, 1766, quoted in Waters, *Otis Family,* 119.

31. Andrew Oliver to Israel Williams, Sept. 30, 1760, Israel Williams Papers; Hutchinson, *History of Massachusetts,* III, 62–64; Waters, *Otis Family,* 118–19.

If Bernard's elevation of Hutchinson divided the politicians of Massachusetts, placing the governor and nonexpansionists on one side and the expansionists and popular party on the other, several issues, stemming in part from imperial questions, reinforced this alignment. During 1761, as expected, the two elite factions battled over the writs of assistance, with James Otis, Jr., leading the attack against the warrants. The court, he thundered, must "demolish this monster of oppression, and . . . tear into rags this remnant of star-chamber tyranny."[32] The popular party applauded Otis's invective, and in May the Boston town meeting elected the fiery lawyer as one of the city's representatives. Chief Justice Hutchinson, however, dismissed his opponents' arguments and declared the writs legal.

Members of the two blocs also crossed swords over the choice of the colony's agent. In April 1762 the expansionists and popular faction finally ousted William Bollan and appointed Jasper Maudit in his stead. "You may rest assured," James Otis, Jr., informed the new agent, "that your election was carried by the friends of liberty, civil and religious, and that . . . this interest are determined at all events to support you."[33] ("I never knew an instance of such mad proceedings," groaned Hutchinson.)[34] Otis cautioned Maudit that "Mr. Secretary [Andrew Oliver] is as much attached to the governor, lieutenant governor [Hutchinson], and to Mr. Bollan, as any of us are to you."[35]

The two groups quarreled over fixing the value of gold and silver and over the right of superior court justices to sit in the legislature. Votes recorded on these questions during the first months of 1762 suggest the strongholds of the opposing blocs. The expansionist–popular party alliance received the support of most Boston members and of many of the poorer communities in the eastern half of the province and in southern Maine. Nonexpansionist delegates came from such prosperous coastal towns as Salem and Marblehead, many of the wealthier settlements near Boston, and the Connecticut Valley.[36]

Another alignment of forces—the two upper-class factions against the lower-class popular party—was also visible during the opening

32. Quoted in Waters, *Otis Family*, 123, and see 133–34; Thomas Hutchinson to Israel Williams, Jan. 21, 1761, Israel Williams Papers; Hutchinson, *History of Massachusetts*, III, 67.
33. Hutchinson, *History of Massachusetts*, III, 69; Waters, *Otis Family*, 121–25, 136; James Otis, Jr., to Jasper Maudit, Apr. 23, 1762, MHS *Cols.*, LXXIV (1918), 30.
34. Thomas Hutchinson to William Bollan, Apr. 24, 1762, Edmund Trowbridge to William Bollan, July 15, 1762, MHS *Cols.*, LXXIV, 32, 66–67.
35. James Otis, Jr., to Jasper Maudit, Oct. 28, 1762, Feb. 14, 1763, Charles Chauncy to Jasper Maudit, Oct. 12, 1762, ibid., 77–80, 95, 73.
36. *Mass. House Journals*, XXXVIII, pt. 2, 224–25, 319–20; Hutchinson, *History of Massachusetts*, III, 71–72; Oxenbridge Thacher to Benjamin Pratt, [1762], MHS *Proc.*, 1st ser., XX (1882–83), 47–48; Waters, *Otis Family*, 139–40; Robert J. Taylor, *Western Massachusetts in the Revolution* (Providence, 1954), 52–74.

years of Bernard's administration. Although the expansionists and the popular party worked together during 1761 and, albeit less consistently, during 1762, they were by no means inseparable. In August 1760, a few weeks after Bernard's arrival but before Hutchinson's elevation to the superior court, the lieutenant governor pointed to the tensions between the popular party, led by Tyng, and the expansionists, headed by the Otises. "If he [Bernard] has shown any greater regard to T–ng and his adherents than to other persons it is not generally known," Hutchinson observed. "It is no small disadvantage to them that the Speaker [James Otis, Sr.] and so many of the principal members of the House dislike them, and he will be convinced that at least for this year he will not want them."[37]

Hutchinson's appointment and such issues as the writs of assistance temporarily drove the expansionists and popular party together but did not end the governor's hope of securing the support of an upper-class alliance. In April 1761 Bernard wrote determinedly, "I shall accomplish my purpose of founding my administration on the broad bottom of a collation."[38] Bernard's patronage policies reflected his intentions, and his resolve was unmistakable in the fall of 1761, when he installed 117 justices of the peace in Suffolk County, the largest set of offices assigned during his administration. He distributed the commissions evenly between the two upper-class factions, offering justiceships to such expansionists as James Otis, Jr., Thomas Cushing, James Bowdoin, and Thomas Hancock, as well as to such nonexpansionists as Andrew Oliver, Jr., James Boutineau, and Richard Clarke. Bernard also allowed James Otis, Sr., his choice of positions in Barnstable County. "The governor flattered himself," Hutchinson observed, "that he should be able to reconcile to him both [Otises], father and son."[39]

Bernard's campaign to cultivate supporters in the two upper-class factions was partially successful. Most significantly, the governor's efforts modified the younger James Otis's partisan loyalties, and in February 1762 the lawyer joined the Hutchinsonians in voting the grant of Mount Desert Island to Bernard. "There is reason to believe our present governor, Mr. Bernard, . . . begins to be convinced whose views are most nearly connected with the true interests of the province," he declared in April.[40] Otis, however, had become a man divid-

37. Thomas Hutchinson to Israel Williams, Aug. 25, 1760, Israel Williams Papers.
38. Gov. Bernard to Thomas Pownall, Apr. 28, 1761, quoted in Waters, *Otis Family*, 139; Gov. Bernard to Lord Barrington, Aug. 7, 1760, *Barrington-Bernard Correspondence*, 15.
39. Whitmore, *Mass. Civil List*, 130–31; Hutchinson, *History of Massachusetts*, III, 69–70; Waters, *Otis Family*, 141–42.
40. Hutchinson, *History of Massachusetts*, III, 70; Gov. Bernard to Lord Barrington, Feb. 20, May 1, 1762, *Barrington-Bernard Correspondence*, 48–49, 52–53; James Otis, Jr., to Jasper Maudit, Apr. 23, 1762, MHS *Cols.*, LXXIV (1918), 30.

ed against himself, and John Adams observed that he "will one time say of the lieutenant governor [i.e., Hutchinson] that he had rather have him than any man he knows in any one office, and the next hour will represent him as the greatest tyrant and most despicable creature living." This inward schism possibly accelerated the mental instability that overwhelmed Otis by the end of the decade.[41]

The governor's efforts to establish an elite "collation" worried many popular party members, who saw their links with the expansionists weakening. Among those gravely concerned was Oxenbridge Thacher, a well-known expansionist lawyer (he had joined Otis in 1761 in arguing against the writs of assistance) with strong ties to the lower-class faction. Thacher wrote to Benjamin Pratt, a Boston politician who had worked with the expansionist–popular party alliance during Pownall's administration and who had left the colony for New York in 1761: "Now as to our brotherhood, I wish that two sentences with which you took leave of us at Dedham had made a more durable impression, to wit, let brotherly love continue, and forsake not the assembling yourselves together.... Come yourself, and dispel all clouds, whatever other variant and inconsistent interests and factions are among us. We shall unite on your return, and make you the head of the union as you were the former of it."[42]

The challenges posed by the new British measures and the economic downturn of the 1760s would restore and strengthen the alliance between the expansionists and the popular party. But the coalition of upper-class politicians, always a possibility, would re-emerge briefly in the early 1770s.

» «

During this era Massachusetts expansionists showed their convictions with words as well as actions. Most utterances focused on the problems at hand, particularly on the conflict with the French and Indians, but some statements made clear that opposition to France did not mean total identification with Great Britain. Thus, in the months that followed Braddock's defeat, Thomas Hancock had little use for the British army. "Give us ships, money, artillery (no regulars), and let us fight [the French] in their own way," he told an English correspondent.[43]

And a few individuals limned a broader vision. Jonathan Mayhew, whose writings are discussed in the Introduction, was perhaps the most outspoken expansionist in Massachusetts during these years,

41. *Diary and Autobiography of John Adams*, ed. L. H. Butterfield et al., 4 vols. (Cambridge, Mass., 1961), I, 226 (June 5, 1762); Waters, *Otis Family*, 177–81.

42. Oxenbridge Thacher to Benjamin Pratt, [1762], MHS *Procs.*, 1st ser., XX (1882–83), 48.

43. Thomas Hancock, 1755, quoted in Baxter, *House of Hancock*, 132.

but others trod similar, daring paths. John Adams told a friend in 1755 that he foresaw the "transfer of the seat of empire into America" and proceeded to detail this prophecy: "If we remove the turbulent Gallics, our people according to the exactest computations, will in another century become more numerous than England itself. Should this be the case, since we have I may say all the naval stores of the nation in our hands, it will be easy to obtain the mastery of the seas, and then the united force of all Europe will not be able to subdue us."[44] Such doctrines helped the expansionists chart their course in the years after 1763, just as contrasting persuasions guided the non-expansionists and popular party. In the revolutionary epoch, each Massachusetts faction remained true to patterns of belief whose origins could be traced back to the beginning of the century.

44. John Adams to Nathan Webb, Oct. 12, 1755, *Papers of John Adams,* ed. Robert Taylor et al. (Cambridge, Mass., 1977–   ), i, 5.

CHAPTER 3

New York:
Traders and Warriors

"All the province was already divided into two parties," remarked William Smith, Jr., in his discussion of New York at the time of Governor William Cosby's accession in 1732.[1] Smith was a highly qualified, if at times partisan, observer of factional struggles. A Yale graduate, lawyer, historian, and active politician, he was born in 1728, the son of another lawyer-politician. He and his father well understood the New York political factions, which were firmly established by the 1730s. In fact, these groups emerged in the second decade of the century and were to be remarkably long-lived, continuing until independence. The expansionists, a party that embraced the Livingstons, Morrises, and Smiths, aggressively defended the colony's interests against a series of external enemies. The nonexpansionist faction, which included such families as the DeLanceys and Philipses, hewed to a more guarded view of colonial growth and eschewed all daring plans to enlarge provincial sovereignty.

» «

The parties that appeared in the late 1710s in New York were shaped primarily by geography and secondarily by religion. For the expansionist faction the firmest pillars of support were the manor lords of the upper Hudson—more particularly, the Livingstons, Van Rensselaers, and Beekmans. These men, living near the lengthy, exposed frontier of New York, realized, as one 1735 petition pronounced, that "their estates would not be near the value they bear at

1. William Smith, Jr., *The History of the Province of New York*, ed. Michael Kammen, 2 vols. (1830; Cambridge, Mass., 1972), ii, 7.

[51]

present" if New France and its Indian allies were left unchecked.[2] Standing first among these great clans were the Livingstons, a family that controlled fiefdoms in both Albany and Dutchess counties and claimed prominent scions in the merchant community of the capital and in the provincial bar. Their political power began with Livingston Manor, which, like Rensselaerswyck, had its own delegate in the twenty-seven-seat legislature. Furthermore, the Livingstons influenced the selection of Albany County's two representatives and were, along with the Beekmans, a potent voice in Dutchess County affairs.[3]

Another wealthy Albany County family, the Schuylers, did not enter the expansionist camp until the 1730s and 1740s. The Schuylers, like the Livingstons, were lords of a sprawling northern barony, but they were also involved in a quasi-illicit trade with Montreal. This commerce, in which English manufactures were exchanged for French peltries, depended on pacific relations with New France. Those involved in this lucrative trade thus were tugged by a strong cord, and usually tied firmly to the nonexpansionist faction. The Schuylers' partisan allegiances, however, changed between 1720 and 1750 as their interests shifted from the Canada trade to the development of their frontier holdings.[4]

The party of the Livingstons and Beekmans could also claim important adherents in other parts of the colony, though its strength was less considerable outside the Hudson Valley. A portion of the New York City elite, particularly such lawyers as James Alexander and William Smith, Sr., and his son, followed the manor lords' lead (and frequently handled their litigation). Some city merchants, if usually a minority of the importing community, stood with the expansionists, and many of the artisans and tradesmen backed the party at the polls and, on occasion, with demonstrations "out of doors." In Westchester County, a nonexpansionist bastion, Livingston's party had the unwavering support of the Morris family. During the 1730s and early 1740s, Lewis Morris, Sr., along with his son and namesake, were unrivaled leaders of the faction. The elder Morris's career had begun in New Jersey, where he worked for the gubernatorial appointment of Andrew Hamilton, an able defender of Britain's larger goals, and his worldly progress continued in New York, where he became

2. "The Humble Petition of Several of the Inhabitants of the Corporation of Albany" to the N.Y. Assembly, [c. Oct. 1735], Rutherfurd Collection, ii, 139, NYHS.

3. Lawrence H. Leder, *Robert Livingston, 1654–1728, and the Politics of Colonial New York* (Chapel Hill, N.C., 1961), passim; Patricia U. Bonomi, *A Factious People: Politics and Society in Colonial New York* (Tarrytown, N.Y., 1980), 71–73, 187, 213–17, 289; George Dangerfield, *Chancellor Robert R. Livingston of New York, 1746–1813* (New York, 1960), passim.

4. Cadwallader Colden to James Alexander, Nov. 19, 1728, Philip Livingston to James Alexander, Oct. 11, 15, 1735, James Alexander to Lewis Morris, Nov. 6, 1735, Rutherfurd Collection, i, 93, ii, 137, 139, 143. See also note 15.

the protégé of another imperial-minded governor, Robert Hunter. Regular electoral battles in Westchester County against the Philipse family deepened Morris's commitment to the expansionists.[5]

The nonexpansionist faction drew its strength from the southern tier of counties, as well as New York City and the town of Albany. Long Island and Staten Island politicians, who grumbled about expenditures for the frontier, usually sided with this party, and as early as 1717 Samuel Mulford complained that the taxes extracted from Long Island were being wasted on fortifications "up the river."[6] Westchester County, home of the powerful Philipse family, leaned toward the nonexpansionists, as did the west Hudson county of Orange. During the revolutionary era, however, there would be a significant defection from party ranks on Long Island. The large New England population in Suffolk County responded sympathetically to events in Massachusetts and Connecticut and helped swing the eastern end of Long Island into the patriot camp.[7]

Politicians in the two principal towns of the colony also played an important role in the nonexpansionist party. Adherents in New York City included many of the merchants, particularly those individuals like the DeLanceys and Philipses involved in the overland trade with Canada. Support from a large segment of the capital's enfranchised citizenry made for frequent victories in local elections. In Albany the *handlaers*, or great merchants, depended on exchanges with the French and were confirmed nonexpansionists; however, Albany, unlike New York City, Schenectady, and the borough of Westchester, claimed no representatives in the assembly, and the town's burghers were rarely able to dictate the choice of delegates for Albany County.[8]

5. "Names of Those Agreeing to Sustain Col. Morris," [c. Nov. 1734], ibid., II, 75; James Alexander, Memorandum of Evidence Given, Feb. 7, 1734, ibid., I, 189; Stanley N. Katz, *Newcastle's New York: Anglo-American Politics, 1732–1753* (Cambridge, Mass., 1968), 70–73, 137–38; Bonomi, *Factious People*, 69–71, 122, 131; Smith, *History of New York*, II, 312; Leder, *Robert Livingston*, 285; Gary B. Nash, *Quakers and Politics: Pennsylvania, 1681–1726* (Princeton, 1968), 249–50.

6. Mulford quoted in Bonomi, *Factious People*, 100; Katz, *Newcastle's New York*, 85–90.

7. Bonomi, *Factious People*, 42–45, 295–311; Leder, *Robert Livingston*, 247. Among the most important material for determining factional lines are the divisions recorded in *Journal of the Votes and Proceedings of the General Assembly of the Colony of New York, 1691–1765*, 2 vols. (New York, 1764–66), and its successor, *Journal of the Votes and Proceedings . . . from 1766 to 1776 inclusive* (Albany, 1820).

8. C. Colden to Alexander Colden, Jan. 31, 1760, Smith, *History of New York*, I, 318. During the second and third decades of the century Stephen DeLancey was the importer with the greatest involvement in the Canada trade, while Adolph Philipse stood second. Philip Livingston was also a fur trader, but he was not based in New York City, and rather than relying on Montreal, he endeavored to establish a commercial center along the Mohawk which would draw peltries from the West. Thomas Elliot Norton, *The Fur Trade in Colonial New York, 1686–1776* (Madison, Wis., 1974), 85–96. See also the text and the bibliographical discussion in Milton M. Klein, *The Politics of Diversity: Essays in the History of Colonial New York* (Port Washington, N.Y., 1974), 14–15.

Religion played a subordinate role in shaping party lines. Anglicans, who made up about 10 percent of the population but were important beyond their numbers, tended to support the Philipse-DeLancey group, swelling its strength in the capital and adjacent counties. The majority of dissenters probably leaned toward the expansionists, but their partisan loyalties were less uniform than the Anglicans'. Dissenters in Albany County and in the capital usually voted for the faction of the Morrises and Livingstons, and those on Long Island generally remained in the nonexpansionist camp. Religious questions, however, could easily become partisan ones. During the 1750s, in the battle over King's College most nonexpansionists campaigned for the Anglican institution while most expansionists denounced the school, and there was at least a grain of substance to the assertion—often heard after 1763—that the two factions might be labeled "church" and "dissenter."[9]

Finally, there were two prominent New Yorkers—Cadwallader Colden and Sir William Johnson—who stood apart from both factions and evinced instead the outlook of British imperialists. Colden was born in Scotland, received the degree of A.B. from the University of Edinburgh, and studied medicine in London. By 1718 he had settled in New York and soon was appointed the colony surveyor-general and a member of council. Later he would become lieutenant governor and then acting governor, and a loyalist. Colden wanted the empire to grow, but always under London's firm guidance. Before 1763 he often applauded the expansionists' initiatives but drew back when he sniffed any challenge to British prerogative. In that light he explained to James Alexander his quiescence in the political struggles of the 1730s: "I cannot see how any remedy can probably be had here without in effect destroying the design of the King's giving this authority [to the governor]."[10]

William Johnson, whose concern for British interests was similar to Colden's, was born in Ireland and came to New York in 1738 to manage an estate belonging to his uncle, Vice Admiral Sir Peter Warren. Johnson settled on the frontier west of Albany, where he became a prominent landowner and helped oversee Indian relations. Like Colden, Johnson often cooperated with the expansionists before 1763, leading colonial forces against the French and Indians during both midcentury wars. But Johnson resented the criticism the colonists

9. Bonomi, *Factious People*, 18–28, 248–52; Dorothy Rita Dillon, *The New York Triumvirate: A Study of the Legal and Political Careers of William Livingston, John Morin Scott, William Smith, Jr.* (New York, 1949), 32–39.

10. C. Colden to James Alexander, Dec. 3, 1735, May 25, 1736, Rutherfurd Collection, II, 85, 183, and see I, 157; Bonomi, *Factious People*, 152–54.

directed at the royal executives, and in the late 1740s he became, along with Colden, one of Governor Clinton's few allies. The Crown, grateful for Johnson's services, made him a baronet in 1755 and superintendent for Indian affairs in 1756. After 1763 Sir William was an obdurate and outspoken supporter of British policies and was particularly determined to keep the colonists out of the trans-Appalachian region.[11]

» «

Although the colony on the Hudson was involved in the fighting that raged in the New World between 1690 and 1713, factions that differed in their vision of America's future did not emerge until the end of the 1710s. During the war years members of the elite closed ranks to repel a serious social threat to their preeminence. This time of troubles—the Leislerian rebellion and its aftermath—ended only in 1715 when Governor Robert Hunter engineered a broad compromise between the aristocracy and the group of slightly less wealthy citizens who had challenged them. But with much of the imperial conflict on or near New York soil, members of the upper class could not wholly suppress their differences on strategic questions. Robert Livingston, for example, as early as 1690, demanded that the colonies attack Quebec and in 1699 proposed that New York outflank the French by erecting a fort at Detroit (then called Wawyachtenok). Such a post, Livingston averred, would show the Indians "the plenty and cheapness of goods," and they would "bring all their trade thither." Others dissented; Albany's *handlaers* feared that an expedition against Canada might endanger their links with Montreal.[12]

After 1715 the wealthy landholders and merchants of New York advertised their views on imperial issues more willingly. Governor Hunter's political skill prevented irreparable divisions from forming in the 1710s, but in implementing his plans for defense, he worked closely with such expansionists as Lewis Morris and Robert Livingston. Morris became Hunter's spokesman in the house and was rewarded for his fealty with the chief justiceship. In the forefront of the opposition to Hunter were such nonexpansionist merchants as Jac-

11. Katz, *Newcastle's New York*, 179–80; "William Johnson," *DAB*; James T. Flexner, *Mohawk Baronet: Sir William Johnson of New York* (New York, 1959).

12. Livingston's Memorial to earl of Bellomont, Apr. 12, 1699, quoted in Leder, *Robert Livingston*, 138, and see 61–74, 71, 87–95, 120–22, 129–250; Jerome R. Reich, *Leisler's Rebellion: A Study of Democracy in New York, 1664–1720* (Chicago, 1953), 55–126; Irving Mark, *Agrarian Conflicts in Colonial New York, 1711–1775* (New York, 1940), 19–28; Smith, *History of New York*, I, 75, 92–93, 110–57; Bonomi, *Factious People*, 42–45, 75–76; Sung Bok Kim, "A New Look at the Great Landlords of Eighteenth-Century New York," *WMQ*, 3d ser., xxvii (1970), 585–99; Norton, *Fur Trade*, 55–57.

obus Van Cortlandt and Stephen DeLancey (both of whom imported goods for the Montreal trade) and the Long Islanders, who resented the sums spent for the frontier.[13]

Immediately after Hunter's departure in July 1719 the fissure separating the two parties widened precariously. Nonexpansionist Peter Schuyler, who headed the government for fourteen months, purged Hunter's allies from office. He removed Robert Livingston's nephew from the mayor's chair in Albany and installed his own relative Myndert Schuyler. Philip Livingston caustically observed that Myndert had "long since made interest with the Canada traders."[14] Peter Schuyler also expelled Hunter's expansionist appointee from the mayor's office in New York City, setting up in his stead fellow partisan Jacobus Van Cortlandt. Moreover, when the Iroquois denounced the Montreal trade ("We desire you to stop," the sachems pleaded), Schuyler pointedly dismissed the complaints.[15]

The actions of the new governor, William Burnet, who arrived in 1720, determined to strengthen Britain's position in the New World, cast factional lines into still sharper relief. Shortly after taking office, Burnet persuaded the Assembly to ban the sale of blankets, guns, and other Indian goods to the French. The expansionists eagerly supported the governor's tack. Robert Livingston wrote a memorial that provided the basis for the bill, and Lewis Morris introduced the measure into the house. Moreover, the lawmakers, following their lead, voted funds in 1722 for a trading post at Oswego, a step designed to direct the commerce in furs away from French Canada. Not surprisingly, such measures outraged other New Yorkers. William Smith, Jr., who wrote the first volume of his provincial history in the 1750s, observed that "among those who were more immediately prejudiced by this new regulation, the importers of those goods from Europe were the chief, and hence the spring of their opposition to the governor."[16] Such nonexpansionist merchants as Adolph Philipse, Stephen

---

13. Leder, *Robert Livingston*, 211–49; Bonomi, *Factious People*, 84–87; Smith, *History of New York*, I, 137–55, 357.

14. Philip Livingston to Robert Livingston, Mar. 16, 25, Apr. 10, 1724, quoted in Leder, *Robert Livingston*, 277; Bonomi, *Factious People*, 88.

15. Quoted from Leder, *Robert Livingston*, 252. More generally on Schuyler's activities, see Bonomi, *Factious People*, 64–65, 88; Smith, *History of New York*, I, 135–36, 144; Thomas Hutchinson, *The History of the Colony and Province of Massachusetts-Bay*, ed. Lawrence S. Mayo, 3 vols. (Cambridge, Mass., 1936), II, 102–3; "Peter Schuyler," *DAB*. Schuyler held a broader view of imperial affairs than that taken by many of the *handlaers*, and on several occasions, he supported colonial expeditions against the French. But his outlook differed markedly from that of the expansionists, for he argued that commercial cooperation with New France was the best long-term policy for New York.

16. Smith, *History of New York*, I, 166–69, quote on 168; Bonomi, *Factious People*, 88–93; Leder, *Robert Livingston*, 250–56, 267.

DeLancey, and Peter Schuyler denounced Burnet's new policies, and the governor responded by purging Philipse and Schuyler from the council.[17]

Clashes over imperial policies in the 1720s led both parties to strengthen their forces. Deprived of their preeminence in the upper house, the nonexpansionists sought to capture the assembly: Philipse, Schuyler, and DeLancey all secured seats in the lower chamber, and in 1725 Philipse became speaker, replacing the aging Robert Livingston. Success encouraged the nonexpansionists to redouble their efforts to block the governor's schemes. When in 1727 Burnet ordered a fort erected at Oswego to protect the traders there, the house denied him funds, forcing Burnet to finance the project himself. Importers in the Philipse-DeLancey faction also lobbied their British correspondents, arguing that the prohibition against exchanges with New France reduced the sale of manufactures and urging English houses to petition the ministry for repeal. This campaign was crowned with victory in 1729 when the Privy Council disallowed the Indian trade acts.[18]

The expansionists responded to these setbacks by taking steps to coordinate their attack. Cadwallader Colden, who during the 1720s shared some expansionist goals, told James Alexander in 1728: "Now I think the external circumstances are not favorable to us at this present time but they may very soon and therefore in my opinion it is only advisable to prepare things for that time. . . . One reason of our having often failed is that we never concerted our measures together."[19] Alexander echoed these sentiments to Lewis Morris: "It's the duty of those who are or may be aimed at (notwithstanding the fair speeches of A[dolph] P[hilips]e to the contrary) to consult together upon that matter and form some regular scheme to prevent any mischief either to themselves or the government."[20] Alexander, Morris, and Colden cultivated new allies, including Henry Beekman of Dutchess County. Such efforts seemed ever more imperative when Burnet's successor, John Montgomerie, sided with the Philipse-DeLancey group.[21]

The two parties ramified more fully during the administration of William Cosby, who took up the seals of office in 1732 and soon made clear his intention to work with the nonexpansionists. Cosby, with

---

17. [James Alexander] to [Robert Hunter], [c. 1723], Rutherfurd Collection, IV, 15; Bonomi, *Factious People*, 89–90.
18. Smith, *History of New York*, I, 181–89; Bonomi, *Factious People*, 83–94.
19. C. Colden to James Alexander, June 21, 1728, Rutherfurd Collection, I, 51.
20. James Alexander to Lewis Morris, [c. 1728], ibid., 51.
21. C. Colden to James Alexander, June 21, 30, Nov. 19, 1728, ibid., 53, 93.

the help of Stephen DeLancey and Speaker Philipse, secured a five-year salary grant from the assembly, sued senior councillor and expansionist Rip Van Dam for part of the income Van Dam had received as interim head of government, and suspended Lewis Morris from his position as chief justice, installing James DeLancey, Stephen's son, in that post. The expansionists (or Morrisites, as they now were often called) responded to this onslaught with a broad counteroffensive. They vigorously contested local elections, sent Lewis Morris to England in 1734 to secure Cosby's removal, and established an opposition newspaper, the *New York Weekly Journal*. Such efforts met with mixed success. Despite expansionist victories in by-elections, the nonexpansionists (or Cosbyites) retained control of the assembly until the general election in 1737. Morris's mission to London was a failure; Cosby remained governor until his death in 1736. The *Weekly Journal*, however, proved an energetic critic of the executive and his allies, and its young editor, John Peter Zenger, emerged with his reputation enhanced after being acquitted of the charge of seditious libel.[22]

The two groups also clashed over Cosby's Indian policy, more particularly over the governor's support in 1733 for the destruction of the "Albany deed," a document promising the Mohawk that their territorial claims would be respected. While the nonexpansionists supported the executive, the Morrisites charged that Cosby had taken this rash step to facilitate his land speculation and that his actions endangered the frontier. In Albany County, Philip Livingston circulated a petition calling for a reaffirmation of the promises to the Five Nations and warning that "from being our friends [the Indians] may become our mortal enemies." In London, Lewis Morris repeated similar arguments as part of his campaign against Cosby.[23]

Party conflicts gradually lessened during George Clarke's admin-

22. Smith, *History of New York*, II, 3–23; James Alexander to F. J. Paris, Mar. 19, 1733, Alexander to Robert Hunter, Nov. 8, 1733, Alexander to Lewis Morris, Jan. 17, 1735, Alexander, Instructions for Morris, [c. Nov. 1734], C. Colden to Alexander, Aug. 1, 1735, Rutherfurd Collection, I, 159, 163, II, 95, 73–74, 125; Bonomi, *Factious People*, 103–33; Katz, *Newcastle's New York*, 61–90. Several historians have argued that New York's revolutionary parties can be traced back to the 1720s or 1730s. For analyses of factional lines that broadly parallel my discussion of alignments, see Klein, *Politics of Diversity*, 13–17; Leopold S. Launitz-Schürer, Jr., *Loyal Whigs and Revolutionaries: The Making of the Revolution in New York, 1765–1776* (New York, 1980), 7–19; and Norton, *Fur Trade*, 174–97.

23. "The Humble Petition of Several of the Inhabitants of the Corporation of Albany" to the N.Y. Assembly, [c. Oct. 1735], and Philip Livingston to James Alexander, Oct. 15, 1735, Rutherfurd Collection, II, 139; Nicholas Varga, "New York Government and Politics during the Mid–Eighteenth Century" (Ph.D. diss., Fordham Univ. 1960), 39; Bonomi, *Factious People*, 121; Katz, *Newcastle's New York*, 81–82; Lewis Morris to James Alexander, Jan. 11, Feb. 25, 1736, Rutherfurd Collection, II, 171, 177.

istration, which stretched from 1736 to 1743. Although Clarke, who had long been active in New York politics, was linked to the Cosbyites, he gained the sympathy of many expansionists by reinstating lawyers James Alexander and William Smith, Sr., both of whom had been debarred by Cosby during the Zenger affair, and by calling a general election—an important Morrisite demand. The expansionists topped the 1737 poll, and under the leadership of Lewis Morris, Jr., pushed through a series of long-desired reforms, including recorded votes and annual salary grants for the governor. However, the able Clarke sought only to right the extremes of Cosby's injustices to the Morrisites, not to become that group's advocate. He opposed the expansionists' efforts to strengthen their control over the house and soon announced a new election, a ballot that enabled the Cosbyites once more to dominate the assembly. Clarke found cooperating with Philipse and his allies easier than working with Morris and Alexander, and continued the assembly chosen in 1739 until Governor George Clinton arrived in 1743. Serious partisan conflict would not resume until New York was drawn into King George's War in 1745.[24]

Despite the political calm prevailing in the late 1730s and early 1740s, factional lines stood forth boldly when the legislature turned to military questions. In the twenty-second assembly, which lasted from 1739 to 1743, preparedness lay at the heart of three key debates dealing with the construction of a stockade in Mohawk country, the settlement of Highlanders in strategic locales, and the supervision of military stores in New York City. A tabulation of the ballots on these questions makes clear the geographical fault lines underlying party formation. The representatives residing in the upper Hudson county of Albany (including the members for Livingston Manor, Rensselaerswyck, Schenectady, and the two delegates from the county itself) as well as Henry Beekman of Dutchess supported firm policies by a margin of fifteen to one. The legislators from Long Island, Staten Island, Westchester, Orange, and Ulster counties opposed expenditures for defense thirty-five to three. The New York City delegation, which favored the expansionist measures seven to four, struck the only note of compromise (map 2).[25]

24. Smith, *History of New York*, II, 29–45; Bonomi, *Factious People*, 133–36; Katz, *Newcastle's New York*, 147–52; C. Colden to James Alexander, May 21, 1737, Alexander to [Peter Collinson], June 4, 1739, Rutherfurd Collection, II, 187, IV, 63; Philip Livingston to Robert Livingston, Jr., Mar. 24, 1739, Livingston Family Papers, reel 7, FDRL.

25. *N.Y. Votes and Proceedings*. Adolph Philipse led the New York City delegation, which ostensibly was composed of nonexpansionists. The circle around DeLancey noted Philipse's wavering on imperial questions and quickly challenged his ascendancy within the faction. Katz, *Newcastle's New York*, 156n, 183. By the early 1750s Philipse was safely back into the nonexpansionist fold.

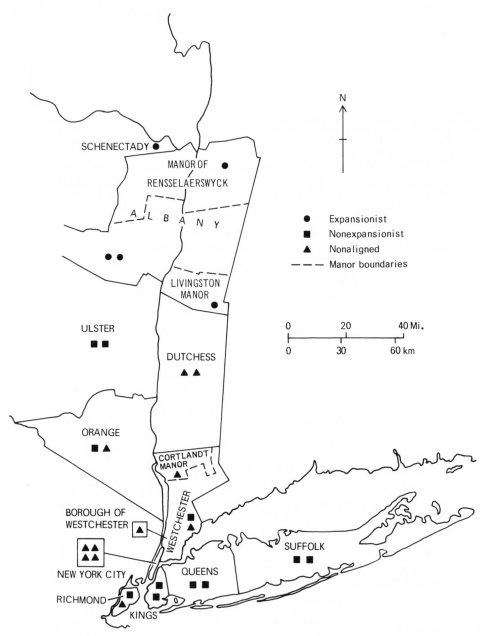

Map 2. New York: Three assembly votes on defense, September 1739–May 1741

SOURCE: *N.Y. Votes and Proceedings,* votes of Sept. 20, 1739 (£600 for fort); Sept. 21, 1739 (delay resettling frontier families); May 23, 1741 (military stores for NYC). Expansionist delegates voted aye, nay, aye; nonexpansionists the opposite; nonaligned representatives adhered to neither pattern.

» «

The distortion of party lines as a result of Governor George Clinton's political ineptitude and the subsequent reemergence of these divisions characterized the next phase in the development of New York factions, 1743 to 1762. When Clinton disembarked in Manhattan in the fall of 1743 the colony was politically tranquil because, as Smith commented, "[Governor] Clarke had crossed the principal zealots of the two parties," and the harmony continued as long as King George's War remained a distant threat to New York frontiers.[26] Thus, during 1744 and most of 1745 the expansionists in the house, under the leadership of Lewis Morris, Jr., cooperated with the imperial-minded Clinton by adopting measures to bolster fortifications while the nonexpansionists offered little opposition. Even James DeLancey, Clinton's closest adviser, approved the initiatives, accepting such measures as part of the price of his elevated position. A pleased Clinton rewarded DeLancey by upgrading his commission as chief justice from "at pleasure" to "on good behavior." It was a favor the governor would soon regret.[27]

With the French and Indian raid on Saratoga in November 1745, New York involvement in the war suddenly intensified, and DeLancey's circle loudly broadcast its opposition to any belligerent plans. Their adamancy soon infected the relationship between DeLancey and Clinton. During the first weeks of 1746 the two men quarreled over strengthening the militia act, and at a dinner party in February they ended any semblance of a working relationship. Both politicians were "in their cups" and spoke freely. The chief justice declared that he would make Clinton's administration "uneasy for the future," while the governor replied roundly that DeLancey "might do his worst."[28] The gulf between the two continued to widen, and in July 1746 DeLancey, along with several of his allies in the council, refused to accompany the governor to an Indian conference at Albany. In August, DeLancey declined Clinton's request that he command an expedition against Canada, excusing himself for

---

26. Smith, *History of New York*, II, 61.

27. Philip Livingston to Robert Livingston, Jr., Mar. 13, 1745, Livingston Family Papers, reel 7, FDRL; William Shirley to duke of Newcastle, Dec. 14, 1745, *Correspondence of William Shirley, Governor of Massachusetts and Military Commander in America, 1731–1760*, ed. Charles Henry Lincoln, 2 vols. (New York, 1912), I, 294. For divisions over defense, see votes on May 5 (2 votes), Aug. 24 (2 votes), Sept. 5, 1744, Apr. 9, May 10, July 4, Aug. 21, 1745, *N.Y. Votes and Proceedings*; Smith, *History of New York*, II, 60–68; Varga, "New York Government," 65–66, 69–75, 84, 282–83, 340; Bonomi, *Factious People*, 149–51; Katz, *Newcastle's New York*, 164–71.

28. Quotations from Varga, "New York Government," 90 (and see 88–93); and from Smith, *History of New York*, II, 72. Also see Katz, *Newcastle's New York*, 169–70.

personal reasons and "for several objections I have to it [the Canadian campaign] in general."[29] From 1746 until the governor's departure in 1753, James DeLancey, with the enthusiastic backing of most
other nonexpansionists, including his brothers Oliver and Peter, led
the attacks against Clinton.[30]

At this juncture, an able governor might have turned for support to
the expansionist faction and so used the party structure of New York
to his advantage. Clinton, however, managed to anger not only the
DeLanceyites but also many of the politicians who shared his views
on fighting the French. Clinton's mishandling of the expansionists is
exemplified by his relations with Philip Livingston. Livingston was a
wealthy estate owner, a councillor, the secretary for Indian affairs,
and probably the most powerful native New Yorker after James De-
Lancey. He was also an outspoken advocate of preparedness and a
firm critic of the opposing faction, lamenting in January 1746, for
example, that "the [assembly] members of the lower counties seem
against doing anything effectually for the frontiers, which is really a
most melancholy case."[31] He journeyed with Clinton to the Albany
conference in the summer of 1746, while DeLancey and his followers
remained at home. Clinton, however, was no better able to work with
Livingston than with DeLancey. The manor lord complained that the
governor was "always out of humor" and unwilling to heed advice
that the expedition set out before the weather grew colder.[32] Clinton,
in turn, reacted angrily to such criticism. He asked the duke of Newcastle in December 1746 to remove Livingston from his post as secretary for Indian affairs, and after Livingston's death in 1749 he frustrated the efforts of Livingston's relatives to keep the secretaryship
within the family.[33]

The governor's impolitic behavior alienated, along with the Livingstons, virtually all the expansionists. Clinton succumbed to fits of
rage, and to the maddened executive the lawmakers were a "stubborn Dutch assembly," Henry Beekman was "that fool," and the
Livingstons were "seditious."[34] At least during his first half dozen

29. James DeLancey to Gov. Clinton, Aug. 30, 1746, quoted in Varga, "New York
Government," 346, and see 99–100, 105–7, 345; Smith, *History of New York*, 72–73.
30. Varga, "New York Government," 232–34, 368–69; Katz, *Newcastle's New York*,
176–84.
31. Philip Livingston to Jacob Wendell, Jan. 14, 1746, quoted in Bonomi, *Factious
People*, 100–1; Norton, *Fur Trade*, 181.
32. Philip Livingston to Jacob Wendell, Sept. 18, 1746, quoted in Bonomi, *Factious
People*, 154.
33. Gov. Clinton to C. Colden, June 30, 1748, Feb. 9, 1750, NYHS *Cols.*, LIII (1920), 69,
189; Varga, "New York Government," 127–28; Katz, *Newcastle's New York*, 180–82;
Bonomi, *Factious People*, 154–55.
34. Gov. Clinton to C. Colden, June 30, 1748, Feb. 9, 1750, James Alexander to C.
Colden, June 13, 1752, NYHS *Cols.*, LIII (1920), 69, 189, 336; C. Colden to Alexander,

years in the colony, the governor seemed completely bereft of the skills needed to build a base of support. "In a province given to hospitality," William Smith, Jr., observed, "he erred by immuring himself in the fort, or retiring to a grotto in the country, where his time was spent with his bottle and a little trifling circle. . . . His manner of living was the very reverse of that requisite to raise a party or make friends."[35] The bipartisan opposition to Clinton, however, never wholly effaced factional lines on the question of war. Expansionist lawmakers continued to back military expenditures despite their personal dislike for the governor, knowing well that undercutting his plans would only endanger their estates. During the last years of King George's War the house appropriated large sums for defense.[36]

Although political allegiances remained askew until the end of Clinton's term, beginning in 1749 several of the expansionists drifted away from the "Faction," as the broad-based opposition to Clinton was called, and into the governor's camp. Any such amalgam as the Faction, which combined expansionists and nonexpansionists, was unnatural in New York. The Morrises, for example, could not long remain in a party containing the Philipses, who were their archrivals in Westchester County, and Lewis Morris, Jr., declared his willingness to assist Clinton if the governor moderated his salary demands. Similarly, James Alexander, an active expansionist since the 1720s, was loath to work with the DeLanceys and became by 1749 a member of Clinton's circle of advisers. Other men, such as William Smith, Sr., a Presbyterian lawyer, found the Faction's politics not to their liking and agreed to cooperate with the executive. Clinton never recruited an extensive following, but he learned to reward his supporters, placing Morris on the admiralty bench and appointing the elder William Smith attorney general. And though the Livingstons maintained their hostility toward Clinton until his departure, his new associates viewed the members of that family as the governor's natural allies in any struggle with James DeLancey. In 1751 Alexander, Smith, and Cadwallader Colden contemplated awarding patronage to Robert R. Livingston, whom they considered a man of "good sense, spirit, and

June 3, 1751, Rutherfurd Collection, IV, 81; Varga, "New York Government," 334; Katz, *Newcastle's New York*, 169.

35. Smith, *History of New York*, II, 138.

36. See defense votes on Jan. 18, 28, Feb. 5, 13, Apr. 7, 9 (4 votes), 23, 24, 1746, *N.Y. Votes and Proceedings*; Smith, *History of New York*, II, 95–101, 114; Varga, "New York Government," 122–28, 153, 160; C. Colden to duke of Newcastle, Mar. 21, 1748, Complaint to the King vs. Oliver DeLancey, July 1749, C. Colden to Gov. Shirley, July 25, 1749, NYHS *Cols.*, LIII, (1920), 22, 117, 120; John Livingston to Robert Livingston, Jr., Aug. 25, 1750, Mar. 25, 1752, Livingston Family Papers, reel 7, FDRL. Clinton's strongest allies were Cadwallader Colden and William Johnson.

independent estate," as well as a politician who "could endeavor to abate" the chief justice's power. Nothing, however, came of these discussions.[37]

The Livingstons did join the other expansionists in the Whig Club, which was founded in 1752. Robert R. Livingston, Peter Van Brugh Livingston, and William Alexander were prominent members of this society, as was the trio of Yale-educated, Presbyterian lawyers who formed the "New York Triumvirate"—William Livingston, John Morin Scott, and William Smith, Jr. Thomas Jones, the loyalist historian, gruffly underscored the continuities in the careers of Whig Club members, "most of whom afterwards engaged, and took active parts in the late, unnatural, unprovoked American rebellion: or were the promoters, the advisers, and counselors in every step taken to, and for a long time after, its actual commencement."[38]

With Clinton's departure, the expansionists and nonexpansionists reemerged as the parties that shaped New York politics. Beginning in 1753 the two groups squabbled publicly over King's College, which the DeLanceys hoped would be a publicly funded Anglican institution. The Morris-Livingston faction (which included most dissenters) viewed the possibility of church control as anathema; the New York Triumvirate were particularly vehement in their opposition. "I exhort, I beseech, I obtest, I implore you," William Livingston declared to his readers, "to expostulate the case with your representatives, and testify your abhorrence of so perilous, so detestable a plot."[39] Inflammatory tracts, however, could not dissuade Anglican James DeLancey, who had become acting governor after Clinton's departure, and the school opened its doors in 1754 with a charter from the executive. The battle over funding continued until 1756 when a compromise was struck, with half the money raised for the college assigned to the construction of a jail and quarantine house and the other half going to the school. Recorded votes in 1754 and 1755 indicate that assemblymen from the expansionist stronghold of Albany County led the fight against the institution, while DeLancey's followers in New York City and in Richmond and Westchester counties campaigned for the school. Long Island, however, proved an exception to the tradi-

37. Smith, *History of New York*, II, 114; Varga, "New York Government," 152–56; Katz, *Newcastle's New York*, 189–91; James Alexander to C. Colden, Dec. 5, 1751, Gov. Clinton to C. Colden, Feb. 8, 1750, NYHS *Cols.*, LIII (1920), 303–4, 189; Robert R. Livingston to Robert Livingston, [Jr.], July 23, 1750, Robert R. Livingston Collection, Box 1, NYHS.

38. Thomas Jones, *History of New York during the Revolutionary War, and of the Leading Events in the Other Colonies at That Period*, 2 vols. (New York, 1879), I, 5–6; Dillon, *New York Triumvirate*, 95.

39. Milton M. Klein, ed., *The Independent Reflector; or, Weekly Essays on Sundry Important Subjects More Particularly Adapted to the Province of New-York, by William Livingston and Others* (Cambridge, Mass., 1963), 214.

tional pattern: dissenters in those counties temporarily abandoned DeLancey's party and voted against the college.[40]

When conflict with New France heated up in the mid-1750s the Morris-Livingston faction once again stood forth as the more determined advocate of preparedness. Such expansionists as James Alexander and William Livingston applauded the Albany Plan of Union, while Governor James DeLancey and his immediate circle rejected the scheme. The groups also squared off over cooperation with the Massachusetts governor, William Shirley, who early in 1755 sent Thomas Pownall to New York to secure aid. "Pownall found Mr. DeLancey and his party rather cold and backward," reported William Smith, Jr., "and applied himself to a party who from various causes were become so considerable as to inspire the lieutenant governor with some awe, and especially as their views corresponded with the recommendations of this ministry."[41] Among the contractors and provisioners who cooperated with Shirley were the scions of the great expansionist families, William Alexander, Lewis Morris III, and Peter V. B. Livingston, for example. Shirley's elevation in 1755 to the post of commander in chief only stiffened the nonexpansionists' reluctance to aid the war. DeLancey refused to lend Shirley cannon for an expedition against Fort Niagara, declaring that the French threat to that outpost was minimal. "Except in New York, or rather a prevailing faction there," commented William Livingston in 1756, "all the colonies hold him [Shirley] in very high esteem."[42] By the end of 1756, however, the promise of large British subventions and the dismissal of Shirley from his military post had helped mute the clash in New York over the war effort. In 1758, 1759, and 1760 lawmakers from both parties voted substantial sums for defense.[43]

Although public debate died down, partisan divisions remained

40. William Livingston to Robert Livingston, Jr., Feb. 4, 1754, Livingston Family Papers, reel 7, FDRL; Smith, *History of New York*, II, 166–68, 207–8; Klein, *Politics of Diversity*, 82–83; Klein, ed., *Independent Reflector*, 28–44, and passim; Dillon, *New York Triumvirate*, 32–38; Bonomi, *Factious People*, 176–77; and see votes on Nov. 26, 28 (3 votes), 1754, June 12, 1755, *N.Y. Votes and Proceedings*.

41. Smith, *History of New York*, II, 181; James Alexander to C. Colden, May 9, 1754, C. Colden to Franklin, June 20, 1754, NYHS *Cols.*, LIII (1920), 441–42, 449; William Livingston, *A Review of Military Operations . . .*, reprinted in MHS *Cols.*, 1st ser., VII (1800), 75–77.

42. Gov. Shirley to Oliver DeLancey, Sept. 29, 1755, Gov. Shirley to Peter V. B. Livingston and Lewis Morris [III], Jan. 5, 1756, Gov. Shirley to J. Erving, William Alexander, and Lewis Morris [III], Apr. 24, 1755, Rutherfurd Collection, III, 69, 131, 55; William Livingston, *A Review of Military Operations*, 160; Gov. Shirley to James DeLancey, June 1, 1755, *Correspondence of Shirley*, II, 184–85, and see 216n; Gov. Shirley to James DeLancey, June 1, 1755, Rutherfurd Collection, III, 63; Smith, *History of New York*, II, 187–89, 196–97; Bonomi, *Factious People*, 175–76.

43. Lord Loudoun to Peter V. B. Livingston, Aug. 23, 1756, Elihu Spence to Peter V. B. Livingston, Aug. 5, 1758, Rutherfurd Collection, III, 131, 175; Alexander Colden to C.

evident between 1757 and 1762. The December 1758 election, which strengthened the expansionist group in the assembly, served in part as a referendum on James DeLancey's efforts to create an Anglican college. "All the arts used to influence the multitude," William Smith observed, "were insufficient to extinguish the flames of jealousy excited by the partial preeminence given to one denomination in the modeling of the college." Four Livingstons, including two from Dutchess County, entered the assembly, and historian Smith commented, "From this time we shall distinguish the opposition under the name of the Livingston party."[44] Yet though, in Jones's words, "a majority of the republican faction were elected," the expansionists did not dominate the legislature; wavering members often decided issues. Moreover, the Livingston family and its allies formed the sort of loose coalition typical of colonial factions. Even the four Livingstons voted together only on a narrow set of partisan questions, such as setting Governor DeLancey's salary.[45]

If perhaps less heatedly, members of both parties continued to affirm their long-held stances on imperial issues. William Livingston, who since the early 1750s had been calling for the conquest of Canada, in 1760 wrote the address in which the house lauded Amherst for accomplishing that goal and, in Smith's words, "made the congratulatory echo louder than the first sound."[46] In 1762 when the Spanish War placed new demands on the colony, expansionists backed appropriations for both provincial troops and the regulars. "But for Mr. Robert R. Livingston, who devised this expedient of a loan," Smith noted, "the credit of that contribution would have been lost, for the house were extremely jealous of raising money to recruit soldiers for the standing army of the nation."[47] The peace treaty of 1763 marked the end of one set of issues that had separated the two factions but also heralded a new era of problems. Britain's attempt to tighten its control over America would widen the fissure dividing New Yorkers.

Colden, Oct. 6, 1757, NYHS *Cols.*, LIV (1921), 196; Smith, *History of New York*, II, 204, 213, 228–29, 234–44; *Historical Statistics of the U.S.*, 1199; and see defense votes on Nov. 9, 24 (2 votes), 1756, Feb. 24, 1757, *N.Y. Votes and Proceedings*.

44. Smith, *History of New York*, II, 236–37; Bonomi, *Factious People*, 178, 230–32, 308.

45. See votes on Mar. 1, 1759 (23 votes), Mar. 21, 1760, *N.Y. Votes and Proceedings*; Jones, *History of New York*, I, 17.

46. Smith, *History of New York*, II, 243–44, 251–53, quotation on 251; C. Colden to John Pownall, Nov. 26, 1761, NYHS *Cols.*, IX (1876), 140; Address of the Legislature to C. Colden, Oct. 29, 1760, ibid., LIV (1921), 367–68.

47. Smith, *History of New York*, II, 243, 255–69, quotation on 269; John Watts to Gen. Robert Monckton, Mar. 30, 1762, MHS *Cols.*, 4th ser., IX (1876), 448–49; Gen. Amherst to C. Colden, Apr. 3, June 7, 1761, C. Colden to Board of Trade, Apr. 7, 1762, Benjamin Pratt to C. Colden, Aug. 22, 1761, NYHS *Cols.*, LV (1922), 24–25, 68, 38, IX (1876), 187.

» «

In the years before 1763 New York partisans gave voice to the outlooks that helped shape their world. As in the other colonies, much of the expansionists' writing emphasized immediate issues, particularly the need for preparedness. In the "Watchtower" essays, the triumvirate of William Livingston, John Morin Scott, and William Smith, Jr., demanded firm steps against the French, while in his *Review of Military Operations* (1756), William Livingston insisted that "Canada must be demolished. *Delenda est Carthago*, or we are undone."[48]

But the most articulate partisans also expounded broader themes. One was a belief in America's abundant resources and potential for growth, a refrain that Livingston, Scott, and Smith wove into their essays in the *Independent Reflector*: "We are, my friends, but just emerged from the rude unpolished condition of an infant colony; there is a large field for improvement open to us. We are set down in a country whose fertility will generously reward the labours of the industrious husbandman."[49] A second chord was the need to defend American rights not only against the designs of enemies like France but also against the craft of the mother country. One of the articles William Livingston proposed for the *Independent Reflector* was to be titled "The equal rights of British subjects in the plantations, to the privileges enjoyed by their fellow subjects in Great Britain, asserted and vindicated."[50]

By contrast, nonexpansionists limned a more narrowly circumscribed vision of America's future. John Watts, a New York City merchant, gave only lukewarm support in 1762 to the idea that Britain might retain Canada. The acquisition, he thought, was "sensible enough" but not of much importance to the colonies: "If Canada be kept or not kept, I imagine our population will be much the same." Moreover, like many nonexpansionists, Watts downgraded provincial troops and elevated the regulars: "Supposing Canada ceded to us, I cannot think it would be safe to trust Quebec and Niagara especially with provincials. They are too negligent a kind of troop for such a service."[51]

---

48. Dillon, *New York Triumvirate*, 85n, discusses the articles published in the *New York Mercury* during 1755. Quote from William Livingston, *A Review of Military Operations*, 163.
49. Klein, ed., *Independent Reflector*, 219, and passim.
50. Ibid., 443.
51. John Watts to Lt. Col. Isaac Barre, Feb. 28, 1762, *Letter Book of John Watts: Merchant and Councillor of New York* (this is NYHS *Cols.*, LXI) (New York, 1928), 25.

CHAPTER 4

Pennsylvania:
Quaker Party Ascendancy

Thomas Willing was furious. "[The] damnable Quaker principle of nonresistance," he sputtered in November 1755, "has spread its influence into our body of representatives, 27 of whom out of 36 are Quakers and others are equally poisoned with their cursed destructive schemes. They are worse than the nobles of Scotland, for they only ruined themselves and these will destroy thousands of better, more honest men."[1] The reluctance of the Pennsylvania assembly to defend the frontier after General Braddock's defeat in the summer of 1755 was enough to madden any expansionist, but for men like Willing the rage had been long building. Ever since 1740, a group of Anglicans, Presbyterians, lapsed Friends, and others had been setting forth a trenchant and frequently acerbic critique of pacifist doctrines—and all too often to no avail. These expansionists, the party of the Willings, William Allen, and Benjamin Franklin, campaigned during the 1740s and 1750s for bellicose measures and would after 1762 become the colony's patriots. Their nonexpansionist opponents, chiefly Quakers but with an admixture of Anglicans and Germans, looked to such leaders as the Pembertons, Isaac Norris, and Joseph Galloway. This group hesitated to arm the province against the French and Indians and would subsequently be reluctant to criticize the mother country.

» «

Because of the colony's relatively sheltered location and the dominance of Quakers in local affairs, Pennsylvanians did not divide over

1. Thomas Willing to [Uncle] Thomas Willing, Nov. 22, 1755, Willing Letterbook, HSP.

their vision of the New World until 1740. The grant young William Penn secured as a haven for the Society of Friends was ideally situated for a sect in search of an earthly peaceable kingdom. The long stretch of the Delaware River leading up to Philadelphia discouraged raids by privateers or warships, while the Appalachian Mountains and the expanses of New York protected the colony from the incursions of the French and their native allies. No overland attack threatened the Quaker Colony until the mid-1750s, when the French marched into the upper Ohio Valley.[2]

Of equal significance, Quaker control of both provincial and local politics discouraged the formation of an expansionist party. Although a minority of the population by 1710, Friends easily dominated the legislature, benefiting from an apportionment that gave the original counties of Philadelphia, Chester, and Bucks eight seats each in a house of thirty members. The Quaker and German settlers in the prosperous, southeastern region consistently returned delegates drawn from the Society of Friends, while the Anglicans and Presbyterians in the city of Philadelphia and the frontier counties could muster but a few spokesmen in the house. Friends also directed the Philadelphia municipal corporation, the closed body that governed the city; as late as the 1730s forty of fifty-nine members of the corporation were Quakers.[3]

The colony's Quaker rulers disagreed bitterly among themselves about such issues as paper money or the distribution of offices, but they were of one mind in eschewing military conflict. Pennsylvanians were not above chicanery in their negotiations with the natives, but unlike politicians in other colonies, they gained new territory through a series of treaties rather than by leveling muskets.[4] Furthermore, requests from other provinces for military aid fell on deaf ears. Pressured by the Crown, the assembly made a single, grudging military appropriation of two thousand pounds in 1711, a decision soon ra-

2. Frederick B. Tolles, *James Logan and the Culture of Provincial America* (Boston, 1957), 100–101, 108, 166–70, 179–83; Gary B. Nash, *Quakers and Politics: Pennsylvania, 1681–1726* (Princeton, 1968), 87.

3. James T. Lemon, *The Best Poor Man's Country: A Geographical Study of Early Southeastern Pennsylvania* (Baltimore, 1972), 42–51, 104; Alan Tully, *William Penn's Legacy: Politics and Social Structure in Provincial Pennsylvania, 1726–1775* (Baltimore, 1977), 3–22, 79–102; Nash, *Quakers and Politics*, 203, and passim; Stephen Brobeck, "Revolutionary Change in Colonial Philadelphia: The Brief Life of the Proprietary Gentry," *WMQ*, 3d ser., xxxiii (1976), 417; Charles P. Keith, *Chronicles of Pennsylvania . . .* , 3 vols. (1917; rpt. Port Washington, New York, 1969), iii, passim. By the mid-1750s the admission of new counties had enlarged assembly membership to thirty-six.

4. Joseph E. Illick, *Colonial Pennsylvania: A History* (New York, 1976), 23–27, 169–70; Frederick B. Tolles, *Meeting House and Counting House: The Quaker Merchants of Colonial Philadelphia, 1682–1763* (Chapel Hill, N.C., 1948), 22–23.

tionalized. "We did not see it inconsistent with our principles to give the Queen money," pronounced one Quaker leader, "notwithstanding any use she might put it to, that being not our part but hers."[5] But such lapses were rare; more typical was the rejection of a request from the Lower Counties (i.e., Delaware) with the comment that there was no danger "but from bears and wolves."[6] Moreover, the Quaker law-makers consistently turned back proposals to create a provincial militia.

» «

The composition of Pennsylvania's expansionist and nonexpansionist parties, which emerged in 1740, primarily reflected religious beliefs and national origins and only secondarily the geography of settlement. The convictions of the Quakers helped polarize local politics. Not all members of the Society of Friends adhered to the gospel of peace so scrupulously as those who during the French and Indian War refused to pay taxes and were subjected "to great straits and difficulties," but most Friends were extremely reluctant to approve a militia act, particularly one that provided for a draft or the discipline of troops, and most were hesitant to take forceful steps to prepare the colony for war. Before the mid-1750s, when strict Friends withdrew from government, the dominant party in the Pennsylvania statehouse was more adamantly opposed to war than was any other nonexpansionist faction in America.[7]

The political strength of the Quakers was far greater than their proportion in the population might have suggested. Although by 1754 only one of every six Pennsylvanians was a Friend, Quakers still filled twenty-seven of the thirty-six seats in the house.[8] Even after many resigned during the French and Indian War, Friends remained the largest religious group in the legislature, if no longer a majority. Leadership of the Quaker forces in the house fell to a series of able individuals. In the 1740s John Kinsey was speaker of the house, and was followed in the 1750s and early 1760s by Isaac Norris. Both men were also active in the Society of Friends. Joseph Galloway, who entered the legislature in 1756, guided the Quaker lawmakers (and the Anglicans who sat with them) after Norris stepped down. Although raised as a Quaker, Galloway belonged to no church.[9]

5. Isaac Norris I to James Logan, Aug. 28, 1711, quoted in Tolles, *James Logan*, 86; Tolles, *Meeting House*, 181–89; Nash, *Quakers and Politics*, 182–99, 249–60, 270–71.

6. *Minutes of Council*, 1689, quoted in Nash, *Quakers and Politics*, 130; Tolles, *James Logan*, 17–19.

7. Nash, *Quakers and Politics*, 130, 201–2, 249; Tully, *Penn's Legacy*, 154.

8. Philadelphia Meeting for Sufferings to London Meeting for Sufferings, Mar. 25, 1760, Letters to and from Philadelphia, I, 25, Friends House Library, London.

9. Tully, *Penn's Legacy*, 54; Edwin B. Bronner, "The Disgrace of John Kinsey, Quaker Politician, 1739–1750," *PMHB*, LXXV (1951), 400–415; John D. Windhausen,

Before 1763 the several denominations that formed Pennsylvania's German community also supported the nonexpansionists. The beliefs of the "sect people"—Moravians, Mennonites, Brethren, and Schwenkenfelders—bore in some respects a striking similarity to the pietistic teachings of Quakerism. These worshipers, who carefully preserved their Old World folkways, were often devout pacifists.[10] Far more numerous, however, were the "church people," Germans who attended the Lutheran and Reformed congregations. This group was bound by no doctrine of peace and melded more fully into the mainstream of colonial life. The church people generally backed the Quakers in the 1740s and 1750s, although a minority of them heartily supported the war effort. During the revolutionary movement, most Lutheran and Reformed Germans came to side with the expansionists. But before 1763 the outlook of the Germans, or "Pennsylvania Dutch," who made up fully 40 percent of the population, angered those who favored a bolder stand on imperial questions. "Why should the Palatine Boors," Benjamin Franklin demanded in 1751, "be suffered to swarm into our settlements, and by herding together establish their language and manners to the exclusion of ours?"[11] And he told Peter Collinson in 1753, "In the last war our Germans showed a general disposition that seems to bode us no good."[12]

The nonexpansionists also received the approval of a portion of the Pennsylvania Anglicans. The Church of England claimed only a small minority of the population in the colony, but it was of notable importance in Philadelphia, where it was probably the largest denomination in the 1740s. Most Anglicans favored the expansionists, but a significant minority backed the Quaker party, seeing in that faction a bulwark against the turbulence of the western settlers. Noting in 1755 that the Anglicans "dread the Presbyterians and Germans," Isaac Norris commented, "The Church of England know they must keep in with the Quakers to keep the others out."[13] Between 1740 and 1755 a few Anglicans, including Thomas Leech and Evan Morgan, sat in the assembly as full-fledged members of the nonexpansionist fac-

"Quaker Pacifism and the Image of Isaac Norris II," *Pennsylvania History*, XXXIV (1967), 346–60; Benjamin H. Newcomb, *Franklin and Galloway: A Political Partnership* (New Haven, 1972), 10–22.

10. Theodore Thayer, *Pennsylvania Politics and the Growth of Democracy, 1740–1776* (Harrisburg, 1953), 41–42; Illick, *Colonial Pennsylvania*, 123, 244, 253, 257.

11. Benjamin Franklin, *Observations Concerning the Increase of Mankind . . .* , 1751, *The Papers of Benjamin Franklin*, ed. Leonard W. Labaree et al. (New Haven, 1959–   ), IV, 234; Tully, *Penn's Legacy*, 54.

12. Franklin to Peter Collinson, May 9, 1753, *Papers of Franklin*, IV, 485.

13. Isaac Norris to Charles Norris, Apr. 29, 1755, quoted in William S. Hanna, *Benjamin Franklin and Pennsylvania Politics* (Stanford, Calif., 1964), 101–2; William Smith to Richard Peters and Franklin, Feb. 1754, Franklin, *Poor Richard's Almanack*, 1750, *Papers of Franklin*, V, 209–10, III, 439; Tully, *Penn's Legacy*, 54–55.

tion. Moreover, after the resignation of the pacifist assemblymen in 1756, several Anglicans—including John Hughes, the future stamp distributor—rushed to fill the vacated seats and made clear their willingness to carry on nonexpansionist traditions, albeit with moderation.[14]

Like the Quaker party, the expansionist faction was a coalition of several religious and national groups. The expansionists could count on the backing of the Presbyterians, who, because of the large Scotch-Irish immigration, claimed over 20 percent of the population in the 1750s. William Allen, one of Pennsylvania's wealthiest men, and Daniel Roberdeau were two Presbyterian leaders who advocated preparedness and would later be active in the revolutionary movement. During the 1740s and 1750s, however, the Presbyterian impact on politics was diminished by a serious schism within the church over the evangelical fervor of the Great Awakening. "The Presbyterians are divided into several sects," gloated Quaker leader Isaac Norris in 1755, "most disliking if not hating one another as is the case between the New and Old Lights, as they call themselves."[15] Despite this internecine conflict, many Calvinists, such as the Reverend Gilbert Tennent, were active in provincial politics before 1763 and worked for expansionist policies. The formal healing of this schism in 1758 laid the basis for the prominent role that the Presbyterians would play in the struggle against Britain.[16]

Most Anglicans, and a scattering of other Pennsylvanians, leaned toward the expansionist faction. Episcopalian merchants—for example, Thomas Willing and Robert Morris—stood in the van of those calling for a vigorous prosecution of the wars against the French and Indians and, subsequently, would be among the leading patriots.[17]

---

14. Ralph L. Ketcham, "Conscience, War, and Politics in Pennsylvania, 1755–1757," *WMQ*, 3d ser., xx (1963), 422; Thayer, *Pennsylvania Politics*, 45n, 58n; Tully, *Penn's Legacy*, 40, 81, 89, 96, 226.

15. Isaac Norris to Charles Norris, Apr. 29, 1755, quoted in Hanna, *Benjamin Franklin*, 102; *Papers of Franklin*, ii, 288n; Tully, *Penn's Legacy*, 54. Daniel Roberdeau has often been labeled an Anglican and indeed was a vestryman of Christ Church. But his connection to the Church of England appears to have been more social than religious. His correspondence makes clear his active involvement in the Presbyterian church. See Roberdeau Letterbook, passim, HSP; Roberdeau Buchanan, *Genealogy of the Roberdeau Family, Including a Biography of General Daniel Roberdeau. . . .* (Washington, D.C., 1876), 49, 53–54.

16. Illick, *Colonial Pennsylvania*, 194; Dietmar Rothermund, *The Layman's Progress: Religious and Political Experience in Colonial Pennsylvania, 1740–1770* (Philadelphia, 1961), 98–108.

17. Willing Letterbook, passim; Brobeck, "Revolutionary Change," 418. On the continuing importance of Anglicans in the revolutionary movement, see Richard A. Ryerson, *The Revolution Is Now Begun: The Radical Committees of Philadelphia, 1765–1776* (Philadelphia, 1978), 74–75.

Such lapsed or disowned Quakers as Samuel Mifflin and John Dickinson buttressed this party, as did Benjamin Franklin, a deist. Franklin, according to his own account, "had been religiously educated as a Presbyterian" but came to prefer his own ideas about God to the teachings of any sect. Franklin was a key figure in Pennsylvania politics and was during this era the best-known expansionist writer in America.[18]

In addition to religious and ethnic affiliations, a secondary influence on factional lines (at least after 1755) was proximity to the frontier. Those settlers who bore the brunt of Indian attacks during the Seven Years' War favored the expansionists, a regional pattern reflected in the votes of the assembly. In 1761 Proprietary Secretary Richard Peters reported to General Robert Monckton the defeat of a bill to enlist four hundred men for the army: "Mr. [William] Allen desires me to mention to you that the members for Cumberland, York, and Lancaster were strenuous for raising the men and did in all respects behave extremely well, not only upon this but all other occasions."[19] In part, the influence of geography related to religious distinctions: Scotch-Irish Presbyterians were strong in the counties William Allen mentioned and were less numerous in the older parts of the colony. Significantly, the sizable German population in Lancaster made that county the least reliable of the three in the west as a base for the expansionists. But the dangers of native incursions helped modify the outlook of the Germans. Thus war-ravaged Northampton County, where the Pennsylvania Dutch formed an overwhelming majority, chose expansionist William Plumstead as its representative in 1756 and 1757. Plumstead, a Philadelphia merchant and a disowned Friend who joined the Anglican church, was a strong critic of Quaker policies.[20]

» «

Factions that differed in their vision of America's future coalesced in 1740 in response to Governor George Thomas's efforts to recruit soldiers for British campaigns in the Caribbean. Thomas's request for support galvanized parishioners in the Presbyterian and Anglican churches—two sects that had grown in wealth and numbers and now felt ready to challenge the Quakers. When the lawmakers refused to

18. *The Autobiography of Benjamin Franklin*, ed. Leonard W. Labaree et al. (New Haven, 1964), 145; Brobeck, "Revolutionary Change," 418–20.

19. Richard Peters to Gen. Monckton, Apr. 27, 1761, MHS *Cols.*, 4th ser., IX (1871), 140.

20. Thayer, *Pennsylvania Politics*, 41–42, 63–64; Lemon, *Best Poor Man's Country*, 49–50.

appropriate funds to aid the English cause except on their own restrictive terms, the affluent non-Quaker merchants subscribed money to outfit several hundred soldiers. Furthermore, the expansionist
faction, or Proprietary party, as it soon came to be called, set up
electoral slates in each county to challenge Quaker domination of the
legislature for the first time in Pennsylvania history. These tickets,
which included such men as William Allen and James Hamilton,
uniformly went down to defeat. The expansionists also forwarded to
the Crown a petition criticizing the assembly and asking that steps be
taken to protect the colony.[21] In response, the Quakers, in Governor
Thomas's words, "immediately entered into consultations, and came
to a resolution to exert their whole power and influence to procure a
considerable majority of their own persuasion to be chosen to oppose
all expense on warlike preparation."[22]

The emergence of the two factions gradually effected a thoroughgo-
ing realignment of Philadelphia social and political institutions. Before the mid-1740s the various clubs and societies of the capital had
mingled Quakers, Anglicans, and Presbyterians. For example, the
rolls of the Library Company in May 1742 show nine members who
can be identified as Friends and nine who adhered to other faiths, and
a similar balance was evident in the Union Fire Company as well as
the Colony in the Schuylkill club.[23] But such informal mixing gradually came to an end. "Our unhappy divisions and animosities of late,"
lamented the directors of the Library Company in 1742, "have too
much interrupted that charitable and friendly intercourse which formerly subsisted among all societies in this place."[24] Quaker functions
began to exclude people of other faiths, and after 1745 Anglicans and
Presbyterians fraternized in organizations rarely attended by pacifists. Among the expansionist conclaves were the Dancing Assembly,
the St. Andrew's Society, the Society of the Sons of St. George, and
(in the 1750s) the Academy and the College of Philadelphia.[25]

21. Board of Trade to Privy Council, July 8, 1742, CO 5/1294/109–13, PRO; Tully,
Penn's Legacy, 23–39, 86, 89–90, 225–27; Thayer, *Pennsylvania Politics*, 17.
22. Gov. Thomas to Board of Trade, Oct. 20, 1740, CO 5/1233/192, PRO; Thayer,
Pennsylvania Politics, 10–19.
23. For Colony in the Schuylkill, see J. Thomas Scharf and Thompson Westcott,
History of Philadelphia, 1609–1884, 3 vols. (Philadelphia, 1884), I, 233. For Anglicans,
see vestrymen lists in *PMHB*, XIX (1895), 518–26. For Union Fire Company and Library
Company, see *Papers of Franklin*, II, 153, 205, 346–47. For religious affiliations, see
Scharf and Westcott, *Philadelphia*, II, 1267–1437. Also consult Daniel Gilbert, "Patterns of Organization and Membership in Colonial Philadelphia's Club Life, 1725–
1755" (Ph.D. diss., Univ. of Pennsylvania, 1952).
24. Directors of Library Company to Proprietors, July 1742, *Papers of Franklin*, II,
348.
25. For Dancing Assembly, St. Andrew's Society, and Sons of St. George, see Scharf
and Westcott, *Philadelphia*, II, 864, 1464–65, 1467. For Academy, see *Papers of Franklin*,
III, 422–23, V, 435, and Franklin to Ebenezer Kinnersley, July 28, 1759, ibid., VIII, 415–
16; Brobeck, "Revolutionary Change," 427.

The emergence of the two parties also transformed certain political institutions. By 1743 the expansionists had secured control of Philadelphia's governing corporation, long an unbreachable redoubt of the Quakers. Included in the reformed city government were Charles Willing, his son Thomas, and William Allen. Furthermore, with the help of Proprietor Thomas Penn's appointments, Presbyterians and Anglicans took control of the provincial council, an advisory chamber traditionally dominated by Friends. After 1741 Penn also began consistently favoring the expansionist faction in the award of commissions of the peace. The corporation, council, and justiceships provided the newly formed party with a base of power and helped balance the strength of the nonexpansionists in the legislature.[26]

Although factional lines had solidified, conflict between the expansionists (or Proprietary party) and the nonexpansionists (or Quaker party) was muted during the mid-1740s. After resounding defeats in the provincial elections of 1740, 1741, and 1742, Anglican and Presbyterian leaders realized, as Secretary Peters explained, that "the people [were under] . . . the power of their adversaries."[27] The expansionists would not again set up full slates for the assembly until 1756. At the same time, the Quaker party, led by Speaker John Kinsey, displayed a notable moderation. Despite the fulminations of root-and-branch Friends like Israel Pemberton, Jr., Kinsey announced that the house was willing to work with Governor Thomas. In 1745 the nonexpansionists yielded to the governor's requests and voted four thousand pounds for various foodstuffs and "other grain" to be shipped to the colonial forces at Louisbourg. With no protest from the assembly, Thomas construed "other grain" as gunpowder. In 1746 the legislature set aside an additional five thousand pounds "for the King's use."[28]

The factional truce came to an end in 1747, however, when the appearance of French and Spanish privateers in the Delaware stirred Pennsylvania's expansionists to demand that local fortifications be strengthened. After the Quaker assembly refused to provide for the colony's defense, Benjamin Franklin issued a tract titled *Plain Truth*, in which he called for the formation of a voluntary militia unit, or "Association." In Franklin's words, the pamphlet "bore somewhat hard on both parties," but he adopted this nonpartisan pose only after consultation with several expansionists. Condemning both factions was, as Richard Peters explained, an "artifice to animate all the

26. For aldermen, common councilmen, and justices of the peace, see Samuel Hazard, ed., *Pennsylvania Archives* (Philadelphia, 1852–1949), 2d ser., ix, 754, 751–52, 700–713; Tully, *Penn's Legacy*, 109, 224; Brobeck, "Revolutionary Change," 419–20.
27. Richard Peters to Thomas Penn, Mar. 4, 1743, quoted in Tully, *Penn's Legacy*, 37.
28. Tully, *Penn's Legacy*, 128–29, 155–57; *Autobiography of Franklin*, 188–90; Tolles, *Meeting House*, 23–24; Thayer, *Pennsylvania Politics*, 19–20.

middling persons."[29] Furthermore, reaction to Franklin's initiative fell along party lines. Men like Presbyterian minister Gilbert Tennent, who had an unbounded view of America's future prospects, extolled Franklin's plan, while nonexpansionists—for example, Christopher Sauer, spokesman for the German "sect people"—castigated the scheme. The Proprietary faction provided almost all the Association's officers as well as the managers of the lottery organized to raise funds for the purchase of cannon.[30]

The formation of the Association in 1747 marked Franklin's full-blown entry into local politics, and in the years up to August 1755 he would continue to present himself as an independent, unaffiliated with either upper-class faction. "An appearance of impartiality in general," he explained to his English friend Peter Collinson, "gives a man sometimes much more weight when he would serve in particular instances."[31] Despite Franklin's spirited advocacy of preparedness, he remained on amicable terms with the Quaker lawmakers, who were happy to befriend the foremost printer in the colony. After his election to the assembly in 1751, Franklin cooperated with the Quaker faction whenever imperial matters were not at stake, and in turn, the legislators frequently made Franklin their penman, sending him to important conferences, such as those at Carlisle and Albany. At the same time, Franklin kept up his close ties with the Proprietary party and sought to foster the rapid development of the New World.[32]

Between 1750 and 1754, Pennsylvania politicians joined battle over several issues. Leading expansionists, including Franklin and William Allen, labored to establish English schools in the German communities and so to encourage those settlers to take a broader view of imperial questions. This scheme, however, begun in earnest in 1754, was at best only a partial success. The Quaker lawmakers refused to vote the schools any funds, and many Germans saw through the inflated rhetoric accompanying the program. The backers of the schools, Christopher Sauer remarked tartly, "care very little for religion or for the cultivation of Germans, they rather want the Germans to stick out their necks by serving in the militia to protect the property of these gentlemen."[33] The two parties were also at odds over a plan of

29. Franklin to Cadwallader Colden, Nov. 27, 1747, Franklin, *Plain Truth . . .* , 1747, *Papers of Franklin*, III, 213, 180–204; Richard Peters to proprietors, Nov. 29, 1747, ibid., 215–17, quotation on 215–16.

30. *Pennsylvania Gazette*, Jan. 5, 1748, has officers, June 2, 1748, has lottery managers; *Papers of Franklin*, III, 184; Illick, *Colonial Pennsylvania*, 194.

31. Franklin to Peter Collinson, Dec. 29, 1754, *Papers of Franklin*, V, 453.

32. On Franklin's affiliations, see Marc Egnal, "The Politics of Ambition: A New Look at Benjamin Franklin's Career," *Canadian Review of American Studies*, VI (1975), 151–64, esp. 152–55.

33. Sauer quoted in Illick, *Colonial Pennsylvania*, 243; Franklin to C. Colden, Aug. 30, 1754, Franklin to Collinson, May 28, 1754, *Papers of Franklin*, V, 427, 333, and see 203–6.

union for the colonies. Franklin had sketched out such a proposal as early as 1751 and was largely responsible for the design adopted at Albany in the summer of 1754. The Quaker party, however, effectively buried the scheme: at the Albany conference, Speaker Isaac Norris joined New York nonexpansionists, the DeLancey faction, in registering his dissent, and once the delegation returned to Philadelphia, the legislature summarily rejected the proposed charter. Expansionists were enraged. "Our vile broad brims here," wrote the Willings, "would not even admit it to be read in the house as hearing 'twas destructive of their peaceable rights and therefore condemned it upon the representation of their Speaker who was one of our company at Albany."[34]

Expansionists and nonexpansionists also differed in their response to French advances in the Ohio Valley. The Assembly party had made its position clear as early as 1749, when it refused to cooperate with Thomas Penn, the chief proprietor, in the construction of a fort in the west. Penn was temporarily forced to concede the colony's trans-Appalachian reaches to the Ohio Company of Virginia, hoping that his proprietary rights would be respected. Expansionists, however, voiced grave concerns about Bourbon aggression. "It is much to be feared," William Allen wrote in 1753, "that in case a new war should break out with France this province that has hitherto been unmolested will be very much annoyed by the French and Indians."[35] George Washington's defeat in 1754 at Fort Necessity heightened such worries. A rash of articles appearing before the October 1754 election called on Friends either to vote funds for defense or to leave office. But the incumbent legislators stood their ground and were easily reelected. "Our people have been so influenced by the Quaker interest at the late election," Charles and Thomas Willing sighed, "that they have returned the same assemblymen through the whole province, and this is so critical a juncture that we dread the consequence."[36]

During the first half of 1755 Britain's decision to mount a major offensive against the French at Fort Duquesne increased the tension between Pennsylvania parties. The Quaker faction viewed the crisis as an opportunity to exact concessions from the proprietors and to tighten its grip on the provincial purse strings; defense of the colony was secondary. "It is a matter of considerable consequence to the

34. Charles Willing & Son to Thomas Willing, Oct. 1754, Willing Letterbook; Franklin to James Alexander and C. Colden, June 8, 1754, *Papers of Franklin*, v, 335–38, and see the documents, 344–90, esp. Thomas Pownall to [?], July 23, 1754, p. 375.
35. William Allen to Mr. Allen, Nov. 15, 1753, CO 5/1233/232, PRO; Thayer, *Pennsylvania Politics*, 30–31.
36. Charles Willing & Son to Thomas Willing, Oct. 1754, Willing Letterbook; *Pennsylvania Gazette*, Sept. 19, 26, 1754.

inhabitants," James Pemberton explained to a London Friend in January 1755, "[that] our liberties are at stake and I think we have as much reason to dread an attack upon them from our proprietors whose ambitious views seem bent on enslaving us as any danger that may be at present thought to threaten us."[37]

Significantly, the expansionists, who would become the patriots of the 1760s and 1770s, were less committed at this juncture to the defense of Whig rights and more concerned that funds be appropriated for the war. Though Franklin disapproved of the proprietors' self-interested actions, he considered an address of January 1755, in which the house set forth its demands, "ill-judged and ill-timed."[38] He managed to persuade the lawmakers to dip into the loan office fund to aid General Braddock, but he was unable to convince them to frame an excise bill incorporating Penn's demands. "I like neither the governor's conduct nor the assembly's," Franklin complained in June, "and having some share in the confidence of both, I have endeavored to reconcile them, but in vain."[39] Thomas Willing and others echoed these sentiments.[40]

» «

Major General Edward Braddock's defeat in July 1755 precipitated climactic changes within the nonexpansionist faction, inaugurating a new phase of party development. The strict Quakers withdrew from the assembly, and a more moderate nonexpansionist party emerged. Conflict continued, but a modicum of wartime cooperation between the two upper-class parties now became possible. More than any other single individual, Benjamin Franklin was the architect of the change.

The printer's decision in August 1755 to abandon his stance as an independent and to side wholeheartedly with the Quaker party marked the first step in the reshaping of the nonexpansionist faction. Franklin was deeply concerned about protecting the colony's frontiers in the aftermath of Braddock's defeat. On August 2 the legislature appropriated fifty thousand pounds for defense, backed by a tax on all landed estates including those of the proprietors. Governor Robert Hunter Morris refused to approve the bill, however, unless the

37. James Pemberton to Hinton Brown, Jan. 15, 1755, Pemberton Papers, HSP; James H. Hutson, "Benjamin Franklin and Pennsylvania Politics, 1751–1755: A Reappraisal," *PMHB*, xciii (1969), 343–56.

38. Franklin to Collinson, June 26, 1755, *Papers of Franklin*, vi, 86.

39. Ibid.; Pa. Assembly, Orders Concerning Provisions, Apr. 2, 1755, Assembly to governor, Mar. 19, 1755, ibid., 6–7, v, 527–31, and see v, 528, vi, 3; Thayer, *Pennsylvania Politics*, 38.

40. Thomas Willing to John Perks, Jan. 15, 1755, Willing Letterbook.

Penns' holdings were exempted. At this juncture, Franklin might have called for a compromise between the legislature and the executive, as he had earlier in the year, but that tack had been unsuccessful, and the lawmakers seemed in no better frame of mind. Instead, Franklin leaped into the front ranks of the Quaker faction and led the campaign against the governor. Morris complained bitterly that the printer "is at the head of these extraordinary measures taken by the assembly, writes their messages, and directs their motions."[41]

Franklin joined the Quaker party not because he accepted its outlook but because he hoped to transform this dominant group into a faction that would adopt the steps necessary for preparedness. He told a friend in August: "To me, it seems that if *Quakerism* (as to the matter of defense) be excluded [from] the house, there is no necessity to exclude *Quakers*, who in other respects make good and useful members."[42] While ardently agreeing with the assemblymen that the fifty thousand pounds appropriated must be adopted on their terms, Franklin persuaded them to support several stopgap measures to check the French and Indians. He had the legislature allot a thousand pounds of its own funds for the defense of the frontier and secured assembly backing for a voluntary subscription to supply warm clothing for the troops at Crown Point. The printer undoubtedly was also pleased when the impasse over the money bill was resolved. In November the lawmakers grudgingly accepted the proprietors' "free gift" of five thousand pounds in lieu of taxes and voted a somewhat enlarged appropriation (sixty thousand pounds) for defense.[43]

From his new position as one of the leaders of the Quaker party, Franklin struggled to secure militia and mutiny acts. In November 1755, "by leave of the house," Franklin introduced a bill to create an armed force. The stricter Friends in the chamber opposed the measure, even though the bill was hedged with restrictions to protect the scrupulous. The act, as signed into law, made enlistments voluntary, explicitly excluded Quakers, and set limits on where troops could be marched. Many Friends, however, feared that this legislation was a step on the road to full-blown conscription. In 1756 one pacifist as-

41. Gov. Morris to Secretary of State Thomas Robinson, Aug. 28, 1755, *Papers of Franklin*, VI, 129–30; John Smith to R. Wells, Aug. 22, 1755, John Smith Correspondence, HSP.
42. Franklin to Collinson, Aug. 27, 1755, *Papers of Franklin*, VI, 171.
43. Franklin to Richard Partridge, Nov. 27, 1755, Franklin to James Read, Nov. 2, 1755, Franklin to Peters, Nov. 5, 1755, Franklin to William Shirley, July 1756, Peters to Franklin, Nov. 5, 1755, Shirley to Franklin, Feb. 4, 1756, ibid., 273, 234–36, 236–37, 477–79, 237, 390–92, and see 165, 537n; James H. Hutson, *Pennsylvania Politics, 1746–1770: The Movement for Royal Government and Its Consequences* (Princeton, 1972), 17–24.

semblyman shuddered, "If a general militia law should be obtained in the manner our high flyers aim at, . . . it would ruin the province."[44] The battle over the mutiny act, which Franklin presented to the house in March 1756, was even more heated. This law, which tightened the rules governing the provincial forces, was adopted only after being voted down and amended several times.[45]

During the second half of 1755 and 1756, pressure from outside the assembly helped Franklin achieve his goal of remodeling the Quaker party. Among those calling for change in the legislature were the leaders of the Proprietary party. In October, William Allen organized a petition asking the king to "interpose your royal authority that this important province . . . may be put into a *posture of defense.*" Allen, William Plumstead, Thomas Willing, Gilbert Tennent, and 106 other expansionists joined their names to the petition.[46] John Kidd, one of the signers, explained to an English correspondent that the colony's troubles were caused by "a stupid party faction that has long prevailed amongst us, which I am afraid nothing can put an end to but an act of Parliament."[47] Many of the same men sent the Pennsylvania legislature a similar protest, a document that the Quaker assemblymen summarily rejected.[48] Settlers living in the backcountry also demanded more forceful policies. In November 1755 about five hundred angry frontiersmen descended on Philadelphia, threatening to "tear the whole members of the legislative body limb from limb, if they did not grant immediate protection."[49]

British officials and English Quakers also urged the Friends in the assembly to yield the reins of power to those with more bellicose views. In March 1756 the Board of Trade, with the hearty approval of its president, the earl of Halifax, argued that the "interposition of an act of the British legislature" was needed to save Penn's Colony from the French.[50] English Friends, concerned to protect their Pennsylvania brethren from the imposition of a test act, added their voices to

44. William Callender to John Fothergill, June 2, 1756, Misc. Corresp., 20/27, Friends House Library; *Autobiography of Franklin*, 230; Franklin, "A Dialogue Between X, Y, and Z . . . ," Dec. 18, 1755, *Papers of Franklin*, vi, 295–306, and see 266–73.
45. *Papers of Franklin*, vi, 433–35.
46. Franklin to R. Partridge, Oct. 25, 1755, ibid., 231–32. Signers of the petition are listed in Charles Stillé, "The Attitude of the Quakers in the Provincial Wars," *PMHB*, x (1886), 283–315.
47. John Kidd to Rawlinson & Davison, Nov. 23, 1755, Kidd Letterbook, HSP; Thomas Willing to Walter Stirling, Nov. 12, 1755, Willing Letterbook.
48. *Papers of Franklin*, vi, 245–48.
49. William Smith, *A Brief View of the Conduct of Pennsylvania in the Year 1755*, quoted in Hutson, *Pennsylvania Politics*, 25; John Kidd to Neate & Neave, Nov. 25, 1755, Kidd Letterbook.
50. Board of Trade to Privy Council, Mar. 3, 1756, CO 5/1295/99–106, quotation on 106; Thayer, *Pennsylvania Politics*, 56; Hanna, *Benjamin Franklin*, 95–99.

those calling for the pacifists to quit their seats. During March 1756 a delegation of English Quakers talked with a "nobleman in a high station," most probably Earl Granville, head of the Privy Council. He assured the delegation that if the Quakers resigned from the house, "he for one would endeavor to prevent any violent measures from being taken at present."[51] English Friends eagerly embraced this plan and sent a series of letters as well as several emissaries to Pennsylvania to persuade the principled lawmakers to retire from politics.[52]

As a result of Franklin's efforts, the pressure exerted by Pennsylvania expansionists and frontiersmen, as well as the urgings of concerned Englishmen, strict Quakers withdrew from the assembly during 1756. In June, James Pemberton and five other pacifist lawmakers resigned, explaining that the citizenry "call upon us for services in a military way, which . . . we cannot comply with."[53] Benjamin Franklin was pleased by the departure of this "stiff rump" as well as by the news that Governor Morris was leaving. "These changes in both branches," Franklin rejoiced, "promise us some fair weather, which I have long sighed for."[54] Three more Friends refused to stand for reelection in October 1756, and four more left the house later that month. The London Quakers who had come to Pennsylvania to urge these resignations reported in November, "There are now only twelve persons in the house who bear any pretence to our name."[55]

A few expansionists, pleased by Franklin's efforts and eager to be part of a ruling faction, now joined the Quaker party. Daniel Roberdeau, a Presbyterian, entered the house in 1756 under Franklin's banner as an opponent of the Penns. Roberdeau had served as an officer in one of the regiments established by the Militia Act of 1755 and would be a leading revolutionary and a general during the War for Independence. Charles Thomson, another Presbyterian expansionist, also became active in the Quaker party during the late 1750s. George Bryan, a third outspoken Calvinist and a future patriot, joined the

51. Records of the London Meeting for Sufferings, Apr. 9, 1756, xxix, 501–4, Friends House Library; Robert Plumstead to Benjamin & Samuel Shoemaker, Mar. 18, 1756, Robert Plumstead Letterbook, Cambridge University Library, Cambridge, Eng.; *Papers of Franklin*, vii, 249n; R. Hingston Fox, *Dr. John Fothergill and His Friends: Chapters in Eighteenth–Century Life* (London, 1919), 307–8.

52. Robert Plumstead to Abel James, May 31, 1756, Plumstead Letterbook; Records of the London Meeting for Sufferings, June 18, 1756, xxix, 523–27, Friends House Library; Report of John Hunt and Christopher Wilson, Feb. 10, 1756, ibid., xxx, 150.

53. *Votes and Proceedings of the House of Representatives of the Province of Pennsylvania, 1755–56*, quoted in Ketcham, "Conscience, War, and Politics," 416; *Papers of Franklin*, vi, 456n.

54. Franklin to Collinson, June 15, 1756, *Papers of Franklin*, vi, 456–57.

55. Christopher Wilson and John Hunt to [London Meeting for Sufferings], Nov. 4, 1756, Misc. Corresp., 21/45, Friends House Library; *Papers of Franklin*, vii, 10n.

Franklinists but soon found the faction too conservative and left it before the end of the 1750s. John Nixon and a scattering of other outward-looking individuals also accepted the printer's lead.[56]

Despite these changes, the Quaker party remained firmly in the hands of the nonexpansionists, if moderate ones, while most expansionists stayed in the opposition faction. The line of schism Richard Peters traced in the Anglican community indicates that only those with a cautious view of imperial questions gravitated to the Assembly party: "The poison has never reached the Plumsteads, the Inglises, the McCalls, nor those who live in the south part of town, . . . but the old Churchmen, Evan Morgan, Jacob Duche, Thomas Leech and others and their friends and relatives are infected; they are mere Franklinists."[57] The first group, those who maintained their allegiance to the Proprietary party, had long criticized Quaker policies, while the Franklinists came from the Anglican coterie that had cooperated with the assembly majority before 1755.[58]

There were other indications of the continuing predominance of nonexpansionists in the remodeled Assembly faction. Isaac Norris's long tenure as speaker of the assembly, from 1750 to 1764, suggests that the changes of the mid-1750s were evolutionary rather than radical. Moreover, the continuing presence of a dozen Quaker assemblymen, most of them, as the visiting London Quakers noted, "acknowledged members of the Society [of Friends]," shows that the majority party still made room for those who combined principles and practicality.[59] Furthermore, the October 1756 election demonstrated that very few expansionists would be welcomed into the Quaker party fold. Before the election, Franklin conferred with several Proprietary party leaders, including William Allen and James Hamilton, and agreed to support a compromise slate for Philadelphia County. He reckoned without the voters, however, who refused to elect any individuals with ties to the opposing faction, and the proprietary portion of the compromise ticket went down to defeat. In short, the efforts of Franklin and his allies (although these men would have proceeded further) eliminated the Quaker obstructionists and transformed this

56. Buchanan, *Roberdeau Family*, 46–48; J. Edwin Hendricks, *Charles Thomson and the Making of a New Nation, 1729–1824* (Rutherford, N.J., 1979), 3–32; Petition for Royal Government, 1764, Privy Council 1, bundle 50, PRO; Ryerson, *Revolution Is Now Begun*, 239–40, 279.

57. Peters to Thomas Penn, June 1, 1756, quoted in Hanna, *Benjamin Franklin*, 104.

58. Tully, *Penn's Legacy*, 40, 81, 89, 96; Ketcham, "Conscience, War and Politics," 422.

59. Christopher Wilson and John Hunt to [London Meeting for Sufferings], Nov. 4, 1756, Misc. Corresp., 21/45, Friends House Library; Thomas Wendel, "The Speaker of the House: Pennsylvania, 1701–1776," *PMHB*, xcvii (1973), 3–21.

hard-line religious faction into one that resembled the nonexpansionist groups in the other colonies.[60]

From the fall of 1756 to the end of 1762 Pennsylvania politics was shaped by the clash between a moderate nonexpansionist party and an expansionist faction. The new, more flexible approach of the majority party in the assembly was soon evident. In November 1756 the legislators, with little debate, renewed the mutiny act that had occasioned so much dissension the previous March. Furthermore, the pressing needs of war, the impassioned requests of several generals, and the promise of parliamentary subventions encouraged the lawmakers to approve a series of generous supply acts: thirty thousand pounds in 1756 and hundred thousand pounds acts in 1757, 1758, 1759, and 1760. The Quaker party may not have lived up to Galloway's glowing description ("Every kind of assistance has been given to the service that our circumstances would permit," he boasted in 1758, "so that 'tis hoped . . . Quaker government and Quaker influence be terms buried in oblivion and no more remembered")[61] but even critical Proprietary men were pleased with the steps taken. "Everything seems carried on with vigor," observed Thomas Willing and his new partner, Robert Morris, in 1758.[62]

Despite this wartime "common front," which prevailed to some extent in all the colonies, conflict between the two Pennsylvania factions continued. In December 1756 Quaker party lawmakers refused to help quarter British soldiers, turning aside Colonel Henry Bouquet's request for accommodations and ignoring General Loudoun's fierce threat: "If the number of troops now in Philadelphia are not sufficient, I will instantly march a number sufficient for that purpose and find quarter to the whole."[63] Only Franklin's leadership was able to defuse the crisis; as Richard Peters observed: "B.F.'s expressing his sentiments in favor of a total compliance, the rest immediately changed their tone."[64] Nevertheless, the larger views Franklin tried to breathe into his adopted party were soon in ever shorter supply. He left in 1757 for England, where he would remain until 1762, depriving the Quaker faction of its most outspoken expansionist.

60. William Logan to John Smith, Oct. 1, 1756, John Smith Correspondence, presents the vote on the two slates. See also *Papers of Franklin*, vii, 10n; Ketcham, "Conscience, War, and Politics," 431–32.

61. Joseph Galloway to Franklin, June 16, 1758, Isaac Norris to Franklin, Apr. 29, 1758, *Papers of Franklin*, viii, 107–8, 54, and see vii, 8; Thayer, *Pennsylvania Politics*, 58–78.

62. Willing & Morris to John Perks, Apr. 27, 1758, Willing Letterbook.

63. Lord Loudoun to Gov. William Denny, Dec. [22?], 1756, *Papers of Franklin*, vii, 38–39, 53, 62n.

64. Peters to Thomas Penn, Dec. 26, 1756, ibid., 62n, and see 64.

(Franklin went to Britain ostensibly to "endeavor a settlement of our disputes" with the proprietors, but there was much truth in the assumption shared by Franklin's foes and close friends and illustrated by his efforts in England that the real purpose of his mission was to secure a royal charter for Pennsylvania and the governorship for himself. His persistence in this quest would have a profound impact on Pennsylvania politics in the mid-1760s).[65]

Clashes between Pennsylvanians with differing views of empire grew more heated in 1757 and 1758. Quaker party meddling at provincial Indian conferences angered expansionists as well as British officials. At the 1757 Easton powwow several assembly party men, led by Joseph Galloway and Israel Pemberton, encouraged the natives to air their grievances against the proprietors. In England, the Board of Trade noted the ill effects: "The part which some members of the Pennsylvania Assembly appear to have had in the transactions with the Indians in July and August 1757 [was] . . . one principle cause for the failure of these measures."[66] The October 1757 election, in which several frontier counties selected Proprietary party men, threw more fuel on the fires of partisan hostility. The majority faction soon struck back at its opponents by jailing an outspoken Chester County expansionist, William Moore, who had publicly lambasted the legislature on several counts, including its failure to create a militia with compulsory service. The lower chamber also imprisoned the Reverend William Smith for his part in reprinting Moore's writings, and fined Thomas Willing and others for supporting Smith. In June 1758 one Quaker party assemblyman chronicled the "happy effect" of such repressive measures: Those "who were very public in their clamors against the conduct of the house, now communicate their thoughts to each other in whispers under the thistle."[67]

The markedly different outlooks of the two factions remained evident during the first years of the new decade. After the reduction of Canada the Quaker party drew the purse strings tight and rejected British demands for troops to staff the frontier posts. "You may depend on it, sir," Governor James Hamilton informed General Monckton in October 1760, "that they have no intention to grant any more

65. Franklin to Collinson, Jan. 31, 1757, ibid., 114–15. Franklin's quest for the governorship is examined in Egnal, "Politics of Ambition," 151–64.

66. Board of Trade to Privy Council, June 1, 1759, CO 5/1295/129–43, quote on 135, PRO; Thayer, *Pennsylvania Politics*, 49–55; Newcomb, *Franklin and Galloway*, 52–58.

67. Hugh Roberts to Franklin, June 1, 1758, Isaac Norris to Franklin, Feb. 21, 1758, *Papers of Franklin*, VIII, 81–82, VII, 385–86; Thayer, *Pennsylvania Politics*, 68–70; Burton A. Konkle, *George Bryan and the Constitution of Pennsylvania, 1731–1791* (Philadelphia, 1922), 34–36.

money for the service, but in a case of the last necessity."[68] The handful of expansionist lawmakers who represented the newer counties to the north and west, however, consistently supported the requisitions for more men. After 1762 the same factional lines would persist, with expansionists leading the revolutionary movement while the Quaker party eschewed forceful assertions of American sovereignty.[69]

» «

During the 1740s and 1750s the most articulate Pennsylvanians from both factions distinguished themselves by the force and clarity with which they expounded their views. Benjamin Franklin's writings, discussed in the Introduction, broadcast to many Americans the tenets of expansionist thought. No less outspoken were the Quakers, who as a group were firmer in their opposition to war than any other set of nonexpansionists. Although the sectarian nature of Quaker doctrine necessarily restricted its audience, these ideas were of first importance in Penn's colony.

Quaker ideology set forth an elaborate prescription for a Christian commonwealth on earth. "True godliness," declared William Penn, "don't turn men out of the world, but enables them to live better in it, and excites their endeavors to mend it."[70] Quakerism, which emerged from the flood tide of the English Reformation, emphasized the practice of simplicity and equality—even if the opulence of its adherents' worldly estates at times seemed to run against this grain. "Keep to that plainness and simplicity in apparel, speech, and behavior which the spirit of truth led our ancestors into," the 1749 Epistle of the London Yearly Meeting admonished the faithful on both sides of the Atlantic.[71] In that light, Friends castigated playhouses, lotteries, wigs, business chicanery, and smuggling; moreover, Quaker doctrine ramified into a concern for a broad range of charities and a mounting opposition to slavery. After 1743 the elders of the Pennsylvania Monthly Meeting regularly asked traders a set of queries, including "Do Friends observe the former advices of the Yearly Meeting, not to encourage the importation of Negroes, not to buy them after imported?" A hierarchy of assemblies, which began with the

68. Gov. Hamilton to Gen. Monckton, Oct. 18, 1760, Peters to Gen. Monckton, Oct. 31, 1760, MHS *Cols.*, 4th ser., ix (1871), 338–39, 340; Thayer, *Pennsylvania Politics*, 75–76; Hutson, *Pennsylvania Politics*, 68–72.

69. Peters to Gen. Monckton, Apr. 27, 1761, MHS *Cols.*, 4th ser., ix (1871), 410; Hutson, *Pennsylvania Politics*, 72–80.

70. William Penn, *No Cross No Crown* (1669), quoted in Tolles, *Meeting House*, 53.

71. London Yearly Meeting Epistles, I, 265 (May 1749), Friends House Library.

London Yearly Meeting and ended with the individual families, helped further elaborate and enforce this credo.[72]

But few beliefs were more important for New World Friends than the testimony of peace, which members emphasized time and again. For example, during the debate in 1748 over defending Philadelphia, Quaker preacher John Churchman demanded and was granted permission to address the assembly. "If those in authority," he warned the legislators, "do suffer their own fears and the persuasion of others, to prevail with them to . . . enact laws in order to [effect] their own protection and defense by carnal weapons and fortifications, styled human prudence, he who is Superintendant, by withdrawing the arm of his power, may permit those evils they feared to come suddenly upon them, and that in his heavy displeasure."[73] Friends rehearsed a similar pacifism during the French and Indian War. Fair dealings, not force of arms, were judged the proper response to Indian hostility. In 1756 James Pemberton pointed out that "the cause of the Indian dissatisfaction" is "an uneasiness about certain contracts for land of late years."[74] The difficulties of maintaining the peace testimony in an armed state, however, led many Friends to withdraw from public life, and this step had a palpable effect on Quaker beliefs. Colonial Friends embarked in the late-1750s on a lengthy era of "reformation," during which many souls turned from the outer plantation to the inner. But the Quaker persuasion, much like Franklin's expansionism, would continue to have an important impact on Pennsylvania politics after 1762.[75]

72. Quoted in Tolles, *Meeting House*, 73–74, and see 4–11; Pennsylvania and New Jersey Yearly Meeting to London Yearly Meeting, Sept. 1750, Epistles Received, III, 272, Friends House Library; John Reynell to John Sherburne, Mar. 12, 1760, Reynell Letterbook, HSP.

73. Churchman quoted in Richard Bauman, *For the Reputation of Truth: Politics, Religion, and Conflict among the Pennsylvania Quakers, 1750–1800* (Baltimore, 1971), 12–14.

74. James Pemberton to Jonah Thompson, Apr. 25, 1756, portfolio 34, #83; Report of John Hunt and Christopher Wilson on Their Visit to Pennsylvania, Feb. 10, 1758, London Meeting for Suffering, xxx, 150, Friends House Library.

75. Tolles, *Meeting House*, 234–39; Bauman, *For the Reputation of Truth*, 77–183; Rufus M. Jones, *The Later Periods of Quakerism* (London, 1921), 66–73.

CHAPTER 5

Virginia: Rise of
the Northern Neckers

The Potomac River, as some Virginians recognized by midcentury, had a strategic significance that distinguished it from the other waterways of the colony. After exploring the upper reaches of the river George Washington reported to Charles Carter: "I doubt [not] but you will readily concur with me in judging it more convenient, least expensive, and I may further say by much the most expeditious way to the [western] country."[1] This waterway not only pointed to the interior but also connected the residences of various individuals who were discussing daring imperial plans. In the late 1740s many of the planters of the Northern Neck—the strip of counties between the Potomac and Rappahannock rivers—had begun to consider exploiting the Ohio Valley and thwarting French ambitions. Along with the Washingtons, such outward-looking Virginians included the Lees, Carters, and Masons. The strength of the opposing faction lay in the counties south of the Rappahannock and east of the Blue Ridge Mountains, a region more firmly walled off from the interior and the dangers posed by the French. There the Robinsons, Randolphs, Pendletons, and other prominent nonexpansionists made their homes. These two factions, which formed in Virginia in the late 1740s and clashed in the 1750s, would continue to dominate politics after 1762, with the expansionists leading the revolutionary movement and the nonexpansionists more reluctant to oppose the mother country.

1. Washington to [Charles Carter], [c. Aug. 1754], *Writings of George Washington*, ed. J. C. Fitzpatrick, 39 vols. (Washington, D.C., 1931–44), I, 101. Fitzpatrick mistakenly states that the addressee was Thomas Lee, who in fact died in 1750. I am indebted to Frederick H. Schmidt, assistant editor of the Papers of George Washington, for pointing out that the letter "almost certainly" was intended for Charles Carter.

» «

Before about 1747 Virginia's location sheltered it from the military problems that had precipitated party formation in Massachusetts, New York, and South Carolina. The soldiery of New France and New Spain stood far removed, and an Indian war waged in 1675 and 1676 had ended the threat from the natives living nearby. In 1705 Robert Beverley boasted that Virginians "are happy in the enjoyment of an everlasting peace. . . . They have the Indians round about in subjection . . . and for a foreign enemy it can never be worth their while to carry troops sufficient to conquer the country, for the scattering method of their settlement will not answer the charge of an expedition to plunder them."[2] In 1735 William Byrd reiterated these views. Although he was one of the few Virginians troubled by French designs, Byrd recognized no immediate threat to the colony. "We live here in health and plenty in innocence and security," he reported, "fearing no enemy from abroad or robbers at home."[3]

Virginians, moreover, were loath to be entangled in the military problems of their neighbors. In the 1690s the House of Burgesses allotted a small sum to help New York repulse the French but pointedly refused further assistance during the first years of Queen Anne's War. When the Tuscarora War (1711–1713) erupted in the Carolinas, the Virginia legislature set aside only three hundred pounds to help the colonies to the south. "We are sorry and amazed," the South Carolina assembly pronounced, "that they to whom God has given great power and opportunities should be so deficient in giving that assistance."[4] The Old Dominion's contribution to the English cause during King George's War was at best halfhearted. In 1740 Virginia provided over four hundred volunteers for the expedition against Cartagena, and six years later the legislature agreed to support the attack of the northern colonies on New France. But more generally, Virginians stayed one remove from the divisive problems raised by military adventures.[5]

2. Robert Beverley, *The History and Present State of Virginia: A Selection*, ed. David Freeman Hawke (1705; rpt. Indianapolis, 1971), 138; Thomas J. Wertenbaker, *Virginia under the Stuarts* (Princeton, 1914), 160–61; Richard L. Morton, *Colonial Virginia*, 2 vols., consec. pagin. (Chapel Hill, N.C., 1960), I, 301, 310, 332, 335; Edmund S. Morgan, *American Slavery—American Freedom: The Ordeal of Colonial Virginia* (New York, 1975), 250, 263, 268.
3. William Byrd II to Peter Beckford, Dec. 6, 1735, *VMHB*, IX (1901–2), 235.
4. Beverley, *History of Virginia*, 62–63; Morton, *Colonial Virginia*, I, 325–26, 345, 349, 372–73; David A. Williams, "Political Alignments in Colonial Virginia Politics, 1698–1750" (Ph.D. diss., Northwestern Univ., 1959), 24–27, 51–52, 134–38, 145; S.C. legislature quoted in Verner W. Crane, *The Southern Frontier, 1670–1732* (Ann Arbor, 1929, 1956), 159, and see 158–59; Leonidas Dodson, *Alexander Spotswood, Governor of Colonial Virginia, 1710–1722* (Philadelphia, 1932), 29.
5. Williams, "Political Alignments," 293–97, 310–14; Morton, *Colonial Virginia*, II, 526–28, 534–35.

Regional distinctions, however, did begin to appear during this era. Most significantly, by the 1720s the Northern Neck had emerged as a cohesive political entity. There the method of land distribution created a world apart. A series of royal decrees dating back to 1649 defined this area as a separate proprietorship within Virginia; land grants were to be issued by the lords proprietary, not by the governor and council, as was the case in the rest of Virginia. The proprietors, who after 1689 were members of the Fairfax family, proved far more generous to speculators than were the authorities in the provincial capital.[6]

The Fairfaxes' liberal land policy created a society with a wealthy upper class, which was often mistrustful of politicians in the rest of Virginia, and a large, unruly lower class, which formed a potent force when mobilized. At the pinnacle of the social order were the great estate owners, the Carters, Lees, and others, who ruled immense baronies. Robert "King" Carter at the time of his death in 1732 was probably the richest man in the colony. White farmers were encouraged to settle in the Neck, but most became tenants because the elite had taken up the best lands. Hence, tenancy was higher in this area than elsewhere in Virginia. Slave labor was common, though not so widespread as in the planting counties south of the Rappahannock, and this regional pattern would persist throughout the colonial period (map 3). White indentured servants—often former convicts—were always in evidence in the Fairfaxes' domain. Many must have worked for tenant farmers, who found the lease of white workers more affordable than the purchase of slaves. Of all the areas east of the mountains, the Virginia counties north of the Rappahannock were the most dependent on indentured servants (map 4).[7]

Around the 1720s, the wealthy landowners of the Northern Neck emerged as a coherent group at odds with the planters to the south over economic and political questions. The great estate owners in the Neck and many of the smaller farmers criticized the regulatory legislation adopted in Williamsburg. They bridled, for example, at the stint law of 1723, which was designed to raise prices by limiting tobacco production. The act, William Byrd noted, was executed "very sparingly in the Northern Neck."[8] Landowners in the area also offered strong resistance to the tobacco inspection act of 1730 and

6. James B. Gouger III, "Agricultural Change in the Northern Neck of Virginia, 1700–1760: An Historical Geography" (Ph.D. diss., Univ. of Florida, 1976), 54–58, 81; Morton, *Colonial Virginia*, II, 546–48.

7. Gouger, "Agricultural Change," 15, 83–85; Morton, *Colonial Virginia*, II, 498–99; Jackson T. Main, *The Social Structure of Revolutionary America* (Princeton, 1965), 45–46.

8. William Byrd II to Micajah Perry, [c. July 1728], quoted in Williams, "Political Alignments," 227, and see 210–16.

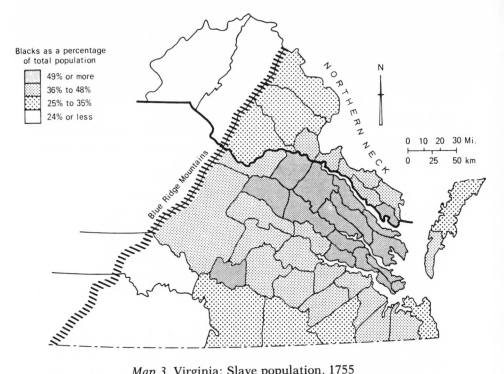

Map 3. Virginia: Slave population, 1755

SOURCES: Evarts B. Greene and Virginia D. Harrington, *American Population before the Federal Census of 1790* (New York, 1932), 150–51; Morton, *Colonial Virginia*, II, 675–76.

burned several government warehouses. During the 1730s and early 1740s the leading men in the Neck supported Thomas Lord Fairfax against those burgesses who endeavored to revoke or curtail the proprietary charter. (Fairfax not only beat back this challenge, but expanded his fiefdom to include the contiguous area west of the Blue Ridge.) And in 1738 and 1742 Northern Neckers joined battle with other burgesses over the speakership.[9]

Observers also commented on the truculence of the white farmers and servants who made up a majority of the free population in the Northern Neck. Governor William Gooch lamented to the bishop of

9. Williams, "Political Alignments," 242–44, 289–318; John M. Hemphill, *Virginia and the English Commercial System, 1689–1733: Studies in the Development and Fluctuations of a Colonial Economy under Imperial Control* (Ph.D. diss., Princeton Univ., 1964; pub. New York, 1985), 150–73. Allan Kulikoff, *Tobacco and Slaves: The Development of Southern Cultures in the Chesapeake, 1680–1800* (Chapel Hill, N.C., 1986), 110–12, presents a map depicting Virginia opposition to the 1730 inspection act.

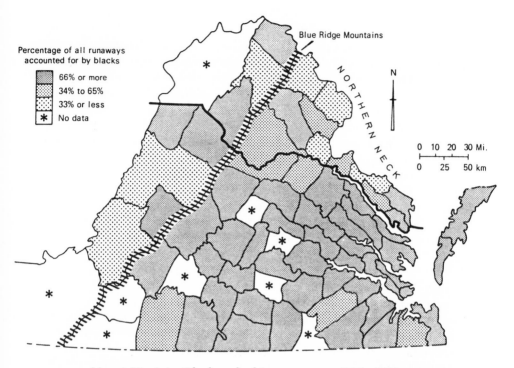

Map 4. Virginia: Black and white runaways, 1751–1780

SOURCES: Data are tabulated from advertisements for runaway slaves and indentured servants in every extant issue of Purdie and Dixon's *Virginia Gazette* and Rind's *Virginia Gazette*, 1751–1780. Each runaway is counted only once regardless of how many times the advertisement reappeared. The same regional pattern is evident in the issues of the *Virginia Gazette* during the late 1730s and 1740s. Marilyn Hector compiled these data in "Runaway Servants and Slaves, 1737–1780" (seminar paper, York Univ., 1976).

London that "in the Northern Neck . . . drinking and boxing is too much in fashion." To the Board of Trade he reported that the Neck was "a part of the country remote from the seat of government, where the common people are generally of a more turbulent and unruly disposition than anywhere else, and are not like to become better by being the place of all this dominion where most of the transported convicts are sold and settled."[10] The "turbulent and unruly disposition" of the white population would be most evident in the years after 1762 and would strengthen the hands of the upperclass expansionists who opposed British measures.

10. Gov. Gooch to bishop of London, July 8, 1735, Gov. Gooch to Board of Trade, Oct. 5, 1732, quoted in Morton, *Colonial Virginia*, II, 541, 525–26.

» «

Geography played a crucial role in the formation of the parties that emerged around 1747, with religion decidedly of secondary importance.[11] The principal supporters of the expansionist faction were the planters of the Northern Neck. The transformation of a coherent local group into a party with an aggressive approach to colonial growth occurred after 1745, when these landowners began to recognize that their territorial ambitions conflicted with the French design for North America. The Northern Neckers considered the Potomac the highroad to the interior and set their sights on the upper Ohio Valley, an area the Bourbons also coveted. "The [Indian] trade can be better supplied from the heads of the Potomac than any other way," Lawrence Washington, George's half brother, explained in 1749. Expressing sentiments widely shared in the Neck, he argued, "The further we extend our frontiers the safer we render the interior dominions," because "the French, having possession of the Ohio, might easily invade Virginia."[12]

A second region—the frontier counties lying along the Blue Ridge Mountains south of the Northern Neck—also came to play an important role in the expansionist party. The cooperation of the "frontier members" with the Northern Neckers in the 1750s harbingered an alliance that would solidify during the years before independence. In the 1770s, Thomas Jefferson, James Madison, and other planters living near the mountains, worked closely with the Masons and Lees. But before 1763 the leaders in the western counties outside the Northern Neck were at best inconsistent allies for the expansionists. Often these men were scions of Tidewater families, and during the late 1740s and 1750s, they joined with nonexpansionists of the Tidewater and lower Piedmont in land companies and other ventures.[13]

11. Several works remark on this division within the Virginia aristocracy and describe the same factions, if with different terms. Joseph A. Ernst calls the expansionists a "group of young politicians and Revolutionaries" and the nonexpansionists the "old-line tidewater aristocrats," in *Money and Politics in America, 1755–1775: A Study in the Currency Act of 1764 and the Political Economy of Revolution* (Chapel Hill, N.C., 1973), 175. David Williams terms the nonexpansionists the "Robinson-Randolph clique," in "Political Alignments," 338. Jack P. Greene's discussion of the "ideologues of virtue and independence" (Northern Neckers) and the "pragmatic politicians" (Robinson faction) splits Virginians along identical lines in "Society, Ideology, and Politics: An Analysis of the Political Culture of Mid-Eighteenth-Century Virginia," *Society, Freedom, and Conscience: The American Revolution in Virginia, Massachusetts, and New York*, ed. Richard M. Jellison (New York, 1976), 54–57.

12. Lawrence Washington to [?], Nov. 7, 1749, quoted in Moncure D. Conway, *Barons of the Potomack and the Rappahannock* (New York, 1892), 275.

13. For example, many westerners joined the Loyal Company; Archibald Henderson, "Dr. Thomas Walker and the Loyal Company of Virginia," AAS *Proceedings*, n.s., XLI (1931), 88–89; Kulikoff, *Tobacco and Slaves*, 96–97.

The nonexpansionist faction drew its supporters from the tobacco counties south of the Rappahannock. More particularly, the strength of this party lay in the zone of sprawling plantations with large slave populations between the Rappahannock and James rivers (map 3). Prominent partisans included the Harrisons, Pendletons, and Randolphs, but the unquestioned leader was John Robinson, a canny politician who served as both speaker and treasurer from 1738 to 1766. Geography helped form the pacific outlook of these politicians; their estates, unlike those of the Northern Neck, were well removed from the threat posed by the French. Moreover, when Robinson and his followers staked their claims to the transmontane region, they concentrated on tracts south of the Ohio River and out of the immediate line of the Bourbon advance. Both parties contained avid land speculators, but the location of the nonexpansionists' holdings made them less eager to endorse defense spending.[14]

Since most planters were Anglicans, religious distinctions were of minor importance in party formation. Nonetheless, the expansionists tended to attract the dissenters and those individuals who were more tolerant of non-Anglicans, while the nonexpansionists seemed more determined to defend the established church. In religion as in other matters, the Northern Neckers questioned the policies laid down in Williamsburg. Landon Carter, for example, quarreled during the early 1750s with Robinson and his allies about the wisdom of laying heavy parish duties on western settlers. "It would be cruel to load tender consciences with a greater burden than they could bear," Carter told the burgesses, "for besides this minister's salary they had their own pastors to pay."[15] Lawrence Washington tried unsuccessfully to end the payment of such tithes on the lands held by the Ohio Company. Furthermore, the Presbyterians, who claimed a number of adherents in the Northern Neck and outside it, worked with the expansionists and enthusiastically supported the French and Indian War. Samuel Davies, a prominent Presbyterian minister, delivered a series of spirited sermons to promote enlistment in the provincial forces.[16]

14. *Executive Journals of the Council of Colonial Virginia*, ed. H. R. McIlwaine and W. L. Hall, 5 vols. (Richmond, 1925–45), v, 172–73, 195, 206, 231, 282, 288, 295–97; Morton, *Colonial Virginia*, II, 575–76.

15. *The Diary of Colonel Landon Carter of Sabine Hall, 1752–1778*, ed. Jack P. Greene, 2 vols. (Charlottesville, Va., 1965), I, 81 (March 10, 1752), 105 (Apr. 17, 1752).

16. Committee of the Ohio Company, Proposal to Settle Foreign Protestants on Ohio Company Lands, Feb. 6, 1753, *The Papers of George Mason, 1725–1792*, ed. Robert A. Rutland, 2 vols. (Chapel Hill, N.C., 1970), 28–31; Kenneth P. Bailey, *The Ohio Company of Virginia and the Westward Movement, 1748–1792: A Chapter in the History of the Colonial Frontier* (Glendale, Calif., 1939), 80–81; Morton, *Colonial Virginia*, II, 583–86,

» «

Between 1747 and 1762 the two parties quarreled over the threat
posed by the French and Indians and, more broadly, over the proper
approach to the development of the West. Both factions formed land
companies to realize their plans. Governor Gooch and the council
gave the first grants west of the mountains to the nonexpansionists,
bestowing vast baronies upon the Robinsons, Blairs, and other planters who resided south of the Rappahannock. In 1747 a group of
Northern Neck planters, who had been excluded from the earlier
awards, along with several Marylanders and Londoners created the
Ohio Company and requested a patent for 200,000 acres near the
Forks of the Ohio. Among the men who were or would soon become
members of the company were George Mason, Robert Carter, and
several Washingtons and Lees. With few exceptions, the Virginians
participating in the Ohio Company lived in the Northern Neck (map
5).[17]

Northern Neckers envisaged the Ohio Company as more than a
vehicle for trade and land speculation. The guiding spirit in the formation of the company was Thomas Lee, a wealthy Northern Neck
planter and one of the few expansionists on the governor's council. Lee
argued that the company would become an agency of imperial growth
and that it would allow Virginians, who were the colonists best prepared to repulse the French, to dominate the West. In 1748 Lee explained to a friend: "We propose to settle a trade on the branches of the
Mississippi and make our settlement at the mouth of the Monongahela." Such a step was needed, he added, to forestall the Pennsylvania traders, for "those rascally fellows . . . by lies and treachery will
be the authors of much bloodshed and in consequence give the French
possession of the trade."[18] Lee stated his view of the Bourbons more
simply in 1750: "The French are intruders into this America."[19]

The treatment of the Ohio Company request for an extensive tract
reflected the difference between the imperial designs of the Northern
Neckers and the simpler desire for land speculation of planters living
south of the Rappahannock. Gooch refused to approve the Ohio Com-

---

593–96, 677; John R. Alden, *Robert Dinwiddie, Servant of the Crown* (Charlottesville, Va.,
1973), 21–22; Rhys Isaac, *The Transformation of Virginia, 1740–1790* (Chapel Hill, N.C.,
1982), 150–54.

17. Thomas Lee to Conrad Weiser, Jan. 9, Apr. 2, 1746, Lee Family Papers, microfilm
at CWF; Bailey, *Ohio Company*, 35–60, 80–81; Alfred P. James, *The Ohio Company: Its
Inner History* (Pittsburgh, 1959), 22–25, 45–49; *Executive Journals*, v, 172–73, 195, 206,
231, 282, 288.

18. Thomas Lee to Conrad Weiser, Dec. 11, 1748, Lee Family Papers.

19. Thomas Lee to Board of Trade, Sept. 29, 1750, quoted in Bailey, *Ohio Company*,
38.

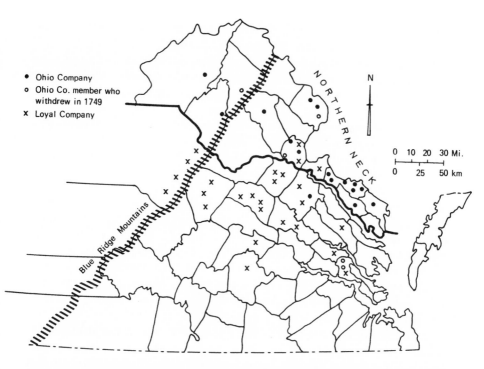

Map 5. Virginia: Members of the Ohio and Loyal land companies, 1747–1770

SOURCES: Members of the two land companies are located by their residence or by the county in which they were politically active. The list of partners in the Ohio Company is drawn from Bailey, *Ohio Company*, 47–49; and James, *Ohio Company*, 35–60. These two works are also the most valuable sources for residences of Ohio Company members. *Executive Journals*, v, 296–97, list participants in the Loyal Company. Information about the home counties of Loyal Company members is given there and in Morton, *Colonial Virginia*. The homes of all the Virginia members of the Ohio Company and twenty-six of the forty members of the Loyal Company were located. (Gov. Dinwiddie and men residing outside the colony are considered non-Virginians.)

pany petition—the first request for transmontane lands he turned down. Arguing that the grant was enmeshed in nettlesome imperial questions, he referred the case to the Privy Council for advice. Moreover, after the British authorities approved the petition, Gooch imposed special conditions on the company, obligating it to erect and garrison a fort and to settle one hundred families within seven years. By contrast, on the same day Gooch and the council announced the Ohio Company grant, July 12, 1749, they gave away to planters residing south of the Rappahannock 1,350,000 acres of western land unencumbered by onerous restrictions. The largest single grant, consisting of 800,000 acres near the Virginia-Carolina border, was bestowed upon the Loyal Company, which included Edmund Pendleton and other associates of Speaker Robinson (map 5).[20]

The activities of the several land companies between 1749 and 1754 exemplify the contrasting plans of the two factions. The expansionists at the helm of the Ohio Company plunged ahead with their ambitious schemes. In 1749 Thomas Lee commissioned young George Washington to survey the upper reaches of the Potomac, and the company soon followed up Washington's efforts with the construction of a trading post. In 1752 it built a fort on the Monongahela, cutting a road through to that river; settlers soon followed the traders along this route. And when, during the first months of 1754, the company erected a stockade at the Forks of the Ohio, Lee's dream of wresting the West from the French, as well as from interloping Pennsylvanians, seemed on the verge of accomplishment. By contrast, the nonexpansionist land companies erected no forts, constructed few roads, and generally contented themselves with the sale of western tracts. The outbreak of the French and Indian War, however, checked these sales and administered a rude shock to the far-reaching plans of the Ohio Company.[21]

Once the French presence in the upper Ohio Valley became unmistakable, the expansionists led the struggle to strengthen Virginia defenses. First to react to the danger posed by Bourbon plans were the Northern Neckers and their ally Governor Robert Dinwiddie. In October 1753 Dinwiddie sent George Washington on a mission to western Pennsylvania to gauge French intentions. The governor had both private and public motives. A partner in the Ohio Company, he had confessed the previous year, "I have the success and prosperity of the Ohio Company much at heart."[22] In his eyes, the area to which he sent Washington was of vital concern both to the corporation and to the province. Similarly, Washington, who had long worked with the company, although he was never a shareholder, was cognizant that the Virginians in the area were all associated with the Ohio Company. He reported back accurately that the French were determined to root out the English from the lands west of the mountains.[23]

20. Bailey, *Ohio Company*, 25–27, and consult the several documents reprinted, 307–12; Williams, "Political Alignments," 333–37; Henderson, "Dr. Thomas Walker," 88–89; *Executive Journals*, v, 295–98. Thomas P. Abernethy, *Western Lands and the American Revolution* (New York, 1937), 5–11, discusses land companies and their links with Virginia factions.
21. George Mason to Lawrence Washington, May 27, 1750, *Papers of Mason*, I, 11; Morton, *Colonial Virginia*, II, 576, 607, 636–47; Bailey, *Ohio Company*, 74–75, 150–55; Washington to Col. Henry Bouquet, Aug. 2, 1758, *Writings of Washington*, II, 252–53; Henderson, "Dr. Thomas Walker," 90–94.
22. Gov. Dinwiddie to Col. Thomas Cresap, Jan. 23, 1752, *The Official Records of Robert Dinwiddie . . .* , ed. R. A. Brock, 2 vols. (1883–84; rpt. New York, 1971), I, 17–18.
23. Washington to Gov. Horatio Sharpe, Apr. 27, 1754, *Writings of Washington*, II, 44; Morton, *Colonial Virginia*, II, 639–44.

Washington's report provoked a quarrel between the expansionists and nonexpansionists in the House of Burgesses in February 1754, and only after a bitter struggle did the assembly vote funds for defense. Expansionist Landon Carter noted in his diary: "When the £10,000 was granted, it was so disagreeable a subject that much art was used to get one penny raised for the defense of the country. And, although we had then certain intelligence our enemy had taken our lands, no steps were to be taken to endeavor to stop them."[24] Northern Neckers backed the funding. For example, Landon's brother, Charles Carter, reminded Washington, "You are a witness to the share I had in promoting the bill for defending our frontiers."[25] The nonexpansionists opposed the appropriation, largely because they believed such spending was designed to help the Ohio Company. In a letter sent to the earl of Loudoun in 1757, Washington recalled: "After I was sent out in December 1753 and brought undoubted testimony even from themselves [the French] of their avowed design, it was yet thought a fiction and a scheme to promote the interest of a private company, even by some who had a share in the government. These unfavorable surmises caused great delay in raising the first men and money."[26]

The burgesses' partisan wrangling and the resulting halfhearted defense measures gravely hurt the English cause. In April 1754 the French captured the Ohio Company stockade at the Forks of the Ohio. In June or early July they destroyed the c mpany storehouse on the Monongahela, and in July they defeated Washington's troops at Fort Necessity, thereby dislodging the Virginians from their toehold on the western side of the Alleghenies.[27]

Against the background of these gloomy tidings, the struggle between the two factions over defense spending resumed in August 1754. The expansionist burgesses, led by Landon Carter, grappled with Robinson's followers, who seemed strangely unperturbed by the gravity of the situation. Landon Carter chronicled the clash: "Observing something like a party that were not for laying anything, I got up and moved that the committee [of the whole] should resolve that the sum of £20,000 should be levied for the defense of the country. As soon as this was seconded, the Speaker, very strongly supported, moved that the question should be put upon £10,000, alleging that he

24. *Diary of Landon Carter*, I, 123 (May 14, 1755); Morton, *Colonial Virginia*, II, 643–44.

25. Col. Charles Carter to Washington, June 5, 1754, *Letters to Washington and Accompanying Papers*, ed. Stanislaus M. Hamilton, 5 vols. (Boston, 1898–1902), I, 2.

26. Washington to earl of Loudoun, [Jan.] 1757, *Writings of Washington*, II, 7.

27. Morton, *Colonial Virginia*, II, 646–56; Bailey, *Ohio Company*, 154–55, 213–17; Hayes Baker-Crothers, *Virginia and the French and Indian War* (Chicago, 1928), 28.

did not imagine any sum we could raise would be sufficient and therefore . . . he was [for] throwing away the least sum."[28]

Carter managed to persuade the committee of the whole to accept a bill for twenty thousand pounds, but his victory did not end the fight over the defense bill; not until October did the assembly approve the appropriation. The August session adjourned without appropriating any funds because the nonexpansionists burdened Carter's proposal with conditions unacceptable to the governor. Moreover, the nonexpansionists were unwilling to give Dinwiddie a free hand when the money was finally voted in October. The assembly established a panel, which was dominated by the speaker and his friends, to oversee the disbursement of funds.[29]

After Braddock's defeat in July 1755 and for the balance of the French and Indian War, expansionists and nonexpansionists worked together, if occasionally with misgivings. In 1756 the Reverend James Maury noted, "It is a very pleasing consideration to observe the general spirit of patriotism, and the resentment against the common enemy, which seems to have diffused itself through every rank of men."[30] In a series of appropriations the assembly granted over two hundred thousand pounds for defense, generally with little partisan wrangling.[31] Unsurprisingly, Northern Neckers warmly supported the campaigns. Washington, who commanded the Virginia forces, easily combined the self-interested goals of the Ohio Company with a determination to oust the French from the West. He urged the British commanders to use the old company road rather than cut a new path across Pennsylvania for the attack on Ford Duquesne. "A road that has been so long opened," he told Colonel Henry Bouquet in 1758, "so well repaired and so often, must be much firmer and better than a new one."[32] To Washington's chagrin, General John Forbes chose to lead his forces through Pennsylvania. Other Northern Neckers also

28. *Diary of Landon Carter,* I, 108–12 (Aug. 22, 1754), quotation on 111; Alden, *Robert Dinwiddie,* 26–31.

29. *Diary of Landon Carter,* II, 112–15 (Aug. 22, Oct. 17, 1754); Gov. Dinwiddie to James Abercromby, Sept. 1, 1754, *Official Records of Dinwiddie,* I, 298–301; Morton, *Colonial Virginia,* II, 659–60; Alden, *Robert Dinwiddie,* 32–33; Baker-Crothers, *French and Indian War,* 53–54.

30. James Maury to John Fontaine, June 15, 1756, *Memoirs of a Huguenot Family . . . ,* ed. Ann Maury (1853; rpt. Baltimore, 1967), 406; Morton, *Colonial Virginia,* II, 684–735.

31. Baker-Crothers, *French and Indian War,* 99–102; Morton, *Colonial Virginia,* II, 706, 726–32.

32. Washington to Bouquet, Aug. 2, 1758, Washington to Gov. Fauquier, Sept. 2, 1758, *Writings of Washington,* II, 253, 281; Robert Munford to Col. Theodorick Bland, Sr., Aug. 4, 1758, *The Bland Papers: Being a Selection from the Manuscripts of Colonel Theodorick Bland, Jr. . . . ,* ed. Charles Campbell, 2 vols. (Petersburg, Va., 1840–43), I, 13.

were active in opposing the French, and as early as August 1755 Colonel William Fitzhugh formulated plans for an attack on Fort Duquesne. Various planters, including the Carters, gave Washington noteworthy support.[33]

Nonexpansionists also backed the defense effort, if with varying degrees of enthusiasm. Robinson endorsed most military appropriations during the second half of the 1750s and was lauded by the new governor, Francis Fauquier. "I believe I owe the supply I have obtained this year of men and money," Fauquier stated in 1759, "to the strong support of himself [Robinson] and his friends."[34] But other nonexpansionists were more qualified in their enthusiasm for the English cause. Richard Corbin and a few other councillors felt that the colony overspent on the war, and some members of Robinson's circle coupled votes for preparedness with criticisms of the westerners. Edmund Pendleton, for example, observed in 1756: "I am greatly concerned for the distressed situation of our unhappy frontiers, though can't help saying those distresses in the northern part have been greatly owing to the cowardice or at least imprudence of the inhabitants of Frederick, who upon the approach of the serpents, either stayed singly with their family exposed to the enemy's butcheries, or run off."[35]

Reacting to this less-than-total support, a few Northern Neckers maintained their mistrust of the opposition party. George Mason disliked the panel established to oversee mil :ary expenditures, a body dominated by Robinson and his followers. "I hope I shall not have anything to do with the . . . C[om]m[itt]ee," he groused to Washington in 1756, "for though I have no objection to any of the gentlemen in their private [capacity], yet they are the last people in the world I should choose to have concern with in their public capacity!"[36] And when Richard Henry Lee entered the assembly in 1758, he called upon his fellow burgesses to end Robinson's tenure as speaker,

33. Gov. Dinwiddie to Col. William Fitzhugh, Aug. 30, 1755, *Official Records of Dinwiddie,* II, 180; Landon Carter to Washington, Apr. 21, 1756, Col. Charles Carter to Washington, Apr. 22, 1756, Capt. William Peachey to Washington, Aug. 22, 1757, *Letters to Washington,* I, 223, 226, II, 181–182.

34. Gov. Fauquier to Board of Trade, Apr. 10, 14, 1759, CO 5/1329/134–35, 121–22, quotation from Apr. 10, transcripts at CWF; Speaker John Robinson to Washington, Jan. 27, Nov. 16, 1756, *Letters to Washington,* I, 181, II, 1: Washington to Gov. Dinwiddie, May 23, 1756, *Writings of Washington,* I, 386–87.

35. Edmund Pendleton to William Preston, May 12, 1756, *The Letters and Papers of Edmund Pendleton, 1734–1803,* ed. David John Mays, 2 vols. (Charlottesville, Va., 1967), I, 8; Richard Bland to Washington, June 7, 1757, Peachey to Washington, Aug. 22, 1757, *Letters to Washington,* II, 87–88, 181–82; James Maury to [?], Jan. 10, 1756, and [c. 1756], *Huguenot Family,* 394, 431.

36. George Mason to Washington, Sept. 13, 1756, *Papers of Mason,* I, 40; Alden, *Robert Dinwiddie,* 37.

thus breathing new life into a campaign started by his father, Thomas Lee.[37] But for the most part the expansionists welcomed the "popular front" that developed during the war years, and several Northern Neckers reassured Washington of the good intentions of the speaker and his circle. For example, in 1756 Augustine Washington confided to his half brother that Robinson was among "those who wishes you well," and the following year Colonel William Fairfax informed Washington that the speaker "and most of the committee [overseeing expenditures], if not all, are your friends."[38]

Within this picture of wartime factional cooperation, the forward role played by the frontier counties must be underscored. The activity of westerners in the second half of the 1750s foreshadows the alliance that emerged after 1770 when these counties joined the Northern Neck in the van of the revolutionary movement. During the French and Indian War western petitions for additional troops and money were a constant prod to the burgesses. Moreover, the militia from such Blue Ridge counties as Augusta and Orange shouldered a disproportionate amount of the fighting when compared with the forces from the lower Piedmont and Tidewater. And on certain military questions western votes proved critical; in 1759, for example, the Blue Ridge counties demanded protection against Indian raids, which had persisted even after the fall of Fort Duquesne. As Governor Fauquier noted in April, "An augmentation of 500 [men] . . . was carried by the coming in of the frontier members."[39]

The factional lines that emerged in the Old Dominion after 1747 and divided planters during the French and Indian War would continue during the revolutionary era. In the turbulent years after 1762 the expansionists would remain outspoken advocates of a stronger, more sovereign America.

» «

During the 1750s Virginia expansionists frequently voiced their views on imperial questions. Many of these statements, to be sure, went little beyond support for the war effort and castigation of the French. "Hope you will soon make those cruel men know that num-

37. Alexander White to Richard Henry Lee, [1758], Lee Family Papers.

38. Augustine Washington to Washington, Oct. 13, 1756, Landon Carter to Washington, Apr. 21, 1756, Col. Charles Carter to Washington, Apr. 22, 1756, Col. William Fairfax to Washington, Jan. 22, 1757, May 4, 1756, *Letters to Washington*, I, 375–76, 223, 226, II, 40, I, 243.

39. Gov. Fauquier to Board of Trade, Apr. 14, 1759, CO 5/1329/121–22, transcript at CWF; *Diary of Landon Carter*, I, 113 (Aug. 22, 1754); James Maury to John Fontaine, June 15, 1756, *Huguenot Family*, 404; Douglas S. Freeman, *George Washington*, 6 vols. (New York, 1948–54), II, 125–40, 189–91, 201–3.

bers can't support an unrighteous cause," Charles Carter told Washington in 1754. "God grant you may be blessed with the like success and drive them out of our colony."[40] In addition, the expansionists favored closer ties between the American colonies. "Nothing I more sincerely wish," pronounced Washington in 1756, "than a union to the colonies in this time of imminent danger."[41] Furthermore, these partisans praised the colonial troops and criticized—the words are Washington's—the "dastardly behavior of the English soldiers."[42]

But a few expansionists sketched a broader picture of America's glorious future. James Maury, a minister and schoolteacher, stood among the westerners helping to mobilize the colony in the struggle against the Bourbons. His vision of a bountiful America would later be echoed and amplified by two of his pupils, Thomas Jefferson and Dabney Carr. Maury was particularly intrigued by the possibility of a link between the Potomac and Ohio rivers. "What an exhaustless fund of wealth would be opened superior to Potosi and all the other South American mines!" he exclaimed in 1756. Maury noted that he was "ever dwelling with pleasure on the consideration of whatever bids fair for contributing to extend the empire and augment the strength of our mother island . . . and at the same time aggrandizing and enriching this spot of the globe." He added, "Were I only to enumerate in a concise manner such of the important benefits only of the country watered by the Ohio, which is but one branch of the Mississippi, as occur even to myself, . . . my letter would swell to an enormous size."[43] After 1762 this belief in the rich potential of the New World would help place the expansionists in the forefront of opposition to Britain, while a more cautious line of thought would make most of the nonexpansionists reluctant revolutionaries.

40. Col. Charles Carter to Washington, June 5, 1754, *Letters to Washington*, i, 2.

41. Washington to Gov. Robert Hunter Morris, Apr. 9, 1756, *Writings of Washington*, i, 309; James Maury to [?], Aug. 9, 1755, *Huguenot Family*, 382.

42. Washington to Gov. Dinwiddie, July 18, 1755, *Writings of Washington*, i, 149; James Maury to [?], Aug. 9, 1755, James Maury to Moses Fontaine, June 19, 1760, *Huguenot Family*, 383, 416–17.

43. James Maury to [?], Jan. 10, 1756, *Huguenot Family*, 392–94; Morton, *Colonial Virginia*, ii, 575–77. On Dabney Carr, see Dumas Malone, *Jefferson the Virginian* (Boston, 1948), 160–61, 170–71; William Wirt, *Sketches of the Life and Character of Patrick Henry* (1836; rpt. Freeport, N.Y., 1970), 105–7.

CHAPTER 6

South Carolina:
Factions Times Two

"I think the people have done with their former animosities," a South Carolina cleric remarked in 1730, "and have been in an indifferent, easy, quiet condition."[1] The story of South Carolina expansionist and nonexpansionist factions is unique in that two successive party systems appeared during the eighteenth century. The first, which emerged in response to threats from the French, Spanish, and Indians, lasted from about 1700 to 1725 and had vanished by the time the Reverend Daniel Dwight made his comments. The second party system, which coalesced after 1755, was much different from the first because of sweeping social changes in South Carolina. It is this second pair of factions that is central to an understanding of the Revolution. Individuals such as Henry Laurens and Christopher Gadsden, who promoted preparedness during the French and Indian War, would become patriots, and those, for example, William Wragg and William Bull, Jr., who were reluctant to endorse defense spending in the late 1750s and early 1760s would also hesitate to oppose the home government after 1762.

» «

Before 1700 the infant colony experienced no grave military threats, and expansionism remained a peripheral issue. In 1680 Carolinians secured two decades of peaceful relations with the local Indians by defeating the Westoes, a tribe dwelling near the coast. The

---

1. Daniel Dwight to secretary of Society for the Propagation of the Gospel, Dec. 21, 1730, quoted in M. Eugene Sirmans, *Colonial South Carolina: A Political History, 1663–1763* (Chapel Hill, N.C., 1966), 165.

Spanish attacked the colony only once during its early decades, launching in 1686 an expedition that destroyed the settlement at Port Royal, fifty miles south of Charleston; however, a "wonderfully horrid and destructive" hurricane prevented the invaders from reaching the capital and forced them to return to Florida. South Carolinians were not free from factionalism during these years, but such struggles as existed split the settlers along religious lines, Anglican versus dissenter, rather than according to their views of growth.[2]

Around 1700 threats to South Carolina security divided local politicians into expansionist and nonexpansionist parties. The emergence of these groups signaled not so much an end to religious feuds (Anglicans and dissenters continued to battle at least until 1712, when organized opposition to the established church ceased) as the appearance of new issues that precipitated new alignments. Many Carolinians were understandably alarmed in 1698 when France established the colony of Louisiana on the lower Mississippi and began a campaign to turn the Indians against the English. Equally ominous were the efforts of the Spanish in Florida to extend their control over the Creek Indians and the outbreak of a new war among the European powers.[3]

The expansionist party that emerged in response to these dangers embraced three groups: the large landowners living near the southern border, a majority of the planters residing in the older parishes, and a portion of the merchant community of Charleston. The rice planters who had recently carved out estates in Colleton and Granville counties (to the south and west of Charleston) formed a bulwark against invaders from the south. These planters included outspoken Thomas Nairne, who enunciated his broad vision in 1708 in an address to the secretary of state. Nairne enclosed a map "to the end your noble Lordship may at one view perceive what part of the continent we are now possessed of, and what not, and procure the articles of peace to be formed in such a manner that the English American

2. Sirmans, *Colonial South Carolina*, 24–54, 76–100; Alexander Hewatt, *An Historical Account of the Rise and Progress of the Colonies of South Carolina and Georgia*, 2 vols. (1779; rpt. Spartanburg, S.C., 1971), 51–144.

3. Verner W. Crane, *The Southern Frontier, 1670–1732* (1929; rpt. Ann Arbor, 1956), 47–74. Sirmans's account of the period from 1700 to 1712 emphasizes the continuation of religious parties from the earlier epoch but also records divisions in both the Anglican and dissenter parties which are not well explained by a sectarian paradigm. For example, the "dissident Anglicans" led by Thomas Nairne played an important, if sporadic, role during these years. I argue that on strictly sectarian matters such coreligionists as Anglicans James Moore and Nicholas Trott worked together. On imperial questions, however, religious groups often divided; expansionist Moore and nonexpansionist Trott, for example, opposed each other on the regulation of the Indian trade. Sirmans, *Colonial South Carolina*, 75–100; Hewatt, *Historical Account*, 150, 164.

empire may not be unreasonably cramped up."[4] John Barnwell, one of Nairne's disciples, echoed Nairne's views in discussions with the Board of Trade in 1720; Barnwell also originated the "township system," a plan implemented in the 1730s to encourage the settlement of frontier communities.[5]

Numerically more important than the frontier magnates were two other groups of expansionists: the planters living in the older, settled areas and the outward-looking traders. Most of the established landowners shared the goals of Nairne and Barnwell, and because planters from the wealthier parishes dominated the Commons House of Assembly, the expansionists usually controlled the legislature. Many importers, for example, John Fenwick and Alexander Parris, also supported this faction. These merchants, it seems, had larger investments in plantations and slaves and were more integrally involved in the colony's growth than were the traders in the opposing party.

The nonexpansionist faction drew its adherents from a minority of the wealthy estate holders in the older parishes and from a portion of the Charleston merchant community. A few prominent planters, including John Ash and Ralph Izard, belonged to this party. The most consistent backing, however, came from such importers as William Rhett and Benjamin de la Conseillere. These traders appear to have been less directly involved in the rice boom than those in the expansionist party and were less eager to defend the rising colony.

Although self-interest was the most important determinant, religion also influenced party makeup. There was, to be sure, no direct link between the Anglican and dissenter groups and the factions that emerged over the issue of growth: between 1700 and 1710 both the expansionist and nonexpansionist parties could point to Anglicans, Presbyterians, and other sectarians in their ranks. After 1710, however, the nonexpansionists drew closer to the proprietors, who were strong supporters of the Church of England. As a result, few dissenters were active in this party in the second decade, although Anglicans and dissenters continued to be important members of the expansionist faction.[6]

During the first years of the century the expansionists urged that

4. Thomas Nairne to secretary of state, July 10, 1708, cited in Crane, *Southern Frontier*, 93–94; Peter H. Wood, *Black Majority: Negroes in Colonial South Carolina from 1670 through the Stono Rebellion* (New York, 1974), 142–55; U.S. Bureau of the Census, *Historical Statistics of the United States, Colonial Times to 1970*, 2 vols., consec. pagin. (Washington, D.C., 1975), 1168, 1192.

5. *Biographical Directory of the South Carolina House of Representatives*, vol. II: Walter B. Edgar and N. Louise Bailey, eds., *The Commons House of Assembly, 1692–1775* (Columbia, S.C., 1977), 52–54.

6. Edgar and Bailey, *Biographical Directory: Commons House;* Sirmans, *Colonial South Carolina*, 104–11.

forceful steps be taken to make the colony more secure. James Moore, a South Carolinian who served as governor from 1700 to 1702, called for the close regulation of dealings with the Indians and also demanded an attack on Florida. "The taking of St. Augustine before it be strengthened with French forces," he told the Commons House in 1702, "opens to us an easy and plain way to remove the French . . . from their settlement on the south [*sic*] side of the Bay of Apalache [in Florida]."[7] Some South Carolinians enthusiastically supported Moore's projects, but the nonexpansionists fiercely opposed them. Assemblyman John Ash, for example, castigated Moore's proposed expedition as "a project of freebooting under the specious name of war."[8] The nonexpansionists were able to thwart Moore's efforts to strengthen the colony's control over the Indian trade, but the expansionists in the house managed to appropriate funds for a military expedition, despite the fulminations of "the party who opposed the enterprise." In October 1702 Moore led an army that razed the town of St. Augustine, though it failed to capture the Spanish fortress.[9]

Conflict between the two groups continued during the first decade. Moore and other expansionists worked closely with the new governor, Sir Nathaniel Johnson, and in 1704 secured legislative approval for a campaign against the pro-Spanish Apalache Indians. The opposing party, however, tacked on a proviso that no public funds be used for the expedition, forcing Moore to finance the march through the sale of Indian slaves and other booty. Although men from both factions came together in 1706 to defend the province against a Spanish invasion, this amity soon faded. In the last years of the decade the expansionists advocated still bolder measures, including an attack on the French at Mobile, but were unable to implement their designs.[10]

During the 1710s the factions quarreled over the conduct of two Indian wars. Between 1711 and 1713 the expansionists in the Commons House called for the vigorous prosecution of the campaigns against the Tuscarora, while two members of this party, James Moore, Jr. (the governor's son), and John Barnwell, led the South Carolina forces. Moreover, most expansionists accepted the need for an expanded currency to finance the war. By contrast, the nonexpansionists showed little enthusiasm for the fight against the Tuscarora and were opposed to printing more treasury notes. Similar factional

7. *Commons House Journals*, Aug. 20, 1702, cited in Crane, *Southern Frontier*, 75.
8. John Ash, *Present State of Affairs*, cited in Sirmans, *Colonial South Carolina*, 84; Crane, *Southern Frontier*, 93.
9. Sirmans, *Colonial South Carolina*, 85–86; Crane, *Southern Frontier*, 93; Hewatt, *Historical Account*, I, 145–55, quotation on 155.
10. Hewatt, *Historical Account*, I, 179–87; Sirmans, *Colonial South Carolina*, 86–87, 93.

divisions marked participation in the Yamasee War, which lasted from 1715 to 1717.[11]

The financial burdens imposed by the two clashes with the Indians precipitated a bitter factional dispute over the role of the proprietors. Earl Granville and his associates had sent the colony little aid during the Tuscarora War, and when fighting with the Yamasee broke out in 1715, the Commons House, now firmly under expansionist control, expressed its fears that "the Lords Proprietors are not capable of supporting us in a war of this nature."[12] The nonexpansionists, who questioned the wisdom of costly campaigns against the natives and who shared the proprietors' aversion to paper money, defended the colony's owners. Lucrative offices further strengthened these partisans' ties to the proprietors: Nicholas Trott, for example, served as chief justice, while William Rhett was receiver general of the quit rents.[13]

The expansionists' criticism of the proprietors' miserliness culminated in the "Revolution of 1719" and the establishment of royal government. Granville and his colleagues were unwilling to strike any compromise and dismissed all opposition in South Carolina as the "business of a faction and party." Rumors of a Spanish attack in 1719 provided the expansionists with an excuse for action; the members of the party met in a convention, declared an end to proprietary rule, installed James Moore, Jr., as governor, and implored the Crown to take the colony under its protection. The resistance of the nonexpansionists was short-lived, and the rebellion was carried through with but a single skirmish and a single casualty—William Rhett, who was wounded by gunfire. In 1720 the new government sent John Barnwell to England as its agent. Barnwell's arguments about the strategic importance of South Carolina persuaded the Privy Council to accept the revolt and make South Carolina a royal colony.[14]

During the 1720s the expansionist and nonexpansionist parties gradually disappeared. An important cause of factional conflict was eliminated as South Carolina grew more secure. Success in the Yamasee War had significantly reduced the danger posed by the

11. Hewatt, *Historical Account*, I, 202–10; Sirmans, *Colonial South Carolina*, 109–11; Crane, *Southern Frontier*, 158–61.

12. Petition of Commons House, Aug. 1715, cited in Sirmans, *Colonial South Carolina*, 116, and see 111, 116–17; David McCord Wright, ed., "Petitioners to the Crown against the Proprietors, 1716–1717," *SCHM*, LXII (1961), 88–95.

13. Sirmans, *Colonial South Carolina*, 105–11.

14. Address of the Commons House, 1716, cited ibid., 118, and see 118–28; Crane, *Southern Frontier*, 216–34; Richard Waterhouse, "South Carolina's Colonial Elite: A Study in the Social Structure and Political Culture of a Southern Colony, 1670–1760" (Ph.D. diss., Johns Hopkins Univ., 1973), 118.

nearby tribes, while the construction of Fort St. George at the mouth of the Altamaha River bolstered provincial defenses against any incursion from Florida. More generally, relations between South Carolina and Spain's New World colonies improved, particularly after the rumored Spanish invasion, which had frightened South Carolinians in 1719, failed to materialize. In addition, the new royal governor, Francis Nicholson, worked to bring the parties together, carefully distributing appointments between the two groups. Factional lines remained evident only in squabbles over paper money, with such expansionists as John Fenwick defending moderate increases in currency, while Benjamin de la Conseillere and others fought any new issues. But even this partisan feud soon subsided.[15]

» «

The lack of stable factions in South Carolina between 1725 and 1754 was, in part, the result of the greater security the colony enjoyed. Relative calm in Europe muted New World rivalries, and the founding of Georgia in 1732 provided South Carolina with an important buffer against attacks from the south. Moreover, the township scheme, begun in the 1730s established a series of strategically located settlements in the backcountry. Between 1725 and 1740 the province undertook only a single campaign, burning a Yamasee village in 1728 in retaliation for raids upon the colony. The issues troubling South Carolinians—a squabble over the production of naval stores in the 1720s, for example, or a conflict over patents and surveys in the 1730s—gave rise to only ephemeral divisions.[16]

During King George's War, a soul-wrenching depression kept the colonists united. The conflict cut the province off from its best markets in Europe, hurting South Carolina more than any of the commonwealths to the north; planters and merchants with one voice lamented "the entire decay of the rice trade."[17] Hard times dampened enthusiasm for bold ventures, and South Carolinians took an active part in the war only during the first years of fighting; in 1740 they contributed a small force to General James Oglethorpe's army,

15. Hewatt, *Historical Account*, I, 295–319; Sirmans, *Colonial South Carolina*, 134–38, 144–53; Crane, *Southern Frontier*, 163, 185, 193–203, 229–47, 259–68, 282–83.
16. Sirmans, *Colonial South Carolina*, 154–82; Crane, *Southern Frontier*, 248–51, 268–72; Hewatt, *Historical Account*, II, 1–15.
17. Governor, Council, and Assembly to king, May 11, 1745, George Dunbar to duke of Newcastle, Aug. 24, 1743, *SCPR*, XXII, 92, XXI, 166, SCA; Charles Boschi to secretary of Society for Propagation of the Gospel, Oct. 30, 1745, *SCHM*, L (1949), 183; Eliza Lucas [Pinckney] to George Lucas, July 25, 1740, Sept. 8, 1742, *The Letterbook of Eliza Lucas Pinckney, 1739–1762*, ed. Elise Pinckney (Chapel Hill, N.C., 1972), 9, 55; Sirmans, *Colonial South Carolina*, 210–16; Hewatt, *Historical Account*, II, 111–222.

which tried and failed to capture St. Augustine, and in 1742 they helped repel a Spanish invasion of Georgia. But the Commons House rejected Governor James Glen's ambitious plans for an attack on Louisiana and refused to appropriate funds for a fort in Cherokee country, despite a treaty that encouraged the colonists to build one. The downturn provided South Carolinians with a common cause: rice growers joined traders in begging the Crown for relief, seeking additional paper money, and restricting the importation of slaves.[18]

During the early 1750s South Carolina was outside the theater of imperial conflict and remained politically quiescent. With the end of the wartime depression the Commons House relaxed its tight grip on the purse strings and in 1752 voted three thousand pounds for the construction of a fort near the Cherokee villages. But military activity remained minimal: the legislature refused to shoulder the expense of rebuilding Charleston's fortifications after a destructive hurricane in 1752 and did little to aid the other colonies during the opening skirmishes of the French and Indian War. The lawmakers accepted Governor Glen's argument that the conflict between Virginia and the French in the upper Ohio Valley reflected nothing more than a desire to "get a large share in the Indian trade."[19]

Between the mid-1720s and 1754 changes in South Carolina ensured that any parties emerging after 1755 would not closely resemble the factions flourishing before 1725. The area of rice planting spread, lessening the relative importance of those parishes, such as St. James Goose Creek and St. Paul, which had been the mainstay of the first expansionist party. Between 1724–1726 and 1753–1756 exports of rice increased fivefold from an annual average of 8.4 million pounds to 41.9 million pounds, with some of the most noteworthy gains in output recorded in the sprawling parish of St. Bartholomew. Moreover, the awesome rise of indigo production, which had been nonexistent as a cash crop in 1725, provided the basis for a new set of affluent planters in the parishes on both sides of the Santee River. Spurred in the 1740s by Eliza Lucas Pinckney's experimentation as

18. Gov. Glen to Board of Trade, May 28, 1745, Apr. 28, 1747, George Morley and James Wedderburn to Board of Trade, received Oct. 13, 1747, *SCPR*, xxii, 101–7, 272–75, 316–21; Sirmans, *Colonial South Carolina*, 258–62, 265–76; John R. Alden, *John Stuart and the Southern Colonial Frontier: A Study of Indian Relations, War, Trade, and Land Problems in the Southern Wilderness, 1754–1775* (1944; rpt. New York, 1966), 23–29, 34; Stuart O. Stumpf, "Implications of King George's War for the Charleston Mercantile Community," *SCHM*, lxxvii (1976), 161–88.

19. Gov. Glen to Secretary of State Thomas Robinson, Aug. 15, 1754, SCPR, xxvi, 84–105, quotation on 92; Gov. Glen to Robert Dinwiddie, June 21, 1753, ibid., xxv, 320; Sirmans, *Colonial South Carolina*, 276, 295–300; Alden, *John Stuart*, 35–37; Carl Bridenbaugh, *Cities in Revolt: Urban Life in America, 1743–1776* (New York, 1955), 19, 22–23; Lewis C. Gray, *History of Agriculture in the Southern United States to 1860*, 2 vols., consec. pagin. (Washington, D.C., 1933), 1030; Gov. Glen to Board of Trade, Aug. 26, 1754, SCPR, xxvi, 112.

well as by a British bounty, indigo exports skyrocketed, and by the mid-1750s were valued annually at over a hundred thousand pounds sterling, equal in some years to the worth of the province's rice shipments. Such changes in staple production transformed the assembly's planting bloc, which after 1755 drew its leadership from a broader area than it had early in the century.[20]

Second, the remarkable battening of the merchant community meant that the traders, instead of being subordinate to the planters as they had been at the beginning of the century, would be of equal importance to the landowners, if not preeminent, in any new set of parties. Although importers had begun to play a larger role in the economy with the upturn in the slave trade around 1700, only after 1725 did their power become evident. The large traders who benefited from the booming commerce in rice, indigo, and blacks, solidified their position by channeling much of their wealth into the purchase of plantations and laborers. Biographies of the principal importers—the Manigaults, Henry Laurens, Miles Brewton, and others—detail a pattern of extensive investment; moreover, tax returns for the 1760s reveal that Charlestonians laid claim to over a quarter of the slaves working outside the capital and to nearly one-third of the taxed rural land in the province. By comparison, during the first decades of the century important traders often had few or no holdings outside Charleston.[21]

The breathtaking surge in mercantile fortunes helped assure importers a more prominent political position. In the 1720s 67 percent of the assemblymen were planters, 25 percent importers. By the 1750s the proportion of estate owners in the Commons House had slid to 50 percent, while the merchants' share had ballooned to 36 percent, with several parishes near Charleston regularly sending importers to the lower chamber. Traders were even more in evidence among leaders in the house, and again they rose in importance. In the 1720s, of sixteen "first-rank" leaders, based on committee assignments, 5 men were merchants (31 percent) and 7 were planters (44 percent)

20. Thomas Thompson to secretary of Society for the Propagation of the Gospel, May 1, 1736, Aug. 16, 1743, William Langhorne to secretary of Society for the Propagation of the Gospel, Aug. 22, 1752, SCHM, L (1949), 178, 181–82, 200; Wood, Black Majority, 142–55; Waterhouse, "South Carolina's Colonial Elite," 214, 236; George Hunter to Board of Trade, Oct. 31, 1743, Gov. Glen to Board of Trade, Mar. 12, 1744, Gov. Glen to duke of Newcastle, Feb. 11, 1746, enclosure in Gov. Glen to Board of Trade, Jan. 29, 1752, SCPR, XXI, 175–77, 245–47, XXII, 134–35, XXV, 10–13; Historical Statistics of the U.S., 1168, 1184, 1189, 1192; Sirmans, Colonial South Carolina, 154–56; H. Roy Merrens, ed., The Colonial South Carolina Scene: Contemporary Views, 1697–1774 (Columbia, S.C., 1977), 144–63, 250–51; Jerome J. Nadelhaft, The Disorders of War: The Revolution in South Carolina (Orono, Me., 1981), 22.

21. Edgar and Bailey, Biographical Directory: Commons House, passim. The 1768 tax account is presented in Merrens, ed., Colonial South Carolina Scene, 248–52.

and one was a merchant-planter (6 percent). By the 1750s, of twenty-four "first-rank" men, fourteen were importers (58 percent) and three were planters (13 percent). Lawyers, doctors, and placemen accounted for the other leaders.[22]

Further emphasizing the discontinuity between the first and second party system, most of the affluent traders in the 1750s were "new men" whose forebears had not been prominent in overseas commerce or politics during the first decades of the century. John Guerard was the son of a trader, but relatively few other merchants flourishing during the French and Indian War could point to a father who had made his wealth importing. Most had either advanced beyond their fathers' professions—Henry Laurens was the son of a saddler, Miles Brewton the son of a goldsmith—or, like John Lloyd, were recent immigrants from Great Britain.[23]

» «

As the pressure of the French and Indian War gradually forced South Carolinians to define their positions on imperial questions, the new factions emerged. Self-interest was the primary determinant of party lines, with national origin and religion of secondary importance.[24]

The expansionist faction enjoyed the support of the wealthier Charleston merchants, most of the rice planters, and the indigo growers of the eastern low country. This broad base justly suggests the lineaments of a dominant party. Yet before the climactic 1765 election, the loyalties of these groups had not hardened, and many affluent districts sent wavering or unaligned delegates to the Commons House. Within the importing community the correlation between wealth and a buoyant view of America's future was strong. With few exceptions, the upper stratum of traders owned large tracts of land whose value depended on secure frontiers; self-interest, there-

22. Waterhouse, "South Carolina's Colonial Elite," 188–90. For "first-rank" leaders, see Jack P. Greene, *The Quest for Power: The Lower Houses of Assembly in the Southern Royal Colonies* (Chapel Hill, N.C., 1963), 475–88; Sirmans, *Colonial South Carolina*, 140n, 152n, 247n, 314.

23. Edgar and Bailey, *Biographical Directory: Commons House*; W. Robert Higgins, "Charles Town Merchants and Factors Dealing in the External Negro Trade, 1735–1775," *SCHM*, LXV (1964), 204–17.

24. Several recent works present a different approach to South Carolina factions, accepting the presence of religious divisions in the province's early history but asserting that later splits were ephemeral or insignificant. Robert Weir's outlook is aptly summed up in his title, " 'The Harmony We Were Famous For': An Interpretation of Pre-Revolutionary South Carolina Politics," *WMQ*, 3d ser., XXVI (1969), 473–501. Weir argues that Carolinians were virtually unanimous in their support for Whig principles. Greene, *Quest for Power*, and Sirmans, *Colonial South Carolina*, emphasize the colonists' solidarity in opposing the royal governors. For a firm statement of the presence of parties in the revolutionary era, one must go back to a contemporary chronicler, Hewatt, *Historical Account*, II, 254–329.

Table 1. Loyalty of Charleston firms active in
the slave trade between 1750 and 1775

Rank among slave traders	Patriots	Tories
1–19	11	0
20–149	36	9
150–405	9	21

SOURCES: Higgins, "Charles Town Merchants," 205–17. On loyalties, see sources cited in the Appendix.

NOTES: This table depicts the loyalties of *firms.* Hence, individuals who were partners in several houses are counted more than once. Thirty-one individual merchants were expansionist slavers, and twenty-three were tories. Unknowns are excluded. Also excluded from this compilation are firms that imported no slaves after 1750, although their rank numbers were retained in determining the groupings.

fore, engendered forceful attitudes toward the colony's enemies, as Lieutenant Colonel James Grant reported to Amherst in 1761. The accompanying table which presents data on slave traders in Charleston, underscores the connection between the size of a firm and expansionism. Six of the seven largest trading houses had at least one partner who distinguished himself by his active support of defense during the Seven Years' War. Henry Laurens and Gabriel Manigault are typical of these merchant princes who were slavers, landowners, lawmakers, ardent warriors, and patriots. Christopher Gadsden, another outspoken partisan, owned a plantation near Georgetown and five ships. These traders helped provide the foundation for the large expansionist bloc in the forty-eight-seat Commons House. In addition to the six seats Charleston could claim in 1760, parishes that fell within the capital's orbit and frequently elected traders offered another nine places. In their outlook and in their commitment to the economic development of the province these businessmen were the spiritual (if rarely the lineal) descendants of the expansionist merchants in the first factional system.[25]

25. Lt. Col. James Grant to Gen. Amherst, Jan. 7, 1761, cited in Alden, *John Stuart,* 125; members of the Commons House are listed in *Biographical Directory of the South Carolina House of Representatives,* vol. I: *Session Lists, 1692–1973,* ed. Joan S. R. Faunt and Robert E. Rector with David K. Bowen (Columbia, S.C., 1974); David R. Chesnutt, "South Carolina's Penetration of Georgia in the 1760s: Henry Laurens as a Case Study," *SCHM,* LXXIII (1972), 194–208. For the merchants' political activity during the Seven Years' War, consult Petition of Merchants, Traders . . . and Others . . . , Dec. 21, 1756, and Public Subscription, Nov. 17, 1759, *The Papers of Henry Laurens,* ed. Philip

Although traders formed a crucial group within the expansionist phalanx, in the last years of the colonial period their revolutionary fervor at times remained a rung below that of the faction's planters. The political awakening of Charleston artisans in the 1760s frightened the merchants more than it did the rural elite, and moderated the patriotism of many wealthy Charlestonians. Hence, the importers lagged behind the planters in pushing for nonimportation against the Townshend Acts ("You cannot expect the merchants will begin this matter themselves," one editorialist commented in 1769),[26] in denouncing the Tea Act, and in undertaking protests in the months before the First Continental Congress. Nonetheless, the distinction between the behavior of the merchants and that of the planters was one of degree, not ideology, and was always far less pronounced than the yawning rift separating expansionists from their nonexpansionist opponents.

As in the other provinces, the wealthy landowners most immediately threatened by the Indians or the French developed an aggressive approach to the growth of an American empire. In the South Carolina of the 1750s and early 1760s, with its lawless backcountry and warlike Indian neighbors, a broad run of prosperous parishes adjoining or lying near the backcountry had cause to feel uneasy. Four rice-growing parishes, stretching from St. Bartholomew to St. John Berkeley and all bordering on the up-country, usually offered most of their thirteen seats to the expansionists (map 6). William Moultrie and Rawlins Lowndes were among the prominent politicians from this region. Farther east in the low country was another party bastion: a set of four parishes in which indigo was relatively more important and rice less predominant. Leading planters in this area—George Gabriel Powell and Thomas Lynch among them—had long records of support for the expansionist cause, and taken together, these eastern parishes added seven delegates to the expansionist bloc. In all, the party's planting and mercantile constituencies could command an insurmountable thirty-four seats in the lower chamber.[27]

The nonexpansionists marshaled a different and, over the long run, much less powerful alliance of South Carolinians. In the rice colony

M. Hamer et al. (Columbia, S.C., 1968–), II, 378–80, III, 16–17; Higgins, "Charles Town Merchants," 205–27; Volunteers to Gov. William Henry Lyttelton, Oct. 31, 1759, *The Writings of Christopher Gadsden, 1746–1805*, ed. Richard Walsh (Columbia, S.C., 1966), 12–13; Edgar and Bailey, *Biographical Directory: Commons House*, passim.

26. *South Carolina Gazette*, June 1, 1769, quoted in Arthur M. Schlesinger, *The Colonial Merchants and the American Revolution, 1763–1776* (New York, 1919), 141–42.

27. George C. Rogers, Jr., *The History of Georgetown County, South Carolina* (Columbia, S.C., 1970), 9–104; Edgar and Bailey, *Biographical Directory: Commons House.*

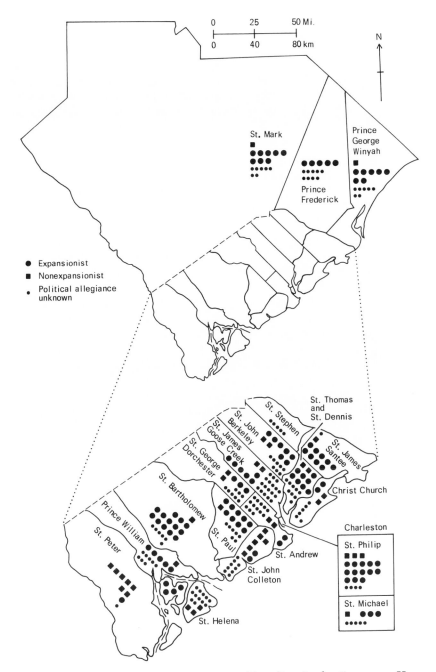

Map 6. South Carolina: Future patriots and loyalists in the Commons House of Assembly, 1757–1762

Source: This map is based on the information in Edgar and Bailey, *Biographical Directory: Commons House.* Individuals who left South Carolina for East Florida in the 1760s and subsequently made their careers in that new British possession have been excluded.

the two parties were less evenly balanced than in Virginia or the commercial provinces; thus while 103 members of the Commons House became patriots, only 28 remained true to the Crown. Before the October 1765 election, however, nonexpansionist lawmakers in conjunction with independent-minded members frequently gained the upper hand.[28]

As the table suggests, many of the lesser merchants supported this cautious party. Most were figures of little consequence, either politically or economically, and many were, as will be discussed, Scots. Martin Campbell and John Johnson, for example, stood well outside the circle of the largest importers: Campbell ranked 199th among slave trading firms and Johnson 210th. Although both were engaged in business during the French and Indian War, neither notably aided the military efforts of the colony, and both would become loyalists.[29]

The nonexpansionists also enjoyed the backing of planters in the coastal lands and Sea Islands—an area that included Christ Church Parish and, more especially, St. John Colleton and St. Helena. Compared to their neighbors, these three districts sent a disproportionate number of nonexpansionists to the Commons House, although together they could control only eight seats (map 6). The pacific outlook of these coastal estate owners, much like the views of the nonexpansionists in other provinces, was shaped by their distance from the perils of the frontier. Although a French or Spanish naval attack remained a theoretical possibility, the palpable burdens of appropriations for the backcountry helped foster a spirited opposition to defense. William Wragg, who represented St. John Colleton from 1758 to 1768, became the faction's most articulate spokesman and was a strong critic of the war against the French and Indians. The distinctive political role played by these coastal parishes was underscored by Governor Charles Montagu's abortive efforts in 1772 to move the seat of government from Charleston to Beaufort, a port town in St. Helena. "The principle promoters of opposition [to the Crown]," Montagu informed the ministry, "reside in or near Charleston."[30] Montagu emphasized the advantages of relocating the

28. Factional continuities are suggested by other data. Of the 103 patriot members of the Commons House, 22 (or 21 percent) actively supported the war effort between 1755 and 1761. Of 28 tory members, only 2 (or 7 percent) favored war. See Edgar and Bailey, *Biographical Directory: Commons House.* Individuals who permanently left South Carolina in the 1760s (for example, those resettling in East Florida) are excluded from this and other tabulations.

29. Humble Address of Merchants of Charles Town, Mar. 22, 1760, *Papers of Laurens,* III, 30–34; Edgar and Bailey, *Biographical Directory: Commons House,* 568; Higgins, "Charles Town Merchants," 205–17; W. O. Moore, Jr., "The Largest Exporters of Deerskins from Charles Town, 1735–1775," *SCHM,* LXXIV (1973), 144–150.

30. Gov. Montagu to Hillsborough, July 27, 1772, SCPR, XXXIII, 167–68.

capital: "The members for [the] Beaufort part of the province residing there would be always on the spot at different meetings of the assembly, ready to seize an opportunity in the absence of the violent party either to exclude them by a vote of non-attendance, or to dispatch the business out of hand before they would arrive at Beaufort."[31]

Finally, the nonexpansionists could count on the backing of many of the less wealthy settlers who lived outside the region of intensive rice and indigo production. The small farmers of St. Peter, which lay between St. Helena and the Georgia border, frequently sent nonexpansionists to the legislature. Beginning in the mid-1760s husbandmen in the rapidly growing backcountry voiced criticism of the expansionist elite and sympathy for the nonexpansionists. This western region, which as early as 1760 could claim half the white population of South Carolina, never spoke with one voice; however, these settlers resented the expansionist aristocracy's opposition to their demands for courts and roads and welcomed the support of men like William Wragg, who eagerly embraced any enemy of the dominant faction. But until the provincial meetings and congresses of 1774 and 1775, an unjust apportionment limited these westerners to the role of outsiders in provincial politics.[32]

National origin also played a noteworthy, if subordinate, role in party formation. Scots were prominent in the nonexpansionist faction from its formation; the contemporary chronicler Alexander Hewatt, who was himself a Scot and a loyalist, detailed the controversy over the behavior of Scottish commander James Grant during the Cherokee War. "From this period," Hewatt observed, "a party-spirit appeared in Carolina. All the malicious aspersions and inflammatory accusations against the inhabitants of North Britain, which were at this time wantonly and wickedly published in England, were greedily swallowed by one party in the province and industriously propagated."[33]

Several well-known Scots were in the thick of partisan ructions and invariably sided with the nonexpansionists. Between 1758 and 1775 Robert Wells, publisher of the *South Carolina and American General Gazette*, offered a rallying point for the party and fostered an outlook that sharply contrasted with that of rival printer Peter Timo-

31. Gov. Montagu to Hillsborough, Sept. 24, 1772, ibid., 173–80, quotation on 176.
32. Peter Manigault to Benjamin Stead, Sept. 14, 1765, "The Letterbook of Peter Manigault, 1763–1773," ed. Maurice A. Crouse, *SCHM*, LXX (1969), 87; Richard M. Brown, *The South Carolina Regulators* (Cambridge, Mass., 1963), 3, 182; Joseph A. Ernst, "Another View of the South Carolina Election of 1768 and the Regulators: A Comment," Patricia U. Bonomi, ed., *Party and Political Opposition in Revolutionary America* (Tarrytown, N.Y., 1980), 87–97; *Biographical Directory: Session Lists*.
33. Hewatt, *Historical Account*, II, 255.

thy. Wells, as his son later recollected, was desperate to preserve the family's national identity: "Fearing that I should become tainted with disloyal principles which began immediately after the peace of 1763 to prevail throughout America, [my father] obliged me to wear a tartan coat, and a blue Scotch bonnet, hoping by these means to make me consider myself a Scotchman."[34] Another Scot, John Stuart, who was a councillor and superintendant for Indian affairs in the South, nettled expansionists with his heavy-handed enforcement of royal policies, while Grant, the commander who helped defeat the Cherokee, outraged such partisans as Christopher Gadsden by his reputed slights of colonial officers.[35]

The Scottish nonexpansionists were largely concentrated in the merchant community of Charleston. Of twenty-three slave importers who became tories, at least half were Scots. (By contrast, of the thirty-one patriot slavers, none, it would seem, was from North Britain.) Some of these cautious merchants—Alexander Rose was one—served as assemblymen for those parishes that sought a nonexpansionist spokesman. Throughout the decade before independence, patriots commented on Scottish opposition to the revolutionary movement; for example, in 1769 Peter Manigault remarked that "only thirty-one persons in Charleston have refused to sign it [the boycott], most of them Scotchmen."[36] Few Scottish nonexpansionists, however, resided in the planting parishes. The "Caledonians," Christopher Gadsden observed, "though they have some little influence in *town* from their numbers and more so from their secret artifices, . . . never were of the least importance in any manner in the country."[37] In any case, the significance of national origin must be kept in perspective. Scots formed only a minor, if highly visible, component of one party. Most low-country politicians were of English extraction, and other identifiable groups, such as the Huguenots, had no clear partisan bias.[38]

34. Wells quoted in Christopher Gould, "Robert Wells, Colonial Charleston Printer," *SCHM*, LXXIX (1978), 27–28; Alden, *John Stuart*, 164, 169–70.

35. Alden, *John Stuart*, passim; *Writings of Gadsden*, 14–15; David Duncan Wallace, *The Life of Henry Laurens, with a Sketch of Lieutenant-Colonel John Laurens* (1915; rpt. New York, 1967), 104–5.

36. Peter Manigault to Ralph Izard, Oct. 4, 1769, "Letterbook of Manigault," 180; *South Carolina Gazette*, Apr. 5, 1770, cited in Leila Sellers, *Charleston Business on the Eve of the American Revolution* (Chapel Hill, N.C., 1934), 210; Higgins, "Charles Town Merchants," 205–17. Forrest McDonald and Ellen Shapiro McDonald, "The Ethnic Origins of the American People, 1790," *WMQ*, 3d ser., XXXVII (1980), 192–94, present a list of surnames that allows an estimate of the proportion of Scots in the population.

37. Christopher Gadsden to James Pearson, Feb. 13, 1766, "Two Letters by Christopher Gadsden, February 1766," ed. Robert M. Weir, *SCHM*, LXXV (1974), 172.

38. McDonald and McDonald, "Ethnic Origins," 188, 196–197, lists Irish and Welsh surnames. For other groups, see Edgar and Bailey, *Biographical Directory: Commons House*, passim.

Finally, religion was of minor importance in shaping the second set of imperial factions. In the rural areas the data suggest no sectarian difference between parishes that elected expansionist assemblymen and those supporting the nonexpansionists. Expansionists enjoyed strong support in such parishes as St. James Goose Creek and St. John Berkeley, where Anglicans dominated, as well as in St. Bartholomew, which had a large Presbyterian minority. Only in the capital was a religious alignment evident, and even there a key group—the Anglicans—was divided. Early in 1775 Lieutenant Governor William Bull offered revealing comments about the observance of a patriotic fast day: "In Charleston the assembly with the speaker preceded by the mace went to St. Philip's [Anglican] Church, where a sermon was preached by Mr. Smith, the rector. . . . In the New England or Independent meeting there was also a full congregation. But in St. Michael's [Anglican] Church, of which Mr. Cooper is rector, only the usual service of prayers on Fridays was performed. And in the Scotch Presbyterian meeting there was no divine service that day."[39] Above all else, self-interest, which was embodied in regional divisions and in the several strata within the merchant community, shaped party membership; national origin and religious distinctions had less impact.

The new set of factions emerged with the advent of war in the mid-1750s. In 1755 those who strongly believed in the growth of America applauded legislative appropriations for Braddock's expedition and for fortifying Charleston. "It will give us great pleasure to see it [the town's fortification] completed," the firm of George Austin & Henry Laurens remarked.[40] Urging vigorous measures against the French, the partners declared, "There is no dealing with that ambitious, deceitful people, but at the muzzle of our guns."[41] Charles Pinckney, who served as one of the colony's agents in London, echoed these views.[42]

The divisions within South Carolina became clearer in 1756. Worried by English setbacks in the northern colonies, many citizens boosted the need for preparedness. In the spring a group of mer-

39. Lt. Gov. William Bull to Dartmouth, Feb. 22, 1775, SCPR, xxxv, 21; William Langhorne to secretary of Society for the Propogation of the Gospel, Aug. 22, 1752, *SCHM*, L (1949), 200; *Atlas of Early American History: The Revolutionary Era, 1760–1790*, ed. Lester J. Cappon et al. (Princeton, N.J., 1976), 39.

40. Austin & Laurens to Devonsheir, Reeve, & Lloyd, July 31, 1755, *Papers of Laurens*, I, 305; Bridenbaugh, *Cities in Revolt*, 23.

41. Austin & Laurens to Sarah Nickelson, Aug. 1, 1755, *Papers of Laurens*, I, 309.

42. Eliza L. Pinckney to Lady Carew, Aug.–Sept., 1755, *Letterbook of Eliza Pinckney*, 84; Frances Leigh Williams, *A Founding Family: The Pinckneys of South Carolina* (New York, 1978), 15.

chants lent the province two thousand pounds sterling to speed the construction of a fort in Cherokee country, and that summer the expansionists pushed through a tax bill to cover the costs of this fort and to repay the loan. An opposing group, with William Wragg at its head, decried these expenditures. Wragg, a member of the council, whom Governor William Henry Lyttelton considered "an insolent and litigious spirit," tried to block passage of the revenue measure and also denounced as an "illegal act" the embargo designed to prevent provisions from reaching the French. Furthermore, according to Lyttelton, Wragg "warmly opposed the act for the distribution of the Acadians . . . although it had been pursued in deference to his majesty's commands concerning these people." Fearing that the councillor "might create new disturbances" in the legislature, Lyttelton in November removed him from the upper chamber.[43]

The threat of a French invasion in 1757 only intensified partisan conflict. During June and July lawmakers with differing views of colonial defense locked horns over a proposal to raise £44,300 and enlist seven hundred men for the defense of Charleston. Lyttelton complained, "This bill met with great opposition, and the sum for fortifications was carried only by two votes in the assembly."[44] During these months a coterie of Charleston expansionists made its support for the war effort unmistakable. Particularly prominent in this group were three importers who were also legislators—Henry Laurens, Christopher Gadsden, and Benjamin Smith. Working together, the three ordered military supplies for the province. Moreover, Laurens sponsored a bill to establish a volunteer artillery company, while Gadsden helped organize the corps and became its first commander. When the regulars arrived that fall, Smith, who was speaker of the house, cooperated with Colonel Henry Bouquet in finding quarters for the troops. Another outspoken expansionist, Peter Timothy, printer of the *South Carolina Gazette*, urged the province to strengthen its ties with the Chickasaw to counter the threat posed by the French and hostile Indians. During 1758 factional tensions lessened as fears of a French attack faded.[45]

43. Gov. Lyttelton to Board of Trade, June 19, Dec. 6, 1756, June 11, 1757, SCPR, xxvii, 107–11, 201–4, 278–81; Sirmans, *Colonial South Carolina*, 308.

44. Gov. Lyttelton to Board of Trade, July 12, 1757, *SCPR*, xxvii, 287–89, quotation on 288.

45. Benjamin Smith, Christopher Gadsden, and Henry Laurens to William Allen, Oct. 27, 1757, *Papers of Laurens*, ii, 537–38; Sirmans, *Colonial South Carolina*, 322; Jack P. Greene, "The South Carolina Quartering Dispute, 1757–1758," *SCHM*, lx (1959), 193–204. Lyttelton responded to this help by recommending Gadsden for a seat on the council; the Board of Trade, however, did not accept his suggestion. Gov. Lyttelton to Board of Trade, Sept. 15, Nov. 30, 1757, SCPR, xxvii, 297, 337; *Papers of Laurens*, iii, 557; Alan Calmes, "The Lyttelton Expedition of 1759: Military Failures and Financial Successes," *SCHM*, lxxvii (1976), 28–33; Sirmans, *Colonial South Carolina*, 322–23.

The Cherokee War, which began in the fall of 1759 and lasted until 1762, once more fanned the coals of partisan hostility. During October and November 1759 expansionists broadcast their support for Governor Lyttelton's proposed campaign against the Indians. Many well-known citizens, including Christopher Gadsden and Francis Marion, volunteered to march with the governor, and nine merchant houses, embracing fourteen men (Henry Laurens and Gabriel Manigault among them), subscribed a loan of forty-five thousand pounds currency for the cause. Similarly, expansionist lawmakers made clear their sentiments, although during these months expansionists were in the minority, and the Commons House appropriation fell far short of the governor's request. "I am sensible there are several among you," Lyttelton told the assemblymen, "whose love of their country has made them wish to see me supported in that emergency with a more liberal hand, but their voices could not prevail."[46]

Nonexpansionists criticized the governor's decision to attack the Cherokee rather than negotiate. "Some think there was no necessity for the expedition," complained Speaker Benjamin Smith in November.[47] One of the leading opponents of the campaign was William Bull, Jr., who was a member of the council and lieutenant governor of the colony. Bull, as the historian Alexander Hewatt reported, urged South Carolinians to consider "the happy consequence of an agreement before more blood was spilt." Bull argued that the province should continue to use its control of the Indian trade as a weapon and should seek a lasting peace by treating with a delegation of Cherokee recently arrived in the capital. Three councillors supported Bull, while four backed the governor.[48]

Feuding between the two parties continued unabated in the aftermath of Lyttelton's expedition, which failed to secure peace. Lyttleton wrote to Amherst for aid and once again requested support from the Commons House. The nonexpansionists remained angry at the governor for the demands he had made the preceding fall, and with the help of some members of the opposing party, adopted on February 7, 1760, an address censuring the executive for his attacks on the "birthright of British subjects."[49] The danger posed by the

---

46. *Commons House Journals*, Oct. 1, 1759, cited in Calmes, "Lyttelton Expedition," 13–14; Volunteers to Gov. Lyttelton, Oct. 31, 1759, *Writings of Gadsden*, 12–13; Public Subscription, Nov. 17, 1759, *Papers of Laurens*, III, 16–17.

47. Smith, letter of Nov. 10, 1759, in "Extracts of Letters from the Speaker of the Assembly in South Carolina to Mr. Wright the Agent," read by Board of Trade, Feb. 1, 1760, SCPR, XXVIII, 266.

48. Ibid.; Hewatt, *Historical Account*, II, 217.

49. Gov. Lyttelton to Board of Trade, Feb. 20, 1760, SCPR, XXVIII, 311–16, quotation on 314; Carl J. Vipperman, *The Rise of Rawlins Lowndes, 1721–1800* (Columbia, S.C., 1978), 93.

Cherokee steadily mounted, however, and the expansionists were at last able to push through an appropriation for one thousand troops; Laurens and Gadsden were among those "on the side of the majority." This grant, Lyttelton remarked, was "violently opposed by those who had been principals in carrying through the message of the 7th."[50]

The steadily worsening situation in the backcountry, coupled with the arrival of Colonel Archibald Montgomery and twelve hundred regulars in April 1760, brought a temporary halt to the clash of factions. William Bull, Jr., who now took up the seals of office (Lyttelton had been translated to the government in Jamaica), worked with members of both factions to assist Montgomery. The British forces, however, did not quell the Cherokee revolt; although the regulars burned several Indian settlements, they were unable to reach the "middle" towns, which lay farther from the colony, and they suffered heavy losses in an ambush. Despite these setbacks, Montgomery pronounced his mission complete and withdrew most of his forces in August. Expansionists believed that Montgomery had seriously erred by turning back before roundly thrashing the Indians.[51]

Politicians from the two groups heatedly debated the proper course of action in the wake of Montgomery's failure. The renewed Cherokee threat helped swell the expansionist ranks in the house, and in August this party secured legislation to raise seven companies of rangers and a regiment of a thousand foot soldiers. Among those accepting commissions in this corps was Henry Laurens, who became a lieutenant colonel. But Governor Bull and other nonexpansionists still hesitated to fight. Bull argued that South Carolina should make peace with the Indians, even on "terms that perhaps may not be thought suitable, according to the rules of honor among Europeans." He opined that "spirited measures . . . are justifiable only when recourse is had to them as the dernier resort."[52] The governor at first refused to raise the authorized regiment. Only in October, after the Cherokee had massacred one of the frontier garrisons, did he agree to

50. Gov. Lyttelton to Board of Trade, Feb. 20, 1760, SCPR, xxviii, 311–16, quotation on 314; Laurens, "A Letter Signed Philolethes," [Mar. 2, 1763], Papers of Laurens, iii, 290, 312–13.

51. Eliza L. Pinckney to Mrs. King, July 19, 1760, Letterbook of Eliza Pinckney, 155; Lt. Gov. Bull to Board of Trade, May 8, 1760, Lt. Gov. Bull to Col. Montgomery, July 12, 1760, SCPR, xxviii, 334–38, 381; Sirmans, Colonial South Carolina, 335–37; Alden, John Stuart, 112.

52. Lt. Gov. Bull to Board of Trade, Aug. 31, 1760, SCPR, xxviii, 394–400, quotations on 396–97 and 400; Laurens, Commission as Lieutenant Colonel, Sept. 16, 1760, Papers of Laurens, iii, 46–47; Sirmans, Colonial South Carolina, 337; Alden, John Stuart, 113–14; Hewatt, Historical Account, ii, 235–36.

enlist the troops and also to ask General Amherst to supply additional aid.[53]

Factional conflict in 1761 and 1762 turned on how severely the Cherokee should be punished. At least initially, men from both parties backed the new British commander, Lieutenant Colonel James Grant, who arrived in Charleston with sixteen hundred regulars early in 1761. Bull labored to secure supplies for Grant, while various expansionists, including Laurens, John and William Moultrie, and Francis Marion, agreed to serve as field officers in the provincial regiment accompanying Grant's forces. These South Carolina commanders, according to a contemporary historian, were "there trained to further and greater services in the cause of their country. They all served in the revolutionary war [as patriots]."[54] Grant's campaign in June and July was a success: he marched into the middle towns and burned the crops, thereby reducing the Cherokee to destitution and forcing them to sue for peace. Despite these manifest "accomplishments," some legislators, such as Gadsden, whose expansionism was heavily compounded with racism, considered Grant's tactics to be overly cautious. The Commons House demanded that the troops continue to fight until they "destroy as many of their people as we can."[55] These lawmakers also insisted that a vindictive treaty be imposed on the Indians, delaying the signing of a pact. Only in December, after Bull had rejected the harsh proposals of the Commons House, did the South Carolina negotiators and the Cherokee approve a definitive peace treaty.[56]

The expansionist lawmakers' castigation of Lieutenant Colonel Grant had another noteworthy effect: it temporarily alienated Henry Laurens from the main body of that faction. Laurens resented the calumnies that Gadsden and others had directed toward Grant. In an article in Timothy's *Gazette* and in a pamphlet that appeared in the spring of 1762, Gadsden charged that the peace was "without advantage," that Grant was cowardly in not "cutting as many throats as possible," and that the British commander had slighted the head of the provincial forces, Thomas Middleton.[57] These attacks on Grant, a

53. Lt. Gov. Bull to Board of Trade, Oct. 21, 1760, SCPR, xxviii, 409–17; Sirmans, *Colonial South Carolina*, 337–42.

54. David Ramsay, *History of South Carolina from Its First Settlement in 1670 to the Year 1808*, 2 vols. (Newbury, S.C., 1858), i, 105–8, quotation on 105n; *South-Carolina Gazette*, Feb. 7, 1761, *Papers of Laurens*, iii, 59.

55. *Commons Journals*, Sept. 18, 1761, cited in Sirmans, *Colonial South Carolina*, 339.

56. Sirmans, *Colonial South Carolina*, 340–42; Alden, *John Stuart*, 130–32.

57. "The Philopatrios Essays on the Cherokee Wars," Dec. 18, 1761, and "Some Observations," 1762, An Abstract, *Writings of Gadsden*, 14–15.

Scot, and his soldiers, many of whom were highlanders, soon became entangled with the anti-Scottish sentiments held by some expansionists. Laurens, who had become the lieutenant colonel's friend, denounced Gadsden and justly pointed out that Grant's campaign and the ensuing treaty had ended the Cherokee menace. Laurens, a strong-willed, hot-tempered individual, fully threw himself into this dispute, as he would into so many others. His anger was only heightened when his Charleston constituents temporarily denied him an assembly seat in 1762. During the next several years he fumed at Gadsden and cast a harsh eye at that merchant's strident patriotism. More than once in his career Laurens allowed personal animosities to influence his view of larger issues; he would rejoin his old expansionist allies only after 1767, when a feud with local customs officials mightily reinforced his distaste for British policies.[58]

» «

Between the mid-1750s and 1762 a few of South Carolina expansionists enunciated the beliefs that made up their world view. Austin & Laurens, for example, extolled the virtues of using provincial forces rather than regulars to fight in the New World, observing, "Our ministry would do well to prosecute a war in America with Americans."[59] In defending his friend Lieutenant Colonel James Grant, Henry Laurens muted but never wholly backed away from these sentiments. Austin & Laurens also called upon "the several provinces to unite their strength" in a colonial union against the French.[60] Charles Pinckney, who was in London during the early years of the war, noted the colonists' larger goals. He stressed to the Board of Trade the danger that the French and their Indian allies posed to South Carolina and argued the necessity of securing the large expanse occupied by the Creek Indians. These lands were valuable, Pinckney explained, "not only as they supply a great part of the skin trade and consume great quantities of the British manufactures, but chiefly as by reason of the fertility of the soil, the happiness of the climate and the situation in regard to and affording one of the best rivers and harbors in the Gulf of Mexico."[61] After 1762 the expansionist and nonexpansionist persuasions would help define responses to the new parliamentary measures.

58. Hewatt, *Historical Account*, II, 246–55; Laurens, "To the *South-Carolina Weekly Gazette*," [Feb. 28, 1763]; Laurens, "A Letter Signed Philolethes," [Mar. 2, 1763], Laurens to Gov. James Grant, Dec. 22, 1768, *Papers of Laurens*, III, 270–72, 275–355 (and see 83n), VI, 233–34; Wallace, *Henry Laurens*, 109.

59. Austin & Laurens to James Cowles, Aug. 20, 1755, *Papers of Laurens*, I, 321.

60. Laurens, "A Letter Signed Philolethes" [Mar. 2, 1763], Austin & Laurens to Devonsheir, Reeve, & Lloyd, Aug. 20, 1755, ibid., III, 350–51, I, 322.

61. Charles Pinckney, Representation to the Board of Trade, Dec. 2, 1756, SCPR, XXVII, 182–91, quotation on 188; Williams, *Founding Family*, 15.

PART TWO

Revolutionary Politics, 1763–1770

Between 1763 and 1770 in each province two groups of wealthy individuals, with markedly different visions of America's development, clashed over the proper response to British measures and over the steps needed to reinflate the local economy. These factions, which had emerged by the 1750s, were little changed in their makeup from earlier decades. The challenges they faced were new, however. Britain replaced France and Spain as the chief adversary, and economic questions now loomed larger than military ones.

In keeping with their faith in the strength and bountiful future of the New World, the expansionists displayed a steadfast resolve in countering ministerial schemes and in tackling postwar economic problems. These upper-class patriots pushed in 1763 and 1764 for a denunciation of the new, oppressive British proposals; they marched in the van of the forces battling the Stamp Act; and they headed the opposition to the Townshend Acts. These partisans also distinguished themselves by their enthusiasm for nonimportation as a means of relieving glutted markets and easing the burden of debt crushing the colonies. The nonexpansionists, by contrast, were reluctant to support or were bitterly hostile to such protests. Although these individuals would have preferred that Britain adopt more lenient policies and although they too groaned under the weight of the postwar slump, their belief in the relative weakness of America and its necessary dependence on the mother country kept them from endorsing defiant measures.

During the stormy 1760s the success of the expansionists varied from colony to colony. In South Carolina and Massachusetts the revolutionary movement helped them gain effective control over local politics. South Carolina expansionists secured an unshakable grip over the lower house with the October 1765 election, while in the Bay Colony, affluent patriots, working closely with the lower-class popular party, achieved a similar victory in May 1766. In New York and Pennsylvania the nonexpansionists displayed greater strength. The two elite factions of New York alternated in power, although the decade ended, significantly, with the cautious DeLanceys dominating the lower chamber and provincial politics in general. The Quaker party maintained its hold on the Pennsylvania legislature throughout these years, frequently retarding, though never wholly blocking, the revolutionaries' programs. In Virginia nonexpansionists were the majority party in the House of Burgesses and could claim the leading grandees in most of the province; however, in the Old Dominion, where the danger posed by a restless urban lower class was absent, nonexpansionists were more open to the suasions of the patriots.

While both upper-class parties welcomed the support of the common people, and while both pulled back from popular excesses, as a broad generalization, during this decade the expansionists strengthened their ties with the less wealthy citizens, and particularly with the artisans in the port towns. Mechanics and, to a lesser extent, farmers had their own reasons for supporting the revolutionary movement: they regarded the struggle against Britain as an opportunity to amplify their voice in society, and they often shared the economic grievances the expansionists addressed. But upper-class patriots were democrats by necessity, not by inclination, and were quick to condemn riotous behavior. Restless backcountry settlers in South Carolina received little sympathy from the revolutionary elite, and in New York the 1766 tenant rebellion briefly complicated provincial politics when it forced patriot manor lords to look to the British army for aid. In Massachusetts, where the less wealthy formed a vigorous third faction, the power of the popular party had become awesome by the end of the decade, and the expansionists temporarily severed their ties with that group. Moreover, during this period lower-class militance and consciousness rose markedly—a development of no small import for the struggles of the 1770s.

As in earlier years, the coherence and formal structure of the elite parties differed from one colony to the next. The sharpest definition of factional lines appeared in Pennsylvania and New York, where tickets were announced and party affiliations often well known. By contrast, such outward signs were rarely present in Virginia and South Carolina and only occasionally evident in Massachusetts. There, during much of the decade, the popular party and expansionists were yoked together as the Friends of Liberty. In every province, however, politically active individuals discussed the role of factions and were aware of allegiances.

Finally, members of both parties enunciated their outlooks. Most, it is true, showed their convictions by their consistent behavior over time or with brief pronouncements about the issues at hand. But some of the most outspoken partisans, particularly in the expansionist camp, drew from a rich palette to depict their vision of America's future course. With the Bourbons driven from North America and colonial population soaring, the elaborations of the expansionist persuasion became ever more confident and daring. Far from unnerved by the clash with the mother country, articulate patriots in every province argued that Britain would be the one to suffer in any test of wills. The writings of the nonexpansionists underwent no comparable flowering and often seemed merely reactive. Many granted the expansionists' contentions about the rapid growth of the New World but asserted that the burgeoning colonies must be subordinate to London lest discord and confusion reign supreme.

CHAPTER 7

The Depression
of the 1760s

"Having taken into our most serious consideration the present state of the trade of this colony," the 1769 Virginia nonimportation pact intoned, "and of *American* commerce in general, [we] observe with anxiety that the debt due to Great Britain is very great, and that the means of paying the debt in the present situation of affairs are likely to become more precarious."[1] The Old Dominion's resolves, drawn up by expansionists George Washington and George Mason, exemplified the concern of the wealthy patriots for the health of the economy—a concern heightened by the hard times that oppressed every colony during the 1760s. For the affluent revolutionaries this resolve to counter the postwar slump stood second only to their determination to protest the new ministerial programs; indeed, in the late 1760s the problems of indebtedness and glutted markets held center stage. Despite the universality of the downturn, conditions differed perceptibly from one province to the next and between city and countryside, and these distinctions helped shape local responses. Consequently, along with the familiar litany of parliamentary enactments, an examination of the depression that followed the French and Indian War forms a crucial backdrop to the agitation of this era.

» «

Two long-term developments, both produced by fluctuations in the pace of British growth, made the hard times in the 1760s especially severe. The first of these changes was the constriction in the flow of British funds to the New World after 1760. From 1745 to 1760 the

1. Virginia Nonimportation Revolves, May 17–18, 1769, *The Papers of Thomas Jefferson*, ed. Julian P. Boyd et al. (Princeton, 1950–), I, 28.

amount of credit the mother country extended to America increased remarkably, reflecting the broad expansion of business activity in Britain. English shippers grew ever more willing to trust marginal traders with goods and gradually stretched the credit period granted to colonial importers beyond the six-month term typical in the mid-1740s; by 1760 a Philadelphia importer could state firmly, "From London we have twelve months' credit for our goods."[2] Similarly, Glasgow houses also offered more liberal terms in their trade with the tobacco colonies, establishing chains of stores that provided the smaller planters with a new source of dry goods and financing.[3]

As long as British merchants were willing to pile loan upon loan, as they were between 1745 and 1760, the colonists benefited handsomely; such funds allowed Americans to make their estates more productive and to acquire more of the comforts of life. "Within these 25 years," a Virginia trader observed in 1766, "£1000 due to a merchant was looked upon as a sum immense and never to be got over. Ten times that sum is now spoke of with indifference. . . . Luxury and expensive living have gone hand in hand with the increase of wealth. In 1740 I don't remember to have seen such a thing as a Turkey carpet in the country except a small thing in a bedchamber. Now nothing are so common as Turkey or Wilton carpets, the whole furniture of rooms elegant and every appearance of opulence. All this is in a great measure owing to the credit which the planters have had from England."[4] New Yorker Cadwallader Colden summed up the changes more succinctly: "The manner of living among all ranks of people is now at a much higher rate than formerly."[5]

But ever more generous extensions of British credit only staved off the ultimate reckoning, and by the 1760s the colonies owed a staggering sum to shippers in the mother country. Barlow Trecothick, a

2. On long-term trends, see Marc Egnal, "The Economic Development of the Thirteen Continental Colonies, 1720 to 1775," *WMQ*, 3d ser., xxxiii (1975), 191–222. This discussion of British economic growth generally follows Phyllis Deane and W. A. Cole, *British Economic Growth, 1688–1959: Trends and Structure* (Cambridge, England, 1962), chaps. 1–3; James & Drinker to John Lindoe, Aug. 26, 1760, James & Drinker Letterbook, HSP. On marginal traders, see Marc Egnal and Joseph A. Ernst, "An Economic Interpretation of the American Revolution," *WMQ*, 3d ser. xxix (1972), 15–16.

3. Marc Egnal, "The Pennsylvania Economy, 1748–1762: An Analysis of Short-Run Fluctuations in the Context of Long-Run Changes in the Atlantic Trading Community" (Ph.D. diss., Univ. of Wisconsin, 1974), 121–29, 238–42; Jacob M. Price, "The Rise of Glasgow in the Chesapeake Tobacco Trade, 1707–1775," *WMQ*, 3d ser., xi (1954), 177–99.

4. John Wayles to Farrell & Jones, Aug. 30, 1766, John M. Hemphill ii, ed., "John Wayles Rates His Neighbors," *VMHB*, lxvi (1958), 305.

5. Cadwallader Colden to Board of Trade, Aug. 9, 1764, NYHS *Cols.*, ix (1876), 341–42.

leading "North American" merchant in London, reported to the House of Commons in 1766:

> The Committee of the Merchants of London trading to North America . . . do unanimously authorize me to give it as their opinion, that at the lowest compilation there is due the merchants of London only £2,900,000
>
> The agent for the merchants in Bristol authorizes in the same manner to say that there is due that town 800,000
> Ditto from Glasgow (Virginia and Maryland only) 500,000
> Ditto from Liverpool 150,000
> Ditto from Manchester 100,000
> £4,450,000
>
> Besides sums due to Lancaster, Whitehaven, Birmingham, Sheffield, Leeds, Norwich, Wakefield, Halifax, and other manufacturing towns, which must considerably augment the balance due from North America.[6]

The crunch for the colonies came after 1760, when the British economy entered a long period of slow growth, and the swollen flow of credit to the New World gradually shrank to an uncertain stream. British houses no longer considered extending the credit period but instead discussed returning to a shorter term and, in general, grew more cautious about financing new correspondents. Retrenchment was the watchword of the day. This long-term slowdown exacerbated the depression of the 1760s and muted the recovery between 1769 and 1771. Only after 1783 would the British economy embark upon a new wave of expansion.[7]

A second long-term development—the slackening of West Indian growth after 1760—also deepened the slump, oppressing, most particularly, the inhabitants of the port cities and New England farmers. Traders had long relied on profits from the sugar islands to aid them during downturns in the dry goods trade and had reveled in favorable conditions in the Caribbean between 1745 and 1760. However, the gradual slowdown in Britain after 1760 dampened growth in the islands, and northern merchants soon discovered that the sugar planters were unable both to cover the rising cost of such provisions as flour and bread and to allow exporters a respectable profit. "Since this time two years," Thomas Clifford of Philadelphia complained to a West Indian correspondent in 1766, "[with] almost every adventure I have shipped the accounts have been closed with a loss."[8] Mer-

6. "Trecothick's Observations on the Merchants' Petition," 1766, Add. MSS 33,030, fol. 215, BM.
7. Egnal, "Economic Development," 217; Egnal and Ernst, "Economic Interpretation," 3–32.
8. Thomas Clifford to Roach & Niles, Apr. 5, 1765, Clifford Letterbook, HSP; Marc

chants responded to such adversity by venturing cargoes less frequently and shipping more often on a commission basis.[9]

The slow growth of the island economies also worsened the depression of the 1760s for New England farmers and fishermen because their products were destined so overwhelmingly for West Indian markets. Consequently, while prices (and demand) for lumber, livestock, and fish had strengthened between 1745 and 1760, quotations for these goods remained level after 1760. The slowdown in the Caribbean had less impact on the grain growers of the middle colonies, for although much of their harvest went to the islands, a sizable portion after 1760 went to southern Europe, and demand from that quarter helped push up prices throughout the Atlantic trading world.[10]

» «

Although long-term changes aggravated the slump of the 1760s, the immediate cause of this depression in the New World was the short-term difficulty the British economy had in righting itself after the Seven Years' War. Unemployment, decreased domestic demand, and the overextension of mercantile credit battered English businesses. These firms in turn tightened the screws on colonial debtors, many of whom were grossly overextended for goods purchased in the heady days of the war. Viewed more closely, economic conditions in Britain and the colonies during the generally depressed decade of the 1760s described two subcycles. In America the first subcycle lasted from 1760 to 1766, with 1765 the worst year and 1766 a time of mild recovery. The second and harsher span stretched from 1766 to 1770 and touched its nadir in most provinces in 1768. Only in 1769 and 1770 did business activity in Great Britain rebound and help foster better times in the New World.[11]

Egnal, "The Changing Structure of Philadelphia's Trade with the British West Indies, 1750–1775," *PMHB*, xcix (1975), 155–66.

9. Egnal, "Changing Structure," 166–79; William S. Sachs, "The Business Outlook in the Northern Colonies, 1750–1775" (Ph.D. diss., Columbia Univ., 1957), 170–77; W. T. Baxter, *The House of Hancock: Business in Boston, 1724–1775* (Cambridge, Mass., 1945), 272.

10. Sachs, "Business Outlook," 172, 175–77, 185–87; Anne Bezanson et al., *Prices in Colonial Pennsylvania* (Philadelphia, 1935), app.; Arthur H. Cole, *Wholesale Commodity Prices in the United States, 1700–1861: Statistical Supplement* (Cambridge, Mass., 1938); David Klingaman, "Food Surpluses and Deficits in the American Colonies, 1768–1772," *JEH*, xxxi (1971), 553–69.

11. On conditions in Great Britain, see T. S. Ashton, *Economic Fluctuations in England, 1700–1800* (Oxford, 1959); Richard B. Sheridan, "The British Credit Crisis of 1772 and the American Colonies," *JEH*, xx (1960), 174–85. Valuable primary material is contained in letters received, Wharton MSS, HSP; *The Beekman Mercantile Papers, 1764–1799*, ed. Philip L. White, 3 vols., consec. pagin. (New York, 1956), 728; and in Feb. 1766 testimony before Parliament, Add. MSS. 33,030, BM.

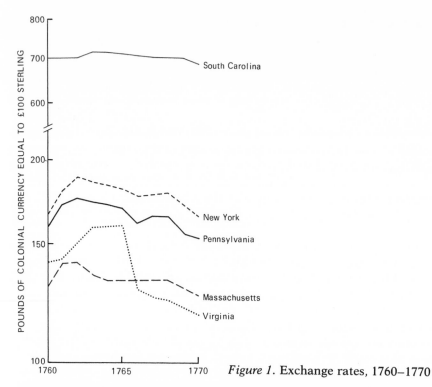

Figure 1. Exchange rates, 1760–1770

SOURCE: John J. McCusker, *Money and Exchange in Europe and America, 1600–1775: A Handbook* (Chapel Hill, N.C., 1978). McCusker's Pennsylvania figures have been supplemented by the series in Egnal, "The Pennsylvania Economy," 307–10. Mc-Cusker's data for South Carolina have been corrected using the quotations in *The Papers of Henry Laurens*, ed. Philip M. Hamer et al. (Columbia, S.C., 1967–   ), vols. III–VII.

The weight of the depression fell unevenly on the different groups that composed urban and rural America but pressed nowhere so hard as upon the inhabitants of the northern cities—Boston, New York, and Philadelphia. In these centers the first hints that wartime prosperity would yield to a postwar slump appeared as early as the summer of 1760. The fall of Canada led to a sharp reduction in military requisitions, as well as to an increase in the cost of sterling bills of exchange, which American merchants used to pay British creditors (figure 1). Traders began to complain about a "scarcity of money," shorthand for the difficulties the colonists encountered in paying off their debts to one another and to the British. Despite such ill auguries, between 1760 and 1762, importers in the northern cities benefited from the relative affluence of the countryside; continued, if reduced, military purchasing; and the specie that had entered the

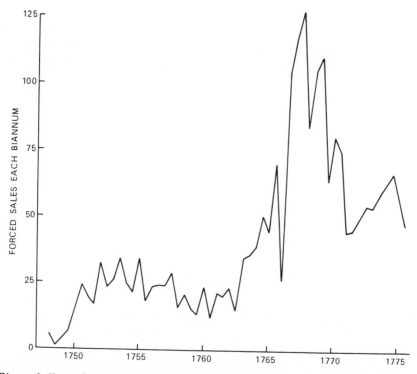

Figure 2. Forced sales of property in the Philadelphia area, 1748–1775

SOURCES: This series, now deposited in Scott Library, York University, records all forced sales of property listed in the *Pennsylvania Gazette,* 1748–75. Each sale was counted only once—at its first listing. While the breakdown varied from year to year, roughly 50 percent of these bankruptcies were in the city and county of Philadelphia, and a total of 85 percent were in Bucks, Chester, and Philadelphia (city and county). The remaining actions were scattered through backcountry Pennsylvania, western New Jersey, and Delaware.

colonies during the preceding five years. There were few bankruptcies in the early 1760s, few forced sales of property (figure 2), and comparatively favorable conditions in urban real estate markets.[12]

The clouds of economic depression began to darken in 1763 as the pressure of English houses on colonial importers and of importers on local shopkeepers took its toll. "Money is become so scarce among

12. James & Drinker to William Neate, Oct. 22, 1761, James & Drinker to Neate & Pigou, July 1, 1762, James & Drinker Letterbook; Egnal, "Pennsylvania Economy," 227–53; John Rowe to Lane & Booth, Feb. 24, 1762, *Letters and Diary of John Rowe . . . ,* ed. Anne R. Cunningham (Boston, 1903), 415; Invoice, July 10, 1762, Dana Papers, 1674–1769, MHS: John J. Waters, Jr. *The Otis Family in Provincial and Revolutionary Massachusetts* (Chapel Hill, N.C., 1968), 127–29; U.S. Bureau of the Census, *Historical Statistics of the United States, Colonial Times to 1970,* 2 vols., consec. pagin. (Washington, D.C., 1975), 1176–77.

us," said New Yorker Gerard Beekman, and John Kidd of Philadelphia explained to a London correspondent, "The many shocks the trade of this place has met with for this two years past has put it out of my power to make your remittance."[13] At least six Quaker City houses closed their doors in 1763, including Scott & McMichael, whose debts totaled over thirty thousand pounds sterling ("the greatest break ever known on this side the water," observed one firm).[14] Forced sales of land and property climbed. Before 1763 creditors had initiated in the New York mayor's court no more than sixteen suits in any one year; in 1763 they commenced forty-six such actions, generally for small sums. Similarly, in Pennsylvania sheriff's sales rose to new heights, with about 40 percent of these distraints in the city and county of Philadelphia (figure 2).[15]

By 1764 the pattern of a worsening urban depression had become clear. The downturn exacerbated the problems of poverty in the cities. The complaint of overseers of the poor in Philadelphia was typical: "Into rooms but ten or eleven feet square, . . . [we] have been obliged to crowd five or six beds."[16] In every city the number of individuals dependent on public charity and the amount of money devoted to relief soared well above the levels recorded earlier. Moreover, the nascent money market in the colonies virtually dried up. "We are in a distressed condition," Richard Waln, Jr., of Philadelphia explained; "all the silver and gold is shipped to England."[17] Other traders complained of the near impossibility of borrowing money on interest.[18]

The hard times also slowed the sale of dry goods. John Hancock

13. Gerard G. Beekman to Thomas Cranston, Feb. 17, 1763, *Beekman Papers*, 431; John Watts to Gen. Monckton, July 23, 1763, MHS *Cols.*, 4th ser., IX (1871), 482–83; John Kidd to Rawlinson, Davison, & Newman, Oct. 17, 1763, Kidd Letterbook, HSP; James & Drinker to Preeson Bowdoin, Dec. 10, 1763, James & Drinker Letterbook.

14. James & Drinker to Neate & Pigou, Dec. 10, Mar. 7, 1763, James & Drinker Letterbook.

15. Gerard G. Beekman to Samuel Fowler, Dec. 6, 1763, *Beekman Papers*, 452; Sachs, "Business Outlook," 132–33; James & Drinker to Edward Pancoast, Oct. 17, 1763, James & Drinker Letterbook; John Watts to Lascelles, Clark, & Dalin, May 13, 1763, *Letter Book of John Watts, Merchant and Councillor of New York* (NYHS *Cols.*, LXI) (New York, 1928), 143; Joseph A. Ernst, *Money and Politics in America, 1755–1775; A Study in the Currency Act of 1764 and the Political Economy of Revolution* (Chapel Hill, N.C., 1973), 3–17.

16. Quoted in Gary B. Nash, "Poverty and Poor Relief in Pre-Revolutionary Philadelphia," *WMQ*, 3d ser., XXXIII (1976), 13–14.

17. Richard Waln, Jr., to Nicholas Waln, Mar. 10, 1764, Waln Collection, Box H, HSP; John Watts to Scott, Pringle, Cheap, & Co., Feb. 5, 1764, *Letter Book of Watts*, 228; Gary B. Nash, "Urban Wealth and Poverty in Pre-Revolutionary America," *Journal of Interdisciplinary History*, VI (1976), 555–67.

18. Gerard G. Beekman to John Hurd, Feb. 21, 1764, *Beekman Papers*, 461; James & Drinker to W. Sitgreaves, Jan. 17, 1764, James & Drinker Letterbook.

complained of "the dullness of trade" in Boston, while New Yorker John Watts observed that "commerce is so stagnated here that little or nothing sells, and payment for what does sell keeps the same dull pace."[19] Reflecting a brief spate of prosperity in England, the value of exports shipped in 1764 from the mother country to the northern colonies rose to the highest level (£1,456,000) it would reach in the depressed 1760s. The short-lived respite in Britain's demand for remittance was of limited benefit to the colonists, however, and the flood of manufactures worsened conditions in already glutted markets. Looking out at Philadelphia's harbor, Thomas Clifford sighed: "The ships from London have brought vast quantities of goods, some of which I think they never will get paid for as that branch is quite overdone."[20] Profit margins on the sale of various fabrics had fallen well below the merchant's break-even point before the end of 1760, and these markups would remain extraordinarily low until the last years of the decade. Figure 3 presents the *gross* profit on the sale of textiles in Philadelphia. This calculation deducts from the local selling price the first cost, as well as charges for freight, insurance, and exchange. Figure 4 shows *net* profit, which includes the deductions made for gross profit but also subtracts a sum for the estimated loss through depreciation and the cost of salaries, storage, and local shipping.

In 1765 the first subcycle sounded its trough, and conditions were nowhere so bad as in Boston, whose hinterland had, for several decades, grown less rapidly than those of the middle colony ports. In January, Nathaniel Wheelwright, a Boston importer with outstanding debts of £170,000 sterling announced his bankruptcy, frightening the town's trading community and touching off a series of other failures. Hancock bewailed this "most prodigious shock."[21] Liquidation was also the order of the day in New York, where John Watts observed: "Business is here very languid. The weak must go to the wall: frequent bankruptcies and growing more frequent."[22] Even

19. John Hancock to Devonshire & Reeve, Dec. 7, 1764, *John Hancock: His Book*, ed. Abram English Brown (Boston, 1898), 57; John Watts to William Brymer, May 15, 1764, *Letter Book of Watts*, 254.
20. Thomas Clifford to Isaac Cox, Apr. 7, 1764, Clifford Letterbook; John Reynell to Francis Rybot, May 30, 1764, Reynell Letterbook, HSP; Gerard G. Beekman to David & William Ross, Feb. 13, 1764, Gerard G. Beekman to John Hurd, Feb. 21, 1764, *Beekman Papers*, 460, 461.
21. John Hancock to Barnard & Harrison, Jan. 21, Feb. 7, Apr. 18, 1765, *Hancock: His Book*, 61, 63, 67; Sachs, "Business Outlook," 131–32.
22. John Watts to Sir William Baker, Aug. 11, 1765, *Letter Book of Watts*, 368; Peter R. Livingston to Robert Livingston, Jr., Jan. 7, 1765, Livingston Family Papers, reel 7, FDRL; Gerard G. Beekman to David & William Ross, Mar. 7, 1765, *Beekman Papers*, 481.

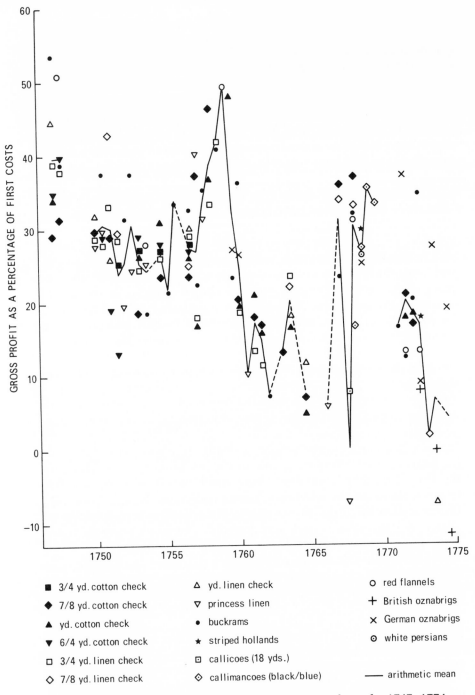

Figure 3. Gross profits in the Philadelphia dry goods trade, 1747–1774

those traders who remained afloat found remittances ever more difficult to obtain. "Money is much scarcer here at present than it hath
been some years past," Quaker Thomas Clifford reported, and Daniel
Roberdeau, another Philadelphian, remarked, "I have no more expectation of raising the money than I have of drawing blood out of a
flint."[23] In his pamphlet *The Late Regulations*, written at the end of
1765, John Dickinson painted a grim picture of the economy of the
commercial provinces: "Trade is decaying, and all credit is expiring.
Money is become so extremely scarce that reputable freeholders find
it impossible to pay debts which are trifling in comparison to their
estates. . . . Thus the consumers break the shopkeepers; they break
the merchants; and the shock must be felt as far as *London*."[24] The
staggering burden of debt and the excessive inventories of unsold
wares encouraged merchants from both parties to support a boycott
of British goods.

The economy of the northern cities showed some slight improvement in 1766, bringing the first subcycle to a close. The nonimportation agreements adopted in the three port cities restricted the influx
of goods during the first months of the year and reduced the total

23. Thomas Clifford to Nathaniel Green & Co., Sept. 17, 1765, Clifford Letterbook;
Israel Pemberton to John Pleasants, Nov. 11, 1765, Pemberton Papers, HSP; Daniel
Roberdeau to Meyer & Hall, Oct. 21, Nov. 9, 1765, Roberdeau Letterbook, HSP.

24. John Dickinson, *The Late Regulations*, in *The Writings of John Dickinson*, ed. Paul
L. Ford (vol. XIV of HSP *Memoirs*) (Philadelphia, 1895), 227–28.

SOURCES: Figure 3. This graph plots gross profit for specific fabrics based on the
following formulas:

$$\text{gross profit} = \frac{\text{sterling receipts} - \text{total sterling cost}}{\text{total sterling cost}} \times 100$$

$$\text{total sterling cost} = (\text{Eng. sterling unit price}) \times (1 + \text{freight} + \text{insurance} + \text{commission} + \text{charges})$$

$$\text{sterling receipts} = \frac{\text{Pa. currency unit price}}{0.01 \times \text{exchange rate}}$$

Deposited in Scott Library, York University, are the following sets of data compiled by
the author from merchant record books: the English sterling prices that the British
shipper charged the colonial merchant, the Pennsylvania currency price that the colonial merchant charged the shopkeepers, insurance, and freight rates for London-Philadelphia shipments. Figures for exchange rates are presented in McCusker, *Money and
Exchange*, 185–86. Commissions were typically 2.5 percent of value, while sundry
charges added another 1 percent. Computations are based on half years, with the
English costs drawn from the *preceding* half year.

NOTE: The line connects arithmetic mean of individual transactions. A solid line
indicates that information is available for successive biannums, while a dashed line is
used where a single half year is missing. In the computation of profits Pennsylvania
prices were interpolated where a single biannum was missing.

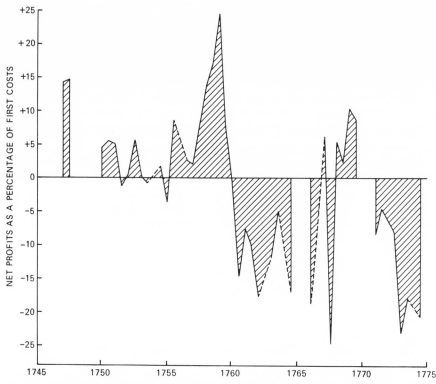

Figure 4. Net profits in the Philadelphia dry goods trade, 1747–1774

SOURCE: This graph uses the data for gross profits plotted in figure 3, but subtracts 25 percent to provide a curve for net profits. A solid line connects data for successive half years; a dashed line has been used where a single biannum is missing. This 25 percent reduction reflects charges for overhead, salaries, unsalable or damaged inventory, local transportation costs, and losses due to bad debts. This figure (admittedly an estimate) is based on the comments of various merchants about their profits and costs. See particularly the following: James & Drinker to John Clitherall, July 16, 1761, James & Drinker to David Barclay & Sons, Nov. 4, 1761, James & Drinker to Neate & Pigou, Jan. 30, 1762, James & Drinker to John Clayton, Mar. 15, 1762, James & Drinker Letterbook; Thomas Willing to John Perks, Jan. 4, 1757, Robert Morris to Coddington Carrington, Jan. 28, 1756, Thomas Willing to Snee, Steer, & Berkin, Nov. 21, 1755, Willing Letterbook, HSP; James & Drinker to John Clitherall, June 4, 1771, Henry Drinker Letterbook, HSP; William Pollard to Thomas Earle, June 19, 1772, Pollard Letterbook, HSP.

imports for 1766 to the lowest levels of the period between 1764 and 1768. The repeal of the Stamp Act also offered an encouraging note. "The happy consequences resulting from so glorious an event," rejoiced New Yorker John Broome, "will doubtless be sensibly felt by all who have embarked in a mercantile bottom."[25] Finally, the "pro-

25. John Broome to Mr. Lloyd, May 30, 1766, quoted in Sachs, "Business Outlook," 194; *Historical Statistics of the U.S.*, 1176–77.

digious demand for wheat for the London market" made sterling bills more available, facilitating remittances to England and dropping exchange rates in Philadelphia and New York to the lowest levels since 1760 (figure 1).[26]

The improvement evident in 1766 can easily be exaggerated, however. The demands of British creditors, who were caught in the grip of hard times at home, did not lessen, and colonial merchants all too frequently echoed New Yorker Gerard Beekman's observation that "money is scarce and times very bad."[27] Returns on dry goods sales in the Quaker City remained low (figures 3, 4). Moreover, the urban poor continued to bear the brunt of the downturn, with hundreds of individuals in every city relying on public relief. A Philadelphia grand jury reported that many of "the laboring people, and others in low circumstances, . . . who are willing to work, cannot obtain sufficient employment to support themselves and their families."[28]

With the slowdown in economic activity in 1767 the second subcycle was underway; moreover, because the deepening depression in Britain made English houses press American debtors ever more closely, the second half of the decade was a more troubled time for the colonists than the first half. Sheriff's sales in Pennsylvania rose to new heights, and in every port importers scrambled to preserve their liquidity. "The situation of our trade and the scarcity of money is such that I have almost come to a resolution to suspend the importation of goods for a year or two," John Hancock announced, and James Beekman of New York informed an English correspondent, "I expected to have made you remittance for what has been due, but the dullness of trade and scarcity of cash has prevented me. . . . Instead of receiving cash for debts due, I am obliged to take bonds, . . . [which], although good, will not pay debts due to you."[29] Several Philadelphia houses failed, including Baynton, Wharton, & Morgan, which stopped payment on obligations totaling over sixty thousand pounds sterling. Dry

26. Daniel Roberdeau to Abraham Chalwill & Co., Nov. 25, 1766, Roberdeau Letterbook.

27. Gerard G. Beekman to David & William Ross, Jan. 14, 1766, Gerard G. Beekman to David Beekman, June 17, 1766, Gerard G. Beekman to Samuel & Thomas Fludyer, Nov. 26, 1766, *Beekman Papers*, 490, 500, 708; John Reynell to Henry Groth, May 27, 1766, Reynell Letterbook; John Hancock to Barnard & Harrison, Oct. 15, 1766, *Hancock: His Book*, 134.

28. Quoted in Nash, "Poverty and Poor Relief," 21n; Nash, "Urban Wealth," 556–67.

29. John Hancock to Harrison & Barnard, July 29, 1767, John Hancock to Harrison, Barnard, & Sprag, Oct. 16, 1767, John Hancock to George Haley, Oct. 16, Dec. 15, 1767, *Hancock: His Book*, 139, 143–44, 146, 150–51; James Beekman to Thomas Harris, Apr. 3, 1767, James Beekman to Peach & Pierce, Sept. 24, 1767, James Beekman to Thomas Owen, Dec. 2, 1767, *Beekman Papers*, 777, 867, 847; John Reynell to Henry Groth, Apr. 27, 1767, Reynell Letterbook; Thomas Riche to Smyth & Sudler, Nov. 5, 1767, Riche Letterbook, HSP.

goods profits in the Quaker City, however, while ranging widely for different fabrics, suggest some improvement (figures 3, 4).[30]

In Boston, New York, and Philadelphia 1768 marked the nadir of the second subcycle. The value of British exports entering the three ports attained the highest levels recorded from 1766 to 1770, while the worsening glut of dry goods, which encouraged importers to contemplate nonimportation, fostered the growth of vendues—public auctions at which manufactures were sold at low rates. These sales often imported goods directly from England, as well as disposing of wares that established merchants found impossible to sell. In Boston advertisements for the auctions reached a decadal peak in 1768; that year New Yorker James Beekman reported, "Goods . . . are a mere drug with us, and are sold out of stores at very little advance, but at the daily vendues may be bought for less than prime cost."[31] Vendues also troubled Philadelphia merchants, although the problem was perhaps less grave there than in the other cities.[32]

The small, if palpable, difference in the impact of the depression on the northern ports helps explain the timing of each city's decision to enter the nonimportation agreements during 1768 or early 1769. Boston expansionists, who confronted the worst economic situation of the three ports, were the boldest advocates of a boycott, proposing in March 1768 a coordinated agreement embracing the three towns and, when that fell through, concluding on August 1 a noncontingent pact. In New York, where conditions were only slightly better, traders backed the abortive March proposal, and then in late August followed the Bostonians' lead by signing an independent agreement. Philadelphia importers, however, were buoyed by the comparative prosperity of the city's extensive grain-growing hinterland; they scuttled Boston's initial plan and joined merchants in the other two ports only in February 1769.

Whatever slender good fortune the upper classes in any of the cities could claim during the second subcycle—and most merchants rode out the storms of these years—there was no respite for those dependent on public charity until the end of the decade. In Philadelphia the bettering house and the hospital for the indigent between them tended to over seven hundred individuals in 1768; the city poor law rates

30. John Reynell to Mildred & Roberts, Oct. 3, Nov. 20, 1767, John Reynell to Henry Groth, Nov. 5, 1767, Reynell Letterbook; Thomas Riche to Cornelius Low, Dec. 6, 1767, Riche Letterbook.
31. James Beekman to Peach & Pierce, Feb. 18, 1768, James Beekman to Pomeroys & Hodgkin, May 4, 1768, James Beekman to Thomas Harris, May 5, 1768, *Beekman Papers*, 867–68, 916, 796; Dave Hutchinson, "A Quantitative Approach to Business Cycles in Massachusetts, 1763–1774" (seminar paper, York Univ., 1971); *Historical Statistics of the U.S.*, 1176–77.
32. Thomas Clifford to William Smith, Dec. 12, 1768, Clifford Letterbook.

climbed to six pence per pound of assessable estate—the high-water mark of the colonial period. Similar reports were filed in New York and in Boston, where one petition noted that "the town for a long time has been devising means to employ the great numbers of poor women and children that are in it."[33] More generally, levies for those on relief and admissions to the almshouses demonstrate that for the lowest stratum of society the last half of the 1760s was far grimmer than the first half.[34]

Gradually during 1769 and 1770 the urban economies of the north recovered. The end of hard times in England meant less pressure on colonial traders, while the nonimportation agreements allowed American merchants to collect debts more readily and remit to Britain. Throughout the North the cost of sterling exchange fell sharply in 1769 and 1770, reflecting the improving balance of payments in the colonies (figure 1). "Instead of being debtors," Bostonian Samuel Cooper boasted to a London friend in the summer of 1770, "we are becoming creditors to your merchants, and some of us have ordered money instead of goods to be remitted."[35] The boycotts also helped importers clear their shelves of old dry goods. "The clerks tell me more than half the stores in town will be quite clear in a short time," Thomas Clifford reported from Philadelphia in November 1769, and letters in 1770 testify to the scarcity of most imported wares.[36] While urban poverty seemed less susceptible to dramatic improvement, there were at least some signs of amelioration at the end of the 1760s. Admissions to the Philadelphia bettering house dropped, allowing the city to halve its poor rate from six pence to three. And throughout the northern cities the boycotts encouraged local manufacturing, removing some poor from the public rolls.[37]

Buttressed by the gains from rice, indigo, and slave sales, Charlestonians suffered less severely from the depression of the 1760s than did the urbanites of the North. A careful balance must characterize any depiction of the Charleston economy, for while many individuals,

33. Subscribers for Manufactory, Mar. 15, 1768, Ezekiel Price Papers, MHS; Gerard G. Beekman to Samuel Fowler, Jan. 11, 1768, *Beekman Papers*, 505; Ernst, *Money and Politics*, 254; Nash, "Poverty and Poor Relief," 20–23; Carl Bridenbaugh, *Cities in Revolt: Urban Life in America, 1743–1776* (New York, 1955), 321.

34. Nash, "Poverty and Poor Relief," 9–25; Nash, "Urban Wealth," 560–63.

35. July 2, 1770, "Letters of Samuel Cooper to Thomas Pownall, 1769–1777," *AHR*, VII (1902–3), 320; Thomas Clifford to Parr & Bulkeley, Apr. 26, 1770, Clifford Letterbook.

36. Thomas Clifford to Lancelot Cowper, Nov. 8, June 26, 1769, Dec. 20, 1770, Clifford Letterbook; John Reynell to Benjamin Lightfoot, Apr. 25, 1770, Reynell Letterbook.

37. Nash, "Poverty and Poor Relief," 20–23; J. Thomas Scharf and Thompson Westcott, *History of Philadelphia, 1609–1884*, 3 vols. (Philadelphia, 1884), I, 262.

particularly among the lower classes, suffered from the contraction, most large importers easily weathered the rigors of the decade. As a consequence, merchants in Charleston rarely showed the same alacrity as their northern brethren in endorsing economic protests.[38]

During the first phase of the downturn, 1760 to 1766, city traders confronted an array of problems similar in kind though not in severity to the ones encountered in the North. As early as 1761 John Guerard announced that "bills [of exchange] . . . are very scarce," and in 1763 Henry Laurens remarked, "I find payments both from planters and merchants come in too slack to serve my own engagements."[39] But Laurens also noted that even the newly established planters rarely defaulted on their debts. "If I were to tell you the total loss that we have sustained in that way," he informed a London house, "you would be pleased on our account to find it so small."[40] And though exchange rates rose above par between 1763 and 1765, the increase was far less than that observed in the northern ports (figure 1). Moreover, although traders complained about overstocked dry goods inventories, the problem never reached the proportions evident in the North, and Charlestonians showed little desire to join the commercial colonies in the boycotts of 1765–1766.[41]

Charleston merchants did undertake one step during the first subcycle to preserve their own and their customers' liquidity: in 1765 they adopted a three-year ban, to commence January 1, 1766, on the importation of slaves. The fate of Middleton, Liston, & Hope, a local house that defaulted on some of its payments in the summer of 1765 and collapsed the following year with outstanding debts of over forty-five thousand pounds sterling, illustrated the dangers that lay in wait for an improvident slave-trading firm. Most merchants backed the three-year prohibition, although few displayed any inordinate caution. Eyeing the prosperous countryside, importers compensated for the anticipated dearth by bringing record numbers of blacks into the colony in 1765. Governor Bull reported in December 1765 that this importation had "in great measure defeated the salutary end pro-

38. *Historical Statistics of the U.S.*, 1192–93; Cole, *Wholesale Commodity Prices: Statistical Supplement*, 15–69.

39. John Guerard to Robert & William Stebbing, June 15, 1761, Round Papers, D/DRc B26, Essex Record Office, Chelmsford, Eng.; Henry Laurens to Grubb & Watson, July 14, 1763, Laurens to Joseph Bower, Jan. 13, 1763, Laurens to John Knight, Feb. 14, 1763, Laurens to Alexander & James Baillie, Apr. 28, 1763, *The Papers of Henry Laurens*, ed. Philip M. Hamer et al. (Columbia, S.C., 1968–), III, 489, 216, 252, 429.

40. Laurens to Richard Oswald & Co., Feb. 15, 1763, *Papers of Laurens*, III, 260.

41. John J. McCusker, *Money and Exchange in Europe and America, 1600–1775* (Chapel Hill, N.C., 1978), 224; Laurens to Joseph Bower, Jan. 13, 1763, Laurens to John Knight, Feb. 14, 1763, Laurens to William Fisher, Jan. 9, 1764, Laurens to Isaac King, Sept. 6, 1764, *Papers of Laurens*, III, 216, 252–53, IV, 128, 403.

posed, as above 8000 [Negroes] have been imported this year, being nearly equal to three years' importations."[42]

Only the mechanics and laborers, who could not profit directly from the rice boom and who had few resources to insulate them from the deepening contraction, seemed hard hit by the downturn during this period. In 1766 the Fellowship Society, an artisan group formed earlier in the decade, applied to the Commons House for incorporation, announcing that it wanted "to afford relief to many poor distressed persons" who were without the benefit of "regular advice, attendance, lodging, diet and medicine." The assembly agreed to this request and also increased to eleven thousand pounds currency the portion of taxes earmarked for relief.[43]

Despite the vicissitudes of the poor, Charleston's good fortune impressed most visitors during the first half of the decade. "The city . . . has increased with sumptuous brick houses in very great number," exclaimed a New England trader in 1764. "One cannot go anywhere where one does not see new buildings and large and small houses started, half finished, and almost finished. To me who comes from poor, humble Rhode Island, it seems to me a new world. In spite of so much new building, I never knew the rent of houses so high."[44]

For the upper classes the second half of the decade was again marked by signs of prosperity, even if the problems associated with the slump were somewhat more severe than they had been before 1766. Laurens was not alone in complaining about a glut of dry goods. "The goods per *Fanny* come to an overstocked market in every article," he remarked in 1768.[45] Moreover, Charleston importers joined the nonimportation movement of 1768–1770, although they entered into their pact well after the northern cities and set forth an agreement that was looser than those signed in the other centers. Yet observers now as earlier in the 1760s underscored Charleston's economic good fortune rather than hardships. "We are regulating our port and harbor, going to build a sumptuous exchange and custom house, extending fine streets and laying out new ones . . . and many

---

42. Lt. Gov. William Bull to Board of Trade, Dec. 17, 1765, SCPR, xxx, 300; Laurens to Isaac King, Sept. 30, 1767, Laurens to William Reeve, Oct. 2, 1767, *Papers of Laurens*, v, 320, 323–24; *Historical Statistics of the U.S.*, 1173; *Biographical Directory of the South Carolina House of Representatives*, vol. II: Walter B. Edgar and N. Louise Bailey, eds., *The Commons House of Assembly, 1692–1775* (Columbia, S.C., 1977), 460–61.

43. Richard Walsh, *Charleston's Sons of Liberty: A Study of the Artisans, 1763–1789* (Columbia, S.C., 1959), 29–30.

44. Moses Lopez to Aaron Lopez, May 3, 1764, Thomas J. Tobias, ed., "Charlestown in 1764," *SCHM*, LXVII (1966), 67–68.

45. Laurens to James Habersham, Jan. 25, 1768, Laurens to James Grant, May 27, 1768, Laurens to John Tarleton, Dec. 27, 1768, *Papers of Laurens*, v, 564–66, 708, VI, 241.

other good things," boasted Laurens in 1767.[46] The following year printer Peter Timothy told his friend Benjamin Franklin: "I do not suppose there is a colony on this continent in so flourishing and promising a situation as South Carolina at present. . . . The exchange is begun, and will be an elegant structure. A new hospital is in some forwardness, and the old is to be converted into a proper workhouse. . . . The lawyers, doctors, and planters get rich apace; the merchants do not in general [do] so well."[47] For the affluent citizens of Charleston, the recovery of 1769–1770 brought to an end not a decade of misery but one of genuine, if at times spotty, prosperity.

For the common folk of Charleston, however, adversity mounted during the second subcycle. In 1767 the vestrymen requested permission to lodge the indigent in army barracks because of overcrowding in the workhouse and associated hospital, and the following year the lawmakers, in response to worsening conditions, voted funds for a new almshouse and revised the poor laws. Circumstances may have improved for the lower classes in 1769 and 1770 as British firms grew more generous with their credit, although several prominent artisans declared bankruptcy during these two years.[48]

» «

The depression of the 1760s also bore down upon rural America, although not always with the same severity as upon the cities. Massachusetts farmers, who scratched a living from rocky soils and lacked a lucrative staple, were among the groups hardest hit by the slump. The prices received for livestock and lumber, which were destined chiefly for the weak West Indian market, did not rise after 1760, while the climb in wheat and flour quotations hurt rather than helped the colony, since it was a net importer of these foodstuffs. Nor did any surge in earnings from the fishery aid the residents of coastal Massachusetts; the value of the catch remained stable or declined slightly during the 1760s. Because of such oppressive conditions, the rural citizens of Massachusetts were more involved in the "economic" protests of the decade than were their counterparts in the middle colonies.[49]

46. Laurens to James Grant, Mar. 23, 1767, ibid., v, 238–39.
47. Peter Timothy to Franklin, Sept. 3, 1768, *The Papers of Benjamin Franklin*, ed. Leonard W. Labaree et al. (New Haven, 1959–   ), xv, 201–2.
48. Walsh, *Charleston's Sons of Liberty*, 42; Bridenbaugh, *Cities in Revolt*, 322–23; Laurens to James Grant, Mar. 23, 1767, *Papers of Laurens*, v, 238–39.
49. Cole, *Wholesale Commodity Prices: Supplement*; Bezanson et al., *Prices in Colonial Pennsylvania*, app.; *Historical Statistics of the U.S.*, 1195; Sachs, "Business Outlook," 175–77, 185–88; Robert J. Taylor, *Western Massachusetts in the Revolution* (Providence, 1954), 58–59; Douglas Lamar Jones, "The Strolling Poor: Transiency in Eighteenth-Century Massachusetts," *Journal of Social History*, viii (1975), 28–54.

For farmers in New York and Pennsylvania, strong southern European and, in some years, English demand for grain helped blunt the impact of the postwar downturn. Prices of wheat, flour, and bread rose, as did the quantities shipped; flour exports from Pennsylvania, for example, swelled more than 60 percent from 1759–1761 to 1769–1771. Therefore, the contraction caused Pennsylvania and New York farmers little hardship before 1767. Forced sales of property in rural Pennsylvania remained at relatively low levels (figure 2), while data for acreage warranted in Cumberland and Lancaster counties, Pennsylvania, indicate a strong demand for new homesteads. New Yorker John Watts observed in 1763 that "the country has gained such strength by the continued high price of all kinds of produce . . . that it will be some time before the farmer can be brought to bend to his old standard."[50] Indentured laborers were in demand. "If the servants are chiefly what you expect them to be," a Philadelphia house informed its London correspondent, "we have very little doubt of their answering."[51]

After 1766 the decade-long contraction grew more severe, and reports from rural New York and Pennsylvania became mixed, with both prosperity and adversity in evidence. Those farmers who had kept their burden of indebtedness low were able to profit from the favorable world market for grain and to avoid the vicissitudes of an ever-greater "scarcity of money." Thus a Philadelphian in 1769 could favorably compare the husbandman's well-being with the city dweller's: "This [is] the best country in the world for laborers and handicrafts, and the worst for what may be called half-breed gentlemen with a capital."[52] But for other middle-colony landowners, the second half of the decade was punctuated by ever more insistent duns and, in some instances, by the threat of a sheriff's sale. Foreclosures soared in Pennsylvania (figure 2), and Henry Moore, governor of New York, reported in 1768 that there were "numberless instances of suits against farmers whose estates have been sold upon execution."[53] The

50. Sachs, "Business Outlook," 170–92; Bezanson et al., *Prices in Colonial Pennsylvania*, appendix; Helen L. Klopfer, "Statistics of Foreign Trade of Philadelphia, 1700–1800" (Ph.D. diss., Univ. of Pennsylvania, 1936); John Watts to Scott, Pringle, Cheap, & Co., Aug. 31, 1763, *Letter Book of Watts*, 178–79; James T. Lemon, *The Best Poor Man's Country: A Geographical Study of Early Southeastern Pennsylvania* (Baltimore, 1972), 68.

51. James & Drinker to Neate, Pigou, & Booth, Sept. 24, 1764, James & Drinker Letterbook.

52. Benjamin Fuller to Joseph Fuller, July 8, 1769, Benjamin Fuller Letterbook, HSP; Thomas Clifford to George Stockham, Nov. 26, 1767, Thomas Clifford to Lancelot Cowper, May 17, 23, 1768, Thomas Clifford to Capt. James Russell, Dec. 7, 1768, Clifford Letterbook; Richard Smith, Jr., to John Smith, Dec. 7, 1768, John Smith Correspondence, HSP.

53. Gov. Henry Moore to earl of Hillsborough, May 14, 1768, quoted in Ernst, *Money and Politics*, 254.

amount of new land taken up in Lancaster and Cumberland counties plummeted after 1766, and rural shopkeepers increasingly complained of financial stringency. "The scarcity of money is the reason that I cannot send you the balance just now," a Lancaster trader told his Philadelphia correspondent, while an Albany storekeeper explained to New Yorker James Beekman, "The declining condition of trade and the scarcity of money here is not to be expressed."[54]

Only in 1770 did conditions improve as the contraction eased. In Pennsylvania forced sales of property fell, and the acreage claimed by settlers rose once more.[55] But in general, middle-colony farmers seem not to have suffered as much as those in New England, and partly for that reason, during the 1760s they rarely gave formal support to the nonconsumption movement or gathered in provincial conventions as did their brethren in New England.

Because the demand for tobacco was weak, the depression hit Virginia planters with special severity. Prices for the weed, although fluctuating, increased little during the decade while colonial tobacco exports (about two-thirds of which came from Virginia and most of the rest from Maryland) climbed slowly, rising only 22 percent between 1759–1761 and 1769–1771. A run of short crops also hurt planters; between 1763 and 1769 tobacco shipments declined from ninety-eight million pounds to seventy million. Hard times led Virginians to advocate various measures of economic protest, such as nonimportation, even though the decentralized nature of the colony often frustrated these efforts.[56]

The first half of the decade seems to have been as difficult for the gentry of Virginia as the second half. Virginians "are greatly in debt to the mother country, which debt is daily increasing," Governor Fauquier observed as early as 1762, and by 1764 the unmistakable pallor of depression had settled over the Chesapeake.[57] "Poor Virginia," lamented one trader in that year, "what art thou reduced to,

54. Christian Wirtz to John Steinmetz, Oct. 10, 1769, Aubrey Roberts to John Steinmetz, Feb. 4, 1769, William & Young Keene to John Steinmetz, Feb. 13, 1769, John Steinmetz Mercantile Correspondence, HSP; Richard Waln, Jr., to Harford & Powell, Nov. 1769, Richard Waln Letterbook, HSP; Gerrit Lansing, Jr., to James Beekman, Apr. 24, 1769, *Beekman Papers*, 973; C. Colden to earl of Hillsborough, July 11, 1769, quoted in Carl Becker, *The History of Political Parties in the Province of New York, 1760–1776* (Madison, Wis., 1909), 79n; Sachs, "Business Outlook," 240.

55. Lemon, *Best Poor Man's Country*, 68.

56. *Historical Statistics of the U.S.*, 1198, 1189–91; Robert Beverley to Samuel Athawes, Sept. 6, 1769, Robert Beverley Letterbook, Library of Congress, microfilm at CWF.

57. Francis Fauquier to Board of Trade, Nov. 3, 1762, quoted in Calvin B. Coulter, "The Virginia Merchant" (Ph.D. diss., Princeton Univ., 1944), 227.

held in scorn and derision by the merchants of Great Britain and torn to pieces by their and our country law suits."[58] Nor was there a letup in 1765. "Things wear but a gloomy aspect," cried one storekeeper, "for the country is so excessively poor that even the industrious frugal man can scarcely live, and the least slip in our economy would be fatal."[59]

The economic disease in Virginia, during the first half of the 1760s, had several worrisome symptoms. Between 1762 and 1765 the exchange rate reached new heights, reflecting the difficulty planters found in securing remittances of any sort, as well as, more particularly, the disappearance of specie (figure 1). "I made it my business to collect all the gold and silver and was assisted by several merchants and the whole was £180 sterling," reported a merchant who left Virginia for Britain in the summer of 1765.[60] Slave sales also fell off. "The African trade to Virginia," an importer prophesied in 1764, "must soon be at an end, for the people will not soon pay for the Negroes they have already bought."[61] The purchase of slaves declined after 1762 and would remain at low levels until the last years of the decade.[62]

Some slight improvement was evident in 1766, marking the end of the first phase of the downturn. The cost of sterling exchange began to fall in November and December 1765 and continued its slide in 1766, a drop precipitated by the cessation of debt proceedings during the Stamp Act crisis. Many Virginia expansionists urged for economic reasons that the courts be kept shut until the abhorred measure was repealed. Virginians also benefited from a decline in the level of imports to the low point of the decade. Nonetheless, if muted at times, the rigors of the contraction still pervaded the Old Dominion's economic life. "I have several thousand due me for the great part of which I have brought suits above two years ago . . . but have not yet got judgments," a planter remarked. "Others I have not sued but entreated and persuaded but to no purpose, as money was so

58. John Baylor to John Norton, Sept. 18, 1764, *John Norton & Sons, Merchants of London and Virginia, Being the Papers from Their Counting House for the Years 1750 to 1795*, ed. Frances N. Mason (Richmond, 1937), 11–12; John Pleasants to Israel Pemberton, May 7, 1764, Pemberton Papers; George Washington to Robert Cary & Co., Aug. 10, 1764, *Writings of George Washington*, ed. J. C. Fitzpatrick, 39 vols. (Washington, D.C., 1931–44), ii, 416.

59. Peter Fontaine, Jr., to John Fontaine, July 8, 1765, James Maury to John Fontaine, Dec. 31, 1765, *Memoirs of a Huguenot Family . . .* , ed. Ann Maury (1853; rpt. Baltimore, 1967), 374–75, 430.

60. Testimony of Mr. Balfour, Feb. 12, 1766, Add. MSS 33,030, f. 114, BM; *Historical Statistics of the U.S.*, 1172.

61. Jerman Baker to Duncan Rose, Feb. 15, 1764, *WMQ*, 1st ser., xii (1903), 242.

62. *Historical Statistics of the U.S.*, 1172; Alan Kulikoff, *Tobacco and Slaves: The Development of Southern Cultures in the Chesapeake, 1680–1800* (Chapel Hill, N.C., 1986), 67.

scarce it could not be got by them. Nay, if they sold their estates (as some offered to do) they could not expect above half price."[63]

Economic adversity remained an ever-present reality in Virginia during the second half of the decade. "If you will have recourse to the public gazettes," George Washington told a neighbor in 1767, "you may perceive by the number of estates which are continually advertising for sale that you are not the only one under misfortune and that many good families are retiring into the interior parts of the country for the benefit of their children."[64] The letterbooks of local merchants who served as factors for British houses overflow with complaints about the difficulty of collecting from debtors. "The slow payments here with the necessity there appears to be for quick remittances . . . gives me great uneasiness," remarked a Caroline County storekeeper in 1768, and a York County trader told his London correspondent in 1769, "I now shall be compelled to bring several suits which perhaps may prejudice my trade here. Money is so scarce, and law so tedious that I have been able to get in but a small part of the debts due."[65]

Many landowners endeavored to counter the depressed conditions during the 1760s by shifting their acreage from tobacco to wheat. Although rising grain prices sparked a new interest in the crop throughout the colony, the change to wheat—an experiment that for some Virginians had begun well before 1760—was most evident in the Northern Neck. "I have no tobacco on this river," Washington reported in 1769 from his Potomac estate, "having made none for two or three years past, and believe I never shall again."[66] Planters, particularly the expansionists, also hoped to lighten their burden of indebtedness by joining in nonimportation during 1769 and 1770. British firms, however, ignored the weak boycott and sharply increased their shipments to the Chesapeake in 1769 and 1770.

63. Col. Thomas Moore to George Washington, Oct. 21, 1766, *Letters to Washington and Accompanying Papers*, ed. Stanislaus M. Hamilton, 5 vols. (Boston, 1898–1902), III, 288; McCusker, *Money and Exchange*, 211.

64. George Washington to Capt. John Posey, June 24, 1767, *Writings of Washington*, II, 459–60.

65. John Hook to [William?] Donald & Co., May 29, 1768, John Hook Papers, Virginia State Library, Richmond, microfilm at CWF; Thomas Adams to William Byrd III, Apr. 10, 1768, William Byrd III to Peter Russell, Dec. 4, 1769, *The Correspondence of the Three William Byrds of Westover, Virginia, 1684–1776*, ed. Marion Tinling (Charlottesville, Va., 1977), 774–75, 776–77, and see 610–13; David Jameson to John Norton, Dec. 8, 1769, Robert Carter Nicholas to John Norton, Jan. 13, 1769, *John Norton & Sons Papers*, 113, 82; Robert Beverley to Samuel Athawes, Sept. 6, 1769, Robert Beverley Letterbook.

66. George Washington to Robert Cary & Co., July 25, 1769, *Writings of Washington*, II, 513–14; Gouger, "Agricultural Change," 105–9; George Washington to George Mason, Apr. 5, 1769, *Writings of Washington*, II, 500–4; *Historical Statistics of the U.S.*, 1176–78.

Despite swelling imports, the economy of the Old Dominion strengthened in 1770, bringing the postwar depression to a close. Harvests were satisfactory, and tobacco and grain prices moved upward; moreover, generous extensions of British credit helped reduce the exchange rate to the lowest point in over forty years (figure 1). Significantly, the preface to the revised nonimportation agreement of June 1770 dropped the catalogue of economic complaints included in the May 1769 pact. Though some continued to complain about the difficulty of collecting debts, a note of optimism crept into the pronouncements of many Virginians. One shopkeeper, Roger Atkinson, enthusiastically boosted the colony in his correspondence with a set of wealthy Englishmen who hoped to purchase land in America. "I would most certainly prefer Virginia," he told them. Along with "the very valuable staple of tobacco . . . the article of wheat, a kind of second staple, is a prodigious addition. It will enrich the people and add greatly to the value of their lands."[67] And a Richmond merchant reported, "The principal planters from the great prices they have lately got for their commodities are entirely out of debt."[68]

Prosperity rather than adversity left its imprint on South Carolina planters and small farmers during the 1760s, even though the province did not wholly escape the vicissitudes of the postwar downturn. Strong demand for rice, supplemented by steady markets for indigo, deerskins, Indian corn, and naval stores underpinned the economy. One result was that the rice planters were less forward than the merchants of the North or the gentry of Virginia in advocating nonimportation, nonconsumption, and local manufacturing.

Landowners generally enjoyed favorable conditions between 1760 and 1766. Substantial earnings from rice, indigo, and corn allowed Henry Laurens in 1762 to predict another burst of prosperity for South Carolina: "These successes together I think will put both planter and merchant out of debt and set the province in general upon an advantageous footing."[69] "Middling" farmers as well as wealthy estate owners basked in the prosperity. "We have now a large field for trade opening in these colonies," Laurens boasted in 1763, "and a vast number of people setting down upon our frontier lands, and that with a little management will take off insensibly a

67. Roger Atkinson to William Hicks, Sept. 4, 1770, *VMHB*, xv, 349–50; McCusker, *Money and Exchange*, 211–12; Virginia Nonimportation Resolutions, May 17–18, 1769, June 22, 1770, *Papers of Jefferson*, i, 27, 31, 43–48.
68. Thomas Adams to Perks, Buchanan, & Brown, Mar. 22, 1770, quoted in Jacob M. Price, *Capital and Credit in British Overseas Trade: The View from the Chesapeake, 1770–1776* (Cambridge, Mass., 1980), 129.
69. Laurens to Augustus & John Boyd, Dec. 16, 1762, *Papers of Laurens*, iii, 193–94.

cargo [of slaves] by one or two in a lot."[70] But South Carolina agriculturists also had to contend with the press of creditors, particularly with the problems of paying for recently purchased slaves. "The sale of Negroes is pretty good," Laurens remarked in 1763, "and if an extraordinary number is not imported will continue so through the present year, but I should think that people must be put to some difficulties to make proper remittances."[71] The failure of Middleton, Liston, & Hope, pointed to problems in the countryside as well as in the city; the insolvent firm had supplied large numbers of blacks to the planters living in the booming region near Port Royal and had folded when payments from the countryside faltered. Planters joined merchants in supporting the decision in 1764 to impose for three years, beginning January 1766, a prohibitive duty on slave imports.[72]

For rural South Carolinians, the economic climate remained much the same during the second half of the decade: favorable skies were only occasionally clouded by the duns of mercantile creditors. The prohibition of slave imports aided those large landowners who had been dangerously overextended, enabling Laurens to remark in 1767, "Our planters are pretty well out of debt." The following year he could say that "our country is in general in flourishing circumstances and our numbers increase daily."[73] In 1769, however, the ports were reopened to slavers, more than forty-six hundred blacks entered the colony, and a new surge of indebtedness engulfed the planting community. Henry Laurens predicted a change: "Our Charleston merchants have been kept very poor, and none more distressed than myself, which is ever the case when the planter's produce gains the ascendant of imports. The case will probably be otherwise after the sale of five thousand Negroes."[74] And indeed, the financial relationship between planters and importers quickly altered. Both planters and merchants demanded that the prohibition of slave sales be incorporated into the 1769 nonimportation agreement, and by 1770 slave imports had dropped a full two-thirds.[75]

70. Laurens to Richard Oswald & Co., Feb. 15, 1763, ibid., 260.

71. Laurens to John Knight, Aug. 17, 1763, Laurens to John Rutherford, June 23, 1763, Laurens to Willing, Morris, & Co., Aug. 26, 1763, ibid., 529, 480, 541.

72. Laurens to Thomas Mears, Aug. 24, 1764, Laurens to Rossel & Gervais, Sept. 4, 1764, Laurens to George Appleby, Oct. 18, 1764, Laurens to Isaac King, Sept. 30, 1767, Laurens to William Reeve, Oct. 2, 1767, ibid., IV, 381–83, 396, 479, 320, V, 322–27.

73. Laurens to William Stork, Nov. 21, 1767, Laurens to Ross & Mill, Dec. 24, 1768, Laurens to Campbell & Hays, Dec. 2, 1768, Laurens to Benjamin Addison, May 26, 1768, ibid., V, 466, VI, 240–41, 220–21, V, 702–3.

74. Laurens to Andrew Turnbull, Oct. 28, 1769, ibid., VII, 177.

75. *Historical Statistics of the U.S.*, 1173; Arthur M. Schlesinger, *The Colonial Merchants and the American Revolution, 1763–1776* (New York, 1919), 140–47.

The deepening contraction also hurt small farmers, many of whom could not profit directly from the rice boom. Debtor grievances formed one facet of the Regulator movement, which commanded a strong following among the western landowners. Lieutenant Governor Bull explained, "Our back settlers . . . persist in their resolution not to be drawn down to Charleston by lawsuits, where by high fees and unprofitable sale of their lands and chattels so far from their homes they are often ruined without being able thereby to pay their creditors."[76] Not all up-country farmers were burdened by such problems, however, and many reports during the late 1760s emphasized that the "back settlements have been . . . greatly improved" and trumpeted the quantities of tobacco, linen, hemp, lumber, and flour produced.[77]

Paralleling the recovery elsewhere in the mainland colonies, the economy of rural South Carolina strengthened in 1770. Shutting the port to "Guinea" vessels aided the large landowners, and Laurens reported, "Our planters are out of debt, and in general have large funds for purchasing Negroes, which they will do very eagerly whenever an importation takes place."[78] More generous British credit policies—reflected in the fall of exchange rates—also helped the countryside (figure 1), as did favorable markets for most of the colony's crops. For South Carolina farmers the decade ended on a strongly upbeat note.[79]

Thus, the downturn of the 1760s, which holds such importance for any analysis of this era's protests, fell harshly upon some groups while brushing others only lightly. The inhabitants of the northern cities, the tobacco planters, and the New England farmers were hardest hit; the planters and merchants of the South Carolina and those who worked the land in the middle colonies were shielded from the worst effects of the contraction. In all colonies, however, the depression, particularly as it worsened during the second half of the decade, presented the expansionists with a challenge almost as grave as the one posed by British measures.

76. Laurens to Capt. Robert Dodson, Sept. 13, 1768, *Papers of Laurens*, VI, 110–11; Lt. Gov. William Bull to earl of Hillsborough, Sept. 7, 1769, SCPR, XXXII, 101.

77. "News from the Back Settlements, 1768," H. Roy Merrens, ed., *The Colonial South Carolina Scene: Contemporary Views, 1697–1774* (Columbia, S.C., 1977), 247; Laurens to Andrew Turnbull, Oct. 28, 1769, *Papers of Laurens*, VII, 177–79.

78. Laurens to Richard Oswald, Sept. 10, 1770, Laurens to Ross & Mill, Apr. 14, 1770, *Papers of Laurens*, VII, 359–60, 283.

79. Laurens to Ashburner & Hind, Oct. 18, 1770, Laurens to Lachlan McIntosh, Mar. 3, 1769, May 10, 1770, Laurens to William Fisher, Aug. 10, 1769, ibid., VII, 382, VI, 397, VII, 290, 119; *Historical Statistics of the U.S.*, 1176, 1178. McCusker, *Money and Exchange*, 224, presents South Carolina exchange rates for 1769 and 1770, but these figures must be corrected with data from *Papers of Laurens*, VI, VII, passim.

CHAPTER 8

Massachusetts:
Patriot Alliance

Never in Massachusetts history had an election dealt so grave a blow to any party as did the 1766 balloting to the nonexpansionists. "Several gentlemen of respectable characters, considerable property, and heretofore of uninterrupted authority [in] their towns were flung out," lamented Governor Francis Bernard after the May poll, "and ignorant and low men elected in their stead."[1] A vigorous campaign to purge thirty-two Hutchinsonians (whose names were prominently displayed in the *Boston Gazette*) capitalized on provincewide resentment of the nonexpansionists' halfhearted opposition to the Stamp Act and with one stroke reduced this group to a mere rump in the assembly. Only within the judiciary and, after Thomas Hutchinson's elevation, in the governor's office would this conservative faction retain any semblance of its former strength.

The years from 1763 to 1770 thus were marked by a sea change in the relative weight of parties in Massachusetts. Nonetheless, even with the weakening of the nonexpansionists in 1766, three coherent groups continued to shape Bay Colony politics, much as they had since the beginning of the century. Throughout most of the decade the expansionists, a faction led by the Hancocks and Otises, and the lower-class popular party, with Samuel Adams at its fore, linked arms as the Friends of Liberty. This potent alliance, however, was always fraught with an undercurrent of tension, and in 1770 the two partners temporarily split. These factions were opposed by the nonexpansionists, whose leaders, the Hutchinsons, Olivers, and Sewalls,

1. Gov. Bernard to John Pownall, May 30, 1766, quoted in Merrill Jensen, *The Founding of a Nation: A History of the American Revolution, 1763–1776* (New York, 1968), 193–95.

long pessimistic about the future of a sovereign American nation, did their best to counter the patriots' forceful schemes.

» «

During 1763 and 1764 the Hutchinsonians' strength in the legislature frustrated efforts to censure the new British measures and place the Bay Colony in the forefront of the protest movement. As the war wound down, nonexpansionists strengthened their hold on many of the more affluent communities in eastern Massachusetts and were bolstered by the unwavering support of the Connecticut Valley towns. Although the river gods had earlier cooperated with the Otises and Hancocks in defending the colony, once Canada fell to the English the foremost concern of these westerners became social stability.

The 1763 election further enlarged the nonexpansionist contingent in the assembly. When the new house convened, the lawmakers reelected a Hutchinsonian, Timothy Ruggles, as speaker; ousted Edes & Gill from its post of official printer, charging the firm had broadcast "Mr. Otis's libels"; and replaced the chaplain because he "was supposed to be connected with Otis."[2] Moreover, early in 1764 nonexpansionists blocked the plan of James Otis, Jr., to include Jasper Maudit's brother Israel in the agency, a proposal designed to give the patriot bloc a louder voice in London. Even in defeat, however, the Friends of Liberty retained a sizable minority of seats and significantly, controlled the capital delegation. Three of Boston's four representatives, Otis, Oxenbridge Thacher, and Thomas Cushing, were expansionists, and the fourth man, Royal Tyler, on occasion backed the revolutionaries.[3]

Effective organization helped the patriot factions maintain their grip on Boston politics during these difficult months. In his diary John Adams described the Caucus Club, which during the early 1760s was the popular party's most important steering body: "This day learned that the Caucus Club meets at certain times in the garret of Tom Dawes. . . . There they smoke tobacco till you cannot see from one end of the garret to the other. There they drink flip, I suppose, and there they choose a moderator, who puts questions to the vote

2. John J. Waters, Jr., *The Otis Family in Provincial and Revolutionary Massachusetts* (Chapel Hill, N.C., 1968), 147; William H. Whitmore, *The Massachusetts Civil List for the Colonial and Provincial Periods, 1630–1774* (Albany, 1870), 67.

3. *Diary and Autobiography of John Adams*, ed. L. H. Butterfield et al., 4 vols. (Cambridge, Mass., 1961), I, 234 (Feb. 1, 1763); Thomas Hutchinson, *The History of the Colony and Province of Massachusetts-Bay*, ed. Lawrence S. Mayo, 3 vols. (Cambridge, Mass., 1936), III, 76; Waters, *Otis Family*, 146–48; James Otis, Jr., to Jasper Maudit, Feb. 14, 1763, MHS *Cols.*, LXXIV (1918), 95–96.

regularly, and selectmen, assessors, collectors, wardens, firewards, and representatives are regularly chosen before they are chosen in the town." Prominent in this gathering was John's distant cousin Samuel Adams. Furthermore, the popular party cooperated closely with the expansionists. Remarked John, "They send committees to wait on the Merchants' Club and to propose, and join in the choice of men and measures."[4]

During the first months of 1764 the patriots won a minor victory when they thwarted Hutchinson's attempt to go to London as the colony's standard bearer. The lieutenant governor's friends proposed that he present the merchants' memorials against the renewal of the Molasses Act. The opposition parties, led on this occasion by Oxenbridge Thacher, feared that once in England Hutchinson might undermine the colonists' liberties and in February voted to keep the lieutenant governor at home. The division was a familiar one: the wealthier inland communities near Boston, several of the port towns, and the Connecticut Valley backed Hutchinson, while the expansionist–popular party bloc received the votes of a broad arc of poorer farming communities from Essex County to Barnstable County, as well as the support of Boston's four representatives.[5]

The Hutchinsonians, however, succeeded in moderating the remonstrance against the new parliamentary enactments. The debate on a memorial to Parliament began in the spring and continued into the fall sessions. The Friends of Liberty endorsed a forceful statement, with the "lawyers upon the Boston seat" particularly vehement on the question.[6] But the nonexpansionists marshaled an effective opposition, and the lawmakers settled upon a mild document emphasizing the colony's privileges rather than its rights. "Our session has ended better than I expected," Hutchinson rejoiced in November, "with a pretty decent address to the House of Commons."[7]

» «

In the struggle over the Stamp Act the upper-class patriots, with strong support from the popular party, finally ended the nonexpan-

4. *Diary and Autobiography of John Adams*, I, 238 (Feb. 1763); Thomas Cushing to Samuel Phillips Savage, Aug. 27, 1764, Samuel P. Savage Papers, 1751–1829, MHS; *A Report of the Record Commissioners of the City of Boston Containing the Boston Town Records, 1758 to 1769* (Boston, 1886), 88; Thomas Hutchinson to William Bollan, Nov. 7, 1764, MHS *Cols.*, LXXIV (1918), 168n.

5. Hutchinson, *History of Massachusetts*, III, 76–77; *Mass. House Journals*, Feb. 1, 1764.

6. Jensen, *Founding of a Nation*, 86.

7. Ibid., 82–87; Hutchinson, *History of Massachusetts*, III, 81–84; Thomas Hutchinson to Israel Williams, Nov. 5, 1764, Israel Williams Papers, MHS.

sionists' power within the lower house. Before the 1766 election, however, the Hutchinsonians retained the upper hand in the assembly, affirming their position in the May 1765 balloting. When the new house met in the spring of 1765 to select the upper chamber, the Friends of Liberty were unable to prevent the legislators from elevating Thomas Hutchinson and his brother-in-law, Andrew Oliver, who secured a council seat despite the news that he was to be the stamp distributor. The revolutionaries persuaded the house to send delegates to the Stamp Act Congress, but they were piqued by the choice of delegates: Oliver Partridge, Timothy Ruggles, and James Otis, Jr. "Two of the three," Governor Bernard gloated, "are fast friends to government of Great Britain."[8] He might have added that the third, Otis, was at best an uncertain patriot. During the first months of 1765 Otis had renewed his flirtation with the nonexpansionists and had written a pamphlet supporting the right of Parliament to tax America. The Hutchinsonians also beat back the efforts of the patriot factions to gain a strong set of resolutions against the ministry's plans, and the revolutionaries were left to applaud the Virginia resolves in private. "They are men," affirmed Oxenbridge Thacher.[9]

The strength of the Hutchinsonians was abundantly clear in the legislative struggles that fall. During September the Friends of Liberty defeated by only a single vote Governor Bernard's suggestion that the lawmakers formally accept the Stamp Act while petitioning for its repeal. In October the house firmly denounced Parliament's attempt to tax the colonies, but the revolutionaries failed to secure a measure instructing government offices to resume business after November 1, the date the hated act went into force.[10]

Frustrated in the assembly, the upper- and lower-class patriots took to the streets of Boston to demonstrate their passionate opposition to the Stamp Act. During the summer of 1765 a group of popular party leaders, calling themselves the Loyal Nine, recruited Ebenezer Mackintosh, a shoemaker who customarily directed the South End mob in the annual Pope's Day celebration. With Mackintosh at its head, a Boston crowd on August 14 razed a building that, according to rumor, Andrew Oliver planned to use as a Stamp Office and went

8. Bernard quoted in Jensen, *Founding of a Nation*, 108; Thomas Hutchinson to Israel Williams, Apr. 26, 1765, Israel Williams Papers; Edmund S. Morgan and Helen M. Morgan, *The Stamp Act Crisis: Prologue to Revolution* (Chapel Hill, N.C., 1953; rev. ed., New York, 1962), 139; Hutchinson, *History of Massachusetts*, III, 97–98.

9. *Mass. House Journals*, Feb. 1, 1765; Waters, *Otis Family*, 132, 153–55; Morgan and Morgan, *Stamp Act Crisis*, 134–35, quotes Thacher.

10. Hutchinson, *History of Massachusetts*, III, 96–97; *Diary and Autobiography of John Adams*, I, 262–66 (Dec. 18, 19, 1765); *Mass. House Journal*, Jan. 23, 1766; Jensen, *Founding of a Nation*, 134–35.

on to threaten Oliver's residence; chastened by this violence, Oliver promptly resigned his post. August 26 Mackintosh led a far more violent demonstration, which destroyed the homes of a member of the admiralty court, the comptroller of customs, and Thomas Hutchinson.[11]

Wealthy expansionists, as well as Boston artisans, shopkeepers, and sailors, encouraged the riots of August 14 and 26. "It is said that there were fifty gentlemen actors in this scene," Hutchinson noted of the first incident, "disguised with trousers and jackets on."[12] Fewer members of the elite, it appears, took part in the fury of August 26, but Bostonians agreed that Jonathan Mayhew's sermon on August 25 heightened tensions in the town. To a "crowded audience" Mayhew had expostulated on the theme, "I would they were cut off which trouble you, for brethren you have been called unto liberty."[13] Upper-class revolutionaries also protested Mackintosh's arrest after the demonstration, as Hutchinson recorded: "The sheriff was immediately surrounded by a number of merchants, and other persons of property and character, who assured him, that if he apprehended Mackintosh, not a man would appear in arms, as had been proposed for the security of the town the next night. The sheriff released him."[14]

From the fall of 1765 through the early months of 1766 the patriots continued their extralegal efforts to nullify the Stamp Act. Hutchinson noted the uneasy calm that prevailed on Pope's Day, November 5, 1765: "The liberty party said the disposition of the body of the people was to be judged from this orderly behavior. . . . The government party inferred that this was an evidence of the influence the mob was under, and that they might let loose, or be kept up, just as their keepers thought fit."[15] In December the Loyal Nine, now more commonly called the Sons of Liberty, contemplated an attack on the customs house as a means of persuading officials to clear vessels

11. Henry Bass to Samuel P. Savage, Dec. 19, 1765, CSM *Pubs.*, xxvi (1924–26), 355–56; *Diary and Autobiography of John Adams*, i, 294 (Jan. 15, 1766), 259–61 (Aug. 15, 1765); Jensen, *Founding of a Nation*, 145–46; Hutchinson, *History of Massachusetts*, iii, 88–92; Gov. Bernard to Lord Barrington, Nov. 23, 1765, *The Barrington-Bernard Correspondence and Illustrative Matter, 1760–1770*, ed. Edward Channing and Archibald Gary Coolidge (Cambridge, Mass., 1912), 102; Morgan and Morgan, *Stamp Act Crisis*, 160–63.

12. Thomas Hutchinson to earl of Halifax, Aug. 15, 1765, quoted in Arthur M. Schlesinger, *The Colonial Merchants and the American Revolution, 1763–1776* (New York, 1919), 71.

13. Jonathan Mayhew to Thomas Hollis, Oct. 1, 1765, MHS *Procs.*, 3d ser., lxix (1947–50), 180–81; Andrew Eliot to Thomas Hollis, Aug. 27, 1767, MHS *Cols.*, 4th ser., iv (1858), 407; Bernard Bailyn, "Religion and Revolution," *Perspectives in American History*, iv (1970), 113–16.

14. Hutchinson, *History of Massachusetts*, iii, 88–91.

15. Ibid., 97; Jensen, *Founding of a Nation*, 147–148.

without stamps. Instead, the Sons brought two thousand people into the streets, forcing Oliver to another public resignation and frightening the customs men, who agreed to allow shipping to move through the port. The Sons also helped plan and control the celebrations that greeted the repeal of the Stamp Act.[16]

Throughout the months of protest against the Stamp Act, the lower-class popular party and the upper-class expansionists worked together but never lost their separate identities. In March 1766 Hutchinson described Boston's stratified politics to a friend: "It will be some amusement to you to have a more circumstantial account of the model of government among us. I will begin with the lowest branch, partly legislative, partly executive. This consists of the rabble of the town of Boston, headed by one Mackintosh . . . ; but since government has been brought to a system, they are somewhat controlled by a superior set, consisting of the master-masons and carpenters & ca. . . . When anything of more importance is to be determined, as opening the customs house or any matter of trade, these are under the direction of a committee of merchants, Mr. [John] Rowe at their head." The two groups came together in the town meeting. Business of a "general nature," Hutchinson observed, "is proper for a general meeting of the inhabitants of Boston, where Otis, with his mob-high eloquence, prevails in every motion."[17]

With the May 1766 elections the patriot coalition captured a new, all-important base of power, the lower house. The events of the preceding twelve months had altered the outlook of many farmers who long had sided with the nonexpansionists; consequently, voters retired nineteen of the thirty-two Hutchinsonians listed in the *Gazette*, reducing the nonexpansionist lawmakers to a small coterie with strength only in Hampshire County to the west and in coastal towns such as Salem and Marblehead. In Boston the patriots further strengthened their hold on local politics, unseating the one delegate, Thomas Gray, who had shown sympathy for the nonexpansionists.[18]

The four men Boston sent to the General Court in 1766 are of spe-

16. *Diary and Autobiography of John Adams*, I, 294 (Jan. 15, 1766); Thomas Hutchinson to Israel Williams, Feb. 20, 1766, Israel Williams Papers; Henry Bass to Samuel P. Savage, Dec. 19, 1765, CSM *Pubs.*, XXVI (1924–26), 355–56; Jensen, *Founding of a Nation*, 135–36, 189.

17. Thomas Hutchinson to [?], Mar. 8, 1766, James K. Hosmer, *The Life of Thomas Hutchinson* (1896; rpt. New York, 1972), 103–4.

18. *Boston Gazette*, Mar. 31, 1766; *Boston Evening Post*, Apr. 28, 1766; Jensen, *Founding of a Nation*, 193–98. This list of thirty-two individuals from thirty different towns provides contemporary corroboration for the partisan divisions presented in map 1. Of the twenty-seven nonexpansionist communities on the map, the 1766 list names thirteen; of the six Connecticut Valley towns, two. However, of the thirty-three settlements that were loyal to the popular party or expansionists of eastern Massachusetts, only two are on the 1766 list.

cial note because they illustrate the continuities of personnel and belief that marked the inner circles of the parties. Three of the delegates were expansionists. John Hancock, chosen to replace Gray, had inherited not only his uncle Thomas's business but his political views: a firm opposition to any power that threatened the growth of the New World. Thomas Cushing was also the scion of a politically active merchant family whose members had long worked for America's ascendancy; Cushing's father, after whom he was named, had been speaker in the 1740s and had been among the expansionists most willing to cooperate with the popular party on political and monetary questions. James Otis, Jr., hailed from a line whose aggressive defense of colonial interests dated back to the turn of the century. Boston's fourth delegate, Samuel Adams, head of the popular party, trod in the footsteps of a father who had been an active leader of the common people in the 1730s and 1740s. These four men would represent Boston for the balance of the 1760s and, all but Otis, who went insane, until 1774.[19]

One other figure deserves particular mention, John Adams, who as lawyer and publicist was active in the patriot cause during these years and who in 1770 replaced Otis as delegate for Boston. Adams's professional training, his eloquent affirmations of American destiny ("I always consider the settlement of America with reverence and wonder, as the opening of a grand scene and design in Providence"), and his belief in a hierarchical society would seem to group him with the upper-class revolutionaries.[20] But Adams also nursed a bitter, remarkably personal hatred for the Hutchinsonians and for ministerial schemes. Of the Stamp Act, for example, he wrote, "This execrable project was set on foot for my ruin as well as that of America in general."[21] Such anger turned him from the balanced program of the expansionists toward the more strident and consistent protests of the popular party. Consequently, John drew ever closer to his cousin Samuel Adams, and between 1763 and 1776 he became a familiar figure at the caucuses of the popular party. Only on the eve of independence, with that longed-for goal in sight, did John Adams pull away from the lower-class faction and begin to redirect part of his formidable energies to the preservation of an elitist social order.[22]

The new, militant assembly majority clashed with Governor Bernard and his supporters when the chamber convened at the end of

19. *Diary and Autobiography of John Adams,* I, 271 (Dec. 23, 1765), 293 (Jan. 14, 1766); Hutchinson, *History of Massachusetts,* III, 211–15.

20. John Adams, "A Dissertation on Canon and Feudal Law," Feb. 1765, *Diary and Autobiography of John Adams,* I, 257.

21. Ibid., 265 (Dec. 18, 1765).

22. Ibid., 305 (Mar. 11, 1766), 329 (Dec. 24, 1766), 343 (Sept. 3, 1769), II, 39 (June 22, 1771), III, 326–27 ("Autobiography").

May 1766. The legislators elevated James Otis, Jr., to the speaker's chair and chose Samuel Adams as clerk. When Bernard vetoed Otis, the house selected another expansionist, Thomas Cushing, in his stead. In the balloting for the upper house the patriots purged several prominent nonexpansionist councillors, including Hutchinson and Andrew and Peter Oliver. Bernard fumed over this "ill-judged and ill-timed oppugnation," and he in turn vetoed six of the house's choices, among them James Otis, Sr., and Nathaniel Sparhawk.[23] Bernard now tried a different tack and proposed a compromise to bring the upper-class factions together and isolate the popular party. He let it be known that "he should be glad to see Colls. Otis and Sparhawk at the Board provided his 4 friends might return." The patriots, in the words of one expansionist merchant, knew "a trick worth two of his" and refused the offer.[24]

Factional disputes lessened during the second half of 1766. Patriots and nonexpansionists quarreled over compensation for the victims of the Stamp Act riots and over customs enforcement, but such clashes rarely stirred the people "out of doors." As John Adams noted at the end of the year,"the repeal of the Stamp Act has hushed into silence almost every popular clamour, and composed every wave of popular disorder into a smooth and peaceful calm."[25] Only with the intertwined problems of the Townshend Acts and a worsening economy would partisan conflict intensify once more.

During the agitation over the Stamp Act, men of all factions acted with an eye to economic problems as well as to political tyranny. With relative unanimity Boston merchants followed the example set by traders in New York and Philadelphia and in December 1765 covenanted not to import any wares from Britain, save a few items used in manufacturing and in the fishery. Most of the city's merchants and shopkeepers, two hundred and fifty individuals in all, signed the pact. Hard times and the burdensome Stamp Act were argument enough; no force was deemed necessary to recruit the few recalcitrants or to keep the signers obedient. Hutchinson observed, "Such as did not join in it became unpopular; but, at this time, there was no compulsion." The traders of Salem, Marblehead, Plymouth, and Newbury entered into similar boycotts. The repeal of the Stamp Act ended the agreements after they had been in force less than six months.[26]

23. Ibid., I, 313 (May 28, 29, 1766); Hutchinson, *History of Massachusetts*, III, 107; Jensen, *Founding of a Nation*, 196, quotes Bernard.

24. Samuel A. Otis to [Joseph Otis], June 17, 1766, Waters, *Otis Family*, 159–60; Hutchinson, *History of Massachusetts*, III, 129.

25. *Diary and Autobiography of John Adams*, I, 324 (Nov./Dec. 1766); Thomas Hutchinson to Israel Williams, Dec. 7, 1766, Israel Williams Papers; Hutchinson, *History of Massachusetts*, III, 107–8, 113–15; Waters, *Otis Family*, 170.

26. Hutchinson, *History of Massachusetts*, III, 99–100; Schlesinger, *Colonial Merchants*, 78–80.

» «

Between 1767 and 1770 the union of expansionists and popular party men backed a series of increasingly forceful political and economic protests, outraging the Hutchinsonians and creating tensions that would eventually shatter the alliance of upper- and lower-class patriots. Many of the political problems that revolutionaries in Massachusetts and in the other colonies encountered during the last part of the decade stemmed from the Townshend Acts, a set of three measures adopted in the summer of 1767. The Revenue Act of 1767 placed duties on paper, glass, white and red lead, painter's colors, and tea, and was unequivocally a tax; the proceeds were to be used to salary royal governors, judges, and other officials in America. Another law created the American Board of Customs Commissioners to oversee the enforcement of acts of trade. The third initiative, of less concern than the others to Bay Colony citizens, suspended the New York assembly until it agreed to provide for the British troops stationed in that province. Colonial newspapers published the wording of the legislation in July, although the measures did not go into effect until the fall.[27]

The initial response of Massachusetts patriots, and particularly the expansionists, was cautious. The patriots raised only mild protests against the establishment of the American Board of Customs Commissioners, even though the ministry selected Boston for its headquarters. Collection of the duties began in Boston, as elsewhere, without commotion, and most merchants, including outspoken expansionists like John Hancock, paid the new taxes. Moreover, expansionist lawmakers questioned the wisdom of sending an epistle to rouse the other colonies and early in 1768 helped vote down such a proposal. Governor Bernard boasted in January: "Otis himself has given up the question and says it is to no purpose any longer to oppose me. And some of his colleagues have already made peace with me."[28]

Gradually during the first months of 1768 the wealthy patriots, prodded by Samuel Adams and other popular party leaders, came to accept the wisdom of a more spirited response. In February the legislature adopted a circular letter denying Parliament's right to tax Americans and calling on the several provinces to "harmonize with each other." At the same time the victorious patriots expunged from

27. Hutchinson, *History of Massachusetts*, III, 124–25; Jensen, *Founding of a Nation*, 223–28, 240–41.
28. Gov. Bernard to Lord Barrington, Jan. 26, 28, 1768, *Barrington-Bernard Correspondence*, 132, 137–39; Jensen, *Founding of a Nation*, 245–46; Hutchinson, *History of Massachusetts*, III, 131; Schlesinger, *Colonial Merchants*, 96, 106.

Massachusetts 159

the assembly journals all record of the earlier refusal to approve the epistle.[29] Moreover, when Secretary of State Hillsborough attacked the circular letter, the revolutionaries closed ranks, and in June they defied the order to rescind by a vote of ninety-two to seventeen. This ballot highlighted the pockets of nonexpansionist strength: most of the seventeen rescinders hailed either from the western part of the province or from coastal Essex County, including the ports of Ipswich, Marblehead, and Salem. Governor Bernard dissolved the house, and bewailed his defeat: "Now I see that popular leaders and popular measures will wholly prevail in that body in which I have hitherto boasted that I have kept the enemy from prevailing."[30]

During the spring and summer of 1768 the common people once again took to the streets to protest British policies and to defend their merchant allies against the customs officers. In March the populace celebrated the repeal of the Stamp Act (and St. Patrick's Day) by hanging in effigy one of the customs commissioners and the inspector general. A more serious incident followed the seizure on June 10 of John Hancock's sloop, the *Liberty*, on the charge that the merchant had smuggled wine. In what was Boston's worst disturbance since August 1765, the crowd roughed up Collector Joseph Harrison, his son, and the comptroller of customs and thoroughly frightened the members of the Board of Customs Commissioners. Four of the five commissioners fled to the British warship *Romney* and did not return for several months. Samuel Adams defended the outburst: "When the people are oppressed, when their rights are invaded . . . in such circumstances, while they have the spirit of freedom, they will *boldly assert* their freedom; and they are to be justified in so doing."[31] The Hutchinsonians, however, were furious. Attorney General Jonathan Sewall, scion of the famous nonexpansionist family, launched a suit against Hancock and five associates, although he eventually dropped the proceedings for want of evidence.[32]

In the fall of 1768 Boston's upper- and lower-class protestors backed a convention to help mobilize the province against the forthcoming arrival of British troops. News of Hillsborough's decision to

29. Gov. Bernard to Lord Barrington, Feb. 7, 20, 29, 1768, *Barrington-Bernard Correspondence*, 143–44, 145–46; Andrew Eliot to Thomas Hollis, Jan. 5, 1768, MHS *Cols.*, 4th ser., IV (1858), 422; Jensen, *Founding of a Nation*, 249–50.
30. Gov. Bernard to Lord Barrington, July 30, 1768, *Barrington-Bernard Correspondence*, 170; *Mass. House Journals*, June 30, 1768.
31. Joseph Harrison to Rockingham, June 17, 1768, D. H. Watson, "Joseph Harrison and the *Liberty* Incident," *WMQ*, 3d ser., xx (1963), 594; Jensen, *Founding of a Nation*, 255, 281–83, 347; Samuel Adams, Article Signed "Determinatus," Aug. 8, 1768, *The Writings of Samuel Adams*, ed. Harry A. Cushing, 4 vols. (New York, 1904–8), I, 240.
32. Carol Berkin, *Jonathan Sewall: Odyssey of an American Loyalist* (New York, 1974), 54–67, and passim; *Diary and Autobiography of John Adams*, I, 355–56 (July 1, 1770).

send several regiments to Massachusetts to check growing violence in Boston came at a time when the dissolution of the house deprived the colonists of their forum. An extralegal assembly was a natural response; however, the two revolutionary factions differed in their expectations for the body. The expansionists hoped the conference would temperately protest the arrival of the troops; thus, James Otis cautioned the convention against any violent initiatives, and Cushing, who headed the irregular assembly, assured a correspondent that the delegates' "determinations will be moderate, and their sessions short, and that they will not attempt any acts of government."[33] By contrast, popular party men hoped the gathering would organize a firm opposition to the British forces. This time, the 120-odd delegates followed the lead of the expansionists, endorsed a set of tame resolves, and disbanded before the soldiers landed in Boston on October 1.[34]

In 1768 the expansionists also made their control of the council clear. Although the purge of Hutchinson and the Olivers in 1766 had wrested the upper chamber from the nonexpansionists, the body seemed slow to abandon its traditional proadministration stance. Only in 1768 did the more outspoken expansionists on the board persuade the majority to call for Governor Bernard's removal. Bernard sighed, "I am no longer to depend upon the council for the support of the small remains of royal and parliamentary power now left."[35] The denunciation of the governor was a sweet victory for James Bowdoin, who in the 1750s had been one of the few expansionists in the upper house. Now, according to Hutchinson, Bowdoin "obtained a greater influence over the council than his predecessor [Hutchinson] ever had; and, being united in principle with the leading men in the house, measures were concerted between him and them."[36]

The May 1769 elections further strengthened the patriot alliance in the assembly, which then expelled from the upper chamber the few

33. Jensen, *Founding of a Nation*, 289–94; Committee of Boston Sons of Liberty to John Wilkes, Oct. 5, 1768, *Papers of John Adams*, ed. Robert Taylor et al., 2 vols. (Cambridge, Mass., 1977), I, 220–23; Andrew Eliot to Thomas Hollis, Sept. 27, Oct. 17, 1768, Thomas Cushing to Dennys DeBerdt, Jan. 19, 1769, MHS *Cols.*, 4th ser., IV (1858), 428–29, 430, 352–55; Waters, *Otis Family*, 175.

34. Convention of Mass. Towns to Dennys DeBerdt, Sept. 27, 1768, *Writings of Samuel Adams*, I, 244–45; Hutchinson, *History of Massachusetts*, III, 152; Richard D. Brown, "The Massachusetts Convention of Towns, 1768," *WMQ*, 3d ser., XXVI (1969), 94–108.

35. Gov. Bernard to Lord Barrington, July 30, 1768, *Barrington-Bernard Correspondence*, 169–70; Jensen, *Founding of a Nation*, 255–56.

36. Hutchinson, *History of Massachusetts*, III, 113; Gov. Bernard to Hillsborough, Nov. 30, 1768, MHS *Procs.*, 1st ser., VIII (1864–65), 86–87; Whitmore, *Mass. Civil List*, 62.

remaining councillors with nonexpansionist sympathies. "They have turned out of the council 4 gentlemen of the first characters, the only men of disposition and ability to serve the crown left in it," Bernard lamented.[37] The governor replied to the assembly by vetoing eleven of its nominees for the upper house, including John Hancock, James Bowdoin, and James Otis, Sr. Bernard also transferred the meeting place of the assembly to Cambridge, to remove it from the contagion of Boston's lower orders. But such tactics were of little avail, and Bernard, who had long despaired of stemming the tide that ran against him and British policy, retired to England, leaving Hutchinson as acting governor.[38]

In 1770 the upper-class revolutionaries, largely because of the bitter conflict over nonimportation, grew increasingly reluctant to continue their alliance with the popular party. Although the boycott was now the focus of attention, part of the story remained more narrowly political. Hoping to establish his administration upon an alliance of the elite factions, Hutchinson carefully avoided disputes with the wealthy patriots, and in May turned down only two councillors, accepting James Bowdoin and James Otis, Sr., back into the upper chamber.[39] "By this artful piece of policy," one observer noted, "he took off a number of leading members from the lower house, some of whom . . . proved staunch friends to him in the upper house."[40] A tilt toward the governor and away from the popular party was also evident in the countryside; in December, Hutchinson could comment happily, "In almost every town a great part of the people say they have been deluded and abused."[41] A fuller understanding of the changes in partisan behavior in 1770, however, requires an examination of the struggles over nonconsumption and nonimportation.

Between 1767 and 1770 expansionists and popular party men took the lead in pushing for a series of economic protests—measures designed to counter the depression as well as to pressure the mother country into repealing its recent legislation. The artisans and trades-

37. Gov. Bernard to Lord Barrington, May 30, 1769, *Barrington-Bernard Correspondence*, 203–4; Hutchinson, *History of Massachusetts*, iii, 166, 169.

38. Gov. Bernard to Lord Barrington, May 30, 1769, *Barrington-Bernard Correspondence*, 205; Hutchinson, *History of Massachusetts*, iii, 169; Jensen, *Founding of a Nation*, 351.

39. Hutchinson, *History of Massachusetts*, iii, 210–11.

40. William Palfrey to John Wilkes, Oct. 23–30, 1770, CSM *Pubs.*, xxxiv (1937–42), 420.

41. Thomas Hutchinson to Israel Williams, Dec. 10, 1770, Israel Williams Papers; Stephen E. Patterson, *Political Parties in Revolutionary Massachusetts* (Madison, Wis., 1973), 68–69.

men of Boston, who formed one of the most battered links in the tightening chain of credit, were the first to suggest collective action. In October 1767 the town meeting approved a nonconsumption agreement, in which the signers promised not to purchase a long list of imported goods, including loaf sugar, household furniture, shoes, snuff, and chinaware. Significantly, the pact mentioned none of the items on which the Townshend Revenue Act had placed duties; the protest targeted an economic, not a constitutional problem. The covenant received strong support from the lower classes of Boston, and the boycott quickly spread to the countryside, where farmers and others faced problems similar to those of the city dwellers. By January 1768 twenty-four towns had followed the capital's lead, with only Salem, a nonexpansionist stronghold, openly rejecting the agreement. Although the upper classes remained at arm's length from the protest, the turn to frugality had an impact on the traders. James Bowdoin, for example, in December 1767 rejected the blandishments of a British print dealer, stating: "You will clearly see therefore the spirit of economy, so necessarily prevalent here, will not allow our importing such kind of articles."[42]

The downturn was too steep and the wealthy patriots too concerned about restoring prosperity for the protests long to remain the exclusive province of the common people. In March 1768 a committee dominated by expansionist traders, including John Hancock and John Rowe, proposed a boycott of wares imported from Britain and drafted a pact that was contingent upon similar action in New York and Philadelphia. The ensuing campaign for signatures revealed the fault line dividing Boston's elite. The initial group of signers, thirty-one in all, was drawn almost exclusively from the expansionist camp. The next and larger list of individuals agreeing to support the pact was mixed in its factional loyalties. But the sixty-three traders who either refused to sign or stated that they would add their names only if the agreement became general, were overwhelmingly nonexpansionists. This group included many—the Hutchinsons, for example, and Theophilus Lillie—whose loyalty to that faction (or whose parents' allegiance) dated back to the 1740s and earlier.[43]

42. Andrew Eliot to Thomas Hollis, Dec. 10, 1767, MHS *Cols.*, 4th ser., IV (1858), 418–19; Schlesinger, *Colonial Merchants*, 106–10; Jensen, *Founding of a Nation*, 245, 266–69; James Bowdoin to John Lane, Dec. 13, 1767, MHS *Cols.*, 6th ser., IX (1897), 84–85; Thomas Cushing to Dennys DeBerdt, Apr. 18, 1768, Miscellaneous Bound, MHS; Samuel Adams to Dennys DeBerdt, May 14, 1768, *Writings of Samuel Adams*, I, 217.

43. Gov. Bernard to Lord Barrington, Mar. 4, 1768, *Barrington-Bernard Correspondence*, 147–48; Reports of Committee of Merchants, Mar. 4, 9, 1768, New York Merchants' Committee to Boston Merchants' Committee, Apr. 13, 1768, Savage Papers, 1751–1829.

The motivation for the boycott was largely economic. At their first meeting in March, the merchants resolved that nonimportation was imperative "in order to extricate the trade from the heavy load of debt due to the merchants in England and prevent a general bankruptcy, which must inevitably ensue if so great an importation of goods from G.B. is continued."[44] In April, Thomas Cushing offered a similar explanation: "I believe the gentlemen in trade are one and all convinced that it will be to no good purpose for them to import English goods as usual under the present distressed and embarrassed state of the trade. They despair of ever selling them and consequently of ever being able to pay for them." Further underscoring the economic (as distinct from the constitutional) reasons for the pact, the agreement drawn up in March was to last for one year, regardless of the status of the Townshend Acts.[45]

New York agreed to the boycott, but Philadelphia did not; so in August Boston's patriot importers set forth a new, noncontingent agreement. They were determined to restrict the flow of goods, even if they had to act unilaterally. The preamble to the new accord discussed British taxes only as part of a catalogue of economic woes and emphasized "the scarcity [of] money which is daily increasing for want of other remittances to discharge our debts in Great Britain." Like the abortive March pact, the August agreement was to last one year and was not dependent on the repeal of the Townshend Acts. A meeting at Faneuil Hall on August 1 ratif ed the boycott, and while most merchants signed, once again about seventy-five nonexpansionist traders refused to participate fully.[46]

In order to keep the Hutchinsonians in check, the patriot importers conceded to Sam Adams's followers during 1769 an ever louder voice in shaping and policing the pact. When a merchant committee discovered in April that twenty-six nonsigning firms had brought in goods, the Boston town meeting broadcast the information in handbills, castigating a group that included the lieutenant governor's sons, Thomas and Elisha Hutchinson, and Theophilus Lillie. The common people also played a key role at a gathering convened July 26 in response to the news that most of the Townshend duties would be repealed. "Men who had no concern in trade had the greatest influence at the meeting," Hutchinson groused. Those present de-

44. Meeting of Boston Merchants, Mar. 1, 1768, Ezekiel Price Papers, MHS.
45. Thomas Cushing to Dennys DeBerdt, Apr. 18, 1768, Miscellaneous Bound, MHS; Meeting of Boston Merchants, July 28, 1768, Ezekiel Price Papers.
46. Meeting of Boston Merchants, July 28, 1768, Ezekiel Price Papers; Schlesinger, *Colonial Merchants*, 120–21; Hutchinson, *History of Massachusetts*, III, 145–46; Jensen, *Founding of a Nation*, 283–84.

nounced the ministry's move as insufficient and said it "would by no means relieve the trade from its difficulties."[47] Self-interest played a role in fanning ardor for the pact. Artisans, one editorialist noted, "find it their interest to proscribe foreign commerce because they can better dispose of the articles they make at any extravagant price."[48] Together the expansionists and popular party made the boycott effective. Imports from Britain to New England (chiefly Massachusetts) fell from £431,000 sterling in 1768 to £224,000 in 1769, and the exchange rate, which reflected the demand for remittances, slid from £133.33 to £126.67.[49]

The decision at the merchants' meeting in October 1769 to extend nonimportation beyond January 1, 1770, and to tie it to the complete repeal of the Townshend duties, forced the patriot traders to rely still more heavily on the populace to counter the mounting opposition of the Hutchinsonians. "By what I can learn," Andrew Eliot wrote in December, "there is greater opposition to it [nonimportation] in Boston than there is in any of the provinces that have come into the agreement."[50] In January a gathering at Faneuil Hall, crowded with artisans and workingmen as well as importers, denounced the traders who refused to abide by the pact and sent delegations to treat with each of the defiant importers. Furthermore, the merchant meeting, which during 1769 had at least nominally overseen the agreement, was now replaced by the "Body," an assembly that was in "every way a town meeting except in the mode of calling it."[51]

The popular party, stridently enforcing the designs of upper-class patriots, reigned supreme in Boston, and the nonexpansionists complained loudly. "I had rather be a slave under one master," Theophilus Lillie declared, "for if I know who he is, I may perhaps be able to please him, than a slave to a hundred or more who I don't

47. Meeting of the Committee to Examine into the Importation of Goods from Great Britain, Apr. 27, 1769, Ezekiel Price Papers; Thomas Cushing to Dennys DeBerdt, Jan. 19, 1769, MHS *Cols.*, 4th ser., IV (1858), 352; Hutchinson, *History of Massachusetts*, III, 181–82, 185–86; James Bowdoin to Thomas Pownall, Dec. 5, 1769, MHS *Cols.*, 6th ser., IX (1897), 158; Schlesinger, *Colonial Merchants*, 122, 158–59, 162–64; Resolutions to Support Non-importation, July 31, 1769, Large Collection, MHS.

48. Patterson, *Political Parties*, 66–68; *Boston Chronicle*, Feb. 5, 1770, quoted in Schlesinger, *Colonial Merchants*, 175.

49. *Historical Statistics of the U.S.*, 1176–77; John McCusker, *Money and Exchange in Europe and America, 1600–1775* (Chapel Hill, N.C., 1978), 142.

50. Andrew Eliot to Thomas Hollis, Dec. 25, 1769, MHS *Cols.*, 4th ser., IV (1858), 446–47; Schlesinger, *Colonial Merchants*, 174.

51. Patterson, *Political Parties*, 68; Hutchinson, *History of Massachusetts*, III, 191–93; Samuel Adams, Article Signed "Determinatus," Jan. 8, 1770, *Writings of Samuel Adams*, II, 7; *Letters and Diary of John Rowe . . .* , ed. Anne R. Cunningham (Boston, 1903), 197–98; Schlesinger, *Colonial Merchants*, 175–77.

know where to find nor what they will expect from me."[52] The crowd drove John Mein, editor of the *Boston Chronicle* and a strong-willed opponent of the boycott, out of town, and freely expressed its resentment of the troops stationed in Boston. Rattled by the jeers of the populace, soldiers on March 5 opened fire, killing five individuals in an event soon known as the Boston Massacre. Only Hutchinson's swift action in arresting the soldiers involved and removing the two regiments to Castle William in Boston Harbor averted further violence. Although he conducted himself with commendable restraint, the lieutenant governor excoriated his lower-class opponents. "In this province," Hutchinson stated in July, "the faction is headed by the lowest, dirtiest, and most abject part of the whole community."[53]

In the fall, however, wealthy revolutionaries separated themselves from the popular party and joined the nonexpansionists to end the boycott. The upper-class patriots had begun to fear the dangers of mob rule. Moreover, the defections of New York in July and Philadelphia in September isolated the Boston traders. In addition, during 1770 New Hampshire and Rhode Island merchants imported quantities of dry goods, undercutting the Bay Colony's efforts: shipments from Britain to New England rose from £224,000 sterling in 1769 to £417,000 in 1770. More important, nonimportation (along with the expansion of British credit) had helped to end the depression, and many traders no longer saw a need for the cessation of commerce. Hutchinson observed in August: "Many who at first were zealous among the merchants against importation, are now as zealous for it."[54] The expansionists now turned a deaf ear to the suasions of the popular party leaders. "There happened during this time," Hutchinson reported in September, "to be a very grand meeting of merchants and tradesmen upon the subject of importation, where [Samuel] Adams made an attempt to inflame them, declaring that I had given up the Castle [i.e., the fort in Boston Harbor] and would give up the

52. Schlesinger, *Colonial Merchants*, 171–85, quotation on 171; John Powell to Christopher Champlin, Feb. 12, 1770, John Powell Papers, MHS; Hutchinson, *History of Massachusetts*, III, 207; Thomas Hutchinson to John Pownall, Mar. 26, 1770, Hosmer, *Thomas Hutchinson*, 189; Bernard Bailyn, *The Ordeal of Thomas Hutchinson* (Cambridge, Mass., 1974), 157–58.

53. Edward Payne to Boston Committee of Merchants, May 26, 1770, Ezekiel Price Papers; Andrew Eliot to Thomas Hollis, June 28, 1770, MHS *Cols.*, 4th ser., IV (1858), 451–52; Jensen, *Founding of a Nation*, 352–53, 361–62; Thomas Hutchinson to Mr. Silliman, July 28, 1770, Hosmer, *Thomas Hutchinson*, 194–95.

54. Hutchinson, *History of Massachusetts*, III, 237–38; Schlesinger, *Colonial Merchants*, 157, 226, 231; *Historical Statistics of the U.S.*, 1176–77; Thomas Hutchinson to Gov. Bernard, Aug. 28, 1770, Hosmer, *Thomas Hutchinson*, 195–96; Andrew Eliot to Thomas Hollis, Jan. 26, 1771, MHS *Cols.*, 4th ser., IV (1858), 457–58.

charter. But some of the merchants declared that was not the business of the meeting and repeatedly stopped him from going on." October 12 the importers met at the British Coffeehouse and unanimously voted to resume trade.[55]

The immediate legacy of nonimportation was the enmity the wealthy patriots, as well as nonexpansionists, displayed toward the popular party. Governor Hutchinson encouraged this sentiment and quietly constructed an upper-class coalition to support his administration. Not until the end of 1772 would Samuel Adams and other popular leaders reforge the links between their faction and the upper-class revolutionaries.

» «

Between 1763 and 1770 some members of the three Massachusetts factions spelled out their beliefs more fully and discoursed on their vision of the future. Not cowed by ministerial plans, expansionists affirmed their faith in the ascendancy of America. British repression, Thomas Cushing observed in 1763, "though at first very grievous and irksome, it's apprehended by some, will prove a wholesome severity, a means of our becoming in the course of years a frugal, industrious, opulent, and independent people."[56] James Otis, Jr., was similarly confident. "I am and have been more concerned for Great Britain than the colonies," he informed an English correspondent in 1768. "You may ruin yourselves but you cannot in the end hurt the colonies. Our fathers were a good people and have been a free people, and if you will not let us remain so any longer, we shall be a great people."[57] James Bowdoin echoed these sentiments: "America, however (if at all), will suffer the least of the two, and in the long run will probably be greatly benefited by the dispute."[58] Speaking more broadly, John Adams declared that liberty "will reign in America over hundreds and thousands of millions at a time. . . . Man shall make his true figure upon this continent."[59]

The upper-class revolutionaries counterposed to Britain's idea of a hierarchical empire, the concept of an English-speaking imperium

55. Thomas Hutchinson to Gov. Bernard, Sept. 15, 1770, quoted in Patterson, *Political Parties*, 69; William Palfrey to John Wilkes, Oct. 23–30, 1770, CSM *Pubs.*, xxxiv (1937–42), 421–22; Schlesinger, *Colonial Merchants*, 233; *Papers of John Adams*, I, 246.

56. Thomas Cushing to Jasper Maudit, Oct. 28, 1763, MHS *Cols.*, lxxiv (1918), 133.

57. James Otis, Jr. to Arthur Jones, Nov. 26, 1768, MHS *Procs.*, 3d ser., xliii (1909–10), 205.

58. James Bowdoin to Thomas Pownall, May 10, 1769, MHS *Cols.*, 6th ser., ix (1897), 139; Samuel Cooper to Franklin, Aug. 3, 1769, *Papers of Franklin*, xvi, 183.

59. John Adams, Fragmentary Notes for "A Dissertation on the Canon and Feudal Law," May–Aug. 1765, *Papers of John Adams*, I, 106.

based on equality. Thomas Cushing told the colony's agent in 1767, "As to improving duties so long as they are confined to the regulation of trade and so conducted as to be of equal advantage to all parts of the empire, no great exception could be taken to it, but when duties are laid with a view of raising a revenue out of the colonies and the revenue also to be applied to establish a civil list in America . . . this is looked upon to be unconstitutional."[60]

During the years following the French and Indian War the inner circle of the popular party, as well as prominent nonexpansionists, also enlarged on their long-standing beliefs. As far back as the 1690s the lower-class faction had defended democratic rights, and this commitment now readily translated into a passionate opposition to British "tyranny." In terms reminiscent of many earlier addresses, the Sons of Liberty in 1768 assured English dissident John Wilkes of their belief in the "dignity of a freeman" and in "the importance of defending his minutest privileges against the determined invasion of the most formidable power on earth."[61] Sam Adams's ardent expression of such sentiments, led the assembly to make him its penman. Meanwhile, such nonexpansionists as Thomas Hutchinson and the Reverend Andrew Eliot, expatiated on the necessary dependence of the colonies upon the mother country and underlined the dangers inherent in any confrontation between the two.[62]

60. Thomas Cushing to [Dennys DeBerdt], May 9, 1767, Miscellaneous Bound, MHS.
61. Joseph Warren probably drafted this letter. Committee of the Boston Sons of Liberty to John Wilkes, Oct. 5, 1768, *Papers of John Adams*, I, 220–23; House of Representatives [Samuel Adams] to governor, Oct. 23, 1765, Samuel Adams to John Smith, Dec. 19, 1765, *Writings of Samuel Adams*, I, 21, 54–55.
62. Hutchinson, *History of Massachusetts*, II, 342; Andrew Eliot to Thomas Hollis, Dec. 10, 1767, MHS *Cols*, 4th ser., IV (1858), 420.

CHAPTER 9

New York: Reluctant
Revolutionaries

For Lieutenant Governor Cadwallader Colden, whose involvement in New York affairs dated back to the late 1710s, when expansionist and nonexpansionist factions had first emerged, the presence of parties in the Hudson Colony was simply a fact of life. "From the different political and religious principles of the inhabitants," he observed in 1770, "opposite parties have at all times [existed], and will exist in this province." These groups, continued Colden, "at different times have taken their denominations from some distinguished person or family who have appeared at their head."[1] Acknowledging the prominence of two great clans in the years following the French and Indian War, New Yorkers often called the expansionist party the Livingstons and the nonexpansionist faction the DeLanceys.[2] In this era, as during earlier decades, the two groups alternated in power, with the Livingstons controlling the lower house from 1763 to 1769 and the DeLanceys dominant at the decade's end.

---

1. Cadwallader Colden to [?], July 7, 1770, NYHS *Cols.*, x (1877), 223–24.
2. On the names of the two factions, see Patricia U. Bonomi, *A Factious People: Politics and Society in Colonial New York* (Tarrytown, N.Y., 1980), 229–30. More broadly, authors have taken several approaches to the partisan battles of the 1760s. Roger Champagne, "Family Politics Versus Constitutional Principles: The New York Assembly Elections of 1768 and 1769," *WMQ*, 3d ser., xx (1963), 56–72, argues that politicians threw all consistency to the winds in a battle between the ins and the outs. Bernard Friedman, "The New York Assembly Elections of 1768 and 1769: The Disruption of Family Politics," *New York History*, xlvi (1965), 3–24, offers a critique of Champagne. Bonomi, *Factious People*, 229–78, views the DeLanceys as "popular Whigs" and the Livingstons as "moderate Whigs" but admits that the labels "lose their significance after the fall of 1769." Leopold S. Launitz-Schürer, Jr., *Loyal Whigs and Revolutionaries: The Making of the Revolution in New York* (New York, 1980), 1–96, sees the differences between the two parties as ones of personality and style.

Broadly viewed, New York politics in the 1760s was marked by a struggle between patriotic expansionists and more conservative non-expansionists. However, lower-class dissent and, more particularly, an uprising of tenant farmers in 1766 complicated partisan battles, unnerving many of the expansionist manor lords and temporarily making them reluctant to initiate bold protests. Consequently, during 1766, 1767, and 1768 the DeLanceys often appeared more ardent in their opposition to Britain than did the Livingstons.

» «

Expansionists took the lead in opposing the ministerial measures announced in 1764. "The stamp duty . . . is resolved," Robert R. Livingston exclaimed angrily in July, "and they think of no other yet but a duty on Negroes, a poll tax which I think will make Negroes of us all."[3] William Smith, Jr., argued that the legislature should be reconvened to consider Parliament's initiatives, and when the lower chamber finally met in September the Livingston majority roundly declared the colony's exclusive right to tax itself. In sharp contrast, nonexpansionist John Watts called this declaration "ill digested," and Colden said it was "disrespectful and even indecent."[4]

During the fall the expansionists broadened their attack on British policies. The New York Triumvirate drafted a set of memorials which the assembly forwarded to the British government; Smith wrote the address to Commons, John Morin Scott the petition to the king, and William Livingston the memorial to the House of Lords. These statements went a step farther than the pronouncements issued by any other province and insisted that New Yorkers "nobly disdain the thought of claiming that exemption [from British taxation] as *a privilege*. They found it on a basis more honorable, solid, and stable; they challenge it, and glory in it as their right."[5] The lawmakers also enlarged the mandate of a house committee headed by Robert R. Livingston, empowering it to communicate with the other assemblies about British policies and to deal with New York's London agent.[6]

3. Robert R. Livingston to Henry Beekman, July 13, 1764, Livingston Family Papers, 1755–1775 (Letters to His Wife), NYPL; John Watts to Col. Barre, Jan. 21, 1764, John Watts to Gen. Monckton, Aug. 11, 1764, *Letter Book of John Watts, Merchant and Councillor of New York* (NYHS *Cols.*, LXI) (New York, 1928), 218, 281; Merrill Jensen, *The Founding of a Nation: A History of the American Revolution, 1763–1776* (New York, 1968), 91–93.

4. John Watts to Gen. Monckton, Sept. 22, 1764, *Letter Book of Watts*, 291; C. Colden to Edward Sedgwick, Sept. 21, 1764, NYHS *Cols.*, IX (1876), 364; *Historical Memoirs from 16 March 1763 to 25 July 1778 of William Smith*, ed. William W. Sabine, 2 vols. (1956, 1958; rpt. New York, 1969), I, 23.

5. *Memoirs of Smith*, I, 24; *N.Y. Votes and Proceedings*, Oct. 18, 1764.

6. *N.Y. Votes and Proceedings*, Oct. 18, 1764.

» «

In the struggle against the Stamp Act the Livingstons continued to spearhead the protests, but grew increasingly more cautious. New Yorkers broadly acknowledged the role of the expansionist lawyers in opposing British measures during 1765. "I am fully persuaded," Colden remarked, that "some of the most popular lawyers are the authors of the seditious papers and have been countenanced by some of the judges and others in the highest trust in the government." Captain John Montressor, who was posted with the British forces in the city, observed that everyone condemned the lawyers as "hornets and firebrands of the constitution, the planners and incendiaries of the present rupture."[7] The expansionists' revolutionary tracts helped persuade the New York stamp distributor, James McEvers, to step down in August. McEvers explained his resignation by pointing to the Boston riots and to "the inflammatory papers lately printed in the colonies."[8] The Livingston party also played an active role at the Stamp Act Congress, which met in New York City in October. Exercising its power to handle intercolonial affairs during assembly recesses, the committee of correspondence, which included Robert R. and Philip Livingston, became the New York delegation to the gathering. Moreover, William Smith, whom Colden caustically described as a "volunteer," lobbied the representatives attending the sessions.[9]

When the lower house convened in November 1765, expansionists, most notably Robert R. Livingston, steered the deliberations. Livingston introduced and secured approval for the resolves of the Stamp Act Congress, reported on correspondence with the colony's London agent, and headed committees to draft addresses to Governor Henry Moore and to the House of Lords. "By the enclosed printed minutes of the assembly," Colden complained to the ministry in December, "it appears that Mr. Justice [Robert R.] Livingston, one of the judges of

7. C. Colden to Secretary of State Henry Conway, Sept. 23, 1765, C. Colden to Amherst, Oct. 10, 1765, C. Colden, State of Province of New York, Dec. 6, 1765, NYHS *Cols.*, x (1877), 36, 44, 71; Dorothy Rita Dillon, *The New York Triumvirate: A Study of the Legal and Political Careers of William Livingston, John Morin Scott, William Smith, Jr.* (New York, 1949), 85–92; *Journals of Captain John Montressor*, NYHS *Cols.*, xiv (1881), 339 (Nov. 7, 1765); Gen. Thomas Gage to Conway, Dec. 21, 1765, *The Correspondence of General Thomas Gage with the Secretaries of State, 1763–1775*, ed. Clarence Edward Carter, 2 vols. (New Haven, 1931), i, 78–79; *New York Journal*, Apr. 19, 1770.

8. James McEvers to C. Colden, Aug. 1765, NYHS *Cols.*, lvi (1923), 56–57; Robert R. Livingston to Monckton, Nov. 8, 1765, MHS *Cols.*, 4th ser., x (1871), 559.

9. C. Colden to Lord Mansfield, Jan. 22, 1768, NYHS *Cols.*, x (1877), 150; Robert R. Livingston to Robert Livingston, Jr., Oct. 19, Nov. 2, 1765, Livingston Papers, Bancroft Trans., NYPL; Edmund S. Morgan and Helen M. Morgan, *The Stamp Act Crisis: Prologue to Revolution* (Chapel Hill, N.C., 1953; rev. ed., New York, 1962), 139–52.

the supreme court and heir to one of the largest land estates, has been a principal director in opposition to the [Stamp Act]. . . . Many other incidents confirm this."[10]

But while the Livingstons were leading the revolutionary movement in New York, they were struggling—to a degree that distinguished them from wealthy patriots in the other provinces—to rein in the common people and to keep the protest movement within narrowly defined bounds. For many of the foremost expansionists this circumspection was an outgrowth of their uncertain and, at times, precarious position as lords of a restless tenantry. Bitter landlord-tenant conflict, the result of the small farmers' desire to own land outright and the estate owners' refusal to sell off any of their domain, had reached one peak in the mid-1750s. Clashes in that decade had left the Livingstons, Van Rensselaers, Beekmans, and others fearful for their property and extraordinarily wary of stirring up the populace. Rural troubles in the 1760s would only confirm long-held attitudes.[11]

The lawyer allies of the manor lords fully shared this mistrust of the poorer citizens as well as the determination to make the pace of resistance a measured step. John Morin Scott angered artisans and shopkeepers with his public castigation of Patrick Henry's Virginia Resolves; these resolutions, Scott wrote some years later in an effort to justify his behavior, rested on the dogma "that the Parliament had no right to bind us by any laws whatsoever. This principle I did then . . . and do now hold to be destructive of the weal of the empire."[12] A second member of the triumvirate, William Livingston, was similarly guarded in his behavior. During the first half of 1765 he had been an effective publicist and opponent of Colden, but he quietly withdrew from the fray by the end of the summer just as the protest movement was heating up in the northern colonies.[13]

But perhaps the concern of expansionists to carefully modulate the protest movement in New York was most fully reflected in Robert R. Livingston's actions. At the Stamp Act Congress he fought a bold

10. C. Colden to Conway, Dec. 13, 1765, NYHS *Cols.*, x (1877), 67; L. Jesse Lemisch, "New York's Petitions and Resolves of December 1765: Liberals vs. Radicals," *NYHS Quarterly*, XLIX (1965), 315–17; *N.Y. Votes and Proceedings*, Nov. 20, 21, 26, 29, 1765.
11. Irving Mark, *Agrarian Conflicts in Colonial New York, 1711–1775* (New York, 1940), 118–30; Bonomi, *Factious People*, 179–218. For a different approach, which minimizes the conflict between landlord and tenant, see Sung Bok Kim, *Landlord and Tenant in Colonial New York: Manorial Society, 1664–1775* (Chapel Hill, N.C., 1978).
12. *New York Journal*, Apr. 19, 1770, and see April 12, May 3, 1770; Bernard Friedman, "The Shaping of Radical Consciousness in Provincial New York," *JAH*, LVI (1970), 788–89, quotes Scott.
13. Friedman, "Shaping of Radical Consciousness," 788; Dillon, *New York Triumvirate*, 90.

declaration of colonial rights and fruitlessly urged the gathering to recognize Parliament's power to regulate colonial trade. "It is impossible to suppose," Livingston reasoned, "that she [Britain] would ever give up the point of internal taxes except the other were fully secured and acknowledged. I find all the sensible people in town to agree with me in this but we had some who were much too warm to do any good."[14] Significantly, Livingston's allies in the debate were the few delegates, such as Timothy Ruggles of Massachusetts, who had long questioned the expansionists' cause.[15]

Livingston also played a major role in quieting the populace in New York City. As long as the possibility existed that Governor Colden might enforce the Stamp Act, Livingston accepted the necessity for a series of raucous and sometimes violent demonstrations, including a night of rioting on November 1. But with Colden's declaration on November 2 that he would not attempt to distribute the stamps the judge's attitude changed. On the evening of the second, along with James Duane and a captain "that had commanded privateers" (most assuredly Alexander McDougall), Livingston "went round to every part of town" urging the sailors and others he encountered to return to their lodgings. Two days later he swayed a public meeting with an impassioned speech on the same theme: "I ventured . . . to tell them that it was high time to form a resolution to keep the peace, and to enter into an engagement for that purpose, and set before them in as strong a light as I could all the terrors of a mob government in such a city as this."[16]

During the balance of 1765 prominent expansionists redoubled their efforts to check the popular leaders and their artisan following. At the end of November the Livingstons clashed at a public meeting with those organizers, such as Isaac Sears and John Lamb, who worked with the common people and who more and more frequently were known as the Sons of Liberty or the Liberty Boys. At this gathering, attended by perhaps twelve hundred New Yorkers, the Liberty Boys demanded a complete defiance of the obnoxious act and a resumption of legal proceedings and all other business that required

14. Robert R. Livingston to [?], Nov. 2, 1765, Livingston Papers, Bancroft Trans., NYPL.

15. Morgan and Morgan, *Stamp Act Crisis*, 145–47.

16. Robert R. Livingston to Monckton, Nov. 8, 1765, MHS *Cols.*, 4th ser., x (1871), 559–66; John Watts to Monckton, Sept. 24, 1765, *Letter Book of Watts*, 386; Minutes of Council, Nov. 2, 1765, "To the Freeholders and Inhabitants of the City of New York," Nov. 6, 1765, NYHS *Cols.*, LVI (1923), 64–65, 91; Thomas Ellison, Jr., to Col. Thomas Ellison, Nov. 4, 1765, Ellison Family MSS, NYHS; Roger J. Champagne, *Alexander McDougall and the American Revolution in New York* (Schenectady, 1975), 14–15; Dillon, *New York Triumvirate*, 117–18; *New York Journal*, May 3, 1770.

stamps. Upper-class patriots, however, headed by the triumvirate of Smith, Scott, and William Livingston, took control of the meeting and pushed through a set of resolutions extolling petitions "in the constitutional way." General Thomas Gage, commander of British forces in New York, observed that "the better sort . . . , fearing the consequences of such extremes, by their numbers and influence quashed the attempts of the inferior burgesses, who, seeing themselves deserted by those who had raised them, were obliged to desist."[17]

Although the Livingstons were quick to trim their sails in 1765, they still pursued a more patriotic tack than the DeLanceys. Nonexpansionists bridled at the harsh invective that filled the newspapers and readily ascribed these fulminations to the opposing faction. "You'll observe in Holt's last Thursday's paper a bold stroke at John Bull," John Watts grumbled to a friend in June 1765. "Who is the author I never heard so much as guessed at, but by the sourness and perseverance (for it seems he is not yet done) I should guess him a Presbyterian, and a rash one too, who does not know what he is about, I mean, what risk he runs."[18] Furthermore, the DeLanceys played only a minor role in New York's legislative protests.[19]

Until the very end of the year the Sons of Liberty, despite the buffets they received, felt more comfortable working with the Livingstons than with the DeLanceys. Isaac Sears testified in 1770: "I can call numbers to witness that none of them [DeLanceys] ever did publicly act in opposition to the detestable Stamp Act, or make their appearance at our associations, except once, when I think I saw Mr. John Alsop and Mr. James DeLancey there. The latter opposed all the plans we were going upon, which affronted many so much, that at a meeting of the Sons of Liberty, after the repeal of the Stamp Act, I had much to do to satisfy them and obtain their consent to choose him as our representative." The single "appearance" Sears recalled was probably at the November public meeting, where Alsop and DeLancey supported the moderate resolutions urged by the triumvirate.[20]

Only in December 1765, on a carefully chosen partisan issue, did the nonexpansionists begin to explore the possibility of cooperating

17. Carl Becker, *The History of Political Parties in the Province of New York, 1760–1776* (Madison, Wis., 1909), 37–39; C. Colden to Lord Mansfield, Jan. 22, 1768, NYHS *Cols.*, x (1877), 150; Roger J. Champagne, "Liberty Boys and Mechanics of New York City, 1764–1774," *Labor History*, VII (1967), 121–22; Lemisch, "New York's Petitions," 318–24; Gen. Gage to Conway, Dec. 21, 1765, *Correspondence of Gage*, I, 78.

18. John Watts to Monckton, June 8, 1765, *Letter Book of Watts*, 357–58.

19. *N.Y. Votes and Proceedings*, Nov.–Dec., passim.

20. *New York Journal*, May 10, 1770; Becker, *Political Parties*, 37–38.

with the leaders of the populace. In Sears's words: "Previous to interesting myself in behalf of Mr. [James] DeLancey, he, with several others were chosen a committee to wait on the lawyers and desire them to go on with business as usual, without stamp paper; this service some of the persons chosen refused; but Mr. DeLancey declared that as he was one of the persons entrusted with it, he thought himself obliged and would perform it. This gave me a good opinion of him." Strengthening DeLancey's resolve to pursue his mission was the knowledge that the demands he presented would prove an embarrassment to such expansionist lawyers as John Morin Scott who were reluctant to resume work as long as the Stamp Act was in force.[21]

Had rural New York remained quiet, this balance of forces between a cautious but patriotic Livingston faction leading the protests and a DeLancey faction playing a distinctly subordinate role in the resistance movement might have continued in 1766. But by the first months of the new year, the expansionists found in the "Great Rebellion of 1766" strong reasons for charting a still more conservative course of action. This resurgence of tenant-landlord conflict dated back at least to November 1765 when a group of settlers announced its intention of reinstating those evicted for nonpayment of rent. Revolutionary rhetoric had stirred the countryside as well as the city, and the small farmers soon noted, and pointed out, the disparity between the expansionists' patriotic language and their oppressive local practices. One of the Livingstons, a farmer remarked in his own colorful idiom, "has spoke treasonable words against king and parliament we must rase a Rebellion against the damned stamp act and I wil shed the blood against it and turn us sels tu a free republic as Holland this is the vue of Livingstons familie the robbers and murders of common poor people."[22]

By March 1766 the countryside was in arms, and a mob, variously estimated at from five hundred to two thousand, gathered for a descent on New York City, where several of the rural agitators were jailed. The urban patriots showed the marchers no sympathy. The Sons of Liberty, Captain Montressor cynically remarked, "are of opinion no one is entitled to riot but themselves." And Governor Henry Moore called out the militia, which dispersed the tenant army.[23] Sporadic attacks on manors continued through the summer.

21. *New York Journal*, May 10, 1770; Launitz-Schürer, *Loyal Whigs*, 36–38; Morgan and Morgan, *Stamp Act Crisis*, 224–25; Champagne, "Family Politics," 66.

22. Howenburgh to J. T. Kemp, quoted in Morgan and Morgan, *Stamp Act Crisis*, 236; Mark, *Agrarian Conflicts*, 136.

23. *Journals of Montressor*, 363 (May 1, 1766); Mark, *Agrarian Conflicts*, 137–39; Bonomi, *Factious People*, 221–22.

A crowd of two hundred on the Livingston estate threatened "to murder the lord of the manor and level his house" but was frightened off when a contingent of armed men arrived. At the end of July, Gage dispatched British troops to the countryside, and by fall peace was restored.[24]

The revolt shook such patriot estate owners as the Livingstons to the quick, reminding them of the delicacy of the social order and the need to avoid any unnecessary disruptions. "We have been like the ocean for a long time, tossed with storms and agitated to the very bottom," Robert R. Livingston told John Sargent, the colony's London agent, "and some little time of calm seems necessary before government can regain its authority and the lower sort can be reduced to a due submission." For Livingston, the rural unrest spelled out a lesson in imperial relations: "I hope upon hearing an account of the repeal of the Stamp Act, our disquiet will end, and the greatest harmony will subsist between us and our mother country. Nothing is more certain than that their interests are inseparable, and whatever jealousy may have obtained at our aiming at an Independence, nothing is more foreign from the thoughts of every man of property amongst us, for the confusion and disorder which arise if this was the case would render this country the most disagreeable of any in the universe."[25]

Other expansionist estate owners or those who were closely linked by political ties or bloodlines to the manor lords shared Robert R. Livingston's fears, and for the next two years questions of class rather than empire guided their behavior. Gerard G. Beekman, a merchant and close relative of the Dutchess County Beekmans, complained to an English correspondent about the "tumults in the countryside," adding, "I fear the consequences."[26] Similarly, Robert Campbell Livingston, with his eyes firmly set upon the unruly farmers, welcomed the repeal of the Stamp Act. "I hope the news of it," he told the lord of Livingston manor, Robert Livingston, Jr., "will be a means of subduing and crushing those relentless, disorderly, turbulent disposed miscreants that have lately involved you in so much trouble and anxiety."[27]

24. *Journals of Montressor*, 375 (June 28, 1766); Mark, *Agrarian Conflicts*, 131–63.
25. Robert R. Livingston to John Sargent, May 2, 1766, Livingston Papers, Bancroft Trans., NYPL; Robert Livingston to Robert Livingston, Jr., May 14, 1766, Livingston Family Papers, reel 8, FDRL.
26. Gerard G. Beekman to Richard Sharpe, July 30, 1766, *The Beekman Mercantile Papers, 1764–1799*, ed. Philip L. White, 2 vols., consec. pagin. (New York, 1956), 502.
27. Robert Campbell Livingston to Robert Livingston, Jr., May 29, 1766, Livingston Family Papers, reel 8, FDRL; Gen. Gage to Conway, May 6, 1766, *Correspondence of Gage*, I, 91.

The Great Rebellion mightily reinforced the conservative bent of New York expansionists. Robert R. Livingston, who since the close of the French and Indian War had been wary of strengthening British authority in New York, proposed in 1766 that the house reward the troops involved in suppressing the tenant uprising. This suggestion, which the lawmakers ultimately voted down, also received warm support from Peter Livingston, who represented Livingston Manor. Moreover, the expansionists now drew closer to Governor Moore, who was only too ready to defend their privileges against any challenge from the common people. Assembly divisions over Moore's salary found the Livingstons solidly in the executive's camp.[28]

A different set of forces, however, shaped the outlook of the nonexpansionists. Thus, these partisans did not display the same sharp turn toward moderation that marked the Livingstons' behavior in 1766. Rural and urban discontent were less frightening to the DeLanceys, who could lay claim to fewer of the threatened manors and who had hitherto felt less need to check the capital's artisans and shopkeepers. Furthermore, since the political center of gravity of the nonexpansionist party lay among the merchants of New York City rather than among the manor lords, the depression of the 1760s struck that faction harder than it did the Livingstons, making the nonexpansionist DeLanceys unusually receptive to the need for firm anti-British policies. Such unusual circumstances and a dose of political opportunism *seemed* to make for a brief exchange of roles in New York in the mid-1760s. It must be emphasized, however, that the nonexpansionists' patriotic initiatives were rarely bold, their preeminence within the revolutionary movement was never clear-cut, and not all New Yorkers recognized the reversal of factional positions. Nonetheless, a new state of affairs emerged in 1766 and would continue in 1767 and 1768.[29]

The DeLanceys' increased willingness to work with the popular leaders, coupled with the Livingstons' growing fear of disorder, helped draw into the nonexpansionist camp a sizable bloc—but not all—of the Sons of Liberty. Dissension throughout 1766 over the proper course to steer between the two parties culminated in a formal split in the Sons. Isaac Sears, John Lamb, and most of their compatriots supported the DeLanceys, while Alexander McDougall headed a minority faithful to the Livingstons. An electoral alliance now emerged between the nonexpansionists and the majority of the

---

28. *N.Y. Votes and Proceedings*, Dec. 12, 1766.
29. See the works cited in note 2 for contrasting approaches to these changes in partisan behavior.

Liberty Boys. During the summer, according to a newspaper account, "Mr. I[saa]c S[ea]rs, in a knot of Sons of Liberty," proposed Captain James DeLancey, the late governor's son, for the legislature "although at that time the then assembly had upwards of two years of their limited time of serving unexpired."[30] William Smith noted in his journal that "James DeLancey would probably get into the assembly now as he was among the Sons of Liberty."[31]

In the house the nonexpansionists showed a readiness to court popular favor, although their revolutionary fervor (and the Livingstons' newfound cautiousness) can easily be exaggerated. John Cruger, mayor and nonexpansionist representative from New York City, who, Smith remarked acerbically, "was afraid of his constituents, and urged by instructions from them,"[32] proposed that the colony erect a statue honoring William Pitt. But other actions undercut any simple reversal of party roles. Several nonexpansionists, including Cruger, Frederick Philipse, and Peter DeLancey, readily supported Robert R. Livingston's proposal for rewarding the British troops used against the tenants. Moreover, Philip Livingston in the fall of 1766 led the struggle, if with little success, for a paper money bill, and members of both parties opposed full compliance with Britain's demand that they provision the regulars stationed in the province.[33]

Along with their political protests, adherents of both factions took action on the economic front to chastise Britain and to alleviate the deepening depression. On October 31, 1765, New York traders became the first in the colonies to undertake nonimportation; it was a step that, Robert R. Livingston emphasized, "the merchants of this town . . . unanimously agreed to."[34] The desire to reduce excessive inventories reinforced the other motives for the boycott. "If the merchants should not send for goods as given out," Cadwallader Colden explained in November, "they will raise their price."[35] And he remarked the next month, "Should it [nonimportation] be executed the people in America will pay an extravagant price for old moth-eaten

30. *Pennsylvania Journal*, Mar. 29, 1770; Morgan and Morgan, *Stamp Act Crisis*, 250–51; *Journals of Montressor*, 349–50 (Feb. 14, 15, 1766); Friedman, "New York Assembly Elections," 9; Becker, *Political Parties*, 44n; Champagne, "Family Politics," 74–75.
31. *Memoirs of Smith*, i, 33.
32. Ibid., 32–33.
33. John Watts to James Napier, June 1, 1765, *Letter Book of Watts*, 354; *Memoirs of Smith*, i, 33; James Duane to Robert Livingston, Jr., Nov. 15, 1766, Peter R. Livingston to Robert Livingston, Jr., Nov. 24, 1766, Livingston Family Papers, reel 8, FDRL; *N.Y. Votes and Proceedings*, Dec. 12, 1766; Champagne, "Family Politics," 63.
34. Robert R. Livingston to [?], Nov. 2, 1765, Livingston Papers, Bancroft Trans., NYPL; Robert R. Livingston to Monckton, Nov. 8, 1765, MHS *Cols.*, 4th ser., x (1871), 560.
35. C. Colden to Conway, Nov. 9, 1765, NYHS *Cols.*, x (1877), 62.

goods and such as the merchant could not otherwise sell." The Sons of Liberty enthusiastically enforced the agreement.[36]

Albany merchants, whose strong links with the nonexpansionist cause dated back to the early decades of the century, were slower than their brethren in the capital to enter into the boycott. They refused during the last months of 1765 to cancel their orders for British goods, and no fewer than five traders applied for the post of stamp distributor. In January 1766, however, a group of Sons of Liberty in the upper Hudson city took matters into its own hands, visited several of the most refractory importers, and brought the town into line.[37]

» «

Although the Livingstons by 1769 would resume their customary role as defenders of America's larger goals, their vacillation in 1767 and 1768 lost them much of their popular following, and the decade ended with the DeLanceys firmly in control of the legislature. The year 1767 was a lull between storms in New York politics. The De-Lanceys initiated no protests, and the Livingstons displayed only a continuing preoccupation with agrarian unrest. The consequence of such quiescence was a subdued response to the Townshend program. The act suspending the New York assembly for its failure to vote adequate funds for the regulars caused no commotion because the house had decided well before the news reached the province to comply with the ministry's request for an appropriation. Secretary of State Shelburne agreeably instructed New York to ignore the suspending act. Nor was any protest made against the establishment of an American Board of Customs Commissioners or the imposition of duties on paper, tea, white and red lead, and painters' colors. "You seem to be fearful that we shall have differences about our public affairs," Robert R. Livingston remarked to a cousin in November, "but the governor and assembly harmonize as well as ever."[38]

In the March 1768 election, the Livingstons' timidity was translated into lost seats. The most hotly contested battle was in New York City, where the nonexpansionists concentrated their fire on John Morin Scott and boosted James DeLancey. Poll books, which make

36. C. Colden, State of the Province of New York, Dec. 6, 1765, ibid., 78; Arthur M. Schlesinger, The Colonial Merchants and the American Revolution, 1763–1776 (New York, 1919), 78, 81.

37. Beverly McAnear, ed., "The Albany Stamp Act Riots," WMQ, 3d ser., IV (1947), 486–98; Launitz-Schürer, Loyal Whigs, 38–39.

38. Robert R. Livingston to Robert Livingston, Jr., Nov. 27, Sept. 18, 1767, Robert R. Livingston Collection, Box 1, NYHS; Mark, Agrarian Conflicts, 155–58; Bonomi, Factious People, 208–9; Jensen, Founding of a Nation, 262, 334–46.

possible a detailed analysis of returns in the capital, reveal that lower-class voters, who made up about half the city's electorate, backed DeLancey and rejected Scott. Artisan support also assured the victories of two nonexpansionist merchants, Jacob Walton and James Jauncey. In Dutchess County the small farmers' bitter recollection of the Livingstons' behavior in 1766 helped DeLancey supporters gain two seats. Despite lost places, however, the expansionists retained control of the house and elected Philip Livingston speaker.[39]

Although the election turned in part on the question of which faction was more patriotic, New Yorkers—DeLanceys and Livingstons alike—continued to play a cautious role in imperial affairs during most of 1768. "This colony is grown the quintessence of moderation," John Watts observed early in the year. "All its neighbors are writing inflammatory papers, while our poor printers would starve if it was not for the dirty trade of copying, which they are forced to submit to for want of originals."[40] The city's merchants responded favorably to Boston's appeal for nonimportation, but New Yorkers showed no resolute defiance of British authority comparable to that in Massachusetts, nor did they boast a pamphleteer the equal of Pennsylvanian John Dickinson. Moore's long delay in convening the assembly (it did not meet until the end of October) also helped keep the province quiet.[41]

In the fall session of the legislature, the nonexpansionists hewed to a slightly bolder course, at least in their rhetoric, than did the expansionists. The first skirmish between the two factions came after a demonstration in November against the Townshend Acts. Smith persuaded Governor Moore to issue a proclamation denouncing the riot, but the DeLanceyite councillors hesitated before publicly associating themselves with a condemnation of the mob. "[Oliver] DeLancey, [John] Watts, and [Henry] Cruger grumbled out objections to the proclamation, and [Joseph] Reade muttered on that side," Smith recorded in his journal. "The governor flamed. They then gave way. I came in and coolly urged the reasons why I thought the measure proper."[42] The same slight but palpable difference in partisan behav-

39. Champagne, "Family Politics," 65–67; Thomas Jones, *History of New York during the Revolutionary War and of the Leading Events in the Other Colonies at That Period*, 2 vols. (New York, 1879), I, 18; John Watts to Monckton, Jan. 23, 1768, MHS *Cols.*, 4th ser., x (1871), 599; Champagne, "Liberty Boys," 132; C. Colden to [?], Apr. 25, 1768, NYHS *Cols.*, x (1877), 167–68; Robert R. Livingston to Robert Livingston, Jr., Feb. 21, 1768, Livingston Family Papers, reel 8, FDRL; Thomas Ellison, Jr., to Col. Thomas Ellison, Oct. 29, 1768, Ellison Family MSS; Bonomi, *Factious People*, 263–64.

40. John Watts to Monckton, Jan. 23, 1768, MHS *Cols.*, 4th ser., x (1871), 600.

41. *Memoirs of Smith*, I, 44–46; Jensen, *Founding of a Nation*, 283–85.

42. *Memoirs of Smith*, I, 46–47.

ior was evident in a quarrel over links with other colonies. "James [DeLancey] a few days ago offered a set of resolves and orders in high terms, one of which was for a committee to correspond with all the assemblies on the continent," observed Smith. "Schuyler showed them to the governor. We supplanted them thus. Scott drew another set fuller and yet more temperate. These the house preferred and rejected DeLancey's."[43]

The nonexpansionists also appeared more assertive on the central issue facing the house: the response to the circular letter from Massachusetts. DeLancey, with support from Walton and other members of his party, pushed for a speedy consideration of the document and a firmly worded reply, but as Smith observed, at least some of De-Lancey's ardor was posturing "to gain credit with the Sons of Liberty."[44] When expansionist Philip Schuyler proposed that the house "either agree to answer the letter tomorrow, or not read it at all, or at least defer reading it till after the business is finished," the nonexpansionists found his first proposal (an immediate reply) too radical. Commented Smith, "DeLancey was thunderstruck partly because he lost the honor of the motion, and had the disgrace of opposing it through fear of an instantaneous dissolution."[45] Once other business had been transacted, the assembly, under the Livingstons' leadership, forthrightly declared its support for the Massachusetts epistle. On January 2, 1769, Governor Moore, in obedience to Secretary of State Hillsborough's directive, chastised the lawmakers for approving the circular letter and dissolved the house.[46]

The sixteen ballots recorded by this assembly illustrate the long-standing geographical lines underlying the political divisions, with the upper Hudson counties supporting the Livingstons and those closer to the capital backing the DeLanceys. Map 7 depicts partisan alignments by showing whether a delegate agreed or disagreed with James DeLancey's position.

In the January 1769 provincial election, much as in the March 1768 contest, the DeLanceys registered gains because of the Livingstons' excessive caution and finally took control of the legislature. New York City was the scene of the hardest-fought contests. Expansionists attempted to transform the battle into one of dissenters versus Anglicans, for the latter, long a mainstay of the DeLanceys, formed a

43. Ibid., 47–48.
44. Ibid., 48; *N.Y. Votes and Proceedings*, Dec. 31, 1768; Champagne, "Family Politics," 69–72.
45. *Memoirs of Smith*, I, 48–49, 59–60; Robert R. Livingston to Robert Livingston, Jr., Dec. 12, 1768, Livingston Papers, Bancroft Trans., NYPL.
46. Bonomi, *Factious People*, 246–47.

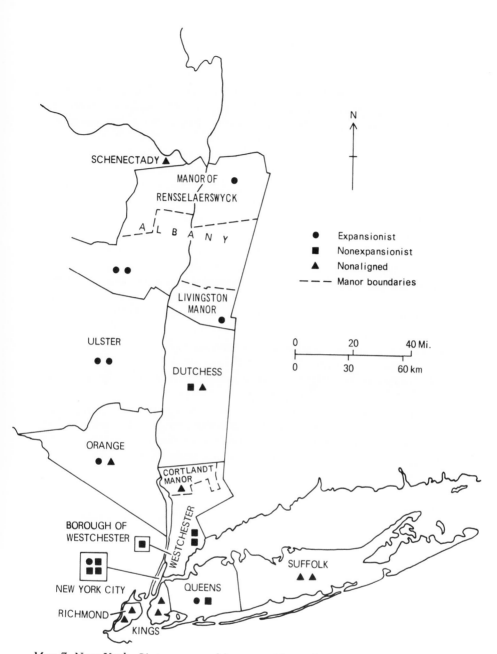

Map 7. New York: Sixteen assembly votes, November–December 1768

Source: *N.Y. Votes and Proceedings*, Nov. 3, 8 (2 votes), 17, 18 (5 votes), 23, Dec. 14, 16 (3 votes), 28, and 31, 1768. Nonexpansionists are those who voted with James De-Lancey two-thirds of the time or more often; expansionists opposed DeLancey two-thirds of the time or more often. Delegates not fitting either of these categories were considered nonaligned.

minority of the population. Religious lines, however, had never been the fundamental determinant of voting in New York, and they did not hold with any firmness. A more decisive factor was the alliance between the majority of the Sons of Liberty and the DeLanceys, and this union helped elect all four nonexpansionist candidates. The capital's lower classes made clear to the Livingstons the price they had to pay for their inconsistent opposition to Britain. In the rural areas, the resentment of the tenants once again meant setbacks for the expansionists. In all, the election was a clear victory for the DeLanceys, and they organized the house when it convened in April, placing John Cruger in the speaker's chair.[47]

The DeLanceys' success at the polls, coupled with the return of calm to the countryside, helped restore to New York politics the traditional pattern of a cautious nonexpansionist faction and a bolder expansionist party. The triumphant DeLanceys soon dropped all pretense of revolutionary activism; the knowledge that with care and circumspection the assembly could well continue for seven years made them hesitant to support any protests. At the same time, the glaring need to rebuild a base of popular support helped reinvigorate the Livingstons' commitment to defend the colonies against British policies. When the new legislature met in April, Philip Livingston proposed a reaffirmation of the previous assembly's constitutional resolves. The DeLancey majority was visibly reluctant to accede. The DeLanceys also voted down several of Philip Schuyler's motions, including the request to appoint special London agents and the demand to set aside a day, wrote William Smith, "to take the state of the colony into consideration with respect to Parliamentary taxation [and] an embarrassed commerce."[48] He noted, "We see now in whom the dread of a dissolution had [?] extinguished the zeal for liberty."[49] Instead of tackling imperial oppression, the majority focused its anger on the Livingstons, expelled both Philip Livingston and Lewis Morris III, and pushed through a bill excluding supreme court judges from the house to prevent Robert R. Livingston from assuming Philip's place.[50]

47. John Jay to Robert R. Livingston, [Jan.?] 1769, William Smith to Robert R. Livingston, Jan. 5, 1769, Robert R. Livingston Collection, Box 2, NYHS; James Duane to Robert Livingston, Jr., June 14, 1769, Livingston Family Papers, reel 8, FDRL; Jones, *History of New York*, 21; Champagne, "Family Politics," 74–76; Bonomi, *Factious People*, 252–57; *Memoirs of Smith*, i, 60; Champagne, "Liberty Boys," 132; John Watts to Monckton, Feb. 4, 1769, MHS *Cols.*, 4th ser., x (1871), 602–3.

48. *Memoirs of Smith*, i, 60–63.

49. Ibid., 63.

50. Peter R. Livingston to Robert Livingston, Jr., Apr. 14, May 15, 1769, Livingston Family Papers, reel 8, FDRL; *Memoirs of Smith*, i, 66; *N.Y. Votes and Proceedings*, Apr. 20, May 12, 1769.

The high-handedness of the DeLanceys accomplished what the vacillation of the Livingstons never had: it united the leaders of the
lower classes against the party in power. Because of a motion offered
by Lewis Morris early in the session, the assembly's galleries were
open to the public, and this access proved disastrous for the DeLanceys. "They are heartily tired of having open doors," Peter R. Livingston remarked, "but know not how to get them shut. They expose
themselves most horribly."[51] Upset by the actions of the nonexpansionists, the Sears and McDougall groups came together in July and
announced the formation of a United Sons of Liberty without regard
to "party distinctions that may have originated from differences in
sentiments in other matters."[52]

In the fall of 1769 the DeLanceys firmly allied themselves with
Colden, who, after Governor Moore's death in September, had once
more taken up the seals of office. "A bargain was struck between
them," Smith commented, "according to which they [the DeLanceys]
were to secure his salary . . . [and] in return for their favor they were
not to lose the present house in which they had a majority."[53] Colden
swiftly displaced a number of Livingston officeholders, installing
nonexpansionists in their stead. For their part, the DeLanceys did
their best to avoid conflicts with Colden or the ministry and approved only perfunctorily ("without giving themselves the trouble of
altering or adding a single syllable," noted Smith) Virginia's resolves
against trying Americans in England; other colonies had appended
strong supporting statements to the resolutions.[54]

Moreover, the DeLanceys pleased Colden but outraged New York
patriots with their willingness to dip into tax revenues and provide
two thousand pounds for the British troops stationed in the colony.
South Carolina and Massachusetts, as New Yorkers knew, had flatly
rejected British demands for such funds, but in the colony on the
Hudson neither party took the forthright stand advocated by patriots
elsewhere. Instead, the battle turned on where the money for the
regulars should come from, with the Livingstons arguing that the
only source should be a proposed loan office, which would issue

51. *Memoirs of Smith*, I, 60–61; Peter R. Livingston to Robert Livingston, Jr., Apr.
24, May 16, 1769, Livingston Family Papers, reel 8, FDRL.
52. Broadside, July 7, 1769, reprinted in Univ. of State of New York, *The American
Revolution in New York* (Albany, 1926), 310–11; Peter R. Livingston to Robert Livingston, Jr., June 15, 1769, Livingston Family Papers, reel 8, FDRL; Champagne, *Alexander McDougall*, 16–17.
53. *Memoirs of Smith*, I, 67.
54. Ibid., 54–55, 68–70; Peter R. Livingston to Robert Livingston, Jr., Dec. 2, 1769,
Livingston Family Papers, reel 8, FDRL; Chief Justice William Allen to Monckton,
Sept. 26, 1767, MHS *Cols.*, 4th ser., x (1871), 533–34.

£120,000 in much-needed paper money, while the DeLanceys countered that at least part of the funds should come from tax receipts. The question was a subtle one perhaps, but it generated much heat. "Great pains have been taken," observed Colden in December, "not only in this town to intimidate the members, but in the counties to procure instructions against granting any money for the troops otherwise than out of the money to be emitted on loan."[55] The DeLanceys, who, in Colden's words, "would willingly have given the whole sum out of the treasury," finally approved what they considered a workable compromise: a measure providing half the two thousand pounds from loan office funds and half from taxes. Colden eagerly accepted this bill, which he felt would raise his standing with the ministry.[56]

The angry popular reaction to the nonexpansionists' troop act strengthened the links between the Livingstons and the common people. On December 15, Alexander McDougall, writing as "A Son of Liberty," issued a broadside charging publicly what many individuals had observed in private: namely, that the appropriation for the regulars was part of a deal between Colden and the DeLanceys, in which the lieutenant governor would "make hay while the sun shines and get a full salary," while the "DeLancey family" would preserve "the ascendancy they have in the present house of assembly . . . [and] prevent a dissolution."[57] McDougall's tract provoked a series of mass meetings in which the reunited Sons of Liberty and the Livingstons loudly denounced the nonexpansionists. The DeLancey majority in the chamber decided to imprison McDougall, inflaming the patriots and, in the eyes of some, transforming the agitator into a martyr, the "Wilkes of North America."[58]

Although the clash over nonimportation came to occupy center stage in 1770, the Livingstons, backed by the Liberty Boys, also fought the DeLanceys over several "political" issues. Leading expansionists as well as the Sons denounced the assembly's attack on McDougall, and the contentious case dragged on through the year, even though the patriot was released from jail in April. William

---

55. *Memoirs of Smith*, I, 54; C. Colden to Hillsborough, Dec. 16, 1769, NYHS *Cols.*, x (1877), 195; Jensen, *Founding of a Nation*, 305, 311–12; Joseph A. Ernst, *Money and Politics in America, 1755–1775: A Study in the Currency Act of 1764 and the Political Economy of Revolution* (Chapel Hill, N.C., 1973), 266–74.

56. C. Colden to Hillsborough, Dec. 16, Oct. 4, 1769, NYHS *Cols.*, x (1877), 195, 188; *Memoirs of Smith*, I, 68–70.

57. *Memoirs of Smith*, I, 66–68, and see lengthy excerpts from [Alexander McDougall], "To the Betrayed Inhabitants of the City and Colony of New York," 71–72; C. Colden to Hillsborough, Oct. 4, 1769, NYHS *Cols.*, x (1877), 188.

58. C. Colden to Hillsborough, Jan. 6, 1770, NYHS *Cols.*, x (1877), 200; James Duane to Robert Livingston, Jr., Feb. 19, 1770, Livingston Family Papers, reel 8, FDRL; Jones, *History of New York*, 28–32; Bonomi, *Factious People*, 267–75; Becker, *Political Parties*, 80–81.

Livingston defended McDougall in print, John Morin Scott served as his counsel, and Philip Livingston and Nicholas Bayard posted his bail. When New York City artisans proposed to erect a liberty pole, expansionists supported them against both the regulars and the city council, which was controlled by DeLancey's supporters. Moreover, the mechanics and shopkeepers now applauded Robert R. Livingston's campaign to reenter the assembly. ("The Sons of Liberty are all on his side," rejoiced Peter R. Livingston.) Finally, many expansionists seconded, if vainly, the lower classes' call for a secret ballot.[59]

Votes recorded in 1769 and 1770 again follow geographical lines. The thirty-four ballots summarized in map 8 chiefly deal with the conflicts over the membership of the house (twenty-two votes) and the provisioning of British troops (six votes). The provincial election of January 1769 was the last held in the colonial period, and with few changes the divisions evident in 1769 and 1770 would continue until the house was dissolved in 1775.

As the depression continued, New York parties fought over economic measures as well as political issues and, more particularly, over nonimportation. In 1768, however, the two factions presented a remarkable picture of harmony on the question of the boycott. Rural unrest had muted the Livingston's ardor, while both political opportunism and the hard times oppressing the merchants (most of whom were associated with the nonexpansionist faction) spurred the DeLanceys. As a result, in New York—alone of the colonies studied here—both factions, rather than simply the expansionists, initiated the boycott movement of 1768–1770. Traders from the two groups responded warmly to Boston's request for a pact embracing the three northern cities. "We have the pleasure to inform you," a bipartisan committee wrote the Bostonians in April 1768, "that we have met with a success therein far beyond what our sanguine hope could have led us to have expected."[60] The enthusiasm of DeLancey's supporters was unmistakable; the New York Chamber of Commerce, which had grown out of the meetings held during the first half of 1768, was top-heavy with nonexpansionist traders.[61]

59. Peter R. Livingston to Robert Livingston, Jr., Dec. 2, 23, 25, 1769, Jan. 22, Feb. 5, 1770, Robert R. Livingston to Robert Livingston, Jr., Dec. 31, 1770, Livingston Family Papers, reel 8, FDRL; C. Colden to Sir William Johnson, Jan. 28, 1770, C. Colden to Hillsborough, Feb. 21, Apr. 25, 1770, NYHS *Cols.*, LVI (1923), 164, x (1877), 210, 217; Bonomi, *Factious People*, 275–76.

60. New York Merchants' Committee to Boston Merchants' Committee, Apr. 13, 1768, Samuel P. Savage Papers, 1751–1829, MHS.

61. Becker, *Political Parties*, 60–61.

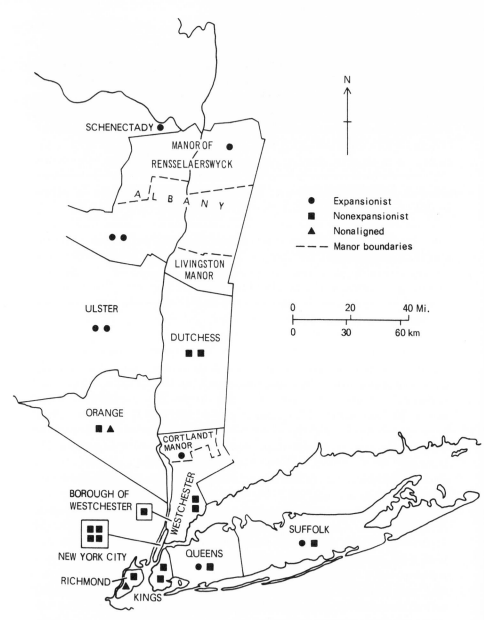

Map 8. New York: Thirty-four assembly votes, April 1769–January 1770

Source: *N.Y. Votes and Proceedings*, Apr. 12 (2 votes), 14 (2 votes), 20 (3 votes), May 12, 17 (3 votes), 18 (2 votes), Nov. 24 (2 votes), Dec. 28, 29 (6 votes), 30, 1769, Jan. 9, 11, 13, 18, 23, 25 (3 votes), 26 (3 votes), 1770. Nonexpansionists are those who voted with James DeLancey two-thirds of the time or more often; expansionists opposed De-Lancey two-thirds of the time or more often. Delegates not fitting either of these categories were considered nonaligned.

Note: Livingston Manor is shown as unrepresented because its delegate, Philip Livingston, was expelled early in the session.

After the efforts to establish a coordinated boycott collapsed because of Philadelphia's refusal to cooperate with the other ports, New York traders, with virtual unanimity, entered into a noncontingent agreement. This pact, signed on August 27, followed Boston's by only a few weeks and interdicted all goods sent from Britain after November 1. Economic motives weighed heavily with the merchants. "I must assure you it [is] very disagreeable to me to owe money when I have a sufficiency, and at the same time [am] unable to pay owing to the great stagnation of trade and scarcity of cash with us," James Beekman explained to a London house in October. "As long as trade remains in this manner, there will be no importers."[62] Several weeks after the importers entered into their accord the artisans and shopkeepers of New York City covenanted to support the boycott. The merchants of Albany also promised to abide by the agreement, though only after contending unsuccessfully that they should be allowed to import wares for the Indian trade.[63]

Both factions continued warm in their support for nonimportation during 1769. In March the merchants established a committee of inspection, with a membership roughly balanced between the two parties and headed by a DeLancey man, Isaac Low. Enforcement was stringent, and British shipments to New York dropped from £491,000 sterling in 1768 to £76,000 in 1769, the steepest slide recorded in any colony. Andrew Oliver of Boston, who visited New York in August, remarked upon the universal support for the boycott among the best citizens. Such behavior he considered "little less than assuming a negative on all acts of parliament which they do not like."[64] The success of the pact helped eliminate many of the importers' problems and so fostered discontent. "New York has kept up to the agreement with the most punctuality, and is consequently the greatest sufferer by it," General Gage commented in December. "Some rich merchants have made advantage, but the traders in general are greatly hurt. Many testify their dissatisfaction, and the country people begin to complain of the dearness of the commodities they stand in need of."[65]

As criticism of the agreement mounted during the first months of 1770, the Livingstons took the lead in blocking efforts to reopen trade. In March the two contending groups separately celebrated the

62. James Beekman to Thomas Harris, Oct. 7, 1768, *Beekman Papers*, 801; Schlesinger, *Colonial Merchants*, 124–25.

63. Schlesinger, *Colonial Merchants*, 125.

64. Ibid., 150, 186–90, quotation on 125; Becker, *Political Parties*, 75–76; Robert R. Livingston to Robert Livingston, Jr., Nov. 17, 1769, Robert R. Livingston Collection, Box 2, NYHS; *Historical Statistics of the U.S.*, 1176–77.

65. Gen. Gage to Hillsborough, Dec. 4, 1769, *Correspondence of Gage*, i, 242.

anniversary of the repeal of the Stamp Act. The DeLanceys, Waltons, Philipses, and Crugers were the guests of honor among the more than two hundred men attending the "Friends of Liberty and Trade" banquet, at which the Livingstons and other expansionists were conspicuous by their absence. The revelers toasted "trade and navigation, and a speedy removal of their embarrassments" and studiously avoided any mention of the imprisoned McDougall. By contrast, at the dinner held by the Sons of Liberty, now firmly allied with the Livingstons, the guests drank to "a continuance of the nonimportation agreement until the revenue acts are repealed" and raised their glasses to their jailed compatriot.[66]

The debate over nonimportation grew ever more strident during the spring and early summer. In May the Albany merchants, who had long displayed their distaste for expansionist schemes, abruptly abandoned their agreement and announced their readiness to import all goods except tea—the one item taxed by the Townshend revenue act after its revision in 1770. After learning that New York City and Boston remained firm, however, the traders of Albany returned to the fold, canceling the orders they had sent. Meanwhile, New York artisans and shopkeepers reaffirmed their commitment to the boycott with several public rallies and a series of tracts. One broadside in praise of the mechanics charged most pointedly that many of the restive traders had undertaken nonimportation only "to collect in their debts, to vend their moth-eaten fragments, and to clear at least fifteen percent."[67]

The fierce partisan struggle ended with a nonexpansionist victory and the decision July 9 to reopen trade, making New York the first of the ports to abrogate its pact. The composition of the opposing sides in the final battle generally followed factional lines, but as in other commercial towns, some of the patriot traders, for narrow economic reasons, joined their nonexpansionist brethren in calling for the resumption of commerce. Although some partisans wavered, such expansionists as the Livingstons and Beekmans circulated petitions insisting the agreement be continued. In contrast, nonexpansionists led the campaign to open the port. "The breaking of the nonimportation agreement in New York," Colden observed, "was a great point carried by the party who favored government [i.e., the DeLanceys]. . . . The members of his majesty's council with a single exception [pre-

66. *New York Journal*, Mar. 29, 1770; *New York Mercury*, Mar. 26, 1770 (these newspapers are also quoted in Becker, *Political Parties*, 86–87); James Beekman to Pomeroys & Hodgkin, Apr. 21, 1770, *Beekman Papers*, 924. *New York Journal*, Apr. 12, 1770, gives a list of those attending the "Friends of Liberty and Trade" dinner on Mar. 18.
67. Quoted in Gary B. Nash, *The Urban Crucible: Social Change, Political Consciousness, and the Origins of the American Revolution* (Cambridge, Mass., 1979), 365; Schlesinger, *Colonial Merchants*, 214–21.

sumably William Smith], and the representatives of the city in general assembly, have zealously exerted themselves for a dissolution of the nonimportation agreement."[68] Other accounts underscore the nonexpansionists' forward role in ending the accord. Members of that faction swelled the list published in the *Boston Gazette* of New Yorkers working to dissolve the agreement. Moreover, in his description of the "victory" parade that celebrated the reopening of trade, Alexander McDougall noted that "DeLancey and Walton headed the importers [marching] from the Coffee House."[69] For the moment the expansionists had been reduced to a dispirited opposition, and they would not seriously challenge the DeLanceys' iron grip on provincial politics until the final imperial crisis of 1774–1776.

» «

New Yorkers from both factions set down their sentiments during these years. If most statements dealt with specific problems, other pronouncements touched on the broader issue of America's future course. Nonexpansionists could not deny their opponents' vision of a burgeoning land but made clear their distaste for the political implications of this ascent. "I really believe some new constitution will be formed in time between the mother country and the colonies," John Watts remarked in 1765 to General Monckton, who was one of the merchant's steady correspondents. Watts for a moment explored the ramifications of rapid growth. "That there should be a supreme power lodged somewhere seems reasonable," he continued, with syntax at times askew, "but as the colonies before a great number of years are elapsed will exceed the mother country in numbers, would it be equally reasonable, the property of the majority should be disposed of by the minority at mere will and pleasure, especially when it is their [Britain's] interest to throw the burden off their own shoulders upon their absent, unrepresented, and, of course, unheard fellow subjects." But Watts bracketed his daring comments with a careful disclaimer: "The injudicious question about the power of Parliament no prudent man would meddle with but among friends as a mere matter of speculation."[70]

Several expansionists also sketched in their vision of the future,

<hr/>

68. Peach & Pierce to James Beekman, Nov. 5, 1770, *Beekman Papers*, 880; Dillon, *New York Triumvirate*, 122; C. Colden to Hillsborough, Oct. 5, Dec. 6, 1770, NYHS *Cols.*, x (1877), 229–30, 251.

69. Alexander McDougall to Joseph Reed, Nov. 21, 1770, quoted in Launitz-Schürer, *Loyal Whigs*, 89; *Boston Gazette*, July 23, 1770; Thomas Ellison, Jr., to Col. Thomas Ellison, July 8, 1770, Ellison Family MSS; James Beekman to Fludyer, Marsh, & Hudson, July 10, 1770, Peach & Pierce to James Beekman, Nov. 5, 1770, *Beekman Papers*, 727, 880; Gen. Gage to Hillsborough, Oct. 6, 1770, *Correspondence of Gage*, i, 274; Bonomi, *Factious People*, 276; Schlesinger, *Colonial Merchants*, 221–27.

70. John Watts to Monckton, Nov. 9, 1765, *Letter Book of Watts*, 400–401.

although the caution that marked the political behavior of their party was evident in these writings. In 1765 Robert R. Livingston's formulations were forceful if rarely rhapsodic. "Here we seem to think it as clear as any proposition of Euclid," he stated in December, "that if America submit to be taxed at the pleasure of the House of Commons the power will be too great and uncontrollable to remain long unabused, and that the abuse of it will naturally render the colonies independent." But Livingston foresaw the decline of the mother country more readily than the rise of the colonies. The question, he remarked, was whether Britain's "empire and trade shall be so extended as to make her the envy of the world, or being debilitated by the universal disaffection of the colonies she shall fall into decay and be finally ruined by the superior power of her European enemies."[71] Similarly, a fear of chaos moderated William Smith's belief in the ascendancy of America; his statements seem but one remove from the expostulations of the DeLanceys. "What a disjointed empire is this!" he observed in 1767. "I am afraid it is too complex for so vast an extent. At all events America must rise. The prosperity and adversity of Britain will conduce to our growth. Would to God we had a little more government here."[72]

Expansionist manifestos, however, were not entirely banished from New York. William Livingston eloquently set forth his creed in a 1768 newspaper article, which was soon republished in a book with other essays. "Liberty, religion, and sciences are on the wing to these shores: the finger of God points out a mighty empire to your sons," he declared. "No possible temper on her [Great Britain's] part, whether kind or cross-grained, will put a stop to this building. There is no contending with Omnipotence, and the *predispositions* are so numerous, and so well adapted to the rise of America that our success is indubitable." Livingston concluded this paean in the same elevated tone: "What an era is this to America! And how loud the call to vigilance, and activity! As we conduct, so it will fare with us and our children."[73]

71. Robert R. Livingston to John Sargent, Dec. 20, 1765, Livingston Papers, Bancroft Trans., NYPL.
72. William Smith, Jr., to Philip Schuyler, May 17, 1767, *Memoirs of Smith* I, 39; Robert R. Livingston to Moses Franks, May 2, 1766, Robert R. Livingston to John Sargent, May 2, 1766, Livingston Papers, Bancroft Trans., NYPL.
73. *New York Gazette*, Apr. 11, 1768, reprinted in *A Collection of Tracts from the Late Newspapers. . . .* (New York, 1768), I, 57–58, quoted in Carl Bridenbaugh, *The Spirit of '76: The Growth of American Patriotism before Independence, 1607–1776* (New York, 1975), 137.

CHAPTER 10

Pennsylvania:
Challenging the Quaker Party

Troubled by the popular unrest surfacing throughout America in 1765, Thomas Wharton found comfort in the Quaker party's role as a counterpoise to the belligerent expansionists. "There are many among us who would go all these lengths" in opposing the Stamp Act, Wharton remarked in November, "but our being at this juncture so split in our politics keeps the C[our]t P[ar]ty and their adherents from [so] engaging."[1] But though the preeminence and resolve of the nonexpansionist faction during the 1760s helped distinguish Pennsylvania from the other provinces studied here, the broad outlines of the partisan struggles in the Quaker Colony were similar to those observable elsewhere. The expansionists, who were variously known as the Proprietary faction, the Court party, New Ticket, or (later in the decade) Presbyterian party, led the fight against Britain and sparked the campaign to reinflate the economy, just as before 1763 they had spearheaded the struggle against France. The nonexpansionists, or Quaker party, were in the 1760s, as earlier, reluctant to endorse any energetic steps to enlarge American sovereignty.

» «

In 1763 and 1764 the strength of the nonexpansionists helped temper the Pennsylvania response to two grave challenges: Pontiac's Rebellion, an Indian uprising that broke out in May 1763 and was not fully quelled until the fall of 1764, and the new British measures, including the Sugar Act, Currency Act, and proposed stamp duty. The Quaker party, which controlled thirty-two of thirty-six seats in

1. Thomas Wharton to Franklin, Nov. 7, 1765, *The Papers of Benjamin Franklin*, ed. Leonard W. Labaree et al. (New Haven, 1959–), XII, 359.

[191]

the assembly, responded to the Indian raids along the frontier with the moderation characteristic of a faction dominated by nonexpansionists. Franklin had reformed the party in 1755–1756, driving out the extreme pacifists and introducing some few expansionists, but he had shifted the group's center of gravity only slightly. In July 1763 the lawmakers, frightened by the ferocity of the Indian war, voted seven hundred men, who were to be paid from funds in the provincial treasury; in October they appropriated twenty-four thousand pounds to maintain these forces (and an additional one hundred soldiers) in the field. But the numbers mustered were inadequate in the face of the widespread attacks, many of the soldiers were unschooled in Indian fighting, and they were prohibited from marching beyond the settled area—and hence were unable to respond to Colonel Henry Bouquet's urgent plea for forces to relieve the seige of Fort Pitt. "Had the design been to have sent so many men to have looked on the ravages that were committed amongst the back settlers without giving them the least assistance," an editorialist wryly observed, "it could not have been more effectually executed."[2] In November 1763 the Reverend Henry Muhlenberg noted ominously that the "country people are becoming embittered because the authorities are taking no adequate measures for defense."[3]

The ongoing debate within the Quaker party between the majority nonexpansionists and the small enclave of expansionists quickened when Franklin, who had returned from England the previous year, resumed his assembly seat in December 1763. "I only fear," Franklin announced, "we shall conclude a new peace before those villains [the Indians] have been made to smart sufficiently for their perfidious breach of the last."[4] Franklin urged compliance with Sir Jeffrey Amherst's request for a thousand men to assist the regulars. "A great deal had been said, with great ingenuity and judgment," in support of raising troops, one legislator recorded, "more particularly by Benjamin Franklin and John Dickinson."[5] The lawmakers agreed in principle to authorize the men but were slow to concur on an appropriation to support the forces. In January 1764 Franklin, again seconded

2. "The Apology of the Paxton Volunteers," *The Paxton Papers*, ed. John R. Dunbar (The Hague, 1957), 189, quoted in James H. Hutson, *Pennsylvania Politics, 1746–1770: The Movement for Royal Government and Its Consequences* (Princeton, 1972), 78n, and see 77–81; John Watts to Gen. Monckton, July 23, 1763, MHS *Cols.*, 4th ser., ix (1871), 483; Richard Waln, Jr., to William Dury, Oct. 8, 1763, Richard Waln Letterbook, HSP; *Papers of Franklin*, x, 362–63.

3. *The Journals of Henry Melchior Muhlenberg*, trans. Theodore G. Tappert and John W. Doberstein, 3 vols. (Philadelphia, 1942–45), i, 709 (Nov. 22, 1763).

4. Franklin to Richard Jackson, Dec. 19, 1763, *Papers of Franklin*, x, 405.

5. "Fragments of a Journal Kept by Samuel Foulke, of Bucks County," *PMHB*, v (1881), 65 (Dec. 23, 1763).

by fellow expansionist Dickinson, advocated an issue of interest-bearing, non-legal-tender paper money to raise funds without angering the proprietors. The Quaker majority turned back this proposal and instead joined battle with the Penns on their demand for preferential treatment in any tax measure. Not until May 30 was a bill for fifty thousand pounds, with major concessions to Penn, signed into law.[6]

Although divided on the question of a military appropriation, the Quaker party was unified in its hostility to the Paxton Boys, a group of frontiersmen who descended on Philadelphia in February 1764, demanding stronger measures for defense and angrily denouncing the legislature. During December 1763 a band of settlers (many from the town of Paxton in Lancaster County) had vented its rage on a tribe of peaceful Indians, killing twenty of them. Friends were shocked by the murders, and were thoroughly frightened by the march on the capital, particularly since nearly all the frontiersmen were Scotch-Irish Presbyterians. Quaker party writers vilified these "Irish rebels" and pointed out that they were of the same faith as the "envious, malicious, hard-hearted Presbyterians" who persecuted Quakers in Massachusetts.[7] Franklin also denounced these protestors. Despite some accord between his aims and theirs, he could not openly agree with the barbs their *Remonstrance* directed at the Society of Friends, nor could he accept their demand that the "frontier counties . . . may be no longer deprived of an equal number" of seats in the house. Any reapportionment would have decisively weakened Franklin's base of support, the Quaker party. Franklin helped organize a volunteer militia to protect the city from the marchers and joined the other legislators in ignoring the protestors' petition.[8]

The warmest sympathy for the demands of the westerners and the strongest critiques of the assembly came from the expansionists allied with the Proprietary party. Richard Peters, an Anglican minister and longtime opponent of the Quaker party, told General Monckton in January that, while he did not approve of the Paxton Boys' crimes, "the government failing to give the people that protection they were bound to do, the compact between them is broke, and . . . the people

6. William Logan to John Smith, Mar. 17, 1764, John Smith Correspondence, HSP; Franklin to R. Jackson, Mar. 14, 1764, *Papers of Franklin*, XI, 105–7, and see 203–7; "Journal Kept by Foulke," 68–69 (Jan. 2, 1764).

7. William Logan to John Smith, Dec. 30, 1763, John Smith Correspondence; *Papers of Franklin*, XI, 25–28; "The Quakers . . . Vindicated," *Paxton Papers*, 392, quoted in Hutson, *Pennsylvania Politics*, 99.

8. Franklin to R. Jackson, Jan. 16, 1764, Franklin, "A Narrative of the Late Massacres . . .," [c. Jan. 30, 1764], Franklin to John Fothergill, Mar. 14, 1764, *Papers of Franklin*, XI, 19, 42–46, 103–4, and see 80–86, 86–87n; George Bryan to [?], Apr. 13, 1764, Burton A. Konkle, *George Bryan and the Constitution of Pennsylvania, 1731–1791* (Philadelphia, 1922), 46–47; "Declaration of Paxton Boys," *Paxton Papers*, 99–110.

are then by the law of nature obliged to preserve themselves."[9] George Bryan concurred. Bryan was a Presbyterian merchant who had joined the Quaker party in 1755 in the first flush of enthusiasm for Franklin's initiative but had soon grown disenchanted with the nonexpansionist domination of the faction and had resumed his ties with the Proprietary party. "Our assembly have adjourned until May," he complained in April 1764, "without making provision for the support of the provincial troops or for entering into the vigorous measures proposed by the king's general in order to bring the shocking calamities our frontier people labor under to a speedy conclusion."[10]

More generally, Presbyterians both in Philadelphia and in the countryside censured the assembly's reticence and hesitated to oppose the march of the Paxton Boys. "All orders of people," a Quaker merchant observed, "showed a steady resolution except the Presbyterians."[11] Even though the religious schism opened by the Great Awakening of the 1740s had been officially healed in 1758, it was the controversy over the defense of the frontier that truly unified Pennsylvania Calvinists and made them a potent political force. In January 1764 Peters reported that "the Presbyterians are kindling fast and, considering themselves as the only people at whom those invectives are aimed, are determined to lay aside the religious animosities subsisting between themselves, and now unite to make the government as disagreeable to the Quakers as they possibly can." The Presbyterians were never the all-powerful, conspiratorial sect that many Quakers (and nonexpansionist Anglicans) imagined. But most upperclass Presbyterians now offered even firmer and more vocal support to the expansionist faction.[12]

The dominant Quaker party also helped assure a temperate response to a second broad challenge faced in 1764: the new parliamentary enactments. The colony's halting steps can be fully understood, however, only in the context of the fight over the royal charter, a

9. [Richard Peters] to Gen. Monckton, Jan. 19, 1764, MHS *Cols.*, 4th ser., x (1871), 510.

10. George Bryan to [?], Apr. 13, 1764, quoted in Konkle, *George Bryan*, 45, and see 34–35; Benjamin H. Newcomb, *Franklin and Galloway: A Political Partnership* (New Haven, 1972), 29–30.

11. Richard Waln, Jr., to Nicholas Waln, Mar. 10, 1764, Waln Collection, Box H, HSP; Dietmar Rothermund, *The Layman's Progress: Religious and Political Experience in Colonial Pennsylvania, 1740–1770* (Philadelphia, 1961), 99n.

12. [R. Peters] to Gen. Monckton, Jan. 19, 1764, MHS *Cols.*, 4th ser., x (1871), 509; George Bryan to [?], July 5, 1758, Konkle, *George Bryan*, 36–37; Benjamin Marshall to John Townsend, May 2, 1764, Marshall to Barnaby Egan, Oct. 5, 1764, "Extracts from the Letter-book of Benjamin Marshall, 1763–1766," ed. Thomas Stewardson, *PMHB*, xx (1896), 206, 207–8.

struggle that made many nonexpansionist politicians exceptionally reluctant to defy the mother country.

In 1764 a group of Quaker party men, led by Benjamin Franklin, called upon the king to revoke the proprietary frame of government and to grant a royal charter. Franklin had been openly working toward this end since 1758 and probably covertly since 1755, when he broadly hinted at his goals. In 1758 he had suggested to Speaker Isaac Norris that "tumults and insurrections that might prove the proprietary government insufficient to preserve order, or show the people to be ungovernable, would do the business immediately."[13] But there was at that time little enthusiasm among Quakers for such a move, which, as Norris observed, could "operate against the people," and Franklin shelved his plans until his return to the province in 1762.[14]

Despite an element of popular support, Franklin's quest for a new charter, which triggered the struggles of 1764, had the earmarks of a personal campaign whose ultimate goal was a royal governorship for Franklin. He was characteristically reticent about his own ambitions, but his intimate friends, as well as his enemies, wrote openly about his quest for the executive post or clearly hinted at it. For example, Joseph Galloway wrote Franklin in 1765, shortly after the printer returned to London, that "the hopes your last letters gave us of a change [in government] give us great joy—and the expectation of seeing you in a station superior to the malice of your unrelenting enemies adds beyond measure to that pleasure."[15] Significantly, Franklin did not relent in his call for a royal government when the ostensible reasons for it disappeared. When the "great riots" and "armed mobs" subsided (the assembly petition Franklin helped draft argued that such disturbances showed the flaw in proprietary rule) or when Penn in the fall of 1764 accepted the house's position on the taxation of his lands (another assembly complaint), Franklin's desire for a change in government remained unabated.[16]

---

13. Franklin to Isaac Norris, Sept. 16, 1758, *Papers of Franklin*, VIII, 157. For a review of the evidence touching on Franklin and the royal governorship, Marc Egnal, "The Politics of Ambition: A New Look at Benjamin Franklin's Career," *Canadian Review of American Studies*, VI (1975), 151–64.

14. Norris to Franklin, Jan. 15, 1759, Franklin to Norris, Mar. 19, 1759, *Papers of Franklin*, VIII, 228, 293–95.

15. Papers from Election Campaign, 1764, William Franklin to Franklin, Nov. 13, 1766, Joseph Galloway to Franklin, July 18, 1765, Thomas Wharton to Franklin, Feb. 9, 1768, ibid., XI, 370, XIII, 501–2, XII, 219, XV, 40–41; George Bryan to [?], Apr. 26, 1764, Konkle, *George Bryan*, 50; Richard Waln, Jr., to Nicholas Waln, Nov. 5, 1764, Waln Collection, Box H.

16. Pennsylvania Assembly to king, May 23, 1764, Franklin to R. Jackson, Mar. 31, 1764, John Dickinson and Others, Protests against the Appointment of Franklin as Agent, Oct. 26, 1764, *Papers of Franklin*, XI, 199, 150–51, 409–11, and see 213–14n.

The campaign divided the traditional constituency of the Quaker party and contributed to the setback it suffered in the October elections. Although most of the Quaker party legislators, who respected Franklin's judgment and who harbored strong animosities toward the Penns, voted in the spring to petition for an end to proprietary rule, outside the house the majority of Friends opposed the change. The Yearly Meeting followed the lead of Israel Pemberton, who declared with some hyperbole that the present charter was "the best frame of government that ever subsisted."[17] Many Germans, already dismayed by the halfhearted defense of the frontier, were further put off by a project that could endanger, as one Schwenkfelder observed, "the celebrated privileges of the said [proprietary] charter."[18] Presbyterians and most Anglicans also opposed the change. Despite a well-organized effort by Franklin's supporters, petitions against a royal charter received over four times as many signatures as those favoring it (fifteen thousand against, thirty-five hundred for), and Franklin's campaign was responsible for the Quaker party losses in the October 1764 election. While the nonexpansionists' grip on the sixteen seats in Bucks and Chester counties remained virtually unshaken, the Proprietary party won eleven or twelve of the other twenty seats, twice its usual complement, and unseated both Franklin and Galloway (map 9).[19]

The struggle over the frame of government helped shape the response of Pennsylvanians to the new British policies. Benjamin Franklin's desire for a new charter and—most possibly—for his elevation as royal governor seriously muted his criticism of the mother country. As for the Sugar Act, Franklin opined, "more is apprehended than will happen," nor did he expect "much inconvenience" from the Currency Act.[20] Franklin even went so far as to suggest items that

17. Israel Pemberton to David Barclay, Sr., Nov. 6, 1764, Pemberton Papers, HSP; Thomas Clifford to Mildred & Roberts, May 12, 1764, Clifford Letterbook, HSP; John Churchman to James Pemberton, June 1764, Pemberton Papers; Richard Waln, Jr., to Nicholas Waln, June 3, 1764, Waln Collection, Box H; John Reynell to Mildred & Roberts, Nov. 23, 1764, Reynell Letterbook, HSP; Pennsylvania and New Jersey Yearly Meeting to London Yearly Meeting, Sept. 1764, Epistles Received, IV, 139–40, Friends House Library, London; Philadelphia Meeting for Sufferings to London Meeting for Sufferings, Sept. 3, 1764, Letters to and from Philadelphia, I, 46, Friends House Library.

18. Christopher Schultze to Israel Pemberton, Apr. 4, 1764, Rothermund, *Layman's Progress*, 181; *Journals of Muhlenberg*, II, 18–19 (Feb. 1, 1764), 19 (Feb. 5, 1764); Papers from the Election Campaign, 1764, Franklin to R. Jackson, Oct. 11, 1764, *Papers of Franklin*, XI, 370, 382, 397, and see 72.

19. Franklin, "Preface to Joseph Galloway's Speech," Aug. 11, 1764, Franklin to R. Jackson, Sept. 25, Oct. 11, 1764, *Papers of Franklin*, XI, 290, 357, 397; William Logan to John Smith, [Oct. 1764], John Smith Correspondence; Hutson, *Pennsylvania Politics*, 125–47.

20. Franklin to R. Jackson, June 25, 1764, *Papers of Franklin*, XI, 234, 238.

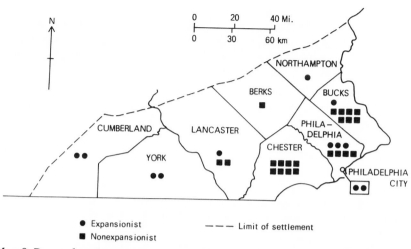

Map 9. Pennsylvania: Five assembly votes on the royal charter, October 1764

SOURCE: *Votes and Proceedings of the House of Representatives of the Province of Pennsylvania,* VII (this is *Evans Imprint* #10124, pp. 11–14): Oct. 15, 20 (3 votes), 25, 1764. Nonexpansionists cast at least four votes for the charter; expansionists voted against it at least four times. Only P. Shepherd of Bucks County was inconsistent, voting against the charter twice and for it once; he was grouped with the expansionists.

Britain might tax ("if money *must* be raised from us") and also indicated a "better mode"—an interest-bearing currency, with receipts to flow to Britain.[21] Franklin was hard put in the public debate to justify a campaign for royal government while the mother country was tightening its controls over the colonies, and his claim that "his Majesty . . . has no views but for the good of the people" had a hollow ring.[22] Franklin's odd moderation would continue until August 1768, when an interview with Secretary of State Hillsborough made it unmistakably clear that Britain would not revoke the proprietary charter. Agile politician that he was, Franklin never wholly espoused the arguments of the nonexpansionists. But many Pennsylvanians during the mid-1760s, with some justification, questioned the printer's patriotism.

The quest for royal government also reinforced the reluctance of the nonexpansionist majority in the house to castigate the policies of the mother country. In the spring the legislators ignored a merchant request that the colony's agent be instructed to protest the proposed revision of the Molasses Act, and the assemblymen's action in Sep-

21. Franklin to R. Jackson, Feb. 11, June 25, 1764, ibid., 76, 236–38.
22. Franklin, "Cool Thoughts on the Present Situation," [Apr.] 1764, ibid., 171.

tember was similarly irresolute. Prodded by a letter from Massachusetts, the house sent agent Richard Jackson a weakly worded directive. The "measures proposed," the lawmakers stated, had a "tendency" to deprive Pennsylvanians of their rights. These instructions also indicated that the assembly had a "plan" for raising money "without . . . infringing [on] the natural and legal rights of the colonies." Though not spelled out, the scheme was Franklin's interest-bearing currency.[23] In October the legislature forwarded to Jackson a somewhat stronger set of resolves. The election of a dozen expansionists had injected a note of vigor, even though nonexpansionists remained in control. The assembly explicitly dropped the proposed "plan" and asserted that any money raised, except by the separate legislatures, was "unequal, oppressive and unjust." The instructions remained silent, however, on the question of the forthcoming Stamp Act.[24]

Finally, the fight over a new charter provided many expansionists with a compelling reason for underscoring the threat posed by the parliamentary measures. In the assembly the opposition to a royal government was led by John Dickinson, a young lawyer and expansionist who had been loosely associated with the Quaker party since he took his seat in 1762. Dickinson broke with Franklin and the Quaker party because he felt a new charter would aggravate the dangers inherent in British policies. "Is not the authority of the Crown full enough exerted over us?" he asked.[25] In May, Dickinson's vote was one of only three cast against the petition for a new form of government. The October elections, however, strengthened his voice by adding to the house such expansionists as George Bryan and Thomas Willing, the new burgesses from Philadelphia. Like Dickinson, Bryan considered Franklin's campaign foolish while the ministry was "devising taxes and funds."[26] These expansionists could not prevent Franklin's appointment as coagent, but they were able to reword the instructions touching colonial policy. And under pressure from the expansionists, the majority in the assembly now agreed to tell the agents to proceed "with the utmost caution" in applying for a new charter.[27]

23. Pa. Assembly, Instructions to Richard Jackson, Sept. 22, 1764, ibid., 347–49.
24. Ibid., 402–3; Merrill Jensen, *The Founding of a Nation: A History of the American Revolution, 1763–1776* (New York, 1968), 81.
25. David L. Jacobson, "John Dickinson's Fight against Royal Government, 1764," *WMQ*, 3d ser., xix (1962), 71–77; *Papers of Franklin*, xi, 193–98; Richard Waln, Jr., to Nicholas Waln, June 3, 1764, Waln Collection, Box H; Newcomb, *Franklin and Galloway*, 87–88.
26. George Bryan to [?], Apr. 13, 1764, quoted in Konkle, *George Bryan*, 49.
27. Pa. Assembly Committee of Correspondence to R. Jackson, Nov. 1, 1764, *Papers of Franklin*, xi, 424.

» «

Although the Quaker party's impressive political muscle helped keep the Pennsylvania response to the Stamp Act comparatively moderate, the expansionists, most of whom were connected to the Proprietary party, made certain the province denounced the measure. "I cannot describe to you the indefatigable industry," Galloway informed Franklin in July 1765, "that have been and are constantly taking by the Proprietary party and men in power here to prevail on the people to give every kind of opposition to the execution of this law."[28] John Dickinson, who had won reelection in 1764 on the Proprietary slate, wrote a series of pamphlets urging a spirited resistance to the act, and in September 1765 adherents of the New Ticket (as the Proprietary party had come to be called) by a single vote secured assembly endorsement for the intercolonial congress at New York. Fear of the Stamp Act, one Presbyterian observed, "even brought over some of their [Quaker party] members in the house to our party by which means they carried the vote."[29] The legislature sent Dickinson, Bryan, and a Quaker party supporter to New York. In October expansionists, including Robert Morris, printer William Bradford, and former Quaker party supporter Charles Thomson, headed the delegation that demanded the resignation of Stamp Distributor John Hughes. And in 1766 the Proprietary party promoted the "illumination" of Philadelphia to celebrate the repeal of the Stamp Act.[30]

Charles Thomson's emergence as a revolutionary leader in 1765 was significant because it revealed that the expansionists who had followed Franklin into the Quaker party after 1755 were now abandoning the majority faction. A few, to be sure, had left earlier: George Bryan's apostasy was evident by the late 1750s, and Dickinson's in 1764. But Thomson, Daniel Roberdeau, and a handful of like-minded individuals had remained with Franklin through the royal charter fight of 1764 and, like the printer, had softened their criticism of British policies. Now these men separated themselves from Galloway and his followers. Thomson not only joined the delegation visiting

28. Joseph Galloway to Franklin, July 18, 1765, ibid., XII, 217–18.
29. John Dickinson, "Address on Stamp Act," *The Writings of John Dickinson*, ed. Paul L. Ford (vol. XIV of HSP *Memoirs*) (Philadelphia, 1859), I, 201–5; Samuel Purviance to Col. James Burd, Sept. 20, 1765, Rothermund, *Layman's Progress*, 185–86; John Hughes to Franklin, Sept. 10, 1765, *Papers of Franklin*, XII, 265; Benjamin H. Newcomb, "Effects of the Stamp Act on Colonial Pennsylvania Politics," *WMQ*, 3d ser., XXIII (1966), 260.
30. John Reynell to Henry Groth, May 27, 1766, John Reynell to Mildred & Roberts, June 4, 1766, Reynell Letterbook, HSP; *Papers of Franklin*, XII, 191–92n; Arthur M. Schlesinger, *The Colonial Merchants and the American Revolution, 1763–1776* (New York, 1919), 73.

Hughes in October, but also led a public meeting in November that again demanded his resignation. And when Franklin counseled "frugality and industry," Thomson gently rebuked him, asking, "Who will labor or save who has not a security in his property?" Thomson added that only force could compel the colonists to obey but that such measures "will beget resentment and provoke to acts never dreamed of."[31]

The import of these new allegiances was not lost on Pennsylvanians: after 1765 most commentators stopped calling the expansionist faction the Proprietary party, and renamed it the Presbyterian party. A group that included Thomson and Roberdeau, who had earlier battled the Penns, could no longer be linked so closely with the colony's owners. Moreover, the new label reflected the vigor and high visibility of the reunited Presbyterians. William Allen and George Bryan (a "red hot Presbyterian," as John Hughes termed him) held assembly seats during these years, and Thomson, Roberdeau, and William Bradford were active in city politics. The "Presbyterian party," however, was never the sole preserve of any single sect. Calvinists worked closely with Anglicans like Willing and Morris and with former Quakers like Dickinson.[32]

Avidly pursuing the royal charter, Franklin, unlike other expansionists, maintained his close ties with the Quaker party in 1765 and 1766 and moderated his criticism of the Stamp Act. Franklin labored for a new frame of government with remarkable persistence, and the optimism filling his letters to Galloway and others ("I am not in the least doubtful of obtaining what we so justly desire," he stated in May 1766) was not dampened by the Privy Council's dismissal of the petition in November 1765.[33] His desire to secure the support of the

31. On George Bryan, see note 10. On Dickinson's ties (and conflicts) with the Quaker party before 1765, see Nicholas Waln to Richard Waln, Jr., July 28, 1764, Waln Collection, Box H; Edward Shippen, Jr., to Edward Shippen, Sr., Oct. 2, 1761, Shippen Papers, vol. II, HSP; Charles J. Stillé, *The Life and Times of John Dickinson, 1732–1808* (Philadelphia, 1891), 37–43; Charles Thomson to Franklin, June 19, Sept. 24, 1765, Dec. 18, 1764, Franklin to Charles Thomson, July 11, 1765, Joseph Galloway to William Franklin, Nov. 14, 1765, *Papers of Franklin*, XII, 183–87, 278–80, quotations on 278 and 280, XI, 521–24, XII, 206–8, 372–73; Petition for Royal Government, 1764, [with accompanying signatures], Privy Council 1, bundle 50, PRO.

32. John Hughes to Stamp Office, Jan. 13, 1766, quoted in Morgan and Morgan, *Stamp Act Crisis*, 321; John Reynell to Capt. James Shirley, May 14, 1765, Reynell Letterbrook, HSP; Gen. Gage to Sec. of State Conway, Jan. 16, 1766, *Correspondence of Gage*, I, 82–83; John Drinker and Stephen Collins to Israel Pemberton, Sept. 25, 1766, Pemberton Papers. Hutson, *Pennsylvania Politics*, 211–13, argues that the Presbyterians formed a separate political party.

33. Franklin to Cadwallader Evans, May 9, 1766, Franklin to John Ross, Feb. 14, June 8, 1765, Samuel Wharton to Franklin, May 27, 1765, Franklin to Samuel Rhoads, July 8, 1765, Thomas Penn to Gov. John Penn, Nov. 30, 1765, Thomas Wharton to Franklin, Dec. 30, 1765, Joseph Galloway to Franklin, Feb. 27, 1766, *Papers of Franklin*, XIII, 269, XII, 67–68, 173, 142, 205, XIII, 179–80n, XII, 420–21, XIII, 179–82, and see XII, 236n.

ministry initially predisposed him to accept the Stamp Act. He sent Thomas Wharton an English pamphlet defending the act, secured the post of stamp distributor for John Hughes, and in August told Hughes to stand firm against the popular outcry: "Your undertaking to execute it may make you unpopular for a time, but your acting with coolness and steadiness and with every circumstance in your power of favor to the people, will by degrees reconcile them."[34]

Only toward the end of 1765, when his Philadelphia correspondents told him his patriotism was widely suspected and when the ministry began considering the expediency of repeal, did Franklin begin even a partial defense of American rights. Even then his positions often would have been unacceptable to the patriots. At first he advocated suspension rather than repeal of the Stamp Act, called for American representatives in Parliament, and urged his scheme for an interest-bearing currency as a source of revenue—a plan that even Galloway later acknowledged would have caused "great clamors" in America.[35] Moderation also marked Franklin's well-publicized appearance before the House of Commons in February 1766. "The ring-leaders of riots in my opinion ought to be punished," he told the honorable members, and he averred that the colonists would pay external taxes though not internal ones like the Stamp Act. But Franklin's performance before Parliament, along with a number of letters from prominent Londoners praising his role in securing repeal, helped convince doubting Pennsylvanians that he was a defender of American rights.[36]

Most members of the Quaker party, while not applauding the Stamp Act, labored—with a measure of success—to moderate the protests. Galloway wrote an article, over the signature "Americanus," designed (as he informed Franklin in July) "to check the

34. Franklin to John Hughes, Aug. 9, 1765, Franklin to David Hall, Feb. 14, June 8, 1765, Thomas Wharton to Franklin, Apr. 27, 1765, Samuel Wharton to Franklin, May 27, 1765, ibid., XII, 234–35, 65–66, 171–72, 113–14, 145–46.

35. Joseph Galloway to William Franklin, Dec. 21, 1766, quoted in Joseph A. Ernst, *Money and Politics in America, 1755–1775: A Study in the Currency Act of 1764 and the Political Economy of Revolution* (Chapel Hill, N.C., 1973), 105; Franklin, "Scheme for Supplying the Colonies with a Paper Currency," Feb. [11–12?], 1765, Franklin to William Franklin, Nov. 9, 1765, Franklin, "Fragments of a Pamphlet," [c. Jan.] 1766, Franklin to [?], Jan. 6, 1766, Franklin to Joseph Galloway, Oct. 11, 1766, *Papers of Franklin*, XII, 47–60, 362–65, XIII, 72–87, 23, 26, 448–49.

36. "Committee on American Papers," Feb. 13, 1766, Add. MSS 33,030, f. 174, BM. For a slightly different version of Franklin's remarks, see "Examination of Benjamin Franklin before the Committee of the Whole of the House of Commons," Feb. 13, 1766, David Hall to Franklin, Sept. 6, 1765, Hugh Roberts to Franklin, Nov. 27, 1765, William Franklin to Franklin, Apr. 30, 1766, James Pemberton to Franklin, May 1, 1766, *Papers of Franklin*, XIII, 124–62, XII, 259, 387, XIII, 254, 261, and see XII, 328–29; Thomas Crowley to Israel Pemberton, Feb. 24, 1766, Pemberton Papers; John Fothergill to James Pemberton, Feb. 27, 1766, Misc. Corresp. 38:85, Friends House Library.

growing mischiefs—by proving the reasonableness of our being taxed."[37] In September, John Hughes reported that "all the sensible
Quakers behave prudently," and he was pleased that the "sober and
sensible part of the people" helped suppress the mob which threatened the homes of the party leaders.[38] The same conservative presence was evident in November, when Thomson tried to raise another
crowd against Hughes, and in May of the following year, when news
of repeal arrived. In general, the Quaker party was able to keep resistance within safe bounds.[39]

An important factor in moderating protests in the mid-1760s was
the willingness of the majority of artisans and small shopkeepers in
Philadelphia to follow the lead of the Quaker faction. Party chieftain
Benjamin Franklin, the model of the successful artisan, remained a
particular object of veneration among the lower classes. Many of the
White Oaks, as a large company of ship carpenters was called, had
signed the petition for a royal charter in 1764, and in September 1765
they were prominent among the eight hundred men who turned out to
protect the homes of Franklin and others. "Every mechanic who
rowed you from Chester to the ship," Samuel Wharton informed
Franklin, helped in suppressing the disturbances.[40] Thomson and
others tried to stir the crowd against Hughes in November, but "everything they proposed," Galloway boasted, "was hissed or opposed by
some of the White Oaks and others of our friends who were there."[41]
Oppressive British policies, however, produced some defections in
this solid support. The Stamp Act, one Proprietary partisan noted,
turns "many of their warm friends out of doors against them."[42]

The divisions in the assembly during the mid-1760s reveal patterns
of partisan support that date back to 1740. The Scotch-Irish Pres-

37. Joseph Galloway to Franklin, July 18, Sept. 20, 1765, *Papers of Franklin*, xii, 218–
19, 269–70; *Pa. Journal*, Aug. 29, 1765.
38. John Hughes to Franklin, Sept. 10–16, 1765, Deborah Franklin to Franklin, Sept.
22, 1765, *Papers of Franklin*, xii, 266, 271–74.
39. Thomas Wharton to Franklin, Nov. 7, 1765, Franklin to David Hall, Feb. 24,
1766, Joseph Galloway to William Franklin, Nov. 14, 1765, ibid., 359, xiii, 169–70, xii,
372–73; John Reynell to Mildred & Roberts, Mar. 30, 1766, Reynell Letterbook.
40. Samuel Wharton to Franklin, Oct. 13, 1765, *Papers of Franklin*, xii, 315–16;
[William Bradford?] to New York Sons of Liberty, Feb. 15, 1766, MSS relating to the
nonimportation agreement, American Philosophical Society; Charles S. Olton, *Artisans for Independence: Philadelphia Mechanics and the American Revolution* (Syracuse, N.Y., 1975), 37–38; James H. Hutson, "An Investigation of the Inarticulate:
Philadelphia's White Oaks," *WMQ*, 3d ser., xxviii (1971), 3–25. Theodore Thayer, *Pennsylvania Politics and the Growth of Democracy, 1740–1776* (Harrisburg, 1953), 95, provides a contrasting argument.
41. Joseph Galloway to William Franklin, Nov. 14, 1765, *Papers of Franklin*, xii, 372–
74.
42. Samuel Purviance to Col. James Burd, Sept. 20, 1765, Rothermund, *Layman's
Progress*, 185–86.

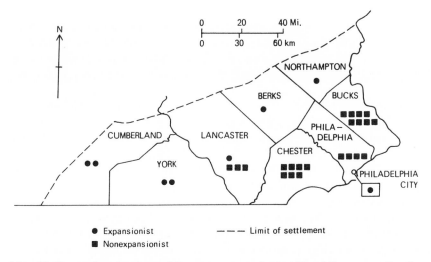

Map 10. Pennsylvania: Assembly vote on appointing Franklin agent, October 15, 1765

SOURCE: *Pa. Votes and Proceedings,* VII (this is *Evans Imprint* #10445, p. 4). Expansionists opposed the appointment and nonexpansionists favored it.

byterians stood solidly behind the New Ticket: the four delegates from York and Cumberland, frontier counties in which immigrants from Northern Ireland predominated, consistently sided with the minority in the house. The Germans, particularly in the newer counties, were divided in their sympathies. The representatives from Lancaster, Berks, and Northampton, where the "Pennsylvania Dutch" were dominant, aligned three to two in favor of the Quaker party after the 1764 election (with one individual not voting), and were split three to three after the polling in 1765. The English formed the mainstay of the Quaker party. The twenty-four delegates from the "original" counties of Philadelphia, Chester, and Bucks, where English settlers, often Quaker or Anglican, formed the single most important group, favored the Quaker party by a margin of twenty to four following the 1764 balloting. The four defections in 1764, however, reflected dissatisfaction with the campaign for a royal charter rather than criticism of the nonexpansionists' imperial policies. Galloway's conservative tack on the Stamp Act did not trouble longtime supporters, and the faction swept all twenty-four of these seats in 1765 and again in 1766 (maps 9, 10).

   In the capital, where no single ethnic or religious group was supreme, the two parties were evenly matched. The Proprietary faction gained both of the city's seats in 1764 (Willing and Bryan), and one in 1765 (Willing). The other delegate in 1765 was James Pemberton, who won his position only after first tying Bryan and then defeating him in a runoff. Quaker party men captured both places in 1766.[43]

During 1765 and 1766 Pennsylvanians also adopted a series of "economic" measures to relieve the hard times weighing upon the colony, as well as to counter the Stamp Act. Although both parties cooperated in these measures, the expansionist faction clearly harbored the bolder spirits. On November 7, a week after New York, Philadelphia traders "unanimously resolved" to enter into a nonimportation agreement and to refuse all British wares arriving after January 1, 1766.[44] A committee established to enforce the pact drew equally from both factions. The boycott enjoyed widespread support, partly because the merchants were eager to ease the glut of foreign manufactures. "We are well convinced," one trader explained, "something of this sort is absolutely necessary at this time from the great much too large importations that have for some time past been made. There will be no want of goods for twelve months."[45] The pact, in addition to pressuring British firms into seeking repeal of the Stamp Act, had a noticeable, if short-lived, impact on the economy. Importations from Britain declined 10 percent from 1765 to 1766, and more significantly, the exchange rate dropped, making remittances easier to obtain.[46]

There was partisan debate in the merchant community, however, over the remonstrance that was to explain the reasons for the boycott to the English traders. One document, apparently drawn up by Presbyterian party men, upset many Quakers, and Galloway took steps to secure a tamer petition. "It being very violent and indiscreet throughout, denying the power of Parliament," he informed Franklin, "at the request of our friends I drew another, every way moderate, and in

43. Thomas Clifford to Harper & Hartshorn, Oct. 8, 1765, Clifford Letterbook, HSP; Joseph Galloway to Franklin, June 7, 1766, *Papers of Franklin*, XIII, 295–96, and see 465n, 521n; Samuel Purviance to Col. James Burd, Sept. 10, 1764, Sept. 20, 1765, Little Ed Burd to James Burd, Sept. 18, 1765, Rothermund, *Layman's Progress*, 182–83, 186–88, 185; James T. Lemon, *The Best Poor Man's Country: A Geographical Study of Early Southeastern Pennsylvania* (Baltimore, 1972), 49–51; Newcomb, *Franklin and Galloway*, 91–92, 98, 124n, 144n; *Pa. Votes and Proceedings*, Oct. 14, 1764, Oct. 14, 1765, Oct. 14, 1766.

44. Richard Waln, Jr., to John Dowell, Nov. 7, 1765, Richard Waln Letterbook; Thomas Wharton to Franklin, Nov. 7, 1765, *Papers of Franklin*, XII, 357–58; Schlesinger, *Colonial Merchants*, 79–81.

45. John Chew to Samuel Galloway, Nov. 7, 1765, Galloway Papers, Library of Congress, quoted in Ronald Hoffman, "Economics, Politics, and the Revolution in Maryland" (Ph.D. diss., Univ. of Wisconsin, 1969), 63–64; J. Thomas Scharf and Thompson Westcott, *History of Philadelphia, 1609–1884*, 3 vols. (Philadelphia, 1884), I, 272; John Reynell to John Southall, Nov. 23, 1765, John Reynell to Francis Rybot, Dec. 14, 1765, Reynell Letterbook, HSP.

46. Gen. Gage to Sec. William Mellish, Dec. 20, 1765, T1/442/219, PRO; U.S. Bureau of the Census, *Historical Statistics of the United States, Colonial Times to 1970*, 2 vols., consec. pagin. (Washington, D.C., 1975), 1176–77; John J. McCusker, *Money and Exchange in Europe and America, 1600–1775* (Chapel Hill, N.C., 1978), 185–86.

decent terms, giving a just account of the distress of our commerce."
The final memorial closely resembled Galloway's draft, and the politician reproached the traders only for adding the word *unconstitutional*
to their discussion of the Stamp Act.[47]

Expansionists also spearheaded an abortive attempt to ease the
currency shortage through a private bank scheme. During the last
months of 1766 eight firms, seven of which adhered to the Presbyterian faction, issued interest-bearing notes worth thirty thousand
pounds. Many traders, however, were wary of such an experiment. In
December over two hundred individuals, drawn from both parties,
signed a statement announcing that they would not accept the bills
"for any payment whatsoever," and the scheme collapsed. Significantly, of the ten Presbyterian party men involved (several of the
firms were partnerships), six would be shareholders in the 1780 Bank
of Pennsylvania. Three of these six, who epitomized the expansionists' sustained concern for a buoyant, autonomous American
economy, were Thomas Willing, Robert Morris, and John Maxwell
Nesbitt.[48]

» «

Between 1767 and 1770 the Quaker party was able to guide protests
into comparatively calm channels, despite the efforts of the Presbyterian party to chart a stormier course. The bitterest, most prolonged battles of these years were over economic rather than political
questions, more particularly, over nonimportation.

In 1767 the initial response of both groups to the Townshend Acts
was restrained, although such discontent as was registered came
from Presbyterian party supporters. During the short session in October, the legislature, firmly in the grip of the Quaker party, made no
protest against the new duties and adjourned until January; party
leader Galloway, who had been elected speaker the preceding year,
even saw advantages in the levies. "Will not this measure assist us in
obtaining the change [to a royal government]?" he asked Franklin.
Galloway reasoned that since Pennsylvanians were now paying more
into British coffers, they would want salaried British officials as rec-
ompense.[49] During these months, expansionists also raised little out-

47. Joseph Galloway to Franklin, Nov. [16–28?], 1765, Joseph Galloway to R. Jack-
son and Franklin, Nov, 29, 1765, *Papers of Franklin*, xii, 377–78, 388–89; "Merchant
Remonstrance," [Nov.] 1765, Morris V. Schappes, ed., *A Documentary History of the
Jews in the United States, 1654–1875* (New York, 1950, 1952), 38–40.

48. *Pa. Gazette*, Dec. 11, 1766; Ernst, *Money and Politics*, 122–24; Samuel Hazard,
ed., *Hazard's Register of Pennsylvania . . .*, 16 vols. (Philadelphia, 1828–35), ii, 260, lists
the men associated with the Bank of Pennsylvania.

49. Joseph Galloway to Franklin, Oct. 9, 1767, *Papers of Franklin*, xiv, 276–77; David
L. Jacobson, *John Dickinson and the Revolution in Pennsylvania, 1764–1776* (Berkeley,
1965), 60.

cry against the new taxes, allowing Thomas Wharton to comment in November: "The watchword among the P[resbyteria]ns is *moderation*."[50] The calm was broken only by John Dickinson's "Letters from a Pennsylvania Farmer," a series of articles, which fiercely attacked the new duties, and which began appearing in Philadelphia newspapers early in December.[51]

Despite the efforts of the Presbyterian party, the Quaker faction kept protests moderate in 1768. In February the assembly instructed Franklin and Jackson to submit a "decent and respectful" petition for the repeal of the Townshend duties if "such application is made" by the other agents.[52] The Quaker party also displayed a studied indifference to the circular letter from Massachusetts. Galloway allowed the request for colonial unity to be read when the house convened in May but adjourned the body before any action was taken. He also penned a tract cautioning against "rash and premature" steps.[53] Dissatisfied with this lethargy, the Presbyterian faction convened a public meeting in July to garner support for stronger measures; Dickinson and Thomson addressed the gathering, urging the importance of the Bay Colony's cause. When the house met in September, it carefully and temperately responded to the plea from Massachusetts. Using language that paralleled the circular letter, the assembly sent off petitions to Britain defending the freedom of Pennsylvania to correspond with other provinces and asserting the colonists' exclusive right to tax themselves. But the legislators did not specifically answer the circular letter and thus did not provoke dissolution.[54]

Partisan energies in 1769 were directed toward the boycott, an issue that initially had little impact on party strength in the legislature. The White Oaks (who had successfully opposed Dickinson's election in 1768 with the cry "No Farmer in the assembly") continued firm in their support of the Quaker party. As in every election since 1765, the expansionists were limited to a handful of seats in the frontier counties.[55]

However, the increasingly heated agitation over nonimportation helped radicalize the common people of Philadelphia, leading in 1770

50. Thomas Wharton to Franklin, Nov. 17, 1767, *Papers of Franklin*, XIV, 307.
51. *Writings of Dickinson*, I, 279–85.
52. Pa. Assembly Committee of Correspondence to R. Jackson and Franklin, Feb. 20, 1768, *Papers of Franklin*, XV, 56–57.
53. Newcomb, *Franklin and Galloway*, 192–93; *Pennsylvania Chronicle*, July 25, 1768.
54. Thomas Clifford to Lancelot Cowper, Aug. 1, 1768, Clifford Letterbook: Pa. Assembly Committee of Correspondence to R. Jackson and Franklin, Sept. 22, 1768, *Papers of Franklin*, XV, 210–14; Jensen, *Founding of a Nation*, 261–62. Hazard, ed., *Hazard's Register*, presents the proceedings of the meeting, VIII, 119–21, and the petitions, 131–34.
55. William Goddard, *The Partnership* [1770], reprinted in *Writings of Dickinson*, I, 283; *Pa. Votes and Proceedings*, Oct. 14, 1769.

to the defection of the artisans from the Quaker party. Printer William Goddard's caustic attack on Galloway in a tract issued before the 1770 balloting also notably influenced the mechanics and tradesmen and made for a set of returns that frightened Quaker party men. "The White Oaks and mechanics, or many of them," Galloway gasped, "have left the Old Ticket [i.e., Quaker party] and 'tis feared will go over to the Presbyterians."[56] The shift ousted Galloway from his Philadelphia County seat, and he barely managed to secure a place in the Quaker stronghold of Bucks. The mechanics' support also allowed Dickinson to gain one of the city's two seats and helped Joseph Parker, a tailor, become a delegate from Philadelphia County.[57]

In these years, too, Benjamin Franklin reemerged as a resolute patriot. In August 1768, Secretary Hillsborough put an end to all hopes for a royal charter. Before that interview Franklin had continued his efforts to ingratiate himself with the ministry. In 1767 he had written a piece for the *London Chronicle* designed "to do some service to the Treasury" by condemning illicit trade and had cautioned Galloway to avoid "rash proceedings on our side."[58] In January 1768 Franklin penned a tract defending Hillsborough, and in July, several months after Hillsborough's name had become anathema to American patriots, he praised the secretary. Once Hillsborough flatly dismissed the idea of a new frame of government, however, Franklin attacked him and sharpened his criticism of British policies.[59]

But even before the August interview with Hillsborough, Franklin's long and deeply held expansionist convictions were leading him to question British policies and to rethink his scheme for a royal charter. His faith in America's growth remained the unshakable bedrock of his beliefs. In 1767 he wrote to a British friend, "America, an immense territory, favored by nature with all advantages . . . , must become a great country, populous and mighty and will in a less time than is generally conceived be able to shake off any shackles that may be imposed on her."[60] In March 1768 he challenged the balanced

56. Joseph Galloway to Franklin, Sept. 27, 1770, *Papers of Franklin*, XVII, 228; Olton, *Artisans for Independence*, 39–55; Samuel Coates to William Logan, Oct. 12, 1770, Coates Letterbook, HSP; Goddard, *The Partnership*, I, 280–83; Newcomb, *Franklin and Galloway*, 214–18.

57. Samuel Coates to William Logan, Oct. 12, 1770, Coates Letterbook; Jacobson, *John Dickinson*, 66–67.

58. Franklin, "On Smuggling," Nov. 21–24, 1767, Franklin to William Franklin, July 2, 1768, Franklin to Joseph Galloway, Aug. 20, 1768, June 13, Aug. 8, 1767, Franklin to William Franklin, Nov. 25, Dec. 29, 1767, *Papers of Franklin*, XIV, 315–19, XV, 162, 189, XIV, 184, 230, 322–23, 349.

59. Franklin, "On the New Office of Secretary of State for the Colonies," Jan. 21, 1768, Franklin to Joseph Galloway, Feb. 17, July 2, 1768, Franklin, "On Absentee Governors," Aug. 27, 1768, ibid., XV, 17–19, 49, 164, 195.

60. Franklin to Lord Kames, Feb. 25, 1767, ibid., XIV, 69–70.

arguments in the "Farmer's Letters" and speculated that either of two extremes was defensible—Parliament could make "*all laws* for us" or "*no laws* for us"—and Franklin indicated his clear preference for the latter position.[61] The corruption he saw in Britain also troubled him. "I have urged over and over the necessity of the change we desire," Franklin told a correspondent in May, "but this country itself being at present in a situation very little better, weakens our argument that a royal government would be better managed and safer to live under than that of a proprietary."[62]

Taken together, the demise of the royal charter scheme and the gradual resurgence of Franklin's expansionist views firmly committed him to resistance. During 1769 and 1770 Franklin repeatedly enunciated his new position that "the King only is sovereign in both countries" and not Parliament, which "has usurped an authority of making laws for [America]."[63] He also urged, in a series of well-publicized letters, that the colonists should adhere to their boycotts "till the end for which they were entered into was *fully* obtained"; partial repeal of the Townshend duties was not sufficient.[64] Franklin viewed nonimportation as a spur to American growth and told a committee of Philadelphia merchants, "The country will be enriched by its industry and frugality, those virtues will become habitual, farms will be more improved, better stocked and rendered more productive by the money that used to be spent in superfluities, our artificers of every kind will be enabled to carry on their business to more advantage."[65] Just as Franklin's cautionary letters had encouraged the Quaker party earlier in the decade, so his patriotic advice strengthened the Presbyterian faction in 1769 and 1770.

Along with their debates over political issues, the two upper-class parties quarreled over the proper response to the economic hardship afflicting Pennsylvania during the last part of the decade. The Quaker party's strength, coupled with the slightly more favorable conditions prevailing in Penn's Colony than in New York or Massachusetts, made the province a laggard partner in the economic protests that swept the northern colonies between 1767 and 1770.

Presbyterian party men first raised their voices for a boycott in

61. Franklin to William Franklin, Mar. 13, 1768, ibid., xv, 75–77.
62. Franklin to John Ross, May 14, 1768, ibid., 129, and see 78.
63. Franklin, Marginalia in *Good Humor*, Franklin to S. Cooper, Apr. 27, 1769, June 8, 1770, Franklin to T. Cushing, Dec. 24, 1770, ibid., xvi, 279, 118–19, xvii, 160–65, 307–8.
64. Franklin to Joseph Galloway, Mar. 21, June 26, 1770, Franklin to Charles Thomson, Mar. 18, 1770, ibid., xvii, 114–19, quotation on 117, 180, 110–13.
65. Franklin to Philadelphia Merchants, July 9, 1769, Franklin to S. Cooper, Apr. 27, 1769, Franklin to Timothy Folger, Sept. 29, 1769, Franklin to William Strahan, Nov. 29, 1769, ibid., xvi, 174–75, 117–19, 208–10, 247.

March 1768, when Philadelphia merchants met to consider Boston's call for a pact. "Numbers were for joining," Thomas Wharton observed, but he added, "I am sure they cannot get the Old Ticket Party into the scheme."[66] Although this first attempt was unsuccessful, expansionists continued during the spring and summer months to press for an agreement; John Dickinson urged the traders to reconsider their decision, and Charles Thomson and other partisans stated the case for a stoppage in a series of newspaper pieces. But Quaker party propagandists effectively countered such efforts, stressing Pennsylvania's relative well-being; the merchants, one editorialist (most possibly Galloway) noted approvingly, "have discovered some secret intentions in the *New England* scheme, that would be very disadvantageous to the trade of this province, and [especially] when we compare the flourishing and great increase of our *trade* with the various accounts we have heard of *their long-declining state.*"[67]

Despite the efforts of the expansionists, Quaker party adherents kept Pennsylvania out of the nonimportation movement during the second half of 1768, as well. In August the traders of Boston and New York agreed to import no more British wares after January 1, thereby putting new pressures on Philadelphia. In response, Presbyterian party supporters formed a seven-member committee "to obtain a general concurrence" in the city. This attempt again proved unavailing.[68] The example of the other commercial cities, however, along with the worsening economy made many merchants contemplate drastic actions, and several large houses sharply curtailed imports in the fall. To stave off a general nonimportation, Quaker party merchants created a new panel and instructed it to draw up a remonstrance listing the traders' grievances. The petition, signed by 208 traders, most of them members of the Quaker party, was then forwarded to London.[69]

66. Thomas Wharton to Franklin, Mar. 29, 1768, ibid., xv, 91–92; *Pa. Gazette*, Mar. 31, 1768; Anne Bezanson et al., *Prices in Colonial Pennsylvania* (Philadelphia, 1935), 281; Schlesinger, *Colonial Merchants*, 116–20.
67. *Pa. Gazette*, June 16, July 21, 25, Aug. 4, 1768; John Dickinson, "Address to Merchants," Apr. 25, 1769, John Dickinson, "Letter from a Gentleman in Virginia," *Writings of Dickinson*, I, 409–16, 439–44, and see 435–36; *Pa. Chronicle*, July 25, 1768.
68. *Pa. Gazette*, Sept. 22, Oct. 20, 1768; Joseph Galloway to Franklin, Oct. 17, 1768, *Papers of Franklin*, xv, 231; Boston Merchants' Committee to Philadelphia Merchants' Committee, Aug. 11, 1768, MSS relating to the nonimportation agreement, vol. II, American Philosophical Society.
69. *Pa. Gazette*, Oct. 20, 1768; Richard Waln, Jr. to Haliday & Dunbar, Oct. 12, Nov. 6, 1768, Richard Waln Letterbook; Merchants' Remonstrance, Nov. 1768, Hazard, ed., *Hazard's Register*, II, 222–23; John Reynell to Welch, Wilkinson, & Startin, Nov. 5, 1768, Reynell Letterbook; Thomas Wharton to Franklin, Nov. 7, 1768, Philadelphia Merchants to Franklin, Nov. 1, 1768, *Papers of Franklin*, xv, 265–66, 266–67; Thomas Clifford to Lancelot Cowper, Nov. 19, 1768, Thomas Clifford to Robert & Nathan Hyde, Dec. 7, 1768, Clifford Letterbook.

Philadelphia merchants, with remarkable, if short-lived, unanimity, signed a conditional nonimportation agreement in February 1769 and finalized it in March. The need to ease the hardships of the depression, even more than Britain's rejection of the petitions sent the previous year, persuaded many houses to support the boycott. "It is a very general wish among the merchants," Quaker importer Richard Waln explained, "that it [nonimportation] may continue at least one year in order that they may dispose of the great quantity of goods on hand and contract their affairs. This is agreeable to my private interest."[70] The committee established to enforce the agreement drew its members from both factions, including such expansionists as Charles Thomson and Robert Morris and such nonexpansionists as Henry Drinker and John Reynell.[71]

Cracks in the facade of factional unity were visible, however, even before the end of the year. Israel Pemberton, along with other Friends, complained about the "impudent conduct of the committee" in enforcing the agreement so strictly.[72] By the fall five Quaker party men, including Drinker and Reynell, had stopped attending committee meetings. The very success of the agreement created pressure for its dissolution. Imports from Britain fell fully 54 percent from 1768 (£441,800) to 1769 (£205,000) and would drop another third in 1770 (£139,700). The exchange rate, which measured the cost of sterling bills, also plummeted. Henry Drinker doubted that the merchants would "keep firm to their agreement." He told his partner in December that "interest, all powerful interest will bear down on patriotism."[73]

The debate over the continuation of the boycott grew increasingly heated in 1770. News of the partial repeal of the Townshend duties, coupled with the growing shortages of particular dry goods, encour-

---

70. Richard Waln, Jr., to Harford & Powell, Apr. 18, 1769, Richard Waln Letterbook; John Reynell to John Southall, Feb. 18, 1769, Reynell Letterbook; Thomas Clifford to Walter Franklin, Mar. 11, 1769, Clifford Letterbook; Philadelphia Merchants' Nonimportation Agreement, Mar. 10, 1769, *Letters to Washington and Accompanying Papers*, ed. Stanislaus M. Hamilton, 5 vols. (Boston, 1898–1902), III, 351–52; Schlesinger, *Colonial Merchants*, 128–30.

71. Philadelphia Merchants to Annapolis Merchants, Mar. 15, 1769, *Letters to Washington*, III, 349; Philadelphia Merchants to London Merchants, Apr. 8, 1769, *PMHB*, XXVII (1903), 84–87.

72. Israel Pemberton to John Pemberton, July 24, 1769, Pemberton Papers; John Reynell to William Henry Reynell, May 15, 1769, Reynell Letterbook.

73. Henry Drinker to Abel James, Dec. 9, 1769, Apr. 29, 1770, *PMHB*, XIV (1890), 41, 42–43; Thomas Clifford to Lancelot Cowper, June 21, Aug. 10, 1769, Clifford Letterbook; *Pa. Gazette*, July 20, Aug. 3, 1769, May 10, 1770; Richard Waln, Jr., to Haliday & Dunbar, Aug. 29, 1769, Richard Waln Letterbook; John Pemberton to James Pemberton, Oct. 2, 1769, Pemberton Papers; *Historical Statistics of the U.S.*, 1176–77; McCusker, *Money and Exchange*, 186.

aged members of the Quaker party and some Presbyterian party supporters to demand an end to the agreement. But the backers of nonimportation had important resources to call upon. One was Franklin, who strongly urged that the agreement be continued. Another source of support for the radical importers was the Philadelphia artisans, who in many instances had profited from the ban on British wares. In May they formed a separate caucus "to strengthen the hands of all merchants who were for supporting and continuing the agreement." A series of public meetings in the spring and summer reaffirmed Philadelphia's commitment to nonimportation.[74]

The struggle ended with the dissolution of the pact in September. By the beginning of that month the merchant committee had polarized and each of the component groups had been enlarged by the addition of new, sympathetic members. Reynell, Drinker, Abel James, and others of the Quaker party dominated the portion of the panel asking for "an alteration in said agreement."[75] Adherents of the Presbyterian faction, led by Thomson, Roberdeau, and John Maxwell Nesbitt, continued to support nonimportation. The traders convened at Davenport's Tavern on September 20 and elected Thomas Willing chairman. A trial vote showed a majority of eighty-nine to forty-five in favor of ending the boycott. As in the other commercial colonies, not only the nonexpansionists but also many expansionists had come to feel that continuation of the agreement was unwise. The traders agreed to admit all undutied wares, and within a few days a vessel sailed for London with orders for dry goods.[76] The breakdown of nonimportation signaled a temporary lull in the factional wars. Not until the last months of 1773 and the response to the Tea Act

74. Henry Drinker to Abel James, Feb. 12, Apr. 29, May 26, 1770, *PMHB*, xiv (1890), 41–42, 42–44, 44–45; Thomas Clifford to Thomas Clifford, Jr., Feb. 19, 1770, Thomas Clifford to Lancelot Cowper, May 13, 16, 26, June 14, 1770, Clifford Letterbook; Richard Waln, Jr., to Harford & Powell, May 11, 1770, Richard Waln, Jr., to Harford & Powell and David & John Barclay, May 15, 1770, Richard Waln Letterbook; John Reynell to Mildred & Roberts, June 13, 1770, Reynell Letterbook; Israel Pemberton to Joseph Pemberton, May 22, 1770, James Pemberton to Sarah Pemberton, July 14, 1770, Pemberton Papers; *Pa. Gazette*, Jan. 25, May 24, 31, June 7, 14, July 12, 19, 26, Aug. 2, 16, 24, 23, 1770; Franklin to Charles Thomson, Mar. 18, 1770, *Papers of Franklin*, xvii, 110–13; *Benjamin Franklin's Letters to the Press, 1758–1775*, ed. Vernon W. Crane (Chapel Hill, N.C., 1950), 209–11.

75. *Pa. Gazette*, Sept. 20, 1770; James & Drinker to Lancelot Cowper, Sept. 6, 1770, James & Drinker Letterbook, HSP; Thomas Clifford to Lancelot Cowper, Sept. 15, 1770, Clifford Letterbook; Samuel Coates to William Logan, Sept. 26, 1770, Coates Letterbook.

76. John Reynell and Samuel Coates to Mildred & Roberts, Sept. 21, 1770, Reynell & Coates Letterbook, HSP; John Reynell to Robert & Nathan Hyde, Sept. 22, 1770, Reynell Letterbook; Samuel Coates to William Logan, Sept. 26, 1770, Coates Letterbook; Daniel Roberdeau to Franklin, Sept. 28, 1770, *Papers of Franklin*, xvii, 232; *Pa. Gazette*, Sept. 20, 27, Oct. 4, 11, 1770; Schlesinger, *Colonial Merchants*, 230–32.

would the upper-class patriots once again vigorously set forth their demands for enlarging American sovereignty.

» «

Along with Benjamin Franklin, several Pennsylvanians undertook thoughtful elaborations of the expansionist persuasion during the 1760s. Because of their active involvement in local politics, Charles Thomson and John Dickinson were two thinkers of special importance. Thomson's vision was aggressive, and his gaze was trained upon distant horizons. Although during the late 1750s he had, as a dutiful Quaker party member, written a lengthy tract attacking the proprietors for abusing the Indians, Thomson showed little sympathy for the tribes engaged in Pontiac's Rebellion. "It is to be feared it will require another campaign to bring them to reason," he told Franklin in 1764, and he complained the following year that the colonists had too long "borne the attacks of barbarous savages."[77]

Thomson denounced the Stamp Act not simply for the burdens it imposed but also because it was one of a series of British measures limiting growth. "This country, it must be allowed," he observed in November 1765, "is as well calculated for trade, manufactures, and commerce as any in the world. Our hills abound with iron and other rich minerals, our plains produce the richer verdure. . . . [But] no sooner did the colonies begin to improve these advantages than they were restricted by acts of P[arliament]." Thomson enumerated a host of oppressive decrees, beginning with the navigation acts and the laws prohibiting certain colonial manufactures and culminating in the exactions of 1765.[78]

To help the New World develop its bountiful potential, Thomson and a few friends in 1767 established "the American Society held at Philadelphia for Promoting and Propagating Useful Knowledge," thereby breathing new life into a group that traced its lineage back to Franklin's Junto. On January 1, 1768, Thomson declaimed to the members an ambitious program: "The spirit of enquiry is awake. . . . Why should we hesitate to enlarge the plan of our society, call to our assistance men of learning and ingenuity from every quarter and unite in one generous, noble attempt, not only to promote the interest of our country but to raise her to some eminence in the ranks of polite and learned nations." In 1769 the American Society would amalga-

77. Charles Thomson to Franklin, Dec. 18, 1764, Sept. 24, 1765, Franklin to Israel Pemberton, June 10, 1758, *Papers of Franklin*, xi, 523, xii, 279, viii, 99–100, and see vii, 376–77. J. Edwin Hendricks, *Charles Thomson and the Making of a New Nation, 1729–1824* (Rutherford, N.J., 1979), 3–15, argues that Thompson acted out of deep conviction in defending the Indians during the 1750s.

78. Charles Thomson to Cook, Lawrence, & Co., Nov. 9, 1765, NYHS *Cols.*, xi (1878), 8–11.

mate with a rival group to form the American Philosophical Society.[79]

Unlike Thomson's outlook or the opinions of most expansionists, John Dickinson's vision of America grew more circumscribed during the 1760s. In *The Late Regulations*, written in 1765, Dickinson grounded his opposition to British policies on a buoyant view of economic and territorial growth. After reviewing provincial accomplishments in the production of homespun, he descanted: "In short, so strong a spirit is raised in these colonies by the late measures and such successful efforts are already made among us, that it cannot be doubted that before the end of the century, the modern regulations will teach *America*, that she has resources within herself of which she never otherwise would have thought." He underscored the impact that the restless, burgeoning population of the New World would have on imperial ties. The colonists, he explained, "are daily pushing further and further into the wilderness." Unless Britain rethought its commercial policies, it was certain to forfeit the loyalty of the "remote regions," which had fewer links to the mother country than did the coastal settlements. But with wise decisions, "in *future* times when America shall be more fully peopled, [the benefits] must exceed . . . the warmest wishes of a *British* patriot."[80]

By December 1767, when the first of the "Letters from a Farmer in Pennsylvania" appeared, Dickinson had trimmed his sails. His attack on the Townshend Acts was forthright, it is true, and was well received by expansionists the length of the continent. But this plea was set in the context of a more circumspect view of empire than he had earlier expressed. Possibly the disorders of 1765 had made him more cautious. "The cause of *liberty*," he affirmed, "is a cause of too much dignity to be sullied by turbulence and tumult." He now dismissed the possibility of colonial industry: "This is a country of planters, farmers, and fishermen; not of manufacturers. The difficulty of establishing particular manufactures is almost insufferable." On the question of territorial growth, he declared that "the acquisition [of Canada and Florida] is greatly injurious to these colonies." Moreover, Dickinson insisted that Britain "unquestionably" had the right to regulate colonial trade, and he condemned any thought of independence, noting that "the happiness of these colonies indubitably consists in their connection with *Great Britain*."[81]

The "Farmer's Letters" thus combined a ringing denunciation of

79. Brooke Hindle, *The Pursuit of Science in Revolutionary America, 1735–1789* (Chapel Hill, N.C., 1956), 121–45, quotations on 125–26; Hendricks, *Charles Thomson*, 31–52; Charles Thomson to Franklin, Nov. 26, 1769, *Papers of Franklin*, xvi, 239–40.
    80. *Writings of Dickinson*, i, 234–37, 226–27, 213–14.
    81. Ibid., 324, 319, 360, 312, 386–87.

the new duties with a set of assumptions that many nonexpansionists would have found acceptable. Undoubtedly, such a balance widened the appeal of the letters. The customs commissioners in Boston noted gloomily, "As the author affects moderation and a parade of learning, we consider them of the most mischievous tendency."[82] Franklin was among the expansionists who scored Dickinson for his temporizing, but most seemed happy to welcome his efforts. The several facets of Dickinson's outlook—his heightened concern for colonial sovereignty, his fear of lower-class dissension, and his worries about the ability of the New World to stand on its own—would help make him an important but timorous patriot leader in the final imperial crisis.[83]

82. American Board of Customs Commissioners to treasury lords, Feb. 12, 1768, Add. MSS 38,340, f.207, BM.
83. Franklin to William Franklin, Mar. 13, 1768, *Papers of Franklin*, xv, 75–77. However, Franklin also wrote a preface to the "Letters" and aided their London publication; see "Preface," May 8, 1768, ibid., 110–12.

CHAPTER 11

Virginia:

Conflict and Cooperation

The House of Burgesses in May 1765 was no harmonious conclave of patriots. "I was entertained with very strong debates," recorded a visiting Frenchman after listening to the lawmakers wrangle over Patrick Henry's resolutions. Virginia's two upper-class factions seemed for the moment to be almost precisely balanced; once Henry's resolves against the Stamp Act had squeezed through, Peyton Randolph exclaimed, "By God, I would have given 500 guineas for a single vote." Henry, with vocal support from the Northern Neck, demanded a bold denunciation of the new tax, while Randolph, Speaker John Robinson, and other nonexpansionists, who were shocked to see their control of the chamber so brashly challenged, argued that moderation was the better part of wisdom.[1]

The exchange over Henry's resolutions was but one of several flashpoints in the post-1763 clash between the two parties. The Virginia factions differed from their counterparts in the other colonies only because of their remarkable ability to cooperate. Nonexpansionists in the Old Dominion rarely exhibited the dogged opposition to revolutionary measures displayed by party adherents elsewhere. The comparative weakness of the common people in Virginia sharply undercut a key argument—the fear of social disorder—that led individuals to denounce the revolutionary movement. In Virginia, therefore, the

1. "Journal of a French Traveller in the Colonies, 1765," *AHR*, xxvi (1920–21), 745–46; William Wirt, *Sketches of the Life and Character of Patrick Henry*, 9th ed. (1817; rpt. Philadelphia, 1845), 78–79; Edmund S. Morgan and Helen M. Morgan, *The Stamp Act Crisis: Prologue to Revolution* (Chapel Hill, N.C., 1953; rev. ed., New York, 1962), 120–32; *Journals of the House of Burgesses of Virginia, 1619–1776*, ed. John Pendleton Kennedy, 13 vols. (Richmond, 1905–15), x, 358–60.

nonexpansionists' customary dominance in the legislature did not dampen revolutionary ardor as did a similar imbalance in Pennsylvania.

» «

In 1763 and 1764 men from the Northern Neck, the heartland of the expansionist faction, spurred resistance to British policies. Richard Henry Lee was among the first to raise his voice against the new parliamentary enactments. "Many late determinations of the great, on your side of the water," he told a British correspondent in May 1764, "seem to prove a resolution to oppress North America with the iron hand of power."[2] Then, in 1764 Lee made a serious misstep. In November, pleading a large family and small fortune, he applied for the post of stamp distributor. According to his account two years later, "a few days after [the] letters were sent away," he deeply regretted the move.[3] Lee's recollection probably was accurate; by year's end he was back among the front-rank patriots, demanding that resolute declarations be sent to the king and parliament.[4] With him was another Northern Necker, Landon Carter, who later boasted that he was the man "who opened the breath of liberty to America."[5] Carter helped frame the remonstrances the burgesses adopted in December 1764, and he campaigned with Lee to overcome the stiff opposition to these memorials. The week-long debate over the wording of the petitions was, according to Governor Fauquier, "very warm and indecent." The documents finally approved stated flatly "that the people are not subject to any taxes but such as are laid on them by their own consent."[6]

During 1763 and 1764 Virginians from both parties also supported "economic" protests, in which the expansionists played an especially prominent role. Planters, particularly Northern Neckers, undertook individual actions to counter the downturn; Washington, for example, experimented with new soils and seeds and promoted the exten-

2. Richard Henry Lee to [?], May 31, 1764, The Letters of Richard Henry Lee, ed. James C. Ballagh, 2 vols. (New York, 1911–14), I, 5.

3. R. H. Lee to editor of Virginia Gazette, July 25, 1766, R. H. Lee to [?], July 4, 1765, ibid., 16–18, 9; Merrill Jensen, The Founding of a Nation: A History of the American Revolution, 1763–1776 (New York, 1968), 199–200; Douglas S. Freeman, George Washington, 6 vols. (New York, 1948–54), III, 169–70.

4. R. H. Lee to editor of Virginia Gazette, July 25, 1766, Letters of Lee, I, 17.

5. Jack P. Greene, Introduction to The Diary of Colonel Landon Carter of Sabine Hall, 1752–1778, ed. Greene, 2 vols. (Charlottesville, Va., 1965), I, 7–8, and see II, 1057 (July 14, 1776), 1063 (July 25, 1776); Freeman, George Washington, III, 118–19.

6. Address, Memorial, and Remonstrance of General Assembly to King, Lords, and Commons Respectively, Dec. 18, 1764, William J. Van Schreeven and Robert L. Scribner, eds., Revolutionary Virginia: The Road to Independence (Charlottesville, Va., 1973–), I, 9–14, quotation on 11. Jensen, Founding of a Nation, 96–97, quotes Fauquier.

sive cultivation of wheat. During the 1760s other landowners who shared Washington's enthusiasms would help transform the Neck from a tobacco- to a grain-growing region. The change demonstrated the progressiveness of the Neck's farmers and reaffirmed the area's economic distinctiveness. Still other individuals explored the possibility of domestic manufactures, in the hope, said Lee, that "poverty and oppression . . . may introduce a virtuous industry."[7]

Virginians, once again with expansionists in the fore, also vigorously asserted their right to issue paper money. "Our assembly is suddenly called," George Washington reported in May 1763, "in consequence of a memorial of the British merchants to the Board of Trade representing the evil consequences of our paper emissions, and their Lordships' report and orders thereupon. [All of] which I suppose will set the whole country on flame. This stir of the merchants seems to be ill-timed, and cannot be attended with any good effects."[8] The burgesses told the governor that the currency issues had been necessary to finance the war and that the notes were adequately backed. The house relied on expansionist Richard Henry Lee to draw up a full defense of the colony's monetary practices and promptly forwarded this statement to Britain. But the home government and, consequently, Governor Fauquier were unrelenting in their opposition to any new treasury bills, a firmness that culminated in the Currency Act, adopted in April 1764. Virginians reacted to the ban on new issues of paper money by refusing, during Pontiac's Rebellion, to vote any funds for the troops.[9]

» «

During the Stamp Act crisis expansionists led the protests, while the nonexpansionists opposed or were hesitant to undertake forceful measures. Northern Neckers were Patrick Henry's strongest backers in the May 1765 debate over the resolutions condemning the act. Henry, who hailed from Hanover County, was an exception to the generalization placing expansionists in the Northern Neck or near the Blue Ridge, but his support apparently came from areas long

7. R. H. Lee to [?], May 31, 1764, *Letters of Lee*, I, 7; Freeman, *Washington*, III, 110, 117; Washington to Robert Cary & Co., July 25, 1769, *Writings of George Washington*, ed. J. C. Fitzpatrick, 39 vols. (Washington, D.C., 1931–44), II, 513–14; James B. Gouger III, "Agricultural Change in the Northern Neck of Virginia, 1700–1760: An Historical Geography" (Ph.D. diss., Univ. of Florida, 1976), 105–9; Joseph A. Ernst, *Money and Politics in America, 1755–1775: A Study in the Currency Act of 1764 and the Political Economy of Revolution* (Chapel Hill, N.C., 1973), 194, 236–39.

8. Washington to Robert Stewart, May 2, 1763, *Writings of Washington*, II, 399–400.

9. Address and Representation of the House of Burgesses to Governor Fauquier, May 28, 1763, Van Schreeven and Scribner, eds., *Revolutionary Virginia*, I, 1–8; Washington to Robert Stewart, Aug. 13, 1763, *Writings of Washington*, II, 403–4; Jensen, *Founding of a Nation*, 95–96; Ernst, *Money and Politics*, 68–77.

associated with this faction. For example, as Thomas Jefferson, who was then a student at William and Mary, recalled, "Mr. [George] Johns[t]on of the Northern Neck seconded the resolution[s], and by him the learning and logic of the case were chiefly maintained."[10] The nonexpansionists opposed the resolves but were deprived of their usual comfortable majority, since Henry had set forth his proposals at the end of a session, when many of Speaker Robinson's supporters had gone home. Discomfited by the expansionists' strength, but hardly silenced, Robinson reprimanded Henry for the treasonous tone of his comments, while Peyton Randolph, Robert Carter Nicholas, Richard Bland, and George Wythe did their best to block the proposals. The house nevertheless adopted five resolutions, one of which the nonexpansionists subsequently managed to expunge from the legislative record.[11]

Most Virginians agreed that the stamp distributor, George Mercer, had to step down, but Northern Neckers took their protests a step farther. The justices of Westmoreland, a county that followed Richard Henry Lee's direction, were the first officers in Virginia to resign their posts rather than enforce the pernicious law. Moreover, farmers in the Neck enthusiastically joined the opposition to the tax, and when Archibald Ritchie, a merchant of Hobb's Hole, attempted to secure stamped paper for his vessels the popular response was swift. One local leader wrote Lee, "[I] have now the pleasure of informing you that many are ready at a moment's warning to assist in anything destructive to him [Ritchie] and his intentions . . . and let the fellow know that the north side of the Rappahannock will not be passive."[12] Four hundred individuals marched to Hobb's Hole, formed two lines down the main street, and forced Ritchie to swear he would not use the reviled stamps. "The ringleaders" of the demonstration, Fauquier informed the Board of Trade, "I believe chiefly reside in the Northern Neck."[13]

Nonexpansionists remained at arm's length from such violent proceedings. "For my own part," Edmund Pendleton observed in Febru-

10. Patrick Henry's Resolutions, May 29–30, 1765, Van Schreeven and Scribner, eds., Revolutionary Virginia, I, 15–18; Thomas Jefferson, "Autobiography," The Writings of Thomas Jefferson, ed. Andrew A. Lipscomb, 18 vols. (Washington, D.C., 1903), I, 5–6.

11. Wirt, Sketches of Patrick Henry, 78–79; Morgan and Morgan, Stamp Act Crisis, 120–32. Also see the materials in Edmund S. Morgan, ed., Prologue to Revolution: The Stamp Act Crisis, Sources and Documents (Chapel Hill, N.C., 1959), 46–50, 82–85.

12. Resignation of the Magistrates of Westmoreland County in Protest against the Stamp Act, Sept. 24, 1765, Resolutions of the Westmoreland Association in Defiance of the Stamp Act, Van Schreeven and Scribner, eds., Revolutionary Virginia, I, 19, 22–26; quotation from Samuel Washington to R. H. Lee, Feb. 22, 1766, Lee Family Papers, microfilm at CWF; Jensen, Founding of a Nation, 121–22.

13. Francis Fauquier to Board of Trade, Apr. 7, 1766, CO 5/1331/76–77, transcript at

ary 1766, "I never have or will enter into noisy and riotous companies."[14] Until his death in May 1766, Speaker John Robinson was the voice of moderation. Robinson's demise, Fauquier lamented, "would have been a sensible loss at any time but more particularly so now, as I had promised myself great assistance from him in the next session of assembly to quiet the people and bring them to a just and proper sense of their duty." Fauquier had similar praise for other members of the faction. Peyton Randolph, who later in the year became the new speaker, "has always used his endeavors to induce the assembly to concur with me in all measures which were conducible to the honor and dignity of the crown." George Wythe, the governor noted, "has also exerted himself in support of government."[15] In general, the efforts of these men to preserve the peace were successful. Outside the Northern Neck, only Norfolk—the colony's chief entrepôt—was the scene of organized resistance.[16]

Factional feuding did not subside when news arrived in May of the repeal of the Stamp Act. A scandal that came to light after John Robinson's death kept the two parties at swords' points. Robinson, who had served as treasurer as well as speaker since 1738, had lent to friends some hundred thousand pounds in paper money instead of burning the bills as instructed by law. With but a few exceptions, Robinson had excluded the Northern Neckers and their allies from his largesse and so had stirred up clouds of mistrust and enmity. For several years Richard Henry Lee had suspected Robinson's peculation but had been frustrated in his attempt to expose the most powerful man in Virginia. Now, with the revelation of the extent of the speaker's malfeasance, expansionists bitterly and openly denounced Robinson. This scandal was of such proportions, however, that party lines did not hold rigidly. Those condemning Robinson's actions received unexpected support, for example, from Robert Carter Nicholas, an old Robinson ally who successfully campaigned in 1766 to become the new treasurer.[17]

CWF; Van Schreeven and Scribner, eds., *Revolutionary Virginia*, I, 22–23; Allan Kulikoff, *Tobacco and Slaves: The Development of Southern Cultures in the Chesapeake, 1680–1800* (Chapel Hill, N.C., 1986), 306.

14. Edmund Pendleton to James Madison, Sr., Feb. 15, 1766, *The Letters and Papers of Edmund Pendleton, 1734–1803*, ed. David John Mays, 2 vols. (Charlottesville, Va., 1967), I, 23.

15. Francis Fauquier to Board of Trade, May 11, 1766, CO 5/1331/83.

16. Francis Fauquier to Board of Trade, Apr. 7, 1766, CO 5/1331/76–77; Freeman, *Washington*, III, 156.

17. David Boyd to R. H. Lee, n.d., quoted in Ernst, *Money and Politics*, 191, and see chap. 6; Francis Fauquier to Board of Trade, Sept. 4, 1766, CO 5/1331/146–47; Jensen, *Founding of a Nation*, 201–2; Greene, Introduction to *Diary of Carter*, I, 34. A list of debtors to the Robinson estate is in David John Mays, *Edmund Pendleton, 1721–1803: A Biography*, 2 vols. (Cambridge, Mass., 1952), I, 358–69.

Virginians from both parties made the Stamp Act crisis an excuse for measures to counter the depression. Again, the expansionists urged the more daring solutions. Politicians north and south of the Rappahannock called upon the citizenry to limit its consumption of foreign "geegaws" and to expand local production, and these appeals met with a favorable response. "This I know," James Maury reported in December 1765, "that the orders for goods from Great Britain have greatly decreased, wherever I am acquainted, as well as the consumption of them within these few months, [and] that the number of wheels, looms, &c. have increased to an amazing degree."[18]

Expansionists also proposed that Virginia courthouses be kept shut while the Stamp Act was in force, arguing that this step would at least temporarily lighten the colony's enormous burden of indebtedness. The cessation of judicial proceedings prevented British houses from suing the planters and thereby raised the worth of Virginia currency relative to sterling, creating a happy state of affairs the Northern Neckers hoped to perpetuate. Expansionists thus argued for a course of action strikingly different from that urged in the northern colonies (where indebtedness to Britain was limited to the port cities); patriots in the commercial provinces considered the return of the judges to the bench a means of nullifying the act. "I could wish some method were fallen upon," Richard Henry Lee remarked, "to inform the northern colonies that our not following their example, proceeds from no regard for the Stamp Act, but the very different situation of our affairs from theirs with respect to Great Britain."[19] Many of the politicians south of the Rappahannock were reluctant to endorse such a drastic step; Edmund Pendleton, for example, wanted proceedings resumed to "convince the people that there is not a total end of laws."[20] The result of this partisan clash was the reopening of several inferior tribunals but not the superior court. In all, proposals for frugality, manufacturing, and closed courts provided only a minor, temporary measure of relief for the depressed economy.[21]

» «

Between 1767 and 1770, members of the two Virginia factions cooperated in the struggle against Britain. Nonetheless, in both the "political" and the "economic" protests the Northern Neckers dis-

18. James Maury to John Fontaine, Dec. 31, 1765, *Memoirs of a Huguenot Family . . .* , ed. Ann Maury (1853; rpt. Baltimore, 1967), 430; Washington to Francis Dandridge, Sept. 20, 1765, *Writings of Washington*, II, 426.

19. R. H. Lee to Landon Carter, Feb. 24, 1766, *Letters of Lee*, I, 15; John J. McCusker, *Money and Exchange in Europe and America, 1600–1775* (Chapel Hill, N.C., 1978), 211.

20. Edmund Pendleton to James Madison, Sr., Dec. 11, 1765, *Letters and Papers of Pendleton*, I, 20.

21. Morgan and Morgan, *Stamp Act Crisis*, 219, 222–23, 228n, 229.

played more initiative than did the planters residing south of the Rappahannock. Fauquier's failure to convene the assembly between April 1767 and March 1768 only postponed the remonstrances against the Townshend Acts. When the house met in 1768, burgesses from both parties addressed the king, Lords, and Commons, forwarding a set of petitions that roundly affirmed the colony's exclusive right of self-taxation, denounced the Revenue Act of 1767 as "a tax internal to all intents and purposes," and labeled as "alarming" the bill suspending the New York assembly. The lawmakers unanimously directed Speaker Randolph to answer the circular letter from Massachusetts and to inform the Bay Colony "that we could not but applaud them for their attention to American liberty." Finally, the Old Dominion drafted its own epistle to the other provinces, calling on them to "go hand in hand in their opposition to measures which they think have an immediate tendency to enslave them." At other times such steps might have provoked dissolution, but Governor Fauquier had died early in March, and John Blair, Sr., the president of the council, was an indecisive head of state.[22]

Northern Neckers kept up the agitation against British measures during 1768 and the first months of 1769. In the fall Richard Henry Lee quarreled with the "time serving men" over the proper response of the burgesses to another attack on their liberties. Virginians had learned that the new governor, Lord Botetourt, was instructed to lay before the house the Declaratory Act (which stated that Parliament had the right to legislate for the colonies "in all cases whatsoever"). Some planters argued that the colony should make no protest, but Lee strongly disagreed: "Silence in this case must by all the world be deemed a tacit giving up our rights."[23] During these same months Richard Henry Lee was active on another front. After his brother Arthur wrote a series of essays castigating the new regulations, Richard Henry brought these pieces and Dickinson's "Farmer's Letters" together in booklet form, adding a spirited preface of his own. He had the pamphlet printed at Williamsburg in 1769 and tirelessly promoted its sale.[24]

22. Address, Memorial, and Remonstrance of the General Assembly to King, Lords, and Commons Respectively, Apr. 16, 1768, Van Schreeven and Scribner, eds., *Revolutionary Virginia*, I, 52–63, quotations on 57–59. On assembly divisions in 1767, see Francis Fauquier to earl of Shelburne, Apr. 27, July 30, 1767, CO 5/1345/182–83, 190–91; Jensen, *Founding of a Nation*, 251–52; Lucille Griffith, *The Virginia House of Burgesses, 1750–1774*, rev. ed. (University, Ala., 1970), 41; Freeman, *Washington*, III, 197–200.

23. R. H. Lee to John Dickinson, Nov. 26, July 25, 1768, *Letters of Lee*, I, 30–31, 29; Jensen, *Founding of a Nation*, 251, 300–301.

24. R. H. Lee to [?], Mar. 27, 1768, R. H. Lee to Arthur Lee, Apr. 5, 1770, *Letters of Lee*, I, 26–27, 42; R. H. Lee, "Preface to Williamsburg Edition," *The Writings of John Dickinson* (vol. XIV of HSP *Memoirs*) (Philadelphia, 1895), 289–92, and see 284–85.

The two factions came together to support still another set of resolves when burgesses met in May 1769. To the surprise of some, Botetourt disobeyed his instructions and delivered a conciliatory opening address, making no mention of the Declaratory Act. The lawmakers, however, ignored this olive branch and bitterly denounced British policies. Four resolutions, which were unanimously approved, once again reaffirmed the legislature's "sole right of imposing taxes," condemned efforts to transport Americans to Britain for trial, and defended Virginia's right to petition the king and to consult other colonies.[25] Some expansionists, it should be noted, had come to question the worth of such pronouncements. "Addresses to the throne and remonstrances to Parliament," Washington remarked to George Mason a month before the opening of the session, "we have already, it is said, proved the inefficacy of." But Botetourt did not take this protest lightly; he promptly dissolved the house.[26] During the balance of 1769 and 1770 the planters focused their efforts on economic measures, most notably on nonimportation.

As the depression of the 1760s worsened, Virginia expansionists agitated for a boycott of British goods both to ease the hard times and to chastise the mother country. During the first months of 1769 Washington and Mason pored over the Philadelphia nonimportation agreement as well as the exchanges between the Quaker City and Annapolis. They quickly agreed that a similar pact should be introduced into the Old Dominion. "There are private as well as public advantages to result from it," Washington emphasized. "The former certain, however precarious the other may prove." He elaborated the economic benefits of a boycott: "That a scheme of this sort will contribute more effectually than any other I can devise to emerge the country from the distress it at present labors under, I do most firmly believe, if it can be generally adopted." The "penurious man," Washington observed, will have additional reasons for living within his means. "The extravagant and expensive man has the same good plea to retrench his expenses. He is thereby furnished with a pretext to live within bounds, and embraces it."[27]

Together Washington, Mason, and possibly a third Northern Neck-

25. Resolves of the House of Burgesses, May 16, 1769, Van Schreeven and Scribner, eds., *Revolutionary Virginia*, I, 68–71.

26. Washington to George Mason, Apr. 5, 1769, *Writings of Washington*, II, 501; Jefferson, "Autobiography," 6.

27. Washington to George Mason, Apr. 5, 1769, *Writings of Washington*, II, 500–504; *The Papers of George Mason, 1725–1792*, ed. Robert A. Rutland, 2 vols. (Chapel Hill, N.C., 1970), I, 94–96.

er, Richard Henry Lee, drew up a plan to be presented to the burgesses in May. Acknowledging the exiguity of local manufactures, Mason observed, "It is plain that in the tobacco colonies we can't at present confine our importations within such narrow bounds as the northern colonies."[28] The proposal, therefore, allowed for a lengthy list of exceptions, including spices and inexpensive cloth. A spirited preamble emphasized the hard times oppressing the province, and as a further step toward retrenchment, the accord prohibited the importation of slaves. Mason lobbied for the agreement with a lengthy article that appeared early in May in both Virginia newspapers.[29]

On May 18, the day after Botetourt dissolved the assembly, the burgesses met in the Apollo room of the Raleigh Tavern and entered into an association that closely followed the Northern Neckers' proposal. The legislators further emphasized their economic rather than principled concerns by allowing cheaper grades of paper (a dutied article) to be imported. Planters from both factions swore their resolute support for the pact and had high hopes for its efficacy. "I like the association," one gentleman told his London correspondent, "because I think it will repeal the disagreeable acts of Parliament, open the eyes of the people with you, and must certainly clear us of our debts."[30] Nonexpansionist Robert Carter Nicholas, who described himself as "a friend to decency and moderation," announced, "I am resolved to import nothing I can possibly do without, and believe this is the resolution of most."[31] "The flame of Liberty," Northern Necker Richard Henry Lee stated proudly, "burns bright and clear."[32]

Despite the planters' initial enthusiasm, the agreement had serious shortcomings that soon vitiated its effectiveness. The pact was a mare's nest of prohibitions and exceptions, which at times bedeviled even the most ardent patriots. Washington in despair sent his London correspondent a copy of the accord, remarking that possibly he had "wrote for some things unwittingly which may be under these cir-

28. George Mason to Washington, Apr. 5, 23, 1769, *Letters to Washington and Accompanying Papers*, ed. Stanislaus M. Hamilton, 5 vols. (Boston, 1898–1902), III, 342–44, 345–46. On Lee's possible authorship, see *Papers of Mason*, I, 95–96.

29. Draft of Virginia Association, [c. Apr. 1769], *Letters to Washington*, III, 346–49; [George Mason?], Letter of "Atticus," May 11, 1769, *Papers of Mason*, I, 106–9.

30. John Page, Jr., to John Norton, May 27, 1769, *John Norton & Sons, Merchants of London and Virginia, Being the Papers from Their Counting House for the Years 1750–1795*, ed. Frances N. Mason (Richmond, 1937), 94; Virginia Nonimportation Resolutions, May 17–18, 1769, *The Papers of Thomas Jefferson*, ed. Julian P. Boyd et al. (Princeton, 1950–), I, 27–31.

31. Robert Carter Nicholas to John Norton, May 31, 1769, *John Norton & Sons Papers*, 96–97; Robert Carter Nicholas to Arthur Lee, May 31, 1769, Lee Family Papers.

32. R. H. Lee to Arthur Lee, May 19, 1769, *Letters of Lee*, I, 34.

cumstances."[33] More significantly, the association did not regulate merchants, who were free to respond to the direction of their parent firms in Britain, nor did the pact make any provision for policing the landowners. Leaders in at least three of the Northern Neck counties made sure that the agreement was widely signed and that the citizenry was fully informed about the resolves, but elsewhere the association seemed to rest on no more than the good intentions of the local magnates. As a result, English and Scottish exports to Virginia actually increased in 1769, and in 1770 recovery in Britain and new, liberal extensions of credit pushed shipments to record heights.[34]

During 1770 the two factions quarreled over whether to abandon or strengthen the agreement. In May the associators formed a committee of twenty to revise the accord, but the panel was soon bitterly divided. "Some of them are full as hearty as I thought they would be," Landon Carter reported. But Robert Carter Nicholas "is at last found out to be the man I always took him, a noisy declaimer on nothing or next akin to it. He and Pendleton [are] at the head of a party who were for meeting the Parliament half [way], as they call this partial repeal of the acts."[35] Carter, Mason, Washington, Lee, and other Northern Neckers adamantly opposed the nonexpansionists, and called for a stricter agreement. For example, George Mason urged that "the names of such persons as purchase or import goods contrary to the association should be published, and themselves stigmatized as enemies to their country," and he added, "The interest too of the importer may be made subservient to our purpose."[36]

The revised pact adopted in June represented a compromise between the two parties. The agreement broadened the definition of an associator to include merchants as well as planters and ordered the counties to establish five-member committees to police the accord. The pact, however, gave the local boards few powers of enforcement and enlarged the already lengthy list of permitted goods. "It was the best that the friends to the cause could obtain here," Washington

33. Washington to Robert Cary & Co., July 25, 1769, *Writings of Washington*, II, 512–13.

34. Washington to Burwell Bassett, July 18, 1769, ibid., 512; Thomas Everard to John Norton, Aug. 2, 1769, *John Norton & Sons Papers*, 101; William Cunningham & Co. to William Henderson, Mar. 3, 1770, William Cunningham Letterbook, microfilm, CWF; R. H. Lee to William Lee, July 7, 1770, *Letters of Lee*, I, 45–46; *Historical Statistics of the U.S.*, 1176–78.

35. *Diary of Carter*, I, 418 (May 29, 1770).

36. George Mason to R. H. Lee, June 7, 1770, *Papers of Mason*, I, 116–20; *Diary of Carter*, I, 418 (May 29, 1770); Martha Goosley to John Norton, June 13, 1770, *John Norton & Sons Papers*, 136; Draft of the Resolves of the Virginia Association, [June?] 1770, Lee Family Papers; R. H. Lee to William Lee, July 7, 1770, *Letters of Lee*, I, 45–46; Washington to George William Fairfax, June 27, 1770, *Writings of Washington*, III, 17.

observed.[37] More pointedly a merchant in Falmouth commented, "As it stands at present it will not be of great prejudice to the trading part of the colony."[38] Many of the panels in the Northern Neck performed diligently, but outside this region supervision was ineffective or non-existent. In July the Norfolk committee was unable to prevent a local firm from receiving debarred goods and publicly conceded its powerlessness in a statement published in Rind's *Virginia Gazette*.[39]

Despite the efforts of the Northern Neckers, the voices demanding an end to the covenant grew louder during the second half of 1770. In December the expansionists mustered their forces at a meeting held in Williamsburg. Landon Carter wrote a "sharp paper" supporting the boycott, and Richard Henry Lee angrily charged that Scottish merchants were behind the efforts to reopen trade.[40] But clearly the support for nonimportation had dwindled, and only the lack of a quorum kept the meeting from terminating the accord. The body scheduled another meeting for the summer of 1771, and in July the associators formally ended their pact.[41]

» «

Between 1763 and 1770 several individuals in each faction explored the broader ramifications of their views. Faith in America's bountiful future ran like a bright thread through the writings of the expansionists. George Washington derided all obstacles to growth in the transmontane West; he regarded the Proclamation of 1763, which prohibited settlement in the region, "as a temporary expedient to quiet the minds of the Indians and [which] must fall of course in a few years."[42] The Potomac, he felt sure, would become "the channel of conveyance of the extensive and valuable trade of a rising empire"

37. Washington to the Reverend Jonathan Boucher, July 30, 1770, *Writings of Washington*, III, 21–22; Virginia Nonimportation Resolutions, June 22, 1770, *Papers of Jefferson*, I, 43–48.

38. William Cunningham & Co. to David [Matthew], July 11, 1770, William Cunningham Letterbook.

39. Arthur M. Schlesinger, *The Colonial Merchants and the American Revolution, 1763–1776* (New York, 1919), 199; Donald M. Sweig, "The Virginia Nonimportation Association Broadside of 1770 and Fairfax County: A Study in Local Participation," *VMHB*, LXXXVII (1979), 316–25.

40. *Diary of Carter*, I, 529 (Dec. 9, 1770); R. H. Lee to William Lee, Jan. 8, 1771, *Letters of Lee*, I, 52–53.

41. George Mason to [George Brent?], Dec. 6, 1770, Committee of the Associators in Fairfax County to Peyton Randolph, July 18, 1771, *Papers of Mason*, I, 127–30, 132–34; William Nelson to John Norton, May 17, 1771, *John Norton & Sons Papers*, 158; Thomas Jefferson to Thomas Adams, June 1, 1771, *Papers of Jefferson*, I, 71; Washington to Robert Cary & Co., July 20, 1771, *Writings of Washington*, III, 60.

42. Washington to William Crawford, Sept. 21, 1767, *Writings of Washington*, II, 469; Freeman, *George Washington*, III, chaps. 6–12, passim.

in the West.[43] Moreover, his hopes were not limited to territorial expansion. He was concerned, as he told a London house in 1767, that "the commercial system of these colonies [be] put upon a more enlarged and extensive footing" and was also an enthusiastic supporter of domestic manufacturing.[44]

Richard Henry Lee echoed Washington's optimism and linked America's rising population and wealth to enhanced national sovereignty. He observed in 1764, "Generous and manly sentiments . . . , when in future they become supported by numbers, may produce a fatal resentment of parental care being converted into tyrannical usurpation."[45] And in his preface to the Williamsburg edition of the "Farmer's Letters," Lee spelled out the political consequences of America's rich endowment. "The nature of the climate, the soil, and its various produce, point out the ease and extent with which manufactures may be conducted here," Lee remarked. "These things are mentioned as proof . . . that the bountiful Author of nature has furnished his creatures with the means of securing their proper rights."[46]

Such bold sentiments contrasted with the nonexpansionists' more cautious view of the future. Council president John Blair regarded the settlers violating the Proclamation of 1763 as "banditti" who would provoke an Indian war and "open afresh those sluices of blood." Edmund Pendleton appears to have been similarly critical of the frontiersmen moving into the territory assigned to the natives.[47]

43. Washington to Thomas Johnson, July 20, 1770, Washington to Capt. John Posey, June 24, 1767, *Writings of Washington*, III, 20, II, 458–60.
44. Washington to Capel and Osgood Hanbury, July 25, 1767, ibid., II, 466; Freeman, *Washington*, III, 110, 144, 179, 243–44, 263.
45. R. H. Lee to [?], May 31, 1764, *Letters of Lee*, I, 7.
46. R. H. Lee, "Preface to Williamsburg Edition," I, 291.
47. *Papers of Mason*, I, 92. Pendleton's consistent outlook on the frontier is suggested by Edmund Pendleton to Joseph Chew, June 20, 1774, Edmund Pendleton to William Preston, May 12, 1756, *Letters and Papers of Pendleton*, I, 94, 8.

CHAPTER 12

South Carolina:
Triumphant Patriots

"The minds of the freeholders," remarked one observer of the October 1765 election in South Carolina, "were inflamed . . . by many a
hearty damn of the Stamp Act over bottles, bowls, and glasses."[1] The
balloting, much like the parallel contest in Massachusetts that following spring, signaled a permanent shift in the legislature. With the
October poll the party of the Pinckneys, Manigaults, Christopher
Gadsden, and Henry Laurens seized an unquestionable ascendancy
in the Commons House. Secure in this redoubt, the expansionists
now could turn the rice colony into a bu' vark of the revolutionary
movement. Moreover, after 1765 the wealthy, low-country patriots
were able to defy not only the royal governors but also the fractious
western farmers, even though such policies heightened backcountry
disaffection. In contrast to the ascent of the upper-class revolutionaries, the ability of the nonexpansionists to affect policy was sharply
diminished. Although long a minority in the legislature, the party of
William Wragg, William Bull, and the Scottish importers of Charleston had on more than one occasion gained the upper hand with the
support of wavering or unaligned members. After the Stamp Act
crisis, most nonexpansionists were forced to the political sidelines
and could but futilely protest the patriots' resolute course.

» «

During 1763 and 1764 the twenty-sixth royal assembly, with its
sizable minority of nonexpansionists, was comparatively restrained
in its response to the new British policies. In this legislature, which

1. Quoted in Robert M. Weir, *"A Most Important Epocha": The Coming of the Revolution in South Carolina* (Columbia, S.C., 1970), 17.

had been elected in 1762, fully 30 percent of those whose future allegiances can be traced became loyalists. The members of this house, instead of tackling imperial policies, devoted their energies to a quarrel with Governor Thomas Boone over legislative privilege.[2]

Consequently, South Carolina issued only the most mild censure of ministerial plans. In September 1764 the Commons House instructed agent Charles Garth "to make all opposition you possibly can . . . in the laying of a stamp duty, or any other tax by act of Parliament," but it adopted no remonstrance or set of ringing resolves, as did the legislatures of Massachusetts, New York, and Virginia. Moreover, the lower chamber reminded Garth that it would "submit most dutifully at all times to acts of Parliament."[3] Tory historian Alexander Hewatt observed that at this time only "a few discontented persons, who are commonly to be found in every legislature, joined the disaffected colonists of New England."[4]

» «

The Stamp Act quickened the expansionists' ardor and helped them tighten their grip on the Commons House. The twenty-sixth royal assembly, however, which continued until the fall of 1765, remained moderate in its opposition to the mother country. In July the lawmakers responded to the Massachusetts call for an intercolonial congress by selecting three wealthy patriots, Christopher Gadsden, Thomas Lynch, and John Rutledge, as delegates to the New York meeting. But there were, according to one account, five dissenting votes cast against this decision. Moreover, the speaker of the Commons House, Rawlins Lowndes, although an expansionist, was an unsteady one, who only occasionally stood among the more fervent party leaders. His less-than-resolute behavior during these months would be sharply criticized later in the decade. In a newspaper exchange in 1769, an opponent put these words into Lowndes's mouth: "Perhaps some lucky hit, some happy occasion, similar to the *Stamp-Act*, may present itself, and give me an opportunity of ingratiating

2. *Biographical Directory of the South Carolina House of Representatives*, vol. I: *Session Lists, 1692–1973*, ed. Joan S. R. Faunt and Robert E. Rector with David K. Bowen (Columbia, S.C., 1974), 127–30; vol. II: Walter B. Edgar and N. Louise Bailey, eds., *The Commons House of Assembly, 1692–1775* (Columbia, S.C., 1977), passim; Jack P. Greene, "The Gadsden Election Controversy and the Revolutionary Movement in South Carolina," *MVHR*, XLIV (1959–60), 469–92.

3. Commons House to Charles Garth, Sept. 4, 1764, Robert W. Gibbes, ed., *Documentary History of the American Revolution . . .* , 3 vols. (New York, 1853–57), I, 1–6.

4. Alexander Hewatt, *An Historical Account of the Rise and Progress of the Colonies of South Carolina and Georgia*, 2 vols. (1779; rpt. Spartanburg, S.C., 1971), II, 314.

myself again into your good graces, and wiping away the foul reproach my then conduct brought upon me."[5]

The election that October was a crucial victory for the patriot party. Peter Timothy's *South Carolina Gazette* urged the citizenry to oust the "politicians" and to choose men who would defend the liberties handed down by "our forefathers."[6] The balloting firmly established expansionist supremacy in the house. In the twenty-seventh royal assembly (which lasted from 1765 to 1768) the share of the tory contingent plummeted from 30 percent to a mere 12 percent, the lowest level recorded since parties emerged in the mid-1750s. Nonexpansionist lawmakers, such as Scottish merchant Alexander Rose and planter William Blake, failed to find seats, and such patriots as Arthur Middleton and Miles Brewton entered the house for the first time. The coastal parish of St. John Colleton, however, long a bastion of the nonexpansionists, once more returned William Wragg.[7]

The triumphant faction was quick to show its mettle. When the new house convened late in October, the lawmakers broke with precedent and refused to reelect the incumbent speaker, Rawlins Lowndes, instead selecting Peter Manigault, who was judged more resolute in his opposition to ministerial schemes. With only William Wragg opposing, the assemblymen adopted a set of resolves along the lines of those drawn up by the Stamp Act Congress. The lawmakers made the South Carolina resolves even stronger, excluding any acknowledgment of "due subordination" to Britain. Furthermore, the house informed its agent that "in taxing ourselves and making laws for our own internal government or police we can by no means allow our provincial legislatures to be subordinate to any legislative power on earth."[8] The patriots also directed their fire against two placemen, Chief Justice Charles Shinner and Attorney General Egerton Leigh, who supported the Stamp Act. The lawmakers began a campaign to oust Shinner from the bench and bitterly criticized Leigh for simultaneously holding the posts of councillor, surveyor general, admi-

5. *South Carolina Gazette and Country Journal*, Mar. 23, 1769, quoted in Maurice A. Crouse, "Cautious Rebellion: South Carolina's Opposition to the Stamp Act," *SCHM*, LXXIII (1972), 60–61; *The Writings of Christopher Gadsden, 1746–1805*, ed. Richard Walsh (Columbia, S.C., 1966), xx; George C. Rogers, Jr., *Evolution of a Federalist: William Loughton Smith of Charleston (1758–1812)* (Columbia, S.C., 1962), 43–45.

6. *South Carolina Gazette*, Sept. 28, Oct. 5, 1765, quoted in Merrill Jensen, *The Founding of a Nation: A History of the American Revolution, 1763–1776* (New York, 1968), 137.

7. *Biographical Directory: Session Lists*, 131–33.

8. *Commons House Journals*, quoted in Weir, "A Most Important Epocha," 18–19; Rogers, *Evolution of a Federalist*, 44–45; Carl J. Vipperman, *The Rise of Rawlins Lowndes, 1721–1800* (Columbia, S.C., 1978), 110–11.

ralty court judge, and attorney general. An angry Commons House told its agent, "The incompatibility of some of the offices held by Mr. Leigh . . . is so striking that it cannot escape your notice."[9]

As was the case in the other colonies, South Carolina's upper-class opponents of the Stamp Act received support from the common people. Whether the patriot elite directly instigated the popular demonstrations is not certain, but two individuals in a position to know believed that wealthy revolutionaries were spurring the mob. Lieutenant Governor Bull asserted that "considerable men who stood behind the curtain" fomented the initial set of public protests in mid-October, and Henry Laurens, using the same metaphor, remarked that he saw in the public violence the presence of Christopher Gadsden, "acting behind the curtain, who could be reached only by suspicion."[10] Unmistakable, however, was the popular respect for the rights of persons and property, a socially conservative stance that pleased the wealthy revolutionaries. Laurens was gratified that the "jacks [i.e., sailors] and townsmen" who descended on his house when rumor spread that he harbored stamps "did not do one penny damage to my garden . . . and not 15/ damage to my fence, gate, or house." Moreover, once he had assured these intruders that he had no stamps, Laurens testified, they "praised me highly, and insisted upon giving me three cheers, and then retired with, 'God bless your honor, good night, Colonel.'"[11] Later that month seven thousand Charlestonians peacefully gathered to hear the stamp distributor and inspector announce that they would not execute their offices.[12]

Crowd activity in 1766 was again directed to expansionist ends. In January a broadside urged the Liberty Boys to force open the port, which had been closed since November for want of stamps. Lieutenant Governor Bull quickly caved in to this demand. There "being now near 1400 [sailors] in this port lying idle," he explained to his superiors, "and though hitherto tolerably well governed, now beginning to grow licentious, . . . the public tranquility . . . was threatened and

9. Committee of Correspondence to Charles Garth, July 2, 1766, *SCHM*, xxviii (1927), 228; "An Account of the Proceedings of the Chief Justice . . .," enclosed in Gov. Montagu's letter, Aug. 6, 1766, SCPR, xxxi, 87–142; Gadsden to William Samuel Johnson, Apr. 16, 1766, *Writings of Gadsden*, 69–70; Crouse, "Cautious Rebellion," 70.

10. Lt. Gov. Bull to Board of Trade, Nov. 3, 1765, SCPR, xxx, 281–89, quotation on 286; Laurens to Joseph Brown, Oct. 22, 1765, *The Papers of Henry Laurens*, ed. Philip M. Hamer et al. (Columbia, S.C., 1968–   ), v, 27–28.

11. Laurens to James Grant, Nov. 1, 1765, Laurens to Joseph Brown, Oct. 28, 1765, *Papers of Laurens*, v, 35, 39–40, 30–31; Pauline Maier, "The Charleston Mob and the Evolution of Popular Politics in Revolutionary South Carolina, 1765–1784," *Perspectives in American History*, iv (1970), 174–77.

12. Laurens to Joseph Brown, Oct. 28, 1765, *Papers of Laurens*, v, 32; George Saxby and Caleb Lloyd to Lt. Gov. Bull, Oct. 29, 1765, SCPR, xxx, 279–80.

greatly endangered."[13] In May the crowd compelled all Charlestonians to illuminate their homes in honor of repeal; and in the fall Gadsden brought together a group of artisans under the Liberty Tree and harangued them about the dangers of the Declaratory Act.[14]

Christopher Gadsden's position within the expansionist party was noteworthy. By 1765 his militance and links with the Charleston mechanics placed him at one extreme within the faction. His mercantile wealth and family ties suggest that he should have been more fully in step with his fellow partisans, but his ardent commitment to the revolution (he "leaves all New England Sons of Liberty far behind," a northern patriot observed)[15] made him impatient with the course of moderation. He grew particularly disenchanted with the balanced programs pushed by the expansionist importers, who often lagged a pace behind the planters. Increasingly, Gadsden associated himself with the artisans and chided his fellow traders for succumbing to their "private interest." Reinforcing Gadsden's separation from the other merchants was the nature of his business activity; he concentrated on the sale of country produce to the shippers, rather than on overseas trade. Significantly, Gadsden's affection for the common people never extended to the dissident backcountry farmers, who were critical of the low-country patriots, nor did it persist for long after independence.[16]

A comparatively small group of nonexpansionists publicly opposed the revolutionaries during the Stamp Act crisis. Lieutenant Governor William Bull attempted to enforce ministerial policies, but he was too wise a politician to join an impossible battle with the majority in the Commons House. Instead, he strove to maintain a working relationship with the patriots, just as earlier, during the Cherokee War, he had tried to find common ground with the lawmakers who rejected his advice. Such temporizing, which allowed Bull to preserve a

13. Lt. Gov. Bull to Sec. of State Conway, Feb. 6, 1766, SCPR, xxxi, 23–24; Jensen, *Founding of a Nation*, 137–38.

14. Laurens to John Lewis Gervais, May 12, 1766, *Papers of Laurens*, v, 129; Benjamin Smith to the Reverend William Smith, May 21, 1766, Smith-Carter Papers, MHS; Lt. Gov. Bull to Chief Justice Shinner, May 5, 1766, SCPR, xxxi, 131. A list of those meeting under the Liberty Tree is presented in Gibbes, ed., *Documentary History*, i, 10; Jensen, *Founding of a Nation*, 205.

15. Silas Deane to Mrs. Deane, Sept. 7, 1774, *Letters of Members of the Continental Congress*, ed. Edmund C. Burnett, 8 vols. (Washington, D.C., 1921–36), i, 18. Also see "Journal of Josiah Quincy, Junior, 1773," ed. Mark A. D. Howe, MHS *Procs.*, xlix (1915–16), 452 (Mar. 19, 1773); Lt. Gov. William Bull to Hillsborough, Dec. 5, 1770, SCPR, xxxii, 416.

16. Gadsden, "To the Planters, Mechanics, and Freeholders . . . ," June 22, 1769, Gadsden to "Sylvanus," Mar. 28, 1769, Gadsden to Peter Timothy, June 8, 1778, *Writings of Gadsden*, 78–79, 74–76, 130; George C. Rogers, Jr., "The Charleston Tea Party: The Significance of December 3, 1773," *SCHM*, lxxv (1974), 156, 160–61.

modicum of popularity, did not suit all the assemblymen. Gadsden
tartly observed, "Our Lt. Governor . . . is and always has been the
weakest and most unsteady man I ever knew, so very obliging that he
never obliged. The regard for him as a private gentleman has had too
great weight with many in our house."[17]

A very few members of the reformed legislature also stood by the
nonexpansionist standard. William Wragg's consistent partisanship,
like William Bull's, stretched over several decades, although Wragg,
unlike the lieutenant governor, rarely showed a desire to accommo-
date his opponents. During 1765 and 1766 Wragg was the single outspoken nonexpansionist in the Commons House; his was the only
vote against the resolutions condemning the Stamp Act, and he found
no seconder for his motion in 1766 to erect a statue of George III
rather than (as the majority decreed) one of William Pitt. William
Henry Drayton, a nephew of William Bull's and delegate from the
parish of St. Andrew, apparently opposed the patriotic protests, for
some years later General Charles Lee sneered at him as an "advocate
for the Stamp Act" and stated that no show of patriotism would
"ever wash away the stain." Yet Drayton, who would be so vocal an
opponent of the boycott in the late 1760s, seems to have added little
to the public debate in 1765–1766.[18]

The Scots in the capital also demonstrated their sympathy for the
British cause. "You cannot possibly be too much on your guard
against the Sc——h representations from this place," Gadsden warned a British correspondent in February 1766. "Those gents have in
Georgia caused the stamps to be taken there, and by every artifice
labored to give them an entrance here, but hitherto to no purpose."[19]
Scottish gazetteer Robert Wells agreed to pay the duty imposed on his
newspaper. (Patriot Peter Timothy at first concurred in this step but, it
appears, soon recanted and emerged as a leader of the Sons of Liberty.)[20]

17. Gadsden to William Samuel Johnson, Apr. 16, 1766, *Writings of Gadsden*, 71; Lt.
Gov. Bull to Board of Trade, Dec. 17, 1765, SCPR, xxx, 298–99.

18. Lee quoted in William M. Dabney and Marion Dargan, *William Henry Drayton &
the American Revolution* (Albuquerque, N.M., 1962), 28; Laurens to John Lewis Gervais,
May 12, 1766, *Papers of Laurens*, v, 128–29; Rogers, *Evolution of a Federalist*, 44–45.

19. Gadsden to James Pearson, Feb. 20, 1766, "Two Letters by Christopher Gadsden,
February 1766," ed., Robert M. Weir, *SCHM*, lxxv (1974), 173; Gadsden to William
Samuel Johnson and Charles Garth, Dec. 2, 1765, *Writings of Gadsden*, 66.

20. Timothy later stated that he remained in disfavor throughout the Stamp Act
period. See Peter Timothy to Franklin, Sept. 3, 1768, *The Papers of Benjamin Franklin*,
ed. Leonard W. Labaree et al. (New Haven, 1959–   ), xv, 200–201. Laurens, however,
testified that Timothy was a leader of the popular forces against the Stamp Act. See
Laurens to James Grant, Nov. 1, 1765, Laurens to John Lewis Gervais, Jan. 29, 1766,
Papers of Laurens, v, 36, 52, and see 28n.

Henry Laurens, continuing his flirtation with the nonexpansionists, called for a "humble and dutiful acquiescence to an act of Parliament however oppressive it may be until by proper representations and remonstrances a repeal of that act can be obtained."[21] His moderation was at least partly motivated by his unabated hostility toward Christopher Gadsden, with whom he had publicly quarreled in 1761 and 1762 over the merits of Lieutenant Colonel James Grant's Cherokee War campaign. Laurens recorded one pointed encounter with a "townsman" when the crowd entered his house in October 1765: "One of them holding my shoulders said they loved me, and everybody would love me if I did not hold sway with one Governor Grant. This provoked me not a little as it exhibited to me the cloven foot of a certain malicious villain [i.e., Gadsden]."[22] Late in 1766, once the passions of the Stamp Act subsided, Laurens began to rethink his position on imperial politics and drew closer to his old expansionist allies. Typically, however, it was not until he feuded with the local customs collector that Laurens vehemently denounced British policies.[23]

Backcountry farmers also offered a measure of support to the nonexpansionists. During the early 1760s men of loyalist inclination had begun to cultivate these westerners as allies and had railed at the expansionist majority in the house for not providing the back settlers with much-needed courts, roads, schools, churches, and representation. And though the western farmers were not monolithic in their views, many responded favorably to such attention and listened with undisguised skepticism to tirades against British tyranny. "I am very glad to hear that your neighbors are not quite so much the Sons of Liberty in the reigning misapplication of that noble characteristic, as some of our illegitimate brothers have bragged of," Laurens told a western settler. "I hope your Loyal Frontier-Friends-Club (of which I beg to be admitted a member when I come your way) will be able to prevent or defeat any irregular steps by the misinformed."[24] After 1766 backcountry resentment, focused in the Regulator movement, would present a still more serious challenge to the expansionists.

» «

Between 1767 and 1770 wealthy patriots, strengthened by the 1765 election, stepped up their campaign against British measures while

21. Laurens to Joseph Brown, Oct. 11, 1765, *Papers of Laurens*, v, 24.
22. Laurens to Joseph Brown, Oct. 28, 1765, ibid., 30.
23. Laurens to John Lewis Gervais, Sept. 1, 1766, ibid., 182–84.
24. Laurens to John Lewis Gervais, Jan. 29, 1766, ibid., 52–53.

wrestling with the challenge posed by dissident western settlers. Conflict between South Carolina and the mother country might have been relatively subdued in 1767, as protests were in most other colonies, had it not been for Henry Laurens's feud with the new venal collector of the port, Daniel Moore. Alleging certain technical infractions of the law, Moore seized two of Laurens's coasting vessels and then declared himself willing to accept a bribe. Laurens, a fair trader, was outraged at such blatant harassment and assaulted the collector when they chanced upon one another. "The act of wringing his nose was unpremediated," the merchant explained. "It was thought of, and executed as quick as thought."[25] Laurens also wrote an angry tract detailing Moore's behavior, and he circulated a remonstrance addressed to the local British naval commander, asking for a return to the customary practices in the coastal trade. The patriotic merchants of Charleston eagerly signed Laurens's petition and welcomed the strong-willed importer back into the expansionist camp. "All those folks," Laurens wryly observed, "who through party heat in 1761 and 1765 affected to be very angry are now upon good terms with me."[26]

Laurens's dispute, which heightened local resentment against British policies, continued in 1768, despite Collector Moore's departure from Charleston. George Roupell, who had earlier served as Moore's assistant, seized another of Laurens's ships, hoping to intimidate the merchant into dropping a suit begun the previous year against the harbor officials. Laurens only broadened his onslaught, compiling another lengthy tract, in which he attacked not only Roupell but also Attorney General Egerton Leigh, who had supported the customs officers. To the excitable Laurens, Leigh was "that POLE CAT," and a "greedy, coarse, and filthy wretch." Despite such vehemence in his squabbles with these officials, Laurens would remain a moderate figure within the inner circle of expansionists. He was hesitant to applaud the most daring protests, he retained his sympathy for the backcountry, and he never quite got over his dislike of Christopher Gadsden.[27]

25. Laurens to James Habersham, Oct. 14, 1767, ibid., 366; Jensen, *Founding of a Nation*, 307–8.

26. Laurens to James Habersham, Sept. 5, 1767, Laurens to James Grant, Aug. 12, 1767, Laurens, "A Representation of Facts . . . ," Nov. 16–23, 1767, Remonstrance to Mark Robinson, Dec. 4, 1767, *Papers of Laurens*, v, 296–98, 277–79, 391–464, 491–94.

27. Laurens quoted in Jensen, *Founding of a Nation*, 308–10; Laurens to Richard Oswald, Apr. 27, 1768, Laurens to William Fisher, May 28, 1768, Seizure of the *Ann*, June 18, 1768, Laurens to William Freeman, July 13, 1768, Laurens to Egerton Leigh, July 28, 1768, Laurens to William Cowles & Co. and William Freeman, Mar. 2, 1769, Laurens, "Extracts from the Proceedings . . . ," 1768, 1769, Laurens, "Appendix to the Extracts . . . ," 1769, Laurens to James Grant, Oct. 1, Dec. 22, 1768, the Reverend

While the expansionists were attempting to defend South Carolina against what they viewed as British oppression during 1767, 1768, and 1769, they also had to deal with a revolt of western farmers, the Regulator movement. Secure in their control of the Commons House, the wealthy revolutionaries felt little need to make any serious concessions to the backcountry settlers until the uprising dragged into its third year. As a result, this conflict, which was played out within the matrix of factional politics, alienated many up-country farmers from the patriot cause.[28]

Although sectional hostility in South Carolina could be traced back at least to midcentury, animosity between the West and the dominant expansionist elite in the low country took a new turn in the fall of 1767 when backcountry vigilante groups, which had emerged to preserve order, came together in a loose organization, calling themselves the Regulators. In November four western leaders presented to the Commons House a lengthy remonstrance demanding courts, jails, schools, and churches and bewailing the lack of representation. The petition noted ominously, "Many sober persons among us are become almost desperate in seeing the nonattention given to these and other matters of serious concern."[29] Some assemblymen wanted to imprison the delegation, but the threat of a march by several thousand Regulators made for second thoughts. Thoroughly frightened, the patriot-dominated house appointed nonexpansionist William Wragg to head a committee on western grievances. Wragg had long been known as a friend of the backcountry, a section he and others in his faction viewed as a potential ally against the revolutionary elite. Within twenty-four hours Wragg's panel reported back, recommending the creation of county and circuit courts. The proposal temporarily mollified the

---

Charles Woodmason to Laurens [1768 or 1769], *Papers of Laurens*, v, 669, 710, 722–23, 751, 760–61, vi, 393–94, 184–216, 287–383, vii, 2–114, vi, 119–20, 233–34, 603–8; Robert M. Calhoon and Robert M. Weir, "The Scandalous History of Sir Egerton Leigh," *WMQ*, 3d ser., xxvi (1969), 47–74; David Duncan Wallace, *The Life of Henry Laurens, with a sketch of Lieutenant-Colonel John Laurens* (1915, rpt. New York, 1967), 167.

28. For a contrasting view of the Regulator movement, consult Richard M. Brown, *The South Carolina Regulators* (Cambridge, Mass., 1963), esp. 135–42. Brown minimizes the conflict between the West and the low-country aristocracy. David R. Chesnutt presents a similar argument in "Greedy Party Work: The South Carolina Election of 1768," Patricia U. Bonomi, ed., *Party and Political Opposition in Revolutionary America* (Tarrytown, N.Y., 1980), 70–86. Ernst, "Another View," ibid., 87–97, disputes Chesnutt's conclusions.

29. "The Remonstrance," Nov. 1767, Richard J. Hooker, ed., *The Carolina Backcountry on the Eve of the Revolution: The Journal and Other Writings of Charles Woodmason, Anglican Itinerant* (Chapel Hill, N.C., 1952), 213–46, quotation on 223; Gov. Montagu to Board of Trade, Nov. 10, 1767, SCPR, xxxi, 423–24; Brown, *South Carolina Regulators*, 35–41.

angry westerners, but once the immediate threat was defused, a "junto" of lawyers (as the backcountry preacher, Charles Woodmason described the opposition) voted down these suggestions, and the house struck new committees.[30]

During 1768 the wealthy patriots took no meaningful steps to satisfy Regulator demands and only further angered these settlers. In March the Commons House adopted a bill establishing circuit courts in the backcountry, but this measure incorporated a controversial clause on judicial tenure and so was assured of (and received) a royal veto. Many of the upper-class revolutionaries excoriated the rebellious farmers. John Rutledge called the westeners a "pack of beggars," and Rawlins Lowndes, then acting chief justice, reported that he had had the pleasure of imprisoning "some of the principal actors in that scene of Regulating."[31] Christopher Gadsden lectured the Reverend Mr. Woodmason on political priorities, asserting that internal problems must not "divert us from the grand *common* concern, at this momentous crisis, of all British America."[32] By contrast, nonexpansionist William Bull was openly sympathetic to the Regulators' demands. He told Hillsborough, "I feel it is best to treat the backcountry with moderation and to give their complaints attention." Meanwhile, angry farmers strengthened their forces against the eastern patriot elite, forming a "Plan of Regulation," which elevated local tribunals and denied the "jurisdiction of the courts holden in Charlestown" over the western reaches.[33]

Only in 1769 did the expansionists take a first halting step to redress western grievances. The Regulators had made clear to the aristocracy that it was in danger of losing its control over the West. "Our back settlers," Bull reported in 1769, "lately upon the appearance of four marshal's men among them have again obstructed those officers from doing their duty, and persist in their resolution not to be drawn down to Charleston by lawsuits."[34] In July the wealthy patriots in the Commons House adopted a circuit court act without the contentious

30. Charles Woodmason, "Notes to 'Remonstrance,'" [c. 1768], Charles Woodmason, "Letter to an English Friend," Mar. 26, 1770, Hooker, ed., *Carolina Backcountry*, 237, 191, 204; Ernst, "Another View," 94.

31. Regulators to John Rutledge, [c. 1768], Hooker, ed., *Carolina Backcountry*, 273; Vipperman, *Rawlins Lowndes*, 135; Henry Middleton to Arthur Middleton, Sept. 22, 1768, "Correspondence of Hon. Arthur Middleton, Signer of the Declaration of Independence," ed. Joseph H. Barnwell, *SCHM*, xxvii (1926), 110; Brown, *South Carolina Regulators*, 49–77; Chesnutt, "Greedy Party Work," 72–74.

32. Gadsden, "Reply to Sylvanus," Mar. 28, 1769, *Writings of Gadsden*, 75–76.

33. Lt. Gov. Bull to Hillsborough, Sept. 10, July 18, 1768, SCPR, xxxii, 40, 14–15; Brown, *South Carolina Regulators*, 49–52.

34. Lt. Gov. Bull to Hillsborough, Sept. 7, 1769, SCPR, xxxii, 101.

judicial tenure clause. They did not address the myriad other back-country demands, however, and they rejected a proposal that the circuit court system commence its operations immediately. Judicial hearings would begin only after the courthouses were completed, and consequently the first sessions in the up-country did not take place until the fall of 1772. With the adoption of this measure much of the more violent discontent in the West subsided. Nevertheless, during the Revolutionary War many westeners would remember their years of frustration at the hands of the expansionists and would side with the British.[35]

Unlike the situation in New York, the rebellion of western farmers in South Carolina did not make the wealthy revolutionaries fear for the social fabric and so moderate their participation in the revolutionary movement. Consequently, during the second half of 1768 the dominant expansionist elite felt few constraints in reaffirming the revolutionary course of South Carolina. In July, Speaker Peter Manigault wrote to the Massachusetts and Virginia assemblies informing them that their circular letters would be closely considered when the Commons House next met. And when Lieutenant Governor Bull dissolved the legislature and promulgated writs of election, both parties worked hard to shape the new assembly and, with it, provincial policy.[36]

The patriots confirmed their position in the legislature by winning a solid victory in the October 1768 balloting, but they had to overcome challenges from several quarters, including the Regulator movement. Although only three parishes, with one representative each, lay in the West, backcountry settlers were technically entitled to vote in several low-country districts, and in the 1768 election many of the angry farmers determined to do just that. In all, the impact of the populous up-country on the makeup of the fifty-two-seat assembly was slight, even though western voters helped select a few representatives, generally with nonexpansionist leanings. The Sea Island and coastal planters, who traditionally favored the nonexpansionists, provided a second source of opposition for the patriots. When John Mackenzie, a fiery revolutionary, instructed the readers of Timothy's *Gazette* to choose unwavering defenders of American liberty, William Wragg announced to his constituents in St. John Colleton that he was happy to stand on his record, and he was reelected, along with a like-minded assemblyman, John Freer. The artisans and shopkeepers of Charleston joined in challenging the upper-class patriots, although in

35. Brown, *South Carolina Regulators*, 96–111; Ernst, "Another View," 96–97.
36. Lt. Gov. Bull to Hillsborough, Sept. 10, 1768, SCPR, xxxii, 36; Vipperman, *Rawlins Lowndes*, 142.

this instance the demand was not for moderation of the revolutionary protests but for greater receptivity to the views of the common people. The mechanics posted a list of the "proper persons to represent them at this important juncture," recommending the reelection of Gadsden and the retirement of more elitist patriots like Laurens and Charles Pinckney. Laurens and Pinckney, as well as Gadsden, nevertheless gained seats. In all, the wealthy revolutionaries achieved an indisputable majority, although men of loyalist leanings increased their proportion among the identifiable delegates from 12 to 24 percent.[37]

The patriot victory in the 1768 provincial election made approval of the circular letters a foregone conclusion; hence, assemblymen sympathetic to the crown chose not to attend the November session. Six of them, including William Wragg and John Freer, appeared before the house, but pointedly refused to "qualify" for their seats. Rawlins Lowndes, the moderate expansionist who had been ousted from the speakership in 1765, was also among the six; Lowndes had been acting as chief justice since Shinner's death in February, and was hoping—in vain, as it turned out—that such discretion would secure him a permanent appointment. Thirteen other delegates failed to assume their places, and though this group embraced several patriots who had been unable to reach Charleston, it also included such outspoken nonexpansionists as Moses Kirkland, a leading Regulator. The twenty-six men who formed the house were, with few exceptions, dedicated revolutionaries; many of them had been expansionists since the 1750s.[38]

The new assembly was defiantly patriotic, if short-lived. It approved the letters from Massachusetts and Virginia, despite stern admonitions from the governor, Lord Charles Montagu, who dissolved the chamber after it had sat for only three days. Timothy's *Gazette* proudly listed the members of the legislature and observed that "since the dissolution the prevailing toast is the UNANIMOUS TWENTY-SIX."[39]

37. *S.C. Gazette*, Oct. 3, 1768, *Papers of Laurens*, VI, 122–23; Laurens to James Grant, Oct. 1, 1768, William Drayton to James Grant, Oct. 29, 1768, ibid., 119–20, 141n; Lt. Gov. Bull to Hillsborough, Sept. 10, 1768, SCPR, XXXII, 37–38; Chesnutt, "Greedy Party Work," 72–82; *Biographical Directory: Session Lists*, 134–35.

38. Rogers, *Evolution of a Federalist*, 49–50; Vipperman, *Rawlins Lowndes*, 137–39; *Biographical Directory: Session Lists*, 134–35. In 1768 the Commons House had fifty-two seats. Twenty-six members sat; nineteen delegates were elected but did not serve; and two districts with five representatives between them never voted. Two parishes elected men who had already secured a seat in the house. Before the 1772 election the number of seats was reduced to forty-eight.

39. *S.C. Gazette*, Nov. 21, 1768, *Papers of Laurens*, VI, 173–76; Laurens to Edward Jones, Nov. 22, 1768, ibid., 176, and see 141n, V, 47; Resolutions of Commons House, Nov. 19, 1768, SCPR, XXXII, 62–64; D. E. Huger Smith, "Wilton's Statue of Pitt," *SCHM*, XV (1914), 27; Chesnutt, "Greedy Party Work," 79–81.

In the ensuing provincial election, held in March 1769, low-country South Carolinians registered their clear disapproval of Montagu's action and their warm appreciation for the expansionist lawmakers' firmness. All but one of the "unanimous twenty-six" were reelected, while only nine of the nineteen nonattenders regained their seats. A sudden renewal of violence in the back settlements distracted the Regulators from their resolve of once more participating in the polling and helped swell the expansionists' electoral victory. Westerners angrily pointed out that the decision of low-country law officials—a few days before the election—to arrest several Regulator leaders had diverted the attention of the settlers from the balloting. Woodmason commented, "The people hearing that their houses were plundered . . . instantly marched back again to secure their families. This was the aim of those below. And hereby they carried the elections in their own way."[40]

The wealthy patriots dominating the twenty-ninth royal assembly (which was to last from June 1769 to November 1771) enlarged upon the revolutionary tradition set down by the previous two houses. In August 1769 the lawmakers refused to provide funds for the British troops stationed in the colony and approved the Virginia resolves against transporting Americans to Britain for trial. Lieutenant Governor Bull reluctantly accepted these votes, well aware that a dissolution and new election would only strengthen the patriot party. "A repetition of such marks of displeasure," he explained to the secretary of state, "had not produced any good effects of changing men or measures . . . but had tended rather to furnish the more turbulent and factious with popular arguments to keep up their clamors and feed their discontent."[41]

In December the Commons House undertook what was perhaps its boldest move. Without seeking the consent of the council or the governor, the legislators instructed the treasurer to forward fifteen hundred pounds sterling to the Bill of Rights Society, a group associated with the English politician and gadfly, John Wilkes. For South Carolina patriots, this grant, which the compliant treasurer readily delivered, was a heady initiative. It not only helped a fellow opponent of ministerial tyranny but also seemed to affirm the exclusive control of

40. Charles Woodmason: "A Letter to an English Friend," March 26, 1770, Hooker, ed., *Carolina Backcountry*, 207–8, and see 183; *Biographical Directory: Session Lists*, 136–39. Some Regulators, however, did vote in the low-country parishes and helped determine the outcome of several contests. See Chesnutt, "Greedy Party Work," 82; Brown, *South Carolina Regulators*, 91–92, 206–7.

41. Lt. Gov. Bull to Hillsborough, Aug. 28, 1769, quoted in Jensen, *Founding of a Nation*, 312; Gov. Montagu to Hillsborough, June 30, 1769, Resolves of Commons House, Aug. 17, 1769, SCPR, xxxii, 80, 97–99; Edward McCrady, *The History of South Carolina under the Royal Government, 1719–1776* (1899; rpt. New York, 1969), 619–21.

the lower house over the purse strings. It was equally exhilarating to realize that the measure had been of their own devising and was not merely an echo of plans set forth in Virginia or the commercial provinces. Declared Peter Timothy, "In this instance it cannot be said *we* have followed the example of the northern colonies."[42] Seven representatives, however, voted against the appropriation, and while this group possibly included some of the few nonexpansionists in the house, it certainly embraced several moderate revolutionaries. Although Henry Laurens was not present at the division, upon hearing the news he "passed his censure in very plain language." Charles Pinckney and Rawlins Lowndes were conspicuously absent from the group of lawmakers selected to implement the decision.[43]

The battle with the governor over the grant to Wilkes continued in 1770. The expansionist assemblymen hoped to use tax revenues to replace the money that had been drawn from the public treasury and sent to England. In April, however, Secretary of State Hillsborough issued a stern directive allowing the adoption of money bills only if the funds were directed to local services and only if the measure was approved by both governor and council. Confronted with this ukase, the expansionists closed ranks; observed Bull, "Many who wish it [the grant to Wilkes] had never passed, are nevertheless very averse to rescind or censure it."[44] Positions hardened on both sides: Whitehall's instructions gave acting Governor Bull little room to maneuver, and the expansionists were adamant in their demand for control of the public treasury. As a result of this deadlock, no revenue measures would be signed into law after 1769 and no legislation whatsoever would be adopted after 1771—a state of affairs that lasted until the Revolutionary War.[45]

At the decade's end South Carolina expansionists also turned their attention to the need to buoy the economy, and they joined the other provinces in a boycott of British wares. In 1768, however, relative prosperity in the rice colony made the wealthy patriots, who were among the leaders of America's "political" protests, more reluctant

42. *S.C. Gazette*, Dec. 8, 1769, quoted in Jack P. Greene, "Bridge to Revolution: The Wilkes Fund Controversy in South Carolina, 1769–1774," *JSH*, xxix (1963), 22; Lt. Gov. Bull to Hillsborough, Dec. 12, 1769, SCPR, xxxii, 132; Benjamin Smith to Isaac Smith, Dec. 12, 1769, Smith-Carter Papers.

43. Wallace, *Henry Laurens*, 167; Greene, "Bridge to Revolution," 23. Peter Manigault also expressed reservations about the gift to Wilkes, in Peter Manigault to David Blake, Oct. 19, 1770, "Letterbook of Manigault," 187.

44. Lt. Gov. Bull to Hillsborough, Aug. 23, 1770, SCPR, xxxii, 317–18; Laurens to William Fisher, Sept. 6, 1770, *Papers of Laurens*, vii, 335–36; Greene, "Bridge to Revolution," 32; Wallace, *Henry Laurens*, 166.

45. Lt. Gov. Bull to Hillsborough, Apr. 15, 1770, SCPR, xxxii, 256–59; Jensen, *Founding of a Nation*, 378.

than their northern brethren to adopt any far-reaching economic measures. Estate owners benefited from the ban imposed on slave imports between 1766 and 1768 as well as from high prices for their produce. "The planters are full of money," remarked Henry Laurens in December 1768, "and their rice commands money, wherefore 'tis probable that the sales of slaves will be very advantageous at this market until we are overstocked or interrupted by any broils with king's officers."[46] The merchants also enjoyed comparatively favorable conditions and evinced little interest in joining the boycotts that were taking root in the North. Lieutenant Governor Bull reported to Hillsborough in the fall that "a letter from Boston . . . has lately been received here and communicated to several of the principal merchants. I have the pleasure to acquaint your lordship that it met with no countenance, having been handed from man to man with silent neglect."[47]

During the first half of 1769 the patriot planters, as well as the lower classes in the capital, began to raise a cry for nonimportation. Changed conditions in the countryside, brought on by large purchases of slaves, drained the rice growers' cash surpluses and made the planters more receptive to the idea of a boycott of imported manufactures and servants. In March, Laurens reported that "a very sensible publication lately appeared in one of our gazettes dissuading the planters from purchasing Negroes, and I am told it is much regarded in the country."[48] Meanwhile, Gadsden, Peter Timothy, and other writers, noting the lethargy of the merchants, urged Charleston artisans to join the planters in taking up the cause of nonimportation. Gadsden underscored his ties with the mechanics and the benefits of local manufacturing by appearing at his wife's funeral in a suit of blue homespun. In June, Gadsden and Timothy set forth in the *Gazette* the details of a proposed agreement.[49]

The expansionist importers proved somewhat more hesitant than the planters to enter into a boycott. The key difference between the two groups lay not in their relative prosperity but in the merchants' deep concern about the newfound militance of the urban lower classes, a concern not fully shared by those who lived outside the capital. The "mechanics' ticket" proposed in the 1768 election had unnerved many

46. Laurens to Ross & Mill, Dec. 24, 1768, *Papers of Laurens*, VI, 240; Arthur H. Cole, *Wholesale Commodity Prices in the United States, 1700–1861: Statistical Supplement* (Cambridge, Mass., 1938), 15–69.

47. Lt. Gov. Bull to Hillsborough, Oct. 18, 1768, SCPR, XXXII, 56–57.

48. Laurens to Ross & Mill, Mar. 11, 1769, *Papers of Laurens*, VI, 407–8.

49. Gadsden, "To the Planters, Mechanics, and Freeholders . . .," *Writings of Gadsden*, 77–88; Arthur M. Schlesinger, *The Colonial Merchants and the American Revolution, 1763–1776* (New York, 1919), 140–42.

importers, and in 1769 at least a few traders roundly condemned the effort of the artisans and planters to draw up an agreement, calling it "an unjust attempt of one part of the community . . . to throw a burden on the rest, more grievous than ever was conceived by the most arbitrary minister of the most despotic king."[50] Gadsden, in turn, sharply criticized the "importers of *European* goods." Acknowledging that "*some* of them" had shown a "firm attachment to the true interest of this province," he asked in June why such men were not able to "procure even one meeting of the *importers of European goods* to consult what they could and might do."[51]

The differences between the several patriot groups—planters, merchants, and artisans—must not be exaggerated, however, and in July individuals from all three callings agreed on a boycott, leaving only the nonexpansionists in opposition. Unsurprisingly, the mechanics and planters convened first. On July 3 and 4 they signed a pact that prohibited the importation of British wares, except a very few items (such as workmen's tools); barred the introduction of slaves after January 1, 1770; and encouraged local manufacturers. On July 7 the merchants announced their own accord, which was similar to that of the planters and artisans but with a longer list of permitted imports and with no provision to boost the efforts of South Carolina craftsmen. At the behest of the traders, delegates from the three groups came together and hammered out a new agreement, which Gadsden presented to an enthusiastic mass meeting on July 22. This pact encouraged local producers but exempted a lengthy catalogue of British wares (such as cheap cloth and artisan's supplies). The accord also interdicted the slave trade, and it was to run until all the reviled Parliamentary acts were repealed. The associators acknowledged occupational distinctions (as well as the enhanced role of the common people) with the creation of a general committee of thirty-nine, comprising equal numbers of planters, merchants, and mechanics.[52]

Only a small group of nonexpansionists publicly opposed the boycott. William Wragg denounced the pact, as did William Henry Drayton, the wealthy twenty-seven-year-old nephew of Lieutenant Governor Bull. Drayton, who came by his nonexpansionist views through his family and through a lengthy residence in Britain during his adolescence, decried the association's strictures as "illegal restraints

50. "The Merchants of Charles-Town," *South Carolina & American Gazette*, July 13, 1769, quoted in Schlesinger, *Colonial Merchants*, 144.

51. Gadsden, "To the Planters, Mechanics, and Freeholders . . .," *Writings of Gadsden*, 78–79.

52. Leila Sellers, *Charleston Business on the Eve of the American Revolution* (Chapel Hill, N.C., 1934), 207–9; Schlesinger, *Colonial Merchants*, 143–46; Richard Walsh, *Charleston's Sons of Liberty: A Study of the Artisans, 1763–1789* (Columbia, S.C., 1959), 48–50. McCrady, *South Carolina*, 651n, lists the thirty-nine committee members.

upon the free wills of free men," and he bristled at lower-class involvement in the boycott, complaining, "I see no reason why I should
allow my opinion to be controlled by theirs." Early in 1770 he fled to
England to escape the social and economic ostracism that confronted
him in South Carolina.[53] Charleston Scots also set themselves
against the agreement. Christopher Gadsden and Peter Manigault
reprobated this group in their correspondence, and an editorialist in
Timothy's *Gazette* remarked that most of the nonsigners were "little
Scotch shopkeepers of no consequence."[54] Scottish printer Robert
Wells put his press at the disposal of boycott opponents. But the
South Carolina tory party—at least the portion that dared raise its
head—was weak. Several hundred individuals soon signed the boycott, and Timothy reported in September 1769 that only thirty-one
persons, excluding royal officials, had deliberately withheld their
names.[55]

The patriots rigorously enforced the nonimportation agreement.
Imports from Britain plummeted from £315,000 sterling in 1769 to
£151,000 in 1770, the lowest level in almost two decades, while the
number of slaves landed in Charleston fell during these two years
from 4,652 to 1,596. Observers from both factions commented on the
strict, effective execution of the resolves. In addition, the associators
sent circular letters to the other colonies urging them not to weaken
in their resolves and suggesting that they join South Carolina in
extending nonimportation until the customs board was dismantled
and the vice-admiralty courts removed. Unsurprisingly, many of
those overseeing the association had long histories of support for the
expansionist cause.[56]

By the end of 1770 the defection of the commercial provinces, as

53. Drayton's comments in *S.C. Gazette*, Sept. 21, 1769, quoted in Schlesinger, *Colo-
nial Merchants*, 204, and see 143–47, 203; Rogers, *Evolution of a Federalist*, 51;
Gadsden, "Letters of Freeman," 1769, *Writings of Gadsden*, 89–90; Lt. Gov. Bull to
Hillsborough, Sept. 25, Dec. 5, 1769, SCPR, xxxII, 103, 121; Dabney and Dargan,
William Henry Drayton, 26–37; Sellers, *Charleston Business*, 209.

54. *S.C. Gazette*, Apr. 5, 1770, quoted in Sellers, *Charleston Business*, 210, and see
214; Vipperman, *Rawlins Loundes*, 146; Gadsden: "To the Planters, Mechanics, and
Freeholders . . . ," *Writings of Gadsden*, 84; Peter Manigault to Ralph Izard, Oct. 4,
1769, "Letterbook of Manigault," 180.

55. Schlesinger, *Colonial Merchants*, 203; Walsh, *Charleston's Sons of Liberty*, 51.

56. Lt. Gov. Bull to Hillsborough, Mar. 6, Dec. 5, July 16, Oct. 20, 1770, SCPR, xxxII,
200–201, 415–16, 298, 342–43; Laurens to James Habersham, Jan. 27, 1770, Laurens to
Bush & Elton, Apr. 2, Sept. 10, 1770, Laurens to Richard Oswald, Sept. 10, 1770, *Papers
of Laurens*, vII, 225–26, 266, 349, 360; Benjamin Smith to Isaac Smith, Dec. 12, 1769,
Isaac Smith, Jr., to the Reverend Isaac Smith, Feb. 3, 1769, Thomas Smith to Isaac
Smith, Jr., Aug. 1, 1770, John Mackenzie to [?] July 27, 1770, Smith-Carter Papers,
MHS; Isaac Smith, Jr., to Joshua Green, Feb. 8, 1770, Samuel A. Green Papers, 1700–
1835, box 1, MHS; U.S. Bureau of the Census, *Historical Statistics of the United States,
Colonial Times to 1970*, 2 vols., consec. pagin. (Washington, D.C., 1975), 1173, 1176–77;
Schlesinger, *Colonial Merchants*, 214, 235.

well as the boycott's success in reducing indebtedness and mercantile inventories, helped divide the expansionist camp in both city and countryside and thus brought the agreement to an end. During the first week of December, Lieutenant Governor Bull limned the splits within the patriot bloc: "The merchants in town, many of whom have long felt the stagnation of their trade and lament their empty stores, now resolve to disregard the association against importation, declaring it folly in this province to stand out alone. And many planters are of the same sentiment, but several of them still suffer themselves to be deluded by a phantom of a mistaken point of honor. And other merchants, powerful by influence and [with] stores filled with goods, are for continuing the resolutions."[57] On December 13 Laurens chaired a public meeting that listened to the impassioned appeals of several revolutionaries who wanted the colony to prolong the boycott of British wares and to open instead a free trade with Holland. But the gathering, after voting down these suggestions, formally ended the boycott and then, with little sense of irony, formed committees to promote local manufacturing and to reprimand the northern colonies for their apostasy.[58]

» «

In the 1760s several South Carolina expansionists elaborated their vision of an American empire, with few of them pushing their horizons back farther than did Christopher Gadsden. At the Stamp Act Congress and again in South Carolina, Gadsden emphasized the shared interests binding the sundry colonies, exclaiming in 1765, "There ought to be no New England man, no New Yorker, etc., known on the continent, but all of us Americans."[59] Gadsden saw America's future in a world of dynamic commercial nations, not within the narrow confines of the British empire. During the winter of 1765–1766 he hoped that South Carolina planters would undertake nonexportation as a step toward securing broader markets: "Will they not readily undergo any disadvantages for a twelve-month or two or even a longer time with the hopes that the result may be a free and open trade with all the powers of Europe, instead of the present limited and restricted one both inwardly and outwardly with the discontented, monopolizing, selfish Great Britain." He apostrophized the rewards for such daring: "What a boundless and allur-

57. Lt. Gov. Bull to Hillsborough, Dec. 5, 1770, SCPR, XXXII, 415.
58. Lt. Gov. Bull to Hillsborough, Dec. 13, 1770, ibid., 434–35; Papers of Laurens, VII, 411, 414.
59. Gadsden to William Samuel Johnson and Charles Garth, Dec. 2, 1765, Writings of Gadsden, 67.

ing prospect of advantages must even the most distant idea of an open trade to all Europe, nay to all the world, be to the Americans."[60]

By 1769 Gadsden was openly flirting with the idea of securing foreign allies and establishing an independent New World nation. He opened his argument with a review of South Carolina mercantile exchanges: "Are not several trading powers of Europe better customers . . . than she [Britain] is? For instance, what an insignificant part of our main staple, rice, is consumed in Great Britain?" From such economic links with countries outside the empire, it was only a short step to more substantive ties. Can Britain, Gadsden asked, "be so blind, or absurd, as to think, that if distress, despair, and self-interest, should cooperate with any fair and safe opportunity, that in the course of some future war, maybe given a better customer, who possibly may then have *more* than *two* regiments ready to land in America, that such dastardly wretches as we are insinuated to be, may not only be afraid to refuse, but glad to jump at a change that we are sure, in such circumstances cannot be for the worse?"[61]

Henry Laurens also enunciated an expansionist credo, although during the early part of the decade his spat with the inner circle of patriots seemed to introduce a qualifying note into his outlook. Laurens applauded the mother country's acquisition of new territory in 1763, but he wondered about the ability of British North America to populate and fully absorb these reaches. "The preliminary articles of peace promise great advantages to these southern provinces," he opined in 1763, pleased that Florida was now in English hands. "And the accession of territory which we are to gain thereby will open a vast field for trade, if we have people enough to improve it."[62] Any additional conquests, he remarked, "would be only an imaginary gain dissipating our strength and exposing us to ruin by means of our own successes."[63]

By the closing years of the decade, Laurens's deepening hostility toward British officials and their programs more than outweighed his differences with local revolutionaries, and his expansionism grew ever bolder. In 1769 he sharply contrasted the troubled future of Great Britain with the gathering strength of America. "They seem *yonder side* to be at their last shifts," he observed in May, "while the Americans are growing wiser and more powerful by all their blun-

60. Gadsden to James Pearson, Feb. 20, 1766, Weir, ed., "Two Letters," 174–75.
61. Gadsden, "To the Planters, Mechanics, and Freeholders . . .," *Writings of Gadsden*, 81–82.
62. Laurens to Isaac King, Feb. 15, 1763, Laurens to John Knight, Feb. 14, 1763, *Papers of Laurens*, III, 258, 253.
63. Laurens to Thomas Mears, Feb. 15, 1763, ibid., 255.

ders."[64] Faith in the ascendancy of the colonies underlay his steady support for nonimportation. "If those unconstitutional burthens are continued," he stated in October, "we shall probably continue our resolutions to run no further in debt for any articles but such as are barely necessary. Great Britain must be essentially hurt by our perseverance, and ourselves must eventually be much benefited."[65]

64. Laurens to James Habersham, May 25, 1769, ibid., vi, 572.
65. Laurens to John Knight, Oct. 23, 1769, Laurens to Isaac King, Oct. 28, 1769, ibid., vii, 172, 181.

PART THREE

The Quiet Years, 1771–1773

CHAPTER 13

The Quiet Years

During 1771, 1772, and 1773 leading expansionists carefully balanced their pronouncements about American relations with Britain. They affirmed the necessary and inevitable rise of the New World but at the same time—sobered by lower-class excesses in the 1760s and buoyed by England's newfound moderation—they hoped the colonists would be circumspect in asserting their rights. The Americans, Benjamin Franklin told his son, "should carefully avoid all tumults and every violent measure, and content themselves with verbally keeping up their claims, and holding forth their rights whenever occasion requires, secure that from the growing importance of America those claims will ere long be attended to and acknowledged."[1] Similarly, Thomas Cushing warned against "prematurely bringing on a contest" and added, "The daily increasing strength *in wealth and numbers* and importance of America to Great Britain must in a little time bring us all we want or can desire, and in peace and safety to both countries."[2]

The "quiet years" at the beginning of the 1770s provide us with a concrete response to a what-if question: what would the expansionists have done if Britain had adopted a conciliatory approach to the New World? The answer is that these affluent partisans would have continued to work for their goal of a "mighty empire" in America but would have granted a due obeisance to the Crown (remarked Franklin, "The king, and not the king, lords and commons collectively, is their [the colonists'] sovereign").[3] They would also have kept the political involvement of the artisans and small farmers to a minimum.

In every colony during these years the expansionists initially dis-

1. Franklin to William Franklin, Oct. 6, 1773, *The Papers of Benjamin Franklin*, ed. Leonard W. Labaree et al. (New Haven, 1959–   ), xx, 437.
2. Thomas Cushing to Arthur Lee, Oct. 1773, MHS *Cols.*, 4th ser., IV (1858), 363.
3. Franklin to William Franklin, Oct. 6, 1773, *Papers of Franklin*, xx, 437.

tanced themselves from the laboring people who had so recently been their allies, and in every province except South Carolina the wealthy revolutionaries commenced a period of relative inactivity. The length of this era of somnolence varied from commonwealth to commonwealth, but nowhere did an upper- and lower-class alliance truly solidify or patriotic fervor reemerge before the protests against the Tea Act in the last months of 1773. For affluent patriots in Massachusetts the first signs of renewed militance came in the second half of 1772 and reflected the prodding of Sam Adams's popular party, whose revolutionary zeal had never flagged; in Virginia such stirrings appeared early in 1773 when the expansionists secured a resolve asking all colonies to establish committees of correspondence. In New York and Pennsylvania wealthy revolutionaries remained irresolute until the last months of 1773; the only indication of ferment in the middle colonies came from the Philadelphia mechanics and shopkeepers, who maintained their spirit, organization, and to some degree, their effectiveness during these quiet months. In South Carolina, however, a dispute over the powers of the legislature kept the expansionists sparring with the ministry and royal governors throughout this period, although the conflict little involved the people "out of doors."

The nonexpansionists applauded the conservative turn and labored to stifle any revival of revolutionary agitation. Their strength varied from colony to colony, reflecting most generally the outcome of the struggles of the 1760s. In Pennsylvania the Quaker party and in New York the DeLanceys dominated their respective legislatures and helped make these provinces among the most moderate. The cautious planters south of the Rappahannock were the stronger faction in the Virginia House of Burgesses, but as in earlier years, they were often willing to cooperate with the expansionists of the Northern Neck and Blue Ridge. In the Bay Colony the Hutchinsonians were a distinct minority, but had the firm backing of the governor, and during 1771 and the first half of 1772 they formed one component of a powerful upper-class coalition that checked the popular party. South Carolina nonexpansionists, however, had become dispirited by the early 1770s, and gubernatorial efforts to revive this faction were unavailing.

The news in the fall of 1773 that the tea ships were on their way galvanized patriots everywhere and set back nonexpansionist hopes for irenic relations with Britain. In the four provinces—Massachusetts, New York, Pennsylvania, and South Carolina—to which the tea was directed, public meetings soon reforged the unions of upper- and lower-class protestors. Despite nonexpansionist efforts, the revolutionaries forced the resignation of the tea consignees and prevented the distribution of the duties tea. In Charleston the crates were securely stored; elsewhere they were sent back or, as in Boston, dumped into the harbor. Virginians took no immediate part in these events but divided along factional lines in their approval or censure of the protests.

Finally, the most articulate individuals in both parties continued to elaborate their sentiments. Outspoken expansionists looked forward to the ascendancy of a prosperous, sovereign America but were willing until the last months of 1773 to consider a slower, evolutionary path. The nonexpansionists warned ever more forcefully about the dangers that lay in a challenge to the mother country.

MASSACHUSETTS

During 1771 and the first half of 1772 Bay Colony expansionists willingly cooperated with Governor Thomas Hutchinson. "The heroes of liberty are some of them seeking a reconciliation," he reported early in the year. "I think it advisable therefore to suspend everything irritating at present."[4] Expansionist votes in 1771 blocked Sam Adams's attempt to become Suffolk County register of deeds and also assured the governor a moderate legislature. "I hear much today and yesterday of the harmony prevailing between the governor and the house," observed a bitter John Adams, whose sympathies during these years lay with the popular party. "Behold how good and pleasant it is for brethren to dwell together in unity. It seems to be forgotten entirely by what means Hutchinson procured the government— by . . . supporting and countenancing all [Governor] Bernard's measures . . . and every other thing we complain of."[5]

Upper-class patriots also frustrated Sam Adams's efforts to draft a defiant reply to the governor in the squabble over returning the legislature, or General Court, to Boston from Cambridge. Although the expansionists agreed with the popular party that the assembly be-

4. Thomas Hutchinson to Israel Williams, Jan. 23, 10, Apr. 1, 1771, Israel Williams Papers, MHS; *Diary and Autobiography of John Adams*, ed. L. H. Butterfield et al., 4 vols. (Cambridge, Mass., 1961), ii, 5 (Feb. 14, 1771), 6 (Apr. 16, 1771); Stephen E. Patterson, *Political Parties in Revolutionary Massachusetts* (Madison, Wis., 1973), 71.
5. *Diary and Autobiography of John Adams*, ii, 34 (June 13, 1771), 10–11 (May 2, 1771); Thomas Hutchinson, *The History of the Colony and Province of Massachusetts-Bay*, ed. Lawrence S. Mayo, 3 vols. (Cambridge, Mass., 1936), iii, 239–43; John J. Waters, Jr., *The Otis Family in Provincial and Revolutionary Massachusetts* (Chapel Hill, N.C., 1968), 178–80; James K. Hosmer, *The Life of Thomas Hutchinson* (1896; rpt. New York, 1972), 191, 203–10.

longed in the capital, where it had been before 1769, they felt that the
question should be argued on the grounds of inconvenience rather
than principle. Commenting on the assembly debates, John Adams
bewailed James Otis's "conversion to toryism" and noted, "[Samuel]
Adams was going on in the old road, and Otis started up and said they
had gone far enough in that way, the governor had an undoubted
right to carry the Court where he pleased, and moved for a committee
to represent the inconveniences of sitting there."[6] With such affluent
patriots as John Hancock and Thomas Cushing supporting Otis, the
assembly hewed to the moderate position.[7]

The expansionists' willingness to abandon their former lower-class
allies delighted the executive and, unsurprisingly, saddened popular
party men. "Hancock and [Samuel] Adams are at great variance,"
Hutchinson exclaimed in December 1771. "Some of my friends blow
the coals and I hope to see a good effect." He gloated to Francis
Bernard that Hancock's "coming over" will "be a great loss to them
as they support themselves with his money."[8] The governor was also
pleased when mental illness temporarily removed James Otis from
the fray; the once-mighty patriot was, in Hutchinson's words, "carried off . . . in a post-chaise bound hand and foot."[9] Hutchinson even
managed to recruit a spy from popular party ranks. In January 1772
Dr. Benjamin Church became a secret "writer on the side of government," and for the next three years he would keep the royal governors
informed of popular party plans.[10] In contrast to Hutchinson's jubila-
tion was the steady plaint that filled John Adams's diary during these
months. Persons "who for a long course of their younger years professed and were believed to be the guardian angels of our civil and
religious liberties," he intoned, now act in "contrast to their former
professions and principles."[11]

Beginning with the second half of 1772 the upper-class patriots
slowly returned to the revolutionary movement and strengthened
resistance to British measures. As the debate over bringing the Gen-

6. *Diary and Autobiography of John Adams*, II, 20 (June 2, 1771), 34 (June 13, 1771);
Hutchinson, *History of Massachusetts*, III, 244.
7. Hutchinson, *History of Massachusetts*, III, 250–51; Hosmer, *Thomas Hutchinson*,
225–27.
8. Thomas Hutchinson to Francis Bernard, Dec. 3, 1771, quoted in Hosmer, *Thomas
Hutchinson*, 224; same to same, Jan. 29, 1772, quoted in Patterson, *Political Parties*, 72.
9. Hutchinson to Bernard, Dec. 3, 1771, quoted in Hosmer, *Thomas Hutchinson*,
224; Hutchinson to Israel Williams, Dec. 2, 1771, Israel Williams Papers; Hutchinson,
History of Massachusetts, III, 248; *Diary and Autobiography of John Adams*, II, 50 (Aug.
22, 23, 1771).
10. Hutchinson to Bernard, Jan. 29, 1771, quoted in Patterson, *Political Parties*, 73;
Hosmer, *Thomas Hutchinson*, 226; Hutchinson, *History of Massachusetts*, III, 255–56.
11. *Diary and Autobiography of John Adams*, II, 59 [c. spring 1772], 49–50 (Aug. 13,
1771).

eral Court back to Boston dragged on, many expansionists gradually came to acknowledge the merits of Samuel Adams's principled stance and helped reverse the previous year's vote. Hutchinson, seeing he could expect no better from the legislature, conceded the issue and moved the body back to the capital. Furthermore, expansionists now supported a remonstrance attacking the ministerial decision to pay the governor's salary. Although the upper-class revolutionaries initially had made "great opposition" to such a protest, they swung behind a firmly worded resolution, which was adopted by a vote of eighty-five to nineteen. Joseph Hawley, one of the few members of the western Massachusetts elite to remain in the expansionist fold after 1760, was the reputed author of the resolve.[12]

During the second half of 1772, however, wealthy men with a buoyant view of the future of America still kept a wary eye on popular party initiatives. Expansionists sought to delay consideration in the Boston town meeting of a new and contentious issue, the ministry's plan to salary the superior court judges. But the popular party would not be checked by such counsels of moderation. In early November the town meeting, following Samuel Adams's lead, broadened the debate and established the Boston committee of correspondence "to state the rights of the colonists and of this province in particular . . . [and] to communicate and publish the same to the several towns in this province and to the world."[13] The leaders of the gathering nominated a set of expansionists to this new body, but of the prominent upper-class patriots proposed only three, including James Otis, who agreed to serve as chairman, accepted. Nine men, among them Hancock and Cushing, rejected places on the panel, alleging that their "private business would not then admit of it."[14] Such leaders of the lower-class faction as Samuel Adams, Joseph Warren, and Thomas Young would dominate the committee during the next several years. Expansionists soon accepted the Boston committee as an ally in the struggle with the mother country but scrutinized its activities, lest popular party leaders once again commit the town to extreme measures.[15]

12. Hutchinson, *History of Massachusetts*, 256–60; Merrill Jensen, *The Founding of a Nation: A History of the American Revolution, 1763–1776* (New York, 1968), 414–16.

13. *Boston Town Records*, Nov. 2, 1772, quoted in Richard D. Brown, *Revolutionary Politics in Massachusetts: The Boston Committee of Correspondence and the Towns, 1772–1774* (Cambridge, Mass., 1970), 57; *Diary and Autobiography of John Adams*, II, 64 (Oct. 27, 1772); Hutchinson, *History of Massachusetts*, III, 261–62.

14. *Massachusetts Gazette & News Letter*, Nov. 12, 1772, quoted in Arthur M. Schlesinger, *The Colonial Merchants and the American Revolution, 1763–1776* (New York, 1919), 257; *Diary and Autobiography of John Adams*, II, 72 (Dec. 24, 1772).

15. Hutchinson, *History of Massachusetts*, III, 264–65; Brown, *Revolutionary Politics*, 59–80.

Gradually, the upper-class revolutionaries realized the need to strengthen popular party stratagems with their own active opposition to Britain. Members of both revolutionary factions were angered during the first months of 1773 when Hutchinson lectured the assembly on the supremacy of Parliament, and lawmakers from the two groups drew up a forceful reply to the governor. Both patriot parties also applauded the Virginia proposal for a legislative committee of correspondence, and Massachusetts was among the first to establish such a body. In a letter to the House of Burgesses, Speaker Cushing noted pointedly that Britain's goal was "either to lull the colonies into a state of profound sleep . . . or to foment divisions among them."[16] Upper-class patriots also shared complicity in the publication of seventeen purloined letters, written by such men as Hutchinson and Lieutenant Governor Andrew Oliver. Franklin, who was still in London, had sent them to Cushing late in 1772, adding somewhat feebly that they should not be copied.[17]

During 1773 the expansionists again began to promote resistance and to cooperate closely with the popular party, even though the two factions never lost their separate identities. "The conductors of the people are divided in sentiment," observed Hutchinson in October 1773, "some of them professing that they only aim to remove the innovations since the date of the Stamp Act. . . . Others declare they will be altogether independent. . . . Each stands in need of the other, and their mutual interest is sufficient to keep them together. Of the first sort the speaker of the house [Cushing] often declares himself. . . . Those of the latter opinion have for their head one of the members of Boston [i.e., Samuel Adams]."[18]

The alliance between the expansionists and the popular party solidified in the fall of 1773, as both factions responded angrily to the Tea Act. Patriots resented the measure because it furthered the sale of a dutied commodity and because it gave a monopoly to a handful of

16. Speaker Thomas Cushing to the speaker of the House of Burgesses, June 3, 1773, William J. Van Schreeven and Robert L. Scribner, eds., *Revolutionary Virginia: The Road to Independence* (Charlottesville, Va., 1973–), II, 31–33; *Diary and Autobiography of John Adams*, II, 77–78 (Mar. 4, 1773), 77 (Jan. 1, 1773); Hutchinson, *History of Massachusetts*, III, 266–75; Brown, *Revolutionary Politics*, 80–121; Hutchinson to the General Court, Jan. 6, Feb. 16, 1773, quoted in Hosmer, *Thomas Hutchinson*, 363–70, 396–411.

17. *Diary and Autobiography of John Adams*, II, 79–80 (Mar. 22, 1773); Hutchinson to Israel Williams, Oct. 30, 1773, Israel Williams Papers; Hosmer, *Thomas Hutchinson*, 268–81; Jensen, *Founding of a Nation*, 419–21.

18. Hutchinson to Lord Dartmouth, Oct. 9, 1773, quoted in Hosmer, *Thomas Hutchinson*, 289–90; Hutchinson, *History of Massachusetts*, III, 278; Hutchinson to Israel Williams, Apr. 7, July 20, 1773, Israel Williams Papers; John Andrews to William Barrell, June 4, 1773, "Letters of John Andrews, Esq., of Boston, 1772–1776," ed. Winthrop Sargent, MHS *Procs.*, VIII (1864–65), 323.

merchants. The first individuals to urge a resolute opposition to the act were the popular party leaders, who met regularly in the North End caucus. But expansionists were also prominent in the early protests. John Hancock, who argued for a peaceful course of action, chaired several town meetings in November and helped shape Boston's initial response. Reported one observer: "The moderator and people were strongly desirous of preserving the tea untouched for the East India Company. . . . They insisted, therefore, that it should go back in the same bottoms."[19] Unsurprisingly, the East India Company agents, including Thomas Hutchinson's sons, Thomas and Elisha, all came from nonexpansionist families whose partisan loyalties can be traced back many decades. The tea consignees' refusal to resign and Hutchinson's obstinacy in not permitting the tea ships to return to Britain frustrated attempts to oppose the act nonviolently, and the expansionists, with little complaint, yielded the initiative to the popular party. On December 16 several hundred individuals, chiefly artisans and shopkeepers, dumped the consigned tea into the harbor.[20]

Although few merchants or other wealthy men were among the "Mohawks" pitching the tea overboard, most of the upper-class patriots felt the attack was justified and placed the blame for it on the ministry's foolishness and Hutchinson's stubbornness. Hancock, who truthfully stated that he was "not acquainted with" the "particulars" of the mob action, directed his anger against the Tea Act. "No one circumstance could possibly have taken place more effectively to unite the colonies than this maneuver of the tea," he told a London correspondent. "It is universally resented here, and people of all ranks detest the measure."[21] Expansionist trader John Andrews, who "went contentedly home" the evening of the Tea Party, praised the "Indians" for disturbing no property other than the tea and told a correspondent, "You may bless your stars that you have not a H[utchinson] and a board of commissioners resident with you."[22] The destruction of the tea would trigger the next round of escalation in the imperial conflict and would heighten the clashes among the three Massachusetts factions.

19. Dr. Samuel Cooper to Franklin, Dec. 17, 1773, MHS Cols., 4th ser., IV (1858), 374–75; Hutchinson, History of Massachusetts, III, 303–4; North End Caucus minutes, Oct. 23, 1773, in Elbridge H. Goss, The Life of Paul Revere, 2 vols. (Boston, 1891), II, 641.
20. Thomas Cushing et al. to Arthur Lee, Dec. 21, 1773, MHS Cols., 4th ser., IV (1858), 377–79; Benjamin W. Labaree, The Boston Tea Party (New York, 1966), 141–45.
21. John Hancock to Haley & Hopkins, Dec. 21, 1773, John Hancock: His Book, ed. Abram English Brown (Boston, 1898), 178.
22. John Andrews to William Barrell, Dec. 18, 19, 1773, "Letters of Andrews," 326, 327; Hutchinson to Israel Williams, Dec. 23, 1773, Israel Williams Papers; John Scollay to Arthur Lee, Dec. 22, 1773, MHS Cols., 4th ser., IV (1858), 379–86.

NEW YORK

Until October 1773 neither elite party in New York was inclined to disturb what General Gage praised as the province's "domestic tranquility."[23] The Livingstons, whose ardor was dampened even though they had recovered from the 1766 tenant rebellion, mounted few protests, and the DeLanceys, with their unshakable control over an assembly whose term under law could run to 1776, tried not to antagonize either the local politicians or the ministry. The nonexpansionists abandoned their efforts to prosecute Alexander McDougall and treated all partisan sniping with a withering disdain. "Enclosed are three of the best written papers against the majority," John Jay told a friend in 1772. "Though wrote with poignancy, they occasioned little noise and by being left unanswered escaped that attention which opposition and recrimination always excite."[24] With little to fear from the subdued upper-class patriots, nonexpansionist lawmakers pushed through annual grants for British troops and turned a deaf ear to pleas for intercolonial cooperation. New York was one of the few colonies to delay a response to the Virginia appeal for committees of correspondence. Not until January of 1774 would the house appoint a committee.[25]

During the last months of 1773 news that the East India Company was consigning dutied tea to New York helped shake the patriots out of their doldrums. Beginning in mid-October, McDougall, a longtime associate of the Livingstons, along with Isaac Sears and John Lamb, whose links with the upper-class patriots dated from the summer of 1769, organized several public meetings against the act. By contrast, the nonexpansionists held back from these protests; remarked William Smith early in November, "The DeLanceys wait to see the disposition of the people."[26] The six-person committee that helped

23. Gen. Gage to Barrington, Jan. 17, 1771, quoted in Leopold S. Launitz-Schürer, Jr., *Loyal Whigs and Revolutionaries: The Making of the Revolution in New York* (New York, 1980), 98; Robert R. Livingston to Robert Livingston, Jr., Jan. 7, 1771, Robert R. Livingston to Wife, Jan. 11, 1771, Robert R. Livingston Collection, Box 2, NYHS; Gov. Dunmore to Hillsborough, Mar. 9, 1771, Edmund B. O'Callaghan, ed., *Documents Relative to the Colonial History of the State of New York Procured in Holland, England and France*, 15 vols. (Albany, 1856–87), VIII, 265.

24. John Jay to Peter W. Yates, Mar. 23, 1772, *John Jay: The Making of a Revolutionary. Unpublished Papers, 1745–1780*, ed. Richard B. Morris et al. (New York, 1975), 110; Dorothy Rita Dillon, *The New York Triumvirate: A Study of the Legal and Political Careers of William Livingston, John Morin Scott, William Smith, Jr.* (New York, 1949), 105, 120.

25. Carl Becker, *The History of Political Parties in the Province of New York, 1760–1776* (Madison, Wis., 1909), 95, 108.

26. *Historical Memoirs from 16 March 1763 to 25 July 1778 of William Smith*, ed. William H. W. Sabine, 2 vols. (1956, 1958; rpt. New York, 1969), I, 157 (Nov. 1, 1773); Becker, *Political Parties*, 104; Jensen, *Founding of a Nation*, 445.

guide the demonstrations in November, included five individuals linked to the expansionists and only one DeLanceyite, merchant Isaac Low. By the end of November the protests had forced the tea agents to swear that they would under no condition sell any of the East India Company shipment.[27]

During December the expansionists remained in the forefront of the resistance as New Yorkers debated what to do when the tea arrived: land and store the chests or insist that the ships return with the cargoes unbroken. A letter from Boston early in the month convinced the Livingstons that the proper course of action was to oppose, forcibly if necessary, Governor William Tryon's plan of bringing the tea ashore. The DeLanceys, however, rejected this vigorous proposal and helped scuttle an attempt to form a bipartisan committee of correspondence.[28] Moreover, DeLanceyites Low and Jacob Walton circulated a petition asserting, "We do not conceive it necessary or expedient to hazard the peace of the city by opposing the landing or storing the said tea with force."[29] Despite the Livingstons' preparations, New York protests were long delayed, for no tea ships sailed into the Hudson during 1773. When the East India Company vessels finally arrived in April 1774, crowds persuaded one captain to return and dumped the other master's cargo into the harbor.[30]

PENNSYLVANIA

During the early 1770s Pennsylvania expansionists rarely struck a bold stance, and the Quaker party easily maintained its stifling grip on the legislature. In February 1771 John Dickinson vainly urged his fellow lawmakers to denounce the duty on tea. Through a series of amendments and revisions, the assemblymen transmuted Dickinson's forthright protest into a fulsome memorial, which questioned the tea tax but also strongly affirmed the house's "confidence in your majesty's transcendent goodness." Dickinson sadly observed that "ministerial influence has reached even to our statehouse," and in the fall he retired from the chamber.[31] During these months few other expansionists raised their voices to criticize the plans of the

27. *Memoirs of Smith*, I, 157 (Dec. 1, 1773); Launitz-Schürer, *Loyal Whigs*, 101.
28. *Memoirs of Smith*, I, 157 (Dec. 1, 1773), 162 (Dec. 18, 1773); Launitz-Schürer, *Loyal Whigs*, 102–6.
29. Quoted in Becker, *Political Parties*, 107–8.
30. Ibid., 110; Launitz-Schürer, *Loyal Whigs*, 106–7.
31. John Dickinson, "A Petition from the Assembly of Pennsylvania to the King," Mar. 9, 1771, *The Writings of John Dickinson*, ed. Paul L. Ford (vol. XIV of HSP *Memoirs*) (Philadelphia, 1895), 447–52, quotation on 451; David L. Jacobson, *John Dickinson and the Revolution in Pennsylvania, 1764–1776* (Berkeley, Calif., 1965), 67–68, quotes

Quaker party and its leader, Speaker Joseph Galloway. Acquiescence of the Whig elite allowed Galloway and his followers to stage, in the summer of 1772, a public celebration of George III's birthday—the first such fete since 1766. Moreover, in 1773, with little outcry from the wealthy patriots, the legislature rejected the Virginia appeal and refused to appoint a committee of correspondence, making Pennsylvania one of only three colonies (along with New York and New Jersey) that did not respond favorably before the year's end.[32]

The limited gains that the wealthy revolutionaries could point to during the months from the beginning of 1771 to the fall of 1773 stemmed from the initiatives of the increasingly articulate, self-confident common people of Philadelphia. The mechanics committee formed in 1770 endeavored to strengthen its role in local politics. In November 1771 the members informed Franklin, "Though the mechanics are censured and despised for attempting to judge or intermeddle in any public affairs, yet we are determined to pursue one steady plan . . . [and will resist] every attempt made to oppress us or violate our [rights and liber]ties." They thanked Franklin for his pro-boycott letter, which had helped buttress the resolve of "our noble and patriotic friends among the merchants."[33]

The tradesmen agitated for their immediate needs, securing the defeat, for example, of a leather inspection proposal, but they also took an ever more active part in the factional wars. They fiercely backed the expansionists and denounced the Quaker party. In August 1772 the artisans formed the Patriotic Society, which rallied voters behind a "mechanics' ticket" drafted for the city and county of Philadelphia. Although two of the prominent upper-class revolutionaries on the list, Charles Thomson and John Dickinson, failed to gain seats, the mechanics helped place in office several other men, including Thomas Mifflin, and they ousted Quaker Abel James. Shortly after the balloting a dispirited Galloway observed of the lower-class electorate, "Friends of good order and government . . . express much uneasiness and alarm at the wicked and base conduct of these mad people."[34]

Dickinson's disgruntled response; Benjamin H. Newcomb, *Franklin and Galloway: A Political Partnership* (New Haven, 1972), 233–34; Charles J. Stillé, *The Life and Times of John Dickinson, 1732–1808* (Philadelphia, 1891), 98.

32. Newcomb, *Franklin and Galloway*, 224; Jensen, *Founding of a Nation*, 431, 442.

33. Committee of Philadelphia Tradesmen to Franklin, Nov. 13, 1771, Joseph Galloway to Franklin, Sept. 27, 1770, *Papers of Franklin*, XVIII, 249–50, 228.

34. Joseph Galloway to Franklin, Oct. 12, 1772, Franklin to Abel James, Dec. 2, 1772, ibid., XIX, 331, 431; Broadside, Oct. 1, 1772, Evans Imprints #12387; Charles S. Olton, *Artisans for Independence: Philadelphia Mechanics and the American Revolution* (Syracuse, N.Y., 1975), 54–55; Newcomb, *Franklin and Galloway*, 219–23; James H. Hutson, *Pennsylvania Politics, 1746–1770: The Movement for Royal Government and Its Consequences* (Princeton, 1972), 241–42.

In 1773 the Patriotic Society once again castigated Galloway's party and supported the affluent protestors. "A Mechanic" writing in the *Chronicle* proudly pointed to the "growing interest and importance of the worthy mechanics and manufacturers of this city" and reminded readers of the tradesmen's "spirit of resolution, so vigorously exerted at the two last elections." This editorialist predicted, "Americus [Galloway] and his junto of conspirators against the liberties of their country [will soon] lose the power they have so arrogantly assumed, of treading upon the necks of mechanics and their friends."[35] In October 1773 artisans helped select the absent Franklin as one of the Philadelphia burgesses in place of a Quaker merchant. Moreover, in the elections of these years the common people in Philadelphia quietly gained control of the ten commission seats, which included the posts of warden, street commissoner, tax assessor, and collector. Before 1770 mechanics had, on average, held fewer than three of the ten places, but in 1770 and 1771 they gained four positions, in 1772 six, and in 1773 seven.[36]

During the last months of 1773 British efforts to implement the Tea Act and flood the colonies with duted tea reawakened Pennsylvania expansionists. Early in October, Thomas Mifflin and Charles Thomson, with the cooperation of printer William Bradford, called for an unflinching opposition to East India Company plans. The nonexpansionists for the moment were divided in their response. Even though the tea consignees, including Abel James, Henry Drinker, and Thomas Wharton, Sr., were all drawn from Quaker party ranks, other members of that faction acknowledged the force of Mifflin's and Thomson's arguments. A public meeting in mid-October appointed a twelve-member committee, evenly balanced between the two upper-class groups. Unlike Boston, which had long relied on British supplies of tea, Philadelphia was noted for tea smuggling. Thus, the East India Company scheme threatened an important set of entrenched interests in the Quaker City. As James & Drinker glumly observed to a New York correspondent, "Philadelphia leads the way, . . . [despite] the character its inhabitants formerly had among men . . . Boston but feebly follows our heroes, . . . [and] your city seems greatly behind both the others."[37]

As pressure for firmer action mounted, expansionists unmistakably

35. *Pa. Chronicle*, Sept. 27, 1773, quoted in Olton, *Artisans for Independence*, 56–57.
36. Ibid., 50–51, 57; Newcomb, *Franklin and Galloway*, 223.
37. James & Drinker to Pigou & Booth, Nov. 18, Sept. 29, 1773, Henry Drinker Letterbook, HSP; Richard A. Ryerson, *The Revolution Is Now Begun: The Radical Committees of Philadelphia, 1765–1776* (Philadelphia, 1978), 34–35; Labaree, *Boston Tea Party*, 36, 50–52, 97–102, 331.

came to the fore. John Dickinson entered the fray in November with a strong appeal for opposition to landing the tea. No one, he instructed, should "touch the accursed trash." Spokesmen for the mechanics vehemently seconded such pleas, strengthening the expansionists' hand. At the end of November the October committee was doubled in size and given a clear expansionist majority with the addition of such men as Thomas Mifflin as well as Presbyterians Charles Thomson and Joseph Reed. Under the leadership of these wealthy revolutionaries Philadelphians prepared for the tea ship and were able to persuade Captain Ayres when he brought the *Polly* up the Delaware at the end of December to return to England rather than risk a violent outburst. The committee also sent a letter to Boston applauding the Tea Party. The nonexpansionists, however, continued to argue for a more cautious approach, and the Quaker party adherents on the enlarged committee refused to sign the letter. "Old Ticket" leader Thomas Wharton called for landing the tea in Philadelphia but observed resignedly, "It's to little purpose to oppose the voice of the multitude."[38]

VIRGINIA

During the first seven months of 1771 planters from the Northern Neck of Virginia futilely labored to continue the nonimportation agreement. Early in the year Richard Henry Lee pronounced himself pleased that in 1770 he had helped counter "a North British scheme for the abolition of the association."[39] George Washington and George Mason reported in July that they were rigorously enforcing the pact, but they and the other members of the Fairfax County committee were struck by the inequities that had come to exist under the agreement. The panel warmly seconded a merchant petition that observed, "Quantities of goods [are] imported into different parts of the colony diametrically opposite both to the spirit and the letter of the articles entered into," and the committee urged the provincial

38. John Dickinson, "Two Letters on the Tea Tax," Nov. 1773, *Writings of Dickinson*, 453–463, quotation on 462; Thomas Wharton to Samuel Wharton, Jr., Jan. 1, 1774, Thomas Wharton to Thomas Walpole, May 2, 1774, *PMHB*, XXXIII (1909), 323, 328–29; William Pollard to Benjamin & John Bower, Nov. 18, 1773, Pollard Letterbook, HSP; William Rickman to John Pemberton, Dec. 6, 1773, Pemberton Papers; Thomas Clifford to Thomas Franks, Jan. 1, 1774, Clifford Letterbook; Joseph Reed to Dartmouth, Dec. 22, 27, 1773, William B. Reed, *Life and Correspondence of Joseph Reed . . .*, 2 vols. (Philadelphia, 1847), I, 52–53, 54–55; Ryerson, *Revolution Is Now Begun*, 36–37, 70.

39. Richard Henry Lee to William Lee, Jan. 8, 1771, *The Letters of Richard Henry Lee*, ed. James C. Ballagh, 2 vols. (New York, 1911–14), I, 52–53.

association to take steps to "put all the members upon an equal footing."[40] Reports from south of the Rappahannock revealed few efforts to police the merchants. "The spirit of association hath grown very cool of late," a Yorktown planter remarked in May, "and I believe will shortly come to nothing." That prediction was fulfilled; on July 15 a general meeting of the associators ended the agreement, leaving only a prohibition against dutied tea.[41]

The balance of 1771 and 1772 were placid years politically for Virginians of both parties. Planters and merchants ignored the ban on tea, and more of this commodity was imported into the Chesapeake colonies in 1772 than ever before. Local matters replaced imperial questions on the burgesses' agenda, and Washington was not alone when he complained about a "tiresome, and in my opinion very unimportant session" of the legislature.[42] Thomas Jefferson recollected in his "Autobiography" that his "countrymen seemed to fall into a state of insensibility" during these months.[43] Economic problems also distracted the planters. In the summer of 1772 a severe, if brief European credit crisis led British houses to press their Virginia creditors closely.[44]

The reinvigoration of opposition to Britain came early in 1773, and as in the past the expansionists took the lead. The immediate stimulus was the news that the British had established an all-powerful tribunal in Rhode Island to investigate the burning of the customs vessel *Gaspee*. Angered by this assertion of the prerogative, Richard Henry Lee opened a correspondence with Samuel Adams and told another colonial leader, probably Massachusetts Speaker Thomas Cushing, that the Old Dominion would take steps to defend the rights of the colonists. In March a coalition of planters from the Northern Neck and from the counties near the Blue Ridge seized the initiative.

40. Committee of the Associators in Fairfax Country to Peyton Randolph, July 18, 1771, *The Papers of George Mason, 1725–1792*, ed. Robert A. Rutland, 2 vols. (Chapel Hill, N.C., 1970), I, 132–34.
41. William Nelson to John Norton, May 17, 1771, *John Norton & Sons, Merchants of London and Virginia, Being the Papers from Their Counting House for the Years 1750–1795*, ed. Frances N. Mason (Richmond, 1937), 158; Thomas Jefferson to Thomas Adams, June 1, 1771, *The Papers of Thomas Jefferson*, ed. Julian P. Boyd et al. (Princeton, 1950–), I, 71; George Washington to Robert Cary & Co., July 20, 1771, *Writings of George Washington*, ed. J. C. Fitzpatrick, 39 vols. (Washington, D.C., 1931–44), III, 60; Douglas S. Freeman, *George Washington*, 6 vols. (New York, 1948–54), III, 277.
42. Washington to the Reverend Jonathan Boucher, May 4, 1772, *Writings of Washington*, III, 80; Edmund Pendleton to John Baylor, Feb. 4, 1772, *The Letters and Papers of Edmund Pendleton, 1734–1803*, ed. David John Mays, 2 vols. (Charlottesville, Va., 1967), I, 68–69; Labaree, *Boston Tea Party*, 331.
43. Thomas Jefferson, "Autobiography," *The Writings of Thomas Jefferson*, ed. Andrew A. Lipscomb, 18 vols. (Washington, D.C., 1903), I, 6–7.
44. Richard B. Sheridan, "The British Credit Crisis of 1772 and the American Colonies," *JEH*, xx (1960), 161–86.

"Not thinking our old and leading members up to the point of forwardness and zeal which the times required," recounted Jefferson,
"Mr. Henry, Richard Henry Lee, Francis L. Lee, Mr. [Dabney] Carr
and myself agreed to meeting in the evening in a private room of the
Raleigh to consult on the state of things." The result was a set of
resolutions that called for the creation of a legislative committee of
correspondence and urged the other provinces to strike similar
boards. Virginia nonexpansionists, who were more cooperative than
their counterparts in the other colonies, accepted the proposals,
which passed *"nem. con."* The burgesses then established a committee roughly balanced between the two factions.[45]

Although Virginia was not one of the colonies singled out for con-
signments of East India Company tea, the planters avidly followed
events in the other provinces; their reactions to the Boston Tea Party
generally fell along factional lines. Expansionist Richard Henry Lee
told Samuel Adams that the tea had met a "well deserved fate," and
Jefferson pronounced, "An exasperated people, who feel that they
possess power, are not easily restrained within limits strictly regular."[46] Philip Fithian, a tutor who resided in the Northern Neck,
drew on his contact with local landowners when he observed that
"gentlemen here in general applaud and honor our northern colonies
for so manly and patriotic [a] resistance."[47] By contrast, nonexpansionist Robert Carter Nicholas was critical of such "acts of violence,"
as was Robert Beverley, and Edmund Pendleton stated flatly, "The
Bostonians did wrong in destroying the tea." Northern Necker
George Washington, who reproved the Bostonians for their actions,
was an exception to this factional pattern.[48]

45. Jefferson, "Autobiography," I, 7–8; R. H. Lee to Samuel Adams, Feb. 4, 1773, R.
H. Lee to John Dickinson, Apr. 4, 1773, *Letters of Lee*, I, 82, 83; *John Norton & Sons
Papers*, 293; Resolutions of the House of Burgesses, Mar. 12, 1773, Van Schreeven and
Scribner, eds., *Revolutionary Virginia*, I, 89–92; R. H. Lee to [Thomas Cushing], Feb. 13,
1773, cited in Jensen, *Founding of a Nation*, 430.

46. R. H. Lee to Samuel Adams, Apr. 24, 1774, *Letters of Lee*, I, 107; Thomas Jefferson, *A Summary View of the Rights of British America*, 1774, in *Tracts of the American
Revolution, 1763–1776*, ed. Merrill Jensen (Indianapolis, Ind., 1967), 266.

47. *Journal and Letters of Philip Vickers Fithian, 1773–1774: A Plantation Tutor of the
Old Dominion*, ed. Hunter D. Farish (Williamsburg, Va., 1965), 59 (Jan. 24, 1774).

48. Robert Carter Nicholas, *Considerations on the Present State of Virginia Examined*,
[c. Aug. 25, 1774], Van Schreeven and Scribner, eds., *Revolutionary Virginia*, I, 261;
Edmund Pendleton to Joseph Chew, June 20, 1774, *Letters and Papers of Pendleton*, I, 93;
George Washington to George William Fairfax, June 10, 1774, *Writings of Washington*,
III, 223; Robert Beverley to William Fitzhugh, July 20, 1775, Robert M. Calhoon, ed.,
"A Sorrowful Spectator of These Tumultuous Times: Robert Beverley Describes the
Coming of the Revolution," *VMHB*, LXXIII (1965), 47–48. In the summer of 1774 Din-
widdie, Hanover, and Middlesex counties—all located south of the Rappahannock—
criticized Boston's destruction of the tea, Van Schreeven and Scribner, eds., *Revolutionary Virginia*, I, 109–68.

SOUTH CAROLINA

Unlike their counterparts in the other commonwealths, South Carolina expansionists remained active and assertive in the early 1770s. Until the last months of 1773, however, the common people, whose cooperation had been crucial in enforcing the boycott of 1769–1770, were not involved in the disputes. Josiah Quincy, Jr., a Massachusetts patriot who visited South Carolina in March 1773, was struck by the near exclusion of the less wealthy from provincial politics. "The middling order in the capital are odious characters," he remarked. Quincy noted that the South Carolinians "have a house of assembly: but who do they represent? The laborer, the mechanic, the tradesman, the farmer, husbandman, or yeoman? No. . . . The members of this house are all very wealthy."[49] Also "unrepresented" (along with women and the black majority) were the nonexpansionists, whose power had been dramatically reduced by patriot victories in 1765 and in subsequent elections.

The series of squabbles that marked the months from January 1771 to the fall of 1773 reflected the ongoing conflict between the wealthy revolutionaries and a succession of governors over the fifteen hundred pounds sterling granted in 1769 to English agitator John Wilkes. The governors, as instructed by Whitehall, insisted that the Commons House acknowledge its mistake in extending funds to Wilkes, while expansionist legislators tried various stratagems to assert their exclusive control over the purse strings. For example, late in 1771 the Commons House, without the concurrence of the council, directed the provincial treasurers to pay the silk manufactory three thousand pounds and then, after the two financial officers refused to comply, the lawmakers with "but one dissenting voice" ordered them jailed. (Laurens, who closely followed these proceedings during his visit to England, at first felt the legislators "had done a violent and provoking act" but soon decided that "they have not done amiss.")[50] In response the governors vetoed all resolves and repeatedly prorogued, or dissolved, the offending houses. Governor Lord Charles Montagu, for example, dismissed the assembly and issued new writs of election

49. "Journal of Josiah Quincy, Jr.," 454–55 (Mar. 25, 1773).
50. Laurens to James Laurens, Dec. 26, 1771, *The Papers of Henry Laurens*, ed. George C. Rogers et al. (Columbia, S.C., 1968–   ), VIII, 125–26; Gov. Montagu to Hillsborough, Nov. 13, 1771, SCPR, XXXIII, 89–90; Jack P. Greene, Introduction to *The Nature of Colony Constitutions: Two Pamphlets on the Wilkes Fund Controversy in South Carolina by Sir Egerton Leigh and Arthur Lee*, ed. Greene (Columbia, S.C., 1970), 18–22. Greene's introduction is an excellent survey of the legislative battles of the early 1770s.

no fewer than four times between November 1771 and his departure for England in March 1773.[51]

Montagu's most desperate gamble was his effort in the fall of 1772 to breathe life into the moribund nonexpansionist faction by moving the capital from Charleston to Beaufort, the port town in the Sea Island parish of St. Helena. Until the late 1760s, when the expansionists swept all before them, lawmakers from St. Helena and the neighboring parishes of St. John Colleton and St. Stephen had provided a notable if weak counterpoise to the majority party. On the advice of his council (itself an amalgam of placemen and nonexpansionists), Montagu directed the new house to meet that October at Beaufort and, at least initially, was heartened by the response of the local leaders. "They have gone so far as to declare that they would at their private expense build a provincial house for the governor had they any reason to believe the assembly would continue there," he told Hillsborough in September, adding, "I do not doubt of their forming a party there, which they cannot form in Charleston."[52] But the low-country patriots made sure that the lawmakers elected were committed revolutionaries who would guide the Beaufort session much as they had directed the meetings in Charleston. The *South Carolina Gazette* remarked that the electors were "determined . . . to vote for no gentlemen but who are on the spot and can give their personal attendance." The result was a body no less firm than its predecessors, and after three days Montagu gave up his attempt and reconvened the house in Charleston.[53]

Invigorated by their victory over Montagu in the capital fight, the expansionists soon reaffirmed both their unity and their commitment to the revolutionary cause. When Peter Manigault resigned the speakership because of ill health, patriot firebrand Christopher Gadsden nominated Rawlins Lowndes, long one of the party's most conservative members. In a remarkable display of factional solidarity, Gadsden lauded his fellow representative as one who "had formerly been speaker of the house . . . and had acquitted himself in that office to the general satisfaction of the assembly"; Gadsden conveniently forgot that Lowndes had been ousted from the chair in 1765

51. Gov. Montagu to Hillsborough, Apr. 27, 1772, SCPR, xxxiii, 140–41; *Biographical Directory of the South Carolina House of Representatives*, vol. i: *Session Lists*, ed. Joan S. R. Faunt and Robert E. Rector with David K. Bowen (Columbia, S.C., 1974), 136–48.
52. Gov. Montagu to Hillsborough, July 27, Sept. 24, 1772, SCPR, xxxiii, 167–68, 174–76.
53. Quoted in Greene, ed., *Colony Constitutions*, 25–26; Laurens to John Laurens, Dec. 15, 1772, *Papers of Laurens*, viii, 501–2; Robert M. Weir, "Beaufort: The Almost Capital," *Sandlapper*, ix (Sept. 1976), 43–44.

for a display of excessive caution.[54] Lowndes, who received unanimous approval, quickly proved himself worthy of his colleagues' trust and defended the rights of the assembly in a series of jousts with the governors. With the same defiant spirit, South Carolina lawmakers in 1773 responded favorably to the Virginia call for legislative committees of correspondence; the house struck a panel of nine and thanked the burgesses "for their steady attention to the general interests of America."[55]

The political quarrels during the first part of 1773 were also notable for catalyzing the transformation of William Henry Drayton, who had been one of the few outspoken nonexpansionists in the province and now quite remarkably became a leader of the patriot party. Drayton, who had fled to England in 1770 to escape the public outrage raised by his opposition to the boycott, returned early in 1772 to assume a seat on the royal council and at first seemed little changed. He supported Montagu that fall against the Commons House, leading one wag to suggest in the *South Carolina Gazette* that Drayton's epitaph should include the verse "PREROGATIVE was my whole aim / Whilst I had spirits to declaim."[56] But early in 1773 Drayton was made personally aware of how British policies could frustrate the plans of a wealthy American. John Stuart, the southern superintendent of Indian affairs, persuaded the council to deny Drayton's petition for 140,000 acres in Indian territory. Stuart argued that this fiefdom defied the royal policy of mollifying the Indians. The wealthy, land-hungry Drayton, who had been steadily acquiring land since the early 1760s, was enraged. In the fall he disassociated himself from the majority in the council, calling its defense of the prerogative "fatal to the freedom of our country." And by 1774 this erstwhile tory would be among the foremost revolutionaries.[57]

The controversy over the Tea Act during the last months of 1773

---

54. *Commons Journal*, Oct. 28, 1772, quoted in Carl J. Vipperman, *The Rise of Rawlins Lowndes, 1721–1800* (Columbia, S.C., 1978), 165–67.

55. Rawlins Lowndes, speaker of the Commons House of Assembly, to Peyton Randolph, speaker of the House of Burgesses, July 9, 1773, Van Schreeven and Scribner, eds., *Revolutionary Virginia*, II, 38–39; Gov. Montagu to Dartmouth, Jan. 21, 1773, Lt. Gov. Bull to Dartmouth, Mar. 30, 1773, SCPR, XXXIII, 204, 225–28; Greene, ed., *Colony Constitutions*, 26–28.

56. *South Carolina Gazette*, Nov. 19, 1772, quoted in Greene, ed., *Colony Constitutions*, 27 and 27–28n; Lt. Gov. Bull to Dartmouth, Sept. 18, 1773, South Carolina Council to king, Sept. 11, 1773, Charles Garth, Petition to king, Dec. 15, 1773, SCPR, XXXIII, 303–10, 311–16, 340–49.

57. Statements by Drayton and the council are presented in the *S.C. Gazette*, Aug. 30, Sept. 2, 13, 1773, and are quoted in Greene, ed., *Colony Constitutions*, 31; William M. Dabney and Marion Dargan, *William Henry Drayton & the American Revolution* (Albuquerque, N.M., 1962), 40–44.

brought Charleston's lower classes back into provincial politics and also revealed the divisions within the large expansionist faction; once again the merchants proved the more reluctant patriots. Fired up by newspaper articles appearing in November, Charleston revolutionaries responded angrily to the arrival of the tea ship on December 2 and circulated handbills "inviting all the inhabitants without exception, particularly the landholders, to assemble" the next day.[58] The result was a meeting crowded with artisans and planters but with relatively few merchants; George Gabriel Powell, an estate owner and an expansionist of long standing (he had marched with Lyttelton against the Cherokees, helped suppress the Regulators, and been active against the Townshend Acts) was called to the chair. The gathering secured the resignation of the three tea consignees, resolved against landing any dutied tea, and formed a committee of five to visit all the merchants and secure their cooperation. Reflecting the new alliance of patriot forces, this panel comprised three individuals—Colonel Charles Pinckney, Charles Cotesworth Pinckney, and Thomas Ferguson—connected to the planting community and two—Christopher Gadsden and a wealthy carpenter, Daniel Cannon—with links to the mechanics.[59]

The expansionist merchants as well as some nonexpansionist traders denounced this bold demarche. Since the late 1760s, when the artisans had emerged as an independent force, the patriot traders had added a tincture of circumspection to their support for revolutionary protests. On the day following the December 3 meeting Henry Laurens's brother James remarked, "I hear many are offended at some severe reflection that Mr. G[adsden] let drop against that body [the merchants] in his warmth of declamation yesterday."[60] Many importers rebuffed Gadsden's committee, and on December 9 the traders met and formed the Charleston Chamber of Commerce. The makeup of the chamber's twenty-one-member steering body suggests the cooperation at least briefly evident between the patriot majority and nonexpansionist minority in the merchant community. Of the sixteen members whose loyalties can be traced, four, including the

58. *S.C. Gazette*, Dec. 6, 1773, quoted in George C. Rogers, Jr., "The Charleston Tea Party: The Significance of December 3, 1773," *SCHM*, LXXV (1974), 157; Lt. Gov. Bull to Dartmouth, Dec. 24, 1773, SCPR, XXXIII, 350–54; Schlesinger, *Colonial Merchants*, 295–96.

59. George C. Rogers, Jr., *Evolution of a Federalist: William Loughton Smith of Charleston (1758–1812)* (Columbia, S.C., 1962), 75–76; Rogers, "Charleston Tea Party," 157–61; Schlesinger, *Colonial Merchants*, 296; *Biographical Directory of the South Carolina House of Representatives*, vol. II, Walter B. Edgar and N. Louise Bailey, *The Commons House of Assembly, 1692–1775* (Columbia, S.C., 1977), 538–39.

60. James Laurens to Laurens, Dec. 2, 4, 1773, *Papers of Laurens*, IX, 190–91.

president, John Savage, would become tories, and twelve, among them such well-known patriots as Gabriel Manigault and Roger Smith, would be faithful to the American cause. At a public meeting on December 17 the merchants blocked efforts to interdict the landing of the tea, and as a consequence, the customs officers a few days later brought the chests ashore and stored them in the Exchange.[61]

Popular agitation in South Carolina, unlike the demonstrations in the commercial provinces, did not subside after the initial protests against the Tea Act. A public meeting in mid-January 1774 resolved that the "East India Company's tea shall not be moved from its present lodgement except to be reshipped."[62] Fears that South Carolina patriotism was in question led to calls for a gathering in mid-March. The mechanics caucused before the meeting; "upon *their* present conduct," declared a broadside, depends "whether this hitherto respectable province shall preserve its reputation or sink into disgrace and contempt."[63] The March gathering resolved against the importation of any tea and also established a forty-five-member "standing general committee," whose makeup reaffirmed the broad base of the revolutionary movement. The new panel included merchants from the Chamber of Commerce, artisans, and planters; more generally, it embraced not only the center but also both extremes of the expansionist faction. For the moment the patriots had formed themselves into a single phalanx, although the events of the coming months would sorely test this show of unity.[64]

CONFLICTING PERSUASIONS

Although the 1770s were quiet years politically, the more vocal partisans continued to reflect upon and map their conflicting persuasions. Leading expansionists extolled America's remarkable destiny,

---

61. Letter from New York Sons of Liberty, *Country Journal*, Feb. 1, 1774, quoted in Rogers, "Charleston Tea Party," 162–64; Schlesinger, *Colonial Merchants*, 297–98; John Drayton, *Memoirs of the American Revolution, from Its Commencement to the Year 1776 Inclusive . . .*, 2 vols. (1821; rpt. [New York?], 1969), I, 97–99. *Rules of the Charleston Chamber of Commerce* (Charleston, 1774) (Evans imprint #13194) lists the members of the steering committee. The loyalists were John Savage, John Smyth, Alexander Inglis, and William Ancrum. The patriots were Manigault, Edmund Head, George-Abbot Hall, James Laurens, John Edwards, John Dawson, Alexander Gillon, Andrew Lord, Roger Smith, Peter Bacot, John Neufville, and David Deas. According to Professor David R. Chesnutt, Miles Brewton—once an outspoken patriot—had become a loyalist by the time of his death in August 1775.

62. The quotation is from Henry Laurens's summary of the resolves. See Laurens to George Appleby, May 4, 1774, *Papers of Laurens*, IX, 428.

63. Handbill quoted in Rogers, "Charleston Tea Party," 164–65.

64. Committee members are listed in Gadsden to Samuel Adams, June 14, 1774, *The Writings of Christopher Gadsden, 1746–1805*, ed. Richard Walsh (Columbia, S.C., 1966),

but they played down the need for vigorous protests and emphasized the ineluctable effects of burgeoning population and riches. John Adams, for example, reported on a dinner party in 1772 where the Reverend Charles Chauncy told the guests "that in 25 years there would be more people here than in the three kingdoms" of Great Britain. Chauncy remarked further that America would become "the greatest empire on earth. Our freeholds would preserve us for interest would not lie."[65] Another outward-looking Bay Colonist, Josiah Quincy, Jr., concluded his journal of a tour through the colonies, with a paean to the New World triumphant. "Were I to breathe a wish," he wrote in the spring of 1773, "it would be that the numerous and surprisingly increasing inhabitants of this extensive, fertile and amazing continent may be thoroughly attentive and suitably actuated by the blessings of Providence, the dangers which surround them, and the duties they owe GOD, themselves and posterity."[66]

The views of the expansionists in the South also exuded confidence. "No people that ever trod the stage of the world have had so glorious a prospect as now rises before the Americans," remarked an editorialist in the *Virginia Gazette*.[67] Henry Laurens openly rejected the Proclamation of 1763, which limited colonial settlement to the area east of the Appalachians. "My sentiments with regard to purchases from Indians," Laurens observed in 1772, "differ widely from the scope and tendency of his majesty's proclamation inhibiting such purchases, and widely from what the ministry would endeavor to make the public believe."[68] And George Washington's writings in the early 1770s displayed the same aggressive view of westward growth that the members of the Ohio Company had propounded in the late 1740s. Washington urged Virginians and Marylanders to cooperate in deepening the Potomac's channel "because I think the opening of the Potomac will at once fix the trade of the western country, at least till it may be conducted through the Mississippi (by New Orleans) . . . and end in amazing advantages to these two colonies."[69]

But perhaps no expansionist gave such careful consideration to America's future as did Benjamin Franklin, who now resided in London and by 1771 served as agent for Pennyslvania, Massachusetts,

98–99. The panel included twenty-one planters, ten merchants, seven artisans, six lawyers or lawyer-planters, and one whose occupation is unknown. See Gadsden to Samuel Adams, May 23, 1774, ibid., 92–94; Rogers, "Charleston Tea Party," 165.

65. *Diary and Autobiography of John Adams*, II, 70 (Dec. 16, 1772).

66. "Journal of Josiah Quincy, Jr.," 481 (May 17, 1773).

67. *Virginia Gazette* (Purdie & Dixon), Nov. 11, 1773, quoted in Jensen, *Founding of a Nation*, 432.

68. Laurens to Elias Vanderhorst, Mar. 6, 1772, Laurens to Alexander Garden, May 24, 1772, *Papers of Laurens*, VIII, 214–15, 327.

69. Washington to Thomas Johnson, May 5, 1772, *Writings of Washington*, III, 83.

New Jersey, and Georgia. Franklin urged upon his many correspondents a combination of steadfastness and moderation in the defense of America's cause. For example, in 1771, he told Speaker Cushing: "I hope the colony assemblies will show by frequently repeated resolves that they know their rights and do not lose sight of them. Our growing importance will ere long compel an acknowledgment of them and establish and secure them to our posterity."[70] And while he praised the Virginia call for legislative committees of correspondence, speculating further that "it is natural to suppose . . . if the oppressions continue, a congress may grow out of that correspondence," he also censured all "violent spirits who are for an immediate rupture."[71]

Franklin, however, was increasingly concerned not only about the pace of the revolutionary movement but also about the nature of the "empire" that would arise in the New World. During the 1760s Franklin had applauded the writings of the French physiocrats, particularly their critiques of British mercantilism; the physiocrats' belief in the primacy of agriculture and their condemnation of any society that rested on the export of manufactures reinforced and focused ideas the printer had long held. In the early 1770s Franklin expanded upon this view of political economy, actively proselytizing his American friends. A tour in 1771 through several British manufacturing districts only confirmed Franklin's opinions. If the colonists, he told a Rhode Islander, "should ever envy the *trade* of these countries, I can put them in a way to obtain a share of it. . . . Let them with the generality of the common people of Scotland go barefoot, then may they make large exports in shoes and stockings, and if they will be content to wear rags like the spinners and weavers of England, they may make cloths and stuffs for all parts of the world."[72]

At the same time that Franklin condemned manufacture for export, he praised artisanal production for the local market and, more broadly, underscored the virtues of "industry and frugality." He told one Pennsylvanian, "If our country people would well consider that all they save in refusing to purchase foreign geegaws, and in making their own apparel, being applied to the improvement of their plantations, would render those more profitable, as yielding a greater produce, I should hope they would persist resolutely in their present commendable industry and frugality."[73] He informed Cushing that

70. Franklin to Thomas Cushing, Feb. 5, 1771, *Papers of Franklin*, xviii, 27.

71. Franklin to Thomas Cushing, July 7, 1773, Franklin to John Winthrop, July 25, 1773, ibid., xx, 273, 330.

72. Franklin to Joshua Babcock, Jan. 13, 1772, ibid., xix, 7; Drew R. McCoy, *The Elusive Republic: Political Economy in Jeffersonian America* (Chapel Hill, N.C., 1980), 52–59.

73. Franklin to Humphrey Marshall, Apr. 22, 1771, *Papers of Franklin*, xviii, 81–82.

"family manufactures will alone amount to a vast saving in the year; and a steady determination of buying only of your own artificers wherever they can supply you, will soon make them more expert in working, so as to dispatch more business, while constant employment enables them to afford their work still cheaper." A reliance on agriculture and local crafts coupled with an avoidance of large-scale production would, Franklin argued, allow Americans to postpone to a far distant era the decline that was the inevitable fate of all empires.[74]

Just as Franklin was the leading spokesman for the expansionists, so few nonexpansionists were as thoughtful or influential as Thomas Hutchinson. In the early 1770s he elaborated his views in letters and speeches, and his public pronouncements often received broad coverage in the colonial press. Hutchinson acknowledged America's remarkable rise and indeed regarded that ascent as the source of imperial friction. "The prevalence of a spirit of opposition to government in the plantation," he told a correspondent, "is the natural consequence of the great growth of colonies so remote from the parent state, and not the effect of oppression in the king or his servants."[75] Even independence was no impossibility, though in the near term, Hutchinson argued, it was a foolish goal. During the first half of 1773 he engaged Massachusetts lawmakers in a public debate over the wisdom of opposing Britain. "But should we finally succeed" in gaining independence, he asked in summary, "how many thousands must have lost their lives in the attempt, and how much greater a number must have been rendered miserable? . . . A few individuals may attain to greater degrees of dignity and power, but the inhabitants in general will never enjoy so great a share of natural liberty as they would have done if they had remained a dependent colony."[76]

74. Franklin to Thomas Cushing, June 10, 1771, ibid., 126; McCoy, *Elusive Republic,* 60–67.
75. Hutchinson to Mr. Robertson, Dec. 28, 1773, quoted in Hosmer, *Thomas Hutchinson,* 304.
76. Hutchinson, *History of Massachusetts,* iii, 255; Hosmer, *Thomas Hutchinson,* 229; Brown, *Revolutionary Politics,* 85–91.

PART FOUR

The Expansionists Prevail, 1774–1776

Between 1774 and 1776 expansionists altered their tactics but not their goal of hastening America's rise in a world of conflicting nation-states. Before 1774 affluent patriots had kept their protests against Britain within well-defined bounds; memorials, nonimportation, sporadic street demonstrations, and a single brief intercolonial meeting, the Stamp Act Congress, marked the limits of their program. Furthermore, these partisans had long regarded independence as no more than a distant, if likely, ramification of the burgeoning of the New World. The events of the final imperial crisis, which began with the news of the Boston Port Act in May 1774 and included the fighting at Lexington and Concord, gradually convinced the upper-class revolutionaries that more forceful initiatives were needed to defend their vision. Although profoundly concerned about the dangers of agitating the common people, these wealthy patriots now endorsed the active involvement of the poorer farmers, a regularly constituted continental assembly, commercial nonintercourse, and the creation of armed forces. And slowly but inexorably the expansionists came to agree that the growth of America must take place outside the confines of the British empire.

To gain their ends, the upper-class protestors had to wage two successive battles against domestic opponents. The first contest was joined with the nonexpansionists, who labored to stem the tide of revolution, and the victory of the wealthy patriots in this struggle marked the culmination of an internecine conflict dating back many decades. The duration and intensity of this final clash between the two elite groups varied from province to province. It was most prolonged in the middle colonies, where the nonexpansionists—the De-

Lanceys of New York and the Quaker party of Pennsylvania—were firmly entrenched in the legislatures. Not until the outbreak of fighting in April 1775 were these tories driven from their redoubts. In Massachusetts and South Carolina nonexpansionist strength was less considerable, and as early as midsummer 1774 patriots had secured control of local institutions. Virginia was a special case. There, the lack of a serious lower-class challenge made for more tolerant nonexpansionists and a degree of partisan cooperation unknown in the other colonies. Hence in the Old Dominion this period of elite conflict, which stretched to the summer of 1775, resulted in the ouster from local politics of only the fraction of the nonexpansionist party that opposed resolute protests.

In this clash with the tories, the wealthy patriots mobilized the common people in the towns and countryside, transforming the dynamics of revolt. Popular participation had been a facet of the revolutionary movement since the Stamp Act, but never before 1774 had the efforts to involve the less affluent been so extensive, nor had so much attention ever been paid to the settlers in the rural areas. The expansionists' success in gaining the affections of the populace was far from uniform. Small farmers in Massachusetts, Pennsylvania, and Virginia generally applauded the patriot stand, but in New York and South Carolina much of the rural citizenry nursed long-standing grievances against the expansionists and became loyalists. In the cities the lower classes, with few exceptions, backed the revolution.

Once the expansionists had driven their affluent opponents from the field, they crossed swords with the less wealthy patriots, who continued to serve as crucial allies in the struggle with Britain but who increasingly demanded a voice in directing revolutionary politics. Upper- and lower-class patriots fought over the extent of democratic reforms and over the timing of independence, with the wealthy revolutionaries defending hierarchical institutions and opposing any rush to separation, lest a precipitous step rend the social fabric. The strength of these contending forces differed from one province to the next. In Pennsylvania the patriotic farmers and mechanics forged a strong alliance and compelled a stubborn set of expansionists to accept far-reaching changes. In New York, South Carolina, and Massachusetts the farmer-artisan coalitions, although potent, were weaker than in Pennsylvania. The loyalism of many New York and South Carolina farmers lessened their impact on patriot politics, while in the Bay Colony, the British occupation of Boston temporarily silenced the artisans and shopkeepers who long had been a local power. In Virginia the lack of a first-rank city and the broad spread of plantation society hindered the emergence of coherent popular opposition. Nonetheless, beginning in the second half of 1775 rebellious slaves and assertive small farmers provided an increasing challenge to the elite.

The expanionists' reluctance to hasten independence because of their fears of the common folk should not be confounded with a hesitance to support the colonial cause. Throughout 1775 and the first half of 1776 wealthy patriots who bridled at an immediate break were active in policing the loyalists, organizing the armed forces, and more generally, guiding the newly formed committees and congresses. Many of these individuals worked to secure foreign alliances and establish new state and national constitutions, seeing such radical steps as necessary preconditions for separation from Britain. Moreover, in the one colony, Virginia, where the small farmers and mechanics posed the least threat, the expansionists became early advocates of independence. Nonetheless, many upper-class patriots dragged their heels on this issue, and within the Continental Congress the Virginia delegation, which included such firebrands as Thomas Jefferson and Richard Henry Lee, found its most ardent allies in the campaign for independence among those like Samuel Adams of Massachusetts who were associated with the "lower orders."

The result of the clash between the richer and poorer revolutionaries was a set of compromises. The Declaration of July 4 came neither as soon as many farmers and artisans desired nor as late as a majority of the merchants and planters wished. Moreover, in each commonwealth some measure of democratization occurred; the new statutes and state constitutions strengthened the lower houses, weakened the executives, disestablished churches, reapportioned the legislatures, and expanded the number of elected local officials. Everywhere nonelite citizens were more involved in decision making than ever before. But in all provinces the patriot upper classes preserved their wealth and remained the most important participants in the new state governments. Relatively few expansionists were so frightened by the disruptions of these years that they abandoned the revolutionary standard for neutrality or loyalism.

Unsurprisingly, the final imperial crisis provoked not only vigorous actions but also an outpouring of words from members of the elite parties as well as from the populace. As earlier, most statements addressed issues of the moment—the burdens of a recent British enactment or the merits of a particular course of colonial resistance. Nonetheless, some members of each group cast their eyes to the future and discussed their views in broader terms. More clearly than ever, wealthy patriots saw the glorious destiny of a New World nation, while nonexpansionists glimpsed ever more darkly the terrors of a conflict with Britain. Artisans and small farmers also loudly voiced their demands, and suggested their transcendent vision of a more democratic American commonwealth.

CHAPTER 14

Northern Colonies:
Antagonists High and Low

John Adams's trip in August 1774 to the First Continental Congress took him from Boston through New York City and on to Philadelphia. "I find that there is a tribe of people here," he observed after arriving in the Quaker City, "exactly like the tribe in the Massachusetts, of Hutchinsonian addressers. There is indeed a set in every colony."[1] Adams's firsthand acquaintance with Massachusetts, New York, and Pennsylvania helped underscore for him the similarities that marked the revolutionary movement in the several American colonies. If all the provinces shared common patterns, the commercial colonies resembled one another still more closely. In each of these three commonwealths the nonexpansionists formed a potent, determined group, and in each of them there was a populous port city with fractious shopkeepers, mechanics, and sailors as well as an extensive hinterland with many small farmers—the raw material for a strong lower class.

Such similarities should not, however, obscure the significant differences demarcating politics in the three commonwealths during the months from the announcement of the Boston Port Act to independence. The first struggle of this period—the conflict between the upper-class patriots and the "Hutchinsonians"—was more intense and prolonged in New York and Pennsylvania, where the nonexpansionist parties were strong, than in the Bay Colony, where the nonexpansionists had been decisively weakened during the Stamp Act Crisis. Moreover, the second battle of this era—the clash between the

---

1. *Diary and Autobiography of John Adams*, ed. L. H. Butterfield et al., 4 vols. (Cambridge, Mass., 1961), II, 119 (Sept. 1, 1774).

expansionists and their lower-class allies—also varied in nature from province to province. Nowhere was the farmer-artisan alliance so effective as in Pennsylvania; by contrast, in Massachusetts the British occupation of the capital and in New York extensive rural loyalism vitiated the power of the lower class.

MASSACHUSETTS

News in mid-May 1774 of the Boston Port Act, which closed the harbor until the tea was paid for, quickened the resistance movement, and during the next three months Massachusetts expansionists battled the Hutchinsonians and drove them out of provincial politics. In this campaign, the upper-class patriots had the support of the artisans and farmers, who proved crucial, if restless, allies. Once the nonexpansionists were routed, the wealthy protestors locked horns with the popular party over the course of the revolutionary movement.

During May and June 1774 the nonexpansionists, although outnumbered by the patriots, remained determined opponents, firmly resolved to slow or reverse the course of American resistance. In May more than 120 Bostonians, including several Olivers and Sewalls, presented a pair of farewell addresses to Governor Hutchinson, who had announced his intention of going to England; the petitioners declared that "making restitution for damage done to the property of the East India Company or to the property of any individual [injured] by the outrage of the people, we acknowledge to be just."[2] Boston nonexpansionists offered a similar salute to General Thomas Gage when he took up the seals of office in June. Hutchinsonians thronged the town meetings, arguing that the province should pay for the tea destroyed and urging the dissolution of the Boston committee of correspondence. These tories indicated their willingness to support the royal government and accepted seats in the appointed council established in June by parliamentary decree.[3]

2. Merchants and Others of Boston to Governor Hutchinson, May 28, 1774, Peter Force, ed., *American Archives*, 4th and 5th ser., 9 vols. (Washington, D.C., 1837–53), 4th ser., I, 361–62; Thomas Hutchinson, *The History of the Colony and Province of Massachusetts-Bay*, ed. Lawrence S. Mayo, 3 vols. (Cambridge, Mass., 1936), III, 332; Thomas Hutchinson to Israel Williams, May 14, 1774, Israel Williams Papers, MHS.

3. Col. Williams to Gen. Thomas Gage, Aug. 10, 1774, Gen. Gage to Lord Dartmouth, Aug. 25, 1774, MHS *Cols.*, 4th ser., X (1871), 715–16, 714; Hutchinson to Israel Williams, Sept. 29, 1774, Israel Williams Papers; John K. Wiggin, "A List of 'Protestors' and 'Addressers,'" MHS *Procs.*, 1st ser., II (1869–70), 392–95; James H. Stark, *The Loyalists of Massachusetts and the Other Side of the American Revolution* (Boston, 1910), 124–33; Albert Mathews, ed., "Documents Relating to the . . . Massachusetts Royal Council, 1774–1776," CSM *Pubs.*, XXXII (1937), 461–86.

Before the wealthy protestors could fully engage these tories, they had to rein in their lower-class allies, who had been driven to fury by the Port Act. After a brief period of indecision, the expansionists opposed Sam Adams's call for an immediate, continentwide nonimportation agreement. News that the provinces to the south had all rejected this brash proposal strengthened their hand. Expansionists also disassociated themselves from Adams's "Solemn League and Covenant," a plan to interdict the consumption of all British wares in Massachusetts. Adams conceded, "The merchants importing goods from England, a few excepted, were totally against the Covenant. They complained of it in our town meeting as a measure destructive to their interests." Because of the opposition of the affluent revolutionaries, the Solemn League was a dead letter, at least in Boston, by summer's end.[4]

More significantly, the expansionists and popular party worked together during these months to defeat the Hutchinsonians. In June the revolutionaries dealt their opponents a series of grave setbacks. Despite the efforts of Gage and his supporters, the assembly selected representatives for the upcoming intercolonial congress (a gathering first suggested by the New Yorkers), appointing a balanced delegation of two popular party adherents, John and Samuel Adams, and three expansionists, including Thomas Cushing. Moreover, the Boston town meeting flatly turned down all suggestions that the colonists pay for the tea. And at the climactic gathering of June 27 Boston patriots overwhelmingly defeated the Hutchinsonians' proposal to "censure and dismiss" the committee of correspondence.[5]

Outside the capital the anger of the populace complemented the firmness shown in Boston and helped reduce the nonexpansionists to onlookers in Bay Colony politics. The militance of rural crowds frightened the tories, and many of these Hutchinsonians fled to the capital where the regulars provided an element of security. By fall General Gage's power in rural Massachusetts had disappeared. The tories remained in occupied Boston, forming in 1775 three companies of "Loyal American Associators." And when the British forces under

---

4. Samuel Adams for Boston Committee of Correspondence to Colrain Committee of Correspondence, *The Writings of Samuel Adams*, ed. Harry A. Cushing, 4 vols. (New York, 1904–8), III, 145; John Andrews to William Barrell, May 18, June 12, July 22, 1774, "Letters of John Andrews, Esq., of Boston, 1772–1776," ed. Winthrop Sargent, MHS *Procs.*, VIII (1864–65), 327, 329, 331–32; Samuel Adams to James Warren, May 14, 1774, MHS *Cols.*, 4th ser., IV (1858), 390–92; Stephen E. Patterson, *Political Parties in Revolutionary Massachusetts* (Madison, Wis., 1973), 80–97; Arthur M. Schlesinger, *The Colonial Merchants and the American Revolution, 1763–1776* (New York, 1919), 311–14.

5. John Andrews to William Barrell, July 22, 1774, "Letters of Andrews," 331; Patterson, *Political Parties*, 82–85; Schlesinger, *Colonial Merchants*, 321–25.

General William Howe left the Bay Colony in the spring of 1776, a
familiar roll call of nonexpansionist families accounted for a sizable
portion of the 927 civilians accompanying the troop ships.[6]

With the nonexpansionists out of the political mainstream after
August 1774, the wealthy patriots began their struggle against the
artisans and small farmers for control of the revolutionary movement.[7] During the summer and fall of 1774 the conflict between the
two groups of patriots broadened as county conventions fully involved the rural citizenry in the protests. In Worcester and Plymouth
counties poorer farmers quickly gained control of the conventions
and adopted a series of forthright resolves. The Plymouth gathering,
for example, declared that "it is justifiable and proper for the people,
at such a time as this to prevent any [court from] sitting."[8] The
expansionists, however, with their strength in the wealthier eastern
towns, dominated the Essex and Suffolk assemblies and emphasized
orderly procedures. Suffolk's resolutions, while denying the legit-
imacy of officials loyal to Governor Gage, instructed the populace
"not to engage in any routs, riots, or licentious attacks upon the
property of any persons whatsoever."[9] In the western counties of
Berkshire and Hampshire affluent revolutionaries ruled the first set
of conventions, which unseated the tory river gods; however, during
the next months upper- and lower-class patriots clashed with each
other, and by the end of 1774 the poorer farmers had seized control of
county affairs in the west.[10]

The clash between wealthier and less affluent revolutionaries continued during the winter of 1774–1775, with the two groups disagree-
ing on the wisdom of establishing a provincial army. Expansionists
opposed the popular party's call for mobilization, fearing that such a
step would only increase the self-assertiveness of the small farmers.
Expansionist strongholds in the east raised the loudest outcry against
the proposal. "In Essex County so many delegates dissented," explained one observer, "that the project, as is supposed, must be laid

6. Loyal American Associators are listed in Edward A. Jones, *The Loyalists of Massachusetts: Their Memorials, Petitions and Claims* (London, 1930), 311–12; Stark, *Loyalists of Massachusetts*, 133–36, enumerates the evacuees.
7. On divisions in Massachusetts during this period, see Marc Egnal, "Society and
Politics in Massachusetts, 1774 to 1778" (M.A. thesis, Univ. of Wisconsin, 1967).
8. Plymouth's resolves are reprinted in *The Journals of Each Provincial Congress of
Massachusetts in 1774 and 1775, and of the Committee of Safety, with an Appendix* . . .
(Boston, 1838), 624–25, and for Worcester's resolutions, 635.
9. For Suffolk's resolves, ibid., 601–5, for Essex's, 616–17.
10. The resolves of the western counties are in ibid., 619–21, 652–54; Col. Williams to
Gen. Gage, Aug. 10, 1774, MHS *Cols.*, 4th ser., x (1871), 715–16; Egnal, "Society and
Politics," 19–20.

aside or referred to the continental congress."[11] Only after the battle on Lexington Green in April 1775 did expansionists join popular party supporters in demanding the creation of a provincial army.[12]

Despite the protests of the common people, the affluent patriots during 1775 and 1776 reinstituted a conservative frame of government. Once Gage's power had been nullified and the 1691 charter rendered inoperative, the popular party urged a reversion to the relatively democratic 1629 compact or the creation of a new and more liberal constitution. The richer revolutionaries balked at these suggestions, however, and with the support of the Continental Congress, secured in July 1775 the resumption of the 1691 frame. The expansionist-dominated council at once claimed the "absent" executive's powers of appointment and attempted to reestablish the court system, which had vanished in the storm of popular protest the previous year. Many of the poorer farmers denounced this bold assertion of the prerogative and forced the expansionists to grant a series of postponements so that most courts did not reopen until the second half of 1776. Lower-class militance also defeated the expansionists' attempt to select militia officers; pronounced one western town, "If the right of nominating to office is not invested in the people, we are indifferent who assumes it, whether any particular persons on this or the other side of the water."[13] The expansionists, however, led by a group from Essex County, secured a signal victory in May 1776 with the passage of a reapportionment act that gave more weight to the populous eastern counties.[14]

11. *The Diary of William Pynchon of Salem*, ed. Fitch E. Oliver (Cambridge, Mass., 1890), 43, quoted in Patterson, *Political Parties*, 116–17; *Diary and Autobiography of John Adams*, II, 159–60 (Nov. 5, 1774); Gen. Gage to Cadwallader Colden, Feb. 26, 1775, NYHS *Cols.*, LVI (1923), 266–67; Samuel Freeman to John Adams, Apr. 23, 1776, Adams Papers, MHS, microfilm; John Andrews to William Barrell, Aug. 31, Sept. 2, Oct. 29, 1774, "Letters of Andrews," 350, 351–52, 380–81; Joseph Hawley to Thomas Cushing, Feb. 22, 1775, MHS *Cols.*, 4th ser., IV (1858), 393–97.

12. John Hancock to Committee of Safety, Apr. 24, 1775, *John Hancock: His Book*, ed. Abram English Brown (Boston, 1898), 197; John Pitts to Samuel Adams, Oct. 25, 1775, Samuel Adams Papers, NYPL [microfilm courtesy of Merrill Jensen]; Egnal, "Society and Politics," 20–31; Patterson, *Political Parties*, 122–32; Jensen, *Founding of a Nation*, 587–88.

13. Petition of Pittsfield, Dec. 26, 1775, Robert J. Taylor, ed., *Massachusetts, Colony to Commonwealth: Documents on the Formation of Its Constitution, 1775–1780* (Chapel Hill, N.C., 1961), 19; Merrill Jensen, *The Founding of a Nation: A History of the American Revolution, 1763–1776* (New York, 1968), 672–73.

14. James Warren to John Adams, May 8, 1776, *Warren-Adams Letters*, 2 vols. (MHS *Cols.*, LXXII, LXXIII [1917, 1925]), I, 240–41; Dr. Winthrop to John Adams, May 23, 1776, [?] to John Adams, May 6, 1776, Adams Papers; Committee of Correspondence of Chesterfield to Committee of Correspondence of Northampton, Mar. 4, 1776, Joseph Hawley Papers, NYPL [microfilm courtesy of Merrill Jensen]; Jensen, *Founding of a Nation*, 674–75.

The wealthy revolutionaries, while buttressing resistance to Britain, sought to postpone independence, fearing that a sudden break would only further excite the populace. During the spring of 1776 the upper-class patriots endorsed measures to apprehend suspected tories and "secure" their estates, agreed to drop the king's name from all proceedings, and bolstered the newly issued paper money. But they firmly opposed all proposals for an immediate break with the mother country. A parallel struggle went on within the congressional delegation, where expansionists John Hancock and Thomas Cushing kept the Adamses from committing the colony to precipitate steps. "It is very hard to be linked and yoked eternally with people who have either no opinion or opposite opinions," complained John Adams.[15] Using their potent influence, the Adamses engineered Cushing's replacement by a more pliant representative. Once back in Massachusetts, however, Thomas Cushing only continued the activities that had so enraged them. Cushing guided the upper house and helped delay a proposal to poll the towns on independence. As a result, not until July 3 did the two chambers call for breaking ties with Britain.[16]

After independence, expansionists remained the dominant group in Massachusetts, although the political power and consciousness of the less wealthy citizens clearly had grown. In Boston popular protests against economic enemies—individuals who tried to "engross" or monopolize a product—became commonplace, and in the western counties of Hampshire and Berkshire many farmers withheld their allegiance from what they viewed as an oppressive state government. Shays's Rebellion in 1786 was only the continuation of lower-class fermentation that never subsided during the war or after. Nonetheless, the affluent patriots retained a firm grip on most offices of state and gained in 1780 a conservative constitution with a strong execu-

15. John Adams to James Otis, Sr., Nov. 23, 1775, *Papers of John Adams*, ed. Robert Taylor et al., 2 vols. (Cambridge, Mass., 1977), III, 313; John Pitts to Samuel Adams, Oct. 25, Nov. 12, 1775, Samuel Adams Papers; Elbridge Gerry to James Warren, Mar. 26, 1776, James T. Austin, *The Life of Elbridge Gerry*, 2 vols. (Boston, 1828–29), I, 174; James Warren to John Adams, Apr. 3, 1776, *Warren-Adams Letters*, I, 219; Joseph Hawley to Samuel Adams, Apr. 1, 1776, Samuel Cooper to Samuel Adams, Apr. 18, 1776, Samuel Adams Papers; Egnal, "Society and Politics," 68–76.

16. James Warren to Samuel Adams, Dec. 19, 1775, *Warren-Adams Letters*, II, 430; John Hancock to Thomas Cushing, Jan. 17, 1776, MHS *Procs.*, LX (1926–27), 98–99; *Diary of Pynchon*, 3–4 (Feb. 12, 1776); Samuel Cooper to Samuel Adams, May 13, 1776, Benjamin Kent to Samuel Adams, May 24, 1776, Samuel Adams Papers; *Records of the Town of Plymouth*, vol. III: *1743 to 1783* (Plymouth, 1903), 314–315; *Boston Town Records*, XVIII, 236–38; Patterson, *Political Parties*, 146–52; Jensen, *Founding of a Nation*, 676–77.

tive and an upper house representing property. Because of their ability to contain the threat from below, virtually none of the Massachusetts expansionists bolted to the British as did some wealthy revolutionaries in the colonies to the south.[17]

NEW YORK

As was the case in the other colonies, news of the Boston Port Act accelerated the revolutionary movement in New York, and the expansionists there began the first of two prolonged battles. From May 1774 to April 1775 the upper-class patriots (or Livingston party), with the assistance of many mechanics and farmers, fought and eventually routed the nonexpansionists (or DeLancey party). After April 1775 the Livingstons confronted a new opponent—the working people, who sought democratic reforms as well as revolution.

Despite the efforts of the expansionists, the DeLanceys initially seized control of New York protests. They directed the May 16 public meeting that had been convoked to discuss a response to the Port Act. Observed Alexander McDougall, "The DeLancey faction . . . were at great pains all day to collect every tool who was under their influence, as well as those in trade as out of it."[18] Isaac Low chaired the Committee of Fifty-one established by the gathering, and DeLanceyites dominated this board. During the next weeks the cautious committee directed the protests, informing Boston that no further steps should be taken until an intercolonial congress assembled and rejecting a Livingston proposal to give the committee of mechanics a voice in the selection of representatives to the congress. However, the expansionists scored a minor victory in July when the Fifty-one agreed to send a balanced delegation to Philadelphia. Only two of the five individuals selected—Isaac Low and John Alsop—were firm DeLanceyites. One man, Philip Livingston, was an expansionist, and two delegates—John Jay and James Duane—encouraged the affections of both parties. Both remained on friendly terms with the De-

17. Egnal, "Society and Politics," 121–45; Patterson, *Political Parties*, 158–247; Robert A. East, "The Massachusetts Conservatives in the Critical Period," in Richard B. Morris, ed., *The Era of the American Revolution* (New York, 1939), 349–91.

18. McDougall, Political Memorandums, May 1774, quoted in Leopold S. Launitz-Schürer, *Loyal Whigs and Revolutionaries: The Making of the Revolution in New York* (New York, 1980), 109; John Watts to Monckton, May 30, 1774, MHS *Cols.*, 4th ser., x (1871), 710; Lt. Gov. Colden to Dartmouth, June 1, 1774, *Documents Relative to the Colonial History of the State of New York Procured in Holland, England and France*, ed. Edmund B. O'Callaghan, 15 vols. (Albany, 1856–87), VIII, 433.

Lanceys but had married Livingstons and would eventually become patriot leaders.[19]

In the fall the need to implement the decisions of the Continental Congress gave expansionists a much-needed boost. The mechanics' committee, which for many months had resented the DeLanceys' hesitant leadership, argued vehemently that the existing panel should not guide the next stage of resistance. The result was a hasty meeting of the artisans and the Fifty-one and the formation of the Committee of Sixty. The Livingstons, whose numbers in the supervisory body soared, were the direct beneficiaries of the change. The members, observed Smith, are "such a set as the most active Liberty Boys approve."[20] Most counties also struck bodies to enforce the Continental Association, with the support for the intercolonial assembly's resolves strongest in the traditional bastions of expansionist strength, such as Albany County, and weakest in the DeLanceyite strongholds around New York City. The one striking exception to the longevity of political allegiances in rural New York was patriot Suffolk, an area whose outlook was shaped by the provenance of its residents. As Cadwallader Colden explained, this "county in the east end of Long Island . . . was settled from Connecticut and the inhabitants still retain a great similarity of manners and sentiments."[21]

When the legislature convened early in 1775 the nonexpansionists struggled to stem the tide of revolution. Although the expansionists in the body strongly urged resolute measures, the DeLancey majority rejected the initiatives of the Continental Congress, declined to thank New Yorkers for their "patriotic conduct" in observing nonimportation, and refused to appoint representatives to the Second Continen-

19. *Diary and Autobiography of John Adams*, II, 105–7 (Aug. 22, 1774); Dartmouth to Lt. Gov. Colden, Nov. 2, 1774, NYHS *Cols.*, LVI (1923), 254; John Jay to Robert R. Livingston, Jan. 1769, Robert R. Livingston Collection, Box 2, NYHS; James Duane to Robert Livingston, Jr., May 17, June 14, 1769, Livingston Family Papers, reel 8, FDRL; Robert R. Livingston to Monckton, Nov. 8, 1765, MHS *Cols.*, 4th ser., X (1871), 559–66; Roger Champagne, "New York and the Intolerable Acts, 1774," *NYHS Quarterly*, XLV (1961), 197–200. Carl Becker, *The History of Political Parties in the Province of New York, 1760–1776* (Madison, Wis., 1909), 117–21, 133–34n, lists the "Fifty-one" (originally the "Fifty"). See also Lt. Gov. Colden to Dartmouth, July 6, June 1, 1774, *Documents Relative to the Colonial History of N.Y.*, VIII, 469–70, 433–34.

20. William Smith to Philip Schuyler, Nov. 22, 1774, *Historical Memoirs from 16 March 1763 to 25 July 1778 of William Smith*, ed. William H. W. Sabine, 2 vols. (1956, 1958; rpt. New York, 1969), I, 203; *Diary and Autobiography of John Adams*, II, 158 (Oct. 31, 1774); Peter R. Livingston to Robert Livingston, Jr., Feb. 19, 1775, Livingston Family Papers, reel 8, FDRL; Launitz-Schürer, *Loyal Whigs*, 121; Becker, *Political Parties*, 165–67.

21. Lt. Gov. Colden to Dartmouth, Aug. 2, Oct. 5, 1774, *Documents Relative to the Colonial History of N.Y.*, VIII, 486, 493; Becker, *Political Parties*, 169–73.

tal Congress. Colden boasted to the ministry that these actions "have tended to preserve this government from the dangerous and extravagant plans which are formed in almost every other part of the continent."[22] The divisions in the chamber illustrate the stable patterns of New York politics: Frederick Philipse of Westchester County, like his forebears, helped lead the nonexpansionists, and he was warmly seconded by James DeLancey and the New York City delegation. The patriot minority included Peter R. Livingston, who represented the family manor; Philip Schuyler of Albany County; and Abraham Ten Broeck, the delegate from Rensselaerswyck. The Livingstons responded to the assembly's recalcitrance by convening a provincial convention, which selected a slate of steadfast congressmen. Among these representatives were Robert R. Livingston, Jr., and Lewis Morris III, a scion of the illustrious Westchester family.[23]

The news of fighting at Lexington and Concord finally allowed the Livingstons to shoulder the nonexpansionists out of the mainstream of New York politics. The widespread commotion during the last week in April led the Sixty to propose its own dissolution and the formation of a new body, the Committee of One Hundred; balloting for members once again (as in the change from the Fifty-one to the Sixty) reduced the percentage of DeLanceyites on the panel. Moreover, the able maneuvering of the Livingstons and the fervor of the populace squelched nonexpansionist hopes that the ministry's recent peace proposals would provide the basis for their resurgence. "There never was a more total revolution at any place than at New York," an observer in Philadelphia noted with excusable hyperbole. "The tories have been obliged to fly, the province [is] arming, and the governor dares not call his prostituted assembly to receive Lord North's foolish plan."[24] The Committee of One Hundred summoned a provincial congress to replace the legislature, which was the DeLanceys' last

22. Lt. Gov. Colden to Dartmouth, Apr. 5, Feb. 1, 1775, *Documents Relative to the Colonial History of N.Y.*, VIII, 566, 532; *Memoirs of Smith*, I, 208 (Jan. 10, 1775). *N.Y. Votes and Proceedings*, Jan. 26, Feb. 21, 23, 1775, presents these divisions.
23. Becker, *Political Parties*, 171–93; Launitz-Schürer, *Loyal Whigs*, 152–54; Lt. Gov. Colden to Dartmouth, May 3, 1775, *Documents Relative to the Colonial History of N.Y.*, VIII, 571–72; *Memoirs of Smith*, I, 222 (Apr. 29, 1775); Becker, *Political Parties*, 194. *Votes and Proceedings*, Jan. 13, Feb. 16, 17, 1775.
24. Richard Henry Lee to Francis Lightfoot Lee, May 21, 1775, *The Letters of Richard Henry Lee*, ed. James C. Ballagh, 2 vols. (New York, 1911–14), I, 137–38; Minutes of the Council of N.Y., May 1, 1775, NYHS *Cols.*, LVI (1923), 287; James Beekman to Fludyer, Marsh, Hudson, & Streatfield, May 6, 1775, *The Beekman Mercantile Papers, 1764–1799*, ed. Philip L. White, 2 vols. consec. pagin. (New York, 1956), 756–58; Lt. Gov. Colden to Dartmouth, May 3, 1775, *Documents Relative to the Colonial History of N.Y.*, VIII, 571–72; *Memoirs of Smith*, I, 222 (Apr. 29, 1775); Becker, *Political Parties*, 194.

redoubt, and by the end of May this new body, safely in the hands of upper-class patriots, had assumed the responsibility of governing New York.[25]

The remarkable strengthening of the Livingstons' position after the outbreak of fighting in New England reduced the DeLanceys to the role of captious critics or forced them into open professions of loyalty to the Crown. After April, nonexpansionists did not wholly abandon participation in the extralegal bodies; John DeLancey, Isaac Low, and Abraham Walton were all members of the first provincial congress. But they had become little more than obstructionists, if vociferous ones; in August the body formally reprimanded DeLancey for "having insulted [J. M.] Scott, a member in this house, while the congress was sitting, by calling him a scoundrel, and attempting to run his fist in his face." The November elections for the second provincial congress excluded the prominent members of the De-Lancey party.[26]

In growing numbers nonexpansionists in the capital and surrounding counties declared their allegiance to Britain. James DeLancey, Myles Cooper (the president of King's College), and a few others fled to the warships or to the mother country in the immediate aftermath of Lexington and Concord, but most other loyalists remained in the province, making no secret of their sympathies. "The counties [of] Westchester, Dutchess, Kings, Queens, and Richmond had the bulk of their inhabitants well affected to government and some friends in all the other counties," Governor William Tryon told Secretary of State Dartmouth in November. "They call for protection as the enemies to government are daily insulting and disarming them."[27] Before the end of the year tories in Queens County were receiving arms from the British fleet. Moreover, when English soldiers arrived in July 1776 to begin what would be a seven-year occupation, many New Yorkers warmly applauded their presence. During the Revolutionary War leading nonexpansionists would command troops against the patriots, and New York would provide about 23,500 men to the British army, almost half the total American contribution to the regular forces.[28]

25. Robert C. Livingston to Robert Livingston, Jr., May 29, 1775, Livingston Family Papers, reel 8, FDRL. Becker, *Political Parties*, 195–200, lists the One Hundred and analyzes their allegiances.

26. Provincial Congress Minutes, Aug. 4, 1775, quoted in Max M. Mintz, *Gouverneur Morris and the American Revolution* (Norman, Okla., 1970), 55. Becker, *Political Parties*, 206–11, discusses the membership of the provincial congress, and see 229–33.

27. Gov. Tryon to Dartmouth, Nov. 11, 1775, *Documents Relative to the Colonial History of N.Y.*, VIII, 643; *Memoirs of Smith*, I, 223 (Apr. 29, 1775), 269 (Mar. 11, 1776).

28. Catherine S. Crary, "Guerrilla Activities of James Delancey's Cowboys in Westchester County: Conventional Warfare or Self-Interested Freebooting," Robert A. East

Having forced the DeLanceys from the foreground of provincial
politics, the Livingstons commenced a struggle with the lower classes
over the direction of the revolutionary movement.[29] In the turbulent
weeks following the news of Lexington and Concord the expansionists took steps to channel the energies of the populace. Despite
the participation of artisans in the selection of the One Hundred, only
four members of the new body belonged to the mechanics' committee; rich patriots predominated. Moreover, soon after assembling, the
One Hundred, at the suggestion of J. M. Scott and McDougall, directed all citizens to sign an "Association," drawn up by Duane and
Jay; signatories to this declaration vowed not only to oppose "oppressive acts of the British Parliament" but also to follow "in all
things . . . the advice of our General Committee respecting the purposes aforesaid, the preservation of peace and good order, and the
safety of individuals and private property."[30]

During the remainder of 1775 the expansionists assiduously pursued their goals of advancing the revolutionary movement and keeping the common people in check. The tug of these antithetical aims
was evident in several areas, including the task of providing the colony with an armed force. Some wealthy revolutionaries considered the
formation and strict regulation of private militia companies the best
means of assuring that the citizen soldiers did not become disruptive.
James Duane heartily approved this tack; after hearing that the
Livingstons were raising men, he confided to Robert Livingston, Jr.,
"Licentiousness is the natural effect of a civil discord, and it can only
be guarded against by placing the command of the troops in the
hands of men of property and rank."[31] Other expansionists directed
their efforts toward the creation of a strong, well-disciplined corps
under the national or provincial banner. Philip Schuyler, for example, served as a general with the continental troops, and Alexander

---

and Jacob Judd, eds., *The Loyalist Americans: A Focus on Greater New York* (Tarrytown,
N.Y., 1975), 14–24; Esmond Wright, "The New York Loyalists: A Cross-Section of
Colonial Society," ibid., 79; Becker, *Political Parties*, 238. Bernard Mason, *The Road to
Independence: The Revolutionary Movement in New York, 1773–1777* (Lexington, Ky.,
1966), 91–94, argues, however, that the New York contribution to the British forces
was significantly less than 23,500.

29. The Progressive historians in their depiction of these months assert that the true
leaders of New York's revolution were the "radicals" or "lower orders" or "popular
party," who compelled the upper classes to break from Britain. See Becker, *Political
Parties*, passim; Schlesinger, *Colonial Merchants*, 327–41, 447–55, 489–93; Jensen,
Founding of a Nation, 532–33, 593–95.

30. Becker, *Political Parties*, 196, quotes the "Association"; *Memoirs of Smith*, I, 223
(Apr. 29, 1775); Launitz-Schürer, *Loyal Whigs*, 159–62.

31. James Duane to Robert Livingston, Jr., June 7, 1775, Livingston Family Papers,
reel 8, FDRL; Mintz, *Gouverneur Morris*, 55–57.

McDougall (who remarked, "I fear liberty is in danger from the licentiousness of the people") commanded a New York regiment.[32]

A related challenge during these months was the need to prevent excesses while enlisting the aid of lower-class patriots in policing the growing legion of loyalists. The wealthy revolutionaries oscillated between the poles of repression and laxity. In the spring of 1775 the One Hundred and the provincial congress resolved to disarm those favoring Britain's cause but, significantly, failed to follow up their bold declaration with any concrete plan for enforcement. Similarly, while the upper-class patriots denounced the activities of tory gazetteer James Rivington, they also rebuked Isaac Sears, who headed an armed band that destroyed Rivington's press.[33]

A similar vacillation marked the Livingston party approach in 1775 to the question of reconciliation with the mother country. During the summer the wealthy revolutionaries steering the provincial congress not only voted to raise troops and strike paper money but also forwarded to the New York delegates in Philadelphia a "Plan of Accommodation between Great Britain and America." Fear of social change underlay this proposal; the letter accompanying the document noted pointedly, "Contests for liberty, fostered in their infancy by the virtuous and wise, become sources of power to wicked and designing men."[34] Although this scheme, which promised Britain voluntary contributions if the colonies were guaranteed the exclusive right of self-taxation, was never formally presented to the Continental Congress, expansionist congressmen from New York voiced similar arguments; Duane, Jay, and Robert R. Livingston, Jr., aided the Canadian campaign and the efforts to strengthen Washington's forces but also stood with the delegates who grasped at each olive branch waved by Britain.[35]

The same desire to make a revolution with a minimum of social

32. Alexander McDougall to John Jay, Mar. 20, 1776, Oct. 30, 1775, Robert R. Livingston, Jr., to Jay, July 17, 1775, *John Jay: The Making of a Revolutionary. Unpublished Papers, 1745–1780*, ed. Richard B. Morris et al., 2 vols. (New York, 1975), I, 237, 174, 158; Battalion of Independent Foot Companies, [c. summer 1775], *Documents Relative to the Colonial History of N.Y.*, VII, 601–3; Jensen, *Founding of a Nation*, 612, 617.

33. Gov. Tryon to Dartmouth, Dec. 6, 1775, *Documents Relative to the Colonial History of N.Y.*, VIII, 645–46; Jay to Alexander McDougall, Dec. 4, 1775, *Jay Papers*, I, 188.

34. Provincial Congress to Delegates, June 28, 1775, quoted in Jensen, *Founding of a Nation*, 662; Mintz, *Gouverneur Morris*, 48; Becker, *Political Parties*, 217–18; Launitz-Schürer, *Loyal Whigs*, 161.

35. *Diary and Autobiography of John Adams*, II, 209–10 (Oct. 20, 1775), 238 (May 13–15, 1776); James Duane to Robert Livingston, Jr., Oct. 23, 1775, Livingston Family Papers, reel 8, FDRL; John Jay, Proofs that the Colonies Do Not Aim at Independence, n.d. [after Dec. 11, 1775], James Duane to Jay, May 18, 1776, Robert R. Livingston, Jr., to Jay, June 4, 1776, *Jay Papers*, I, 198–201, 266, 273; Becker, *Political Parties*, 210–15.

disruption marked the expansionists' behavior during the first half of 1776 and helped make New York (along with Pennsylvania) one of the more laggard colonies in the revolutionary struggle. Early in the year the provincial congress arrested a group of Queens County loyalists but subsequently released them, in what General Charles Lee called "an act of absolute idiotism." Only in June, with the establishment of a panel that included Gouverneur Morris, who was a half brother to Lewis Morris III, and John Jay did the province begin to move resolutely against the tories.[36]

In the debate over independence, wealthy revolutionaries in New York struggled to preserve their social and political preeminence while encouraging a slow march toward separation. "The first thing therefore in my opinion to be done," pronounced Jay in April, "is to erect good and well-ordered governments in all the colonies, and thereby exclude that anarchy which already too much prevails."[37] Gouverneur Morris presented an elaborate design to advance American sovereignty without agitating the common people. "I would send ambassadors to the European courts and enter into treaties with them," he told the provincial congress in May. "Everything like Independence should form secret articles; the rest I would give to the world as soon as it was completed. This measure will both discourage and preclude impertinent enquiry. And when the people of this country enjoy the solid advantages which arise from our measures, they will thank us for the deception."[38] Because of such cautiousness and despite the pleas of the mechanics' committee, New York delegates in Philadelphia remained uninstructed when Congress voted for independence on July 2. Only a week later did the Hudson commonwealth formally support the break from Britain.[39]

After independence the expansionists remained dominant in New York but increasingly had to share power with the common people. Reflecting a measure of success in the social conflict, almost all members of this elite faction remained faithful to the American cause;

36. General Charles Lee to Joseph Reed, Feb. 28, 1776, William B. Reed, *Life and Correspondence of Joseph Reed . . .*, 2 vols. (Philadelphia, 1847), I, 161; Leonard Gansevoort et al. to William Smith, June 27, 1776, *Memoirs of Smith*, I, 278; Mintz, *Gouverneur Morris*, 51; Becker, *Political Parties*, 244–46, 263–65; Launitz-Schürer, *Loyal Whigs*, 162.

37. Jay to Alexander McDougall, Apr. 11, 1776, Dec. 23, 1775, Mar. 23, 1776, *Jay Papers*, I, 254, 213, 243; John Patterson to Robert Livingston, Jr., Nov. 6, 1775, Robert Livingston, Jr., to [Gen. Montgomery], Nov. 15, 1775, Livingston Family Papers, reel 8, FDRL.

38. Oration on the Necessity of Declaring Independence from Britain, [c. May 1776], quoted in Mintz, *Gouverneur Morris*, 57–60.

39. *Jay Papers*, I, 263–64; Becker, *Political Parties*, 265–74; Robert Champagne, "New York Politics and Independence, 1776," *NYHS Quarterly*, XLVI (1962), 295–97.

William Smith, who argued that "the meditated revolution tends to light up a civil war, and the miseries of it will probably exceed those which the people have been accustomed to endure," and who eventually joined the British side, was the most significant exception to the larger pattern.[40] During the war years, the British occupation of the capital eliminated one center of lower-class agitation and, so, strengthened the position of the wealthy revolutionaries within the state. The 1777 constitution, drafted in large part by Robert R. Livingston, Jr., Jay, Duane, and Gouverneur Morris, included restrictive property qualifications and a cumbersome council of revision, which could block the initiatives of the lower house. Nonetheless, the revolution had transformed the political landscape. Small farmers frequently dominated the local committees and would grow more powerful during the early 1780s. Even the 1777 constitution mirrored the changing balance, for along with its hierarchical features it included a fairer apportionment and a far greater number of representatives than had been the case before 1775.[41]

PENNSYLVANIA

News of the Boston Port Act in May 1774 quickened the revolutionary movement in Pennsylvania, and for the next twelve months expansionists battled Joseph Galloway's Quaker party, gradually ousting these nonexpansionists from their position of political supremacy. During this year the mechanics and farmers served as all-important, if at times bumptious, allies for the wealthy patriots. With the Quaker party defeated, the expansionists embarked on a second struggle—this one against their lower-class allies—over the extent of the social change that would accompany the revolution.[42]

Initial response to the ministry's attack on Boston involved a com-

40. *Memoirs of Smith*, I, 271 (June 9, 1776), and see 6–11; William Smith to Gov. Tryon, Dec. 17, 1775, *Documents Relative to the Colonial History of N.Y.*, VIII, 653–54; Virginia D. Harrington, *The New York Merchant on the Eve of the Revolution* (New York, 1935), 348–51.

41. Jay to Robert R. Livingston, Jr., May 29, 1776, *Jay Papers*, I, 271; Mason, *Road to Independence*, 213–49. Several studies emphasize the social and political changes accompanying the Revolution: Staughton Lynd, "Who Should Rule at Home? Dutchess County, New York, in the American Revolution," *WMQ*, 3d ser., XVIII (1961), 330–59; Edward Countryman, *A People in Revolution: The American Revolution and Political Society in New York, 1760–1790* (Baltimore, 1981); Alfred F. Young, *The Democratic Republicans of New York: The Origins, 1763–1797* (Chapel Hill, N.C., 1967).

42. The Progressive historians argue that in Pennsylvania between 1774 and 1776 a democratic lower class led the revolutionary movement and struggled against a conservative aristocracy. Charles H. Lincoln, *The Revolutionary Movement in Pennsylvania, 1760–1776* (Philadelphia, 1901); Schlesinger, *Colonial Merchants*; Jensen, *Founding of a Nation*. The author of the most recent detailed account of events in Pennsylvania

promise between the two upper-class parties: the expansionists publicly reaffirmed the supremacy of the Quaker party but at the same time secured the creation of a patriot committee. On May 20 Charles Thomson, John Dickinson, Thomas Mifflin, and Joseph Reed carefully orchestrated a gathering of wealthy Philadelphians. The affluent protestors urged Galloway's supporters to approve a balanced set of proposals, lest hotheads insist upon rash measures. This tack was successful, and members of the two factions, with comparative unanimity, endorsed the program set forth by John Dickinson. Expansionists were pleased by the establishment of a new body, the Committee of Nineteen, in which they formed a majority; board members included Dickinson, Thomson, Reed, Mifflin, and J. M. Nesbitt. Nonexpansionists, in turn, were assured that the committee's first order of business, as two Quakers present at the meeting reported, was "to wait upon the governor, and request that he would immediately call the assembly to take the matter into consideration."[43] Nonexpansionist Thomas Wharton rejoiced, "Every step which appeared to have a tendency to inflame was entirely set aside."[44]

When Governor Penn rejected the request for a session of the legislature, the wealthy patriots determined to broaden their base of support and called for the election of a new and larger committee. This appeal served as a tocsin for the mechanics, who had been excluded from the initial set of deliberations. On June 9, twelve hundred tradesmen met in the statehouse yard and appointed their own panel "to cooperate with the committee of merchants [i.e., the Nineteen] and to strengthen their hands."[45] Nine days later several thousand people assembled in response to the expansionists' request and, following the directives of cochairmen Thomas Willing and John Dickinson, approved a slate of committeemen and a list of moderate resolves. Many of the artisans present, however, grumbled at the temperate stratagems. "It was with difficulty that a division and

explicitly groups himself with the neo-Whig school; see Richard A. Ryerson, *The Revolution Is Now Begun: The Radical Committees of Philadelphia, 1765–1776* (Philadelphia, 1978), esp. 1–5. This work makes little attempt to relate ideas to action, however, and remains a political study in which revolutionary conflict is defined by "radicals," "moderates," and "conservatives"—groups whose membership and whose focal issues are constantly changing.

43. Reynell & Coates to Little & Greenleafe, May 21, 1774, Reynell-Coates Letterbook, HSP; James & Drinker to Pigou & Booth, May 24, 31, 1774, Henry Drinker Letterbook, HSP; "Charles Thomson's Account of Opposition to the Boston Port Bill" [c. 1778], *PMHB*, ii (1878), 413–15; "Joseph Reed's Narrative," NYHS *Cols.*, xi (1878), 269–72.

44. Thomas Wharton to Thomas Walpole, May 31, 1774, *PMHB*, xxxiii (1909), 337; *Pa. Gazette*, June 8, 1774; Ryerson, *Revolution Is Now Begun*, 42, 183.

45. *Pa. Gazette*, June 15, 1774, quoted in Charles S. Olton, *Artisans for Independence: Philadelphia Mechanics and the American Revolution* (Syracuse, N.Y., 1975), 60–61; "Charles Thomson's Account," *PMHB*, ii (1878), 416–67.

much confusion was prevented," noted one Quaker observer. Along with its expansionist majority, the new Committee of Forty-three included a few mechanics, several nonexpansionists, and a handful of Germans. The meeting instructed the board to make certain that the colony was represented at the forthcoming intercolonial congress.[46]

Buoyed by the creation of the Forty-three, the expansionists took steps to ensure that a hostile governor and a potent nonexpansionist party did not check Pennsylvania participation in the revolutionary movement. The new panel elected Thomas Willing chairman and Charles Thomson secretary and then called a provincial convention for July 15. Moreover, during the last week in June, Thomson, Mifflin, and Dickinson "under color of an excursion of pleasure," as Thomson later recalled, "made a tour through two or three frontier counties in order to discover the sentiments of the inhabitants and particularly the Germans." In July the provincial convention, with Thomas Willing in the chair, assembled and announced its support for commercial nonintercourse (urging the forthcoming congress, however, to try first the "gentler mode" of petitioning). The convention also proposed that expansionists Willing, Dickinson, and James Wilson be included among the congressmen.[47]

In the face of this rising tide of revolution, the Quaker party endeavored to keep Pennsylvania the epitome of political caution. A frightened Governor Penn reversed himself and summoned the assembly to meet on July 18. When the lower house convened, the Quaker party bowed to the inevitable and seconded the call for a continental congress. But the Old Ticket legislators ignored the provincial convention's suggestions for representatives and instructions and instead nominated a group of nonexpansionists headed by Galloway. Moreover, the lawmakers "strictly charged" the delegates "to avoid everything indecent or disrespectful to the mother state."[48]

In the fall of 1774 the upper-class patriots, with support from the

46. James & Drinker to Benjamin Booth, [c. June 21, 1774], Henry Drinker Letterbook; Thomas Clifford to Thomas Franks, June 21, 1774, Clifford Letterbook; Resolves of Meeting of Freeholders and Freemen, June 18, 1774, William J. Van Schreeven and Robert L. Scribner, eds., *Revolutionary Virginia: The Road to Independence* (Charlottesville, Va., 1973–   ), II, 122–23; *Pa. Gazette*, June 22, 1774; Ryerson, *Revolution Is Now Begun*, 49–52, 268.

47. "Charles Thomson's Account," 416–17; Summary of Governor Penn to Dartmouth, July 5, 1774, MHS *Cols.*, 4th ser., x (1871), 702–3; Chairman Thomas Willing, on behalf of the committee, to the mechanics, July 11, 1774, quoted in Olton, *Artisans for Independence*, 67; Schlesinger, *Colonial Merchants*, 351.

48. Assembly Votes and Proceedings, July 23, 1774, quoted in Ryerson, *Revolution Is Now Begun*, 62; Provincial Convention, Commencing July 15, 1774, Instructions of Provincial Convention, July 21, 1774, Van Schreeven and Scribner, eds., *Revolutionary Virginia*, II, 145–48, 148–155; "Charles Thomson's Account," 418.

common people, dealt Galloway's faction a series of telling blows. In the October 1 poll, Dickinson and Thomson gained assembly seats, and Thomas Mifflin was reelected by a solid margin, a turn of events that profoundly disturbed cautious men. "To what shamefully depraved state are we arrived," Quakers Abel James and Henry Drinker sighed, noting that "the lower class of people yesterday were generally mustered by the Presbyterian Party."[49] The lawmakers read the handwriting on the statehouse wall, ended Galloway's eight-year reign as speaker, and promptly made Dickinson a congressman, thus allowing the Pennsylvania Farmer to combat Galloway within the national body. The nonexpansionists suffered a further setback in November when the wealthy patriots and their mechanic backers created the Committee of Sixty-six to replace the Forty-three. The new panel, formed to enforce the trade boycott, included a familiar core of expansionists but excluded those Old Ticket backers who had sat on the Forty-three. It also had far more mechanics (seventeen, or 26 percent) than the previous board (three, or 7 percent).[50]

During the winter of 1774–1775 and the following spring the expansionists, while keeping their lower-class allies in check, continued their combat with the Quaker party. In January, the Sixty-six convened a second provincial convention to coordinate the work of the county committees that had sprung up to enforce the Continental Association. At this gathering Joseph Reed, who chaired the body, along with Dickinson, Thomson, Mifflin, and Wilson, entered the lists against the more militant farmers and artisans. Certain delegates, Reed observed, "intended to take some steps towards arming and disciplining the province, a measure which I opposed both publicly and privately." Ultimately the delegates adhered to Dickinson's advice that they restrict themselves to "commercial opposition" and blocked all proposals that would have put Pennsylvanians under arms.[51] More bitter still was the battle waged against Galloway's followers. In March, patriot lawmakers defeated, twenty-two to fifteen, the nonexpansionists' call for an address to George III and so

49. James & Drinker to Benjamin Booth, Oct. 4, 1774, James & Drinker to Pigou & Booth, Aug. 4, 1774, Henry Drinker Letterbook; James Pemberton to Daniel Mildred, July 22, 1774, James Pemberton to Dr. William Sandiford, Oct. 8, 1774, Pemberton Papers, HSP; *Diary and Autobiography of John Adams*, II, 147 (Oct. 4, 1774).

50. Israel Pemberton to John Pemberton, Oct. 19, 1774, Pemberton Papers; "Charles Thomson's Account," 418–19; Joseph Reed to Josiah Quincy, Jr., Nov. 6, 1774, Reed, *Joseph Reed*, I, 86; *Pa. Gazette*, Nov. 16, 1774; Ryerson, *Revolution Is Now Begun*, 91–96, 179–89, 270–71.

51. Joseph Reed to Dartmouth, Feb. 10, 1775, Joseph Reed to Charles Pettit, Jan. 31, 1775, Reed, *Joseph Reed*, I, 93–95, 92; Dickinson quoted in Charles J. Stillé, *The Life and Times of John Dickinson, 1732–1808* (Philadelphia, 1891), 150; Geoffrey Seed, *James Wilson* (Millwood, N.Y., 1978), 7–11; Ryerson, *Revolution Is Now Begun*, 101.

ended the last concerted effort of the Old Ticket to reverse the course of the revolution. Galloway was left with a bloc of eight delegates from Quaker-dominated Bucks County and seven assemblymen from Philadelphia, Chester, and Lancaster counties, representing, it seems, districts where Friends and German sectarians were predominant.[52]

The arrival of the news of Lexington and Concord on April 24 sealed the fate of the nonexpansionists and confirmed the triumph of Dickinson's faction, at least within the framework of elite politics. As late as the first week in April, Galloway was confidently dismissing his opponents as "but one-fourth part of our people" and boasting of his abilities to check "the Pennsylvania Farmer and his old assistant Charles Thomson."[53] Reports of fighting in Massachusetts ended all such hopes. Militia units formed throughout the province, and during the first weeks in May the expansionists in the house erased their opponents' timorous instructions, appointed three expansionist congressmen, and accepted Galloway's resignation from the Continental Congress. The Quaker party chieftain retired to his country estate and made no further attempts to rally his followers.[54]

After April 1775 the nonexpansionists were reduced to leaderless obstructionists or, more commonly, to forlorn bystanders, witnessing with bewilderment the torrent of revolution. The October 1775 election limited them to ten of the forty-one assembly seats, and the formation of a new government in the summer of 1776 ended their legislative role. Galloway and some others fled to the British lines, but most remained in Pennsylvania, ineffectually complaining about the directives of local officials. The patriots restricted the civil liberties of many and in 1777 exiled twenty-one of them. Among the exiles were such prominent Friends as Thomas Wharton, Abel James, Henry Drinker, and three Pembertons. "We have been and are subject to many trials, exercises, and sufferings," Philadelphia Quakers intoned in 1778. The German sectarians also felt the revolutionaries' fury; Schwenkfelder Christopher Sauer, whose links with the Quaker party went back to the 1750s, was one of several well-known Germans "attainted of high treason."[55]

52. Joseph Galloway to William Franklin, Mar. 26, 1775, *New Jersey Archives*, 1st ser., x (1886), 579–85, presents an analysis of ethnic and religious divisions in Pennsylvania; Ryerson, *Revolution Is Now Begun*, 109–10.

53. Joseph Galloway to Samuel Verplanck, Apr. 1, 1775, *PMHB*, xxi (1897), 482.

54. Benjamin H. Newcomb, *Franklin and Galloway: A Political Partnership* (New Haven, 1972), 278–82; Ryerson, *Revolution Is Now Begun*, 117–21.

55. Philadelphia Meeting for Sufferings to New England Meeting for Sufferings, Feb. 19, 1778, quoted in Richard Bauman, *For the Reputation of Truth: Politics, Religion, and Conflict among the Pennsylvania Quakers, 1750–1800* (Baltimore, 1971), 165; James Donald Anderson, "Thomas Wharton, Exile in Virginia, 1777–1778," *VMHB*, lxxxix (1980), 425–47. "Attainted tories" are presented in *Black List: A List of Those Tories . . .* (Philadelphia, 1802).

Once they had defeated the nonexpansionists, the affluent patriots, like their counterparts in the other colonies, began a new phase of the conflict: a clash with the less wealthy citizens over the direction of the revolutionary movement. Because the common people of Philadelphia were spirited and articulate, however, and because they and the backcountry farmers created a formidable union, the well-to-do protestors of Pennsylvania were less successful than the other patriot elites in controlling local affairs.

Between May and October 1775 the expansionists kept a firm grip on the campaign against Britain, even if the rumblings of lower-class discontent grew increasingly audible. Dickinson and his followers pursued a balanced set of policies, voting funds for the troops but resisting such demands as the cry for a universal draft. Moreover, upper-class patriots filled most of the new posts that emerged in a commonwealth preparing for war. Expansionists dominated the officer corps that the militiamen (or "associators") elected in May; they held the majority of seats in the Committee of Safety, which the house established in June; and in August they secured control of the successor to the Sixty-six—the One Hundred—even though mechanics now made up fully 34 percent of the new panel. But signs of dissatisfaction mounted. In August the associators rejected the Committee of Safety's "Rules for Establishing Rank and Procedure," and the next month the rank and file formed the Committee of Privates to push for their demands. Wealthy James Allen, who had joined one of the batallions ("I believe discreet people mixing with them may keep them in order"), noted that the soldiery "have refused to be bound by any articles and have no subordination." He added, "With all my zeal for the great cause we are engaged in, I frequently cry out—dreadful times."[56]

Despite their initial successes in checking the common people, many of the leading expansionists chose to sidestep fractious provincial issues and to concentrate their energies on the national level. Franklin, who returned to Philadelphia early in May 1775, stayed above the grit of local politics and finally, toward the end of 1776, sailed once more to Europe, this time as ambassador to France. Charles Thomson devoted himself to his duties as secretary of Congress, and Thomas Mifflin left the province in the summer of 1775 to serve as Washington's quartermaster general. James Wilson, the backcountry lawyer who had apprenticed under Dickinson, was another outward-looking individual who considered Congress his prop-

56. "Diary of James Allen, Esq., of Philadelphia, Counsellor-at-Law, 1770–1778," *PMHB*, ix (1885), 186 (Oct. 14, 1775), 184–85 (July 26, 1775); "Charles Thomson's Account," 420–22; Ryerson, *Revolution Is Now Begun*, 118–23, 130–34, 181, 197.

er forum, even though he kept a wary eye on provincial matters. Wilson was active in Indian affairs and stridently but vainly urged the national body to make Detroit one of the objectives of the 1775 campaign. Similarly, Thomas Willing and Robert Morris made their first priority providing the new nation with much-needed supplies, an enterprise in which they thoroughly mixed profit with patriotism. (Fumed one congressman, "£14 [a barrel] we are to give [Willing and Morris] if we get the powder, and £14 if we don't get it.") Though some of these men would denounce the course Pennsylvania politics took in 1776, they never wavered in their efforts to help the American cause.[57]

By November 1775 battle lines were more tightly drawn in Penn's Colony, with the expansionists and lower-class revolutionaries sharply differing over the question of an immediate declaration of independence. Both sides recognized the close connection between an imminent break from Britain and another fundamental issue: the reform of Pennsylvania's political institutions. In November the expansionist lawmakers under Dickinson's guidance directed the colony's delegation to "dissent from and utterly reject any propositions, should such be made, that may cause, or lead to a separation from our mother country, or a change of the form of this government."[58] Opposition to a hasty declaration, it must be emphasized, was for most upper-class patriots a tactic to lessen social change, not a sign of sympathy for Britain. Thus these wealthy lawmakers readily appropriated eighty thousand pounds for defense and penalized nonassociators. During these same months, those who spoke for the populace broadcast their support for independence *and* political change. No one enunciated this outlook more effectively than Tom Paine in his tract *Common Sense*, which appeared in January 1776. Along with his call for the speedy establishment of a New World republic, Paine urged the "necessity of a large and equal representation" in each province and pointedly criticized the unjustness of Pennsylvania government.[59]

57. *Diary and Autobiography of John Adams*, II, 184 (Sept. 24 [25], 1775), 188 (Oct. 3 [4], 1775); Franklin, "Sketch of Propositions for a Peace," [c. Sept.–Oct., 1776], *The Writings of Benjamin Franklin*, ed. Albert H. Smyth, 10 vols. (New York, 1905–7), VI, 452; Seed, *James Wilson*, 5–11; Eugene R. Slaski, "Thomas Willing: A Study in Moderation, 1774–1778," *PMHB*, C (1976), 491–506; J. Edwin Hendricks, *Charles Thomson and the Making of a New Nation, 1729–1824* (Rutherford, N.J., 1979); Ryerson, *Revolution Is Now Begun*, 125.

58. Pennsylvania Assembly, Resolution of Nov. 9, 1775, quoted in Jensen, *Founding of a Nation*, 641; "Joseph Reed's Narrative," 273.

59. Thomas Paine, *Common Sense*, in Harry H. Clark, ed., *Thomas Paine: Representative Selections with Introduction, Bibliography and Notes* (New York, 1961), 3–44, quotation on 41; Eric Foner, *Tom Paine and Revolutionary America* (New York, 1976), 71–106; Ryerson, *Revolution Is Now Begun*, 141–44.

In the February 1776 elections the Philadelphia mechanics and shopkeepers gained control of the Committee of One Hundred and ever more fiercely challenged the preeminence of the upper-class patriots. New committee leaders Benjamin Rush, Timothy Matlack, and such popular spokesmen as Tom Paine and James Cannon soon developed close ties with the rural county committees. Together these representatives of the artisans and farmers called for independence, compulsory military service, and a more democratic charter. The expansionists responded by offering a broad set of concessions, while damning all proposals to replace the legislature with a new body. "We shall endeavor to get the assembly to amend the [military] associa-tion, take off the instructions [against independence] from the dele-gates, and increase the representation," Joseph Reed remarked early in March. "I hope we shall succeed in all, but some violent spirits have obstructed our measures by calling a convention or attempting to do so before we know what the assembly will do."[60] During March and early April, expansionist lawmakers voted eighty-five thousand pounds for defense, added seventeen new seats, and further penalized nonassociators. But despite the suggestions of a few, they refused "by a great majority" to alter the directives against independence, and they made clear their dislike of any alternative body.[61]

Encouraged by the Continental Congress, spirited Pennsylvania mechanics and farmers pushed aside the expansionist-dominated as-sembly and established a new frame during the summer and fall of 1776. Many in the national body had come to see Dickinson's party as a major stumbling block on the path to independence; these con-gressmen backed John Adams's May 10 resolution calling for each province to form a "government sufficient to the exigencies of their affairs" and a few days later added to the resolve a forceful preamble, which stated that all regimes deriving their authority from the Crown "should be totally suppressed." Protested James Wilson, "In this province, if that preamble passes, there will be an immediate dissolution of every kind of authority."[62] Wilson's fears were well

60. Joseph Reed to Charles Pettit, Mar. 3, 1776, Reed, *Joseph Reed*, I, 153. "Charles Thomson's Account," 421–22, presents an excellent, retrospective statement of the expansionists' position. See also David F. Hawke, *In the Midst of a Revolution* (Phila-delphia, 1961), 18–22, 102–7. For the activities of the lower-class leaders, consult *Passages from the Remembrancer of Christopher Marshall . . .* , ed. William Duane, Jr. (Philadelphia, 1839).

61. *Pa. Votes and Proceedings*, Apr. 6, 1776, quoted in Ryerson, *Revolution Is Now Begun*, 166, and see 158–66.

62. Wilson quoted in Notes of Debates, May 13–15, 1776, *Diary and Autobiography of John Adams*, II, 239–40. The resolve and preamble are quoted in Jensen, *Founding of a Nation*, 684; "James Allen Diary," 186–87 (May 15, 1776); Hawke, *Midst of a Revolu-tion*, 119–24.

founded; following the affirmative congressional vote on the preamble, the One Hundred at once took steps to secure a new charter. Concessions made by Dickinson and his adherents in the house—abandoning the oath to the king and allowing the delegation a free vote on independence—were deemed insufficient. In June a provincial conference met, declared the colony's support for separation from Britain, and prepared for the constitutional convention to meet the following month. By fall a new government with a broad suffrage, an apportionment favorable to the west, and a powerful single chamber ruled in Pennsylvania.[63]

This successful attack on the hierarchical institutions presented the expansionists with a set of difficult choices. A few upper-class revolutionaries, such as George Bryan and Daniel Roberdeau, responded by wholeheartedly acclaiming the cause of the artisans and farmers. Another group fled to the British lines or attempted to sit out the British-American struggle. "The madness of the multitude," sighed James Allen in the spring of 1776, "is but one degree better than submission to the Tea Act."[64] Because of the unusual militancy of the Pennsylvania populace, more expansionists defected from the patriot ranks in Pennsylvania than in any of the other colonies studied here, with the possible exception of South Carolina. Most affluent protestors in the Quaker commonwealth, however, neither backed the lower classes nor became tories. Men like Dickinson, Robert Morris, and Joseph Reed labored both to restrain the poorer citizens and to aid the struggle against Britain. Dickinson, for example, opposed independence but, within days after that decision was made, led Pennsylvania troops against the British. That November he entered the new assembly and campaigned, in vain, for a second constitutional convention.[65]

63. "James Allen Diary," 187–88 (June 16, 1776); Hawke, *Midst of a Revolution*, 59–60, 84–85, 127–37, 139–45, 156–75; J. Paul Selsam, *The Pennsylvania Constitution of 1776* (Philadelphia, 1936).

64. "James Allen Diary," 186 (Mar. 6, 1776). The small, wealthy proprietary clique, largely defined by membership on the governor's council, shared the outlook of vacillating expansionists like Allen. Members of this circle, which included James Hamilton, Benjamin Chew, and Edward Shippen, Jr., typically became "neutrals" after 1776. See Ryerson, *Revolution Is Now Begun*, 12; Hawke, *Midst of a Revolution*, 26–30, 137. Owen S. Ireland, "The Ethnic-Religious Dimension of Pennsylvania Politics, 1778–1779," *WMQ*, 3d ser., xxx (1973), 423–44, shows that within the elite, Presbyterians (like Bryan and Roberdeau) were the most sympathetic to the common people.

65. "Speech of John Dickinson Opposing the Declaration of Independence, July 1, 1776," ed. J. H. Powell, *PMHB*, lxv (1941), 458–81; Joseph Reed to Robert Morris, July 18, 1776, Morris to Reed, July 20, 1776, Reed, *Joseph Reed*, i, 199, 200–202; Robert A. East, *Business Enterprise in the American Revolutionary Era* (New York, 1938), 126–48; John F. Roche, *Joseph Reed: A Moderate in the American Revolution* (New York, 1957); Stillé, *John Dickinson*, 201–11; "James Allen Diary," 188–96 (Jan. 25, 1777).

Although the influence of the farmers and artisans was greater in Pennsylvania than in the other commonwealths, the upper-class patriots gradually reasserted their dominance. The 1776 constitutional convention stopped well short of a social revolution. It voted down, for example, a resolution anathematizing rich men (the rejected plank stated "that an enormous proportion of property vested in a few individuals is dangerous to the rights . . . of mankind"); and though this gathering removed Willing and Dickinson from the congressional delegation, it reappointed Robert Morris and James Wilson.[66] In 1778 Joseph Reed was chosen governor, or more precisely, "President of the Executive Council," and he was followed in this office by Dickinson and Franklin, each of whom served three-year terms. Moreover, in 1781 the legislature (along with the Continental Congress) chartered the Bank of North of America, whose list of directors and subscribers reads like a who's who of the Philadelphia upper class. Thus, in the stormy years following independence, the difference between Pennsylvania and the other states, where dominant expansionists wrestled with the newly aroused farmers and mechanics, was more of degree than of kind.[67]

CONFLICTING PERSUASIONS

During the final revolutionary crisis many outspoken expansionists, nonexpansionists, and members of the populace elaborated their world views. The wealthy and articulate patriots in the commercial provinces were not of one mind in their approach to the future. A minority, while never wholly abandoning its vision of New World ascendancy, grew ever more moderate in the face of the mounting social turmoil. "This country must rise," sighed William Smith in 1774. "I wish we had a spirit more favorable to our interests."[68] During the months before independence, he hoped against hope that the worldly progress of America might continue within the framework of a London-centered imperium. He confided to his journal his prayer that Britain would display "a wise and liberal system of administration for retarding that catastrophe [i.e., independence] until the gradual transfer of her wealth and inhabitants has reared an

66. Proceedings of the constitutional convention are quoted in Foner, *Tom Paine*, 133.

67. Thomas M. Doerflinger, *A Vigorous Spirit of Enterprise: Merchants and Economic Development in Revolutionary Philadelphia* (Chapel Hill, N.C., 1986), 296–310; Jacob E. Cooke, *Tench Coxe and the Early Republic* (Chapel Hill, N.C., 1978), 86–92.

68. William Smith to Schuyler, n.d. [c. July 1774], *Memoirs of Smith*, I, 190.

empire for her in the western hemisphere superior to what she enjoys in the east."[69]

Like Smith, John Dickinson (whose ideological vacillation was already evident in the 1760s) grew ever more circumspect as the prospect of independence loomed larger. Dickinson's faith in America was unmistakable when he addressed the New Jersey assembly in the spring of 1775, urging that chamber not to forward a separate petition to Britain: "The eyes of all Europe are upon us. Until this controversy the strength and importance of this country were not known." He added that "the nations of Europe look with jealous eyes on the struggle. Britain has natural enemies, France and Spain. France will not sit still and suffer Britain to conquer," and he called on the lawmakers not to "break our Union."[70] But the strengthening of the popular forces in America unnerved Dickinson and cast a shadow across his vision of a mighty nation. On July 1, 1776, he urged his fellow congressmen to delay independence: "When our enemies are pressing us so vigorously, when we are in so wretched a state of preparation, when the sentiments and designs of our expected friends are so unknown to us, I am alarmed at this declaration being so vehemently presented." Dickinson continued, "I should be glad to know whether in twenty or thirty years this commonwealth of colonies may not be thought too unwieldy, and Hudson's River be a proper boundary for a separate commonwealth to the northward. I have a strong impression on my mind that this will take place."[71]

But most wealthy patriots were bolder than Smith, who belonged to that small group of expansionists who sided with the Crown, and most were less daunted by lower-class demands than Dickinson. Mercy Otis Warren, James Otis's sister, stood perhaps at the other end of the continuum. An early advocate of independence, she lectured John Adams in the fall of 1775, "It is time to leap into the *theater*, to unlock the bars, and open every gate that impedes the rise and growth of the American republic."[72] More typical of the affluent revolutionaries was Gouverneur Morris, who in May 1776 admonished the New York provincial convention to proceed toward separation with great care and secrecy lest the farmers and artisans be aroused, while in the same breath he painted a glowing picture of the nation he felt would soon emerge. Population would skyrocket, Morris pronounced, for "free republican states are always most thickly inhabited." Western settlements would complement those along the coast, commerce and

69. Ibid., 277 (June 9, 1776).
70. Stillé, *John Dickinson*, 151n.
71. "Speech of John Dickinson," 458–81, quotations on 480–81.
72. James Warren to John Adams, Nov. 14, 1775, *Warren-Adams Letters*, I, 184.

education would spread, and America would become an "asylum from oppression" for all peoples.[73]

In contrast, the nonexpansionists projected a grim future, in which the new American nation states would be bedeviled by rapacious foreign powers and endless, internecine warfare. Gazing into the future, Thomas Hutchinson opined: "After all, a new independent state may be added to the empires of the world, with perhaps the name of a free state; a few individuals may attain to greater degrees of dignity and power; but the inhabitants in general will never enjoy so great a share of natural liberty as they would have done if they had remained a dependent colony."[74]

Joseph Galloway, who in 1774 and the first months of 1775 stood forth as America's most articulate and outspoken nonexpansionist, also feared the trials awaiting independence. In *A Candid Examination of the Mutual Claims of Great Britain and the Colonies*, issued in February 1775, he argued that the mounting conflict with England would soon rend the social fabric: "The unthinking, ignorant multitude, in the east and west, are arming against the mother state, and the authority of government is silenced by the din of war." Moreover, an American victory would lead only to a new set of problems. Internal conflicts, Galloway remarked, "can only be decided by the sword, there being no other power to appeal to. The northern colonies, inured to military discipline and hardships will, in all probability, be the first to enter the list of military controversy; and, like the northern Saxons and Danes carry devastation and havoc over the southern." The one path to liberty, Galloway concluded, was his Plan of Union, which combined an American legislature with a governor appointed by the Crown.[75]

Other nonexpansionists echoed these dour prophecies, underscoring their lack of faith in the future of an independent America and the need for continuing ties with Britain. Jonathan Sewall of Massachusetts predicted that after separation either "a set of petty tyrants" would govern with "a rod of iron" or Americans would "live in a state of perpetual war with your neighbours, and suffer all the calamities and misfortunes incident to anarchy, confusion, and bloodshed."[76] His fellow colonist Chief Justice Peter Oliver warned that

73. Mintz, *Gouverneur Morris*, 58–59.
74. Hutchinson, *History of Massachusetts*, III, 255.
75. Galloway's pamphlet is reprinted in Merrill Jensen, ed., *Tracts of the American Revolution, 1763–1776* (Indianapolis, Ind., 1967), 350–99, quotations on 375, 386–88.
76. Jonathan Sewall as "Phileirene," in *Massachusetts Gazette and Boston Weekly News-Letter*, Jan. 16, 1775, quoted in Janice Potter, *The Liberty We Seek: Loyalist Ideology in Colonial New York and Massachusetts* (Cambridge, Mass., 1983), 34–35. The

"foreign powers will step in and share the plunder that remains, and those who are left to tell the story will be reduced to a more abject slavery than that which you now dread."[77] And Thomas Bradbury Chandler, an Anglican cleric from New York, supported such arguments by asserting that Britain was the vital source of North American well-being: "The colonies have hitherto flourished beyond example. They have become populous, both by natural increase and the yearly influx of foreigners. . . . And were they to pursue the same path which has brought them thus far, there is no doubt but that they would go on to flourish and prosper in the same proportion."[78]

Members of the lower classes, who were involved in the revolutionary movement as never before, also articulated their views and enunciated two broad contentions. First, they insisted, government must be democratized. The Reverend Thomas Allen, a spokesman for the farmers of western Massachusetts, observed in March 1776, "It concerned the people to see to it that while we are fighting against oppression from the King and parliament, that we did not suffer it to rise up in our own bowels."[79] In a similar vein, the town of Pittsfield exhorted the Massachusetts legislature: "We have always been persuaded that the people are the fountain of power. . . . A representative body . . . being but servants of the people cannot be greater than their masters and must be responsible to them."[80] Tom Paine lambasted the Pennsylvania oligarchs and demanded a frame of government more responsive to the common people. "Let the assemblies be annual with a president only," he declared. "The representation [must be] more equal."[81]

Second, some members of the populace, particularly the urban artisans, applauded the rise of a New World empire. This outlook, which dovetailed with expansionist beliefs, dated back to the me-

---

three quotations in this paragraph are drawn from the many statements Potter uses to support her contention that "the Loyalists depicted the colonies as potentially unstable, very different, heterogeneous communities with a history of trade rivalries, and boundary disputes, unable to unite even in the face of a common foe. The British Empire could provide the unity, sense of direction, and order which the colonies lacked" (171).

77. Peter Oliver, "An Address to the Soldiers of Massachusetts Bay . . .," *Massachusetts Gazette and Boston Weekly News-Letter*, Jan. 11, 1776, quoted in Potter, *Liberty We Seek*, 35–36.

78. Thomas B. Chandler, *A Friendly Address to All Reasonable Americans* (New York, 1774), quoted in Potter, *Liberty We Seek*, 171–72.

79. Affidavit of Thomas Allen, Mar. 2, 1776, Taylor, ed., *Massachusetts, Colony to Commonwealth*, 25.

80. Petition of Pittsfield, May 1776, ibid., 27–28.

81. Paine, *Common Sense* (1776), in Clark, ed., *Thomas Paine*, 3–44, quotation on 31. Foner, *Tom Paine*, 71–106, presents a perceptive analysis of the tract.

chanics' support of the boycotts of the late 1760s. Paine's tract urged a set of policies that would assist in the creation of a towering American commonwealth. Free trade was one pillar for the edifice: "Our plan is commerce, and that well attended to will secure us the peace and friendship of all Europe." A powerful navy would be a cornerstone for the new realm, while the national debt would form a durable cement: "No nation ought to be without a debt. A national debt is a national bond." Paine noted that the wealth contained in the western lands "may be hereafter supplied not only to the discharge of the present debt but to the constant support of government. No nation under heaven hath such an advantage as this." Rising above all else would be a "continental form of government," which would "keep the peace of the continent and preserve it inviolate from civil wars."[82]

Although most small farmers clamored for a greater voice in the government and seemed less concerned about the course of empire, the behavior of the working people in the cities was shaped by these two strands. Tom Paine's American career is a case in point. During the late 1770s, with the support of Philadelphia mechanics, he lobbied for price fixing and the close regulation of the merchants, but he reemerged in the 1780s as a propagandist for Robert and Gouverneur Morris's nationalist schemes. Similarly, the tradesmen in the northern cities, after a period of democratic ferment, became enthusiastic backers of the movement for a new federal constitution and then of a Jeffersonianism that promised both democratic reform and continental development.[83]

82. Paine, *Common Sense*, in Clark, ed., *Thomas Paine*, 3–44, quotations on 22, 29, 36, 39.

83. Foner, *Tom Paine*, 145–209; Olton, *Artisans for Independence*, 81–120; Alfred F. Young, "The Mechanics and the Jeffersonians," *Labor History*, v (1964), 247–76.

CHAPTER 15

Southern Colonies:
Maintaining Control

During the spring and early summer of 1776 Virginia expansionists were exceptional in their forthright advocacy of independence. On June 7 Richard Henry Lee introduced in the Continental Congress a resolution calling for a formal break, and a few weeks later Thomas Jefferson presented an elegant first draft of a supporting declaration.[1] By contrast, wealthy patriots in South Carolina, like their counterparts in the middle colonies and Massachusetts, struggled to make separation the last and not the first of the series of steps undertaken by the united provinces. "A declaration of independence, the form of a confederation of these colonies, and a scheme for a treaty with foreign powers will be laid before [Congress]," Edward Rutledge told New Yorker John Jay. "Whether we shall be able effectually to oppose the first and infuse wisdom into the others will depend in a great measure upon the exertions of the honest and sensible part of the members."[2]

Virginia and South Carolina, despite their obvious similarities—both relied on slave labor, and both shipped their staples to the mother country—cannot be grouped together as neatly as can the commercial provinces. The relative docility of the poorer farmers in Virginia emboldened the affluent patriots and helped create a set of nonexpansionists willing to cooperate with their factional opponents in daring measures. The outspokenness of South Carolina's common

1. Jefferson, "Original Rough Draught" of the Declaration of Independence, June 11–July 4, 1776, *The Papers of Thomas Jefferson*, ed. Julian P. Boyd et al. (Princeton, 1950–), I, 423–28.
2. Edward Rutledge to John Jay, June 29, 8, 1776, *Letters of Members of the Continental Congress*, ed. Edmund C. Burnett, 8 vols. (Washington, D.C., 1921–36), I, 517, 476–77.

people, however, made politics in the rice colony more akin to the bitter class and party wars found in the northern commonwealths. As in every province, during the months between the Boston Port Act and independence, expansionists in Virginia and South Carolina joined two battles: the first against the nonexpansionists and the second with the revolutionary lower classes. In the Old Dominion the first phase was characterized by a remarkable spirit of compromise, while in the rice colony the patriots offered their enemies no quarter. During the second clash the poorer citizens of South Carolina proved to be far more dogged antagonists than did the small farmers of Virginia.

VIRGINIA

News of the Boston Port Act revivified the struggle between the Virginia expansionists and nonexpansionists. Learning in May 1774 of the ministerial decision to punish Boston, Northern Necker Richard Henry Lee prepared a spirited set of resolutions but was, as he explained to Samuel Adams, "prevented from offering them by many worthy members, who wished to have the public business first finished."[3] Rebuffed in this effort, Lee and his fellow expansionists attempted a different tack. "The lead in the house on these subjects being no longer left to the old members," observed Thomas Jefferson in his "Autobiography," "Mr. Henry, R. H. Lee, Fr[ancis] L[ightfoot] Lee, three or four other members whom I do not recollect, and myself, agreeing that we must boldly take an unequivocal stand in the line with Massachusetts, determined to meet." The result of this caucus was the proposal of a "day of general fasting and prayer" for June 1.[4] The nonexpansionists in the lower chamber accepted this suggestion and allowed the resolution to pass unanimously, but the wealthy planters in the council, who epitomized the minority of nonexpansionists opposed to the revolutionary movement, condemned the resolution. Governor Dunmore, fully in sympathy with the sentiments of the upper house, dissolved the assembly.[5]

3. Richard Henry Lee to Samuel Adams, June 23, 1774, *The Letters of Richard Henry Lee*, ed. James C. Ballagh, 2 vols. (New York, 1911–14), I, 111.
4. Jefferson, "Autobiography," in *The Writings of Thomas Jefferson*, ed. Andrew A. Lipscomb, 18 vols. (Washington, D.C., 1903), I, 9–11, quotation on 6; Lord Dunmore to Dartmouth, May 29, 1774, *Writings of George Washington*, ed. J. C. Fitzpatrick, 39 vols. (Washington, D.C., 1931–44), III, 215n; George Mason to Martin Cockburn, May 26, 1774, *The Papers of George Mason, 1725–1792*, ed. Robert A. Rutland, 2 vols. (Chapel Hill, N.C., 1970), I, 190.
5. *The Diary of Colonel Landon Carter of Sabine Hall, 1752–1778*, ed. Jack P. Greene, 2 vols. (Charlottesville, Va., 1965), II, 818 (June 3, 1774); Jefferson, "Autobiography," I, 10.

Defying his dictum, the burgesses reconvened as an extralegal body, and with little dissent agreed to support Boston's cause by boycotting East Indian commodities and by endorsing the call for an intercolonial congress. Richard Henry Lee regretted only that the resolves were not still stronger, commenting that the "conduct of the members was surely much too feeble."[6] After this assembly disbanded, letters requesting aid arrived from Boston. Most of the burgesses had left town, but Speaker Peyton Randolph on May 31 managed to convene twenty-five lawmakers. This rump, which included prominent members of both factions, declared itself too small to make policy but requested that members of the last house assemble August 1 to determine a course of action.[7]

During the summer months, the Northern Neckers and their allies took the lead in advocating a spirited resistance to Britain, adopting, for example, a more daring position than the nonexpansionists in the debate over paying British creditors. In the county meetings held to instruct the delegates to the August convention, such expansionists as George Mason, Patrick Henry, Richard Henry Lee, and Landon Carter argued that Virginia should close its courts and so halt debt payments to British firms. Landon Carter countered the assertion that "private justice obliges the payment of our debts" by stating that "public happiness in this case is against either private justice or private [happiness]."[8] Six of the eight counties calling for the end of debt proceedings were located in the Northern Neck. By contrast, nonexpansionists insisted that the planters honor their obligations. Edmund Pendleton averred that closed courts could "introduce anarchy and disorder," and Robert Beverley insisted that nonpayment was "full of cruelty and injustice." Despite the reservations of planters residing south of the Rappahannock, the county judiciaries through Virginia quietly ended debt proceedings.[9]

6. R. H. Lee to Samuel Adams, June 23, 1774, *Letters of Lee*, I, 112; An Association Signed by 89 Members of the Late House of Burgesses, May 27, 1774, *Papers of Jefferson*, I, 107–8.

7. Peyton Randolph and Others to Members of the Late House of Burgesses, May 31, 1774, *Papers of Jefferson*, I, 111–12; Washington to George William Fairfax, June 10, 1774, *Writings of Washington*, III, 222–24.

8. *Diary of Carter*, II, 946 (Sept. 20, 1775), 822 (June 8, 1774), 847 (Aug. 8, 1774); James Parker to Charles Steuart, June 17, 1774, cited in Emory G. Evans, "Planter Indebtedness and the Coming of the Revolution in Virginia," *WMQ*, 3d ser., XIX (1962), 530–31.

9. Edmund Pendleton to Ralph Wormeley, Jr., July 28, 1774, *The Letters and Papers of Edmund Pendleton, 1734–1803*, ed. David John Mays, 2 vols. (Charlottesville, Va., 1967), I, 97; Robert Beverley to Landon Carter, Aug. 28, 1774, quoted in Evans, "Planter Indebtedness," 530, and see 530–31. The proceedings of the counties during June and July 1774 are reprinted in William J. Van Schreeven and Robert L. Scribner,

Expansionists were also more active in encouraging popular demonstrations by what one editorialist called the "middling and lower classes of people."[10] The fast day resolution, initiated by the Northern Neckers and their supporters, was designed, in Jefferson's words, to arouse "our people from the lethargy into which they had fallen."[11] Moreover, in response to the exhortations of the local elite, the populace in the Northern Neck continued to be the most militant in the province. David Wardrobe, a schoolteacher, reported in June: "In the county of Richmond about ten days ago, I saw an elegant effigy of Lord North hanged and burnt in the midst of a vast concourse of people. . . . Then [a member of the gentry] . . . mounted on an eminence, and harangued the people, acquainting them of all the efforts Parliament had made to abridge them of their liberties." Wardrobe described similar events in Westmoreland County: "Yesterday we had a meeting of freeholders of this county at our courthouse, where there were some of the greatest men in the colony encouraging the common people to a like steady adherence to [a plan of nonintercourse]."[12] Northern Necker Landon Carter also spoke at his local courthouse "to convince the people that the case of the Bostonians was the case of all America." He noted happily, "There seemed to be an assent to all I said."[13]

South of the Rappahannock the local proceedings during May, June, and July appeared more orderly, and leaders were less quick to rouse the small farmers to defiant action. Few observers reported popular demonstrations, and the outlook of many of the less wealthy citizens seems aptly described by a merchant who stated that "honest 6 hogshead planters downward know little or nothing of this

---

eds., *Revolutionary Virginia: The Road to Independence* (Charlottesville, Va., 1973–   ), I, 109–68; Merrill Jensen, *The Founding of a Nation: A History of the American Revolution, 1763–1776* (New York, 1968), 476–77. The two significant exceptions to this factional pattern were Washington, who opposed closing the courts, and Robert Carter Nicholas, who apparently favored it. On Washington, see his letters to Bryan Fairfax, July 4, 20, 1774, *Writings of Washington*, III, 229, 234. On Nicholas, see Evans, "Planter Indebtedness," 530–31, but also Robert Carter Nicholas, *Considerations on the Present State of Virginia Examined*, [c. Aug. 25, 1774], Van Schreeven and Scribner, eds., *Revolutionary Virginia*, I, 279.

10. *Virginia Gazette* (Purdie), July 14, 1776, quoted in Rhys Isaac, "Dramatizing the Ideology of Revolution: Popular Mobilization in Virginia, 1774 to 1776," *WMQ*, 3d ser., XXXIII (1976), 369.

11. Jefferson, "Autobiography," I, 9–11, quotation on 6; *Diary of Carter*, II, 818 (June 3, 1774).

12. David Wardrobe to Archibald Provan, June 30, 1774, Van Schreeven and Scribner, eds., *Revolutionary Virginia*, II, 135–36.

13. *Diary of Carter*, II, 821–22 (June 8, 1774); *Journal and Letters of Philip Vickers Fithian, 1773–1774: A Plantation Tutor of the Old Dominion*, ed. Hunter D. Farish (Williamsburg, Va., 1965), 111 (May 31, 1774), 122 (June 18, 1774).

accursed dispute."[14] In Norfolk the meeting of the freeholders in July urged that local committees should consist only of "respectable men, fixed and settled inhabitants of their respective counties."[15] Attorney General John Randolph was even more outspokenly elitist, declaring that the "ignorant vulgar" were unfit to "manage the reins of government."[16] Randolph ultimately would side with the British, but even those nonexpansionists untainted by loyalist leanings adopted a moderate stance; the county meetings held south of the Rappahannock (and east of the row of Blue Ridge counties) were far more likely than their expansionist counterparts to reaffirm their loyalty to the Crown and condemn the Bostonians for dumping the tea and were less likely to call for nonexportation or the end of debt proceedings.[17]

Despite their real differences, the two upper-class Virginia factions cooperated more readily than the parties in the other colonies studied here, and this amity made possible a bold common front in the late summer and fall of 1774. The Williamsburg convention, meeting at the beginning of August, adopted a set of forceful initiatives that outdistanced most other provinces. Although the majority at the gathering refused to sanction the de facto closing of the courts, the convention agreed to the nonimportation of British wares and slaves after November 1, 1774, and the nonexportation of Virginia produce after August 10, 1775. Counties were instructed to strike committees, which would make certain that all merchants and planters complied with the association. The resolves electrified patriots. "Saw the Virginia paper," John Adams remarked. "The spirit of the people is prodigious. Their resolutions are really grand."[18] The convention also selected a balanced slate of four nonexpansionist congressmen, including Peyton Randolph and Edmund Pendleton, and three expansionists, Washington, Richard Henry Lee, and Patrick Henry. Whatever differences separated these seven individuals, their fervor compared favorably to that of other delegations, where nonexpansionists flatly opposed the revolutionary movement. Exclaimed

14. Quoted in Emory G. Evans, *Thomas Nelson of Yorktown: Revolutionary Virginian* (Charlottesville, Va., 1975), 37; Marquis de Chastellux, *Travels in North America in the Years 1780, 1781, and 1782*, trans. Howard C. Rice, Jr., 2 vols. (Chapel Hill, N.C., 1963) II, 429 (Apr. 26, 1782).

15. Norfolk County and Borough Meeting, July 9, 1774, Van Schreeven and Scribner, eds., *Revolutionary Virginia*, I, 150.

16. John Randolph, *A Plea for Moderation*, [c. early July 1774], ibid., 206; Robert Beverley to [?], Sept. 6, 1774, Robert Beverley Letterbook, microfilm at CWF.

17. Van Schreeven and Scribner, eds., *Revolutionary Virginia*, I, 109–68.

18. *Diary and Autobiography of John Adams*, ed. L. H. Butterfield et al., 4 vols. (Cambridge, Mass., 1961), II, 109 (Aug. 23, 1774); Resolutions and Association of the Virginia Convention of 1774, Aug. 1–6, 1774, *Papers of Jefferson*, I, 137–41.

Adams, "These gentlemen from Virginia appear to be the most spirited and consistent of any."[19]

The ability of the two parties to work together was evident also in the strong support for the continental association. The nonintercourse pact of the Continental Congress copied, with some modifications, the Virginia resolves, and the planters enthusiastically welcomed the accord. Most counties soon formed committees of observation, and instances of enforcement on both sides of the Rappahannock are plentiful. The panels strictly policed nonimportation, which began November 1, and, more generally, scrutinized the behavior of the citizenry. Acts of public contrition became the order of the day; for example, in Caroline County, one Andrew Leckie apologized to the committee and to an assembled crowd: "I was so unguarded and imprudent, as to address myself to a Negro boy who was present [while a petition was being circulated], in this indecent manner, 'Piss Jack, turn about my boy and sign.' "[20]

The traders, however, who overwhelmingly were factors for British and particularly Scottish houses, would prove refractory. The merchants' first response to the pact was conciliatory; the body of traders meeting at Williamsburg in November (according to a newspaper account, "supposed to be between 4 and 500" strong) "voluntarily and generally" signed the association. Nevertheless, many planters suspected, and with justice, that the majority of these individuals had little intention of keeping their word.[21]

Despite such cooperation, partisan differences remained apparent during the fall of 1774 and the ensuing winter. Expansionists took the lead in efforts to arm the commonwealth; the Fairfax County committee, guided by Washington and Mason, became in September the first panel to recruit a patriot company. During the next months the Fairfax board remained in the vanguard, appealing in January 1775 to the other counties to raise men and assuming the power of taxation to help pay for war materiel. Other Northern Neck counties, such as Prince William, Richmond, and possibly Northumberland, were active, as was the frontier region, where many individuals had taken

19. *Diary and Autobiography of John Adams*, II, 120 (Sept. 2, 1774); Convention of 1774, The Election of Deputies to Attend a General Congress, Aug. 5, 1774, Van Schreeven and Scribner, eds., *Revolutionary Virginia*, I, 227–29.

20. Caroline County Committee, Oct. 13, 1774, Van Schreeven and Scribner, eds., *Revolutionary Virginia*, II, 161, and more generally, see the county proceedings reprinted 159–247.

21. *Virginia Gazette* (Purdie), Nov. 10, 1774, quoted in Jensen, *Founding of a Nation*, 523–24; Arthur M. Schlesinger, *The Colonial Merchants and the American Revolution, 1763–1776* (New York, 1919), 509–10.

part in an Indian war during 1774. By contrast, south of the Rappahannock and east of the mountains few districts drilled soldiers before March 1775. When Virginians met in convention at Richmond that month, the delegates pronounced the province, on balance, ill prepared for war: "The legal and necessary disciplining of the militia has been much neglected, and a proper provision of arms and ammunition has not been made, to the evident danger of the community in case of invasion."[22]

The debate between the two upper-class factions over forming county militias came to a head at the Richmond gathering. Patrick Henry, seconded by Richard Henry Lee and supported by such expansionists as Washington and Jefferson, offered a set of resolutions that began, "A well-regulated militia, composed of gentlemen and yeomen, is the natural strength and only security of a free government" and concluded with a recommendation that "this colony be immediately put into a posture of defense."[23] Nicholas, Pendleton, Peyton Randolph, George Wythe, and other nonexpansionists opposed the resolves. According to most observers Henry's impassioned oratory ("I know not what course others may take; but as for me, give me liberty or give me death") made the difference, and the resolutions were adopted by a narrow margin, reportedly sixty-five to sixty. With the conciliation typical of factional warfare in Virginia, the defeated nonexpansionists agreed to help implement Henry's resolves.[24]

Even the leading patriots, however, were divided in the spring of 1775 on the wisdom of an armed clash with royal troops, and some expansionists joined the opposing faction in counseling caution after Governor Dunmore on April 21 moved powder from the Williamsburg magazine to a warship. Nonexpansionist voices were the loudest urging a peaceful response; Pendleton, Nicholas, and Peyton Randolph persuaded the populace to remain calm and called on the

22. Proceedings of Convention, Mar. 25, 1775, Van Schreeven and Scribner, eds., *Revolutionary Virginia*, II, 374–75, and see the proceedings of the counties, 163–321; William Black to Boston Committee, n.d., Washington to William Milnor, Jan. 23, 1775, Gov. Dunmore to Dartmouth, Dec. 24, 1774, *Writings of Washington*, III, 247n, 266, 248n; Fairfax County Militia Association, Sept. 21, 1774, Remarks on Annual Election for the Fairfax Independent Company, [c. Apr. 17–26, 1775], *Papers of Mason*, I, 210–12, 229–32; *Diary and Autobiography of John Adams*, II, 117 (Aug. 23, 1774); Douglas S. Freeman, *George Washington*, 6 vols. (New York, 1954), III, 400–402; Rhys Isaac, *The Transformation of Virginia, 1740–1790* (Chapel Hill, N.C., 1982), 256–58.

23. Proceedings of Convention, Mar. 23, 1775, Van Schreeven and Scribner, eds., *Revolutionary Virginia*, II, 366–70, quotation on 366.

24. Proceedings of Convention, Mar. 23, 1775, ibid., 366–70, quotation on 369; William Wirt Henry, *Patrick Henry: Life, Correspondence, and Speeches*, 3 vols. (New York, 1981), I, 255–75; Jefferson, Appendix to "Autobiography," *Writings of Jefferson*, I, 168.

independent companies that were preparing for a descent on Williamsburg to return home. Northern Neckers Washington and Richard Henry Lee seconded this advice, although not all expansionists were willing to countenance so tame a reaction. Patrick Henry, fired up by the governor's move and by the news that reached Virginia April 29 of fighting at Lexington and Concord, led an armed band to Williamsburg, halting only when a frightened Dunmore agreed to pay for the powder. James Madison, a rising young politician in the Blue Ridge county of Orange, also favored firm measures and was outraged that some "gentlemen below . . . discovered a pusillanimity little comporting with their professions or the name of Virginian."[25] Moreover, a majority of the militias responding to the challenge came from the areas linked to the expansionists. Several Northern Neck districts mustered, and a soldier at Fredericksburg justly noted, "All the frontier counties of Virginia were in motion."[26]

The increasing firmness of resistance to Britain convinced Governor Dunmore and the minority of nonexpansionists with loyalist leanings that they no longer had a place in the mainstream of provincial politics. As early as December 1774 most members of the faculty of the College of William and Mary made clear their dislike of the continental association. In March 1775 Attorney General John Randolph refused to attend the Richmond Convention because of his dissatisfaction with the revolutionaries' actions. And the majority in the upper house took a similarly dark view of the escalating protests; when Henry marched on the capital, the councillors declared their "detestation of that licentious and ungovernable spirit that is gone forth and misleads the once happy people of this country."[27] For these tories, Governor Dunmore's decision in June to abandon the government meant the disappearance of their last pillar of support. Dunmore had reconvened the burgesses June 1 hoping the lawmakers would prove conciliatory, but they rejected Lord North's most recent

25. James Madison to William Bradford, May 9, 1775, *The Papers of James Madison*, ed. William T. Hutchinson and William M. E. Rachal (Chicago, 1962–   ), i, 145; David John Mays, *Edmund Pendleton, 1721–1803: A Biography*, 2 vols. (Cambridge, Mass., 1952), ii, 14–16; Richard R. Beeman, *Patrick Henry: A Biography* (New York, 1974), 68–70; Edmund Pendleton to William Woodford, May 30, 1775, *Letters and Papers of Pendleton*, i, 103.

26. Michael Wallace to Gustavus Brown Wallace, May 14, 1775, quoted in Mays, *Edmund Pendleton*, ii, 355, and see 14–15; Independent Company of Spotsylvania to Washington, Apr. 20, 1775, Independent Company of Prince William to Washington, Apr. 26, 1775, Independent Company of Albemarle to Washington, Apr. 29, 1775, *Letters to Washington and Accompanying Papers*, ed. Stanislaus M. Hamilton, 5 vols. (Boston, 1898–1902), v, 162, 163–64, 165.

27. Councillors quoted in Beeman, *Patrick Henry*, 71; Schlesinger, *Colonial Merchants*, 509; Freeman, *George Washington*, iii, 402.

proposal, refused to reopen the courts, and demanded the key to the public magazine in Williamsburg. The governor, condemning the "blind and unmeasurable fury" of the patriots, slipped aboard HMS *Fowey*.[28]

With Dunmore's departure from Williamsburg, Virginia's pro-British nonexpansionists found their path rocky. Some individuals, such as John Randolph, emigrated to England. Others, including councillors Richard Corbin and Ralph Wormeley, retreated to their plantations and in general lived unmolested. Robert Beverley, who in July 1775 pronounced himself "a sorrowful spectator of these tumultuous times," pursued a similar passive course. William Byrd III, who that same month complained, "The moderate are awed into silence, and have no opportunity to show their allegiance," anguished about his position and on New Year's Day 1777 shot himself.[29] Still others joined Dunmore's forces and assisted his efforts to reconquer Virginia. In all, the nonexpansionists who stood apart from the revolutionary movement were a comparatively small group, numbering in the dozens rather than the hundreds, as was the case in the other colonies studied here.[30]

One other group that would ultimately side with the mother country—the British merchants resident in Virginia—seemed less immediately affected by Dunmore's fall. These factors maintained a facade of cooperation with the revolutionaries at least until the autumn of 1775. But for many traders such amity was often little more than hypocrisy, and their private letters bristled with anger. "Everything is managed by committee," one Scot groused to his partner early in 1775, "selling and pricing goods, inspecting books, forcing some to sign scandalous concessions, and by such bullying conduct they expect to bring government to their own terms."[31] Another merchant noted that the factors had accepted a document drafted by the county committee because they "thought it expedient, not from any conviction, but from notions of self-preservation with peace and quietness

28. Dunmore quoted in Evans, *Thomas Nelson*, 47–48.
29. Robert Beverley to John Backhouse, July 12, 1775, Calhoon, ed., "A Sorrowful Spectator," *VMHB*, LXXIII (1965), 42; William Byrd III to Sir Jeffrey Amherst, July 30, 1775, *The Correspondence of the Three William Byrds of Westover, Virginia, 1684–1776*, ed. Marion Tinling (Charlottesville, Va., 1977), II, 812, and see 613; Isaac S. Harrell, *Loyalism in Virginia: Chapters in the Economic History of the Revolution* (Durham, N.C., 1926), 49; Mary Beth Norton, ed., "John Randolph's 'Plan of Accommodations,'" *WMQ*, 3d ser., XXVIII (1971), 104.
30. Wallace Brown, *The King's Friends: The Composition and Motives of the American Loyalist Claimants* (Providence, R.I., 1965), 177–91, 329–32; Harrell, *Loyalism in Virginia*, 33–53.
31. James Parker to Charles Steuart, Jan. 27, 1775, quoted in William M. Dabney, "Letters from Norfolk: Scottish Merchants View the Revolutionary Crisis," in Darrett B. Rutman, ed., *The Old Dominion: Essays for Thomas Perkins Abernethy* (Charlottesville, Va., 1964), 188; Harrell, *Loyalism in Virginia*, 33, 47.

to sign it."[32] By the end of 1775 the hostility between the traders and patriots would be fully in the open.

With the ousting of Virginia tories from all positions of power in the early summer of 1775 the second phase of the revolutionary crisis began: the expansionists increasingly turned their attention to the restless lower classes—both black and white. As earlier, the Northern Neckers and their allies led the continuing protests against Britain, and the two elite factions worked together on crucial issues.

During the second half of 1775 Dunmore's efforts to reconquer Virginia temporarily united the two parties around a plan of stout resistance. Dunmore began his campaign with a series of harassing raids. "Where he finds a defenseless place," a Norfolk resident explained, "he lands, plunders the plantation, and carries off the Negroes."[33] In response to these attacks, the provincial convention, which succeeded the House of Burgesses, raised two regiments, struck paper money, and created a powerful committee of safety that included both expansionists, such as George Mason and Thomas Ludwell Lee, and nonexpansionists, for example, Carter Braxton and Edmund Pendleton. This committee energetically opposed Dunmore's efforts to establish a mainland base of operations in the Norfolk area, where many tory-leaning merchants made their home. Although the governor was victorious in a skirmish in mid-November, the provincial army roundly defeated him early in December, ending his control of any Virginia soil. The committee of safety also finally took steps to expel foreign merchants, many of whom had revealed their true colors after Dunmore's November triumph.[34]

Men from both parties were particularly incensed by the governor's efforts to liberate slaves and servants. During the summer and early fall of 1775 Lord Dunmore pursued an informal policy of welcoming any blacks who reached his fleet. Then after his victory in mid-November he broadcast a proclamation declaring "all indented servants, Negroes, or others (appertaining to rebels), free" if they would bear arms for the Crown.[35] Several hundred slaves rushed to the governor's standard, underscoring for upper-class Virginians the grave danger in Dunmore's scheme. Nonexpansionist Robert Carter Nicholas anxiously wrote the Virginia delegates that the "infamous

32. Quoted in Mays, *Edmund Pendleton*, I, 302–3.
33. Letter of Oct. 28, 1775, quoted in Benjamin Quarles, "Lord Dunmore as Liberator," *WMQ*, 3d ser., XV (1958), 497.
34. Edmund Pendleton to R. H. Lee, Nov. 27, 1775, Edmund Pendleton to William Woodford, Dec. 7, 1775, *Letters and Papers of Pendleton*, I, 132–33, 137; Mays, *Edmund Pendleton*, II, 36; Beeman, *Patrick Henry*, 75; Jensen, *Founding of a Nation*, 644.
35. Proclamation, Nov. 7, 1775, quoted in Quarles, "Dunmore as Liberator," 494, and see 497–501; John Page to Jefferson, Nov. 24, 1775, *Papers of Jefferson*, I, 265.

proclamation" was "an object worthy the most serious attention of the congress," and expansionist George Washington exclaimed to a correspondent that Dunmore must be "instantly crushed," adding "that which renders the measure indispensably necessary is the Negroes. For if he gets formidable, numbers will be tempted to join."[36] Fortunately for the planter class, Dunmore's defeat in December drove him from the mainland, making access for runaways difficult. Moreover, disease swept through Dunmore's "Ethiopian regiment," decimating the corps of black soldiers supporting the royal cause.[37]

During the first half of 1776 the upper-class parties confronted a challenge from another quarter: the increasingly self-aware and assertive yeomanry. The new reality in Virginia was lower-class anger directed not just at England but also at the gentry. "I need only tell you of one definition that I heard of Independency," Landon Carter informed Washington. "It was expected to be a form of government that by being independent of the rich men, every man would then be able to do as he pleased."[38] Dr. George Gilmer devoted much of his address to the Albemarle County freeholders to a refutation of the small farmers' complaints. As he put it, "Some declare the gentlemen have more at stake and ought to fight to protect it, but that none enter the service but as officers."[39] In April a wealthy correspondent of Jefferson's wondered, if adversity mounted, how long the populace would remain peaceful: "Might they not be induced to give up the authors of their misfortunes, their leaders, who had led them into such a scrape, and be willing to sacrifice them to a reconciliation?"[40]

Few Virginia expansionists, however, construed the grumbling of the populace as a reason for muting the struggle against Britain or for backing away from a measure that seemed ever more necessary: independence. Soon after the appearance of Thomas Paine's *Common Sense*—a tract that sent shudders down the spines of those who feared social change—Washington praised its "sound doctrine and unanswerable reasoning," and Richard Henry Lee declared himself a

36. Robert Carter Nicholas to Virginia Delegation in Congress, Nov. 25, 1775, *Papers of Jefferson*, I, 267; Washington to Joseph Reed, Dec. 15, 1775, Washington to R. H. Lee, Dec. 26, 1775, *Writings of Washington*, IV, 167, 186.

37. Members of Virginia Committee of Safety to Maryland Convention, Dec. 29, 1775, *Letters and Papers of Pendleton*, I, 144; Quarles, "Dunmore as Liberator," 503–6.

38. Landon Carter to Washington, May 9, 1776, Peter Force, ed., *American Archives*, 4th and 5th ser., 9 vols. (Washington, D.C., 1837–53), 4th ser., VI, 390; Francis Lightfoot Lee to Landon Carter, Apr. 9, 1776, *Letters of Congress*, I, 417; *Diary of Carter*, II, 1030–31 (May 1, 1776).

39. George Gilmer, Address to Inhabitants of Albemarle, n.d. [c. early 1776], Virginia Historical Society *Collections*, n.s., VI (1887), 123–24.

40. John Page to Jefferson, Apr. 26, 1776, *Papers of Jefferson*, I, 288.

"prodigious admirer" of the pamphlet.[41] Similarly, Jefferson was a vigorous advocate of separation and saw no reason to fear popular opinion on the questions of the day. "When at home I took great pains to enquire into the sentiments of the people on that head [independence]," he remarked in May. "In the upper counties I think I may safely say nine out of ten are for it."[42] George Mason and Patrick Henry were also enthusiastic supporters of a New World republic. The one notable exception to this rule was Northern Necker Landon Carter, who became increasingly worried about lower-class dissension, loudly condemned the "absurd arguments" in *Common Sense*, and wondered whether Virginia "might fall into a worse situation from internal oppression and commotions than might have been obtained by a serious as well as cautious reconciliation."[43]

By contrast, nonexpansionists argued that the democratic ferment strengthened the case for slowing the rush to independence. In April, Carter Braxton remarked, with an eye on the Old Dominion, that if independence "was to be now asserted, the continent would be torn in pieces by intestine wars and convulsions."[44] Speaking from a similar viewpoint, Richard Bland labeled the author of *Common Sense* a "blockhead and ignoramus," and Edmund Pendleton argued that Britain had "met so many rubs" that it was earnestly seeking compromise.[45] Planters residing south of the Rappahannock acted as a brake within the committee of safety and within the congressional delegation. As John Adams recollected, "Jealousies and divisions appeared among the delegates of no state more remarkably than among those of Virginia. . . . Mr. Samuel Adams and myself were very intimate with Mr. [Richard Henry] Lee, and he agreed perfectly with us in the great system of our policy and by his means we kept a majority of the delegates of Virginia with us, but [Benjamin] Harrison, Pendleton, and some others showed their jealousy of this intimacy plainly enough at times."[46]

41. Washington to Joseph Reed, Jan. 31, Feb. 10, 1776, *Writings of Washington*, IV, 297, 321; *Diary of Carter*, II, 1007 (Mar. 29, 1776); R. H. Lee to Patrick Henry, Apr. 20, 1776, *Letters of Lee*, I, 176–77.

42. Jefferson to Thomas Nelson, May 16, 1776, *Papers of Jefferson*, I, 292.

43. *Diary of Carter*, II, 1046 (May 29, 1776), 980–81 (Feb. 14, 1776), 1041 (May 18, 1776), 1050 (June 14, 1776); George Mason to R. H. Lee, May 18, 1776, *Papers of Mason*, I, 271. Henry, however, also argued that confederation should precede independence. See Patrick Henry to John Adams, May 20, 1776, Henry, *Patrick Henry*, I, 412–13.

44. Carter Braxton to Landon Carter, Apr. 14, 1776, *Letters of Congress*, I, 420–21; Joseph Reed to Washington, Mar. 15, 1776, *Writings of Washington*, IV, 455n.

45. Charles Lee to R. H. Lee, Apr. 5, 1776, Letters to R. H. Lee, microfilm at CWF; Edmund Pendleton to R. H. Lee, April 20, 1776, *Letters and Papers of Pendleton*, I, 163.

46. *Diary and Autobiography of John Adams*, III, 367–68 (Autobiography); Charles Lee to R. H. Lee, Apr. 5, 1776, Letters to R. H. Lee; Charles Lee to Washington, Apr. 5, 1776, *Writings of Washington*, IV, 451n.

Despite the hesitation of the nonexpansionists during the first months of 1776, the two parties came together in May to support independence. The common people, for all their fractiousness, never manifested the strength or coherence of the less wealthy citizens in other provinces, and most members of the planter elite could risk separation from Britain without fearing wrenching change. The provincial convention that met May 6 elected Pendleton chairman and after several days of routine matters turned to the question of independence. Patrick Henry then introduced and eloquently argued for a resolution that Virginia congressmen "be enjoined in the strongest and most positive manner to exert their ability in procuring" a declaration of independence.[47] The ensuing debate turned not on substance but on the subtleties of wording, and the next day the convention, toning down Henry's language, agreed that the delegates "be instructed to propose" separation and also to support the establishment of foreign alliances and a plan of confederation.[48] Only Robert Carter Nicholas spoke against independence but, in the characteristic fashion of the majority of Virginia nonexpansionists, "declared that he would rise or fall with his country." Cooperation between the two elite factions had once again helped place Virginians squarely in the forefront of the revolutionary movement.[49]

In the May and June debates over a new state constitution the two factions were separated by a definite but never unbridgeable gap, with the nonexpansionists leaning toward more elitist models and the expansionists advocating more popular plans. Pendleton, for example, favored a senate composed of "people of great property" serving for life, and Carter Braxton set forth an autocratic scheme designed to prevent the "tumult and riot incident to simple democracy."[50] In contrast, expansionist Richard Henry Lee denounced Braxton's charter for its "aristocratic pride," and Patrick Henry called it "a silly thing."[51] But in the place of Braxton's scheme the two men

47. Henry, *Patrick Henry*, I, 386–95, quotation on 395; Edmund Randolph, *History of Virginia*, ed. Arthur Shaffer (Charlottesville, Va., 1970), 250.
48. Resolutions of the Virginia Convention Calling upon Congress for a Declaration of Independence, May 15, 1776, *Letters and Papers of Pendleton*, I, 178–79; Patrick Henry to John Adams, May 20, 1776, Henry, *Patrick Henry*, I, 412, and see 394–401; Mays, *Edmund Pendleton*, II, 106–11.
49. Randolph, *History of Virginia*, 251. On Nicholas's outlook, see Isaac, *Transformation of Virginia*, 238–39.
50. Edmund Pendleton to Jefferson, Aug. 10, 1776, Edmund Pendleton to Carter Braxton, May 12, 1776, *Letters and Papers of Pendleton*, I, 198, 177; Braxton quoted in Jensen, *Founding of a Nation*, 665; Thomas Ludwell Lee to R. H. Lee, June 1, 1776, quoted in *Papers of Mason*, I, 275; Virginia Declaration of Rights, May–June, 1776, ibid., 274–91; Randolph, *History of Virginia*, 253.
51. R. H. Lee to Edmund Pendleton, May 12, 1776, *Letters of Lee*, I, 190; Patrick Henry to John Adams, May 20, 1776, Henry, *Patrick Henry*, I, 413; William Fleming to Jefferson, July 27, 1776, *Papers of Jefferson*, I, 475.

elevated John Adams's *Thoughts on Government,* a plan that most northerners aptly considered far from democratic. Thomas Jefferson's proposed reforms—including broader suffrage, local election of sheriffs, proportional representation, and the distribution of property to the landless—marked him as an extremist within his own party. Unsurprisingly, given the comparative weakness of the yeomanry, the document adopted by the convention made few concessions in the direction of democracy. The new frame of government enhanced the power of the planter-legislators by creating a weak executive, left the restrictive colonial voting requirements intact, and preserved the distribution of seats which denied the frontier counties an equal voice in the house.[52]

Not only did the Virginia upper class remain firmly in control after independence, but also (uniquely among the commonwealths studied here) the two elite factions continued relatively intact. Indeed, the partisan groups that had emerged in the late 1740s would still be discernable in the conflicts of the 1780s, 1790s, and early nineteenth century. For example, the fight over religious freedom, which culminated in 1786 with the passage of Jefferson's bill disestablishing the Anglican church, pitted expansionists Mason, Madison, and Jefferson against nonexpansionists Nicholas, Braxton, and Pendleton. Moreover, in Virginia the Federalist and Democratic-Republican parties of the early national period built upon the divisions of the colonial era.[53]

SOUTH CAROLINA

News of the Boston Port Act reached Charleston at the end of May 1774, quickening the revolutionary movement. As in the other commonwealths, the wealthy patriots engaged in successive battles with the nonexpansionists and then the artisans and farmers. Following the reports of Parliament's onslaught against the Bay Colony, the expansionist-dominated general committee, which had been formed in South Carolina during the protests over the Tea Act, reconvened and called a "general meeting of the inhabitants of this colony" for July 6. The committee also sent letters to leading men throughout the

---

52. Patrick Henry to John Adams, May 20, 1776, Patrick Henry to R. H. Lee, May 20, 1776, Henry, *Patrick Henry,* I, 412–13, 411; R. H. Lee to Charles Lee, Apr. 22, 1776, *Letters of Lee,* I, 183; Jefferson, Three Drafts of Virginia Constitution, [c. June 1776], Constitution as Adopted by the Convention, June 29, 1776, Jefferson to Edmund Pendleton, Aug. 26, 1776, *Papers of Jefferson,* I, 329–65, 377–86, 504–5.

53. *Papers of Mason,* I, 318–19; Jackson Turner Main, *Political Parties before the Constitution* (Chapel Hill, N.C., 1973), 244–67; Norman K. Risjord, "The Virginia Federalists," *JSH,* xxxiii (1967), 486–517.

province instructing them to select representatives for the gathering.[54] Meanwhile, Charleston newspapers published a spate of articles exhorting the citizenry to "join with our sister colonies in a determined proper opposition to tyranny."[55]

South Carolina nonexpansionists responded to this upwelling of patriotic fervor much as they had reacted to all similar outbursts since the late 1760s—they grumbled privately but avoided any forceful display of opposition which might bring down the wrath of the majority. Members of this cautious faction took no part in the July general meeting; one observer at the gathering commented, "The set of advocates for the present misguided administration, whose chains had often been heard to clatter in private companies, were all struck dumb and kept aloof from the public debates."[56] The 104 delegates attending the meeting came from all areas of the province except five parishes that were traditional nonexpansionist strongholds. Not sending representatives to Charleston were the coastal districts of Christ Church, St. John Colleton, and St. Helena, as well as two parishes near Georgia—Prince William and St. Peter. Other South Carolinians testified during these weeks to the timidity of the nonexpansionists. Noting the "universal shout of jealousy against Great Britain," Lieutenant Governor Bull remarked in July, "Few who think otherwise are hardy enough to avow it publicly."[57]

Though the nonexpansionists caused no dissension at the July general meeting, the wealthy revolutionaries at the gathering confronted and annealed a rift in their own ranks. The fault line lay between most of the Charleston merchant community, which had grown cautious in the face of mounting lower-class activity, and the majority of the planters, who for the moment enjoyed the support of the patriot farmers and tradesmen. A series of compromises helped bring the two groups together. On the question of trade with Britain, the Chamber of Commerce had resolved "not to accede to any measure of nonexportation or nonimportation."[58] The gathering, however, pick-

54. Article, June 13, 1774, Force, ed., *American Archives*, 4th ser., I, 408.

55. Articles, June 4, July 4, 1774, ibid., 382–84, 508–12, quotation on 384; Gadsden to Samuel Adams, June 14, 28, 1774, *The Writings of Christopher Gadsden, 1746–1805*, ed. Richard Walsh (Columbia, S.C., 1966), 97, 99; Schlesinger, *Colonial Merchants*, 373–75.

56. "A Letter Received in Boston, Dated Charlestown, S.C., July 11, 1774," Force, ed., *American Archives*, 4th ser., I, 533.

57. Lt. Gov. Bull to Dartmouth, July 31, 1774, SCPR, XXXIV, 177–78, SCA; Gadsden to Samuel Adams, June 5, 1774, *Writings of Gadsden*, 95; Mr. Farr to Ralph Izard, Aug. 8, 1774, Edward Rutledge to Ralph Izard, Oct. 29, 1774, *Correspondence of Mr. Ralph Izard of South Carolina*, ed. Anne Izard Deas (1844; rpt. New York, 1976), 7, 23–24; John Drayton, *Memoirs of the American Revolution, from Its Commencement to the Year 1776 Inclusive . . .* , 2 vols. (1821; rpt. [New York?], 1969), I, 126.

58. Drayton, *Memoirs of the American Revolution*, I, 131.

ing its words carefully, empowered the South Carolina delegation to Philadelphia to agree to all "legal measures." The selection of congressmen also marked out a middle ground; the delegation included the outspoken—Christopher Gadsden and Thomas Lynch—and the more conservative—Henry Middleton and John Rutledge. Finally, the meeting established a new general committee, chaired by lawyer Charles Pinckney and composed of revolutionaries of various persuasions. The most active group within the ninety-nine-member panel was the carefully balanced Charleston contingent, which consisted of fifteen merchants, fourteen artisans, and Pinckney.[59]

By August the strength of the united, affluent patriots was evident to all, and the ability of the royal governor and the nonexpansionists to check or even openly to criticize the revolution had ended. On August 2 the Commons House convened at eight o'clock in the morning, "on account of the excessive heat of the weather at this season," as a newspaper account drolly explained. Rushing through their business before Bull awoke and arrived to prorogue them, the lawmakers endorsed the resolves of the general meeting and voted a generous fifteen hundred pounds sterling to defray the expenses of the congressmen. Bull lamented to Dartmouth, "Your lordship will see by this instance with what perseverance, secrecy, and unanimity they form and conduct their designs."[60] That same month the expansionists delivered a stern reproof to the Reverend John Bulman, the assistant minister at St. Michael's Church in Charleston, for daring to preach a sermon on "the Christian duty of peaceableness." The foolhardy Bulman had lambasted "every silly clown and illiterate mechanic [who] will take upon him[self] to censure the conduct of his prince or governor." Even though St. Michael (in contrast to St. Philip, the other Charleston parish) had a large aggregation of tories, the vestry voted forty-two to thirty-three to dismiss the assistant rector, and he soon fled to England.[61]

With the patriots so clearly in control, the nonexpansionists were reduced to silence. Some wealthy tories left the province before independence, but most remained and grudgingly signed the loyalty oath

---

59. Ibid., 129–32. Force, ed., *American Archives*, 4th ser., i, 525–28, presents the Charleston members of the general committee, and see Extract of a Letter Received in New York, dated July 8, 1774, Charlestown, S.C. (525), A letter received in Boston, dated Charleston, S.C., July 11, 1774, (531–34), and Miles Brewton to Josiah Quincy, Jr., July 12, 1774, (534); Edward Rutledge to Ralph Izard, July 21, 1774, *Correspondence of Izard*, 3–5.

60. Lt. Gov. Bull to Dartmouth, Aug. 3, 1774, SCPR, xxxiv, 188–89; Article, Aug. 3, 1774, Force, ed., *American Archives*, 4th ser., i, 672.

61. Bulman quoted in Richard Walsh, *Charleston's Sons of Liberty: A Study of the Artisans, 1763–1789* (Columbia, S.C., 1959), 71; Drayton, *Memoirs of the American Revolution*, i, 142–45; Brown, *King's Friends*, 227.

circulated in the summer of 1775. The defeat of the backcountry loyalists in 1775 and of a British naval force in 1776 were further arguments for tory reticence. Most British sympathizers revealed their true colors only with Cornwallis's capture of Charleston in May 1780. Several hundred "people of the first fortunes" signed addresses welcoming Generals Clinton and Cornwallis and offered aid to the regulars. The patriot assembly struck back with measures that confiscated the estates of 237 loyalists and levied a punitive tax on other holdings. When Charleston was evacuated in December 1782 nearly four thousand whites (not all residents of South Carolina) left with the fleet.[62]

With the nonexpansionists stilled and the governor a helpless bystander, the wealthy patriots, merchant and planter alike, commenced in the fall of 1774 a second and much lengthier struggle with their lower-class allies over the direction of the revolutionary movement. These less affluent citizens never gained the strength that their brethren in Pennsylvania displayed, in part because of the widespread loyalism in the up-country and in part, perhaps, because of the dangers posed to a disunified white population by the black majority. "We are a weak colony," intoned Gadsden in 1774, "from the number of Negroes we have amongst us."[63]

The general committee broadened the conflict between the upper- and lower-class patriots when in November 1774 it called for a provincial congress with a relatively democratic apportionment to assemble the following January. The committee's directive expanded the total number of seats from 48 in the last royal assembly to 187 in the new body and sharply inflated backcountry representation from 6

62. Alexander Innes to Dartmouth, June 10, 1775, B. D. Bargar, ed., "Charles Town Loyalism in 1775: The Secret Reports of Alexander Innes," *SCHM*, LXIII (1962), 132; Gov. William Campbell to Gen. Gage, July 1, 1775, George Milligan's Report, Sept. 15, 1775, SCPR, XXXVI, 14–15, XXXV, 229–44; Arthur Middleton to William Henry Drayton, Apr. [Sep.] 15, 1775, Joseph Barnwell, ed., "Correspondence of Hon. Arthur Middleton, Signer of the Declaration of Independence," *SCHM*, XXVII (1926), 114; Drayton, *Memoirs of the American Revolution*, I, 313–17; Jerome J. Nadelhaft, *The Disorders of War: The Revolution in South Carolina* (Orono, Me., 1981), 45–85; *Biographical Directory of the South Carolina House of Representatives*, vol. II: Walter B. Edgar and N. Louise Bailey, eds., *The Commons House of Assembly, 1692–1775* (Columbia, S.C., 1977), 83, 125, 517–18, 732–33. Fully 136 Charlestonians would memorialize the Loyalist Claims Commission. When considered as a percentage of urban population, these tories made the South Carolina capital the most loyal of the major American ports. Three-fourths of this group detailed losses of over five hundred pounds sterling. See Brown, *King's Friends*, 218, 253–55, 290–344.

63. Gadsden to Samuel Adams, May 23, 1774, *Writings of Gadsden*, 93. Also see Howe, ed., "Journal of Josiah Quincy, Jr., 1773," MHS *Procs.*, XLIX (1915–16), 454–57 (Mar. 25, 1774); Pierce Butler to [Arthur Middleton], Mar. 21, 1776, "Middleton Correspondence," 140.

percent (3 places) to 33 percent (61 seats). The call for new slates also encouraged Charleston tradesmen to change the makeup of the capital delegation. Voters increased the number of artisans in the assembly and reduced the clout of the traders, who had formerly made up 88 percent of the assemblymen (seven of eight places) and now accounted for only 32 percent of the total (eight of thirty seats). Lamented Henry Laurens, "No man is now supposed to be unequal to a share in government. I see trouble and confusion in prospect."[64]

Despite the mounting strength of the common people, affluent patriots remained dominant at the January gathering, which discussed the proceedings of the First Continental Congress. Members of the elite triumphed in the debate over the special status the South Carolina delegation had secured for rice, the only grain excluded from the nonexportation that was to cut off shipments to the British West Indies and Britain after September 10, 1775. John Drayton, William Henry Drayton's son and the author of a detailed chronicle of this period, observed, "This exception had given so general a disgust that the whole interior of the province considered their interests as sacrificed to the emolument of the rice planters."[65] Despite such opposition, the rice planters and their merchant allies prevailed in the vote on the exemption, eighty-seven to seventy-five. The January meeting acknowledged the rising strength of the lower-class patriots by establishing a new general committee, consisting of the thirty members of the Charleston delegation and any other representatives then in town. The preceding general committee had included among its thirty active members, ten traders from the Chamber of Commerce; by contrast, the new panel claimed only four, and in all the merchant contingent was reduced from fifteen to nine. And while expansionists retained considerable influence, the new committee boasted thirteen mechanics, as well as such fiery patriots as Gadsden and the Reverend William Tennent.[66]

64. Laurens to John Laurens, Jan. 4, 1775, Laurens Papers, roll 5, SCHS. *Biographical Directory of the South Carolina House of Representatives*, vol. I: *Session Lists, 1692–1973*, ed. Joan S. R. Faunt and Robert E. Rector with David K. Bowen (Columbia, S.C., 1974), 150–62, provide data on apportionment. Nadelhaft, *Disorders of War*, 24, offers slightly different statistics. And see Walsh, *Charleston's Sons of Liberty*, 64–65.

65. Drayton, *Memoirs of the American Revolution*, I, 167–75, quotation on 168; Edward Rutledge to Ralph Izard, Oct. 29, 1774, *Correspondence of Izard*, 23–24; Laurens to Richard Oswald, Jan. 4, 1775, Laurens to John Laurens, Jan. 4, 1775, Laurens Papers, roll 5; Laurens to John Laurens, Jan. 8, 1775, *SCHM*, IV (1903), 273.

66. Drayton, *Memoirs of the American Revolution*, I, 169, 172–75, 182–87, 221–28; Laurens to John Laurens, Jan. 18, 1775, Laurens Papers, roll 5; Lt. Gov. Bull to Dartmouth, Mar. 28, 1775, SCPR, xxxv, 80–82; Schlesinger, *Colonial Merchants*, 527–28; Proceedings of the Provincial Congress, Jan. 1775, Force, ed., *American Archives*, 4th ser., I, 113; David Duncan Wallace, *The Life of Henry Laurens, with a Sketch of*

After the arrival of the news of Lexington and Concord, South Carolina expansionists supported still more vigorous steps, always seeking that balance by which the populace would be involved but not excessively agitated. Reports of fighting in the Bay Colony reached Charleston early in May, and the general committee immediately reconvened the provincial congress. Once assembled, the provincial body divided along class lines in debates over several issues. Particularly contentious was a proposed loyalty oath; reported one observer, "The opulent and sensible wish to avoid such desperate measures, . . . but they are powerfully opposed by a numerous body of the low and ignorant, led by a few desperate incendiaries, who have nothing to lose, and some hot-headed young men of fortune."[67] Though they could not block the act, Laurens, Brewton, and Lowndes were able to soften the wording of the oath. With comparable circumspection, the expansionists agreed to raise about two thousand troops but made certain that the captains and lieutenants were drawn from the elite. One visitor from the North noted, "The officers are chiefly gentlemen possessed of much property."[68] Finally, the congress created the Council of Safety to act as a provincial executive. Laurens chaired the body, and moderate expansionists occupied most of the seats.[69]

With the quickening of the revolutionary movement in the summer of 1775 the upper-class patriots grew increasingly concerned about the loyalty of backcountry farmers. Western resentment of expansionist policies, evident in the Regulator movement of the 1760s, had never wholly subsided. In August, William Henry Drayton and the Reverend William Tennent, at the behest of the Council of Safety, set out on a tour of the up-country to gain support for the revolution. They soon encountered opposition; enmity was especially fierce in the area between the Broad and Saluda rivers and in the Ninety-Six

Lieutenant-Colonel John Laurens (1915; rpt. New York, 1967), 204; Rules of the Charleston Chamber of Commerce (Charleston, 1774) (Evans Imprint #13194); Biographical Directory: Session Lists, 156.

67. Alexander Innes to Dartmouth, June 3, 1775, Bargar, ed., "Charles Town Loyalism," 131; Drayton, Memoirs of the American Revolution, I, 246–47.

68. Gen. John Armstrong to James Wilson, May 7, 1776, Gratz Collection, HSP; Drayton, Memoirs of the American Revolution, I, 254–55, 262–63; William E. Hemphill and Wylma A. Wates, eds., Extracts from the Journals of the Provincial Congresses of South Carolina, 1775–1776 (Columbia, S.C., 1960), 46 (June 11, 1775), 47–48 (June 12, 1775), list the provincial officers; provincial association, June 3, 1775, Force, ed., American Archives, 4th ser., II, 897. Laurens's speech of June 4, 1775, is reprinted in Wallace, Henry Laurens, 207–10; Carl J. Vipperman, The Rise of Rawlins Lowndes, 1721–1800 (Columbia, S.C., 1978), 185.

69. Drayton, Memoirs of the American Revolution, I, 255, 265, 318; David Ramsay, History of South Carolina from Its First Settlement in 1670 to the Year 1808, 2 vols. (Newbury, S.C., 1858), I, 135.

District. After a force of nineteen hundred tories compelled a patriot garrison to surrender its stockade, the Council of Safety raised an army of over four thousand men, with Colonel Richard Richardson, a hero of the Cherokee War, at its head. Richardson quickly routed his opponents, and by January 1776 Laurens could rejoice to his son, "The heads of the faction in that part, except three who narrowly escaped by flight, are in prison—the common people whom they had deluded . . . declare their willingness to join their brethren in America in defense of their common rights." The backcountry would remain relatively quiet until the British invasion of 1780 reignited bitter civil strife.[70]

Patriots, both wealthy and less affluent, also worried about the faithfulness of the black majority. In response to a rumor that the ministry was going to "grant freedom to such slaves as should desert their masters and join the king's troops," the general committee in May 1775 mounted an evening patrol of one hundred men.[71] Laurens told the provincial congress in June that "there are just grounds to apprehend an insurrection of the slaves . . . instigated by the tools of a wicked administration"; moreover, that month the patriots ordered two men tarred and feathered for spreading the "good news" that arms were to be "distributed among the Negroes, Roman Catholics, and Indians."[72] In August the Council of Safety executed Jerry, a free Negro pilot, for vowing that he would guide the royal fleet into the harbor, and during the fall and winter months the revolutionaries reprobated the commanders of the British war vessels for welcoming runaways. Few slaves, however, managed to reach the royal navy, and no uprising occurred in the colony. This relative quiescence made possible William Henry Drayton's comment in July: "As to our apprehensions of the Negroes and Indians, they have all passed over." And a smug Thomas Lynch could remark in November: Behold "our slaves remaining faithful against the promise even of liberty, dearest, best of all rewards."[73]

70. Laurens to John Laurens, Jan. 16, 1776, *SCHM*, v (1904), 142; Laurens to Robert Deas, Jan. 8, 1776, Laurens Papers, roll 5; Arthur Middleton to W. H. Drayton, Aug. 22, 1775, "Middleton Correspondence," 133–34; Drayton, *Memoirs of the American Revolution*, II, 118–20, 131–35, 321–31, 351–81; Ramsay, *History of South Carolina*, I, 137, 144–47; Edgar and Bailey, *Biographical Directory: Commons House*, 557–60; Gov. Campbell to Dartmouth, July 19, 20, 1775, SCPR, XXXV, 148–49.
71. Alexander Innes to Dartmouth, May 16, 1775, Bargar, ed., "Charles Town Loyalism," 128.
72. Drayton, *Memoirs of the American Revolution*, I, 252–53, 300–302.
73. W. H. Drayton to South Carolina Delegation, July 4, 1775, Robert W. Gibbes, ed., *Documentary History of the American Revolution . . .*, 3 vols. (New York, 1853–57), I, 118; Thomas Lynch to Ralph Izard, Nov. 19, 1775, *Correspondence of Izard*, 154; Peter Timothy to W. H. Drayton, Aug. 22, 1775, "Middleton Correspondence," 132; M. Foster Farley, "The South Carolina Negro in the American Revolution," *SCHM*, LXXIX (1978), 75–78.

During the second half of 1775 the expansionists, pushed both by the common people and by British escalation, grudgingly approved ever more bellicose steps. "The plebians are still for war," Peter Timothy explained in August, "but the noblesse [are] perfectly pacific."[74] The conflict between the two sets of patriots quickly translated into a feud between the expansionist-dominated Council of Safety and the general committee, which had become a forum for Charleston mechanics and the most ardent protestors. The council initially rejected the demand of the general committee that Charleston be fortified, but the threat posed by British frigates in the harbor and tories in the backcountry made clear that resolute actions were needed. In September the council ordered provincial forces to take Fort Johnson, which commanded the southern approaches to the port. Governor William Campbell, who had arrived in June, now dissolved the assembly one last time and fled to a warship. In November after British commanders cannonaded an American schooner, the Council of Safety took further steps to defend the capital. "We have been precipitated into measures which in all probability will work our destruction," mourned Laurens, who headed the executive body. "Yet those who struggled hardest against the prosecution of such ruinous measures (I am one of them) are still striving to struggle against the prosecution of more diabolical measures by the British administration, and prefer poverty and death to a tame submission."[75]

Months of wrestling with the lower classes made South Carolina expansionists increasingly reluctant to undertake a step as precipitous as an immediate declaration of independence. By the winter of 1775–1776 a change was evident in the colony's congressional delegation. Recollected John Adams: "Mr. Dickinson himself told me . . . the balance lay with South Carolina. Accordingly all their efforts were employed to convert the delegates from that state. . . . And we soon began to find that Mr. Lynch, Mr. Arthur Middleton, and even the two Rutledges began to waver and clamor about [i.e., against] independence. Mr. Gadsden was either from despair of success never attempted, or if he was he received no impression from

74. Peter Timothy to W. H. Drayton, Aug. 22, 1775, "Middleton Correspondence," 131.

75. Laurens to William Manning, Nov. 26, 1775, Laurens to James Laurens, Oct. 20, Dec. 6, 1775, Laurens Papers, roll 5; Gov. Campbell to Gen. Gage, Sept. 20, 1775, SCPR, xxxvi, 21; Arthur Middleton to W. H. Drayton, Aug. 4, 5, 1775, "Middleton Correspondence," 123, 125; Drayton, *Memoirs of the American Revolution*, i, 319–20, ii, 28, 35, 40, 54–60, 74–88, 161–63; Ramsay, *History of South Carolina*, i, 138–42, Farley, "South Carolina Negro," 77.

them."[76] Similar sentiments were revealed in the provincial congress when in February 1776 Gadsden returned to South Carolina with a copy of *Common Sense* and announced his support for separation. The reaction was uniform and harsh: Lowndes's comments were unprintable; Laurens said Paine's tract was full of "indecent expressions," and he excoriated the proposal; John Rutledge declared "he was willing to ride post by day and night to Philadelphia" to prevent a declaration of independence. Moreover, according to John Drayton, "even the few who wished for independence thought Colonel Gadsden imprudent in thus suddenly declaring for it."[77]

Although anxious to delay a break from Britain, the wealthy patriots pursued the creation of a new provincial government that would stave off what Edward Rutledge called the "demon of anarchy."[78] In the fall of 1775 John Rutledge secured in the Continental Congress a resolution encouraging South Carolina to draft a charter. When the provincial congress convened in February it struck a committee, dominated by such conservative expansionists as Laurens and Lowndes, to draw up such a frame, and in March the legislature approved and proclaimed a new constitution. This charter confirmed the dominance of the expansionists while making certain concessions to the populace. The large lower house, with its relatively democratic apportionment, remained nearly as it had been in the provincial congresses, strikingly different from the more elitist structures of the royal assembly. The new constitution, however, also preserved the colonial property qualifications; allowed the governor autocratic powers; provided for election of the upper house by the lower; and defended the established Anglican church. Moreover, the aristocracy filled all the key offices, beginning with John Rutledge who was chosen president. The prominence of men who had served in the Cherokee War of 1759–1762—for example, Laurens was vice-president and George Gabriel Powell speaker of the upper house—underscores the continuities in the expansionist faction.[79]

In the final tempestuous debate over independence, South Carolina

76. *Diary and Autobiography of John Adams*, III, 316–17, 330 (Autobiography), II, 209 (Oct. 20, 1775); Thomas Lynch to Ralph Izard, Nov. 19, 1775, Edward Rutledge to Ralph Izard, Dec. 8, 1775, *Correspondence of Izard*, 155, 165.

77. Drayton, *Memoirs of the American Revolution*, II, 172–73; Vipperman, *Rawlins Lowndes*, 190; Wallace, *Henry Laurens*, 221, 224–25; Laurens to Robert Deans, Jan. 8, 1776, Laurens Papers, roll 5.

78. Edward Rutledge to Ralph Izard, Dec. 8, 1775, *Correspondence of Izard*, 165.

79. *Diary and Autobiography of John Adams*, III, 356–58 (Autobiography); Drayton, *Memoirs of the American Revolution*, II, 168, 171–72, 176–97, 240–41; Ramsay, *History of South Carolina*, I, 149–50; Nadelhaft, *Disorders of War*, 28–34.

expansionists, concerned about popular disorder, remained among the more cautious patriots on the continent. When in March 1776 news reached South Carolina of the American Prohibitory Act, by which Parliament interdicted colonial commerce, the provincial congress empowered its delegation to concur with the other representatives in all "necessary" acts. Yet the preamble to the new constitution called for "an accommodation" with Britain, and this sentiment was reiterated in April in exchanges between President John Rutledge and the two houses.[80] Moreover, South Carolina congressmen worked with the delegates from the middle colonies to delay independence. In June, Edward Rutledge informed New Yorker John Jay that "the sensible part of the house . . . saw no wisdom in a *declaration* of independence, nor any other purpose to be enforced by it but . . . rendering ourselves ridiculous in the eyes of foreign powers by attempting to bring them into a union with us before we had united with each other. For daily experience evinces that the inhabitants of every colony consider themselves at liberty to do as they please upon almost every occasion."[81] On July 1 South Carolina joined New York, Pennsylvania, and Delaware in opposing separation. The next day, however, "for the sake of unanimity," the rice colony changed its vote.[82]

In the years following independence upper-class patriots ruled South Carolina, but as in the other states, they were forced to deal with a determined lower class. Popular dissatisfaction with the 1776 constitution quickly mounted, and in 1778 the legislature was forced to adopt a new charter, which weakened the power of the executive, disestablished the Anglican church, and provided for the direct election of the upper house. Despite such concessions, the wealthy rebels retained their dominance and when President John Rutledge resigned in a huff, calling the new frame a "simple democracy," another conservative, Rawlins Lowndes, succeeded him. Because of the continuing ascendancy of the elite, the vast majority of expansionists remained patriots even when the British temporarily conquered the state in 1780. A group of revolutionaries, however, including Lowndes, Colonel Charles Pinckney, and Henry Middleton, voluntarily accepted General Clinton's and General Cornwallis's offers of protection, just as a handful of South Carolina expansionists had abandoned the continental standard even before independence.[83]

80. Drayton, *Memoirs of the American Revolution*, ii, 177–81, 189, 244–51, reprints several key documents.
81. Edward Rutledge to John Jay, June 8, 29, 1776, *Letters of Congress*, i, 476–77, 517–18; *Diary and Autobiography of John Adams*, iii, 393 (Autobiography).
82. Jensen, *Founding of a Nation*, 700; *Diary and Autobiography of John Adams*, iii, 396–97 (Autobiography).
83. Nadelhaft, *Disorders of War*, 34–43, Rutledge quoted on 42; Ramsay, *History of South Carolina*, i, 151–60, ii, 77; Drayton, *Memoirs of the American Revolution*, ii, 307–9, 316, 341–44; Brown, *King's Friends*, 214; Farley, "South Carolina Negro," 75.

CONFLICTING PERSUASIONS

The events following the Boston Port Act spurred the more vocal expansionists and nonexpansionists in the plantation provinces to elaborate their views. Partisans committed to a prosperous New World nation extolled the benefits of commercial freedom. In his 1774 tract *A Summary View of the Rights of British America*, Thomas Jefferson denounced the navigation acts as an "unjust encroachment" on "the exercise of a free trade with all parts of the world possessed by the American colonists as of natural right." He urged the king and the British people to "accept of every commercial preference it is in our power to give for such things as we can raise for their use, or they make for ours. But let them not think to exclude us from going to other markets to dispose of those commodities which they cannot use, or to supply those wants which they cannot supply."[84]

Henry Laurens also applauded the rise of America. He emphasized that the true strength of the thirteen colonies lay in their vast interior reaches. Hearing of the Boston Port Act, Laurens observed: Lord North "may possibly fix the badge of slavery upon the sea coast, but this will hasten the beginning of independence out of the reach of fleets and British troops, an independence which might by wisdom be protracted to distant ages."[85] Laurens firmly trusted in the ability of the New World to supply itself with all necessary goods. "If the administration on your side should . . . continue firm in pressing us," he told an English correspondent in December 1774, "we shall be a set of ragged patriots before the expiration of '75 . . . [but] in '76 we shall begin to deck ourselves in woolen, cotton, linen, and silk of our own manufacture."[86] During these months, however, Laurens clung to the hope that some accommodation could be reached. "Independence is not the view of America," he affirmed in 1775. "Not a sober sensible man wishes for it."[87]

William Henry Drayton, who before 1773 had been an arch-tory, now expounded expansionist views with a convert's zeal and argued that God would guide America. "The Almighty created America to be independent of Britain," he pronounced in April 1776. "Let us be-

84. Thomas Jefferson, *A Summary View of the Rights of British America* (1774), Merrill Jensen, ed., *Tracts of the American Revolution, 1763–1776* (Indianapolis, Ind., 1967), 256–76, quotations on 261, 275–76; Jefferson to George Gilmer, July 5, 1775, *Papers of Jefferson*, I, 186; William Lee to George Mason, July 29, 1775, *Papers of Mason*, I, 244.

85. Laurens to John Laurens, Mar. 25, 1774, Laurens to George Appleby, Mar. 10, 1774, Laurens to James Laurens, May 12, 1774, *The Papers of Henry Laurens*, ed. George C. Rogers et al. (Columbia, S.C., 1968–   ), IX, 367, 349, 450.

86. Laurens to William Manning, Dec. 17, 1774, Laurens Papers, roll 5, SCHS.

87. Laurens to Rod Valtravers, May 22, 1775, *Papers of Laurens*, X, 134.

ware of the impiety of being backward to act as instruments in the Almighty hand, now extended to accomplish his purpose." Drayton praised the South Carolina constitution of 1776 because it meshed so fully with his vision of America's upward path. The new frame of government, he rejoiced, "is wisely adapted to enable us to . . . supply our wants at the *cheapest* markets in the universe; to extend our trade infinitely beyond what it has ever been known; to encourage manufacturers among us; and it is peculiarly formed to promote the happiness of the people from among whom, by virtue and merit, *the poorest man* may arrive at *the highest dignity.*"[88]

But Drayton also illustrated another, less appealing facet of expansionist thought, a malevolent racism directed toward the native peoples. "It is expected you make smooth work as you go," Drayton told an officer marching against the Cherokee in 1776, "that is, you cut up every Indian cornfield, and burn every Indian town, and that every Indian taken shall be the slave and property of the taker; that the nation be extirpated, and the lands become the property of the public. For my part, I shall never give my voice for a peace with the Cherokee nation upon any other term than their removal beyond the mountains."[89]

In contrast, nonexpansionists in the planting provinces doubted the ability of the colonies to survive on their own. "We may rise, grow rich, and be happy under the fostering protection of Great Britain," averred Robert Beverley in 1775, "but without her parental aid, must become victims to the first foreign invader. We have [in the southern colonies] neither arms, ammunition, or ships to protect our commerce. We have no resources to conduct war and no artisans to carry on manufactures or improve us in the arts of life. We are an infant country, unconnected in interest and naturally disunited by inclination."[90] A fellow Virginian, William Byrd III, echoed this pessimism. "Everything must proceed from bad to worse," he observed in 1775, "till either we are reduced to punishment by the force of Great Britain, or till the people of America, reduced by their distresses, are brought to search into the cause of their sufferings, and take vengeance on those who deluded them."[91]

88. William Henry Drayton's Charge to the Charleston Grand Jury, Apr. 23, 1776, William Henry Drayton, Address to the Grand Jury, Oct. 15, 1776, Drayton, *Memoirs of the American Revolution*, II, 259–74, 384–85, quotations on 272, 274.
89. W. H. Drayton to Francis Salvador, July 24, 1776, Gibbes, ed., *Documentary History*, II, 29.
90. Robert Beverley to William Fitzhugh, July 20, 1775, Calhoon, ed., "A Sorrowful Spectator," 52.
91. William Byrd III to Ralph Wormeley, Oct. 4, 1775, *Correspondence of the Byrds*, II, 815; John Randolph, "A Plea for Moderation," [ca. early July 1774], Van Schreeven and Scribner, eds., *Revolutionary Virginia*, I, 210; Norton, ed., "Randolph's 'Plan of Accommodations,'" 103–20, esp. 106, 120.

These divergent views help explain why the establishment of a sovereign nation was an exciting prospect for the wealthy patriots, who could look ahead to a succession of new challenges, and why independence was a deeply tragic turn of events for nonexpansionists like Robert Beverley and William Byrd.

CHAPTER 16

Beyond Independence

For James Madison, as for most expansionists, the achievement of independence only accelerated the pursuit of national goals. During the 1780s Madison argued that the young republic should firmly repel the schemes of the Old World colonizers. He urged "retaliating regulations of trade" against Great Britain, and he looked forward to the day when the United States would wrest the Mississippi from Spain. Mixing threat with prophecy, Madison remarked to Jefferson in 1784: "The U[nited] S[tates] are already a power not to be despised by Spain. The time cannot be distant, when in spite of all her precautions, the safety of her possessions in this quarter of the globe must depend more on our peaceableness than her own power."[1]

In the years after 1776 important continuities marked the response of the upper-class patriots to two challenges—one subordinate and one dominant. The first problem stemmed from questions of class, the need to circumscribe the newfound influence of small farmers and artisans. This difficulty was, for the wealthy, a secondary matter, because changes in the social structure had always been incidental to their larger goals; for most expansionists lower-class dissension was an unfortunate by-product of a necessary struggle with Britain. The primary challenge emerged from their long-standing and deeply held concern to buttress the (now independent) nation so that rapid economic growth might resume and so the United States could deal effectively with a hostile world. These priorities help explain political developments in the decades after independence and also provide an

1. Madison to James Monroe, Aug. 7, 1785, Madison to Jefferson, Aug. 20, 1784, *The Papers of James Madison,* ed. William T. Hutchinson and William M. E. Rachal (Chicago, 1962–), VIII, 334, 105–6.

introduction to the larger question of the links between the Revolution and present-day America.

» «

Although the task of restricting the populace was of secondary importance, it was never a minor matter. During the dozen years after 1776 the affluent patriots struggled furiously with the less wealthy citizens, whose self-awareness and political strength had burgeoned with the Revolution. The conflict in each state bore little resemblance to the factional strife evident before 1774. The earlier clashes had pitted against each other two upper-class groups with different views of American growth. But the triumph of the patriots expelled the nonexpansionists from almost all the commonwealths (Virginia was the exception), and a new set of political battles aligned the wealthy revolutionaries of the cities and coastal regions against the poorer inland farmers. This dichotomy characterized the opposing forces in Massachusetts, New York, Pennsylvania, and South Carolina, even if well-heeled individuals often commanded the inland parties and even if one important group—the urban lower classes— gradually shifted its allegiances. (The mechanics first sided with the poorer husbandmen but by the 1780s cast their lot with the merchants' party.) Only in Virginia did the divisions resemble those of earlier years, and only there were class questions muted. During the second half of the 1770s and the 1780s the two sides in each state battled over a series of issues, including taxation, paper money, and debtor-creditor relations. Only occasionally did the common people triumph, but everywhere they threatened the elite as never before in American history.[2]

Fear of the populace was one reason that the affluent revolutionaries came together in 1787 to draw up a new frame of government for the United States. Edmund Randolph voiced widely shared sentiments when he opened the Constitutional Convention: "Our chief danger arises from the democratic parts of our [state] constitutions. It is a maxim which I hold incontrovertible that the powers of government exercised by the people swallows up the other branches. None of the constitutions have provided sufficient checks against the democracy." Other delegates emphatically agreed. Said Elbridge

---

2. See the divisions detailed in Jackson Turner Main, *Political Parties before the Constitution* (Chapel Hill, N.C., 1973). Neo-Whig historians frequently cite the conclusions in Forrest McDonald, *We the People: The Economic Origins of the Constitution* (Chicago, 1958), to show that Americans were not divided along class lines in the 1780s. An examination of McDonald's evidence, however, supports the alignments spelled out in Main.

Gerry, "The evils we experience flow from the excess of democracy." James Madison noted, "Symptoms of a leveling spirit, as we have understood, have sufficiently appeared in a certain quarters to give notice of the future danger." Charles Pinckney of South Carolina called for "a real military force," adding, "The United States had been making an experiment without it, and we see the consequence in their rapid approaches toward anarchy." Even George Mason, who ultimately opposed the document he helped draft because he felt it swung the pendulum too far in the other direction, scored the popular excesses. According to the notes of the debates, "He admitted that we had been too democratic, but was afraid we should incautiously run into the opposite extreme."[3]

While loathing the "excesses of democracy," the upper-class patriots underscored a crucial distinction. The problem lay with the *institutions* and not with the *social structure* of the 1780s; no truly frightening inequality would emerge until America's vast reaches were densely populated and a landless multitude appeared. "The people of the U. States," beamed Charles Pinckney, "are perhaps the most singular of any we are acquainted with. Among them there are fewer distinctions of fortune and less of rank than among the inhabitants of any other nation." Madison agreed, even though he took a slightly more pessimistic view of the present and regarded the distant future grimly: "It was true as had been observed (by Mr. Pinckney) we had not among us those hereditary distinctions . . . nor those extremes of wealth or poverty. . . . We cannot, however, be regarded even at this time as one homogeneous mass, [and] . . . we should not lose sight of the changes which ages will produce. An increase of population will of necessity increase the proportion of those who will labor under all the hardships of life, and secretly sigh for a more equal distribution of its blessings." Gerry rounded out a debate in which all participants shared common assumptions, if with different emphases: "He did not deny the position of Mr. (Madison) . . . [but said] our situation was different from that of G[reat] Britain, and the great body of lands yet to be parceled out and settled would very much prolong the difference."[4]

Hence, if America suffered from no irreconcilable clashes of interest, at least for the present, the expansionists needed only to erect

3. Edmund Randolph, May 29, Elbridge Gerry, May 31, Madison, June 26, Charles Pinckney, Aug. 18, George Mason, May 31, *The Records of the Federal Convention of 1787*, ed. Max Farrand, 4 vols. (rev. ed.; New Haven, Conn., 1937), I, 26–27, 48, 423, II, 332, I, 49.
4. Pinckney, June 25, Madison, June 26, Elbridge Gerry, June 26, ibid., I, 398, 422, 425.

the proper set of structures to check popular enthusiasms. Thoughts of a monarchy or permanent aristocracy were brushed aside; overwhelmingly the delegates agreed with Madison that "the government be strictly republican."[5] The expansionists concurred that ironclad restrictions must be set upon the states and that the federal system must be hedged with elaborate checks and balances. Thus the Constitution forbade the states to issue paper money, to pass legal tender laws (which might allow debtors to pay in kind), or to impair the "obligation of contracts." Moreover, while the populace was allowed to vote directly for the House of Representatives, this chamber was balanced by an indirectly elected president and Senate and by an appointed judiciary. Having erected a government of high walls and elaborate safeguards, the founders could extoll the virtues of popular involvement. James Wilson (who with Madison went so far as to urge a congressional veto on state laws) "contended strenuously for drawing the most numerous branch of the legislature immediately from the people. He was for raising the federal pyramid to a considerable altitude, and for that reason wished to give it as broad a basis as possible."[6]

Fulfilling the hopes of the founders, the Constitution checked the extremes of popular government in the states and thereby helped alter the terms of political discourse in America. Where Shays's Rebellion in 1786 had sent shivers through the hearts of the wealthy, the Whiskey Rebellion of 1794 demonstrated the ability of the federal government to suppress a local demonstration. The Constitutional Convention of 1787 was the last time that American leaders met, or needed to meet, to lament the strength of the people. Once the Constitution was in place, affirmations of popular participation increasingly became the order of the day, and by the 1820s only a few antediluvian figures could be heard grumping about the malevolent lower orders. The elevation of the common man in the 1830s and the ready adoption of democratic rhetoric by both major political parties was a measure of how far the world of American politics had evolved.

In the years after Independence the expansionists addressed themselves to a second, more fundamental undertaking: the need to foster the ascent of the newly independent American "empire." This imperative emerged from a world view that had guided these individuals and their factional forebears for many decades. During the late 1770s and 1780s, dedication to this goal was evident in the deeds and pronouncements of upper-class patriots involved in a myriad of activities. Peace commissioners Benjamin Franklin, John Adams, Hen-

5. Madison, *The Federalist*, no. 39.
6. James Wilson, May 31, *Records of Convention of 1787*, I, 49.

ry Laurens, and John Jay adopted an aggressive stance in their negotiations with Britain. Although America's allies, France and Spain, would have had the independent states acquiesce in the most meager gains, including an Appalachian boundary, the commissioners unrolled their charts far wider. The four diplomats secured the Mississippi River as the new western border, and in the north they established a boundary traversing the St. Lawrence and the Great Lakes. And even though Franklin strove in vain for the acquisition of all of Canada, John Adams made certain that the new nation gained the right to fish in the waters of British North America. He exulted in December 1782, "Thanks be to God . . . that our Tom Cod are safe."[7]

The affluent patriots often disagreed bitterly with one another, but stronger still was their shared desire to promote the growth of America. Robert Morris, who in 1781 assumed leadership of the newly created Department of Finance, had been laboring for expansionist ends since the 1750s when he and his partner Thomas Willing had demanded more spirited defense measures. Finance Minister Morris was rarely given to lengthy disquisitions, but his correspondence was suffused with an unshakable faith in the destiny of the New World. For example, he encouraged Thomas Jefferson to invest in a planned national bank, remarking, "The capital proposed is but small when the extent and riches of the United States are considered, but when put in motion, the benefits from it will be so perceptible that all difficulty about increasing the capital will vanish." For Washington he tallied the copious rewards of free trade and domestic tranquility: "Whenever these measures have their proper force in our governments, the United States will abound with the greatest plenty of their own produce of perhaps any nation in the world; the people are by nature and habit industrious; feeling themselves secure in the possession of their property they will labor incessantly; that labor lays the foundation for commerce."[8]

Similarly, James Madison campaigned in the 1780s for a variety of programs, all designed to gird with steel the newly sovereign nation. He tried to concentrate Virginia commerce in a few key ports, such as Norfolk and Alexandria, arguing for "the utility of establishing a Philadelphia or a Baltimore among ourselves," but was blocked by

    7. John Adams to Elbridge Gerry, Dec. 14, 1782, quoted in Merrill Jensen, *The New Nation: A History of the United States during the Confederation, 1781–1789* (New York, 1950), 18; Richard B. Morris, *The Peacemakers* (New York, 1966).
    8. Robert Morris to Jefferson, June 11, 1781, Morris to Washington, July 2, 1781, *The Papers of Robert Morris*, ed. E. James Ferguson et al. (Pittsburgh, Pa., 1975–   ), I, 143, 214–15.

those planters and local merchants who favored "the old plan of monopoly and credit."[9] Madison also insisted that Virginia's great route to the West, the Potomac River, be improved (Washington seconded the appeal), and he called for the expulsion of Spain from the Mississippi Valley and Britain from the northwest posts. Madison's maledictions against the Spanish exhibited the strain of bellicosity that ran through expansionist thought. If Spain "calculated on the impotence of the U.S. under their dismemberment from the British empire," he wrote, "she saw but little way into futurity; if on the pacific temper of republics, unjust irritations on her part will soon teach her that republics have like passions with other governments."[10] Finally, he repeatedly urged the virtues of a forceful national government, in 1784, for example, telling Richard Henry Lee, "I hold it for a maxim, that the union of the states is essential to their safety against foreign danger and internal contention, and that the perpetuity and efficacy of the present system cannot be confided on."[11]

Such individual efforts to bolster the Republic were focused in the summer of 1787 when delegates from twelve of the thirteen states (Rhode Island sent no representatives) convened in the Constitutional Convention. While concerned about lower-class dissension, the founders took as their polestar the creation of a mighty nation state. Benjamin Franklin, spiritual parent of the gathering, called the delegates to prayer: "If a sparrow cannot fall to the ground without His notice, is it probable that an empire can rise without His aid?"[12] And when debate mired in a slough of special pleading, others returned the representatives to the job at hand. "Among the many provisions which had been urged," according to Gouverneur Morris, "he had seen none for supporting the dignity and splendor of the American empire. It had been one of our greatest misfortunes that the great objects of the nation had been sacrificed constantly to local views."[13] Madison, Gerry, Alexander Hamilton, and others explained the snares that awaited the enfeebled in a world of assertive nation states. The frame emerging from these deliberations established a strong central government, presided over by a powerful executive, who was also commander in chief of the armed forces, and it granted

9. Madison to James Monroe, June 21, 1785, Madison to Jefferson, Aug. 20, 1784, *Papers of Madison*, VIII, 307, 102.
10. Madison to Jefferson, Aug. 20, 1784, Madison to James Monroe, May 29, 1785, ibid., 106, 285.
11. Madison to Richard Henry Lee, Dec. 25, 1784, ibid., 201.
12. Franklin, June 28, *Records of Convention of 1787*, I, 451. Franklin prayed to a "Superintending Providence."
13. Gouverneur Morris, July 7, ibid., 552.

this government control over taxation and trade, two key powers absent from the Articles of Confederation.[14]

The Federalist, the most important of the tracts written to defend the Constitution, expanded upon the reasoning set forth at the convention and insisted that the charter was an absolute necessity if America was to flourish in a hostile world. Madison vigorously countered the traditional wisdom that republican government was suitable only for small states: "The people of America . . . [should not allow] a blind veneration for antiquity, for custom, or for names to overule the suggestions of their own good sense."[15] Hamilton praised the new frame for permitting a large national debt, and Jay listed a plethora of commercial rivalries—such as the competition for the fisheries or for the China trade—that might drag the United States into war and destroy a spineless country. Perhaps nowhere was the call for an American imperium more forceful than in *Federalist* number 11, in which Hamilton urged the citizenry to unite and establish their own commercial system: "It belongs to us to vindicate the honor of the human race, and to teach that assuming brother [Europe] moderation. . . . Let the thirteen states, bound together in a strict and indissoluble Union, concur in erecting one great American system superior to the control of all transatlantic force or influence and able to dictate the terms of the connection between the old and new world!"[16]

The "road to happiness and glory" that Jefferson had discussed in the first drafts of the Declaration of Independence was never a smooth one, nor did all the wealthy revolutionaries choose to travel it in the same manner. Southern planters and northern merchants soon enunciated different approaches to growth and helped foster in the 1790s opposing national parties. But such disagreements should not obscure the adherence of the elite to larger goals or its total acceptance of the social contract drawn up in 1787. Significantly, the transition in 1800 from Federalist John Adams to Democratic-Republican Thomas Jefferson was peaceable, and the support for Jefferson's ex-

14. For example, Madison, July 25, Elbridge Gerry, July 2, Alexander Hamilton, June 18, ibid., II, 109, I, 515, 297–98. Most expansionists avidly supported the Constitution, but there were significant exceptions. For example, by the early 1780s Patrick Henry (whose home south of the Rappahannock made him an anomaly among Virginia expansionists) had joined with his former partisan opponents, and in 1787 he would oppose the new national frame. Also note that a few others who had been not expansionists but popular party leaders—such as Samuel Adams or John Lamb of New York—censured the Constitution because it restricted democratic rights.

15. Madison, *The Federalist*, no. 14, and see no. 10.

16. For Hamilton on the national debt, see *The Federalist*, nos. 15, 30, and Jay discusses commercial rivalries in no. 4.

pansionist policies was widespread. Such shared values would continue to mark the American ruling classes, even during the middle decades of the nineteenth century, when the centrifugal pull of sectional ideologies overwhelmed the common strains, and the expansionists of the North and South took up arms to decide which of two particular incarnations of the national vision would prevail.

» «

What then are the links between the American Revolution and the present? One reading of this book might suggest that a line can now be drawn from the "expansionists" of the eighteenth century, through the nineteenth-century Americans who drove the Indians and Mexicans from their lands, to the twentieth-century politicians (and others) who have encouraged intervention in the Far East, Central America, and, indeed, around the world. Such an analysis, or flattening, of our history is not novel; revisionist historians of American foreign policy have often argued this point of view. "Very simply," writes William A. Williams in *Empire as a Way of Life*, "Americans of the 20th century liked empire for the same reasons that their ancestors had favored it in the 18th and 19th centuries. It provided them with renewable opportunities, wealth, and other benefits and satisfactions including a psychological sense of well-being and power."[17]

This approach to the Revolution, collapsing three centuries to isolate a single thread, is not so much wrong as reductive, and it results in a grave distortion of the struggle with Britain. Drawn through one set of filters the expansionists presented in this book are recognizable as the progenitors of those modern politicans who feel that the world role of the United States is that of police officer. But selecting a different set of characteristics, one might contend that the upper-class patriots were the forebears of present-day reformers or even of third-world revolutionaries. Such polarities cannot be waved away with an arbitrary choice of sides. Rather the resolution of this paradox requires a careful synthesis and a willingness to ground the American revolutionaries in their particular world.

Since the revisionist historians have forcefully presented the connections between the aggressive, America-first schemes of the eighteenth, nineteenth, and twentieth centuries, there is a need—before any summation can be attempted—to elaborate the other half of the

17. William Appleman Williams, *Empire as a Way of Life* (New York, 1980), 13; two essays that examine the revisionist approach to the American Revolution, are Jerald A. Combs, "The Diplomatic Legacy of America's Revolutionary Generation," in Larry R. Gerlach et al., eds., *Legacies of the American Revolution* (Logan, Utah, 1978), 127–50; and Sung Bok Kim, "The American Revolution and the Modern World," ibid., 221–38.

picture, the reformist, liberating thrust of expansionist beliefs and
actions. As scholars such as Douglass Adair and Gary Wills demonstrate, upper-class revolutionaries took a step beyond the world view
limned by John Locke at the end of the seventeenth century; they
were profoundly interested not only in the security of their possessions but also in the "happiness" of the citizenry. The wealthy patriots in the colonies were the children of the Scottish Enlightenment
and its Continental counterparts; in a series of influential works written between the 1720s and 1770s, Francis Hutcheson, David Hume,
Adam Smith, and other Scots had explored the human "moral sense"
and had argued (the words are Hutcheson's) that "the general happiness is the supreme end of all political union."[18] Accepting this
outlook, James Wilson of Pennsylvania declared in a 1774 treatise
that "the happiness of the society is the *first* law of every government," and Jefferson rejected Locke's trinity of "life, liberty, and
property," positing instead "unalienable" rights to "life, liberty, and
the pursuit of happiness."[19]

Other expansionists expressed the same concern for the commonwealth, a concern far broader than mere self-interest. "Upon this
point all speculative politicians will agree," wrote John Adams in
1776, "that the happiness of society is the end of government."[20]
George Washington examined the question at length. "The foundation of our empire was not laid in the gloomy age of ignorance and
superstition," he observed in a letter of 1783 to the state governors,
"but at an epocha when the rights of mankind were better understood and more clearly defined, than at any former period; the re-
searches of the human mind after social happiness have been carried
to a great extent, the treasures of knowledge, acquired by the labors
of philosophers, sages, and legislators, through a long succession of
years are laid open for our use, and their collected wisdom may be
happily applied in the establishment of our forms of government. . . .
At this auspicious period, the United States came into existence as a
nation, and if their citizens should not be completely free and happy,
the fault will be entirely their own."[21]

This desire to promote the well-being of society (Francis Hutch-

18. Garry Wills, *Inventing America: Jefferson's Declaration of Independence* (New
York, 1978), quotation on 252; Douglass Adair, "'That Politics May Be Reduced to a
Science': David Hume, James Madison, and the Tenth Federalist," *Huntington Library
Quarterly*, xx (1957), 343–60.
19. Wilson quoted in Wills, *Inventing America*, 248.
20. John Adams, "Thoughts on Government," Apr. 1776, *Papers of John Adams*, ed.
Robert Taylor et al., (Cambridge, Mass., 1977–), iv, 86–93, quotation on 86.
21. Washington to state governors, June 1783, quoted in Adair, "'That Politics,'"
343–44.

eson's phrase was "the greatest happiness of the greatest number") meshed, it is true, with a determination to restrain the populace and build a strong nation-state.[22] But the concern for public felicity also pushed many expansionists beyond such goals and helped make them advocates of other reforms. Most of the new state constitutions included bills of rights, which extended civil and religious liberties. Moreover, some of the upper-class patriots, such as Jefferson, Madison, and Christopher Gadsden, with support and pressure from the common people, waged prolonged struggles for religious freedom in the 1770s and 1780s. Furthermore, throughout revolutionary America members of the upper class expressed their repugnance for slavery, while in the northern states independence heralded an age of emancipation. A planter, Thomas Jefferson, penned the ordinance prohibiting slavery in the Northwest Territory.[23]

If such reforms were limited, which indeed they were, the radical, liberating nature of the Revolution was clearly perceived both by Americans and by observers in other countries. Thomas Paine remarked in *Common Sense,* "The cause of America is, in a great measure, the cause of all mankind." Benjamin Franklin reported from France in 1777, "All Europe is on our side of the question, as far as applause and good wishes can carry them. Those who live under arbitrary power do never the less approve of liberty, and wish for it. They almost despair of recovering it in Europe; they read the translations of our separate colony constitutions with rapture. . . . Hence 'tis a common observation here that our cause is *the cause of all mankind;* and that we are fighting for their liberty in defending our own."[24] Subsequent generations of revolutionaries have provided further corroboration for Franklin's remarks. Louis Kossuth, leader of the 1848 rebellion in Hungary, pronounced the Declaration of Independence the "noblest, happiest page of mankind's history"; Ho Chi Minh began the Declaration of Independence of the Democratic Republic of Vietnam with the words: "All men are created equal. They are endowed by their Creator with certain unalienable rights."[25]

22. Hutcheson quoted in Wills, *Inventing America*, 250.
23. The classic work on these changes is J. Franklin Jameson, *The American Revolution Considered as a Social Movement* (Princeton, 1926).
24. Paine, "Common Sense," 1776, Harry H. Clark, ed., *Thomas Paine: Representative Selections with Introduction, Bibliography and Notes* (New York, 1961), 3; Franklin to Samuel Cooper, May 1, 1777, *The Papers of Benjamin Franklin*, ed. Leonard W. Labaree et al. (New Haven, 1959–), XXIV, 6–7.
25. Kossuth quoted in Kim, "The American Revolution and the Modern World," 233; Ho Chi Minh, Declaration of Independence of the Democratic Republic of Vietnam, Sept. 2, 1945, Allan W. Cameron, ed., *Viet-Nam Crisis: A Documentary History*, 2 vols. (Ithaca, 1981), I, 52.

Who then were the expansionists and, we may ask again, what are their links with the present? To begin with—and to reiterate the definition used throughout this book—the expansionists were those wealthy individuals who were committed to fostering America's rise to greatness. In each commonwealth they formed a faction within the elite, selected by self-interest, religion, and national origin. From these influences and through the pressures of a series of imperial wars, they developed a deep commitment to the commercial, political, and territorial growth of America. On occasion, they expressed their convictions in ringing perorations; far more often they testified to their credo with a consistency of action that stretched over several decades. Moreover, as members of the elite—chiefly planters, merchants, and lawyers—these citizens viewed class relations from their lofty place in the social hierarchy.

But the trunk of expansionism ramified broadly. These affluent revolutionaries could be racist—America was, after all, a slaveholding nation; ethnocentric with regard to the native civilizations; and commercially and diplomatically aggressive, particularly after independence, in a way that sends shock waves through the historical record. But these same wealthy patriots could also be *reformers* in the fullest sense of that word, conscious, as Thomas Jefferson observed, "that we are acting under obligations not confined to the limits of our own society. It is impossible not to be sensible that we are acting for all mankind."[26] Indeed, these qualities, negative and positive, could easily be joined in a single individual such as Jefferson. Has one side—a self-centered, America-first approach to the world—become in the twentieth century the dominant voice in the councils of the nation, and the other half—a daring belief in human betterment and liberation—become a subordinate theme? Perhaps. We must be careful, however, not to read such an imbalance into the past. With their actions and words the expansionists of the eighteenth century have provided us with a valuable, if potentially dangerous, legacy, and it falls on our shoulders to determine how to continue and refine their vision in today's world.

26. Jefferson to Joseph Priestley, June 19, 1802, quoted in Kim, "The American Revolution and the Modern World," 221.

APPENDIX

Members of the Factions

The lists that follow must be used with care and with an awareness of the vagaries of early American politics. Colonial factions were rarely rigidly defined and often lacked even such rudiments of formal structure as electoral slates or party names. Nonetheless, local politicians recognized the factional nature of provincial politics and worked together in identifiable groups over long periods of time; it is these aggregations that are presented below. In view of the looseness of the parties, expansionists and nonexpansionists must be identified by broad patterns of political commitment rather than absolute, personal consistency. The detailed examination in the text of some of the leaders should make clear that the crosscurrents of personal pique or ambition or changing self-interest could and often did mix with the Gulf Stream of ideological outlook. Similarly, no one of the specific activities tabulated below can be read as a full warrant of membership in a particular party. A preponderance of evidence, rather than a mechanistic approach to any particular set of data, is required.

While this appendix expands the number of names presented in the text, it does not present a complete roster of partisans in the five provinces. The names that follow were selected, at least in part, from a series of worksheets that tabulate data for four to five hundred individuals in each colony. Those seeking to enlarge the present listings should consult these worksheets, which have been deposited in the archives of Scott Library, York University.

Finally, anyone who has wrestled with colonial American orthography realizes the possibilities for error arising from the variant spellings of a single name, identical spellings that turn out to be different persons, or fathers and sons who appear without any hint of Sr. or Jr. Despite such problems (and the mechanical errors that creep into such enterprises) I am satisfied that these lists stand as a reasonably accurate guide to the more prominent members of the factions in the several commonwealths.

Massachusetts, 1700–1776

Expansionists

	Accepts or rejects 1726 charter	Silver banker 1740	Merchant leader of nonimportation 1768	Accepts or rejects seat on committee of correspondence 1772	North End caucus	Patriot or loyalist
John Andrews						P
Israel Ashley*						L
John Ashley*						L
Jonathan Ashley, Jr.*						P
Benjamin Austin				R		
Samuel Austin			x			P
James Bowdoin, Jr.						P
James Bowdoin, Sr.		x				
Rev. Charles Chauncy						P
John Colman	R					
Rev. Samuel Cooper						P
Thomas Cushing I				R		
Thomas Cushing II						P
Paul Dudley	A					
William Dudley	A					
Timothy Dwight*						
John Hancock				R		P
Thomas Hancock						P
Joseph Hawley*						P
Samuel Hewes						
John Higginson			x			
Henderson Inches		x			x	P
John Lowell						P

[340]

Name					
Rev. Jonathan Mayhew					
George Minot				x†	
John Minot					
Joseph Minot					
James Otis, Jr.	P	A			
James Otis, Sr.	P				
John Otis	P				
Joseph Otis					
Samuel A. Otis					
William Phillips	P	R	x		
Edmund Quincy					A
Josiah Quincy, Jr.	P	A			
Josiah Quincy, Sr.				x	
John Rowe	P				
John Scollay	P		x		
Nathaniel Sparhawk	P	R	x		
John Stoddard*					A
Solomon Stoddard*					
Oxenbridge Thacher					A
Penn Townsend					A
Samuel Waldo					
Joseph Waldo					
Arnold Welles	P		x		
Jacob Wendell				x†	
Oliver Wendell	P	A			

[341]

*From western counties of Hampshire and Berkshire.
†Also accepted land bank notes.

continued on next page

Massachusetts, 1700–1776

Expansionists (continued)

	Accepts or rejects 1726 charter	Silver banker 1740	Merchant leader of nonimportation 1768	Accepts or rejects seat on committee of correspondence 1772	North End caucus	Patriot or loyalist
Abijiah Williams*						L
Ephraim Williams*						L
Israel Williams*	A	x†				
Adam Winthrop					x	P
Prof. John Winthrop						
Wait Winthrop						
John Worthington*						L

*From the western counties of Hampshire and Berkshire.
†Also accepted land bank notes.

Nonexpansionists

	Accepts or rejects 1726 charter	Silver banker 1740	Trinity Church member	Opposes nonimportation 1768	Hutchinson or Gage addresser	Patriot or loyalist
Thomas Amory						
John Amory				x		L
Charles Apthorp		x	x			
Thomas Apthorp					x	
William Apthorp		x				L
Robert Auchmuty					x	L

[342]

Name					
James Boutineau			x	x	L
John Boylston					L
Benjamin Clarke			x	x	L
Richard Clarke		x		x	L
Nathaniel Coffin				x	L
William Coffin, Jr.					L
William Coffin, Sr.			x	x	L
Addington Davenport			x		L
Gilbert Deblois		x			L
Lewis Deblois		x			L
William Douglass					
Rev. Andrew Eliot					P?
George Erving					L
John Erving, Jr.				x	L
John Erving, Sr.			x	x	L
Benjamin Faneuil			x	x	L
Dr. Silvester Gardiner				x	L
Harrison Gray, Jr.				x	L
Harrison Gray, Sr.				x	L
Thomas Gray					
Edward Hutchinson	A				
Edward Hutchinson (d. 1806)		x		x	L
Foster Hutchinson					L
[Gov.] Thomas Hutchinson					L
Thomas Hutchinson, Sr.	A				L

[343]

continued on next page

Massachusetts, 1700–1776

Nonexpansionists (continued)

	Accepts or rejects 1726 charter	Silver banker 1740	Trinity Church member	Opposes nonimportation 1768	Hutchinson or Gage addresser	Patriot or loyalist
Thomas Lee		x		x		L
Daniel Leonard						L
George Leonard						L
Theophilus Lillie		x		x	x	L
Byfield Lyde		x			x	
Cotton Mather						
Andrew Oliver		x				L
Daniel Oliver	A					
Peter Oliver						L
Oliver Partridge						
Nathaniel Rogers		x				
John Ruggles						L
Timothy Ruggles						L
Jonathan Sewall						
Samuel Sewall (d. 1730)						
Samuel Sewall (cousin)		x				
Samuel Sewall					x	L
Stephen Sewall						
Jonathan Simpson						L
John Spooner		x		x		L
John Vassal		x			x	L

[344]

Popular Party

Name	Accepts or rejects 1726 charter	Land banker 1740	Accepts or rejects seat on committee of correspondence 1772	North End caucus	Tea Party participant 1773	Patriot or loyalist
Abijah Willard						L
Edward Winslow						L
Isaac Winslow, Jr.		x			x	L
Isaac Winslow, Sr.					x	L
John Winslow, Jr.					x	L
John Winslow, Sr.						L
Joshua Winslow, Jr.		x			x	L
Joshua Winslow, Sr.					x	L
John Adams				x		P
Samuel Adams, Jr.			A	x		P
Samuel Adams, Sr.		x				
James Allen						
Henry Bass				x	x	P
Nathaniel Byfield	R					
John Clark	R					
William Clark	R					
John Colman		x				
Elisha Cooke, Jr.	R					
Elisha Cooke, Sr.						

[345]

continued on next page

Massachusetts, 1700–1776
Popular Party (continued)

	Accepts or rejects 1726 charter	Land banker 1740	Accepts or rejects seat on committee of correspondence 1772	North End caucus	Tea Party participant 1773	Patriot or loyalist
Benjamin Edes				x		
William Greenleaf		x				P
Joseph Greenleaf				x		P
Joseph Hale	R					
Estes Hatch		x				
Joseph Heath						
Ebenezer Mackintosh					x	
William Molineux			A	x	x	P
Oliver Noyes	R					
Thomas Palmer						
William Payne						
William Powell			A			
Paul Revere				x	x	P
John Ruddock		x		x		P
Abiel Ruddock				x		P
William Stoddard		x		x		
Jonathan Stoddard						
John Tyng						
Joseph Warren			A	x		P
Thomas Young				x	x	P

Sources: Note that none of the listed expansionists was a member of Trinity Church, opposed nonimportation, addressed Hutchinson or Gage, was a land banker, or participated in the Tea Party; no listed nonexpansionist was a merchant leader of nonimportation, participated in the Tea Party, the land bank, or the North End caucus, and none either accepted or rejected a seat on the Boston committee of correspondence; none of the listed popular party members was a silver banker, a merchant leader of nonimportation, a Trinity Church member, none opposed nonimportation or addressed Hutchinson or Gage.

On the 1726 charter: Albert Matthews, "Acceptance of the Explanatory Charter, 1725–1726," CSM *Pubs.*, xiv (1913), 389–400.

On silver bankers: Andrew McFarland Davis, ed., "List of Subscribers to the Silver Bank," CSM *Pubs.*, iv (1910), 195–200; on silver bankers who agreed to take land bank notes: Anthony G. Roeber, "'Her Merchandize . . . Shall Be Holiness to the Lord': The Progress and Decline of the Puritan Gentility at the Brattle Street Church, Boston, 1715–1745," *NEHGR*, cxxxi (1977), 189n.

On nonimportation: Report of Committee of Merchants, March 1768, Samuel P. Savage Papers, 1751–1829, MHS.

On the Boston committee of correspondence: Richard D. Brown, *Revolutionary Politics in Massachusetts: The Boston Committee of Correspondence and the Towns, 1772–1774* (Cambridge, Mass., 1970), 59–60.

On patriots: *A Report of the Record Commissioners of the City of Boston Containing the Boston Town Records, 1770 through 1777* (Boston, 1887); Marc Egnal, "Society and Politics in Massachusetts, 1774 to 1778" (M.A. thesis, Univ. of Wisconsin, 1967), chaps. 2, 3, 7.

On Trinity Church: [The Wardens and Vestry of Trinity Church], *Trinity Church in the City of Boston, Massachusetts, 1733–1793* (Boston, 1933), 201–5.

On Hutchinson and Gage addressers: John K. Wiggin, ed., "A List of 'Protestors' and 'Addressers,'" MHS *Procs.*, 1st ser., ii (1869–1870), 392–95; James H. Stark, *The Loyalists of Massachusetts and the Other Side of the American Revolution* (Boston, 1910), 124–32.

On loyalists: Stark, *Loyalists of Massachusetts*, 132–140 (list of those who left with the royal fleet and those banished by the Massachusetts legislature); Edward A. Jones, *The Loyalists of Massachusetts: Their Memorials, Petitions, and Claims* (London, 1930), 311–12 (list of the Loyal American Associators of Boston); more generally, Lorenzo Sabine, *Biographical Sketches of Loyalists of the American Revolution*, 2 vols. (Boston, 1864).

On land bankers: Andrew McFarland Davis, "Alphabetical List of Partners in the Land Bank of 1740," *NEHGR*, l (1896), 187–97, 308–17; Davis, "List of Partners in the Land Bank of 1740," CSM *Pubs.*, iv (1910), 166–94.

On the North End Caucus: Elbridge H. Goss, *The Life of Colonel Paul Revere*, 2 vols. (Boston, 1891), II, 635–44.

On Tea Party participants: Francis G. Drake, *Tea Leaves: Being a Collection of Letters and Documents Relating to the Shipment of Tea to the American Colonies in the Year 1773 by the East India Company* (Boston, 1854), xii–cxiv.

Several individuals not covered by any category are discussed in the text. Also valuable is William H. Whitmore, *The Massachusetts Civil List for the Colonial and Provincial Periods, 1630–1740* (Albany, N.Y., 1870). Whitmore lists councillors, judges, and other provincial appointees. William Pencak, *War, Politics, & Revolution in Provincial Massachusetts* (Boston, 1981), 251–85, presents several useful lists, including assembly leaders and loyalists.

New York, 1719–1775

	Politically active councillor or assemblyman			Committee of Safety 1775	Patriot or loyalist
Expansionists	1719–1739	1740–1759	1760–1775		
James Alexander	C	C			
William Alexander			C		
Nicholas Bayard					
Henry Beekman	A	A			
Abraham Brasher				x	P
George Clinton			A		P
Charles DeWitt			A		P
James Duane			A		P
Francis Lewis					P
Henry Livingston		A	A		P
Peter R. Livingston			A		P
Peter V. B. Livingston				x	P
Philip Livingston (d. 1749)	C	C			
Philip Livingston (d. 1778)		A	A		P
Robert Livingston (d. 1728)	A				
Robert Campbell Livingston					
Robert Livingston, Jr.	A	A			P
Robert R. Livingston		A	A		P
William Livingston		A	A		P
Abram P. Lott		A	A		P
Alexander McDougall				x	P
Gouverneur Morris				x	P
Lewis Morris, Sr.	A				

[348]

	Politically active councillor or assemblyman			Attends March 18, 1770, dinner	Opposes nonimportation 1770	Patriot or loyalist
	1719–1739	1740–1759	1760–1775			
Lewis Morris, Jr.	C	A				P
Lewis Morris III		A				P
Jacobus Myndertse						
Philip Schuyler		A				P
John Morin Scott					x	P
William Smith, Jr.						L
William Smith, Sr.						
Abraham Ten Broeck						P
Pierre Van Cortlandt					x	P
Rip Van Dam	C					
Abraham Van Horne	C	A				
Jeremiah Van Rensselaer	A	A				
John Baptist Van Rensselaer		A				
Nonexpansionists						
John Alsop				x	x	L
Charles Ward Apthorp			C			L
Theophylact Bache				x	x	L
William Bayard					x	L
Stephen Bayard		C				
Christopher Billop			A			L
Benjamin Boothe						L

[349]

continued on next page

New York, 1719–1775
Nonexpansionists (continued)

	Politically active councillor or assemblyman			Attends March 18, 1770, dinner	Opposes nonimportation 1770	Patriot or loyalist
	1719–1739	1740–1759	1760–1775			
Henry Cruger		A	C		x	
John Cruger		A	A	x	x	L?
John Harris Cruger			C	x?	x	L
James DeLancey (d. 1760)	C	C				L
James DeLancey (d. 1800)			C,A	x	x	L
John DeLancey II			A			L
Oliver DeLancey		A	C,A	x		
Peter DeLancey		A	A	x		
Stephen DeLancey	C					
John DeNoyelles			A			L
George Folliot				x	x?	L
Daniel Horsmanden	C	C	C			L
James Jauncey			C,A	x	x	L
James Jauncey, Jr.				x		L
Thomas Jones				x	x	L
Daniel Kissam			A			L
Edward Laight					x	L
Isaac Low				x	x	L
Gabriel Ludlow					x?	L
William McAdam				x		L
Charles McEvers					x	L
John Moore						L
Adolph Philipse	A,C	C,A				L
Frederick Philipse (d. 1751)	A	A				L

[350]

John Rapalaje		A			L
Rem Rapalaje			x		L
Joseph Reade		C			
Peter Schuyler		C,A			
Myndert Schuyler					L
Rev. Samuel Seabury		A			L
Benjamin Seaman					L
Miles Sherbrooke			x		L
John Thurman				x	
Jacobus Van Cortlandt	C				
Philip Van Cortlandt	C				
Alexander Wallace			x	x	L
Hugh Wallace				x	L
Jacob Walton		A	x	x	L
William Walton	C	C,A	x	x	L
John Watts	C	C	x	x	L
Henry White		C		x	L
Richard Yates				x	L

SOURCES: Note that none of the listed expansionists was at the March 18, 1770, dinner of the Friends of Liberty and Trade, and none opposed nonimportation. None of the listed nonexpansionists was on the Committee of Safety.

On politically active councillors and assemblymen: Patricia U. Bonomi, *A Factious People: Politics and Society in Colonial New York* (New York, 1971), 295–316 (list of councillors and legislators), and chap. 7; on divisions in the council: Stanley N. Katz, *Newcastle's New York: Anglo-American Politics, 1732–1753* (Cambridge, Mass., 1968), 87–88, 148–49, 166–68, 179; William Smith, Jr., *The History of the Province of New York*, ed. Michael Kammen, 2 vols. (Cambridge, Mass., 1972), II, 68, 125; William H. W. Sabine, ed., *Historical Memoirs from 16 March 1763 to 25 July 1778 of William Smith*, 2 vols. (1956, 1958; rpt. New York, 1969), I, 46–47; on splits in the assembly: *Journal of the Votes and Proceedings of the General Assembly of the Colony of New York, from 1766 to 1776 Inclusive* (Albany, 1820).

On Committee of Safety: Carl L. Becker, *The History of Political Parties in the Province of New York, 1760–1776* (Madison, Wis., 1909), 211, 234.

On patriots and tories: Useful lists are presented in Becker, *Political Parties*, passim; Virginia D. Harrington, *The New York Merchant on the Eve of the Revolution* (New York, 1935), 348–51; Lorenzo Sabine, *Biographical Sketches of Loyalists of the American Revolution*, 2 vols. (Boston, 1864).

On the Friends of Liberty and Trade dinner: *New York Journal*, Apr. 12, 1770.

On opposition to nonimportation: *Boston Gazette*, July 23, 1770.

Some individuals not covered by the categories in this table are discussed in the text.

Pennsylvania, 1740–1775

Expansionists

	Religion*	Military activity 1748 or 1755	Opposes Quaker legislature 1755	Favors or opposes nonimportation 1770	Bank of Pa. 1780	Patriot, neutral, or loyalist
Andrew Allen	P					L
James Allen	P					L
John Allen	P					L
William Allen	P	x	x			L
Richard Bache	A				x	P
John Benezet	A?			O		P
Philip Benezet	A	x	x			P?
William Bingham	A	x				P
William Bradford	P	x				P
George Bryan	P					P
John Cadwallader	A?			F		P
Samuel Carsan		x				P?
Peter Chevalier	P			F		P
Matthew Clarkson		x			x	P
George Clymer	A			F	x	P
John Cox, Jr.	P			F	x	P
John Dickinson	ex-Q					P
Tench Francis	A			O	x	P
Benjamin Franklin	Deist	x				P
John Gibson	A			F	x	P
James Hamilton	Deist,A					N
Andrew Hodge	P		x		x	P

[352]

Name	Religion				
William Hodge	ex-Q		F	x	P
Samuel Howell	P		F	x	P
Alex Huston	A?			x	
John Inglis		x			P
Henry Keppele, Jr.	L	x			
Henry Keppele, Sr.	L				
John Kidd		x		x	P
Thomas Lawrence	Q or A?	x		x	P
James Loughead			F		P
Benjamin Loxley	B	x			P
William Masters	Q or A?	x	F		P
Archibald McCall	A?			x	
Samuel McCall, Jr.	A?			x	
Samuel McCall, Sr.	A?	x?		x	
George Meade	RC?		F	x	P
James Mease	P			x	P
Samuel Mifflin	ex-Q	x	F	x	P
Thomas Mifflin	ex-Q		F	x	P
William Moore	A	x		x	P
Robert Morris				x	P
John M. Nesbitt	P		F	x	P
John Nixon	A			x	P
Joseph Parker	Q				P
Rev. Richard Peters	A				
William Plumstead	ex-Q,A	x	F	x	P
Joseph Reed	P				P
John Rhea	P	x			P
Daniel Roberdeau	P	x			P
John Ross	A	x			P
William Rush	P	x		x	P?

continued on next page

Pennsylvania, 1740–1775

Expansionists (continued)

Name	Religion*	Military activity 1748 or 1755	Opposes Quaker legislature 1755	Favors or opposes nonimportation 1770	Bank of Pa. 1780	Patriot, neutral, or loyalist
John Shee	A?				x	P
William Shippen	P		x	F		P?
Rev. William Smith	A					N?
Joseph Stamper		x	x			
Amos Strettel	ex-Q,A		x			
Gilbert Tennent	P		x			P
Charles Thomson	P			F	x	P
John Wilco	A		x			
Charles Willing	A					
Thomas Willing	A	x			x	P
James Wilson			x			P

Nonexpansionists

Name	Religion*	Favors or opposes nonimportation 1770	Exiled Quaker 1777	Blacklisted tory	Patriot, neutral, or loyalist
Clement Biddle	Q?	O			N
John Biddle	Q	O		x	L
Phineas Bond	ex-Q,A		x	x	N
Elijah Brown	Q				N
William Brown	Q			x	N

Name					
Thomas Clifford	Q				N
Hugh Donaldson	Q	O			N
Henry Drinker	Q	O			N
John Drinker	Q	O			N
Samuel Emlen, Jr.	Q				N
Jonathan Evans				x	L?
Joseph Fisher	Q				N
Samuel Fisher	Q		x		N
Thomas Fisher	Q		x		N
Joseph Fox	Q	O	.	x	L
Joseph Galloway	ex-Q			x	N
Peter Howard	Q			x	L?
Joshua Howell	A				
John Hughes	A				
Abel James	Q	O		x	N
Owen Jones, Jr.	Q			x	N
Dr. John Kearsley	Q			x	L?
John Kinsey	Q				
Thomas Leech	A				
Thomas Lightfoot	Q			x	N
Randle Mitchell	A	O			
Evan Morgan	A				
Isaac Norris	Q				
Richard Parker	Q	O			N
Israel Pemberton, Jr.	Q		x		
Israel Pemberton, Sr.	Q				N
James Pemberton	Q		x		N

[355]

continued on next page

Pennsylvania, 1740–1775

Nonexpansionists (continued)

	Religion*	Favors or opposes nonimportation 1770	Exiled Quaker 1777	Blacklisted tory	Patriot, neutral, or loyalist
John Pemberton	Q		x		N
Joseph Pemberton	Q				N
Edward Penington	Q		x		N
Samuel Pleasants	Q		x		N
John Reynell	Q	O			N?
Samuel Rhoads, Jr.	Q				N
Daniel Rundle				x	L?
Christopher Sauer, Jr.	D?S?			x	N?
Christopher Sauer, Sr.	D?S?			x	N?
Bertles Shee		O			L
Samuel Shoemaker	Q			x	
John Taylor				x	L?
Richard Waln	Q				N
Jeremiah Warder	Q	O			N
William West, Jr.	Q	O		x	N
Isaac Wharton	Q			x	L
Thomas Wharton, Sr.	Q		x		N
William Wharton	Q				N?

*A, Anglican; D, Dunker; L, Lutheran; P, Presbyterian; Q, Quaker; RC, Roman Catholic; S, Schwenkfelder.

SOURCES: Note that none of the listed expansionists was an exiled Quaker or blacklisted tory; none of the listed nonexpansionists was engaged in military activity in 1748 or 1775, opposed the Quaker legislature, or participated in the Bank of Pennsylvania.
On religion: Thomas H. Montgomery, "List of Vestrymen of Christ Church, Philadelphia," *PMHB*, xix (1895), 518–26 (Anglicans); John Thomas Scharf and Thompson Westcott, *History of Philadelphia, 1609–1884*, 3 vols. (Philadelphia, 1884), II, 1267, 1306–9 (Baptists and Presbyterians);

[356]

William Wade Hinshaw, ed., *The Encyclopedia of Quaker Genealogy* (Ann Arbor, Mich., 1938), and Pennsylvania and New Jersey Yearly Meeting to London Yearly Meeting, Sept. 1764, Epistles Received, IV, 140, Friends House Library, London (Quakers); more generally, John W. Jordan, *Colonial and Revolutionary Families of Pennsylvania*, 3 vols. (New York, 1911); Stephen Brobeck, "Revolutionary Change in Colonial Philadelphia: The Brief Life of the Proprietary Gentry," *WMQ*, 3d ser., XXXII (1976), 410–34; Richard Alan Ryerson, *The Revolution Is Now Begun: The Radical Committees of Philadelphia, 1765–1776* (Philadelphia, 1976), passim, is an important source for members of all denominations.

On military activity, 1748 and 1755: *Pennsylvania Gazette*, Jan. 5, 1748 (officers of the Association); Scharf and Westcott, *History of Philadelphia*, I, 247–48 (officers of the 1755 militia); *The Papers of Benjamin Franklin*, ed. Leonard W. Labaree et al. (New Haven, Conn., 1959–   ), VI, 409 (additional names).

On opponents of the Quaker assembly, 1755: The list of those signing a memorial demanding that the king take steps to remodel the Quaker assembly is presented in Charles Stillé, "The Attitude of the Quakers in the Provincial Wars," *PMHB*, X (1886), 296–97.

On supporters and opponents of nonimportation: Letter from Philadelphia Merchant Committee, Nov. 25, 1769, *Pennsylvania Gazette*, May 10, 1770; Henry Drinker to Abel James, Apr. 29, 1770, "Effects of the 'Non-Importation Agreement' in Philadelphia, 1769–1770," *PMHB*, XIV (1890), 42–44; list of merchants in favor and those opposed, *Pennsylvania Gazette*, Sept. 20, 1770, and see Sept. 27, Oct. 4, 1770; Memorial of Phila. Merchants, Apr. 18, 1769, Franklin Papers, American Philosophical Society; Ryerson, *Revolution Is Now Begun*, 29–33, 77–79.

On Bank of Pennsylvania: Samuel Hazard, ed., *Hazard's Register of Pennsylvania . . .* , 16 vols. (Philadelphia, 1828–1835), II, 260 (list of directors and subscribers).

On patriots, neutrals, and loyalists: "Members of the Patriotic Association of Philadelphia, 1778," *PMHB*, XXIII (1899), 356–59; Scharf and Westcott, *History of Philadelphia*, I, 298, 337, 386–87, 395, 396; Robert A. East, *Business Enterprise in the American Revolutionary Era* (New York, 1938), esp. 124–60. The 1779 tax assessment punished tories and neutrals with a "double tax," *Pennsylvania Archives*, 3d ser. (Harrisburg, 1894–97), XII–XXII. On the distinction between neutrality and loyalism among Quakers, see Wallace Brown, *The King's Friends: The Composition and Motives of the American Loyalist Claimants* (Providence, R.I., 1965), 131–53.

On exiled Quakers: James D. Anderson, "Thomas Wharton, Exile in Virginia, 1777–1778," *VMHB*, LXXXIX (1981), 425–47, and particularly the list on 428.

On blacklisted tories: *Black List: A List of Those Tories Who Took Part with Great Britain in the Revolutionary War and Were Attainted of High Treason, Commonly Called the Black List. To Which Is Prefixed the Legal Opinions of Attorney Generals McKean & Dallas &c.* (Philadelphia, 1802). Several of those not covered by any of the categories in this table are discussed in the text. See also Petition for Royal Government, 1764, Privy Council 1, bundle 50, PRO, which identifies members of the Quaker party. Furthermore, various social organizations paralleled factional lines. See the discussion of these societies in Chapter 4 and in Daniel Gilbert, "Patterns of Organization and Membership in Colonial Philadelphia Club Life, 1725–1755" (Ph.D. diss., Univ. of Pennsylvania, 1952).

Virginia, 1747–1775

		Expansionists			
	Residence*	Member Greenbriar, Loyal, Ohio, or New River land companies	Robinson debtor 1766	Initiates committee of correspondence 1773 or fast day 1774	Patriot, neutral, or loyalist
Dabney Carr	BR			1773	P?
Charles Carter, Jr.	NN		x		P
Landon Carter	NN				P
Robert Carter	NN	O			
Rev. Samuel Davies					
Henry Fitzhugh	NN				P
William Fitzhugh	NN		x		P
Patrick Henry	SE			1773, 1774	P
Thomas Jefferson	BR			1773, 1774	P
George Johnston	NN				P
Arthur Lee	NN			1773, 1774	P?
Francis Lightfoot Lee	NN				P
Philip Ludwell Lee	NN	O			
Richard Henry Lee	NN	O		1773, 1774	P
Thomas Lee	NN	O			
Thomas Ludwell Lee	NN	O			
James Madison	BR	O			P
George Mason	NN	O			P
George Mercer	NN	O?			L
James Mercer	NN				P
John Mercer	NN	O	x		P?
Rev. James Maury	SE	L			

	Residence*	Member Greenbriar, Loyal, Ohio, or New River land companies	Robinson debtor 1766	Opposes Henry's resolves on Stamp Act 1765 or militia 1775	Patriot, neutral, or loyalist
James Scott	NN	O			
John Tayloe	NN	O			
Presley Thornton	NN	O			
Augustine Washington	NN	O			
George Washington	NN	O			P
Lawrence Washington	NN	O			
Nonexpansionists					
John Baylor	SE	L			P?
Robert Beverley	SE				N
William Beverley	SE	G	x		
Richard Bland	SE			1765	P
Carter Braxton	SE		x		
George Braxton	SE		x?		
Armistead Burwell	SE	NR			
Lewis Burwell	SE		x		P?
William Byrd III	SE		x		L
Rev. John Camm	SE				L
George Carrington	SE	NR			P?
Paul Carrington	SE				P?
Archibald Cary	SE		x		
Richard Corbin, Jr.	SE				L
Richard Corbin, Sr.	SE				N

[359]

continued on next page

Virginia, 1747–1775

Nonexpansionists (continued)

	Residence*	Member Greenbriar, Loyal, Ohio, or New River land companies	Robinson debtor 1766	Opposes Henry's resolves on Stamp Act 1765 or militia 1775	Patriot, neutral, or loyalist
Harry Gaines	SE		x		
Benjamin Grymes	SE		x		
John Randolph Grymes	SE				L
Benjamin Harrison	SE				P
Nathaniel Harrison	SE		x		P
Benjamin Hubbard	SE		x		
John Lewis	SE	G,L			
Bernard Moore	SE	NR	x		
Thomas Moore	SE		x		
Thomas Nelson	SE	G			P
Robert C. Nicholas	SE			1765, 1775	P
William Byrd Page	SE				L
Edmund Pendleton	SE	L,NR	x	1775	P
James Power	SE	NR			
John Randolph	SE		x		P
Peyton Randolph	SE	NR		1765, 1775	P
John Robinson, Jr.	SE	G,L		1765	
John Robinson, Sr.	SE	G			
Benjamin Robinson	SE		x		

Name					
John Thorton	SE	L			
Robert Tucker	SE	NR			
Benjamin Waller	SE	NR			
John Wayles	SE		x		
Beverley Whiting	SE		x		
John Whiting	SE		x		
Ralph Wormley	SE		x		
George Wythe	SE			N	1765, 1775
				P	

* *BR*, Blue Ridge counties but not in the Northern Neck; *NN*, Northern Neck; *SE*, south of the Rappahannock and east of the Blue Ridge.

SOURCES: Note that none of the listed expansionists opposed either set of Henry's resolves, and none of the listed nonexpansionists helped initiate the committee of correspondence or the fast day.

On residence: Among the more valuable sources are *Journals of the House of Burgesses of Virginia, 1619–1776*, ed. John Pendleton Kennedy (Richmond, 1905–15); *Executive Journals of the Council of Virginia*, ed. H. R. McIlwaine and Wilbur L. Hall (Richmond, 1925–45), esp. vol. v; Richard L. Morton, *Colonial Virginia*, vol. II: *Westward Expansion and Prelude to Revolution, 1710–1763* (Chapel Hill, N.C., 1970).

On land company membership: Morton, *Colonial Virginia*, 571 (Greenbriar); Archibald Henderson, "Dr. Thomas Walker and the Loyal Company of Virginia," *AAS Proceedings*, n.s., XLI (1931), 77–121, list on 88–89 (Loyal); Morton, *Colonial Virginia*, II, 572, and Lucille Griffith, *The Virginia House of Burgesses, 1750–1774* (University, Ala., 1968, 1970), 130 (New River); Kenneth P. Bailey, *The Ohio Company of Virginia and the Westward Movement, 1748–1792: A Chapter in the History of the Colonial Frontier* (Glendale, Calif., 1939), list on 35–36, and Alfred P. James, *The Ohio Company: Its Inner History* (Pittsburgh, 1959) (Ohio). I have excluded those who dropped out of the Ohio Company shortly after its inception.

On debtors to the estate of John Robinson, Jr.: David John Mays, *Edmund Pendleton, 1721–1803: A Biography*, 2 vols. (Cambridge, Mass., 1952), I, 358–69. Only those whose debt was five hundred pounds or more are noted.

On committee of correspondence and the fast day of 1774: Thomas Jefferson, "Autobiography," in *The Writings of Thomas Jefferson*, ed. Andrew A. Lipscomb, 18 vols. (Washington, D.C., 1903), I, 7–8, 9–11.

On patriots, neutrals, or loyalists: Wallace Brown, *The King's Friends: The Composition and Motives of the American Loyalist Claimants* (Providence, R.I., 1965), 178–91; Isaac S. Harrell, *Loyalism in Virginia: Chapters in the Economic History of the Revolution* (Durham, N.C., 1926); Lorenzo Sabine, *Biographical Sketches of Loyalists of the American Revolution with an Historical Essay*, 2 vols. (Boston, 1864); Jackson T. Main, "The One Hundred," *WMQ*, 3d ser., XI (1954), 354–58; *Journals of the House of Delegates of Virginia, 1776–1790*, 4 vols. (Richmond, 1827–28).

On opposition to Patrick Henry's Stamp Act and militia resolves: William Wirt, *Sketches of the Life and Character of Patrick Henry*, 9th ed. (Philadelphia, 1845 [orig. pub. 1817]), 78–79; Edmund S. Morgan and Helen M. Morgan, *The Stamp Act Crisis: Prologue to Revolution* (Chapel Hill, N.C., 1953, 1962), 120–32; Edmund S. Morgan, ed., *Prologue to Revolution: The Stamp Act Crisis, Sources and Documents* (Chapel Hill, N.C., 1959), 46–50, 82–85; *Proceedings of Convention, Mar. 23, 1775*; William J. Van Schreeven and Robert L. Scribner, eds., *Revolutionary Virginia: The Road to Independence* (Charlottesville, Va., 1973–   ), II, 366–70; William Wirt Henry, *Patrick Henry: Life, Correspondence, and Speeches*, 3 vols. (New York, 1832), I, 255–75; Jefferson, Appendix to "Autobiography," *Writings of Jefferson*, I, 168.

South Carolina, 1700–1725

Expansionists

	Anglican or dissenter	Associate of Thomas Nairne	Supports or opposes proprietors 1719–1720	Favors or opposes paper money
John Barnwell	D	x	O	
Thomas Broughton	A		O	
George Chicken	D	x	O	
Samuel Eveleigh			O	F
John Fenwick	D	x		
Tobias Fitch			O	F
William Gibbon			O	F
Thomas Hepworth				F
Hugh Hext			O	F
Daniel Huger			O	F?
James Kinloch	D		O	F
Arthur Middleton	A		O	F
James Moore, Jr.	A		O	F
James Moore, Sr.	A			
Thomas Nairne	A	x		F
John Raven, Jr.	D		O	F
Benjamin Schenkingh	A?		O	
Alexander Skene	A		O	F
Richard Smith			O	F
Francis Yonge			O	

[362]

Nonexpansionists

	Anglican or dissenter	Opposes Governor James Moore	Supports or opposes proprietors 1719–1720	Favors or opposes paper money
John Ash	D	x		
Stephen Bull	D	x		
Charles Burnham	D	x		
Hugh Butler			S	O
Benjamin De La Conseillere	D		S	O
Abraham Eve	D	x		
Benjamin Godin	D,A		S?	O
Charles Hart	A		S	
Ralph Izard	A		S	O
William Rhett	A		S	
Nicholas Trott	A		S	O
Henry Wigginton	D	x		

SOURCES: Note that none of the listed expansionists opposed Governor Moore, and none of the listed nonexpansionists was an associate of Nairne.

The most valuable single source for identifying South Carolina partisans is Walter B. Edgar and N. Louise Bailey, eds., *Biographical Directory of the South Carolina House of Representatives*, vol. II: *The Commons House of Assembly, 1692–1775* (Columbia, S.C., 1977). This book, which could well be listed under each of the headings that follow, profiles all the individuals listed in this table except Francis Yonge and Charles Hart.

On religion: M. Eugene Sirmans, *Colonial South Carolina: A Political History, 1663–1763* (Chapel Hill, N.C., 1966), 17–163.

On associates of Thomas Nairne: Sirmans, *Colonial South Carolina*, 81.

On support for or opposition to the proprietors: Sirmans, *Colonial South Carolina*, 103–44. Also see the list in Richard Waterhouse, "South Carolina's Colonial Elite: A Study in the Social Structure and Political Culture of a Southern Colony, 1670–1760" (Ph.D. diss., Johns Hopkins Univ., 1973), 118.

On paper money: Sirmans, *Colonial South Carolina*, 86–87, 108–11, 115–16, 120–24, 130.

On opposition to Governor Moore: Sirmans, *Colonial South Carolina*, 75–93.

[363]

South Carolina, 1756–1775

Expansionists

	Small or large slave importer	Supports war 1757–1762	Accepts or rejects place in Nov. 1768 assembly	Leads or opposes nonimportation 1769–1770	Council of Safety 1775	Patriot or loyalist
Miles Brewton*	L	x		L	x	P/L
Thomas Bee*					x	P
David Deas*		x				P
Daniel D'Oyley*†		x		L		P
William H. Drayton*†‡				O	x	P
John Edwards*	L			L		P
Benjamin Elliot*		x	A	L	x	P
Charles Elliot*	S		A	L		P
Barnard Elliot*†		x		L		P
Thomas Evance*	L?		A			P
Thomas Farr, Jr.*	L	x		L		P
Thomas Ferguson*				L	x	P
Christopher Gadsden*	S	x		L		P
Tacitus Gaillard*			A	L		P
John Abbott Hall	L			L		P
Thomas Heyward, Jr.*						P
Benjamin Huger*				L		P
Isaac Huger*		x				P
John Huger*		x	A	L	x	P
Henry Hyrne, Sr.*		x			x	P
Henry Hyrne, Jr.*		x?			x	P

Ralph Izard, Jr.		x			x	P
Henry Laurens*	L	x	A	L	x	P
John Lloyd*	S	x	A			P
Rawlins Lowndes*†		x	R	L	x	P?
Thomas Lynch*			A	L	x	P
John Mackenzie*	L			L		P
Gabriel Manigault*		x	A			P
Peter Manigault*		x				P
Francis Marion		x			x	P
Arthur Middleton*					x	P
Henry Middleton*†		x			x	P
Thomas Middleton*	L	x				P?
Isaac Motte*		x		L		P
William Moultrie*		x	A	L		P
John Neufville	L			L		P
John Parker*				L		P
James Parsons*		x	A	L	x	P
Charles Pinckney (d. 1758)*†		x?				P/L
Charles Pinckney (d. 1782)*		x	A	L	x	P
Charles C. Pinckney*						P
Peter Porcher*		x				P
George G. Powell*		x		L		P
Robert Quash, Jr.*			A			P
Richard Richardson*		x				P
Edward Rutledge*					x	P
John Rutledge*†			A		x	P
Thomas Savage*	L		A		x	P
William Scott*			A			P

continued on next page

South Carolina, 1756–1775

Expansionists (continued)

	Small or large slave importer	Supports war 1757–1762	Accepts or rejects place in Nov. 1768 assembly	Leads or opposes nonimportation 1769–1770	Council of Safety 1775	Patriot or loyalist
James Skirving, Jr.*	L		A			P
Benjamin Smith*	L	x				P
Roger Smith*	S			L		P
Rev. William Tennent*						P
Peter Timothy*		x				P
John Ward, Jr.*		x		L?		P
Benjamin Waring*			A	L		P
William Williamson*					x	P

Nonexpansionists

	Scot	Small or large slave importer	Supports war, 1757–1762	Accepts or rejects place in Nov. 1768 assembly	Leads or opposes nonimportation 1769–1770	Patriot or loyalist
William Ancrum		L				L
William Baker		S				L
William Blake*		S				L
William Bull*†						L
William Bull, Jr.			x?		O	P/L
John Bremar†						L
Rev. John Bulman						L

[366]

Name						
Martin Campbell	x					L
Brian Cape		S				L
Samuel Carne*		S				L
William Carson		S				L
George Cooke		S				L
Robert Cunningham					O	L
William H. Drayton*†‡		S			O	P
Robert Ellis		S				L
John Freer*				R		L
John Gaillard*						L
Theodore Gaillard*				R		L
Dr. Alexander Garden						L
William Glen					O	L
Paul Hamilton*						L
John Harleston*						L
Alexander Hewatt	x					L
Price Hopkins*						L
Daniel Horry*				R	L	P/L
John Johnson		S				L
Moses Kirkland*				R		L
Aaron Loocock*		S		R	L	P/L
Sir Egerton Leigh*†			x			L
Robert Mackenzie	x?	S				L
John Mills		S				L
John Morris		S				L
William Ogilvy		S				L
Henry Peronneau*						L
Hopkins Price*						L

continued on next page

South Carolina, 1756–1775

Nonexpansionists (continued)

	Scot	Small or large slave importer	Supports war, 1757–1762	Accepts or rejects place in Nov. 1768 assembly	Leads or opposes nonimportation 1769–1770	Patriot or loyalist
Thomas Radcliffe		S				L
Alexander Rose*	x	L				L
John Rose	x?	S				L
George Roupell*†		S				L
Robert Rowand	x					L
Jeremiah Savage*				R		L
George Saxby*†						L
John Scott, Jr.	x?	S				L
Thomas Skottowe*†						L
James Smyth		L				L
John Smyth		L				L
John Stuart*†	x	S	x			L
John Watson	x?	S				L
Robert Wells	x					L
Robert Williams, Jr.*						L
William Wragg*				R	O	L

*Elected to Commons House of Assembly, whether he served or not.
†Royal official: attorney general, councillor, governor, lieutenant governor, judge (not justice of the peace), treasurer or customs official.
‡Changed factional allegiance in 1773 and so is listed with both factions.

SOURCES: Note that of the listed expansionists only David Deas is identifiable as a Scot, and no listed nonexpansionist was a member of the Council of Safety. The table excludes those who left South Carolina after the Seven Years' War to settle in East Florida. These individuals, who typically remained loyal to the Crown, operated in a framework much different from that in South Carolina.
As noted, the most important source of information for South Carolina partisans is *Biographical Directory: Commons House*, which might be

included under each of the headings that follow, for it profiles all delegates elected to the Commons House.

On individuals elected to the Commons House: *Biographical Directory of the South Carolina House of Representatives*, vol. I: *Session Lists, 1692–1973*, ed. Joan S. R. Faunt and Robert E. Rector (Columbia, S.C., 1974).

On royal officials: James K. Martin, *Men in Rebellion: Higher Governmental Leaders and the Coming of the American Revolution* (1973; New York, 1976), 218–19.

On slave importers: W. Robert Higgins, "Charles Town Merchants and Factors Dealing in the External Negro Trade, 1735–1775," *SCHM*, LXV (1964), 205–17. Firms that stood among the top 75 were judged large, and those that were between 76 and 406 on the list were small. These divisions differ somewhat from the table in Chapter 6 (which considers firms rather than individuals), but any other points of demarcation would produce comparable results, with the expansionists predominating among the larger slavers and the nonexpansionists among the smaller.

On support for war: W. Bogdani, secretary to the Board of Ordnance, to John Pownal, secretary to the Board of Trade, Jan. 23, 1756, "A Return of the Muster Rolls . . . ," May 4, 1757, SCPR, XXVII, 1–2, 305, SCA; Petition of the Merchants . . . , Dec. 21, 1756, Public Subscription, Nov. 17, 1759, *The Papers of Henry Laurens*, ed. Philip M. Hamer et al. (Columbia, S.C., 1968–), II, 378–80, III, 16; Volunteers to Governor William Henry Lyttelton, Oct. 31, 1759, *The Writings of Christopher Gadsden, 1746–1805*, ed. Richard Walsh (Columbia, S.C., 1966), 12–13.

On the November 1768 assembly: *Biographical Directory: Session Lists*, 134–35. Both those who appeared before the assembly and declined to serve and those who failed to qualify are listed as rejecting a seat.

On nonimportation: leaders are drawn from Edward McCrady, *The History of South Carolina under the Royal Government, 1719–1776* (1899; rpt. New York, 1969), 651n (Committee of Thirty-nine); *Papers of Laurens*, VII, 322–23 (committee appointed in August 1770); Lieutenant Governor William Bull to Hillsborough, Dec. 5, 1770, SCPR, XXXII, 415. For opponents, consult Arthur M. Schlesinger, *The Colonial Merchants and the American Revolution, 1763–1776* (New York, 1918), 202–8; McGrady, *History of South Carolina*, 645–76.

On Council of Safety: Lord William Campbell to [Secretary of State?], July 2, 1775, SCPR, XXXV, 131; *Extracts from the Journals of the Provincial Congresses of South Carolina, 1775–1776*, ed. William E. Hemphill and Wylma A. Wates (Columbia, S.C., 1960), 132 (Nov. 16, 1775).

On patriots and loyalists: Lorenzo Sabine, *Biographical Sketches of Loyalists of the American Revolution*, 2 vols. (Boston, 1864); Wallace Brown, *The King's Friends: The Composition and Motives of the American Loyalist Claimants* (Providence, R.I., 1965), chap. 12.

On Scots: Forrest McDonald and Ellen Shapiro McDonald, "The Ethnic Origins of the American People, 1790," *WMQ*, XXXVII (1980), 192–94, provides a suggestive list of Scottish surnames.

Index

Adair, Douglass, 336
Adams, John, 10, 277; and Bernard's administration, 48–49, 151–52, 156–57; and continental congress, 275, 277, 280, 306–7, 313; and democratic institutions, 314–15; after independence, 332; and independence, 322; outlook of, 50, 156, 166, 267, 334–35, 336; and politics in 1750s, 44; and the quiet years, 250–51
Adams, Samuel, Jr., 20–21; and Bernard's administration, 150, 152, 156–59; and Boston committee of correspondence, 252; and Constitution, 334n; and continental congress, 273, 280, 313; and nonimportation, 163, 165–66; outlook of, 167; and quiet years, 249–53; and Solemn League and Covenant, 277
Adams, Samuel, Sr., 20, 21, 34–35, 38, 40
Agrarian unrest, 14, 272–74, 329, 331; in Massachusetts, 23, 277–80, 331; in New York, 124, 169, 171, 174–78, 182, 255; in Pennsylvania, 80, 193–95, 295, 331; in South Carolina, 233, 235–39, 320–21; in Virginia, 89–91, 218–19, 305–6, 308–9
Albany, N.Y., 43, 53, 55, 56, 61, 76, 77, 178, 187, 188
Albany County, N.Y., 52–54, 58, 59, 64, 282
Albany Plan of Union [1754], 43, 65, 76–77
Albemarle County, Va., 312
Alexander, James, 52, 54, 57, 59, 63–64, 65
Alexander, William, 64–65
Alexandria, Va., 332
Allegheny Mountains, 97
Allen, James [of Massachusetts], 38, 40, 41–42, 43
Allen, James [of Pennsylvania], 293, 296
Allen, Rev. Thomas, 300
Allen, William, 68, 72–77, 80, 82, 200
Alsop, John, 173, 281
Altamaha River, 107

American Board of Customs Commissioners, 158, 159, 178. *See also* Townshend Acts.
American Philosophical Society, 212–13
American Prohibitory Act [1775], 324
Amherst, Gen. Jeffrey, 192
Andrews, John, 254
Anglicans: in Massachusetts, 18, 25, 28; in New York, 18, 54, 66; in Pennsylvania, 18, 68, 69, 71–75, 82, 194, 196, 200, 203; in South Carolina, 103, 104, 117, 323, 324; in Virginia, 93, 315
Annapolis, Md., 222
Apthorp family, 28
Articles of Confederation, 333–34
Ash, John, 104, 105
Association [Pennsylvania militia], 75–76, 293–95
Atkinson, Roger, 147
Augusta County, Va., 100
Austin & Laurens, 19, 117, 122

Bailyn, Bernard, 3–5
Baltimore, Md., 332
Bancroft, George, 3
Bank of North America, 297
Bank of Pennsylvania [1780–81], 205
Baptists, 23
Barnstable, Mass., 25
Barnstable County, Mass., 48, 152
Barnwell, John, 104, 105, 106
Bayard, Nicholas, 185
Baynton, Wharton, & Morgan, 137
Bay of Apalache, 105
Beaufort, S.C., 114–15, 263
Becker, Carl, 2
Beekman, Gerard, 131–32, 137, 175
Beekman, Henry, 57, 59, 62
Beekman, James, 137, 138, 144, 187
Beekman family, 51, 52, 171, 188
Belcher, Jonathan [Gov., Mass.], 34–36, 39

371

Library of Congress Cataloging-in-Publication Data

Egnal, Marc.
  A mighty empire.

  Includes index.
    1. United States—History—Revolution, 1775–1783—Causes. 2. United States—
Politics and government—Revolution, 1775–1783. I. Title.
E210.E27 1988   973.2′7   87-19059
ISBN 0-8014-1932-8 (alk. paper)